Lecture Notes in Computer Science 12706

More information about this subseries at http://www.springer.com/series/7409

Marco Brambilla · Richard Chbeir ·
Flavius Frasincar · Ioana Manolescu (Eds.)

Web Engineering

21st International Conference, ICWE 2021
Biarritz, France, May 18–21, 2021
Proceedings

 Springer

Editors
Marco Brambilla (iD)
Dipartimento di Elettronica
Politecnico di Milano
Milan, Italy

Flavius Frasincar (iD)
Econometric Institute
Erasmus University Rotterdam
Rotterdam, The Netherlands

Richard Chbeir (iD)
E2S UPPA, LIUPPA
Université de Pau et des Pays de l'Adour
Anglet, France

Ioana Manolescu (iD)
Inria Saclay-Île-de-France,
Institut Polytechnique de Paris
Palaiseau, France

ISSN 0302-9743   ISSN 1611-3349   (electronic)
Lecture Notes in Computer Science
ISBN 978-3-030-74295-9   ISBN 978-3-030-74296-6   (eBook)
https://doi.org/10.1007/978-3-030-74296-6

LNCS Sublibrary: SL3 – Information Systems and Applications, incl. Internet/Web, and HCI

This Springer imprint is published by the registered company Springer Nature Switzerland AG
The registered company address is: Gewerbestrasse 11, 6330 Cham, Switzerland

Preface

The Web is 30 years old, and few technologies have withstood the test of time as well as the Web has. Despite its age, the Web is more relevant than ever. Nowadays, few can imagine a life without it. The Web is omnipresent in our daily lives from reading news, buying products, keeping in touch with friends, or doing business, to name a few examples. Due to its undeniable importance, a new discipline aimed at studying the multidisciplinary aspects of the Web has emerged entitled Web Science. Part of this discipline is Web Engineering (WE), which aims to study Web technologies and their applications following rigorous engineering practices. One could claim that this field appeared with the first edition of the International Conference on Web Engineering (ICWE), i.e., 20 years ago, a reason for the WE community to celebrate!

ICWE is the flagship conference for the WE community. Previous editions of ICWE took place in Helsinki, Finland (2020) [virtually], Daejeon, South Korea (2019), Cáceres, Spain (2018), Rome, Italy (2017), Lugano, Switzerland (2016), Rotterdam, the Netherlands (2015), Toulouse, France (2014), Aalborg, Denmark (2013), Berlin, Germany (2012), Paphos, Cyprus (2011), Vienna, Austria (2010), San Sebastian, Spain (2009), Yorktown Heights, USA (2008), Como, Italy (2007), Palo Alto, USA (2006), Sydney, Australia (2005), Munich, Germany (2004), Oviedo, Spain (2003), Santa Fe, Argentina (2002), and Cáceres, Spain (2001).

This volume contains the full research papers, short research papers, posters, demonstrations, PhD symposium papers, tutorials, and extended abstracts for the keynotes of the 21st International Conference on Web Engineering (ICWE 2021), held from May 18–21, 2021, in Biarritz, France [virtually].

ICWE 2021 focused on eight research themes, namely, *Semantic Web, Social Web, Web Modeling and Engineering, Web Big Data and Data Analytics, Web Mining and Knowledge Extraction, Web of Things, Web Programming,* and *Web User Interfaces.*

The ICWE 2021 edition received 128 submissions, out of which the Program Committee selected 22 full research papers (17% acceptance rate) and 13 short research papers (27% acceptance rate). Additionally, the Program Committee accepted six demonstrations, one poster, and three contributions to the PhD symposium. Also accepted were three tutorials: (1) High-level Interaction Design with Discourse Models for Automated Web GUI Generation, (2) Similarity Search, Recommendation and Explainability over Graphs for different domains: Social Media, News, and Health Industry, and (3) Influence Learning and Maximization, and three workshops: (1) 1st International Workshop on Big Data Driven Edge Cloud Services (BECS 2021), (2) 1st International Workshop on Web Engineering in Education (WEE 2021), and (3) 7th International Workshop on Knowledge Discovery on the Web (KDWEB 2021).

The comprehensive program would not have been possible without the support of the many people that contributed to the successful organization of this event. We would like to thank all the Special Issues, Tutorials, Workshops, Demonstrations and Posters, PhD Symposium, Publicity, Website, Local Arrangements, and Finance Chairs for their dedication and hard work. Our thanks goes also to Ricardo Baeza-Yates (Northeastern University, USA), Christos Faloutsos (Carnegie Mellon University, USA), and Fabrizio Silvestri (Sapienza University of Rome, Italy) who accepted to be our keynote speakers. Alessandro Bozzon and Oscar Diaz deserve special thanks for their support and encouragement in setting up ICWE 2021. We would like to also thank André Langer and Martin Gaedke for hosting the conference website. We are grateful to Springer for making possible the publication of this volume. In addition, we thank the reviewers for their hard work that allowed us to select the best papers to be presented at ICWE 2021. Last but not least, we would like to thank the authors that sent their work to ICWE 2021 and all the participants that contributed to the success of this conference.

May 2021   Marco Brambilla
Richard Chbeir
Flavius Frasincar
Ioana Manolescu

Organization

Technical Committee

General Chair

Richard Chbeir   Université de Pau et des Pays de l'Adour, France

Vice-General Chair

Flavius Frasincar   Erasmus University Rotterdam, the Netherlands

Program Committee Chairs

Marco Brambilla   Politecnico di Milano, Italy
Ioana Manolescu   Inria Saclay-Île-de-France and Institut Polytechnique
                         de Paris, France

Special Issues Chair

Yannis Manolopoulos   Open University of Cyprus, Cyprus

Tutorials Chairs

Vassilis Christophides   ENSEA, France
Michalis Vazirgiannis   École Polytechnique, Institut Polytechnique de Paris,
                         France

Workshops Chairs

Maxim Bakaev   Novosibirsk State Technical University, Russia
Cesare Pautasso   University of Lugano, Switzerland

Demonstrations and Posters Chairs

Irene Garrigós   University of Alicante, Spain
Marco Winckler   Université Côte d'Azur, France

PhD Symposium Chairs

Cinzia Cappiello   Politecnico di Milano, Italy
Gustavo Rossi   Universidad Nacional de La Plata, Argentina

Publicity Chairs

Tommaso Di Noia   Politecnico di Bari, Italy
In-Young Ko   Korea Advanced Institute of Science and Technology,
                          South Korea

Website Chairs

Sabri Allani   Université de Pau et des Pays de l'Adour, France
Elio Mansour   Université de Pau et des Pays de l'Adour, France

Local Arrangements Chairs

Philippe Aniorté   Université de Pau et des Pays de l'Adour, France
Philippe Arnould   Université de Pau et des Pays de l'Adour, France
Laurent Gallon   Université de Pau et des Pays de l'Adour, France

Finance Chair

Khouloud Salameh   American University of Ras Al Khaimah, UAE

Steering Committee Liaisons

Alessandro Bozzon   Delft University of Technology, the Netherlands
Oscar Diaz   University of the Basque Country, Spain

Program Committee

Research Program Committee

Ioannis Anagnostopoulos   University of Thessaly, Greece
Myriam Arrue   University of the Basque Country, Spain
Mohamed-Amine Baazizi   Sorbonne University, France
Marcos Baez   University of Trento, Italy
Maxim Bakaev   Novosibirsk State Technical University, Russia
Luciano Baresi   Politecnico di Milano, Italy
Peter Bednár   Technical University of Kosice, Slovakia
Devis Bianchini   University of Brescia, Italy
Matthias Book   University of Iceland, Iceland
Gabriela Bosetti   VeryConnect, UK
Alessandro Bozzon   Delft University of Technology, the Netherlands
Christoph Bussler   Google, USA
Carlos Canal   University of Málaga, Spain
Cinzia Cappiello   Politecnico di Milano, Italy

Oscar Pastor Lopez	Universitat Politècnica de València, Spain
Pankesh Patel	National University of Ireland, Ireland
Cesare Pautasso	University of Lugano, Switzerland
Vicente Pelechano	Universitat Politècnica de València, Spain
Alfonso Pierantonio	University of L'Aquila, Italy
Nicoleta Preda	University of Versailles, France
Raphael M. Reischuk	ETH Zurich, Switzerland
Werner Retschitzegger	Johannes Kepler University Linz, Austria
Filippo Ricca	Università di Genova, Italy
Thomas Richter	Rhein-Waal University of Applied Sciences, Germany
Gustavo Rossi	Universidad Nacional de La Plata, Argentina
Harald Sack	Leibniz Institute for Information Infrastructure and KIT Karlsruhe, Germany
Carmen Santoro	ISTI-CNR, Italy
Andrea Stocco	University of Lugano, Switzerland
Zhu Sun	Macquarie University, Australia
Kari Systä	Tampere University of Technology, Finland
Aikaterini Tzompanaki	CY Cergy Paris University, France
William Van Woensel	Dalhousie University, Canada
Markel Vigo	University of Manchester, UK
Michael Weiss	Carleton University, Canada
Erik Wilde	CA Technologies, USA
Manuel Wimmer	Johannes Kepler University Linz, Austria
Marco Winckler	Université Côte d'Azur, France
Yeliz Yesilada	Middle East Technical University, Turkey
Nicola Zannone	Eindhoven University of Technology, the Netherlands
Gefei Zhang	Hochschule für Technik und Wirtschaft Berlin, Germany
Jürgen Ziegler	University of Duisburg-Essen, Germany

Research Additional Reviewers

Oana Balalau	Hae-Na Lee
Nelly Barret	Andrea Mauri
Luca Berardinelli	Madhulika Mohanty
Russa Biswas	Andrea Morichatta
Yiyi Chen	Mahda Noura
Alexandre Connat	Tarmo Robal
Lorenzo Corti	Martin Sarnovsky
Paolo Cremonesi	Salma Sassi
Evan Crothers	Miroslav Smatana
Marco Di Giovanni	Mary Ann Tan
Antonio Gamendia	Andrea Tocchetti
Alberto González-Pérez	Utku Uckun
Ibrahim Hammoud	Sabine Wolny
Sebastian Heil	Derek Yu
Yu-Jung Ko	

Demonstrations and Posters Program Committee

Devis Bianchini	University of Brescia, Italy
Sven Casteleyn	Universitat Jaume I de Castelló, Spain
Damiano Distante	University of Rome Unitelma Sapienza, Italy
Sergio Firmenich	UNLP and CONICET, Argentina
César González Mora	University of Alicante, Spain
Jose Norberto Mazón	University of Alicante, Spain

PhD Symposium Program Committee

Marcos Baez	University of Trento, Italy
Maxim Bakaev	Novosibirsk State Technical University, Russia
Alessandro Bozzon	Delft University of Technology, the Netherlands
Jordi Cabot	Open University of Catalonia, Spain
Carlos Canal	University of Málaga, Spain
Cinzia Cappiello	Politecnico di Milano, Italy
Oscar Diaz	University of the Basque Country, Spain
Francisco José Domínguez Mayo	University of Seville, Spain
Irene Garrigós	University of Alicante, Spain
Daniela Godoy	ISISTAN Research Institute, Argentina
In-Young Ko	Korea Advanced Institute of Science and Technology, South Korea
Maristella Matera	Politecnico di Milano, Italy
Birgit Pröll	Johannes Kepler University Linz, Austria
Gustavo Rossi	Universidad Nacional de La Plata, Argentina
Marco Winckler	Université Côte d'Azur, France

Sponsors

In Memoriam

In the last year we have lost one of our beloved colleagues, Florian Daniel, a prominent member of the WE community. Few people from the WE field do not know Florian. He is remembered as an enthusiastic fellow, a proficient scientist, a passionate educator, and, above all, an authentic and inspiring person. Florian, you will be dearly missed!

Keynotes

Biases on Web Systems

Ricardo Baeza-Yates [ID]

Institute for Experiential AI, Northeastern University, USA
rbaeza@acm.org

Abstract. Biases on the Web reflects both societal and cognitive biases, emerging in subtler ways. This keynote aims to increase awareness of the potential effects imposed on us all through bias present in Web use and content, coming from different sources: data, algorithms, and our interaction with them. We must thus consider and account for it in the design and engineering of web systems that truly address people's needs.

Keywords: ML-based web systems · bad practices · good practices

Summary

We have already discussed many sources of bias on the Web ?, so here we focus on the biases while we engineer web systems, where today most of the time we use machine learning (ML). In this context, many systems fail to have even one of the properties proposed by the ACM [1].

When we design web systems (and in general), we have many bad practices, similar to the ones we find in ML-based systems [5]:

- We use the available data instead of the data that you need.
- We do not properly check the quality and completeness of the data.
- We use training data that does not cover well all the solution space.
- We learn from the past without checking the difference with the current context, reusing code in unanticipated contexts.
- We learn from human behavior without considering encoded biases and the possibility of malicious training.
- We do not check for spurious correlations or if there are proxies for protected information.

After the system is designed and implemented, we have the tendency to aggressively resist reviews, failing to measure the impact of the deployed system and in many times having inappropriate relationships between the system and the people taking decisions [5].

But going one step further: Do systems reflect the characteristics of the designers and/or the coders? We believe the answer is yes [2]. Indeed, we all have professional biases product of our culture, education and experience. For example, today big data and deep learning are the current focus of the industry, forgetting that most of the institutions in the world will never have big data [3]. Moreover, in [4] it is shown that cultural and cognitive biases of programmers can be transferred to the code.

This is particularly true when we do software evaluation. One clue is the experiment done regarding data analysis, where all 29 teams did something different [6]. This shows the breadth of thought, knowledge and experience of different teams. This affects what experiments we design, the test data that we use, the metrics considered, and the baselines for comparison that we choose.

Hence, what can we do? For the data part, we can:

– Analyze for known and unknown biases, debiasing and/or mitigating when possible.
– Recollect more data for sparse regions of the solution space.
– Do not use features associated directly/indirectly with protected attributes that can produce harmful bias.

For the design and implementation, we need to let experts/colleagues/users contest every step of the process. We can be completely transparent publishing our code in a public repository and at the end registering the algorithm. We can even request an external audit. For the human computer interaction part, we need to make sure that the user is aware of the system's biases all the time and has tools to control it.

What are the good practices then? In my personal opinion, some are:

– Design thinking in people first! (users and society).
– Have a deep respect for the limitations of your system, starting with the fact that you cannot learn what is not in the data.
– Be humble, if your result or prediction is not good, answer "I don't know".
– Do a strong evaluation and cross-discipline validation.
– Have an external ethics board for the process and enforce a *Code of Ethics*.
– Remember that we, humans, should be in *control* and hence *machines are in the loop*.

References

1. ACM U.S. Technology Policy Committee: Statement on algorithmic transparency and accountability (January 2017). https://www.acm.org/ binaries/content/assets/public-policy/2017_usacm_statement_algorithms.pdf
2. Baeza-Yates, R.: Bias on the web. Commun. ACM **61**(6), 54–61 (2018). https://cacm.acm.org/magazines/2018/6/228035-bias-on-the-web/fulltext
3. Baeza-Yates, R.: BIG, small or right data: which is the proper focus? (October 2018). https://www.kdnuggets.com/2018/10/big-small-right-data.html
4. Johansen, J., Pedersen, T., Johansen, C.: Studying the transfer of biases from programmers to programs (December 2020). https://arxiv.org/abs/2005.08231v2
5. Matthews, J.N.: Patterns and anti-patterns, principles and pitfalls: accountability and transparency in AI. AI Mag. **41**(1), 82–89 (2020). https://doi.org/10.1609/aimag.v41i1.5204
6. Silberzahn, R., et al.: Many analysts, one data set: making transparent how variations in analytic choices affect results. Adv. Methods Pract. Psychol. Sci. **1**(3), 337–356 (2018). https://psyarxiv.com/qkwst/

Anomaly Detection in Large Graphs

Christos Faloutsos [ID]

Carnegie Mellon University, Pittsburgh PA, USA
christos@cs.cmu.edu

Abstract. Given a large graph, like who-calls-whom, or who-likes-whom, what behavior is normal and what should be surprising, possibly due to fraudulent activity? How do graphs evolve over time? We focus on these topics: (a) anomaly detection in large static graphs and (b) patterns and anomalies in large time-evolving graphs. For the first, we present a list of static and temporal laws, including advances patterns like 'eigenspokes'; we show how to use them to spot suspicious activities, in on-line buyer-and-seller settings, in Facebook, in twitter-like networks. For the second, we show how to handle time-evolving graphs as tensors, as well as some surprising discoveries such settings.

Keywords: Graph mining · Anomaly detection

Introduction

Graphs appear in numerous settings: who-follows-whom in Twitter, who-buys-what from e-retailers, which machine sends packets to what machine in a computer communication network. The list continues: which protein interacts with what protein; which patient exhibits what symptoms in a medical records setting; which document contains what word.

How do we spot abnormal patterns in such graphs? It turns out that most real graphs tend to obey some recurring patterns, like the 'six-degrees' of separation, power-law degree distributions [3], and several other patterns that we will present in the talk. Patterns that do *not* appear in organic graphs, are the cliques and bi-partite cores - such patterns usually signify organized behavior, and is often malicious, like DDoS (distributed denial of service), or fake twitter followers, fake product reviews. We will present tools to spot such behavior, like the 'eigenspokes' method [7], and related dense-block detection methods (CopyCatch [1], CrossSpot [5], Fraudar [4], D-Cube [8]).

Studying static graphs like the above, is still on-going. But there are even more fascinating patterns when we study time-evolving graphs, like who-calls-whom-and-when. We will present some patterns [2, 9], as well as tools to analyze time evolving graphs, including tensor analysis [6].

References

1. Beutel, A., Xu, W., Guruswami, V., Palow, C., Faloutsos, C.: Copycatch: stopping group attacks by spotting lockstep behavior in social networks. In: International World Wide Web Conferences Steering Committee/ACM (WWW), pp. 119–130 (2013)
2. Costa, A.F., Yamaguchi, Y., Traina, A.J.M., Jr., C.T., Faloutsos, C.: RSC: mining and modeling temporal activity in social media. In: KDD, pp. 269–278. ACM (2015)
3. Faloutsos, M., Faloutsos, P., Faloutsos, C.: On power-law relationships of the internet topology. In: SIGCOMM, pp. 251–262. ACM (1999)
4. Hooi, B., Song, H.A., Beutel, A., Shah, N., Shin, K., Faloutsos, C.: FRAUDAR: bounding graph fraud in the face of camouflage. In: KDD, pp. 895–904. ACM (2016)
5. Jiang, M., Beutel, A., Cui, P., Hooi, B., Yang, S., Faloutsos, C.: A general suspiciousness metric for dense blocks in multimodal data. In: ICDM, pp. 781–786. IEEE Computer Society (2015)
6. Papalexakis, E.E., Faloutsos, C., Sidiropoulos, N.D.: Tensors for data mining and data fusion: models, applications, and scalable algorithms. ACM TIST 8(2), 16:1–16:44 (2017)
7. Prakash, B.A., Sridharan, A., Seshadri, M., Machiraju, S., Faloutsos, C.: Eigenspokes: surprising patterns and scalable community chipping in large graphs. In: PAKDD 2010. LNCS, vol. 6119, pp. 435–448. Springer, Heidelberg. https://doi.org/10.1007/978-3-642-13672-6_42 (2010)
8. Shin, K., Hooi, B., Kim, J., Faloutsos, C.: D-cube: dense-block detection in terabyte-scale tensors. In: WSDM, pp. 681–689. ACM (2017)
9. Zang, C., Cui, P., Faloutsos, C.: Beyond sigmoids: the nettide model for social network growth, and its applications. In: KDD, pp. 2015–2024. ACM (2016)

Neural Databases

Fabrizio Silvestri ⓘ

University of Rome, Italy
fabrizio.silvestri@uniroma1.it

Abstract. We introduce *neural databases*, a class of systems that use NLP transformers as localized answer derivation engines. We ground the vision in NEURALDB, a system for querying facts represented as short natural language sentences. In fact, in this research, we explore the possibility of using neural network architectures to relax the fundamental assumption of database management: the processed data is represented as fields of a pre-defined *schema*. We demonstrate that recent natural language processing models, specifically the ones based on transformers, can answer select-project-join (SPJ) queries if they are given a set of relevant facts. In addition to that, we show experiments proving that a simple transformer-based solution cannot answer queries requiring aggregations, e.g., *min, max, count, avg*. We thus propose an improved NEURALDB architecture that specifically address also this task. It adds a component that enable the use of traditional aggregation operators on top of neural components and is able to effectively match the performance of traditional DBs in a large fraction of the cases.

Keywords: Transformers · Databases · Neural language understanding

Introduction

Neural networks have been successful in many different areas, such as vision and language. In this research, we explore the possibility of using neural network architectures to relax the fundamental assumption of database management: the processed data is represented as fields of a pre-defined *schema*. The question, then, is: *can data and queries be represented as short natural language sentences, and can queries be answered from these sentences?* This research presents a first step in answering that question. We propose NeuralDB, a database system in which updates and queries are given in natural language. The query processor of a NEURALDB builds on the primitives offered by the state-of-the-art Natural Language Processing (NLP) techniques.

Realizing the vision of NeuralDB will offer several benefits that database systems have struggled to support for decades. The first and most important benefit is that a NEURALDB, by definition, has no pre-defined schema. The database's scope does not

---

A longer, and thorough, description of the system described in this abstract can be found in the paper authored by Thorne

need to be defined in advance, and any data that becomes relevant as the application is used can be stored and queried. Also, updates and queries can be posed in various natural language forms, as is convenient to any user. Finally, NEURALDB is based on a pre-trained language model that already contains much knowledge. For example, the fact that London is in the UK is already encoded in the language model. Hence, a query asking who lives in the UK can retrieve people who are known to live in London without having to specify an additional join explicitly. Furthermore, using the same paradigm, we can endow the NEURALDB with more domain knowledge by extending the pre-training corpus to that domain.

By nature, a NEURALDB is not meant to provide the same correctness guarantees of a traditional database system, i.e., that the answers returned for a query satisfy the query language's precise binary semantics. Hence, NEURALDBs should not be considered an alternative to traditional databases in applications where such guarantees are required. Given its benefits, Neural Databases are well suited for emerging applications where the schema of the data cannot be determined in advance and data can be stated in a wide range of linguistic patterns.

One of our contributions is to show that state-of-the-art transformer models [2] can be adapted to answer simple natural language queries. Specifically, the models can process facts relevant to a query independent of their specific linguistic form and combine multiple facts to yield correct answers, effectively performing a join. However, we identify two significant limitations of these models: (1) they do not perform well on aggregation queries (e.g., counting, max/min), and (2) since the input size to the transformer is bounded, and the complexity of the transformer is quadratic in the size of its input, they only work on a relatively small collection of facts.

Another contribution is to propose an architecture for neural databases that uses the power of transformers at its core but puts several other components in place to address the scalability and aggregation issues. Our architecture runs multiple instances of a Neural SPJ operator in parallel. The operator results are either the answer to the query or the input to an aggregation operator, which is done traditionally. Underlying this architecture is a novel algorithm for generating the small sets of database sentences fed to each Neural SPJ operator.

References

1. Thorne, J., Yazdani, M., Saeidi, M., Silvestri, F., Riedel, S., Halevy, A.: Neural databases. arXiv preprint arXiv:2010.06973 (2020)
2. Vaswani, A., et al.: Attention is all you need. In: NIPS, pp. 5998–6008. Curran Associates, Inc. (2017)

Contents

Web Big Data and Data Analytics

Web Mining and Knowledge Extraction

Web of Things

Web Programming

Web User Interfaces

Ph.D. Symposium

Posters and Demonstrations

Semantic Web

Interface to Query and Visualise Definitions from a Knowledge Base

Anelia Kurteva[1(✉)] and Hélène De Ribaupierre[2]

[1] Semantic Technology Institute, Department of Computer Science,
University of Innsbruck, Innsbruck, Austria
`anelia.kurteva@sti2.at`

[2] School of Computer Science and Informatics, Cardiff Univeristy, Cardiff, Wales, UK
`deribaupierreh@cardiff.ac.uk`

Abstract. Linked data is at the core of the Web due to its ability to model real world entities, connect them via relationships and provide context, which could help to transform data into information and information into knowledge. For example, ontologies, which could be stored locally or could be made available to everyone online (e.g. the DBpedia knowledge base). However, both access and usage of Linked Data require individuals to have knowledge in the field of the Semantic Web. Many of the existing solutions are developed for specific use cases such as building and exploring ontologies visually and are aimed at expert users. The solutions that are aimed at non-experts are generic and, in most cases, a data visualisation is not available. In this paper, we present a web application with a user interface (UI), which combines features from applications for both expert and non-experts. The UI allows individuals with no previous knowledge of the Semantic Web to query the DBpedia knowledge base for definitions of a specific word and to view a graphical visualisation of the query results (the search keyword itself and concepts related to it).

Keywords: Linked data · Knowledge base · User interface · Graphical visualisation · Human-computer interaction · Comprehension

1 Introduction

Linked Data is at the core of the web. However, its access and usage is not as straightforward for humans as it is for machines. Search engines such as Google[1], Swoogle [5], Falcons [4] allow one to access and use Linked Data indirectly. With the help of its knowledge graph[2], Google can provide hundreds of sources as an answer to one's query in a matter of seconds. However, most of the information presented on the result's page is in textual and tabular formats, which does not ease one's comprehension and decision making. While machines are able

---

[1] https://www.google.com.
[2] https://developers.google.com/knowledge-graph.

© Springer Nature Switzerland AG 2021
M. Brambilla et al. (Eds.): ICWE 2021, LNCS 12706, pp. 3–10, 2021.
https://doi.org/10.1007/978-3-030-74296-6_1

to comprehend large volumes of information, written in different languages in milliseconds, this is not the case with humans. Humans are visual creatures and look for visual cues such as colors, forms, depth, and movements [3,8]. Reading large volumes of information in textual formats is time-consuming and can cause problems such as information overload [7].

Linked Data can be also queried directly with tools such as Protégé[3] or through application programming interfaces (APIs) such as the DBpedia REST API[4]. However, in order to work with Linked Data directly, for example, to query DBpedia[5], knowledge of OWL[6], RDF[7] RDFs[8] and SPARQL[9] is needed. The query results are, in most cases, still in textual format, follow a triple pattern and can include specific uniform resource identifiers (URIs), which while useful for machines and individuals with expert knowledge of the Semantic Web it is not in favour of non-experts. Further, querying DBpedia, even for a single concept, results in displaying millions of triples thus the issue of information overload [7] arises again.

This paper presents a web application with a user interface (UI) that allows individuals with no previous knowledge of the Semantic Web to query the DBpedia knowledge base for definitions of a specific word and to view a visualisation of the query result (i.e. the search keyword and concepts related to it). The web application combines features from applications for both experts and non-experts and aims to ease one's comprehension. The main research question that this paper aims to answer is:

"Is a visualisation of a knowledge base's query result useful for individuals?".

Our main hypothesis is that a visualisation of the query results, when presented together with a definition of a word, is both useful and interesting to individuals.

The rest of the paper is structured as follows: Related work is presented in Sect. 2. Section 3 outlines the methodology that this research follows. Section 4 provides insights of the implemented solution, while Sect. 5 presents the evaluation results. Conclusions and future work are presented in Sect. 6.

2   Related Work

Existing applications that are powered by Linked Data have interfaces are either too generic or too complex. Applications aimed at professionals such as Protégé (see footnote 3) provide the option to not only explore Linked Data but also to create, edit and visualise it. These options are rarely available in applications developed for non-experts. While it is true that different users have different

---

[3] https://Protege.stanford.edu.
[4] https://wiki.dbpedia.org/rest-api.
[5] https://wiki.dbpedia.org.
[6] https://www.w3.org/2001/sw/wiki/OWL.
[7] https://www.w3.org/TR/2004/REC-rdf-primer-20040210/.
[8] https://www.w3.org/2001/sw/wiki/RDFS.
[9] https://www.w3.org/TR/rdf-sparql-query/.

needs regarding functionality, presenting users with visualisation of data has been proven to be useful as visualisations help ease comprehension, engage one's attention and arouse curiosity [10–12,17].

Online dictionaries such as Lexico[10], Oxford Learner's Dictionaries[11] and Cambridge Dictionary[12] have an interface, which resembles a search engine and could be used by both experts and non-experts. The main focus of these tools is on searching for word's meaning, displaying similar terms and grammar rules. While the Lexico and Oxford Learner's Dictionaries allow one to input a word and hear how it is pronounced, the Cambridge Dictionary allows one to simultaneously search for a word's meaning and its translation in different languages. Regarding the interface design, all three dictionaries resemble each other. The interface is designed as a single page view, which based on the input term is divided into several sections explaining its meaning and providing examples. Although, providing examples of how a term could be used could help one comprehend the meaning of the term better, all of the information is in textual format. Further, depending on how much information is available for a specific term, the result page could require one to scroll several times in order to get to a specific section. Google Search[13], which is powered by a knowledge graph [6], allows one to perform much more complicated search queries. Google's interface is simple and does not require expert knowledge in how Linked Data is structured thus it has turned into the main source of information for many. However, the results of a Google search are still presented in a textual and tabular formats.

Linked Data-powered tools and applications that present information in formats other that textual are developed for experts. The Protégé (see footnote 3) ontology development environment allows one to create, import, export, query and visualise Linked Data structures such as ontologies. Protégé's interface provides the option to customise what fields are shown. Individuals can select from a variety of editing options and can further use plugins such as OntoGraph[14] to view a graphical visualisation of the current ontology. Due to its user-friendly and intuitive interface design, Protégé has become a standard for ontology development. In order to use it, one needs to have knowledge of semantic models and experience with SPARQL (see footnote 9) as one needs to import or create an ontology first in order to explore it visually.

Lohman et al. [14] present VOWL[15] - an application for interactive Linked Data exploration and visualisation, which is available online under the name WebVOWL[16] and as a plugin extension for Protégé (see footnote 3) called ProtégéVOWL[17]. VOWL's interface allows one to import ontologies from a file or via a Uniform Resource Locator (URL). Once imported a scalable vector

---

[10] https://www.lexico.com.
[11] https://www.oxfordlearnersdictionaries.com.
[12] https://dictionary.cambridge.org.
[13] https://www.google.com.
[14] https://protegewiki.stanford.edu/wiki/OntoGraf.
[15] http://vowl.visualdataweb.org.
[16] http://vowl.visualdataweb.org/webvowl.html.
[17] http://vowl.visualdataweb.org/protegevowl.html.

graphics (SVG) visualisation of the whole file is generated with D3.js[18]. The interface gives individuals the options to customize the generated visualisation by filtering and editing data and the colours associated with it. The evaluation of the tool, which was done with five participants (four of which were experts), showed that while helpful VOWL is *"almost showing too much information"*, which had a negative effect on one's comprehension [14].

A similarity that could be found in existing Linked Data tools for experts is their ability to generate a graphical visualisation of the data. This feature could be extremely useful when one wants to view relationships between things and discover more information. Most of the tools such as Protégé (see footnote 3) and VOWL (see footnote 15) require an ontology or schema to be imported or created first. Once such semantic model is available a graphical visualisation is generated for the whole ontology. A graphical visualisation of specific data could be generated only upon inputting special parameters. For example, limiting the number of results a query could return. From an experts perspective, all these options are useful but this does not apply to non-experts. However, non-experts should be given the opportunity to benefit from such visualisation. In order to achieve that, an interface that simplifies the process of Linked Data query and visualisation is needed.

3   Methodology

This work follows the methodology for building interfaces based on Linked Data presented in [13]. The methodology consists of four main steps: (i) gather data, (ii) define use case, (iii) build interface and (iv) use data. Further, we follow the recommendations for UI design by Schneiderman presented in [15]. Our main focus is on reducing one's short-term memory load (i.e. the eight rule of Schnerderman [16]) by building a one screen UI and by using hierarchical visualisations.

This work uses Linked Data that is available through the DBpedia (see footnote 5) knowledge base. The main use case that we focus on is querying definitions of terms and providing a visualisation of the query results (i.e. the definition of a word and concepts related or similar to it). Figure 1 presents this system's architecture and all of its building blocks. The front-end implementation is based on HTML[19], CSS[20] and PHP[21], while EasyRDF[22], SPARQL (see footnote 9) and JavaScript[23] were used on the back-end. The Speak.js[24] library was used for text-to-speech transformation. The visualisation itself was done with D3.js (see

---

[18] https://d3js.org.
[19] https://html.spec.whatwg.org.
[20] https://developer.mozilla.org/en-US/docs/Web/CSS.
[21] https://www.php.net.
[22] https://www.easyrdf.org.
[23] https://www.javascript.com.
[24] https://github.com/kripken/speak.js/.

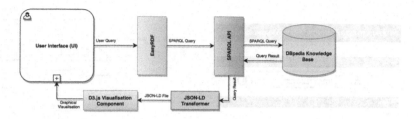

Fig. 1. System architecture

footnote 18). The solution was hosted on a local host provided by the XAMPP[25] tool and was later made public on remote web server in order to be evaluated.

4   Implementation

The implementation of the proposed web application comprises of two stages. Stage 1 focuses on the UI design and implementation, while Stage 2 on the graphical visualisation of the query results. The next sections present an overview of the development at each stage.

4.1   User Interface

The UI (Fig. 2) consist of three main components: a search bar that allows the input of keywords, a "Result" field, which displays the query results in textual format and a "Visualisation" field that presents the graphical visualisation of the query results.

We focus mainly on querying definitions of words from DBpedia (see footnote 5) thus we have predefined a SPARQL (see footnote 9) query that could use any word as its query variable. With the help of the EasyRDF (see footnote 22) library, one's input is sent to the predefined SPARQL query, which takes it as an input variable. The query is then send to DBpedia. The main DBpedia properties we query are *"dbo:abstract"*, *"dbo:thumbnail"*, *"dbo:sameAs"*, *"rdfs:seeAlso"* and *"owl:differentFrom"*. As some concepts have longer abstracts, we limit the queried information to a few sentences in order to avoid information overload when displaying the definition to the user. All query results are stored in JSON-LD format, which allows data to be easily consumed by the D3.js (see footnote 18) visualisation library. Once a query is executed and the result (i.e. the keyword, its definition and its thumbnail) is returned it is displayed in the "Result" field (Fig. 2).

When developing the UI, Human-Computer Interaction [9] was also considered. In order to try to raise one's comprehension and make one feel involved, we focused on interactivity. Components of the UI, such as the graphical visualisation, which we describe in the next section, and the fields themselves can

---

[25] https://www.apachefriends.org/index.html.

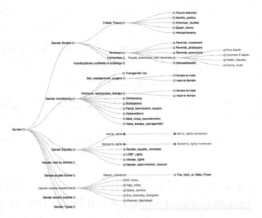

Fig. 2. User interface and graphical visualisation

Fig. 3. Interactive hierarchical tree layout

be expanded and collapsed on demand. Further, the UI provides the option to hear a keyword's pronunciation, which is also available in the LEXICO (see footnote 10) dictionary. Implementing this feature was a challenge as most of the recordings of word pronunciations were not openly available thus a simple text-to-speech functionality was implemented using the Speak.js (see footnote 24) library. We made use of the *textToSpeech()* function, which allows passing a value to it and returning the specified language pronunciation.

4.2 Graphical Visualisation of the Query Result

Viarious graph visualisation layouts such as a Force-Directed Graph [1] and Hierarchical Edge Bundling [2] exist and are widely used. However, each has its own limitation and is suitable for a different use case. For example, a Force-Directed Graph displays all nodes and edges that are available, does not display information about the type relationship between the nodes and does not follow a hierarchy, which can be a challenge for non-experts' comprehension.

Based on this we have selected one of the simplest, most common and intuitive graph layouts - a hierarchical tree (Fig. 3), where one's search term is the root node. All branches coming out of it are directly connected to it based on the relationships queried from DBpedia (see footnote 5). Each branch represents a specific sub-category connected to the main term and has its own sub-divisions. In order to differentiate between the available data types, different colours were used. Nodes that represent individual personas are in green, while contradictions are shown in red. External nodes, which hold hyperlinks, change colour upon hoover. All nodes can be collapsed and expanded with a click. Further, upon hoovering on the root node a tooltip with its definition is shown. The options to zoom in and zoom out via a scroll of the mouse wheel or the equivalent touch pad action are available as well.

5   Evaluation

The evaluation, in the form of different questionnaires[26], was conducted with 10 participants from different educational and ethnic backgrounds. The participants were presented with a system usability questionnaire, which helped evaluate the design and overall experience while using the application, scenarios and were asked to complete several tasks.

The analysis showed that 7 out of the 10 participants strongly agreed that the application was helpful and easy to use, while the rest agreed. When asked if they would use the application frequently, more than the half agreed. Regarding the visualisation itself, half strongly agreed that it was useful, while the other half gave "agree" as an answer. By computing the median values for each question, we were able to see how answers differ through the different categories. The biggest difference in answers was in the category "educational level". Participants with a Postgraduate degree strongly agreed or agreed that they would frequently use the application, while participants with both Undergraduate and High School educational level are on the fence between agree and disagree. Undergraduate users found the application not as easy to use as postgraduates and High School participants did. However, looking at the comments that all participants left on the questionnaire and while completing the given tasks, it was agreed that the application is easy to use, useful and simple. Finally, participants were given the option to describe with their own words the application and their experience. Some of the adjectives that the participants used were: useful, intuitive and accessible. When asked about what they would improve, the participants stated: "bigger font size", "link should be easier to hoover on" and "delay in the return times". In conclusion, the evaluation showed that the application is well-accepted, user-friendly and helpful.

6   Conclusion

In this paper, we presented a web application for querying and visualising Linked Data aimed at non-expert users. The developed solution provides a simple, intuitive user interface, which enables users to perform different tasks such as search for definitions, interact with the graphical visualisation of their query and hear a word's pronunciation. Looking back at the main research question, we believe that the conducted evaluation provides a positive answer and proves our hypothesis.

Future work will be focused on improving the visualisation algorithm, which currently accepts as an input only a specific JSON-LD structure, providing different graph layouts, an option to filter data and allowing multi-word search. In conclusion, although the presented solutions has its limitations, it achieves the task of combining features from Linked Data-powered solutions for both experts and non-experts and presents them to non-experts in an accessible way.

---

[26] https://github.com/aneliamk/research.

Acknowledgements. We would like to thank Simon Tippner for his helpful feedback regarding the graphical visualisation and Midhat Faheem for participating in the discussions that this research inspired.

References

1. Bostock, M.: Force-directed graph (2017). https://observablehq.com/@d3/force-directed-graph
2. Bostock, M.: Hierarchical edge bundling with d3.js (2018). https://observablehq.com/@d3/hierarchical-edge-bundling
3. Brookhaven National Laboratory: visualizing scientific big data in informative and interactive ways (2017). https://phys.org/news/2017-04-visualizing-scientific-big-interactive-ways.html
4. Cheng, G., Qu, Y.: Searching linked objects with falcons: approach, implementation and evaluation. Int. J. Semant. Web Inf. Syst. **5**, 49–70 (2009)
5. Ding, L., Pan, R., Finin, T., Joshi, A., Peng, Y., Kolari, P.: Finding and ranking knowledge on the semantic web. In: Gil, Y., Motta, E., Benjamins, V.R., Musen, M.A. (eds.) ISWC 2005. LNCS, vol. 3729, pp. 156–170. Springer, Heidelberg (2005). https://doi.org/10.1007/11574620_14
6. Google: How google's knowledge graph works. https://support.google.com/knowledgepanel/answer/9787176?hl=en
7. Gross., B.M.: The managing of organizations: the administrative struggle. Ann. Am. Acad. Polit. Soc. Sci. **360**(1), 197–198 (1965). https://doi.org/10.1177/000271626536000140
8. Eisenberg, H.: Humans process visual data better (2014). https://www.t-sciences.com/news/humans-process-visual-data-better
9. Holzinger, A.: Human-computer interaction and knowledge discovery (HCI-KDD): what is the benefit of bringing those two fields to work together? In: Cuzzocrea, A., Kittl, C., Simos, D.E., Weippl, E., Xu, L. (eds.) CD-ARES 2013. LNCS, vol. 8127, pp. 319–328. Springer, Heidelberg (2013). https://doi.org/10.1007/978-3-642-40511-2_22
10. Kolari, S., Savander-Ranne, C.: Why do our students not learn as we wish them to?. In: Proceedings of 2nd Global Congress on Engineering Education, pp. 153–155 (2000)
11. Kolari, S., Savander-Ranne, C.: Will the application of constructivism bring a solution to today's problems of engineering education? Glob. J. Eng. Educ. **4**(3), 275–280 (2000)
12. Kolari, S., Savander-Ranne, C.: Visualisation promotes apprehension and comprehension. Int. J. Eng. Educ. **20**(3), 484–493 (2004)
13. Lindstörm, N., Mainsten, M.: Building interfaces on a networked graph. In: Linked data and user interaction, pp. 85–97. De Gruyter Saur, Berlin/Munich/Boston (2015)
14. Lohmann, S., Negru, S., Haag, F., Ertl, T.: Visualizing ontologies with VOWL. Semant. Web **7**(4), 399–419 (2016). https://doi.org/10.3233/SW-150200, http://dx.doi.org/10.3233/SW-150200
15. Shneiderman, B., Plaisant, C., Cohen, M., Jacobs, S.: Designing the user interface: strategies for effective human-computer interaction. In: SIGB (2016)
16. Shneiderman, B., Plaisant, C., Cohen, M., Jacobs, S.: The eight golden rules of interface design (2016). https://www.cs.umd.edu/users/ben/goldenrules.html
17. White, R.T.: Learning Science. Basil Blackwell, Oxford (1988)

CARDINAL: Contextualized Adaptive Research Data Description INterface Applying LinkedData

André Langer$^{(\boxtimes)}$ ⓘ, Christoph Göpfert ⓘ, and Martin Gaedke ⓘ

Chemnitz University of Technology, Chemnitz, Germany
{andre.langer,christoph.goepfert,martin.gaedke}@informatik.tu-chemnitz.de

Abstract. In the publishing process for research data, common user interfaces for gathering descriptive structured metadata traditionally rely on static free-text input elements. This constitutes an obstacle for interdisciplinary, unambiguous, fine-grained data descriptions. Reusing already existing domain-specific metadata models based on semantic ontologies are a more promising approach, but the careful selection and presentation of relevant properties is not trivial. In this paper, we present the CARDINAL approach, which takes the current research context into consideration to request additional but only meaningful domain-specific characteristics. It generates and presents an adaptive user input interface to the user that allows the structured input of knowledge-domain specific descriptive metadata based on existing ontologies. We show in a proof-of-concept the feasibility of such a contextualized web form for research metadata and discuss challenges in the selection process for relevant ontologies and properties. A web-based survey experiment with 83 participants of varying research domain and expertise shows, that the CARDINAL approach allows to collect additional relevant metadata in a structured way without overstraining the user.

Keywords: Adaptive user interface · Contextualization · Linked data · Research data management · Data publishing · Ontologies

1 Introduction

In the context of OpenScience, researchers are encouraged to publish their research data (also known as research datasets) in common data repositories so that others can find and reuse them. The term research data refers to any "data being a (descriptive) part or the result of a research process". Any kind of research literature is usually excluded when using the term research data, e.g., research articles or papers [4,11].

This research data publishing process shall increasingly be in compliance with the FAIR (Findable, Accessible, Interoperable, Reusable) guiding principles for scientific data management [17]. As digital research data is normally not self-descriptive, a user has to add additional metadata during the research data

© Springer Nature Switzerland AG 2021
M. Brambilla et al. (Eds.): ICWE 2021, LNCS 12706, pp. 11–27, 2021.
https://doi.org/10.1007/978-3-030-74296-6_2

publishing process to explicitly describe all relevant aspects of the contained data to make it findable by search crawlers and other applications.

Nowadays, data repositories primarily focus on administrative, citation, technical and some basic descriptive metadata [9]. Information on particular data characteristics are either collected not at all, in an unstructured way as floating text or only in domain-specific data repositories. This makes it difficult to simplify the discoverability of relevant datasets for researchers from different knowledge disciplines and results in the current situation, that dedicated scientific search catalogs are relying on keyword-based or fuzzy-logic based full-text search operations in this metadata. And their faceted search possibilities are limited to basic entities such as the *knowledge discipline, resource type* or *data license* and certain *provenance* constraints, which is directly in conflict with the FAIR principles to provide rich metadata (F1) in standardized vocabularies (I2) with accurate and relevant attributes (R1).

This is astounding as scientific communities have already yielded domain-specific high-quality, well-structured, controlled vocabularies that contain relevant properties. However, traditional approaches of using static user input interfaces do not take these domain-specific metadata models into account, as static forms are always structured the same way in terms of input elements, neglecting the context of the research artifact being described. A semantic technology-based approach, which focuses on an established metadata representation format and additionally incorporates other relevant vocabularies in such a metadata description, would be a means to improve the interdisciplinary publishing and discovery process.

Within the collaborative research center *Hybrid Societies*[1], we investigated the realization of an adaptive user input interface for collecting structured, descriptive, detailed research metadata as part of the *PIROL* PhD project [8] and provide the following three contributions:

1. We present CARDINAL to demonstrate an approach on how to select and adaptively incorporate domain-specific properties into a web form.
2. We formalize and discuss the contextualization of the research metadata collection in user input interfaces.
3. We show in an online study experiment the acceptance of the approach and the acquisition of additional domain-specific, descriptive metadata.

The results will contribute to the purpose of improving the interdisciplinary findability of published research data.

The rest of the paper is structured in the following way: In Sect. 2, we provide a conceptual problem and requirement analysis based on a comprehensive usage scenario. In Sect. 3, we describe a concept to identify and present relevant properties to a user for metadata input for describing research data. The realization of this process is then shown in Sect. 4 and evaluated in Sect. 5 wrt. acceptance and metadata quality. Section 6 compares our approach with other

---

[1] https://hybrid-societies.org/.

related literature, and Sect. 7 finally summarizes our results and provides an outlook to future work.

2   Problem Analysis

The findability and reusability of research data is interrelated as the relevance of search results depends on its suitability for a new application scenario and the possibility to limit a search to particular characteristics of a dataset. By using general-purpose search applications for research data repositories such as the *OpenAIRE search*[2], *EOSC EUDAT B2FIND*[3] or the *Google Dataset search*[4], users are already accustomed to a keyword-based input with some basic filter possibilities, where they have to review results on the search pages individually and carefully in order to actually find existing, relevant research data that can be reused or repurposed for their own work beside irrelevant search results. Additional available research datasets might be even existing that will not show up in such a result list as there is a mismatch between the terms used in the meta description of the published research data and the keywords that were entered by a user in a search interface.

Search services for scientific data typically still focus on keyword-based search methods[5], and filter possibilities are commonly limited to general entities. Instead, it would be a benefit, if a user can make use of more particular filters for characteristics of research data that the user is looking for. This would require better structured metadata that supports concept-based search approaches, but relevant characteristics vary greatly between different knowledge disciplines and a user might not be willing or able to describe all possibly eligible aspects in a research data meta description. A semantic vocabulary-based approach is promising to improve this situation, especially because a large set of domain-specific controlled vocabularies already exists[6]. Research data repositories have started to add support for additional domain-specific structured metadata descriptions, however, the user interface experience is still weak and requires expert knowledge and manual completion as shown in Fig. 1, thus, its usage is limited in a broader scope.

In the following, we will describe a fictitious scenario to illustrate an adaptive approach, how a user can be encouraged to provide more specific metadata while maintaining or even improving the user interface experience. *John Doe* is a political scientist and conducts research on electoral behavior. Recently, *John* and his colleagues conducted a randomized survey in which they asked *50* people who they would vote for if they had to choose right now. The answers of the survey participants were compiled in a spreadsheet, which shall now be published to a broader scientific community.

---

[2] https://explore.openaire.eu/search/find.
[3] http://b2find.eudat.eu/dataset.
[4] https://datasetsearch.research.google.com/.
[5] https://www.eosc-hub.eu/services/B2FIND.
[6] https://lov.linkeddata.es/dataset/lov/vocabs.

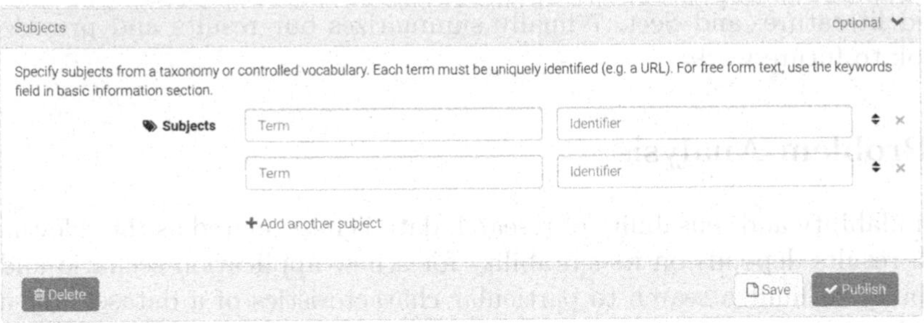

Subjects
optional
Specify subjects from a taxonomy or controlled vocabulary. Each term must be uniquely identified (e.g. a URL). For free form text, use the keywords field in basic information section.
Subjects
Term
Identifier
Term
Identifier
Add another subject
Delete
Save
Publish

Fig. 1. Current situation: provision of domain-specific characteristics, zenodo.org

Depending on the research area which the dataset relates to, further complementary information should be provided. This makes the data easier to interpret and facilitates reuse. In various research areas, there already exist semantic knowledge models about domain-specific concepts in form of ontologies. In the provided scenario, an ontology that models characteristics for survey data could be relevant to *John*, such as the *DDI-RDF Discovery (DISCO)* Vocabulary[7].

There are three user roles to consider for this scenario as shown in Fig. 2: The user who publishes research data together with additional descriptive metadata, users that search for existing datasets in the future, and domain experts that provide a domain-specific ontology and the knowledge which concepts are relevant to describe.

Domain Expert
Research Data Repository
Research Data Description Form
Research Data Search
Research Data Publisher
Researcher

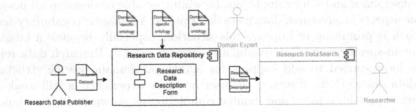

Fig. 2. Conceptual view on the problem scenario

Based on that scenario, we investigate how to design an adaptive submission form for describing a research dataset. Therefore, we identified the following five objectives which also consider the criteria introduced by Paulheim and Probst [12]:

[7] https://rdf-vocabulary.ddialliance.org/discovery.html.

OBJ1 **Metadata acquisition**: In the user input interface, it shall be possible to enter additional structured metadata based on existing domain-specific ontologies which is considered to be of interest for other users in the future.

OBJ2 **Adaptivity**: The form shall be adaptive in the sense that its structure and its components adapt to the context of the research data.

OBJ3 **Research characteristics**: The form shall reuse existing standardized recommendations for properties and concepts to describe research characteristics.

OBJ4 **Usability**: The form shall hide technical data details from the user and not create an unsatisfying user interface experience causing additional user effort.

OBJ5 **Metadata output**: The resulting research data metadata description shall be stored persistently in a machine-readable format, so that it can be easily provided and used in consecutive tool chains, e.g., by corresponding search services.

3   The CARDINAL Approach

The following design is based on three assumptions:

1. A user intends to publish research data, possessing certain attributes that can be related to at least one knowledge domain.
2. Standardized vocabularies / ontologies already exist and are available in this knowledge domain in a structured (OWL) description that reflect relevant concepts to describe research in this discipline.
3. A subset of these properties is relevant for other users to find and reuse this research data.

Input forms are an established means to collect metadata in a manual user input activity. In contrast to static input forms, which are assembled by a developer and commonly present the same input controls to all users, we are heading for an adaptive approach, which will add additional input elements depending on the nature of the resource to describe. Therefore, additional knowledge has to be provided to the application in a first step that can be used to contextualize the further form handling. In a consecutive form building process, relevant ontologies and properties have to be (semi-)automatically selected in order to generate an input form in which a user can then provide and store metadata in a final process step, as shown in Fig. 3.

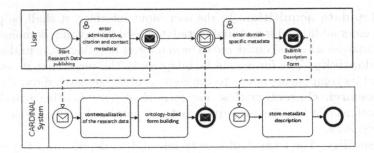

Fig. 3. BPMN process for an adaptive research metadata input form

3.1   Contextualization

In order to tailor the adaptive form to the useful description of particular research data, the context of a published research artifact must be understood. This step is necessary to decide on which domain-specific information is relevant for this research data. We refer to the process of finding a suitable context for an artifact as contextualization.

Referring to context-aware software [15], this can be done based on information explicitly provided by the user, implicitly by processing the provided research data with knowledge extractors if a file artifact is directly provided, implicitly by reusing externally available metadata background information to the dataset if a persistent identifier is already provided, or a combination or variation of the mentioned approaches. For the sake of simplicity, we focus on the first option and reuse meta information that a user might provide anyway when publishing research data (context-triggering actions) independent of a materialized file artifact or identifier.

Contextualization can be related to the classification, characteristics and usage of the investigated object and its origin as well as to spatial or temporal constraints. Attributes that might be used to describe the context of the research data include, for example, the research area(s) which the data can be assigned to, the resource type, or information about the research or application environment in which the data was generated.

Apparently, there exists also a trade-off between the amount of requested metadata for contextualization purposes, the appropriateness of the adaptivity behavior and the effort of the user and the application to achieve the activity result, so these contextualization attributes have to be considered carefully by the application developer.

$$Context\,(dataset) = \{c_i \mid i \in 0, 1, \ldots, c_i \text{ is attribute of dataset with } key\,(c_i) \text{ and } value\,(c_i)\} \tag{1}$$

The provided contextual information can then be used to select the most suitable ontologies for a given research data artifact that contain additional characteristics in the meaning of classes and properties that are worth to describe. This decision-making problem can be tackled by strategies such as using a rule-based approach or a decision tree. It is thereby advantageous to limit the value ranges for the contextualization attributes.

3.2   Ontology Selection

Based on the specified contextual information, relevant ontologies have to be selected which shall be incorporated adaptively into the input form to describe particular characteristics of the research data from the user. Selecting reusable ontologies is not a trivial step. Ontology catalogs can be used to retrieve information about publicly available ontologies in an automated fashion. However, they need to contain tagged metadata to consider them as appropriate for a particular research context.

In our approach, we suggest a weighted sum model as a simple multi-criteria decision making method for selecting relevant ontologies out of a list of classified available ontologies, shown in Eq. (2).

$$
\begin{aligned}
&score(ontology, dataset) \\
&= \sum_{c_i \in Context(dataset)} \omega_{ontology}(c_i) \cdot isMatch\left(value_{ontology}(c_i), value_{dataset}(c_i)\right) \\
&\text{with } isMatch\left(value_{ontology}(c_i), value_{dataset}(c_i)\right) \\
&= \begin{cases} 1 & value_{ontology}(c_i) = value_{dataset}(c_i) \\ 0 & \text{otherwise} \end{cases}
\end{aligned}
\tag{2}
$$

Based on that, an ontology selection component can return all ontologies related to the provided context whose score value exceed a predefined threshold. If no score value exceeds the threshold, an empty list will be returned, thus, the further input form will not be adaptive and not offer additional input fields.

3.3   Form Generation

The previously provided ontology selection is used to build the adaptive section of the input form, which we will refer to as ontology-based form building.

In an ideal case, the structured OWL representation of an ontology can automatically be processed to generate an input interface for its provided classes and properties (Code generation through model transformation [7]). However, in practice it turns out, that a direct reuse of ontology representations is not feasible and that an additional presentation specification is needed.

Domain-specific ontologies are usually developed with focus on modeling knowledge about certain concepts, not necessarily with focus on data acquisition. The structure and content of the ontologies can vary greatly. Furthermore, ontologies might contain classes and properties irrelevant for describing research data. However, it is difficult to automate the process to decide which classes and properties are relevant. Instead, this decision should ideally be made in consultation with an expert of the respective domain. Additionally, it might be necessary to describe further layout, order, nesting and repetition possibilities for a certain property.

As existing approaches are not applicable in this scenario, we rely on a separately introduced representation of ontologies for presentation and reusability purposes, called *OnForm*, which is described in more detail in [6]. *OnForm* specifications for an ontology are also represented in an RDF format and can be read and interpreted by an *OnForm* generation component. For details on the detailed form generation process, we refer to the corresponding publication.

3.4   Metadata Acquisition

After generating a form user interface based on an *OnForm* description, a user can then enter context-specific information into the form fields that will be stored as metadata to describe this research data.

The input elements can make use of additional information provided by the respective ontology, such as an *rdf:type* or *rdfs:range* constraint, in order to render input elements with assistance, entity lookup and auto-completion functionality to increase the user interface experience, hide on a technical level semantic persistent identifiers from the user and nevertheless collect structured, unambiguous information [10].

3.5   Metadata Persistence

Following the completion of an adaptive research data submission form, a serialized metadata description has to be created based on the provided form input data. Using established semantic technologies, this process can then be done in a straight-forward fashion as the user interface itself is already based on RDF classes and properties with corresponding identifiers. The provided values by the user will be taken by a persistency component and stored in a common RDF serialization format such as RDF/XML, JSON-LD or Turtle.

4   Prototypical Design

Based on the concept presented in the previous section and our sample application scenario from Sect. 2, we designed a prototypical CARDINAL application for Creating an Adaptive Research Data Description Interface that applies Linked Data properties and concepts based on existing ontologies.

It realizes an adaptive web form, that is divided in a straight-forward fashion into three sections as depicted in Fig. 4. Each serves a distinct purpose. The first section requires users to provide general literal administrative and citational metadata. The second section requests additional common meta information that constitutes the basis for contextualizing the research data-specific further part of the web form. The third section is then built adaptively depending on the selected *OnForm* ontology.

In this simple form, the user does not have to provide the research data itself or any reference to it, as we do not focus on automated classification and knowledge extraction methods in this paper.

In order to select appropriate attributes for the contextualization section, we carefully reviewed existing user interfaces of established research data repository providers, namely the research data submission forms from *Zenodo, Research-Gate, Mendeley Data, Dataverse* and *B2SHARE*. In all of these application, a dedicated input field for *keywords* and the *file type* is already established and users are used to provide this additional information. Additionally, we add the *research area* as another contextual attribute as this information might be directly related to existing vocabularies established by dedicated communities.

In order to limit the value range of these contextual attributes to mappable characteristics of existing ontologies, we rely on existing classifications schemes for these attribute values. As a basis for suggesting research areas, a comparison of existing librarian classification systems focusing on scientific publications was done. As a result, the German/Dutch Basisklassifikation (BK) was used, which offered a number of 48 main classes and was already available in a structured RDF description, which made it simple to integrate the provided research area resource URI into a meta description. For the file type, our review also resulted in a set of typical data types for our demonstrator, containing *Audio, Code/-Software, Document, Image, Model, Tabular Data, Text,* and *Video* similar to the recommended list for *DCMITypes*. We excluded common generic data types such as *Dataset* or *Publication*, as their usage for contextualization was considered limited. The scope of allowed keywords is difficult to limit in practice. As we focus on identifiable concepts with a persistent mappable identifier, we added an auto-suggestion feature to the keyword input element which retrieves keyword suggestions from a an appropriate terminology, such as *DBpedia*[8], Wikidata[9] and the *WordNet*[10] dump.

Available domain-specific ontologies were retrieved from ontology catalogs, such as *Linked Open Vocabularies (LOV)*[11]. The retrievable ontologies are already tagged with basic category labels that were considered for the ontology selection process in the CARDINAL prototype, in such a way, that we curated a list of relevant ontologies and stored for each of these ontologies a context definition, attribute weight and *OnForm description* as a basic application configuration.

We followed our introductory scenario example and added an *OnForm* representation of the *DISCO* ontology[12] together with matching for research data with keywords, such as *Survey* or *Questionnaire* and a data type *tabular data* or *text*, independent of the research area. Similar rules can, of course, also be defined for other usage scenarios, e.g., for applying a multimedia ontology to describe an *image, video* or *3d model*.

---

[8] https://dbpedia.org/sparql.
[9] https://query.wikidata.org/.
[10] https://wordnet.princeton.edu/.
[11] https://lov.linkeddata.es/dataset/lov/vocabs.
[12] http://purl.org/net/vsr/onf/desc/survey.

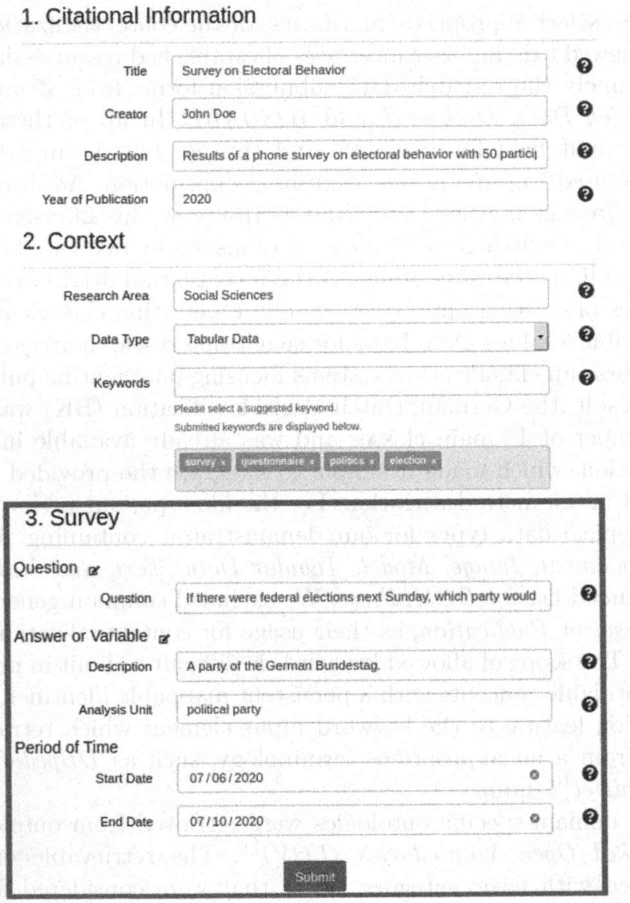

1. Citational Information

Title	Survey on Electoral Behavior
Creator	John Doe
Description	Results of a phone survey on electoral behavior with 50 partici
Year of Publication	2020

2. Context

Research Area	Social Sciences
Data Type	Tabular Data
Keywords	

Please select a suggested keyword.
Submited keywords are displayed below.

survey ×   questionnaire ×   politics ×   election ×

3. Survey

Question

| Question | If there were federal elections next Sunday, which party would |

Answer or Variable

| Description | A party of the German Bundestag. |
| Analysis Unit | political party |

Period of Time

| Start Date | 07 / 06 / 2020 |
| End Date | 07 / 10 / 2020 |

Submit

Fig. 4. Exemplary user interface for a generated adaptive web form

After a user fills out and submits the generated form, all form data is stored and provided in Turtle as an RDF serialization format for download. An example is given in Fig. 5. We emphasize, that the information in the highlighted section is additionally gathered by the adaptive CARDINAL approach in comparison to traditional research data submission forms.

```
 1  @prefix dc: <http://purl.org/dc/elements/1.1/>
 2  @prefix dcterms: <http://purl.org/dc/terms/>
 3  @prefix dctype: <http://purl.org/dc/dcmitype/>
 4  @prefix dbr: <http://dbpedia.org/resource/>
 5  @prefix disco: <http://rdf-vocabulary.ddialliance.org/discovery#>
 6  @prefix ex: <http://www.example.org/>
 7
 8  ex:dataset1
 9      dc:title        "Survey on Electoral Behavior";
10      dc:creator:     "John Doe";
11      dc:description  """Results of a phone survey on electoral behavior with 50 participants""";
12      dc:date         "2020";
13      dct:DCMIType    dctype:Text;
14      dc:subject      dbr:Social_Sciences, dbr:Survey_(human_research), dbr:Questionnaire, dbr:Politics, dbr:Election.
15
16      rdf:type        disco:Questionnaire ;
17      disco:question [
18          rdf:type        disco:Question ;
19          disco:questionText """If there were federal elections next Sunday, which party would you give your vote?"""
20          disco:variable [
21              rdf:type        disco:Variable;
22              disco:description "A party of the German Bundestag." ;
23              disco:analysisUnit "political party"^^disco:AnalysisUnit.
24          ];
25          disco:temporal [
26              rdf:type        disco:PeriodOfTime;
27              ns2:startDate "2020-07-06"^^xsd:date ;
28              ns2:endDate "2020-07-10"^^xsd:date .
29          ];
```

Fig. 5. Exemplary metadata export result in Turtle

5   Evaluation

In order to evaluate our proposed approach, we implemented the designed prototype from Sect. 4 as a proof-of-concept[13] in *Python* based in a straight-forward
fashion on *Django*, *Bootstrap* and *rdflib*.

The demonstrator was then used in an unsupervised online study which contained a web-based survey experiment. The guiding research question for the
survey was, if users provide additional and more specific descriptive research
metadata with limited effort in comparison to a traditional static form-based
approach. We therefore used an A/B test and users had the option to skip irrelevant sections of the presented web form. Our hypothesis was, that users will be
willing to provide additional information as long as this is comprehensive and relevant for them. The survey was realized with *LimeSurvey*[14] and distributed via
university mailing lists and the platform *SurveyCircle*[15]. Based on the objectives
defined in Sect. 2, the online study had the purpose to analyze the feasibility
and acceptance of an adaptive input form approach. We were therefore especially
interested in the extent of the acquired metadata and its data quality characteristics, additional user effort reflected by the time to complete the form as well
as occurring usability issues.

The study was based on a given fictitious initial scenario, similar to Sect. 2. It
was provided to all study participants at the beginning of the survey description
in German or English.

The participants were randomly divided into two groups. The participants of
group A were given a traditional static submission form which did not contain
an additional research data context-specific section whereas the participants of

---

[13] http://purl.org/net/vsr/onf/onform.

[14] https://bildungsportal.sachsen.de/umfragen/limesurvey/index.php/877377.

[15] https://www.surveycircle.com/.

group B saw the adaptive submission form with an additional dynamic form section based on their contextual selection. After participants completed the input procedure, they were asked to fill out a System Usability Score (SUS) questionnaire to evaluate the usability of the system.

The survey took place without incentives over a period of one month between July 2020 - August 2020 and reached 83 participants with 74 full responses[16]. The majority of our participants assigned their primary field of knowledge to Economics (38), Psychology (15) and Social ScienceS (7), but the target group also contained participants from the field of Engineering & Computer Science (6), Medicine (2), and other disciplines with varying age and experience level. 35 participants were assigned to version A, thus, the static submission form, and 39 participants were assigned to version B, the adaptive submission form.

5.1   Acquired Metadata

For test group B, the entered general information from the study participants was used to identify a suitable ontology together with a corresponding *OnForm* description and to display additional input fields in a separate form section to the user. Based on the provided input data, we evaluated the extent, to which the contextualization step worked as expected and if additional metadata was actually entered by the adaptive test group B in comparison to the reference group A.

Identifying a context based on the provided keywords worked very well. Within the experiment, we relied on *WordNet* as a data source and compared the entered keywords with it. A total of 115 keywords were provided. 86 out of 115 keywords were selected from suggestions, so that internally the user input could be mapped to a corresponding resource URI successfully. Surprisingly, explicitly providing a data type for the given scenario was unexpectedly challenging for the participants. Although the scenario description stated to publish an *Excel spreadsheet*, only 23 users actually selected the tabular data option, whereas other participants selected Document (6), Text (6) or even Audio (4). Especially in the last case, the form did not adapt as intended to the context of questionnaire data. In the following form section, participants were then able to specify information based on the context-related *DISCO* ontology. Figure 6 shows which of these input fields participants completed or skipped. A question text was provided by 33 participants. The field for "Analysis Unit" was skipped the most with only 26 participants specifying a value, which might originate in the ambiguous label provided by the ontology and could be resolved easily in the future.

Only two participants decided to skip the second form section entirely.

5.2   User Effort

Additionally, we measured Time to Completion. The adaptive form consisted of 12 fields compared to 4 fields of the static form – therefore, we expected that

---

[16] https://doi.org/10.5281/zenodo.4439700.

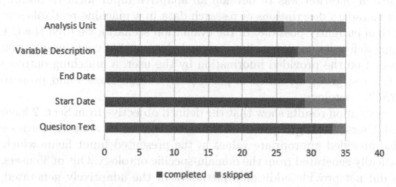

Fig. 6. Number of participants in test group B that provided additional descriptive metadata

the completion time would approximately triple as well, which turned out to be correct as shown in Table 1.

Table 1. Completion times for static form (A) and adaptive form (B)

	Min time	Max time	Avg time
Group A	16 s	314 s	101 s
Group B	58 s	1084 s	286 s

We want to point out explicitly the enhancement, that the adaptive approach will only display input elements to the user that are worth to consider in comparison to an input form which simply displays all imaginable input elements to a user.

5.3 Usability Assessment

We used a System Usability Score (SUS) questionnaire as introduced by Brooke to assess usability [2]. The static form thereby received an average SUS score of 72 (standard deviation 15.88) and the adaptive form a score of 58 (standard deviation 16.95). According to the Sauro-Lewis curved grading scale for the SUS, the static form is located in the 60–64 percentile range and the adaptive form is located in the 15–34 percentile range [14]. In terms of scores, the static form achieved a score of C+, far exceeding the adaptive form, which is rated D. This indicates a below-average user-friendliness.

5.4   Summary and Discussion of Evaluation Results

Our research question was to develop an adaptive input form to obtain more detailed metadata descriptions of research data in a machine-readable semantic format than currently possible. In the evaluation scenario, we used the CARDI-NAL approach to let users describe a research dataset that contains questionnaire data. Based on the provided information by the user, a matching ontology was selected in test group B, which in particularly reused classes and properties of the (*DISCO*) ontology.

The evaluation results show that the defined objective from Sect. 2 have been achieved. Users in test group B did not only work with an adaptive form section; they also provided appropriate values in the presented input fields which were automatically generated from the domain-specific ontology. Out of 35 users, only 2 users did not provide additional metadata in the adaptively generated form section. That means that in 94% of all submission procedures, our approach has led to an improved metadata description of the research data (OBJ1). Our approach requires users to specify additional context metadata to contextualize research data. 31 out of 35 users got a relevant ontology displayed in the adaptive form section based on their specified data type (OBJ2). The classes and properties of the presented ontologies are domain-specific and suitable for describing additional research characteristics (OBJ3). Nevertheless, usability problems do still exist (OBJ4). Users are able to use the adaptive description form efficiently and effectively, but they are evidently not satisfied with it. According to user feedback, this is mostly due to labels and help texts that are incomprehensible to some. We consider this mainly as a UI problem in our CARDINAL prototype. Therefore, focus should be put on improving usability in the future. The provided form input is offered to the user as a json-ld metadata export for download after clicking on the form submit button. This is a functional feature realized in the CARDINAL demonstrator (OBJ5).

6   Related Work

In the field of human-computer interaction, research is conducted on context-aware computing and context-aware software. Schilit et al. [15] use the term in reference to mobile computing by mainly focusing on the physical environment of devices. They state that context-awareness software can be implemented by using simple if-then rules. In contrast, Schmidt et al. [16] argue that the term context refers to more than just the physical environment. They classify contexts into two categories: human factors and physical environment.

There are various suggestions to define the term adaptivity. Preim and Dachselt [13] distinguish three types of adaptivity wrt. the experience of users, perceptual skills and work environments. At present, there are no research data repositories that adapt to the context of a research data artifact. However, a few approaches have been proposed that show how adaptive user interfaces can be designed. Baclawski and Schneider implemented an approach for using ontologies to describe data [1] by annotating their research data with additional metadata.

However, their system relies heavily on user expertise. Users are required to determine themselves which ontology is most suitable for their research data. A similar initial situation is described by Cimino and Ayres [3].

Besides using ontologies to describe data in more detail, Gonçalves et al. have shown an approach on how ontologies can be used to generate web forms. They introduced an "ontology-based method for web form generation and structured data acquisition" [5]. Their system requires two input files to generate a web form which is used to digitize a standardized questionnaire. Firstly, an XML file is used to configure the form layout, as well as bindings of user interface components to entities within the ontology. Secondly, a form specification is used to define the actual content of the form. Paulheim and Probst created an extensive state of the art survey on ontology-enhanced user interfaces [12]. An ontology-enhanced user interface is defined as "a user interface whose visualization capabilities, interaction possibilities, or development process are enabled or (at least) improved by the employment of one or more ontologies".

Although there are currently no research data repositories that employ adaptive user interfaces as defined in this section, the use of adaptive user interfaces can be advantageous to provide users with means to describe their research data in more detail, specifically by using domain-specific terminology. These user interfaces should adapt to the context of a user's research data artifact. With regard to the definition of adaptivity according to Preim and Dachselt, this corresponds in the broadest sense to the adaptivity type with regard to the physical environment. However, we instead refer to the contextual environment of research data and not to the physical environment as in the original definition. As exemplary case studies of [1,3,5] show, emphasis should be placed on data interoperability. For this purpose, ontologies for describing the structure and semantics of data proved to be useful. In contrast to approaches that statically add entity classes and value ranges from particular ontologies to dedicated application input elements, such as [18], the CARDINAL approach is more flexible and provides a dynamic, application-independent adaptive ontology selection mechanism.

7 Conclusion

In this paper, we focused on the description step in research data publishing processes and discussed CARDINAL: an adaptive ontology-based form building approach based on existing, domain-specific ontologies in order to provide research data descriptions with additional context-related structured meta information. By considering general contextual information for the semi-automated selection of relevant ontologies, we relieve the user from filling out extensive research data submission forms with input elements that are not relevant at all as well as the developer who had to manually craft detailed input forms in the past. The additionally acquisitioned metadata can facilitate the interdisciplinary findability and reuse of existing research data based on Linked Data.

We implemented our suggested CARDINAL approach, demonstrated it as a proof-of-concept and additionally evaluated the solution based on an online survey experiment with 83 participants. The results of our user study proved that the prototype could successfully be used for obtaining more detailed metadata descriptions. The results also showed that our prototype fulfills all predefined requirements apart from usability weaknesses, where the survey results already disclosed some issues. We additionally learnt in the evaluation, that the quality of the contextualization depends both on the availability of appropriately tagged ontology classifications, but also on the correct user input for the selection criteria, which was not always given.

As future work, it is necessary to further improve the user interface experience as well as to provide further *OnForm* descriptions for existing domain-specific ontologies. Furthermore, it makes sense to investigate more deeply possibilities to semi-automatically create these *OnForm* representations by applying more sophisticated ontology classification algorithms, property relevance metrics and knowledge extraction methods.

Acknowledgment. This work was funded by the Deutsche Forschungsgemeinschaft (DFG, German Research Foundation) – Project-ID 416228727 – SFB 1410.

References

1. Baclawski, K., Schneider, T.: The open ontology repository initiative: requirements and research challenges. In: Proceedings of Workshop on Collaborative Construction, Management and Linking of Structured Knowledge, ISWC (2009)
2. Brooke, J.: Sus: a quick and dirty usability scale. Usability Evaluation in Industry, vol. 189, November 1995
3. Cimino, J., Ayres, E.: The clinical research data repository of the us national institutes of health. Stud. Health Technol. Inform. **160**, 1299–1303 (2010)
4. Elsevier: Sharing research data (2021). https://www.elsevier.com/authors/author-resources/research-data
5. Gonçalves, R., Tu, S., Nyulas, C., Tierney, M., Musen, M.: An ontology-driven tool for structured data acquisition using web forms. J. Biomed. Semant. **8**(1), 1–14 (2017)
6. Göpfert, C., Langer, A., Gaedke, M.: Ontoform: deriving web input forms from ontologies. In: Web Engineering - 21th International Conference, ICWE 2021, Biarritz, France, May 18–21, 2021, Proceedings. Currently Under Review. Lecture Notes in Computer Science, Springer (2021)
7. Hemel, Z., Kats, L.C., Groenewegen, D.M., Visser, E.: Code generation by model transformation: a case study in transformation modularity. Softw. Syst. Model. **9**(3), 375–402 (2010)
8. Langer, A.: PIROL: cross-domain research data publishing with linked data technologies. In: La Rosa, M., Plebani, P., Reichert, M. (eds.) Proceedings of the Doctoral Consortium Papers Presented at the 31st CAiSE 2019, pp. 43–51. CEUR, Rome (2019)
9. Langer, A., Bilz, E., Gaedke, M.: Analysis of current RDM applications for the interdisciplinary publication of research data. In: CEUR Workshop Proceedings, vol. 2447. CEUR-WS.org (2019)

10. Langer, A., Göpfert, C., Gaedke, M.: URI-aware user input interfaces for the unobtrusive reference to Linked Data. IADIS International Journal on Computer Science and Information Systems, vol. 13, no. 2 (2018)
11. Pampel, H., Vierkant, P., Scholze, F., et al.: Making research data repositories visible: the re3data.org registry. Plos One **8**(11), 1–10 (2013)
12. Paulheim, H., Probst, F.: Ontology-enhanced user interfaces: a survey. Int. J. Seman. Web Inf. Syst. **6**, 36–59 (2010)
13. Preim, B., Dachselt, R.: Interaktive Systeme. Springer, Heidelberg (2010). https://doi.org/10.1007/978-3-642-05402-0
14. Sauro, J., Lewis, J.R.: Quantifying the User Experience, Second Edition: Practical Statistics for User Research, vol. 38. Morgan Kaufmann, Burlington (2016)
15. Schilit, B., Adams, N., Want, R.: Context-aware computing applications. In: 1994 First Workshop on Mobile Computing Systems and Applications, pp. 85–90 (1994)
16. Schmidt, A., Beigl, M., Gellersen, H.W.: There is more to context than location. Comput. Graph. **23**(6), 893–901 (1999)
17. Wilkinson, M.D., Dumontier, M., Aalbersberg, I.J., et al.: The fair guiding principles for scientific data management and stewardship. Sci. Data **3**(1), 160018 (2016)
18. Wolstencroft, K., Owen, S., Horridge, M., et al.: RightField: embedding ontology annotation in spreadsheets. Bioinformatics **27**(14), 2021–2022 (2011)

Publishing Base Registries as Linked Data Event Streams

Dwight Van Lancker[1,3]($\boxtimes$), Pieter Colpaert[1]($\boxtimes$), Harm Delva[1],
Brecht Van de Vyvere[1], Julián Rojas Meléndez[1], Ruben Dedecker[1],
Philippe Michiels[2], Raf Buyle[1,3], Annelies De Craene[3], and Ruben Verborgh[1]

[1] IDLab, Department of Electronics and Information Systems,
Ghent University–Imec, Ghent, Belgium
{dwight.vanlancker,pieter.colpaert,harm.delva,brecht.vandevyvere,
julianandres.rojasmelendez,ruben.dedecker,raf.buyle,ruben.verborgh}@ugent.be
[2] Imec EDiT, Leuven, Belgium
philippe.michiels.ext@imec.be
[3] Flemish Information Agency, Flanders, Belgium
annelies.decraene@vlaanderen.be

Abstract. Fostering interoperability, Public Sector Bodies (PSBs) maintain datasets that should become queryable as an integrated Knowledge Graph (KG). While some PSBs allow to query a part of the KG on their servers, others favor publishing data dumps allowing the querying to happen on third party servers. As the budget of a PSB to publish their dataset on the Web is finite, PSBs need guidance on what interface to offer first. A core API can be designed that covers the core tasks of Base Registries, which is a well-defined term in Flanders for the management of authoritative datasets. This core API should be the basis on which an ecosystem of data services can be built. In this paper, we introduce the concept of a Linked Data Event Stream (LDES) for datasets like air quality sensors and observations or a registry of officially registered addresses. We show that extra ecosystem requirements can be built on top of the LDES using a generic fragmenter. By using hypermedia for describing the LDES as well as the derived datasets, agents can dynamically discover their best way through the KG, and server administrators can dynamically add or remove functionality based on costs and needs. This way, we allow PSBs to prioritize API functionality based on three tiers: (i) the LDES, (ii) intermediary indexes and (iii) querying interfaces. While the ecosystem will never be feature-complete, based on the market needs, PSBs as well as market players can fill in gaps as requirements evolve.

Keywords: Semantic web · Web Apis · Data reuse · Data versioning

1 Introduction

Public Sector Bodies (PSBs) world-wide maintain and open up reference datasets to foster interoperability by advocating the reuse of the identifiers for which

M. Brambilla et al. (Eds.): ICWE 2021, LNCS 12706, pp. 28–36, 2021.
https://doi.org/10.1007/978-3-030-74296-6_3

they are the authoritative source. In Flanders, for example, the Large-scale Reference Database[1] (LRD) contains millions of geospatial objects in the Flemish region [2]. On the one hand, the LRD publishes periodical data dumps or version materializations, which users have to fully download to stay up to date with the dataset. With a querying API, on the other hand, users can query the dataset without first having to download the entire dataset. Trying to meet the needs of their reusers, PSBs will have to provide and maintain an increasing amount of such querying APIs as specific end-user features are solved by creating feature-specific APIs [7]. However both data dumps and querying APIs will never fully meet the needs of their end-users, as a data dump gives a possibly outdated view on the dataset, whereas a querying API provides its client only with a partial view of the dataset.

To avoid synchronization problems with data dumps on the one hand, and maintenance problems of an always increasing amount of querying APIs on the other, trade-offs need to be made. This resulted in the question: "**What is the base API for base registries?**". PSBs must accept they will not be able to implement any querying API on their own, but that there are other organizations with other interests that can take up parts of the processing. In Sect. 2 we discuss the definition of the European term "base registry", the ideas behind Linked Data Fragments and the recent initiative of Streaming Linked Data on which our approach was inspired. In Sect. 3 we design a Linked Data Event Stream (LDES) incrementally by first making sure everyone can download the history and retrieve the latest updates on the data collection. In Sect. 4 we then introduce three generic open-source building blocks for a FAIR [10] ecosystem, where also third parties can build reusable indexes on top of an LDES. Finally we discuss in Sect. 5 the three tiers of base registry management, creating a vision for PSBs to set the priorities when deciding upon their next API.

2 Related Work

The term *base registry* was introduced by the European Commission and is defined as a trusted and authoritative source of information, which can and should be digitally re-used by others. A single organization is responsible and accountable for the collection, use, updating and preservation of information. Authoritative in this context means that a base registry is considered to be the source of information and is thus up-to-date and of the highest quality[2]. In order to publish its base registries for maximum reuse on the Web, the Flemish Information Agency (FIA) embraces Linked Data with the Flemish Interoperability Program called Open Standards for Linked Organizations (OSLO). OSLO develops unambiguous data standards to exchange data in an uniform way [1].

---

[1] https://overheid.vlaanderen.be/en/producten-diensten/large-scale-reference-database-lrd.

[2] http://eurlex.europa.eu/resource.html?uri=cellar:2c2f2554-0faf-11e7-8a35-01aa75ed71a1.0017.02/DOC_1&format=PDF p. 31–32.

The FIA has aligned its base registries with the definition as stated by the European Commission, but extended it with three additional requirements: (i) Base registries are part of a semantic system of uniform identified objects and relations which are in line with the OSLO standards; (ii) The identifiers of objects in a base registry should be re-used in other base registries (or datasets); and (iii) Each base registry is obliged to have life-cycle and history management of their objects [2]. This extended definition is considered to be the *core task* of a base registry.

Today, data controllers publish their data through a querying API, such as the Open Geospatial Consortium (OGC)[3] APIs for example. These APIs build upon the legacy of OGC Web Service standards, of which WFS and WMS are the most known. Although the WFS is a standardised – technical - protocol, it does not provide interoperable data. At the moment, it is impossible to use a dataset described with the principles of Linked Data as a data source in a WFS service, although recent efforts have been made [3]. Furthermore, the processing done by such a service happens fully on the server side, meaning that all costs are for the provider of it.

Instead of publishing their data through a querying API, data controllers also have the possibility to publish a data dump of the dataset. Both interfaces have in common that they only return a *fragment* of the dataset. Given a Linked Data dataset, the result of each request to such interfaces is called a Linked Data Fragment (LDF)[4]. On the axis of LDFs, both data dumps and querying APIs are situated at the extremes, because the workload needed to compute the fragments is divided differently between clients and servers. In the case of a data dump, the processing burden is put on the client-side, but also allows the most flexibility for the client. In the other case, providing a querying API on top of the dataset puts the processing burden on the server, allowing any kind of query and therefore limiting the availability of the API, i.e. a SPARQL endpoint. In order to achieve efficient Web querying, in-between solutions that provide an optimal balance between client and server effort are needed [8]. In-between solutions exist, such as Triple Patterns Fragments, brTPF, Smart KG and subject pages. These in-between solutions shift the needed processing more towards the client and limit the different queries that can be executed on the server.

Publishing data at a high speed has caused a shift in the data landscape, as such that it does not always make sense anymore to use polling-based approaches. Instead, it makes more sense to push this fast-changing (with an acceptable latency of ≤ 10 s), continuously updating dataset to its consumers [9]. In order to manage these streams of data, Stream Processing Engines have come to aid [6]. To counter the problem that a data stream can be in all shapes and sizes, an effort was needed by the Web of Data community. This led to the creation of RDF Stream Processing techniques, which allows to process RDF-based data streams. These ideas were already applied on non-sensor related datasets such

---

[3] https://ogcapi.ogc.org/.
[4] https://linkeddatafragments.org/.

as DBPedia and Wikimedia, where the goal was to query of the latest changes, with the term Streaming Linked Data [6]. However, more general the goal should be to provide the ability to query over a window of updates on top of a stream, which is similar to our goal, as we want to provide everyone as fast as possible with the latest updates.

3   A Base API for Base Registries

A Linked Data Event Stream (LDES) extends the principles of an event stream by publishing interoperable data re-using existing machine-readable data standards. We applied this data publishing strategy to two datasets: for context information, we used the registry of all officially registered addresses in Flanders, using the OSLO data standard[5] to describe them. For a faster updating dataset, we used measurements of air quality sensors, using the Semantic Sensor Network Ontology.

```
<C>  a ldes:EventStream  ;
     tree:shape <shacl.shape>  ;
     tree:member <Observation1> .

<Observation1> a sosa:Observation  ;
     sosa:resultTime "2020..."  ;
     sosa:hasSimpleResult "1" .
```

Listing 1.1: Linked Data Event Streams described with the TREE hypermedia API specification

To describe LDESs, we used a hypermedia specification, called the TREE Hypermedia API specification[6]. Using a hypermedia specification to describe event streams, makes them self-descriptive. There is not really a definition of what an event stream exactly is, which means, in order to replicate the event stream, the links have to be followed. The TREE specification describes an LDES as a `ldes:EventStream` which is an extension of `tree:Collection`, containing not only a collection of objects, but each object is also immutable. Each immutable object, defined as a `tree:member`, has a timestamp that indicates at which time it was created. Furthermore, with `tree:shape` the specification allows to link a SHACL shape [4] to the collection, indicating the content of the immutable objects. The presence of such a SHACL shape is rather an optimization so that autonomous agents know beforehand what the content of the immutable objects is within the collection. An example of the specification is shown in Listing 1.1 and was also applied to air quality observations: https://streams.datapiloten.be/observations.

However when implementing an LDES for data models that do not have the concept of things that live in time, the model must be extended, which is the case for an address or a sensor. It is possible for a sensor to change, take for

---

[5] https://data.vlaanderen.be/ns/adres.
[6] https://treecg.github.io/specification/.

example the Bel-Air project[7] in Flanders, where air quality sensor were fitted to the roof of mail delivery vans. So periodically, not only the observation made by a sensor changes, but it is also possible that the location of a sensor has changed. The stated problem can be solved by using the concept of versions, for example `dcterms:isVersionOf`, as shown in Listing 1.2. This way, we indicate to which object this version belongs. The Dutch NEN3610 standard[8] for example advocates the use of `foaf:isPrimaryTopicOf`. Furthermore, uniquely identifying each version object, makes them individual reusable.

```
<C> a ldes:EventStream  ;
    tree:shape <shacl.shape>  ;
    tree:member <E1> .

<E1> prov:generatedAtTime "2020-01-01T00:00:00Z"  ;
     adms:versionNote "First version of this address"  ;
     dcterms:isVersionOf <AddressRecord1>  ;
     dcterms:title "Streetname X, ZIP Municipality, Country" .
```

Listing 1.2: When a data model does not have the concept of things that live in time, the model must be extended, for example, with the concept of versions. Here, `dcterms:isVersionOf` is used to indicate which address object is affected by this event.

Furthermore, the TREE Hypermedia API specification was also used to describe the metadata of each page. With `tree:relation`, the specification enables users to describe the relation between a specific value and all members on a page linked from the current page. Using this relation, a query agent can automatically discover whether or not it is useful to go to the next page. An interesting fragmentation strategy for an event stream is time-based as the data grows in time. As shown in Listing 1.3, the first page, which always contains the oldest objects, has a `tree:GreaterThanOrEqualToRelation` with the second page, which indicates that all values of page two are greater than or equal to those of page 1. To indicate on what property of the immutable object the relation is based on, the predicate `tree:path` is used. The predicate `tree:value` then contains the value for which all members on the next page are greater than or equal to. In Listing 1.3, `sosa:resultTime` is the property that the relation is based on, and thus all members on `?page=2` have a `sosa:resultTime` that is later than or equal to 2020-12-24T12:00:00Z. The LDES specification is available at https://w3id.org/ldes/specification.

---

[7] https://www.imeccityofthings.be/en/projecten/bel-air.
[8] https://geonovum.github.io/NEN3610-Linkeddata/.

```
<?page=1> a tree:Node ;
          tree:relation [
              a tree:GreaterThanOrEqualToRelation ;
              tree:path sosa:resultTime ;
              tree:node <?page=2> ;
              tree:value "2020-12-24T12:00:00Z"^^xsd:dateTime .
          ] .
```

Listing 1.3: Within the TREE Hypermedia API specification, a relation to another page can be described with `tree:relation`.

4   A Linked Data Event Streams Ecosystem

We implemented three reusable building blocks:

The metadata extractor can be used to read TREE metadata in a page and show the next steps possible from the current page to an app or an intermediary server. The extractor has been written within the Comunica framework [5] and is available at https://github.com/TREEcg/comunica-feature-tree/.

The LDES client reuses the metadata extractor to allow intermediary servers to copy all members of a `tree:Collection`, and subscribe to new updates. A fragment's time to live is retained from its HTTP caching headers. A polling interval can be configured to wait before refetching. Specifically for an LDES, before emitting an immutable member of a collection, a cache can be checked to check whether the object has not been emitted before. This way, consumers only retrieve updated members of a collection. Code is available at https://github.com/brechtvdv/event-stream-client.

The fragmenter reuses the LDES client to keep its own copy in sync and to refragment the LDES based on a configuration. Code is available at https://github.com/hdelva/tree_index.

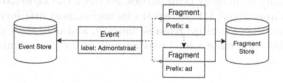

Fig. 1. A schematic overview of the fragmentation process. Values from each individual event are used to place that event into one or more fragments. In this example, the event represents a street labeled as "Admontstraat", and this label is used as the input of a prefix-based fragmenter. The logical links between increasingly specific prefixes are stored in a separate storage layer, which is used to generate the hypermedia descriptions. The events themselves are stored like regular RDF data, and the contents of a fragment are persisted as a set of event URIs.

Applications that require a specific subset of the data can be optimized by consuming only the most relevant data for their use case. For instance, applications that focus on a specific geospatial region are more likely to reuse the published data if they can filter out data from other regions.

To realize this, we have implemented an intermediary server that (re)fragments an existing LDES into multiple smaller ones[9]. Every discovered immutable object is assigned to one or more fragments, as illustrated in Fig. 1. An LDES may be processed using multiple fragmentation strategies, resulting in multiple orthogonal fragmentations, and some strategies can yield multiple fragments for a single event. In the latter case, the fragments can be ordered by increasing specificity such as by prefix length or geospatial granularity. These relations between fragments are stored separately from the events themselves, and are used to generate the hypermedia controls.

5 Conclusion and Future Work

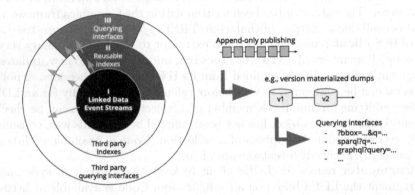

Fig. 2. The three layered shield of base registry data publishing: the core (I) is what must be done by PSBs; the second layer (II) as well as the third layer (III) can be done PSBs, but can equally be done by third parties. As tier 2 can be derived from tier 1 by anyone, and tier 3 from 2 and 1, base registry managers must first focus on the Linked Data Event Stream, then prioritize reusable indexes, and only then prioritize specific querying APIs. This will create a level playing field for an ecosystem of data services on top of this dataset.

With Linked Data Event Streams, this paper sets out a vision regarding the core task of a PSB when publishing a base registry. The LDES, which is an append-only publishing interface, is the last interface that must be removed when austerity would strike. In Fig. 2, a conceptual three layered shield illustrating the entire ecosystem sets out the next priorities. The PSB can bootstrap the ecosystem by building reusable indexes on top of their LDES by using the TREE indexer. This way, consumers – which can be both the PSB itself or third parties – can more efficiently create querying interfaces on top the dataset. When a third party for example needs an OGC API for geospatial querying, a geospatial

---

[9] For example, a prefix fragmentation applied to the LDES of streetnames: https://fast-and-slow.osoc.be/data/streetname/prefix.

fragmentation will allow that third party to fetch the right parts of the dataset just in time, blurring the lines between replication, prefetching and cacheable querying. Compared to the in-between solutions discussed in the related work, an LDES can be used as a basis to create these solutions.

An LDES and its reusable indexes are self-descriptive thanks to the TREE Hypermedia Specification. Every page becomes part of a tree structure, and clients, such as the LDES client or Comunica, can traverse the tree to answer certain queries. Multiple trees or indexes can be traversed in parallel, and the fastest interface for a specific task can by dynamically selected. This makes the ecosystem as a whole more resilient: there are always multiple paths to answer a certain query, in worst case having to replicate the core LDES. Contrary to the core LDES API, derived indexes can evolve faster: when a better geospatial indexes has been thought of, the old geospatial index can be taken offline without any problem.

Future work is to fully implement the TREE specification within the Comunica [5] framework to perform among others SPARQL, GraphQL-LD and auto-completion queries across Linked Data Fragments datasets. Query optimization combining interfaces such as TPF [8] and various TREE views and collections will be a challenge for the coming years.

References

1. Buyle, R., et al.: Open standards for linked organizations. In: Proceedings of the International Conference on Electronic Governance and Open Society: Challenges in Eurasia, pp. 126–134 (2016)
2. Buyle, R., et al.: Raising interoperability among base registries: the evolution of the linked base registry for addresses in flanders. J. Web Semant. **55**, 86–101 (2019)
3. Jones, J., Kuhn, W., Keßler, C., Scheider, S.: Making the web of data available via web feature services. In: Huerta, J., Schade, S., Granell, C. (eds.) Connecting a Digital Europe Through Location and Place. LNGC, pp. 341–361. Springer, Cham (2014). https://doi.org/10.1007/978-3-319-03611-3_20
4. Knublauch, H., Kontokostas, D.: Shapes constraint language (SHACL) (2017). W3C recommendation (2017). https://www.w3.org/TR/shacl/#property-paths
5. Taelman, R., Van Herwegen, J., Vander Sande, M., Verborgh, R.: Comunica: a modular SPARQL query engine for the web. In: Vrandečić, D., et al. (eds.) ISWC 2018. LNCS, vol. 11137, pp. 239–255. Springer, Cham (2018). https://doi.org/10.1007/978-3-030-00668-6_15
6. Tommasini, R., Ragab, M., Falcetta, A., Valle, E.D., Sakr, S.: A first step towards a streaming linked data life-cycle. In: Pan, J.Z., et al. (eds.) ISWC 2020. LNCS, vol. 12507, pp. 634–650. Springer, Cham (2020). https://doi.org/10.1007/978-3-030-62466-8_39
7. Verborgh, R., Dumontier, M.: A Web API ecosystem through feature-based reuse. Internet Computing **22**(3), 29–37 (2018). DOI: https://doi.org/10.1109/MIC.2018.032501515,https://ruben.verborgh.org/articles/web-api-ecosystem/
8. Verborgh, R., et al.: Querying datasets on the web with high availability. In: Mika, P., et al. (eds.) ISWC 2014. LNCS, vol. 8796, pp. 180–196. Springer, Cham (2014). https://doi.org/10.1007/978-3-319-11964-9_12

9. Van de Vyvere, B., Colpaert, P., Verborgh, R.: Comparing a polling and push-based approach for live open data interfaces. In: Bielikova, M., Mikkonen, T., Pautasso, C. (eds.) ICWE 2020. LNCS, vol. 12128, pp. 87–101. Springer, Cham (2020). https://doi.org/10.1007/978-3-030-50578-3_7
10. Wilkinson, M.D., et al.: The fair guiding principles for scientific data management and stewardship. Sci. Data **3**(1), 1–9 (2016)

OntoSpect: IoT Ontology Inspection by Concept Extraction and Natural Language Generation

Mahda Noura[✉][ID], Yichen Wang[ID], Sebastian Heil[ID], and Martin Gaedke[ID]

Technische Universität Chemnitz, Chemnitz, Germany
{mahda.noura,sebastian.heil,martin.gaedke}@informatik.tu-chemnitz.de

Abstract. One of the main challenges in the Internet of Things (IoT) is the lack of semantic interoperability between heterogeneous sources. In the Semantic Web domain, ontologies are one way to achieve semantic interoperability by using a common vocabulary that represents heterogeneous sources. However, recent studies have shown that the amount of concept reuse from existing IoT ontologies is low. As the number of IoT ontologies increases, encouraging users to reuse existing ontologies instead of creating new concepts becomes important. Ontology catalogues are a prominent approach to discover and inspect existing ontologies for reuse. However, such catalogues inspect the ontologies using general criteria which is not enough to understand the content of the ontology. In this paper, we propose a method for automatic ontology inspection (OntoSpect) of IoT ontologies from different application domains based on a generic set of content-related concepts. OntoSpect consists of two main steps: first it extracts the set of IoT concepts, and then generates human-understandable descriptions using a Model-driven Engineering (MDE) approach. We evaluate the quality of concept extraction and natural language description generation with 84 ontologies retrieved from the LOV4IoT catalogue and report on quality metrics. In addition, we conduct an empirical study with 28 ontology users to further assess the quality of the generated descriptions. The results demonstrate the capability of OntoSpect to support ontology users inspecting IoT ontologies.

Keywords: Internet of Things · Semantic Web · Ontology · Concept extraction · Model-driven Engineering · Natural Language Generation

1 Introduction

The vision of the Internet of Things (IoT) is to connect all "Things" (radio-frequency identification, sensors, actuators, etc.) to the Internet, allowing a wide range of innovations and opportunities in different application domains. In spite of the massive growth in this domain, currently "developing a single and global ecosystem of Things that communicate with each other seamlessly is virtually

© Springer Nature Switzerland AG 2021
M. Brambilla et al. (Eds.): ICWE 2021, LNCS 12706, pp. 37–52, 2021.
https://doi.org/10.1007/978-3-030-74296-6_4

impossible" [10]. To achieve the vision of IoT, interoperability at different layers is required [9]. Semantic interoperability describes smart devices according to their data, services, and capabilities in machine readable form using a shared vocabulary (a.k.a ontologies). Ontologies allow developers to reuse and share domain knowledge using a common vocabulary across heterogeneous systems, platforms, environments, etc. Numerous ontologies have been proposed to cover the different IoT application domains. According to LOV4IoT[1], there are over 550 ontology-based research projects which have been categorized into more than 29 application domains. Unfortunately, the wide range of ontologies to represent IoT devices and their produced data hinders the efficient development of cross-platform and cross-domain applications [16]. The analysis in [11,12] demonstrates that many of the ontologies found in existing standardization's and different projects have many redundant concepts and properties redesigned.

What are Existing Solutions Towards IoT Ontology Reuse? One way to encourage the reuse of existing ontologies is to provide a common standard vocabulary. Current efforts such as W3C WoT Description[2], and iot.schema.org[3] are dedicated to provide a common vocabulary for the IoT domain. However, the IoT domain still lacks one comprehensive standard ontology. Another method towards ontology reuse is ontology registries, indexes and catalogues such as LOV4IoT, READY4SmartCities[4], LOV[5], and OpenSensingCity[6]. Such ontology catalogues enable discovering, inspecting and selecting an ontology according to a set of criteria. The catalogues make a high contribution towards discovering the distributed ontologies over the Web for reuse.

What are the Limitations of Existing Solutions? The catalogues have facilitated discovering and providing a high-level overview of an ontology, however, for ontology comparison and selection, additional information within the ontology is required. The existing catalogues inspect the ontologies using general criteria such as quality indicators and metadata which is not enough to understand the content of the ontology. Inspecting the main content-related concepts is time-consuming for IoT *developers* and needs interdisciplinary experts. Moreover, the catalogues put a huge effort on the *catalogue maintainers*. When a new ontology is published, the catalogue maintainer has to inspect the ontology manually to identify the required metadata which is time-consuming and subjective.

What are the Information Requirements of IoT Developers when Inspecting Ontologies? Given the wealth of information described in IoT ontologies and the advantages provided by ontology catalogues, the challenge lies in systematically inspecting IoT ontologies from different application domains based on a similar set of content-related concepts with reduced effort. There are many

---

[1] https://lov4iot.appspot.com/.
[2] https://www.w3.org/WoT/.
[3] http://iotschema.org/.
[4] http://smartcity.linkeddata.es/.
[5] https://lov.linkeddata.es/dataset/lov/vocabs?tag=IoT.
[6] http://opensensingcity.emse.fr/scans/ontologies.

different IoT application domains and each ontology describes the concepts that are essential to that specific domain. Lets assume a developer who wants to develop an IoT application with a set of physical devices and is looking for the most suitable concepts to reuse from the ontologies within the catalogue according to an application scenario. In accordance to a typical IoT application development process, such a developer would start with identifying the concepts defined in the ontologies related to the physical devices or the category of the hardware, represented as the *sensors* and *actuators*. Since, these are the initial information that is available when a developer first starts to query the catalogue. Concepts like sensors and actuators are needed for identifying a candidate set of ontologies. With the shortlisted ontologies, the developer can then have a deeper look at the content to identify the knowledge and the relationships encoded within the ontology. The *rules* defined in an ontology is a common way of representing the logic and the results of an ontology [4]. These concepts are also commonly found in the literature. For instance, the analysis in [11,12] showed that among 46 ontologies from four IoT domains, sensor and actuator are the most frequent concepts designed. Gyrard et al. [2] identified that the IF THEN rules defined within IoT ontologies provide valuable knowledge for interpreting IoT data.

What is Our Contribution? Therefore, we propose a systematic approach, called Ontology Inspection *OntoSpect*, which enables the inspection of IoT ontologies according to a common set of concepts (sensor, actuator and rules). OntoSpect consists of two steps: first it automatically extracts a set of IoT concepts defined in the ontology using a pattern-based approach, and then generates human-understandable description from the extracted rules using a Model-driven Engineering (MDE) approach. To the best of our knowledge, no previous work has proposed such a method incorporating MDE to automatically describe semantic rules in natural language (NL). Moreover, we implement a prototype of the solution which is publicly available online[7] and conduct extensive evaluation on the LOV4IoT ontology catalogue to demonstrate its effectiveness. Our solution especially supports (1) application developers to inspect ontologies based on similar concepts to enable them to choose and reuse the ontologies that might be appropriate for their application scenario (2) ontology catalogues maintainers with a tool that automatically extracts the concepts with lower effort, and (3) IoT standardization efforts (e.g., W3C WoT Working Group (see footnote 2)) to migrate the existing ontologies to new standards, known as Extract Transform Load (ETL) procedure. In addition, OntoSpect also facilitates ontology inspection for researchers and ontology engineers, because they also need to assess, summarize and modify IoT ontologies.

In Sect. 2, we discuss the related work. Then Sect. 3, elaborates on the proposed approach. Section 4 provides the evaluation procedure and obtained results. Finally, Sect. 5 concludes the paper and provides future insights.

---

[7] https://vsr.informatik.tu-chemnitz.de/projects/2019/growth.

2   Related Work

IoT suffers from a lack of semantic interoperability between heterogeneous devices. These challenges are highlighted in [7]. The European Research Cluster on the IoT released IoT semantic interoperability best practices and recommendations [15], but does not refer concrete tools to encourage the reuse of the domain knowledge already designed. Tirado et al. [19] highlight that the lack of standard data models and structures forces developers to create models from scratch. Developers need collaborations with domain experts having the correct background knowledge. Given the absence of a common standard data model, knowledge repositories encourage developers to reuse and share domain knowledge using a common vocabulary across heterogeneous systems [13]. There are several knowledge repositories for the IoT domain like LOV4IoT (see footnote 1), Ready4SmartCities (see footnote 4), and OpenSensingCity (see footnote 6). These repositories make a high contribution towards discovering the distributed ontologies over the Web for facilitating reuse. However, they inspect the ontologies using general criteria such as quality indicators (e.g., online availability, license, etc.) and metadata (authors, syntax, domain, etc.) which is not enough for developers to make targeted comparison over the content. Moreover, the catalogue maintainers manually extract the ontology metadata which is time-consuming and subjective. In contrast, OnstoSpect automatically extracts content-related concepts (sensor, actuator, rules) which complements the existing ontology catalogues to improve their findability and provide the catalogue users an overview about the ontology content.

On the other hand, several researches are proposed in the literature to enhance the reuse of ontologies through knowledge extraction. Sun et al. [18] highlights that one of the requirements for achieving a well-defined data model for the IoT is information extraction. They define a semantic data model which extracts useful information from raw IoT data. However, in this work, we extract useful information modelled within existing ontologies. The KE4WoT proposed in [11,12], analyze the existing IoT ontologies in several sub-domains to identify what are the most important concepts defined within them. The authors use word2vec and k-means algorithm and for each IoT domain the most relevant vocabularies are provided to encourage reuse. They observed that *sensor* and *actuator* are the most frequent concepts designed within IoT ontologies. Therefore, we base our research on the KE4WoT analysis to automatically extract the specific types of sensors and actuators defined in an ontology.

The authors in [2,17] point to the importance of rules for interpreting raw data coming from IoT devices. Rules are logical elements composed of preconditions and postconditions. Preconditions represent a state of the world such that the rule should be applied in order to generate its post conditions [17]. W3C standards such as RuleML[8] and RIF[9] provide interoperability between rule languages, inference systems and knowledge representation paradigms.

---

[8] https://www.w3.org/2004/12/rules-ws/paper/96/.
[9] http://www.w3.org/TR/rif-overview/.

In [4], a set of principles for Linked Rule is proposed to facilitate rule reuse over the web. Maarala et al. [5] provide many approaches that utilize rules for context-awareness in the IoT. The authors of [6] propose a rule-based approach to process and execute rules semantically, concerned with the deductions of rules and semantifying them. In contrast, OntoSpect is not concerned with the execution of the rules and reasoning upon them. This work falls one step before the execution and is concerned with the challenge of automatic rule identification from ontologies and how to present semantically-described rules in a NL form. Sensor-based Linked Open Rules (S-LOR) [2] provide an automated rule discovery approach for IoT applications and its use in smart cities via a rule-based reasoning engine aiming to share, reuse and execute rules for interpreting sensor data. This approach is only automated for developers trying to discover rules and not on the catalogue maintainer side. When there are new rules, the catalogue maintainer has to manually identify the rules from existing ontologies or publications and feed them to S-LOR. OntoSpect helps catalogue maintainers by automatically identifying the rules from ontologies which can then serve as an input for S-LOR.

Faced with the challenge of inspecting IoT ontologies, generating human-understandable description from the rules remains an important issue. Automatic approaches can benefit ontology users to ease and speed up the ontology understanding process. In the literature, many studies have focused on generating NL text of the knowledge encoded in an ontology, which is called *ontology verbalization*. An analysis conducted by Power et al. provides over 600,000 axioms from 203 ontologies to evaluate the feasibility of ontology verbalization [14]. We do not aim to verbalize the entire ontology but rather the rules expressed in them. There are several ontology verbalization approaches in the literature, such as ACE [3] and SWAT [20]. They rely on NL techniques to name symbols of the underlying formalism to construct the content lexicon in which concepts are mapped onto nouns or adjectives and roles map onto transitive verbs. By this means, the underlying semantic operators and constructors are mapped onto NL constructs. However, these approaches cannot verbalize IoT ontologies because they are not able to understand the rules encoded in an ontology. In contrast, our solution aims at performing verbalization of the rules designed for the IoT domain. Moreover, we have not found any MDE-based approach for generating NL descriptions from ontologies.

In the MDE domain, there is a line of research focusing on enabling software developers to locate software artifacts for reuse, which is similar to the problem dealt in this research. The existing works use clustering techniques based on similarity measures e.g. [1] or supervised techniques based on machine learning e.g. [8] for grouping metamodels. In an analogy to OntoSpect, they classify an ontology according to the ontologies metadata. In contrast to our work, we do not intend to classify an ontology, rather we aim to identify knowledge from the ontology content in a human-understandable form.

In summary, there is a lack of approaches for inspecting IoT ontologies, that can extract the sensors, actuators and rules from an IoT ontology, and provide a human-understandable description of the rules. Our approach targets this gap.

3   IoT Ontology Inspection Using OntoSpect

In this section, we present the end-to-end approach that is employed for IoT ontology inspection from IoT sub-domains according to a common set of concepts (sensor, actuator, and IF THEN rules). The main objective is to extract the key concepts from an IoT ontology and to transform the machine-understandable rules into human-understandable descriptions. In particular, this solution can be seen as an interface for *ontology users*—catalogue maintainers, IoT application developers, IoT researchers, and ontology engineers—inspecting IoT ontologies in different IoT application domains.

Figure 1 shows an overview of the workflow as BPMN diagram in the two main stages of our solution: Concept Extraction and Natural Language Generation. The *Concept Extraction* shown on top automatically identifies the main IoT concepts—sensors, actuators, and rules—in the ontology based on pattern-matching. The *Natural Language Generation* shown on bottom transforms the extracted knowledge into human-understandable NL descriptions according to a generative model-to-text approach. The entire process is executed by the *OntoSpect Toolchain*, a system role representing our proposed software toolchain for supporting the ontology users' inspection of a given IoT ontology.

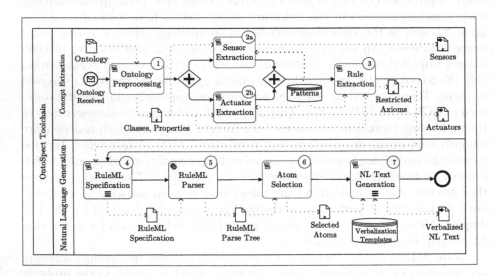

Fig. 1. The OntoSpect process

The OntoSpect process requires two inputs: a repository of extraction patterns and an IoT ontology for inspection. The patterns are an artifact which is created by a domain expert and initialized only once. On the other hand, the ontology is a run-time input artifact provided by the ontology user with the aim of automatic inspection. The *OntoSpect pattern repository* is created through ontology selection and pattern identification. It represents the different ways in which

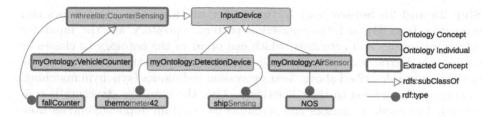

Fig. 2. Sensor identification examples

IoT ontologies describe sensors, actuators and rules. To realize this, we used 37 ontologies from the LOV4IoT catalogue. The ontologies were selected according to the following criteria:

- Citations of the scientific publications describing the ontology (e.g., the SSN[10] ontology V1 has more than 1000 citations).
- Dissemination or scheduled for dissemination by standardization organizations (e.g., W3C SSN/SOSA, W3C WoT ontology).
- Increased impact of ontology-based projects when industrial partners are involved.
- Availability of Ontology code from IoT catalogues.

The domain expert then manually analyzed the selected ontologies to identify the set of patterns used for defining sensors, actuators and rules. These patterns combine reasoning based on well-known concepts with a heuristic NLP-based approach. For that, the patterns have to consider both ontology structure and identifiers as shown in the example in Fig. 4 for Sensor identification. Known concepts from well-known/standardized IoT onotologies like W3C's SSN, WoT (see footnote 2), or M3Lite are used to identify matching ontology concepts by following subclass- and instance relationships: in the example, the myOntology:VehicleCounter concept is identified as sensor due to having mthreelite:CounterSensing in its ancestor graph, the fallCounter individual because of being an instance of an ancestor graph containing mthreelite: CounterSensing. In the absence of such well-known concepts, patterns need to consider the identifiers of concepts and individuals in the inspected IoT ontology. Synonym matching and stemming allows us to identify unknown individuals (e.g. thermometer42, shipSensing) and concepts (e.g. myOntology:AirSensor) based on appearance of character sequences of matching stems in their identifiers. The consideration of ancestry is also applied, allowing to identify NOS as Sensor.

The OntoSpect process consists of the following nine steps:

Step 1 Ontology Preprocessing. The received ontology is first converted into Turtle representation and character encoding is converted from unicode to ASCII for compatibility with the ontology parsers. Then, the ontology is queried to identify its classes, subclasses, and properties as a graph.

---

[10] https://www.w3.org/TR/vocab-ssn/.

Step 2a and 2b Sensor and Actuator Extraction. The set of classes and properties from (1) and the extraction pattern repository are the input for extracting sensors and actuators, which can occur in the ontology as classes or individuals. Extraction starts by the individuals and then the classes according to the patterns described above. Text processing techniques (synonym matching, stemming) are applied to their identifiers. Also, the ontology structure is considered. The resulting sensors and actuators can contain duplicate entries from matching several patterns, which are then removed. The output of this is a list of sensor and actuators represented using their identifiers. These can be used for catalogue maintainers as can be seen in LOV4IoT catalogue[11].

Step 3 Rule Extraction. The rules are designed as property restrictions on classes within an ontology axiom. These restrictions include `owl:allValuesFrom`, `owl:someValuesFrom`, `owl:hasValue`, `owl:cardinality`, `owl:minCardinality`, and `owl:maxCardinality`. OWL ontologies express these in combination with `owl:Restriction` statements. Therefore, the ontology is queried to identify all classes and properties with restrictions. Listing 1.1 shows an example of an extracted rule from Staroch ontology: "if the temperature value is greater than 20.0 and smaller than 25.0 degree-Celsius then it is room temperature". The output of this step is a set of rules represented as restricted axioms.

Listing 1.1. *Room temperature* rule from Staroch ontology in Turtle

```
:RoomTemperature rdf:type owl:Class ;
  owl:equivalentClass [ rdf:type owl:Class ;
  owl:intersectionOf ( :WeatherPhenomenon
    [ rdf:type owl:Restriction ;
      owl:onProperty :hasTemperatureValue;
      owl:someValuesFrom [rdf:type owl:Class ;
      owl:intersectionOf ( [rdf:type owl:Restriction ;
        owl:onProperty muo:measuredIn 1
        owl:hasValue temperature:degree-Celsius ]
      [ rdf:type owl:Restriction ;
        owl:onProperty muo:numericalValue ;
        owl:someValuesFrom [ rdf:type rdfs:Datatype ;
          owl:onDatatype xsd:float ;
          owl:with Restrictions ( [ xsd:min Inclusive "20.0"^^
            ↪ xsd:float ]) ] ]
      [ rdf:type owl:Restriction ;
        owl:onProperty muo:numericalValue ;
        owl:someValuesFrom [ rdf:type rdfs:Datatype ;
          owl:onDatatype xsd:float ;
          owl:withRestrictions ( [ xsd:max Inclusive "25.0"^^
            ↪ xsd:float ]) ] ] ) ] ] ) ] .
```

---

[11] https://linkedopenreasoning.appspot.com/?p=slor.

Step 4 RuleML Specification. The restricted axioms identified in the previous step need to be expressed in NL to facilitate understanding by users. MDE is used to automate this generation process. Step 4 is a model-to-model transformation from OWL to RuleML. We adopt the First Order Logic RuleML (FOL RuleML)[12] specification. In this step, the restricted axioms extracted from step 3 are automatically transformed into a set of FOL-RuleML models using the OWL Trans[13]. The semantic meanings are decomposed into a set of RuleML *atoms* as shown in 1.2, which represent a node in the form of an RDF triple (subject, property, object) and the relationship between nodes are replaced by node IDs. The transformation reduces the structural complexity of the OWL by converting it to a standard language without losing its semantic meaning. This step produces an intermediate artifact in FOL-Rule ML syntax that can be also used when processed with existing tool chains.

Listing 1.2. Extract of FOL-RuleML speicification for *Room temperature* rule

```
<Atom>
<Rel>statement</Rel>
<Ind>N65585</Ind>
<Ind>owl:hasValue</Ind>
<Ind>temperature:degree-Celsius</Ind>
</Atom> ...
```

Step 5 RuleML Parser. This step is the first towards generating a model-to-text transformation from RuleML specification to text. Given the RuleML specification as input, this step parses it according to a Domain Specific Language (DSL) Grammar. The parser is implemented using ANTLR4[14] (Another Tool for Language Recognition). The OntoSpect grammar includes the *lexer grammar* and the *parser grammar*. Listing 1.3 and 1.4 provides a minimal sample of the rules in the grammar. The Ontospect grammar consists of 174 lexer rules and 154 parser rules. The output of this phase is the RuleML parse tree.

Listing 1.3. Ontospect *lexer grammar* extract

```
OWLSVF :  'owl:someValuesFrom ';
OWLAVF :  'owl:allValuesFrom ';
OWLONP :  'owl:onProperty ';
```

---

[12] https://www.w3.org/Submission/FOL-RuleML/.
[13] http://www.ag-nbi.de/research/owltrans/.
[14] https://github.com/antlr/grammars-v4.

Listing 1.4. Ontospect *Parser grammar* extract

```
ruleMLDoc: (selective_atom | unselective_atom)*;
selected_atom: subject selective_functor object;
unselective_atom: subject unselective_functor object;
selective_functor: OWLSVF | OWLAVF | OWLONP;
unselective_functor: RDFTYPE | RDFSCOMMENT;
```

Step 6 Atom Selection. Not all initially extracted restricted axioms in the parse tree represent IF THEN rules. To distinguish such rules, we use the OntoSpect grammar to label those rules as 'unselective_atom' as shown in listing 1.4. Therefore, those nodes will not be considered for NL text generation.

Step 7 NL Text Generation. This step finalizes the model-to-text transformation from the selected atoms in the parse tree to NL descriptions. The text is generated by mapping the nodes in the parse tree to a sequence of placeholders in a matching verbalization template in the pattern repository as demonstrated in Table 1.

The resulting output artifacts created by running the OntoSpect toolchain are the sensors, actuators and NL descriptions of the rules contained in the ontology. These artifacts allow IoT developers when used in combination with the

Table 1. RoomTemperature NL generation process

Selected atom			NL output
Subject	Property	Object	
Room-Temperature	Owl:equivalentClass	N65552	"IF"
N65552	Owl:intersectionOf	Weather-Phenomenon	"WeatherPhenomenon"
N65561	Owl:onProperty	Temperature-Value	"TemperatureValue"
N65561	Owl:someValuesFrom	N65569	"is"
N65575	Owl:onProperty	MeasuredIn	"measuredIn degree-Celsius"
N65569	Owl:intersectionOf	N65585	"and"
N65585	Owl:someValuesFrom	N65590	"is"
N65596	Xsd:minInclusive	20.0	"greater than or equal to 20.0"
N65569	Owl:intersectionOf	N65614	"and"
N65614	Owl:someValuesFrom	N65622	"is"
N65631	Xsd:maxInclusive	25.0	"smaller than or equal to 25.0"
Verbalization Template END clause			"THEN RoomTemperature"

meta-data provided by existing ontology catalogues to evaluate the suitability of an ontology for the application scenario. For catalogue maintainers, the artifacts created by OntoSpect reduce the work effort when adding a newly published ontology to their catalogues.

4   Evaluation

The main goal of our evaluation is to assess the quality of OntoSpect for extracting sensors, actuators and rules from IoT ontologies as well as NL representations of these rules. We describe the evaluation procedure and report on the results.

4.1   Evaluation Procedure and Material

The evaluation consists of two experiments, the first experiment addresses the quality of the concept extraction and the second one the quality of the NL text generated by OntoSpect. To evaluate the quality of the concept extraction, we use ontology samples collected from the LOV4IoT catalogue. LOV4IoT references about 550 ontology-based research projects. However, there is a vast amount of ontologies which are not available anymore or have syntax errors, and thus have been removed from the evaluation dataset. To avoid a very positive bias in the results, the ontologies which were used for creating the OntoSpect extraction patterns as described in Sect. 3 are also excluded from the evaluation. Ultimately, the remaining dataset resulted in 84 ontologies from 22 different IoT sub-domains. The evaluation dataset was then assessed manually by two domain experts to extract the sensors, actuators and rules which forms the ground-truth for the evaluation experiment as described in Table 2. The evaluation dataset is available (see footnote 7) for review and further research. Based on this ground truth, we calculate the precision, recall and F-measure scores of OntoSpect concept extraction.

In the second evaluation experiment, the performance of the generated NL descriptions is evaluated: two domain experts manually wrote the NL descriptions of the rules for each ontology in the evaluation dataset. Then, the Bilingual Evaluation Understudy (BLEU) score is calculated to measure the similarity between the generated descriptions and the ground-truth human-written text. Since automatic metrics may not completely correspond with human judgement, human testing is required to evaluate how natural the generated rule descriptions are. We therefore conducted an additional empirical study to evaluate the quality of the generated text. We invited ontology catalogue maintainers, developers and participants working in IoT ontology standardization like iot.schema.org and W3C WoT. The participants were shown 11 randomly sampled rules in OWL and their NL-equivalents generated by OntoSpect. They were then asked to score each text in terms of readability and accuracy based on a 5-point Likert scale ranging from *very poor* to *excellent*. Here *readability* is defined as whether the text is clearly readable and understandable, and *accuracy* is defined as whether the text contains all the information specified in the semantic rule.

Table 2. Evaluation dataset characteristics, showing the number of concept instances, and ontologies/domains containing the concept

Concept	Number of instances	Ontologies	Domain
Sensor	432	31	11
Actuator	181	16	4
Rule	377	15	7

Table 3. OntoSpect concept extraction evaluation statistics

Concept	$\overline{P}$	$\overline{R}$	$\overline{P_\mu}$	$\overline{R_\mu}$	$\overline{F_1}$
Sensor	0.9489	0.9658	0.9379	0.9585	0.9480
Actuator	0.9548	0.9846	0.8994	0.9157	0.9075
Rule	0.9672	0.9649	0.9155	0.9259	0.9207

Mean Precision $\overline{P}$, Mean Recall $\overline{R}$, Mean Precision (micro-averaged) $\overline{P_\mu}$, Mean Recall (micro-averaged) $\overline{R_\mu}$, and Mean F_1-score (micro-averaged)

4.2 Results and Analysis

Evaluation of the OntoSpect concept extraction on 84 ontologies, containing 432 sensors, 181 actuators, and 377 rules in the ground-truth resulted in the statistics in Table 3. Due to the unbalanced distribution of the concepts across the ontologies—sensor, actuator and rules occur very frequently in some ontologies and rarely in some other ontologies—we also show the micro-average Precision and Recall. While the latter is slightly lower than the macro average, both have a $F_1 > 0.9$ and only display limited differences. The overall $F_1 = 0.94, 0.90$, and 0.92 for sensor, actuator and rule respectively, shows a good performance of OntoSpect in extracting these concepts from IoT ontologies.

To analyze the quality of OntoSpect for generating NL description rules, we report on BLEU scores in terms of their cumulative n-gram precision for different rule lengths. Figure 3 illustrates the NL rule length distribution in the evaluation dataset. The n-gram scores are calculated by counting the number of n-gram matches between extracted tokens by OntoSpect, and the actual tokens by the domain expert. For example, 1-g score is calculated from individual tokens, while the 2-g compares word pairs. We report on these n-gram precision scores for $n \in \{1, 2, 3, 4\}$ in Table 4 which follows the standard practice for evaluation of automatic verbalization. The precision decreases with the increase of the rule length as longer rules introduce more possibilities for error.

To further analyze the quality of the rule verbalization an online questionnaire was taken by 28 subjects. We checked their expertise and asked them to select the role best describing them (multi-selections were possible). Most of the experts were developers (74%), 48.1% had a basic understanding of ontologies, 22.2% had experience with researching ontologies, 18.5% classified themselves as experienced ontology designers and 14.8% were ontology practitioners.

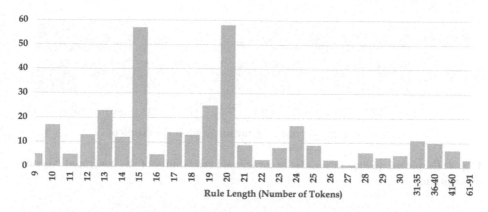

Fig. 3. Frequency distribution of rule length

The evaluation investigates whether the NL descriptions generated by OntoSpect are readable and accurate. The test subjects rated accuracy and readability of the rule verbalizations relatively good (64,3% / 56,2% good or excellent, respectively) with a slightly better rating for accuracy as shown in Fig. 4.

Overall, the experiments show promising result quality, indicating that OntoSpect can be helpful for inspecting IoT ontologies. Further experiments with ontology users are required assess the performance of OntoSpect when embedded within their corresponding work processes.

4.3 Threats to Validity

External Validity. Is limited by the representativeness of the ontology catalogue used in this study, and the overall generealizability of the concept extraction to domains other than IoT. We expect that for other IoT ontology catalogues the quality of the results will be similar, because sensor and actuators are commonly found in all IoT ontologies [11]. Sensor and actuator extraction is restricted to the IoT domain while the rules extraction and NL generation may also work for other domains that follow a similar rule structure.

Table 4. N-gram precision scores for different rule lengths

BLEU type	≤20 Tokens	≤30 Tokens	>30 Tokens	Total
Cumulative 1-g	0.9026	0.8863	0.7579	0.8748
Cumulative 2-g	0.8264	0.8091	0.6755	0.7970
Cumulative 3-g	0.7649	0.7435	0.5861	0.7293
Cumulative 4-g	0.7112	0.6841	0.4908	0.6666
|Rules|	247	312	31	343

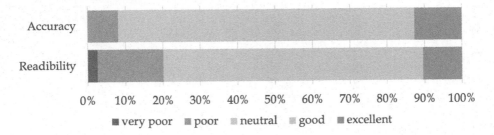

Fig. 4. Empirical quality ratings for accuracy and readability of the generated NL rule descriptions

Internal Validity. A potential threat to internal validity lies in the manual extraction and NL description generation forming the evaluation dataset. To deal with this, two domain experts have performed this with many discussions. The experimental design involves empirical ratings of the text quality that may have introduced a bias by the test subjects. To reduce this, we also computed BLEU scores as an objective quantitative metric. In addition, for evaluating the NL generation, a subset of the rules (11 from 377) was selected. To avoid the selection bias, the rules were randomly sampled.

Construct Validity. Our evaluation focused on result quality and is not a complete user study with ontology users such as catalogue maintainers. This would exceed the scope of this paper, since the different groups have different work processes and requirements necessitating separate evaluation runs per group, which is planned for future work.

5   Conclusion and Future Work

Inspecting IoT ontologies with content-related concepts can encourage developers to reuse existing ontologies and reduce the effort of catalogue maintainers. In this paper, we introduced OntoSpect for automatically inspecting IoT ontologies according to sensor, actuator and rules using concept extraction- and NL generation-based techniques. The prototype of OntoSpect is publicly available (see footnote 7) for use and further research. OntoSpect was evaluated using quality metrics and empirical evaluation. The concept extraction results showed that OntoSpect can extract sensors, actuators and rules with good quality. Also, the generated NL description of the rules are sufficiently readable and accurate. Overall, the evaluation suggested that OntoSpect can be helpful for inspecting IoT ontologies. In the future work, we plan to extend the experiments by allowing different ontology user groups to use OntoSpect tool and to report on the benefits. In addition, we plan to integrate OntoSpect with the LOV4IoT catalogue.

Acknowledgements. We thank the maintainer of LOV4IoT, Amelie Gyrard, for motivating this research and supporting it with basic evaluation data. This work was partially funded by the Deutsche Forschungsgemeinschaft (DFG, German Research Foundation)–Project-ID 416228727–SFB 1410.

References

1. Basciani, F., Di Rocco, J., Di Ruscio, D., Iovino, L., Pierantonio, A.: Automated clustering of metamodel repositories. In: Nurcan, S., Soffer, P., Bajec, M., Eder, J. (eds.) CAiSE 2016. LNCS, vol. 9694, pp. 342–358. Springer, Cham (2016). https:// doi.org/10.1007/978-3-319-39696-5_21

2. Gyrard, A., Serrano, M., Jares, J.B., Datta, S.K., Ali, M.I.: Sensor-based linked open rules (s-lor) an automated rule discovery approach for IoT applications and its use in smart cities. In: Proceedings of the 26th International Conference on World Wide Web Companion, pp. 1153–1159 (2017)

3. Kaljurand, K.: Attempto controlled english as a semantic web language. Ph.D. thesis (2007)

4. Khandelwal, A., Jacobi, I., Kagal, L.: Linked rules: principles for rule reuse on the web. In: Rudolph, S., Gutierrez, C. (eds.) RR 2011. LNCS, vol. 6902, pp. 108–123. Springer, Heidelberg (2011). https://doi.org/10.1007/978-3-642-23580-1_9

5. Maarala, A.I., Su, X., Riekki, J.: Semantic reasoning for context-aware internet of things applications. IEEE Internet Things J. 4(2), 461–473 (2016)

6. Mainetti, L., Mighali, V., Patrono, L., Rametta, P.: A novel rule-based semantic architecture for IoT building automation systems. In: 2015 23rd International Conference on Software, Telecommunications and Computer Networks (SoftCOM), pp. 124–131. IEEE (2015)

7. Murdock, P., et al.: Semantic Interoperability for the Web of Things (White Paper) (2016)

8. Nguyen, P.T., Di Rocco, J., Di Ruscio, D., Pierantonio, A., Iovino, L.: Automated classification of metamodel repositories: a machine learning approach. In: 2019 ACM/IEEE 22nd International Conference on Model Driven Engineering Languages and Systems (MODELS), pp. 272–282. IEEE (2019)

9. Noura, M., Atiquzzaman, M., Gaedke, M.: Interoperability in internet of things infrastructure: classification, challenges, and future work. In: Lin, Y.-B., Deng, D.-J., You, I., Lin, C.-C. (eds.) IoTaaS 2017. LNICST, vol. 246, pp. 11–18. Springer, Cham (2018). https://doi.org/10.1007/978-3-030-00410-1_2

10. Noura, M., Atiquzzaman, M., Gaedke, M.: Interoperability in internet of things: taxonomies and open challenges. Mobile Netw. Appl. 24(3), 796–809 (2018). https://doi.org/10.1007/s11036-018-1089-9

11. Noura, M., Gyrard, A., Heil, S., Gaedke, M.: Concept extraction from the web of things knowledge bases. In: 17th International Conference WWW/Internet (2018)

12. Noura, M., Gyrard, A., Heil, S., Gaedke, M.: Automatic knowledge extraction to build semantic web of things applications. IEEE Internet Things J. 6(5), 8447–8454 (2019)

13. Poveda-Villalón, M., García-Castro, R., Gómez-Pérez, A.: Building an ontology catalogue for smart cities. In: Proceedings of the 10th European Conference on Product and Process Modelling, ECPPM 2014, pp. 1–8 (2014)

14. Power, R., Third, A.: Expressing owl axioms by english sentences: dubious in theory, feasible in practice (2010)

15. Serrano, M., Barnaghi, P., Carrez, F., Cousin, P., Vermesan, O., Friess, P.: Internet of things IoT semantic interoperability: research challenges, best practices, recommendations and next steps. European Research Cluster on the Internet of Things, Technical report, IERC (2015)
16. Serrano, M., Barnaghi, P., et al.: Internet of Things IoT semantic interoperability: research challenges, best practices, recommendations and next steps. Technical report, European Research Cluster on the Internet of Things, AC4 (2015)
17. Seydoux, N., Drira, K., Hernandez, N., Monteil, T.: Edr: a generic approach for the distribution of rule-based reasoning in a cloud-fog continuum. Semantic Web (Preprint), pp. 1–32 (2020)
18. Sun, Y., Jara, A.J.: An extensible and active semantic model of information organizing for the internet of things. Pers. Ubiquit. Comput. **18**(8), 1821–1833 (2014)
19. Tirado, J.M., Serban, O., Guo, Q., Yoneki, E.: Web data knowledge extraction. arXiv preprint arXiv:1603.07534 (2016)
20. Williams, S., Third, A., Power, R.: Levels of organisation in ontology verbalisation. In: Proceedings of the 13th European Workshop on Natural Language Generation, pp. 158–163 (2011)

A File-Based Linked Data Fragments Approach to Prefix Search

Ruben Dedecker[✉][iD], Harm Delva[iD], Pieter Colpaert[iD],
and Ruben Verborgh[iD]

IDLab, Department of Electronics and Information Systems, Ghent University–imec,
Technologiepark-Zwijnaarde 122, 9052 Ghent, Belgium
Ruben.Dedecker@Ugent.be

Abstract. Text-fields that need to look up specific entities in a dataset
can be equipped with autocompletion functionality. When a dataset
becomes too large to be embedded in the page, setting up a full-text
search API is not the only alternative. Alternate API designs that balance different trade-offs such as archivability, cacheability and privacy,
may not require setting up a new back-end architecture. In this paper,
we propose to perform prefix search over a fragmentation of the dataset,
enabling the client to take part in the query execution by navigating
through the fragmented dataset. Our proposal consists of (i) a self-
describing fragmentation strategy, (ii) a client search algorithm, and (iii)
an evaluation of the proposed solution, based on a small dataset of 73k
entities and a large dataset of 3.87 m entities. We found that the server
cache hit ratio is three times higher compared to a server-side prefix
search API, at the cost of a higher bandwidth consumption. Nevertheless,
an acceptable user-perceived performance has been measured: assuming
150 ms as an acceptable waiting time between keystrokes, this approach
allows 15 entities per prefix to be retrieved in this interval. We conclude
that an alternate set of trade-offs has been established for specific prefix
search use cases: having added more choice to the spectrum of Web APIs
for autocompletion, a file-based approach enables more datasets to afford
prefix search.

Keywords: Prefix search · Query evaluation · Linked data fragments ·
Web APIs

1 Introduction

Prefix autocompletion is a common user interface feature in forms. Given a
certain prefix, suggestions are provided that match the prefix to an item in a
collection. This way, a user can recognize the item they are looking for, rather
than recalling the exact identifier it may have in the underlying data. To provide
such functionality, an API can be provided that filters the dataset entities on

© Springer Nature Switzerland AG 2021
M. Brambilla et al. (Eds.): ICWE 2021, LNCS 12706, pp. 53–67, 2021.
https://doi.org/10.1007/978-3-030-74296-6_5

the server-side illustrated by the URL template https://example.org/%7B?query %7D. Such a service requires the server to process all queries for every typed character of every connected client. Another solution is to ship the collection of entities to the client for processing. While feasible for small collections, this quickly becomes problematic when the dataset grows.

Where some data publishers manage to publicly provide such an API for prefix autocompletion for their datasets, others leave this feature up to third parties reusing the data. An in-between solution could add more choice to the spectrum for cases where prefix query evaluation entirely on the server is less desirable. For example,

- for a website builder, shipping a collection of a couple of thousand entities would make a page too heavy, yet setting up a website with a full-text search API requires the maintenance of dynamic server-side functionality;
- for specialized cases where additional information can be incorporated in the autocompletion client, e.g. adding error correction using a list of common mistakes or filtering of geographically irrelevant results.
- for users that do not want to leak their search queries via query logs.

In this paper, we present **a file-based architecture with an acceptable user-perceived performance that enables clients to take control of the prefix query evaluation process**. The contributions are as follows: (i) a hypermedia specification that can describe fragmentation strategies for string search, (ii) a tailored implementation of a B-tree fragmentation described with this hypermedia, (iii) a client search algorithm able to traverse the hypermedia search space, and (iv) an evaluation discussing query performance, cache hit ratio, bandwidth and efficiency.

In Sect. 2 we provide an overview on related work that inspired our work. Evaluating the approach introduced in Sect. 3, in Sect. 4 we used the database of all public transport stops in Belgium, for which we also published a real query-set based on an access log, as well as a subset of OSMNames[1], for which we generated a random query-set. We measure whether clients evaluating prefix queries over the proposed fragmentation strategy experience an acceptable user-perceived performance by analyzing the performance, cache hit ratio, bandwidth consumed and efficiency.

2   Related Work

Research on full-text search, prefix search or autocompletion on one machine has a large history [1]. These techniques have profited from that prior work, resulting in powerful open-source tools such as ElasticSearch. Today, for example, Elastic-Search is the engine behind the autocompletion of Linked Open Vocabularies [7], offering a search engine through all indexed Linked Data vocabularies[2]. Another

---

[1] https://osmnames.org/download/.

[2] The service can be used via the URL template `https://lov.linkeddata.es/data set/lov/api/v2/term/autocompleteLabels{?q}`.

example of a reconciliation tool using ElasticSearch is Pelias[3]. It offers world-wide address autocompletion and geocoding by combining different datasets such as Geonames[4], OpenStreetMap[5], Who's on first[6] and openaddresses.io. There is however no public instance and a user is required to self-host it, or rely on software as a service solutions that come at a pay per use cost. Furthermore, when using the API, there are user experience guidelines to take into account, such as (i) throttling requests, (ii) taking into account possible out of order responses and (iii) using a pre-written client on the front-end if possible.

Triple Pattern Fragments (TPF) [8] is a Linked Data API specification for solving queries using Basic Graph Patterns, introduced as an alternative to hosting a SPARQL endpoint. Instead of answering a full SPARQL query on the server-side, it requires the client to take part in the query execution. The client retrieves the fragments of the dataset required to evaluate the query from the server by requesting Triple Patterns, and evaluates the query over the retrieved fragments. Approximate counts of the specific triple patterns in the full dataset are provided in the retrieved fragments to optimize client query evaluation based on selectivity of certain triple patterns.

Van Herwegen et al. [6] extended the TPF interface with substring filtering on objects using different indexes, such as ElasticSearch or an FM-index. For this part of the query, the client thus relies on the server to fully filter the triple pattern fragment's response and does not explore in-between solutions. These initiatives follow the idea of Linked Data Fragments (LDF)[7] [5].

Finally, in a survey on Query Auto Completion (QAC) [1] the state of the art is discussed. It sketches an elaborate overview of the research trends, among others, heuristic and learning based approaches to raising the relevance of the suggestions, analysis of the computational complexity – yet only on one machine – of different algorithms, or the state of the art in QAC user experience. No alternate Web API designs are discussed where clients could take part in the query execution. Furthermore, in order to test the computational complexity, only the complexity of resolving one prefix is considered, despite the fact that a consecutive QAC query may continue querying from where a previous query left off, and thus have a lower amortized complexity.

3   Dataset Fragmentation and Traversal

Client participation in query evaluation can be easily achieved by sending all data to the client. However, as datasets grow larger, this approach leads to increased bandwidth requirement and application response times, which is undesirable for cases such as mobile applications where bandwidth caps are in place, and stable network reception cannot be guaranteed.

---

[3] https://pelias.io/.
[4] https://www.geonames.org/.
[5] https://www.openstreetmap.org/.
[6] https://whosonfirst.org/.
[7] https://linkeddatafragments.org.

In this section, we propose our strategy to publish datasets by fragmenting the data using search tree structures. With this approach to data publishing, clients are enabled to evaluate prefix queries over remote datasets by only retrieving fragments of the dataset relevant to the client query. In Sect. 3.1 we introduce preliminaries, which we use in Sect. 3.2 to introduce a self-describing fragmentation strategy. Finally, in Sect. 3.3 a generic client-side traversal algorithm is introduced.

3.1 Preliminaries

Given a dataset D, an autocompletion interface provides autocompletion functionality over all entities in D. These entities can have different properties over which autocompletion can be offered, such as a person entity having a first and last name property. To enable fast prefix search lookups in a dataset for a given property, an index can be constructed for that property using a data structure that enables lookups to only retrieve the parts of the dataset relevant to the query. Clients use such an indexing structure to more efficiently find entities in the dataset matching a given prefix value for the indexed properties. Our approach explores generating such indexing data structures, and using them to fragment the dataset into smaller files (fragments). By embedding this tree structure as hypermedia controls in the generated fragments, clients are enabled to only retrieve fragments relevant to the evaluated prefix query from the dataset.

3.2 A Self-describing Fragmentation Strategy

Instead of publishing a dataset as a query interface, or publishing it as a single data dump, an in-between solution was chosen. To enable clients to participate in the prefix query evaluation, clients should be able to retrieve only the data relevant to the evaluated query from the dataset. This requires the dataset to be fragmented, and for the fragments to be structured in a way that enables clients to traverse and prune the search space. In the interest of improving query performance by limiting the amount of HTTP requests necessary for a client to autocomplete a prefix, we took our inspiration from the design of balanced tree structures such as a B-tree [2]. The implementation of the creation algorithm used in this paper makes use of B-tree structures to fragment the dataset. It can be found at https://github.com/Dexagod/linked_data_tree.

To create fragmentations of a dataset, the data publisher first has to deciding the properties over which the dataset entities should be indexed. For each chosen property, a separate fragmentation of the dataset is created.

To create a fragmentation, first an indexing search tree data structure is generated, adding all entities in the dataset using the value of the chosen property as key to add to the data structure (the data publisher decides the extent of a data entity). Upon adding all dataset entities, for each node in the tree structure a dataset fragment is generated, stored as a separate file. Such a fragment contains the node information, its relations to other nodes in the data structure, and the data entities present in the node. To enable the client to traverse the tree structure in the generated fragments, the node and relation data in the fragments are defined in a semantic way as hypermedia controls, using the TREE hypermedia descriptions[8], as depicted in Listing 1.1.

To enable clients to find a dataset and its available fragmentations, this dataset information is published semantically as a **collection** object, as seen in Listing 1.1. The different created fragmentations of the dataset are defined as *views* on this collection object. These view properties point to the root nodes of used tree structure and its containing fragment. An optional *shape* property can be provided, defining the base shape (structure) of all entities in the collection. On publishing this collection object on the Web, a client can discover all available fragmentations of the dataset through the view properties present in the object.

```
1  {
2      "@context": {
3          "tree": "https://w3id.org/tree#"
4      },
5      "@id": "#Dataset",                                     ///D
6      "@type": "tree:Collection",
7      "tree:shape": "shape.shacl",
8      "tree:view": {
9          "@id": "node1.jsonld",                             ///n
10         "tree:relation": [
11             {
12                 "@type": "tree:GreaterThanRelation",  ///defines χ
13                 "tree:path": "foaf:name",              ///p
14                 "tree:value": "Alice",                 ///v
15                 "tree:node": "node2.jsonld",           ///c
16             },
17             ...
18         ]
19     },
20     "tree:member": [ ... ]                                 ///array of e
21 }
```

Listing 1.1. An example of the metadata of a response in JSON-LD. A client encountering this relation knows that all data found following the link to `node2.jsonld` will result in a value that is greater than `Alice` for the `foaf:name` property.

For each node in the created tree structure of the dataset, the generated fragment for that node defines a **node** object. This object stores the relations to its child nodes (and their containing fragments). The dataset entities present in the node of the tree structure are stored in the generated fragment as members of the collection object (dataset) as seen on line 20 of Listing 1.1.

The relations to the child nodes are defined as **relation** objects, as seen on line 10 of Listing 1.1. These semantically define the data found in the subtree of the referenced child node, by specifying the following properties:

1. The relation type, being `LessThanRelation`, `LessThanOrEqualToRelation`, `GreaterThanRelation` or `GreaterThanOrEqualToRelation`. This relation type specifies a comparison operator χ, to to which all entities e_c in the subtree of child node c are evaluated in comparison to the relation value $v_{relation}$;

---

[8] https://treecg.github.io/specification.

2. a node property, being the hypermedia link to the child node c and its containing dataset fragment.
3. an optional path p, that is the property path over which all entities e_c in the subtree of child node c are evaluated, and
4. a value $v_{relation}$.

This relation object semantically defines the entities that can be found in the subtree of child node c. E.g. for a path p of *firstName*, a value $v_{relation}$ of *Alice*, and a relation type of GreaterThanRelation, the relation defines that all data entities e_c in the subtree of c have value greater than *Alice* for the value of their *firstname* property. With this information, a client evaluating a query over the dataset fragmentation can process the available relations, and prune the ones that do not lead to relevant data entities for the evaluated query. Note that multiple relation objects can defined in a node referencing the same child node, further specifying the entities found in the child node and its subtree.

In order to express the property paths, the design of property paths in the Shapes Constraint Language (SHACL) [4] is reused. As the ordering of characters is important for comparing string based values, unicode ordering is used as a default, as defined by the TREE specification. Flags are available to indicate other orderings used to generate the fragmentation, and have to be followed by clients.

As datasets can contain entities with non-unique values for a given property, the tree structure used to fragment the dataset needs to support duplicate key values. In Modern B-tree techniques [3], duplicate key values are stored once, and subsequent entities with the same value are added in a (paged) array-structure. Since however we are not limited to predefined semantics for relations, we adapted the B-tree splitting algorithm to allow entities with duplicate key values to just be stored in the tree structure. In case a node overflows during the creation of the tree structure, and is split between duplicate key values, this is resolved by having the parent node reference the two new nodes using the relation types LessThanOrEqualToRelation and GreaterThanOrEqualToRelation. The client is not required to be aware of this adaptation, as it just requires an understanding of the relation semantics to prune the search space.

3.3 Client Algorithm

In this section we describe the client algorithm used for the evaluation in Sect. 4. A client can be asked to evaluate prefix search queries for a given prefix value v_{query} and property path p_{query} over a dataset D (e.g. the client searches for entities in D where the property p_{query} value of *firstName* matches the prefix v_{query} of *Ali*). For this, the client requires a reference to the collection object of D. Upon retrieving this collection object, the client dereferences the root nodes of the available fragmentations of the dataset through the views defined on the collection. This operation can be done at page load times, and should not slow down lookups when used in Web applications.

At the start of the query evaluation process, the client decides the best fragmentation of the dataset to query over. For all fragmentations, the client checks if the available relations specify a property path $p_{relation}$ that matches the queried property path p_{query} (e.g. the relation specifies it stores relations for the *first-Name* property, and the query searches entities matching a prefix value for the *firstName* property). If a fragmentation is found containing such relations, the client continues to evaluate its query over this fragmentation. If no such fragmentation can be discovered, the client will not be able to prune relations of any of the fragmentations (e.g. when the relations provide information over the stored entities *firstName* property, but the client is querying for entities with a *lastName* property matching the prefix *Bob*). In this case the client can retrieve fragments of a random fragmentation without pruning, until the required amount of results is retrieved for the query.

Now that the client has chosen a fragmentation to evaluate the query over, the **recursive traversal process** is started. On retrieval of a new fragment of the dataset (initially the one containing the root node), the client starts by extracting all tree metadata from the fragment. First, the client emits all data entities in the fragment matching the client query. In case the desired amount of results is retrieved, the client is stopped. This design of incremental results contrasts with evaluating the full query on the server-side, where traditionally results are only emitted when the desired amount of results have been found.

If more results are needed, the relations available in the node of the fragment are evaluated, as seen in Listing 1.1 on line 10. As multiple relations may reference the same child node, and provide additional constraints to the entities stored in the subtree of that child node, the relations are grouped on the child nodes they point to. If any of the relations pointing to a child node can be pruned, all the relations to that child node can be pruned, as the referenced node and its subtree cannot contain results for the client query

A relation is evaluated by matching the relation path $p_{relation}$ to the query path p_{query}. In the case that these paths do not match (e.g. the relations stores entities for the *firstName* property, where the client queries entities based on their *lastName* property), the client can make no assumptions about the entities stored in the node referenced by the relation, and the relation cannot be pruned.

In the case of matching path properties, the client tries to prune the search space. This is done by comparing the queried prefix value v_{query} to the relation value $v_{relation}$ and the comparison operator χ specified by the relation type (e.g. the `GreaterThanRelation` specifies the $>$ comparison operator). In the case of prefix search, the client now evaluates if the queried prefix value v_{query} is contained in the range specified by the prefix of the same length of the relation value $v_{relation}$ and the comparison operator χ defined by the relation type. A query for the prefix *Car* evaluated over a relation of type `GreaterThanRelation` with a value $v_{relation}$ of *Alice*, requires the client to check if $Car > Ali$. If this comparison holds, the client may retrieve entities relevant for the evaluated query by dereferencing the relation child node. For prefix search, the edge cases where the queried prefix and the prefix of the relation value are equal, or where the relation value is smaller prefix of the queried prefix value, the referenced child node may also contain entities relevant to the evaluated query. When all relations referencing a child node cannot be pruned by the algorithm, the child node may contain useful data and the **recursive traversal process** is repeated for the child node fragment.

As the client is in control of the query evaluation process, subsequent evaluated queries for incremental prefix values (e.g. **"A"** → **"Al"** → **"Ali"**) can continue the previous query evaluation, for an updated prefix value, as the results of the updated query are a subset of the results of the previous query. Additional rules can be implemented, such as deciding to not prune relations that provide results within a certain Levenshtein distance of the queried prefix if only few results are found. Different traversal strategies such as breadth-first or depth-first can be implemented and changed during query evaluation depending on the situation. Multithreading can be implemented using a queue system, where a set number of relations can be processed in parallel.

The client implementation used for evaluating the approach can be found at https://github.com/Dexagod/ldtreeBrowser.

4 Experiments and Results

We define a prefix query as the set of the requests that are performed to retrieve 25 results (if available) that start with that prefix. The *query server* approach consists of a client using a query server that returns a page with 25 results from the dataset (if available) for the queried prefix value and path. The *search tree* is the approach introduced in this paper, where a client traverses a published search tree for entities matching the queried prefix value and path. For this evaluation, we assume that a fragmentation is available for the property over which the prefix query is evaluated. In order to understand the effectiveness of the tree approach, we will measure the cacheability of these requests, and how this impacts efficiency and bandwidth, based on the size of a dataset in a real-world environment. Based on this cacheability and the scalability of the depth of the tree, we can deduct what this means for the overall user-perceived performance.

For the experiments, we republished 2 datasets using our approach, and setup a query server interface for these datasets: A dataset of Belgian public transport stops (6 triples per entity, and a total of 72,967 entities), and a subset (BE, FR, NE, LU, DE) of the OSMNames dataset[9] (32 triples per entity, and a total of 3.87 m entities), both published using a fragment size (m) of 25 members (a fragment contains 25 data entities, and relations to the 26 child nodes and their containing fragments). For the Belgian public transport stops dataset, a real-world query log was extracted from a server autocompleting Belgian railway stops. For the OSMnames subset, we did not have access to a real-world query set, so a randomized query set was generated. This randomized query set was generated for 1000 target values distributed over 50 simulated user clients, where for each target a series of prefix queries was created, starting at random length prefix, for a

---

[9] https://osmnames.org/download/.

randomized amount of subsequent prefixes (e.g. "Lou" → "Louv" → "Louvai"). In the case of the query server, the client sends a separate request for every prefix in the query log. The used datasets and query logs are made available on Github[10].

The evaluation consists of a server providing the search tree fragmentation, a server providing the server-sided prefix search query interface and a proxy cache in front of these servers on the same network, and a laptop using Wi-Fi with an average ping of ±20 ms. All servers are dedicated machines with a 2x Dual Core AMD Opteron 270 (2 GHz) CPU, 4 GB Ram and a 80 Gb Hdd. All queries are evaluated on a laptop with a Intel M4800MQ CPU and 16 GB Ram.

4.1 Cache Efficiency

In Fig. 1, we show the server cache hit ratio for a client evaluating the randomized prefix query set over the OSMNames dataset, using an nginx cache at 10% the size of the original dataset. This evaluation was done for the larger dataset, to provide a better overview of the caching behavior. We tested this for both a query server (baseline) as the search tree approach and notice the search tree approach achieves a three times bigger cache hit rate on the server.

As the baseline query server returns results for a specific prefix value, it can only return a cached request in the case of an exact match in requested prefix. In contrast, our approach uses a tree structure to fragment the dataset. A client evaluating a prefix query over a tree structure requires multiple requests for nodes in the tree in contrast to the single request when using the baseline query server. As the client evaluates queries by traversing the tree structure starting from the root node, nodes closer to the root of the tree structure are fewer and therefore have a higher probability of being retrieved for a random prefix query. Because of this, they have a higher probability of being present in the server cache. This explains the higher server cache hit ratio for our approach of evaluating prefix queries compared to the baseline query server.

4.2 Query Performance

As the proposed search tree querying approach enables the autocompletion client to emit results during the traversal process of the tree structure, this experiment was setup to see how many results can be achieved within 150 ms, a time span which feels instantaneous to end-users. As query server interfaces are capable of this, and do not provide incremental results (all results are transmitted at once), we focus on the query performance of the proposed *search tree* approach.

Prefix requests are not isolated events, where often the value of the previous request is a prefix of the current request. Because of this, the performance evaluation is done separately for the first three queries (if available) in each series of prefix queries in the used query sets.

---

[10] https://github.com/Dexagod/Paper_metadata/tree/master/ISWC2021.

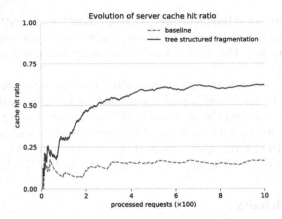

Fig. 1. Average server cache hit ratio evaluating the randomized query set over the OSMNames dataset. The query server stagnates at around 20%, where our proposed approach provides cached result for more than half the requests to the server after an initial warmup period.

The performance is measured as the amount of results the query emits for the evaluation of a prefix query within a 150 ms interval of the client receiving a new prefix value. The results are averaged for all first, second and third requests in all series of subsequent prefix queries in the query logs. For the experiment, the server cache size is set to 10% of the dataset size, and a client cache is set per user that stores all previously retrieved fragments.

In Fig. 2 we can see that for the public transport stops dataset (73k entities), the first evaluated prefix query in a series returns on average just below 15 results in within the 150 ms period. For the subsequent second and third prefix queries, the results can be retrieved faster, producing on average 15 results within a 150 ms interval. For an average query, the first 5 results are shown in a 25 ms interval as a result of server caching, and cached results from previous queries. Subsequent queries in a series returning less results can be explained by the dataset containing less than 15 entities matching the queried prefix.

In Fig. 3, we see that for the subset of the OSMNames[11] dataset (3.87 m entities), the proposed approach results in a slower start for the evaluation of the first prefix queries in a series. This is caused by the randomized nature of the query set used for this dataset. As the first prefix query has a randomized length, it may have results stored deeper in the tree structure of the published dataset fragmentation, requiring a more expensive initial lookup. For subsequent queries in the series, the performance normalizes because of previously cached data, with the second evaluated prefix query returning on average 15 results in the 150 ms interval. A slower average results in the first 25 ms of the query compared to the smaller dataset is caused by the deeper tree structure of the fragmentation.

---

[11] https://osmnames.org.

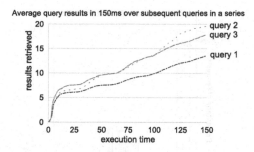

Fig. 2. Increased performance in a series of subsequent prefix queries (e.g. query1: "Lou", query2: "Louv", query3: "Louva") over the transport stops dataset (73k entries) for the proposed approach. First 5 results are shown in a 25 ms as a result of caching and results available from previous queries. Later queries may not have 15 results in the dataset, leading to a lower amount of retrieved results.

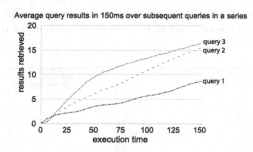

Fig. 3. Slower retrieval of results for the first evaluated prefix query in a series because of randomized length of the first query in the generated query set for the OSMNames dataset (3.87 m entities). Subsequent queries provide 15 results in the 150 ms interval, with a slower start because of the deeper tree structure of the dataset fragmentation.

4.3 Efficiency and Bandwidth

We define the efficiency as "the fraction of data retrieved from the server during the execution of a task over the amount of data required to execute that task" [8]. In a query server approach, developers will aim towards a 100% efficiency. At the cost of efficiency, the search tree approach raises the cacheability. In Fig. 4, we discuss the results for how much efficiency we sacrifice. In Fig. 5 we discuss the bandwidth consumption and the number of HTTP requests that this adheres to.

In the implementation for our approach, we made the decision to allow the data publisher to decide how many data entities can be stored per dataset fragment (identical to the amount of values that can be stored in a node of a generic B-tree implementation). The consequence of this is that the size of a single fragment scales both with the amount of data entities stored in the fragment, as well as with the individual sizes of each of these entities. Because of this, at publication time the average entity size has to be taken into consideration when creating a fragmentation, as this will influence the bandwidth requirement of the interface.

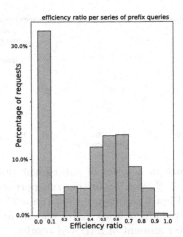

Fig. 4. The efficiency shows a large quantity of 0% queries. This is due to targets that do not result in an answer (not in the collection). For other requests we see the efficiency averages over 50%.

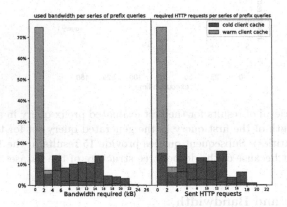

Fig. 5. A max bandwidth of 25kB is consumed for an autocompletion query for this particular dataset and query log. The number of requests for a full query autocompletion range from 0 to 20 requests in worst-case. The y-axis is the % of queries.

4.4 Fragment Sizes

In the prior experiments, we always used a fragment size of 25 entities per page. We selected this page size when comparing the query performance of 25, 50, 75 to 100 entities per page. The results are provided in Fig. 6. We notice longer startup times for the initial queries over larger dataset, and that larger fragment sizes perform better for small datasets, but in turn perform worse for larger datasets. This can be attributed to the trade-off between traversal speed and data locality, where for larger datasets traversal speed becomes increasingly important.

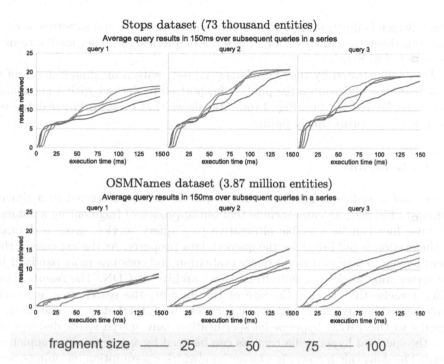

Fig. 6. This figure compares the performance for clients evaluating prefix queries over (Top) the public transport stops dataset (73k entities, 6 triples per entity) and (Bottom) the OSMNames dataset (3.87m entities, 32 triples per entity).

5 Discussion

In contrast to a query server, where the number of HTTP requests stays constant when a dataset grows in size, the amount of HTTP requests needed with the tree approach is proportional to the amount of entities in the dataset. In case of a fragmentation based on a theoretical B-tree, the number of requests necessary to find entities matching a prefix value is decided based on the height of the tree, which can be calculated theoretically for a dataset of n entities as: $r_{max} = \lfloor log_{\lceil m/2 \rceil}(\frac{n+1}{2}) \rfloor$, with r_{max} the maximum number of requests necessary, without counting the root node which can be prefetched, and with m the maximum number of children a node can have. The depth thus defines the number of HTTP requests needed when only the root node of a tree is found, and this is the first time the auto-completion is being ran, so the client cache is cold. With every depth that is added, it takes an exponential (power of $m/2$) number of entities more to result in an increase in worst-case number of requests necessary. Applied to our dataset: with 25 entities per fragment for a total of 10^5 entities, a depth of 4 would be needed (h_{max}), and thus 4 HTTP requests would be needed in worst-case to show results. When a new query shortly thereafter is done, the probability of being able to cache one of the higher-level nodes should become higher, which is illustrated by Fig. 2. Our implementation and experiment confirms this theoretical analysis: for a full series of queries, the experimental results are depicted in Fig. 5.

This is illustrated by the OSMNames dataset, with a maximum depth of 6 for 3.87 million entities, vs. the public transport stops dataset with a maximum depth of 4 for 73k entities. Fig. 3 thus also shows that even for larger datasets, the approach returns timely results.

6 Conclusion

Given that a sufficient number (±15) of results will be retrieved in a timely fashion (±150 ms), we can conclude that our approach of fragmenting a dataset as static files can be a viable alternative to a query service, given a dataset fragmentation is published for the queried data property. At the expense of the client having to take part in the query evaluation and consume more bandwidth, the server may work even fully from cache, archive or CDN. The results show using a cache that is 10% the size of the dataset, the search tree approach implemented in this paper reaches a server cache hit ratio that is ±3 times better. Thanks to the TREE hypermedia specification, any search space design that uses the specified hypermedia controls can be used by a generic autocompletion client. The downside however is a larger bandwidth consumption, meaning query response times will be easier impacted by a bad internet connectivity. While we designed this approach for datasets for which setting up a tool like ElasticSearch or a SPARQL endpoint is not worth the effort, the approach can return results in a timely fashion even for large datasets with millions of entities.

The fragment size itself however is a difficult decision to make, and we do not have a silver bullet approach to decide what the best number per dataset fragment would be. In this paper we tested the approach for one specific use case of prefix autocompletion and came to the conclusion that a size of 25 entities per fragment gave the best response times. However, depending on the dataset, the query set used for the benchmark, the level of privacy you want to guarantee and type of text search query, we believe other fragment sizes may be more interesting. Furthermore, the ideal fragment size will also depend on the type of hypermedia search space one implements. In this paper we chose a B-tree approach to prove that file-based fragmentation strategies can produce and acceptable user-perceived performance, yet we certainly do not rule out other search space designs. Future work will be to come up with specific search space designs such as faster querying by adding important entities higher up in the tree, for substring search with automata, for fuzzy matches by clustering by string distance, with a geospatial bias by first adding a geospatial fragmentation to your dataset, etc.

The new client-server relation for prefix search has an effect on the user experience guidelines of Pelias (cfr. Sect. 2)). (i) Throttling requests can happen differently, as a large amount of requests can be handled from server cache. In a similar way, there is also no danger of out of order responses (ii). As the client controls the query evaluation process, subsequent request can filter the previously retrieved results, and continue the on-going query processing to the next prefix. Finally, (iii) using a pre-written client was a guideline when working with the query server design, and remains our guideline here as well. This pre-written client is given more responsibility for the query evaluation process, giving it more flexibility to implement the autocompletion or any text search feature in the way a developer wants. In the same spirit of the Pelias user experience guidelines, we formulate two additional guidelines for publishing a fragmented interface. A caching is the driver behind the scalability of this approach, probably the most important of these guidelines will be (iv) to set caching headers. Both conditional caching with `etag header`, as setting a `cache-control` header are possibilities in different designs. Next, for public datasets, also (v) Cross Origin Resource Sharing (CORS) headers need to be enabled. This will enable application developers to reuse the dataset from a different domain than where the dataset itself is hosted.

References

1. Cai, F., De Rijke, M., et al.: A survey of query auto completion in information retrieval. Found. Trends Inf. Retrieval **10**(4), 273–363 (2016). https://staff.fnwi. uva.nl/m.derijke/wp-content/papercite-data/pdf/cai-survey-2016.pdf
2. Comer, D.: Ubiquitous b-tree. ACM Comput. Surv. (CSUR) **11**(2), 121–137 (1979). https://dl.acm.org/doi/10.1145/356770.356776
3. Graefe, G., Kuno, H.: Modern b-tree techniques. In: 2011 IEEE 27th International Conference on Data Engineering, pp. 1370–1373. IEEE (2011). https://doi.org/10. 1561/1900000028. http://citeseerx.ist.psu.edu/viewdoc/download?doi=10.1.1.219. 7269&rep=rep1&type=pdf
4. Knublauch, H., Kontokostas, D.: Shapes constraint language (shacl) (2017). W3C recommendation (2017) https://www.w3.org/TR/shacl/#property-paths
5. Taelman, R., Van Herwegen, J., Vander Sande, M., Verborgh, R.: Comunica: a modular SPARQL query engine for the web. In: Vrandečić, D., et al. (eds.) ISWC 2018. LNCS, vol. 11137, pp. 239–255. Springer, Cham (2018). https://doi.org/10. 1007/978-3-030-00668-6_15
6. Van Herwegen, J., De Vocht, L., Verborgh, R., Mannens, E., Van de Walle, R.: Substring filtering for low-cost linked data interfaces. In: Arenas, M., et al. (eds.) ISWC 2015. LNCS, vol. 9366, pp. 128–143. Springer, Cham (2015). https://doi.org/ 10.1007/978-3-319-25007-6_8
7. Vandenbussche, P.Y., Atemezing, G.A., Poveda-Villalón, M., Vatant, B.: Linked Open Vocabularies (LOV): a gateway to reusable semantic vocabularies on the Web. Semantic Web **8**(3), 437–452 (2017)
8. Verborgh, R., et al.: Triple pattern fragments: a low-cost knowledge graph interface for the web. J. Web Semant. 37–38, 184–206 (2016). http://linkeddatafragments. org/publications/jws2016.pdf. https://doi.org/10.1016/j.websem.2016.03.003

Social Web

Assessing the Quality of Online Reviews Using Formal Argumentation Theory

Davide Ceolin[1]([⊠])[iD], Giuseppe Primiero[2][iD], Jan Wielemaker[1][iD], and Michael Soprano[3][iD]

[1] Centrum Wiskunde & Informatica, Amsterdam, The Netherlands
{davide.ceolin,j.wielemaker}@cwi.nl
[2] University of Milan, Milan, Italy
giuseppe.primiero@unimi.it
[3] University of Udine, Udine, Italy
michael.soprano@uniud.it

Abstract. Review scores collect users' opinions in a simple and intuitive manner. However, review scores are also easily manipulable, hence they are often accompanied by explanations. A substantial amount of research has been devoted to ascertaining the quality of reviews, to identify the most useful and authentic scores through explanation analysis. In this paper, we advance the state of the art in review quality analysis. We introduce a rating system to identify review arguments and to define an appropriate weighted semantics through formal argumentation theory. We introduce an algorithm to construct a corresponding graph, based on a selection of weighted arguments, their semantic similarity, and the supported ratings. We provide an algorithm to identify the model of such an argumentation graph, maximizing the overall weight of the admitted nodes and edges. We evaluate these contributions on the Amazon review dataset by McAuley et al. [15], by comparing the results of our argumentation assessment with the upvotes received by the reviews. Also, we deepen the evaluation by crowdsourcing a multidimensional assessment of reviews and comparing it to the argumentation assessment. Lastly, we perform a user study to evaluate the explainability of our method. Our method achieves two goals: (1) it identifies reviews that are considered useful, comprehensible, truthful by online users and does so in an unsupervised manner, and (2) it provides an explanation of quality assessments.

Keywords: Formal argumentation theory · Online reviews · Information quality

1 Introduction

Online reviews can be a valuable source of information, as they allow users to gain from the experience of others who have expressed their opinion about the next product to buy or room to book. Opinions provided by Web users

© Springer Nature Switzerland AG 2021
M. Brambilla et al. (Eds.): ICWE 2021, LNCS 12706, pp. 71–87, 2021.
https://doi.org/10.1007/978-3-030-74296-6_6

are useful insofar as those of higher quality can be identified. Over the past years, research has characterized reviews' trustworthiness in several ways: user reputation and quality assessment are among them. However, while reviews are about specific products or services, they represent often express multifaceted views on the target object. To assess the quality and trustworthiness of a review, it is important to understand which arguments it provides, their strength, and on which aspects of a target product they provide positive or negative evidence.

Reviews can be seen in the form of ratings-descriptions pairs. Such form of reviews, common in many e-commerce sites, indicates a rating (often in a 1–5 Likert scale) for the quality of a given target product, enriched with textual descriptions motivating the score. We analyze these descriptions to identify arguments that support the corresponding scores. Arguments are identified through natural language processing of such descriptions and ranked according to their importance using the textRank algorithm [16]. The quality of the descriptions is quantified through a readability measure [11]. We formulate, implement, and evaluate a rating system based on formal argumentation theory which collects such sets of pairs when they share a given argument but offer opposing ratings. We study it in depth by addressing the following research questions:

R1: Given a set of reviews about the same product, can argumentation reasoning help assessing review quality?
R2: Which quality aspects does argumentation reasoning emphasize?
R3: Can argumentation reasoning be used to explain review quality?

The rest of this paper is structured as follows. In Sect. 2 we first provide some informal preliminaries, then develop a preferential argumentation framework. In Sect. 3 we describe the experimental settings we adopt. In Sects. 4, 5, and 6 we present our approaches to RQ1, 2, and 3, and the related results. We discuss the three evaluations in Sect. 7. In Sect. 8 we present related work, and in Sect. 9 we conclude.

2   Weight Based Preferential Rating Systems

We propose a formal semantics of value-based argumentation that extends the model of Baroni et al. [3] to describe the conflict and support dynamics between topics as arguments within a set of reviews. Let us consider a set of reviews of a given product. We interpret them as nodes of a graph, where edges of the graph express the attack relation between two reviews providing descriptions for at least one common feature of the product, while they assign different scores to it. The semantics of the graph is established by a standard labeling function on vertices:

1. An argument is labeled *in* when all its attackers are *out*;
2. An argument is labeled *out* when at least one of its attackers is *in*;
3. An argument is labeled *undec* if not all its attackers are *out* and no attacker is *in*.

This semantics is aligned with the scores from natural language processing of the reviews and translated in a graph construction algorithm. Topics are grouped using K-means clustering; two reviews with disagreeing ratings attack each other when they share two topics belonging to the same cluster. Attacks follow topic weight ordering and support between arguments is represented indirectly: an argument supports another argument when it attacks its attacker. The weight of the corresponding edge is based on semantic similarity. Grouping reviews per topic allows obtaining a coherent set of reviews identifying the pros and cons of the same item.

Definition 1 (Review). *A review $\mathscr{R}_i(t)$ by an agent $i \in \mathscr{A}$ on a target t is construed as:*

1. *A list of topics: $\mathscr{T} = \{\phi_1; ...; \phi_n\}$;*
2. *A relevance value $r(\phi_i) \in [0, 1]$ for each topic ϕ_i;*
3. *A semantic similarity value $sem\_sim(\phi_i, \phi_j) \in [0, 1]$ defined for each pair of topic for each review;*
4. *A score $sc(\mathscr{R}_i) = \{1, 2, 3, 4, 5\}$;*
5. *A quality value $v(\mathscr{R}_i) \in [0, 1]$.*

Provided a list of reviews $\{\mathscr{R}\}$, we collect all those with the same target object t and denote them as $\{\mathscr{R}(t)\}$. The list of topics $\mathscr{T}$ collects the elements characterizing the review content on the target product: for example, on the target "shoes", topics could be "sole", "upper", but also "comfortable for long walks". The relevance value $r(\phi_i)$ quantifies the importance of topic ϕ_i within the review itself. This is a *de facto* value function from topics to real positive numbers. Likewise, $sem\_sim(\phi_i, \phi_j)$ represents any of the available functions (e.g. based on thesaurus, symbolical representations of word semantics, term probabilistic co-occurrence) for semantic similarity defined for every couple of topics. Given $\{\mathscr{R}(t)\}$ and $\mathscr{T}(t) = \{\phi_1; ...; \phi_n\}$, we cluster any two topics according to a function $sem\_dist(\phi_i, \phi_j)$ defined in the interval $[0, \infty]$. Several implementations are possible for this measure. In our case, we use the Word Mover distance [13] to measure the similarity between topics that are represented through text tokens, that are, in fact, groups of words. To identify the ideal number of clusters, we compute the cluster silhouette for a diverse number of clusters and we select the cluster configuration that maximizes this value, i.e. such that the intra-cluster average distance is minimized. The function $sem\_sim(\phi_i, \phi_j)$ is then computed simply as $\frac{1}{sem\_dist(\phi_i, \phi_j)}$. The score $\mathscr{R}_i$ is the value attributed to the object. We represent the score as an integer from 1 to 5, as it is done in many review systems. We currently consider different values as opposing, and do not consider the absolute difference between them (e.g. treating the difference between $| sc(\mathscr{R}_i) - sc(\mathscr{R}_j) | > | sc(\mathscr{R}_i) - sc(\mathscr{R}_k) |$). Finally, a quality value is used to rank reviews. We especially consider the readability of the review to be an important aspect because: (1) it quantifies how easily a reader might consume it and (2) it might provide a proxy for the quality of the information it contains. In particular, in our experiments, we use the Flesch Kincaid Reading Ease measure [11]. This formula provides reliable scores between 100 (text understandable by 5th graders) and 0 (texts understandable by professionals). Other readability measures will be tested in the future.

Topics within the same cluster are those on which reviews' attacks are defined, as reviews showing semantically distant topics might be considered incomparable:

Definition 2 (Attack). *Review $\mathscr{R}_i$ attacks review $\mathscr{R}_j$ with weight w ($\mathscr{R}_i \rightarrow_w \mathscr{R}_j$) iff*

1. *$\mathscr{R}_i(t) = \mathscr{R}_j(t)$;*
2. *$\{\mathscr{T}(t) \in \mathscr{R}_i \cap \mathscr{T}(t) \in \mathscr{R}_j\} \neq \emptyset$;*
3. *$sc(\mathscr{R}_i) \neq sc(\mathscr{R}_j)$;*
4. *$\sum_{\phi_i \in \mathscr{R}_i}(r(\phi_i) \cdot v(\mathscr{R}_i)) > \sum_{\phi_j \in \mathscr{R}_j}(r(\phi_j) \cdot v(\mathscr{R}_j))$;*
5. *$w = 1/\sum_{\phi_i \in \mathscr{R}_i, \phi_j \in \mathscr{R}_j}(sem\_dist(\phi_i, \phi_j))$*

According to the definition above a review attacks another one if and only if (1) they are about the same target object; (2) they have at least one of the topics of the target object considered in common; (3) their score is different (as mentioned above, we make at this point no granular distinction between differences in scores); (4) the (sum of the) relevance value(s) of the topic(s) of the attacking review weighted by its quality is higher than that of the attacked review; and finally, (5) attacks are weighted on their importance: the weight of an attack is defined as the inverse of the (sum of the) semantic distance(s) of the topic(s) of the reviews involved, hence expressing the fact that an attack on more closely related topics weights more than one involving distant topics. A rating system is now built as a set of reviews and attacks between them, ordered according to a preference relation based on their weights:

Definition 3 (Rating System). *A rating system is a tuple $RS := \langle \{\mathscr{R}(t)\}, R^-, \leq \rangle$ where*

1. *$\{R(t)\}$ is a list of reviews on target t;*
2. *$R^- \subseteq \{R(t)\} \times \{R(t)\}$ is a binary relation of attack between reviews, such that $(\mathscr{R}_i, \mathscr{R}_j) \in R^-$ iff $\mathscr{R}_i \rightarrow_w \mathscr{R}_j$;*
3. *$\leq \subseteq R^- \times R'^-$ is a preference relation such that $R^- \leq R'^-$ if and only if $R^- : \mathscr{R}_i \rightarrow_w \mathscr{R}_j$, $R'^- : \mathscr{R}_k \rightarrow_{w'} \mathscr{R}_l$, $w > w'$ with possibly $j = k$.*

According to this Definition, a rating system contains (1) a set of reviews on the same target, (2) equipped with a set of attack relations, (3) ordered based on their weights. We now define several strategies to establish the attack relations actually included in any given rating system:

Definition 4 (Full Attack Strategy). *$\forall R^-, R^- \in RS$.*

The Full Attack Strategy includes every well-defined attack relation in the graph, i.e. any review attacks any other review with a different score with which it shares a topic within the same semantic similarity cluster and which has a lower weight computed as the relevance of the topic and quality value of the review. From this general case, we offer several pruning strategies on the number of attack relations.

Definition 5 (Heavy Weight Pruning). $R^- \in RS$ iff $\exists R'^-$. $R^- \leq R'^-$.

In the Heavy Weight Pruning, we remove from the rating system the (set of) attack(s) with the lowest weight. By the definition of weight, this reflects the intuition that one removes those attacks based on the reviews having a different score on topics of low relevance, or on semantically distant topics (i.e. the reviews express different views on possibly incomparable aspects of the product). Note that a significant variant of this pruning method consists in removing the attacks with the weight under a certain value, e.g. falling within the last percentile. A more selective pruning strategy is expressed through clustering by semantic similarity:

Definition 6 (Clustering Pruning). $R^- \in RS$ iff $R^- < R'^-$ for some R'^- : $\mathscr{R}_i \rightarrow_{w'} \mathscr{R}_j$ and $w' < n$ such that n is the chosen value for a given clustering algorithm.

According to this method, an attack relation is considered in the graph of the rating system if and only if its weight is above the clustering threshold for the semantic similarity of the topics involved by the attack. Once the clustering is established of what does it mean for two topics to be similar, any attack which picks topics from distinct clusters is removed and no longer considered. In the following, we consider this pruning strategy as our main one. We now define the labeling of a rating system:

Definition 7 (Labelling). *Given a rating system RS*

- $\{\mathscr{S}(t)\} \subseteq \{\mathscr{R}(t)\}$ is conflict-free iff there are no $\mathscr{R}_i, \mathscr{R}_j \in \{\mathscr{S}(t)\}$ such that $(\mathscr{R}_i, \mathscr{R}_j) \in R^-$;
- A review $\mathscr{R}_i \in \{\mathscr{R}(t)\}$ is supported by $\{\mathscr{S}(t)\} \subseteq \{\mathscr{R}(t)\}$ iff for any $\mathscr{R}_j \in \{\mathscr{R}(t)\}$ such that $(\mathscr{R}_j, \mathscr{R}_i) \in R^-$, it exists $\mathscr{R}_k \in \{\mathscr{R}(t)\}$ such that $(\mathscr{R}_k, \mathscr{R}_j) \in R^-$;
- A review $\mathscr{R}_i \in \{\mathscr{R}(t)\}$ is defeated by $\{\mathscr{S}(t)\} \subseteq \{\mathscr{R}(t)\}$ if and only if it $\exists \mathscr{R}_j \in \{\mathscr{S}(t)\}$ such that $(\mathscr{R}_j, \mathscr{R}_i) \in R^-$ and $\mathscr{R}_j$ is supported by $\{\mathscr{S}(t)\}$;
- A review $\mathscr{R}_i \in \{\mathscr{R}(t)\}$ which is neither supported nor defeated is undecided.

A conflict-free RS is possible if and only if every review has the same score for every topic ϕ_i within a given cluster of semantic similarity. The notion of support of a review by a rating system expresses the idea that the score of that review for the given (cluster of) topic(s) is endorsed; the defeat of a review by a rating system expresses the dual idea that the score of that review for the given (cluster of) topic(s) is rejected; an undecided review is one which presents high expected variance on its usefulness in establishing the score of the product.

Definition 8 (Semantics). *Given a rating system RS*

- A conflict free set $\{\mathscr{S}(t)\} \subseteq \{\mathscr{R}(t)\}$ is admissible iff each $\mathscr{R}_i \in \{\mathscr{S}(t)\}$ is supported by $\{\mathscr{S}(t)\}$;
- A preferred extension is an admissible subset of $\{\mathscr{R}(t)\}$ maximal w.r.t. set-inclusion and preference;

- *An admissible $\{\mathscr{S}(t)\} \subseteq \{\mathscr{R}(t)\}$ is a complete extension iff each review supported by $\{\mathscr{S}(t)\}$ is in $\{\mathscr{S}(t)\}$;*
- *The most (with respect to the weight of supported reviews) complete extension is the weighted complete extension.*

We look for the model which maximizes the number of *in*-nodes with higher weight.

3 Experimental Setting

We describe the implementation of the above framework and the dataset adopted.

3.1 Implementation

Figure 1 provides an overview of our implementation,[1] described as follows.

Feature Extraction. Given a set of reviews for product target t, we extract:

1. The set of textual tokens in such reviews to use as the set of topics $\mathscr{T}$ and their importance in the text $r(\phi_i)$ for each topic $\phi_i \in \mathscr{T}$. Textual tokens are estimated using the Spacy library, their importance is estimated through the pyTextRank library implementing the TextRank algorithm, i.e., computing the PageRank of the tokens in the review based on their textual dependency.
2. The readability scores of the review to use as a proxy for $sc(\mathscr{R}_i)$; again we use the Spacy library and, in particular, the Spacy-readability extension.

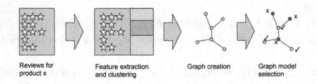

Reviews for product x   Feature extraction and clustering   Graph creation   Graph model selection

Fig. 1. Overview of the graph creation pipeline

Argumentation Graph Building. We proceed as follows:

1. Build the semantic distance matrix of all the tokens in the reviews of that product from each $sem\_dist(\phi_i, \phi_j)$. We use the Word Mover distance [13] implemented in Gensim [19] to this aim;
2. cluster tokens according to their semantic similarity. We use K-means and we identify the optimal number of clusters using the silhouette method;
3. represent an argumentation graph as a NetworkX Directed graph where: (1) nodes represent reviews; and (2) links represent attacks. Reviews attack all other reviews with a lighter score that share the same topic and disagree on the rating.

---

[1] Source code available at: https://github.com/davideceolin/FAReviews.

Graph Solution. In order to identify the models of the graph, we implement a SWISH Prolog-based solver also available as a standalone service accessed via a customized extension of the Python Prolog Pengines library.[2]

3.2 Dataset

We evaluate the above model on the Amazon Review Dataset [15], in particular on the Amazon Fashion 5-core dataset, which consists of 3,562 reviews (3,009 after duplicate removal) provided by 406 users about 31 products. For each review, the dataset reports:

- the id of the review author;
- the timestamp and the text of the review;
- the id of the product reviewed;
- the rating given to the product (on a 1–5 Likert scale);
- the number of upvotes a given review received. Note that users can only indicate whether they found a given review useful, not the contrary.

3.3 Argumentation Graph Building Example

Reviews and their argumentation graph are compared for explainability. Details of the graph construction process are given below in Sect. 4. Here we provide an example:

> Review 1: 'We have used these inserts for years. They provide great support.' (5 stars)
> Review 2: 'This is my 6th pair and they are the best thing ever for my plantar fasciitis and resultant neuromas. Unfortunately, the ones I ordered from SmartDestination must be seconds as they kill my feet. The hard plastic insert rubs on the outside edges of my feet. I am unable to exchange them as I waited one day too late to use them in my walking shoes.' (2 stars).

The two reviews have no textual token in common, however, some of their tokens are semantically related. For example, 'these inserts' (Review 1) and 'hard plastic insert' are semantically close enough to belong to the same cluster. This means that we capture an attack between the two, from Review 1 (readability 102.5) to Review 2 (readability 73.44). The weight of the attack is given by the sum of the importance of all the tokens of the two reviews which co-occur in a cluster, weighted on the semantic similarity between each pair of tokens and on the readability of the review itself. The semantic similarity is computed after stop words removal (the above tokens are 'hard plastic insert' and 'inserts'). This process is repeated with all the tokens shared between two reviews and with all the review pair combinations for a given product.

---

[2] https://swish.swi-prolog.org/p/argue.swinb.

4   RQ1 - Review Quality Assessment Evaluation

We consider here the ability of our system to discriminate reviews' quality.

4.1   Baselines and Evaluation Settings

We created two baselines:

Unsupervised (K-Means). We extract a set of basic textual features from the reviews (e.g., text length) and we cluster them using the K-Means algorithm with $K = 3$.

Supervised (SVC). Using the same features as above, we split the dataset and use the first 30% of reviews to train a Support Vector Classifier to classify the remaining 70%. To allow a fair comparison between the three methods, we convert the number of upvotes into two buckets, to mimic the classification obtained with our method. We provide three variations on this, with thresholds at 1, 5, and 10 upvotes.

We evaluate our framework under three different settings:

Argumentation Framework. We adopt the dataset described in Sect. 3.1.

Argumentation Framework Weighted. We adopt the dataset described in Sect. 3.1, but we apply a decaying function to the number of upvotes based on their age. The decaying function we use is $w(x) = \frac{t_{max} - t_x}{t_{max} - t_{min}}$ where t_{max} and t_{min} are the highest and lowest timestamps in the dataset; t_x is the timestamp of review x. Since the argumentation framework result is compared with a snapshot of the upvotes collected at a given time, this decaying function compensates for the fact that the older reviews had a higher chance to get upvotes than the younger ones.

Argumentation Framework Weighted (Upvotes > 0). Since votes can only be up and not down, we cannot tell whether zero-votes reviews deserve zero votes or negative votes. We focus here on reviews that received at least one upvote.

Table 1. Average number (left) and sum (right) of upvotes received by the reviews in each class. The average of upvotes in the class should be maximized, the average in the *out* class minimized. In Arg. Framework Weighted, a temporal decaying function (see Sect. 4.1) is used. In Arg. Framework Weighted (>0 upvotes), we consider reviews with at least 1 upvote (see Table 3).

Method	Out	In	Method	Out	In
Arg. Framework	2.3	0.5	Arg. Framework	35	**1553**
Arg. Framework Weighted	**0.0**	0.4	Arg. Framework Weighted	0	1210
Arg. Fram. Weigh. (>0 upvotes)	**0.0**	4.2	Arg. Fram. Weigh. (>0 upvotes)	0	1210
Unsupervised (K-Means)	2.5	0.3	Unsupervised (K-Means)	662	926
Supervised (SVC) @1	**0.0**	5.7	Supervised (SVC) @1	26	1165
Supervised (SVC) @5	0.1	10.2	Supervised (SVC) @5	304	765
Supervised (SVC) @10	0.3	**17.7**	Supervised (SVC) @10	610	459

4.2 Results

We run the above algorithm and we obtain a classification of product reviews as *in* or *out*. No review is classified as *undecided*. Table 1 shows the average number and sum of upvotes that the review in given class received. For example, the reviews that are labeled as *out* (i.e., rejected) by the weighted version of our framework got, on average, 4.2 upvotes, and reviews classified as *out* got on average 0.0. We considered the possibility of computing precision and recall of our method. However, precision and recall imply the existence of negative samples, while upvotes are only positive values. Artificially introducing a threshold to split reviews into positive and negative items would be possibly misleading. A "one-size-fits-all" would hardly work in this case: such a threshold could have to vary per product or product type and could have to take into account also temporal aspects. For instance, less popular products could receive fewer reviews and have a smaller chance to get upvotes. Thus, their threshold should be lower than that of popular products. At the same time, the rareness of reviews alone cannot be considered a sufficient reason to set the bar low: those few reviews could get few upvotes because of their poor quality. Therefore, we limit the comparison with the baseline approaches to Table 1. With these considerations in mind, to allow a comparison between our method and SVC, we still introduce the use of thresholds to convert the multivalued classification of SVC into binary values. For this, we use three thresholds, 1, 5, and 10 (the mean number of upvotes received by a review in the ground truth is 0.55, median 0). We deepen these considerations in Sect. 7.

5 RQ2 - Multidimensional Review Quality Assessment

The evaluation of the argumentation theory-based review assessment by correlation with upvotes uses the latter as the only ground truth provided in the dataset at our disposal, but they also show important limitations. First, upvotes collect only positive votes: if a review did not get a high number of upvotes, it could be either of low- or average-quality. Second, the semantics of upvotes is rather vague and broad: since they are the only means for readers to express their endorsement, they can capture appreciation in a too broad sense. Third, upvotes might depend on the order with which reviews are exposed to users and their age. We extend our analysis on the quality of reviews to obtain a more thorough and detailed gold standard. We crowdsource answers to questions regarding quality aspects of a significant number of reviews, as detailed below.

5.1   Crowdsourcing Setting

We collect 380 reviews by first randomly selecting one of the products reviewed, then one of its reviews. This ensures that the products are fairly represented since the dataset is rather skewed. Considering that, in total, the dataset is composed of 3.009 reviews, our sample has a confidence interval of 6.19 with a confidence level of 99%. We ask each worker to evaluate the quality of 10 reviews, and each review is evaluated by 5 workers. Workers are located in the US, and the tasks (which are rewarded 0.9$) are performed through Amazon Mechanical Turk.[3]

Task Description. We present the worker with a product description as provided in the Amazon dataset. Then, we present the review, and we ask the worker to assess the review on a 5-level Likert scale (from −2, completely disagree, to +2, completely agree), across the following quality dimensions:

Truthfulness: measures the overall truthfulness and trustworthiness of the review.

Reliability: the review is considered reliable, as opposed to reporting unreliable information. *Example (label: +2 Completely agree): "They fit great, look great, are quite comfortable and are just what I was looking for!".*

Neutrality: the review is expressed objective terms, as opposed to resulting subjective or biased. *Example (label: −2 Completely disagree): "Love them!!"*

Comprehensibility: the review is comprehensible/understandable/readable as opposed to difficult to understand. *Example (label: +2 Completely agree): "They run big. Order a full size smaller".*

Precision: the review is precise/specific, as opposed to vague. *Example (label: +2 Completely agree): They run big. Order a full size smaller.*

Completeness: the review is complete as opposed to partial. *Example (label: +2 Completely agree): "I actually have 3 pairs of these trainers. They are very comfortable, there is a neoprene sleeve that goes around your ankle that makes them the most comfortable for me compared to normal athletic shoes. They run a little narrow - for me this is perfect, but you may want to round up on the size or try on in the store first if your feet are on the wider side."*

Informativeness: The review allows deriving useful information as opposed to well-known facts and/or tautologies. *Example (label: +1 Agree): "Love these shoes! Needed new running shoes and these are perfect. Light weight and fit great!"*

---

[3] http://mturk.com.

The above dimensions are based on previous work on multidimensional quality assessment [6]. However, with reviews, it is very hard for the workers to determine the truthfulness of information because they need to assess the authenticity of the review itself, which is often subjective. So, we adapt the quality dimensions from the literature to represent more subjective aspects like reliability.

5.2 Results

Assessments were collected and we checked whether the scores in any of the evaluated dimensions showed a correlation with the *in-out* evaluation of the review by our algorithm. Since our classification consists of two labels only, while the crowdsourced data are multidimensional and finer-grained, we performed a set of analyses at diverse levels of aggregation, starting from splitting the reviews into *in* and *out*, obtaining:

- a χ^2 on the two sets review scores: no significant difference is identified;
- a Mann-Whitney test on the average score per dimension: no significant difference between the two sets of reviews is identified;
- t-test or Mann-Whitney test when comparing the raw scores on each dimension: no significant difference is identified.

Then, we aggregate the scores in two ($[-2,0], [1,2]$) and three ($[-2,-1], [0], [1,2]$):

- a χ^2 test on the two sets reviews still does not identify any significant difference in the distribution of scores;
- a Mann-Whitney test on the average score per dimension identifies a significant difference in the distribution of scores;
- at 90% confidence, a significant difference is identified in the distribution of the comprehensibility and the overall truthfulness scores of the two distributions.

In other words, when the crowdsourced scores are expressed on a coarse scale (two- or three-valued), our classification identifies two sets of reviews, where those labeled as *out* have higher comprehensibility and a higher overall-truthfulness than those labeled as *out*. Since readability score plays a role in the argumentation framework, those results might just be linked to the use of those scores. However, the readability score has a correlation of 0.24 with the crowdsourced comprehensibility, and of only 0.02 with the overall truthfulness. Thus, the identification of the review with higher truthfulness can be attributed to the whole framework.

6 RQ3 - Explainability Evaluation

We run an explorative questionnaire[4] to evaluate whether our approach provides informative explanations on the decision taken about the reviews (*in/out* outcome). We select two reviews about the same product, one accepted, and one

---

[4] The questionnaire is available at https://forms.gle/srGJpGyYBzWd9RTaA.

rejected by our system. We show the argumentation graph on which the judgment is based and we ask the respondent whether the graph helps in understanding the underlying reasoning using a 1–5 Likert scale. Users can provide additional feedback. Table 2 shows the distribution of the 31 anonymous responses received, while Fig. 2 shows an example question.

According to these results, the argumentation graph does indeed help in explaining the outcome. Since the outcomes vary from 'poorly informative' (1) 'to very informative' (5), the results are explanatory on both reviews (although for review 2 the signal is stronger). An important aspect of consideration as a possible limitation is that in argumentation-based reasoning arguments are valid until attacked and this translates into reviews accepted because not attacked.

Table 2. Distribution of the answers regarding the helpfulness.

Informativeness	1 (poorly informative)	2	3	4	5 (very informative)
Review 1 (accepted)	0	6	11	12	2
Review 2 (rejected)	0	1	7	15	8

Below, we represent the graph of reviews of product B00OKPIHQ4. Review 1 is accepted because it is not attacked by any other reviews (while it attacks others). It is the one highlighted in the graph.

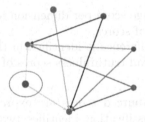

Fig. 2. Example question. Nodes represent reviews, (green *in*, red *out*) for the argument-based review classification, arrows represent attacks, their shade expresses semantic similarity. (Color figure online)

7 Discussion

We now discuss the results related to each research question.

7.1 RQ1 - Given a Set of Reviews About the Same Product, Can Argumentation Reasoning Help Assess Review Quality?

Our method (especially in the improved versions, see rows 2 and 3 of Table 1) *identifies two clusters of reviews where those in have a higher chance of having more upvotes than those out. Also, the method identifies the majority of the reviews that received upvotes.*

The first difference between the unsupervised approach and the proposed argumentation framework concerns labeling. The results reported in Table 1 assume arbitrarily that one of the two classes predicted by the K-means method equals the *out* class, the other the *in* class. However, we do not have any means to label the classes in this respect. So, while the performance of the two methods looks similar when considering the averages in Table 1, this may not be the case. For most of the remaining performance reported in Table 1, our method outperforms K-means. The supervised approaches are those showing the best performance in terms of the distribution of the average number of upvotes. Supervised approaches focus on identifying the peculiarities of reviews that hint at their upvotes. They do so at the dataset level, they make use of labeled data (number of upvotes per review) and can identify those reviews that meet these criteria. These methods achieve high accuracy of the number of upvotes estimated for a given review. However, they do so at the expense of a significant amount of upvotes missed, as the right table of Table 1 shows. Measuring performance as precision and recall would have meant comparing our method on the mere ability to identify reviews having at least n upvotes for an arbitrary threshold n (this step is necessary to transform the number of upvotes in the ground truth into binary values comparable with our classification). This goes beyond our goals and just amplifies the results reported in the left table of Table 1. The correct threshold should depend on the number of reviews received by a given product, etc. We use thresholds to transform SVC in binary outcomes, though, because of the quantitative nature of SVC. SVC predicts the number of upvotes received by a review. Setting a threshold introduces the mentioned limitations but, in this case, performance would have been measured in terms of error of the number of upvotes predicted. Thresholds mainly reduce the granularity of such metrics but necessarily introduce some error: reviews which got n upvotes for $0 < n <$ threshold are labeled as out, thus affecting the performance reported in the right table of Table 1. Also, the good performance of the supervised methods comes with limitations:

- **Need for training data.** Being supervised, SVC craves for labeled data; in production, the system might be affected by the cold start problem.
- **Arbitrary parameters.** When comparing the two methods, we had to convert the estimated number of upvotes into two classes. This is arbitrary because it corresponds to answering a question like "how many upvotes does a review need to receive to be accepted?". This has led to testing the three different parameters.
- **Lack of explanations.** The method is meant to estimate the number of upvotes received by each review. However, when deciding whether to consider a given review or not based on such estimates, it is important to understand how such reasoning was performed. Inspection on the importance would require additional efforts.

These limitations are not shown by our method, which is unsupervised and explainable. Also, from the diverse evaluation settings, we learned the following lessons.

Lesson Learned 1: Time Matters. When inspecting the reviews in the *out* class, the high average is due to just one review labeled as out, despite having received 35 upvotes. This is the oldest review of that product; 6 more reviews, received about 6 years later, had 0 upvotes. Given that these newer reviews got a lower chance to get an upvote because they are more recent, we discounted the number of upvotes based on the age of the review. This improves the system performance (see Table 1).

Lesson Learned 2: Non-attacked Reviews Should Not Necessarily Be Accepted. In formal argumentation theory, arguments are accepted until they are defeated. However, not yet attacked reviews could get zero upvotes for a variety of reasons (e.g., they are out of topic). On a long-tail distributed dataset, this affects the results obtained. This is the reason why the reviews classified *in* have a low average number of upvotes. As shown in the third row of Table 1, the performance on the reviews with at least one upvote is higher. Table 3 provides an overview of the number of reviews per class.

7.2   RQ2 - Which Quality Aspects Does Argumentation Reasoning Emphasize?

The labeling obtained by our argumentation framework is correlated with the comprehensibility and with the overall truthfulness of the reviews. As already pointed out in Sect. 5, the readability scores alone would not be able to point out the reviews having higher overall truthfulness. This result has a twofold consequence. First, it supports the argumentation-based approach and the need for logical reasoning to be performed on top of the ranked arguments to obtain labeling that correlates with overall truthfulness and comprehensibility. Second, it points out other quality aspects that we might consider in future extensions of our framework. E.g., completeness might be correlated to the number of *in* arguments in a review. Here we learned an important lesson.

Table 3. Number of reviews classified as in and out, split on the number of upvotes.

Class	In	Out
Reviews with 0 upvotes	2,706	14
Reviews with at least 1 upvote	288	1

Lesson Learned 3: Granularity and Semantics Matter. While quality is subjective and contextual, it is also possible to define which aspects of quality we are interested in. This is important to allow a more precise understanding of the argumentation outcome. Also, the current implementation of the framework provides a three-valued assessment and, as expected, correlation with crowdsourced ratings emerges only when these are aggregated in buckets. Future extensions of the framework might consider a fine-grained representation of acceptance/rejection of arguments.

7.3   RQ3 - Can Argumentation Reasoning Be Used to Explain Review Quality?

According to the exploratory study described in Sect. 6, *argumentation graphs are useful to explain review assessment.* The study was meant to provide a first indication about the hypothesis that argumentation graphs are useful to explain review assessment. The responders agreed with this idea: 45,2% of them rated informativeness at level 4 or 5 (very informative) for the first question, 73,6% for the second. This will be further explored in the future. "How to better represent attack weights?" and "which level of complexity users can handle?" are examples of questions we will tackle.

8   Related Work

This work falls within the growing family of weighted argumentation frameworks extending standard Dung's setting, including Preferential Argumentation Frameworks [1,2,17] and Value-based Argumentation Frameworks [4,5]. A specific approach is represented by systems defining preferences based on weighted attacks, see [9], establishing that some inconsistencies are tolerated in the set of arguments, provided that the sum of the weights of attacks does not exceed a given value. Weights can be used to provide a total order of attacks, see [14]. This approach can be generalized in several ways: in [8] a different way of relaxing the admissibility condition and strengthening the notion of defense is presented; in [7] different selections on extensions based on the order of weights are proposed. Our work also relies on an ordering on weighted attacks, essential differences being that:

1. the definition of weights is given by the semantic distance between topics;
2. the clustering of attacks is based on weights;
3. the pruning of the graph is based on the order, as distinct from the selection of the model based on the maximization of the weight of accepted arguments.

Research on the assessment of quality and credibility of product reviews has focused mostly on linguistic aspects, e.g. based on readability and linguistic errors [10,12,18,22]. While such approaches can be a source of inspiration for future extensions, the main difference with our approach is the combination of such linguistic aspects with argumentation reasoning. A similar extension can be obtained by looking into credibility factors, as in [21]. Lastly, [23] looks for a junction between natural language processing and argumentation reasoning. While it classifies more thoroughly the diverse tokens as different kinds of arguments, it does so semi-automatically, while we take an automatic unsupervised approach. Refining the characterization of arguments is one aspect we intend to improve in the future. Regarding the crowdsourced assessment of online information, we refer the reader to [20], although their focus is on political statements, and their assessment is mono-dimensional. A multidimensional approach is adopted in [6], where Web documents are assessed by experts (nichesourcing).

9   Conclusion and Future Work

This paper presents a framework for classifying reviews' quality based on a combination of NLP and argumentation reasoning. We evaluate the framework on a real-world dataset showing that this approach partly outperforms baseline unsupervised and supervised approaches, while also providing explainable results. A deeper analysis of the quality of the reviews based on crowdsourcing highlights that the argumentation framework is actually capable of identifying those reviews that the users perceive as more comprehensible and truthful. Also, a two- or three-level scoring of reviews across multiple quality dimensions reveals to be the ideal level of granularity. We also run a user study that confirms the ability of argumentation graphs of providing useful explanations. This argumentation-based framework represents a first step towards a reliable and transparent assessment of the quality of online opinions.

We foresee several future developments for this work. Firstly, the framework should be extended by discounting the weight of the review and its attacks considering the temporal aspect (e.g., using weight $w(x)$ of Sect. 7). Secondly, the model could account for a different semantics of nodes *in* and *out* to prevent that novel reviews be automatically *in*. Thirdly, we will improve the identification of the arguments among the review tokens. Lastly, we plan on analyzing a larger number of datasets and reviews.

Acknowledgements. This work is partially supported by The Credibility Coalition.

References

1. Amgoud, L., Cayrol, C.: A reasoning model based on the production of acceptable arguments. Ann. Math. Artif. Intell. **34**, 197–215 (2002)
2. Amgoud, L., Vesic, S.: Two roles of preferences in argumentation frameworks. In: Liu, W. (ed.) ECSQARU 2011. LNCS (LNAI), vol. 6717, pp. 86–97. Springer, Heidelberg (2011). https://doi.org/10.1007/978-3-642-22152-1_8
3. Baroni, P., Caminada, M., Giacomin, M.: Abstract argumentation frameworks and their semantics. In: Baroni, P., Gabbay, D., Giacomin, M. (eds.) Handbook of Formal Argumentation, Chap. 4. College Publications, London (2018)
4. Bench-Capon, T.J.M.: Value-based argumentation frameworks. In: Proceedings of NMR Workshop, pp. 443–454 (2002)

5. Bench-Capon, T.J.M.: Persuasion in practical argument using value-based argumentation frameworks. J. Logic Comput. **13**(3), 429–448 (2003)
6. Ceolin, D., Noordegraaf, J., Aroyo, L.: Capturing the ineffable: collecting, analysing, and automating web document quality assessments. In: Blomqvist, E., Ciancarini, P., Poggi, F., Vitali, F. (eds.) EKAW 2016. LNCS (LNAI), vol. 10024, pp. 83–97. Springer, Cham (2016). https://doi.org/10.1007/978-3-319-49004-5_6
7. Coste-Marquis, S., Konieczny, S., Marquis, P., Ouali, M.A.: Selecting extensions in weighted argumentation frameworks. In: Proceedings of COMMA. IOS Press (2012)
8. Coste-Marquis, S., Konieczny, S., Marquis, P., Ouali, M.A.: Weighted attacks in argumentation frameworks. In: Proceedings of KR, pp. 593–597. AAAI Press (2012)
9. Dunne, P.E., Hunter, A., McBurney, P., Parsons, S., Wooldridge, M.: Weighted argument systems: basic definitions, algorithms, and complexity results. Artif. Intell. **175**(2), 457–486 (2011)
10. Ghose, A., Ipeirotis, P.G.: Estimating the helpfulness and economic impact of product reviews: mining text and reviewer characteristics. IEEE Trans. Knowl. Data Eng. **23**(10), 1498–1512 (2011)
11. Kincaid, J., Fishburne, R., Rogers, R., Chissom, B.: Derivation of new readability formulas for navy enlisted personnel. Research branch report 8–75. Technical report, Chief of Naval Technical Training: Naval Air Station Memphis (1975)
12. Korfiatis, N., García-Bariocanal, E., Sánchez-Alonso, S.: Evaluating content quality and helpfulness of online product reviews: the interplay of review helpfulness vs. review content. Electron. Commer. Res. Appl. **11**(3), 205–217 (2012)
13. Kusner, M.J., Sun, Y., Kolkin, N.I., Weinberger, K.Q.: From word embeddings to document distances. In: Proceedings of ICML, pp. 957–966. JMLR.org (2015)
14. Martínez, D.C., García, A.J., Simari, G.R.: An abstract argumentation framework with varied-strength attacks. In: Proceedings of KR, pp. 135–144. AAAI Press (2008)
15. McAuley, J.J., Targett, C., Shi, Q., van den Hengel, A.: Image-based recommendations on styles and substitutes. In: Proceedings of SIGIR, pp. 43–52. ACM (2015)
16. Mihalcea, R., Tarau, P.: TextRank: bringing order into text. In: Proceedings of EMNLP, pp. 404–411. ACL (2004)
17. Modgil, S.: Reasoning about preferences in argumentation frameworks. Artif. Intell. **173**(9), 901–934 (2009)
18. Ocampo Diaz, G., Ng, V.: Modeling and prediction of online product review helpfulness: a survey. In: Proceedings of ACL, vol. 1, pp. 698–708. ACL (2018)
19. Řehůřek, R., Sojka, P.: Software framework for topic modelling with large corpora. In: Proceedings of NLP Frameworks Workshop, pp. 45–50. ELRA (2010)
20. Roitero, K., Soprano, M., Fan, S., Spina, D., Mizzaro, S., Demartini, G.: Can the crowd identify misinformation objectively? The effects of judgment scale and assessor's background. In: Proceedings of SIGIR, pp. 439–448. ACM (2020)
21. Wathen, C.N., Burkell, J.: Believe it or not: factors influencing credibility on the web. J. Am. Soc. Inf. Sci. Technol. **53**(2), 134–144 (2002)
22. Wu, P., Van Der, Heijden, H., Korfiatis, N.: The influences of negativity and review quality on the helpfulness of online reviews. In: Proceedings of ICIS, pp. 3710–3719 (2011)
23. Wyner, A., Schneider, J., Atkinson, K., Bench-Capon, T.: Semi-automated argumentative analysis of online product reviews. In: Proceedings of COMMA, pp. 43–50. IOS Press (2012)

Web User Interface as a Message

Power Law for Fraud Detection in Crowdsourced Labeling

Sebastian Heil[1] , Maxim Bakaev[2]([⊠]) , and Martin Gaedke[1]

[1] Technische Universität Chemnitz, Chemnitz, Germany
{sebastian.heil,martin.gaedke}@informatik.tu-chemnitz.de
[2] Novosibirsk State Technical University, Novosibirsk, Russia
bakaev@corp.nstu.ru

Abstract. Web Engineering becomes increasingly hungry for training data, as the application of machine learning (ML) methods in the field intensifies. Human-labeled datasets are particularly indispensable for ML-based validation and design of user interfaces (UIs). The production of such datasets is often outsourced to crowdworkers, who typically have lower motivation and payment compared to in-house staff, so the quality of their work becomes the paramount concern. In our paper, we explore the applicability of the trending fraud detection approach based on fit to power law in crowdsourced web UI labeling. On Amazon Mechanical Turk, 298 crowdworkers labeled over 30,000 UI elements in about 500 university homepage screenshots. We found a significant correlation between workers' precisions and Kolmogorov-Smirnov statistics-based goodness-of-fit between the frequencies of UI elements in a worker's output and power law. The obtained $R^2 = 0.504$ was higher than the $R^2 = 0.432$ baseline for the popular time-on-task parameter. Moreover, the distribution of UI elements' frequencies is much less prone to manipulation by malicious crowdworkers, which is advantageous as a crowdsourced data quality control measure. The findings of our study suggest a certain resemblance between web UIs and natural language texts, in which word frequencies are known to comply with Zipf's law.

Keywords: Data quality · Distribution functions · Crowdsourcing · Amazon Mechanical Turk · Image labeling

1 Introduction

Web Engineering increasingly relies on machine learning (ML) models hungry for human-labeled training data: for information engineering, code and logs analysis, and foremost for engineering human-computer interaction and designing user interfaces (UIs). Abundant and adequate dataset is at least as important as a fine algorithm for solving a task, and training data provision is an outstanding topic in today's AI. *Crowdsourcing* has become a kind of *fast-food* technology for ML, being able to quickly and economically deliver sizable datasets, though of dubious quality and benefit. Indeed, the

---

S. Heil and M. Bakaev—Both authors contributed equally to the work.

M. Brambilla et al. (Eds.): ICWE 2021, LNCS 12706, pp. 88–96, 2021.
https://doi.org/10.1007/978-3-030-74296-6_7

core challenge in crowdsourcing today is obtaining data of appropriate quality, in the light of low wages and motivation of the workers [1]. Crowdplatforms, such as Amazon Mechanical Turk (MTurk), microworkers.com, Yandex.Toloka, struggle to support data quality assessment and control – so, lately, various related tools, such as CDAS, Crowd Truth, iCrowd, DOCS for MTurk, etc., have been introduced [2].

Concerning crowd data-quality control methods, the most widely used and supported in most of the platforms are majority/group consensus (MC) and ground truth (GT). These two methods necessarily imply redundancy, i.e. several workers performing the same task, which means wasting some – up to 67% in case of the MC – of the potentially useful work effort. Non-redundant data quality control methods that have the potential to decrease the share of low-quality or unnecessary data, can involve comparing the workers' output or some secondary parameters to a common sense or a fundamental "truth". An apparent example of a secondary parameter related to worker behavior is **time-on-task**, which is indeed reasonably popular in practical crowdsourcing quality control [1]. Obviously, knowing some expected characteristics that the dataset should comply with to be of desired quality can be even more advantageous.

A corresponding technique long known in financial fraud detection and popularized with the recent political elections is comparing large sets of data to a known distribution. Particularly, *Benford's law*, from the family of *power laws*, that predicts the probability of a specific leading digit in numbers, can be an indicator of numerical data trustworthiness in various fields [3]. Another widely known power law is *Zipf's law* for natural language texts, whose original formulation is "the frequency of any word is inversely proportional to its rank in the frequency table". There is evidence that random texts do not exhibit this phenomenon [4], and the fit to Zipf's law is believed to be one of the factors that search engines use to judge an online text's naturalness.

In our paper, we enquire whether fit to power law can be indicative of crowdsourced data quality in web UI labeling tasks, which are gaining in popularity as computer vision methods are seeing wider application for web UI visual analysis [2]. We base our assumption on the semiotic view that **UI is essentially a message**, since in a human-computer system *"... a human being (the user...) exchanges messages... with the system... using a constrained type of artificial codes"* [5]. Despite this conceptual outlook, to the extent of our knowledge, there were no successful applications of power laws to UIs. In part, this is probably due to the low diversity of the artificial codes (web UI elements) and the insufficient total number of elements in up-to-date web UIs. For instance, in one of our previous works motivated labelers found on average 86.3 visual UI elements in university homepages [2], which is far too little for a straightforward statistical test for fit to power law that is foremost characterized by its "long tail" [6]. In Sect. 2 of the paper, we position our approach within the crowdsourced data quality control and provide some background on the power laws and the testing with goodness-of-fit (GOF) that we employ instead of statistical significance, as a workaround for the small samples in web UIs. In Sect. 3, we analyze the data of the experiment we performed with MTurk workers who labeled over 30,000 UI elements in about 500 university homepage screenshots and show the superiority of the GOF measure compared to the time-on-task baseline.

2 Methods and Related Work

2.1 Data Quality Control in Crowdsourcing

A recent and comprehensive review of quality control methods for crowdsourcing can be found in [1], where the methods are organized into three major groups: individual, group and computation-based. The former two generally imply involvement of humans into assessment of the annotators or of the tasks output, thus suggesting additional overhead in the work effort. As for the methods that can be automatically performed by machines, the comparison of the measurements to some known distributions is described e.g. in the standard ISO 13528:2015 *Statistical methods for use in proficiency testing by interlaboratory comparison* (Chap. 8.4).

Automation in data quality control does not have to imply automated rejections, but should rather support Requester's decisions. In MTurk's own system for controlling fraud and abuse[1], they first use ML to identify suspicious activities, and then humans review them. Correspondingly, regression should be preferred to classification in estimating the crowd data quality. A viable approach is assessing workers, not just their output, for which worker reputation systems were implemented in all major crowd platforms. There are also methods that predict the likelihood of cheating based on workers' behavior in interaction with the task interface and even propose to transfer the predictions to other related tasks [7]. Since the number of elements in a typical web UI has the order of 10^2, we decided to rely on the **assessment of workers** each labeling several UIs, to have enough samples for checking the fit to the power law.

2.2 Power Law Distributions for Fraud Detection

The formulation of the power law is that a quantity x is drawn from a probability distribution.

$$p(x) \propto x^{-\alpha} \tag{1}$$

where α is the scaling parameter [6]. Zipf's law is basically the case when α is close to 1. Benford's law for the leading digit is conceptually similar, but has somehow different distribution and formulation:

$$p(d) = \log_b(1 + 1/d) \tag{2}$$

where d is the digit number (1...9), b is the base (e.g. b = 10).

Both laws essentially deal with frequency distributions, but Benford's law requires numerical attributes, whereas Zipf's does not. Correspondingly, the former's use to detect fraud and invalid data is wider and includes such fields as finance, social and political sciences, biometrics, network traffic analysis, etc. [3]. Zipf's law, even though not being limited to natural language texts – e.g. Halstead's equation for software code is also derivable from the law – sees comparingly less application for validating data quality.

---

[1] https://blog.mturk.com/important-updates-on-mturk-marketplace-integrity-worker-identity-and-requester-tools-to-manage-206e4e90da0c (accessed 18 Jan 2021).

Still, it was reported that the Zipf exponent characterizes the quality of peer reviewers [8], while in SEO they use it to rank copywriting texts, although different related services can provide very different estimations.

Indeed, statistical testing of fit to power law used to be controversial, as least-squares fitting is inaccurate, not being able to distinguish from e.g. exponential or lognormal distributions. In [6] they justify the use of goodness-of-fit tests based on the Kolmogorov-Smirnov (KS) statistic in combination with maximum-likelihood fitting and provide the software implementation (plpva library)[2]. As we have a low diversity of elements in UIs and relatively small samples overall, we cannot expect statistical significance of any power law tests, so we are going to rely on the goodness-of-fit measure alone.

3 Evaluation

The hypothesis in our experimental study was that the degree of compliance with power law can better explain variance in workers' performance than the baseline time-on-task.

3.1 The Experiment Description

Material. The material for the UI labeling was screenshots of homepages of higher educational organizations' (universities, colleges, etc.) websites. Initially, we collected 10,639 screenshots in PNG format using a dedicated Python script crawling through URLs that we acquired from various catalogs (DBPedia, etc.). To ensure better diversity of UI elements, the screenshots were made for full web pages, not just of the part above the fold or of a fixed size. For the current experiment, 495 screenshots were manually selected, as described in our previous related study with the same dataset [2]. The budget allocated for the MTurk experimental session was 300 USD, following our estimation of an average UI labeling task difficulty and the required work effort of 5 min.

Procedure (HIT). The labeling HIT was designed using the Crowd HTML elements provided by MTurk, based on the crowd-form and crowd-bounding-box widgets, with the screenshot URL as input parameter. The MTurk crowd-bounding-box widget renders the screenshot, allows to zoom and pan it, and to create bounding boxes of the given types with keyboard shortcuts available for fast labeling of a larger number of objects. HITs could be previewed and skipped by the crowd workers.

As we require representative frequencies for testing fit to power law, we estimated the desired number of contributions per crowdworker as at least 20. To achieve this objective within our budget of 300 USD, we introduced a second HIT, called set HIT. This HIT was only available to crowd workers with a custom qualification, which we assigned to those workers who successfully completed at least 20 of our labeling HITs. The overall fair reward per screenshot $R = 0.5$ USD was calculated based on a minimum hourly wage of 6 USD and an average labeling time of 5 min. A worker completing 20 screenshots would thus receive $R_{20} = 10$ USD. To incentivize workers to complete at least 20 labeling HITs, this reward was distributed between the labeling and the set HIT with a ratio of 1 to 10, resulting in $R_1 = 0.05$ USD reward for one labeling HIT

---

[2] https://aaronclauset.github.io/powerlaws/

and $R_S = 9$ USD for the set HIT. This setup was pre-tested by the authors in the MTurk sandbox.

Over a period of 44 days from June 29 to August 11 2020, the labeling and set HITs were available on MTurk in 4 batches of 80, 160, 160, and 97 screenshots. Within a batch, workers could submit as many labeling HITs as they wanted. To increase the diversity, however, workers who had successfully labeled 20 or more screenshots in a batch were not allowed to accept labeling HITs in the following batch.

Design. Exactly one label per bounding box and only labels from the list of pre-defined classes could be selected by the crowd workers. There were 10 classes (partially by analogy to 10 digits in Benford's law), focused on the most frequent UI objects: including interactive (*button, check, input, link, dropdown, navigation*), non-interactive (*image, backgroundimage*), and container (*table, panel*) objects.

In order to effectively use our budget and create a crowd-labeled dataset with diverse quality levels of sufficient size, the labeled screenshots submitted by the crowd workers were subject to our quick (5–10 s per screenshot) visual inspection. Using MTurk's results Rejection mechanism, we would reject the contributions:

- of evidently malicious quality – i.e. empty submissions or submissions of a few non-existing objects arbitrary located across the screenshot;
- of workers misunderstanding the labeling task – e.g. only few objects, significantly less than required for complete labeling or labeling of only one object type.

Workers who repeatedly submitted malicious results were excluded from further submissions using the "Block Worker" mechanism. In case of a HIT rejection, an explanation was provided to the workers. All other submissions were approved and received the rewards specified above.

From the UI labeling results and the data recorded by the Amazon MTurk, we derived the following variables for each worker:

- frequency distribution of the classes, i.e. the number of labels in each class: AMT_i;
- KS-based goodness-of-fit of AMT_i to power law (with plpva.r from [6]): GOF_{KS};
- mean time-on-task: ToT;
- precision, reflecting the worker's performance (quality data or fraud):

$$Precision = \frac{accepted\ HITs}{accepted\ HITs + rejected\ HITs} \tag{3}$$

Participants (Crowdworkers). Altogether 298 recorded workers participated in the 4 labeling batches (20 of them we had to block as malicious). According to the IP addresses provided by MTurk and correlated with MaxMind GeoIP2, ¾ of the workers came from the 3 countries: US (44.8%), Brazil (15.5%), and India (13.8%).

3.2 Descriptive Statistics

In total, we collected 31676 labeled UI elements for 488 accepted and 754 rejected HITs. The mean Precision per worker was 0.442 (SD = 0.475). The total amount of time spent on the 1242 HITs by all the workers was 665322 s, and on average a worker devoted 635 s (SD = 481 s) to a UI labeling HIT, the correlation between ToT and Precision being significant ($r_{298} = 0.449$, $p < 0.001$). ANOVA test for the 4 batches of screenshots suggested that there were no significant differences in either mean number of HITs per worker ($F_{3,310} = 2.41$, $p = 0.07$) or in Precision ($F_{3,310} = 1.82$, $p = 0.14$).

The mean ToT turned out to be more than twice as long compared to the 5 min (300 s) that we estimated when planning the crowdsourcing session budget. Interestingly, 22 workers who didn't label a single UI element still spent 188416 s on the HITs, which might suggest that the time-on-task became widely known as a quality control parameter in crowdsourcing and can be manipulated by malicious workers.

On average, a worker attempted to perform 4.17 HITs (SD = 4.50), of which 1.64 (SD = 2.13) would be accepted. Contrary to our expectations, the extra 9 USD award for labeling 20 UIs seemingly did not motivate the workers enough, as only 9 of them have reached this threshold. Our total expended budget for the session was 126.72 USD, which corresponds to 0.26 USD per accepted labeled UI or about 0.69 USD per working (or slacking) hour. Of the 9 workers who took our questionnaire in the set HIT, 6 provided textual feedback (3 positive, 3 satisfied, 0 negative).

3.3 The Testing Set of MTurk Workers

Since the number of crowdworkers who tried to complete at least 20 HITs turned out to be lower than expected, we decided to soften the requirements for inclusion to the testing set. The rule we applied was that *a worker must have attempted at least 10 HITs (accepted or rejected) and have labeled at least 100 UI elements* so that a reasonably representative distribution of classes could be composed. Of all the recorded workers, only 20 (6.71%) have complied with the rule, but it was them who provided 272 (55.7%) of all accepted UIs and 17067 (53.9%) of all labeled elements, spending 169768 s (25.5%) and earning 94.7 USD (74.7%) in total.

In the testing set, the mean Precision has somehow improved: 0.566 (SD = 0.453), but the mean ToT dropped to 408 s (SD = 303 s), which may suggest the effect of training. Each of the 20 workers had on average undertaken 23.85 HITs (SD = 7.11), labeling in total 853 UI elements (SD = 619) or 36.4 elements per UI (SD = 25.3). As we demonstrate in Table 1, neither class was the most popular for all the workers.

Table 1. The frequency distributions in the testing set (20 workers) and the entire MTurk set

Class	Testing set		MTurk set
	Overall frequency	# times most frequent	Overall frequency
link	8604	12	14524
button	3134	2	5933

(*continued*)

Table 1. (*continued*)

Class	Testing set		MTurk set
	Overall frequency	# times most frequent	Overall frequency
image	3036	6	5554
navigation	885		1773
panel	362		838
dropdown	359		943
input	330		1023
backgroundimage	244		659
table	86		239
check	27		190
Total	**17067**	**20**	**31676**

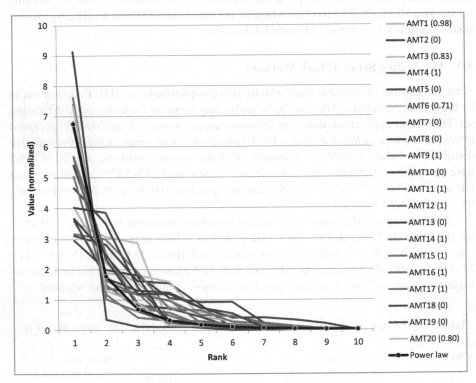

Fig. 1. Frequencies distributions for the workers and the power law (Color figure online)

3.4 Power Law-Based Fraud Detection

In Fig. 1 we show the frequency distributions of the classes for the 20 workers of the testing set (AMT_i) and the overlaid power law distribution ($\alpha = 2.49$) that best fit the overall frequencies. The classes were sorted by frequency for each of the workers, so the ranks on the horizontal axis correspond to **different classes for different workers**. The distributions were normalized by dividing each value by the mean frequency. The Precision values for each worker are given in brackets in the legend, and the lines are displayed in green(Precision = 1), red(Precision = 0) or orange(anything in between). Even before the quantitative analysis, one can notice that the distributions that deviate from the power law the most and/or the ones that have a "bad" shape are red or orange.

Then, for each of the workers, we calculated GOF_{KS} (mean = 0.542, SD = 0.104). In explaining the variance in Precision, the GOF_{KS} factor ($R^2 = 0.504$, $F_{1,18} = 18.3$, $p < 0.001$) turned out to be superior compared to the baseline ToT ($R^2 = 0.432$, $F_{1,18} = 13.7$, $p = 0.002$). In the regression for Precision with the two factors, both GOF_{KS} (Beta = 0.533, $p = 0.003$) and ToT (Beta = 0.445, $p = 0.009$) were highly significant, and the model had further improved $R^2 = 0.670$ ($F_{2,17} = 17.3$, $p < 0.001$):

$$Precision = -0.668 + 1.87 GOF_{KS} + 0.001 ToT \tag{4}$$

4 Discussion and Conclusions

Our results suggest that power laws might be applicable for crowdsourced UI labeling data quality control. GOF_{KS} [6] was able to explain more variance in Precision ($R^2 = 0.504$) than the baseline ToT factor ($R^2 = 0.432$), and had a higher Beta in the joint regression (4). Moreover, time-on-task is easily prone to malicious manipulations, as the crowdworkers seem to be already well aware of its role. In our study, the 22 workers who did not label a single UI element have inflated their overall ToT to 28.3% of all time elapsed by the workers. At the same time, manipulating the output to better fit the frequencies to power law appears problematic and might be even harder than performing the actual crowdsourcing task well.

Arguably the strongest limitation of the proposed approach is that a worker needs to produce enough results to compose a representative distribution of the classes – in our study, at least 100 UI elements labeled in 10 UIs. Indeed, the workers excluded from the testing set had contributed 216 (44.3%) of accepted HITs, which would probably need to undergo different quality control procedures. On the other hand, the UI labeling task has an entry threshold – the workers need to comprehend the classes, read instructions, etc., so the learning effect is a positive thing and fewer workers each performing more HITs should be preferred to the contrary situation.

The results of our study might be applicable for decision-support in web UI labeling quality control. The Requester could order the workers by the predicted quality of output and choose to perform more detailed manual checks for certain workers or HITs, based on the available time and validation resources, the dataset quality requirements, etc. Our theoretical contribution to HCI and Web Engineering – although much more research would be required – is that power laws might be characteristic of web UIs, similarly as for natural language texts. Thus, consideration of UIs as messages in human-computer systems [5] receives additional quantitative reinforcement.

Acknowledgment. This work was funded by RFBR according to the research project No. 19-29-01017 and partially funded by the Deutsche Forschungsgemeinschaft (DFG, German Research Foundation) – Project-ID 416228727 – SFB 1410.

References

1. Florian, D., et al.: Quality control in crowdsourcing: a survey of quality attributes, assessment techniques, and assurance actions. ACM Comput. Surv. **51**(1), 1–40 (2018)
2. Heil, S., Bakaev, M., Gaedke, M.: Assessing completeness in training data for image-based analysis of web user interfaces. In: CEUR Workshop Proceedings, vol. 2500, art. 17 (2019)
3. Iorliam, A.: Application of power laws to biometrics, forensics and network traffic analysis. Doctoral dissertation, University of Surrey (2016)
4. Ferrer-i-Cancho, R., Elvevåg, B.: Random texts do not exhibit the real Zipf's law-like rank distribution. PLoS ONE **5**(3), e9411 (2010)
5. De Souza, C.S.: The Semiotic Engineering of Human-Computer Interaction. MIT Press, Cambridge (2005)
6. Clauset, A., Shalizi, C.R., Newman, M.E.J.: Power-law distributions in empirical data. SIAM Rev. **51**(4), 661–703 (2009)
7. Rzeszotarski, J.M., Kittur, A.: Instrumenting the crowd: using implicit behavioral measures to predict task performance. In: Proceedings of the 24th ACM UIST, pp. 13–22 (2011)
8. Ausloos, M., Nedic, O., Fronczak, A., Fronczak, P.: Quantifying the quality of peer reviewers through Zipf's law. Scientometrics **106**(1), 347–368 (2015)

Conversation Graphs in Online Social Media

Marco Brambilla$^{(\boxtimes)}$ (ID), Alireza Javadian (ID), and Amin Endah Sulistiawati

Dipartimento di Elettronica, Informazione e Bioingegneria, Politecnico di Milano,
Via Giuseppe Ponzio, 34, 20133 Milano, Italy
{marco.brambilla,alireza.javadian,amin.sulistiawati}@polimi.it

Abstract. In online social media platforms, users can express their ideas by posting original content or by adding comments and responses to existing posts, thus generating virtual discussions and conversations. Studying these conversations is essential for understanding the online communication behavior of users. This study proposes a novel approach to retrieve popular patterns on online conversations using network-based analysis. The analysis consists of two main stages: intent analysis and network generation. Users' intention is detected using keyword-based categorization of posts and comments, integrated with classification through Naïve Bayes and Support Vector Machine algorithms for uncategorized comments. A continuous human-in-the-loop approach further improves the keyword-based classification. To build and understand communication patterns among the users, we build conversation graphs starting from the hierarchical structure of posts and comments, using a directed multigraph network. The experiments categorize 90% comments with 98% accuracy on a real social media dataset. The model then identifies relevant patterns in terms of shape and content; and finally determines the relevance and frequency of the patterns. Results show that the most popular online discussion patterns obtained from conversation graphs resemble real-life interactions and communication.

Keywords: Network analysis · Conversation graph · Intent analysis · Social media · Instagram · Discourse analysis · Online conversation

1 Introduction

According to Qualman, 2011 [23], the emergence of social media (SM) has profoundly changed the perspective of communication, which resulted in a revolution in the way people interact with each other. As technology grows and expands the range of communication, SM becomes a vital tool for daily social interactions. The interactions can take the form of various activities, like sharing links about interesting content, public updates on the profile such as location data or current activities, and commenting or liking posts and updates.

To leverage SM data benefits as a key to crucial insights into human behavior, many studies such as [4,7,15,18] have been done to perform analysis on

© Springer Nature Switzerland AG 2021
M. Brambilla et al. (Eds.): ICWE 2021, LNCS 12706, pp. 97–112, 2021.
https://doi.org/10.1007/978-3-030-74296-6_8

SM data by scholars, journalists, and governments. Reasons of people relying on SM platforms include, but are not limited to, interacting within the inner circle of friendship, entertainment purposes, or subscribing to news; also as presented in various work such as [1,26], evolving widely for knowledge sharing purpose on online learning and Q&A platforms. Many companies adopt SM to utilize this growing trend to gain business values [13]. Schreck *et al.* [25] discuss how leveraging massive amounts of SM data presents many challenges. The data is multimodal and ambiguous in its content. Communication patterns also change rapidly among various SM elements. This defies choosing proper approaches to handle the systems' complexity. Various methods can be used for understanding complex SM systems [6,16]. The presence of graph libraries simplifies the intricacy analysis of social networks (SNs), yet the workloads to uncover meaningful values from billions of nodes and vertexes have not diminished.

1.1 Problem Statement

Understanding communication behaviors is an essential awareness. The conversations among SM users are the core of virtual communication that deputizes closely to the real/direct communication. Seeing that most studies on SNs are centralized on a user-to-user relationship, they let through the valuable information from generated conversations in order to conceive online communication behavior. Considering a large dataset from SM platforms with its complex structure, the research questions that lead to this work are as follows:

1. How to build a convenient graph to describe the conversations on SM?
2. How to reconstruct conversations from comments that belong to an SM post that does not follow the *reply* feature?
3. How to assign an appropriate category label to an SM comment that represents the author's intention?
4. What frequent patterns can be found in conversation graphs of online SM?

1.2 Objective

This study proposes a new approach for analyzing online conversations. It consists of two main stages. The first step is **intention analysis** on SM comments reflecting the authors' thoughts. Initially, a list of category names is defined using popular keywords based on set bag-of-words. Then, we perform keyword-based classification to assign a label to each SM comment representing its meaning. Finally, human-in-the-loop techniques are involved in improving the initial keywords. The second stage is **network generation** based on the designed nodes and edges from SM data as well as their attributes. Subsequently, by identifying comments connected by a *reply* edge in the generated network, we automatically generate conversation graphs. Therefore, conversation graphs with labeled comments are produced, portraying patterns of communication behavior between the authors. Finally, we perform statistical and matrix analyses on the conversations. We test the proposed methodology on a real SM event—*YourExpo2015*[1], *i.e.*, a game challenge developed for Expo 2015 Milano event.

1.3 Contribution

This study is designed for companies or organizations that desire to analyze their audiences' *communication behaviors* on SM platforms. Using text classification on SM comments, we can obtain the *most discussed topics*. Accordingly, exploiting the illustrated comment-to-comment relationships, *patterns from conversation graphs* are gained. Considering the obtained patterns, they can better understand the most *frequent conversations*. Moreover, an *automatic reply* feature is possibly generated based on the analysis result.

The rest of the work is as follows. Sect. 2 discusses the related work. Sect. 3 details the methodology. Sect. 4 presents a set of experiments on a real case dataset. Sect. 5 discusses the results. Finally, Sect. 6 concludes the work.

2 Related Work

2.1 Graph Analysis on Social Network

Myers *et al.* [21] investigate the structural characteristics of Twitter's follow graph to understand how such networks arise. Zhao *et al.* [30] formulate a new problem of specialized finding in Q&A platforms. Buntain *et al.* [8] present an identification method to find a social role based on the user interactions' graph on Reddit. McAuley *et al.* [20] develop a model for detecting circles in ego networks. Rao *et al.* [24] propose a new algorithm for community detection using graph techniques. Yang *et al.* [28] model the statistical interaction between the network structure and the node attributes.

2.2 Conversation Graphs on Social Media

Ning *et al.* [22] utilize graph analysis to better support Q&A systems. Aumayr *et al.* [3] explore classification methods for recovering the reply structures in forum threads. Cogan *et al.* [11] propose a method to reconstruct complete conversations around initial tweets. Zayats *et al.* [29] predict the popularity of comments on Reddit discussions. Kumar *et al.* [17] propose a mathematical model for the generation of basic conversation structure to explore the model humans follow during online conversations. Aragon *et al.* [2] investigate the impact of threading the messages instead of linearly displaying them. Work [12,14] show how individuals' contribution increases when they feel unique. *Reply* and *Mention* functions can be employed for this purpose.

---

[1] http://www.socialmediaexpo2015.com/yourexpo/.

2.3 Proposed Network Analysis on Conversation Graphs

This study offers a novel network analysis to learn conversation graphs on SM by automatically detected *reply* comments. Besides, we further perform analysis on users' intentions. Note that intent analysis is different from sentiment analysis (*positive, neutral,* or *negative* [10]), while the proposed intent analysis studies several classes that are most relevant for the comments. Finally, the constructed conversations with labeled members bring exciting information, such as finding common patterns. To analyze networks, we use SNAP [19] and Gephi [5].

3   Methodology

Figure 1 illustrates the main methods implemented in this study. Initially, the data gathering from the Internet is constructed to extract data from SM platforms; afterward, the data is stored in the database. Then, we do text processing to perform intent analysis. The next step is to develop a multigraph network's design to construct conversation graphs.

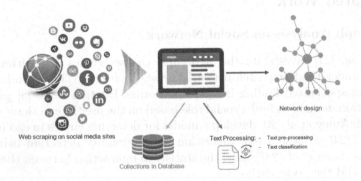

Web scraping on social media sites

Collections in Database

Text Processing: · Text pre-processing
- Text classification

Network design

Fig. 1. High-level overview of the employed methods.

3.1   Text Classification Design

The text preprocessing pipeline consists of two main activities. At first, it applies text cleaning and stemming in order to produce bag-of-words. Then it constructs the TF/IDF to obtain the word/document weight matrix. After preprocessing, as illustrated in Fig. 2, the list of comment categories is initially defined. After we specify the classes' label, we use keyword-based classification to assign each media comment label. Then, we apply Naïve Bayes and SVM to increase our intent analysis accuracy. Finally, human-in-the-loop is involved for validation.

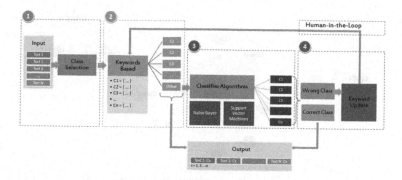

Fig. 2. Intent analysis procedure.

3.2 Network and Conversation Graph Design

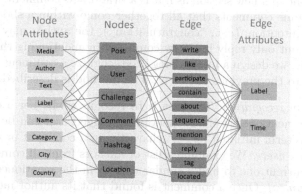

Fig. 3. Network design for Social Media platforms.

In Fig. 3, we present a general SN design representing relationships among all components, such as SM posts, users, comments, locations, *etc.* Figure 4 displays a graph illustration of a post on SM. The path destination is needed, for instance, to describe the relationship between comment nodes within a conversation and to track which comment's sequence. This is the reason for designing a directed multigraph for this study. Meanwhile, a multigraph is selected since there are possibly multiple edges connecting two nodes. Attributes of each node and edge from the graph depict the information needed for our analysis. Finally, the generated graph is stored in a graph file to be used for the analysis.

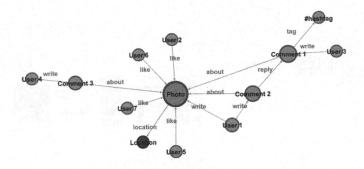

Fig. 4. Graph visualization of a Social Media post from the case study.

To date, most SMs adopt the comment *reply* feature, making it easier to recognize relationships between comments in a post. However, it is possible that the users do not use this feature. They can write a comment intended to reply to the preceding one in a new section as if it is a brand new comment. Also, when a post contains some comments that all together come within a short period and have the same intention, (*e.g.*, "congratulation"), the author may do not reply to them singly but only reply in a new comment by mentioning those users.

In this study, we design a methodology to recognize a comment that is intentionally linked to the previous comment. The method is described as follows.

1. *User mention recognition:* The idea is to recognize whether a comment has one or more mentioned users. A mentioned/tagged user can be extracted by identifying a term initiated by "@" character in a comment or caption.
2. *Search tagged users:* We examine a list of authors from all comments posted before the current one to find a similar user from the mentioned users list.
3. *Reply assignment:* Once a comment is found that its author mentions in the recent comment, the reply edge is assigned between the two comments.

4   Experiments

4.1   Case Study and Data Collection

Expo 2015, hosted in Milan, Italy, was a universal exposition and a part of the International Registered Exhibition. During the six months of the exhibition, 145 countries participated by running their exhibition. The exhibition successfully attracted more than $22M$ visitors and derived many marketing campaigns to promote the event. Also, an SM game challenge—*YourExpo2015* was proposed. The game was based on Instagram posts, which are tagged by specific hashtags published every week by Expo 2015. During the whole challenge cycle of nine weeks, more than $15K$ photos and $600K$ actions were generated. This study is applied to $15,343$ posts containing $98,924$ comments related to the challenge.

4.2 Intent Analysis

After applying the text preprocessing steps, we obtained the bag-of-words. By analyzing the most frequent and interesting words, with a subjective assumption, we conclude that the suitable categories for the contents associated with the case study are: *thank, congratulation, agreement, positive, invitation, food, greeting, question, hashtag,* and *other* which cannot be assigned to any other class.

The initial keywords for each category are constructed based on the obtained bag-of-words. The classification method merely is counting scores for each category's keywords to the comment collection. This method is a simple approach with a consequence of having several comments (20%) being labeled as *other*. Using direct observation to define keyword-based classification's ground truth, 100 random samples are chosen for each category to be validated by humans. The average accuracy is 97.5%. So the implementation of keyword-based classification is reliable. The misplace labeling on keyword-based classification is due to the lack of consideration for keywords dependence or context meaning.

Next, comments labeled as *hashtag* and *other* were used as a new dataset to be classified using Naïve Bayes and SVM algorithms. As we are not provided the ground truth, we employed the previous result to train Naïve Bayes and SVM. The result states that SVM outperforms Naïve Bayes with 97.67% accuracy.

4.3 Network Analysis

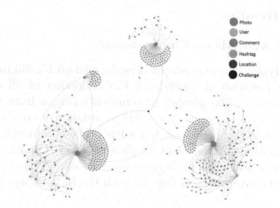

Fig. 5. Graph visualization of three Social Media posts from the case study.

The generated graph is composed of $461,952$ nodes and $1,416,751$ edges. Figure 5 presents the visualization of 3 photos. All photos are connected through the challenges node. All nodes are unique, including users. As we can see, a user can publish, like, and comment on more than a photo. Outgoing edges draw user activities; the more outgoing the edges are, the more active the user is.

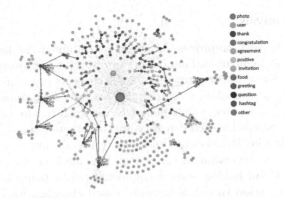

Fig. 6. Visualization of the conversation graphs.

Figure 6 presents an intent analysis in different colors. Generated relationships inside comments from an Instagram photo portray opinion exchange from the author of those comments. A *reply* edge links two comments. The idea to retrieve conversation graphs is to recognize all connected comments node by *reply* link. From the visualization, we observe that there are some interesting patterns. A node that replies to many comment nodes most likely is a *thank* comment, and a *positive* comment is usually followed either by a *positive* or *thank* comment.

5   Analysis Results

5.1   Statistical Analysis on Conversation

Statistical Analysis. The experiment is performed on 15, 343 Instagram posts. Table 1 clarifies a statistical analysis of the collection of all comments and retrieved conversations. The number of comments ranges from 0 to 328. If we exclude photos with no comment, the average number of comments is 7. If we include a comment with no relationship with other comments, the maximum number of conversations extracted in all photos is 177. On average, the size of the conversation is 2 nodes. From all conversations in all photos, we obtain that the most extended conversation is the one with the highest size (*i.e.*, 93 nodes).

Table 1. Statistical analysis of comments and conversations.

	# Comments per post (min 1 comment)	# Conversation per post (1 member include)	Size per conversation (1 member exclude)
Mean	7.45	5.10	2.79
Q1	2	2	2
Q2/Median	4	3	2
Q3	8	6	3
Min	1	1	2
Max	328	177	93

Figure 7 displays the total number of all the conversations. A comment without a relation with others, has the highest frequency. Conversations composed of 2 nodes are the most prevalent ones. The frequency decreases gradually as the size of the conversation increases. Most of the long conversations only occur once.

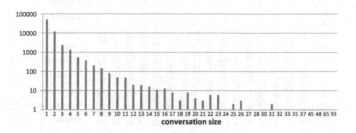

Fig. 7. Frequency for each size of conversation.

Comment Category Distribution. Figure 8 describes the spread of intent categories in the post having at least 30 comments. It shows that *positive* and *thank* comments dominate all conversations. Two other classes that appear almost in all variations of conversation size are *greeting* and *question* types. Comments with invitation and agreement intention are slightly expressed in most conversations, whereas *congratulations* are only mentioned in some discussions.

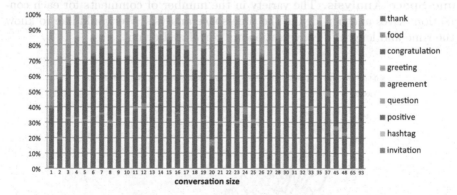

Fig. 8. Distribution of categories on conversations having minimum 30 comments.

As expected, *thank* is not stated in solo conversations, which is most likely in a real discussion. Additionally, *hashtag* comments generally appear in a single comment. In more extended discussions, participants generally talk about *compliments*, *gratitude*, and *salutation*. Considering such online conversations, by investigating the figure, one might conclude that by increasing the conversation size, most of the categories will be dominated by fewer categories. *Food* is the 3rd significant topic; however, it is barely mentioned in extensive conversations. Thus, we investigated photos with 7 to 29 comments.

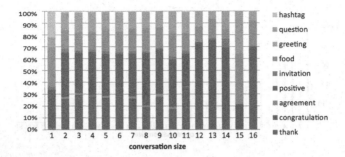

Fig. 9. Distribution of categories on conversations having 7 to 29 comments.

Figure 9 accounts that the fewer comments, the smaller length of conversation is. *Thank, positive,* and *food* categories dominated the overall conversations. Similar to the previous analysis, *agreement, congratulation,* and *invitation* categories have low frequency confirming that *hashtag* comments are only written in a single comment. Oppositely, *gratitude* expression is not mentioned in self conversation.

Time Space Analysis. The variety in the number of comments for each conversation drives another idea in the time-space analysis. We would like to know if the time and length of conversation are correlated or not.

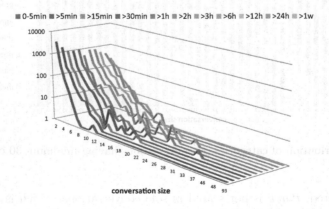

Fig. 10. 3D representation of the conversation size, period, and frequency.

Figure 10 displays conversation size, period, and frequency. The duration of conversations is calculated by subtracting the time of the latest comment and the first one. Durations range from less than 5 min to longer than one week. We were expecting that the smaller conversation takes less time than the longer one. However, the result contradicts our presumption. It visualizes (in logarithmic scale) that generally, conversations occupy a variety of duration. Accordingly, we can conclude that mostly smaller discussions possibly have a longer duration. Conversations with size comments between 2 and 10 have all ranges of duration, while conversations with more than 10 comments tend to narrow the duration.

Figure 11 shows that long discussions with a conversation size greater than 10 positively do not take a duration of fewer than 15 min. It is clearly stated that users involved in the discussion need time to write a comment reply. Another proof states that longer conversations do not take more than 1 day to end the discussion. For instance, a conversation that involves 93 comments takes time between 12 and 24 h. In conclusion, the small discussions can take a longer time to finish, while more extended ones lean to finish discussion within 24 h.

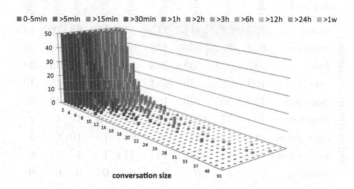

Fig. 11. 3D representation of conversation duration in a smaller frequency range.

5.2   Conversation Patterns Retrieval

The user's intention in a comment is included in the graphs as a category label. To understand the online communication behavior, we analyze the conversations to retrieve the most frequent patterns generated from intent relationships.

Two-Node Patterns. Table 2 illustrates a heat matrix that details the occurrences for each combination of categories. The matrix's left side represents a comment that replies to a previous comment on the matrix's top side.

As expected, *thank → positive* is the most popular pattern; in other words, a *gratitude* action is generally expressed after a *compliment*. Similar rational behaviors which frequently happened are *thank → thank, positive → positive,*

108   M. Brambilla et al.

positive → *greeting*, *thank* → *invitation*, and so on. These virtual characters imitate real-world communications. It also reveals less popular combinations that most likely do not happen in direct communication, such as agreement after a congratulation or congratulation after someone saying an invitation or even asking a question to someone who gives congratulation. Another less possible pattern is *hashtag* comment used to reply to any other types of comments.

In conclusion, with combinations of all intention labels on the two linked comments, we can obtain digital communication behavior that similarly adopts real-life conversation. Both the most and least popular patterns are likely to happen also in daily communication. Therefore, in the next stage of our analysis, we want to know how far we can expand the length of conversation paths.

Table 2. The frequency of the comment-reply relationship for categories.

	Previous comment								
replies to	thank	positive	food	greeting	question	congrats	agreement	invitation	hashtag
thank	1830	9299	1783	1150	397	149	88	790	143
positive	632	2158	997	439	581	27	73	98	95
food	247	924	738	203	546	5	24	36	34
greeting	109	625	180	644	136	8	12	15	13
question	154	409	279	109	182	1	14	49	26
congrats	14	37	11	16	7	19	1	1	2
agreement	21	128	57	37	92	1	10	6	5
invitation	40	82	54	18	114	1	7	31	6
hashtag	2	3	0	1	6	0	0	0	0

(Subsequent comment)

Three- and Four-Nodes Patterns. We take further the analysis patterns into 3 and 4 nodes, and we select the most popular patterns. In this case, we select intent combinations that have more than $1K$ occurrences. They include *thank* → *positive*, *positive* → *positive*, *thank* → *thank*, *thank* → *food*, *thank* → *greeting*.

The next step is to find the pattern in our conversation graphs for all possible combinations of those 5 schemas by adding another comment category before and after the patterns. The results show that the top pattern is *thank* → *thank* → *positive*. It replicates direct communication when a person says a complimentary comment; then, the partner replies to express their gratefulness. Afterward, most likely, the first person replies with another gratitude comment. Other popular patterns are reasonable as well. However, the number of occurrences decreases significantly from the most popular one. From the retrieved patterns, we select top ones composed of 3 and 4 nodes to perform temporal analysis and analyze the number of users involved in the discussions. The first analysis seeks to find how long a user takes time to write a reply comment. We pick *thank* → *thank* → *positive* pattern that has 1,254 occurrences in the conversation graphs. Figure 12 shows the diversity of reply times. The first part of the chart shows the time needed for the last comment to reply to the previous comment, and the second part is the duration of 2nd comment to reply to the 1st comment.

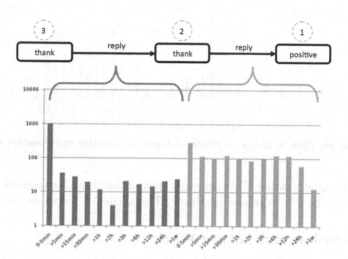

Fig. 12. Reply time in *thank* → *thank* → *positive* conversation pattern.

We observe that the reply time from the 2nd comment to the 1st one mostly takes less than 5 min, as well as periods, need for the 3rd to answer the 2nd one. Yet, some users need more than 1 week to reply to a comment. On average, it takes 12 to 24 h for the 2nd comment to reply to the 1st one, and the period in which the 3rd comment answers the 2nd one is between 6 and 12 h.

The second analysis is applied to top patterns arranged in 4 nodes *thank* → *thank* → *thank* → *positive*. In Fig. 13, the result shows that the time needed for the 2nd comment to reply to the 1st one varies in the range of 5 min to more than a week. However, in other cases, for the 3rd comment to answer the 2nd one and the 4th comment to react to the 3rd comment, the period taken is generally less than 5 min. On average, the 2nd comment takes 6 to 12 h to respond to the 1st one. The 3rd comment requires 30 to 60 min to answer the 2nd one, and the 4th comment needs 3 to 6 h to react to the 3rd one.

Another thing that interests us is how many users are involved in the conversations. We analyze the top patterns with 3 and 4 nodes. We sum up the number of users that join the discussion. Overall, two users participate in the conversations, and in some cases, 3 and 4 users have taken part in the discussions.

In conclusion, it is a natural behavior that when a compliment is presented at the beginning of the talk, the following responses are all gratitude, and two

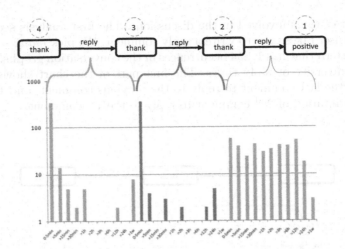

Fig. 13. Reply time in *thank* → *thank* → *thank* → *positive* conversation pattern.

people are communicating. This generally means that the 1st expresses a positive opinion, then the 2nd expresses gratitude. Then, the 1st responds, and so on.

6   Conclusion and Future Work

This study aims at understanding communication behavior on SM discussions compared to real-life. Intent analysis using keyword-based classification is proposed on SM comments. For the case study, we use Instagram photos of the *Your-Expo2015* challenge. Initially, the approach classifies comments into 9 categories, *thank, congratulation, agreement, positive, invitation, food, greeting, question,* and *hashtag,* on each class's defined keywords. Comments that do not contain any keywords are assigned to the *other* category. Then, we perform Naïve Bayes and SVM on the uncategorized comments. Finally, we perform human-in-the-loop to improve keywords from misclassified comments with the algorithms. In the end, our performance shows a significant result with an accuracy of 98%, with the dominant categories being *compliment* expression and *food* talk.

We also utilized a directed multigraph composed of more than $450K$ nodes and $1.4M$ edges representing the collected SM dataset, including intent analysis on the comments. It contains essential information representing relationships among nodes, together with their attribute information. The list of nodes is composed by *posts, comments, authors, locations, comments,* and *hashtags.*

A conversation from a post is constructed by identifying the relationships among all comments on an SM post. A virtual discussion is built from one comment that replies to another and analyzes and checks whether other comments are linked as well. Our proposed approach is also able to recognize comment-reply that does not follow the *reply* feature provided on the SM platform.

The analysis of online discussion is not limited to conversation graph retrieval but also understanding users' intentions. Thus, the study's final stage is mining popular patterns of conversation composed of comments with labels. The most popular obtained patterns resemble real-life conversation, where people tend to say *thank* after others say something positive to them. Another observation about the challenge is that most participants are willing to write compliments in the comment section, even when they talk about food.

Future work concerns a more in-depth analysis of mechanisms, particularly in the intent analysis. Even our proposed intent analysis has high accuracy, we perform a plain way to classify SM comments; thus, in the future, we can perform other text classification methods such as [27] to obtain the ground truth. Since we are involved with SM data in which emoticon symbols mostly appear together with text, another work is the learning of emoticon expressions as studied in [9].

References

1. Al-Atabi, M., DeBoer, J.: Teaching entrepreneurship using massive open online course (MOOC). Technovation **34**(4), 261–264 (2014)
2. Aragón, P., Gómez, V., Kaltenbrunner, A.: To thread or not to thread: the impact of conversation threading on online discussion. In: Proceedings of the International AAAI Conference on Web and Social Media, vol. 11 (2017)
3. Aumayr, E., Chan, J., Hayes, C.: Reconstruction of threaded conversations in online discussion forums. ICWSM **11**, 26–33 (2011)
4. Balduini, M., et al.: Models and practices in urban data science at scale. Big Data Res. **17**, 66–84 (2019)
5. Bastian, M., Heymann, S., Jacomy, M.: Gephi: an open source software for exploring and manipulating networks. In: Proceedings of 3rd ICWSM (2009)
6. Brambilla, M., Sabet, A.J., Hosseini, M.: The role of social media in long-running live events: the case of the big four fashion weeks dataset. Data Brief **35**, 106840 (2021)
7. Brena, G., Brambilla, M., Ceri, S., Di Giovanni, M., Pierri, F., Ramponi, G.: News sharing user behaviour on Twitter: a comprehensive data collection of news articles and social interactions. In: Proceedings of the International AAAI Conference on Web and Social Media, vol. 13, pp. 592–597 (2019)
8. Buntain, C., Golbeck, J.: Identifying social roles in reddit using network structure. In: Proceedings of the 23rd International Conference on World Wide Web, pp. 615–620 (2014)
9. Cha, Y., Kim, J., Park, S., Yi, M.Y., Lee, U.: Complex and ambiguous: understanding sticker misinterpretations in instant messaging. In: Proceedings of the ACM on Human-Computer Interaction, vol. 2(CSCW), November 2018
10. Chakraborty, K., Bhattacharyya, S., Bag, R.: A survey of sentiment analysis from social media data. IEEE Trans. CSS **7**(2), 450–464 (2020)
11. Cogan, P., Andrews, M., Bradonjic, M., Kennedy, W.S., Sala, A., Tucci, G. Reconstruction and analysis of twitter conversation graphs. In: Proceedings of the 1st ACM International Workshop on HotSocial, pp. 25–31 (2012)
12. Dillahunt, T.R., Mankoff, J. Understanding factors of successful engagement around energy consumption between and among households. In: Proceedings of the 17th ACM Conference on CSCW, pp. 1246–1257 (2014)
13. Dong, J.Q., Wu, W.: Business value of social media technologies: Evidence from online user innovation communities. J. Strat. Inf. Sys. **24**(2), 113–127 (2015)

14. Farzan, R., Dabbish, L.A., Kraut, R.E., Postmes, T.: Increasing commitment to online communities by designing for social presence. In: Proceedings of the ACM 2011 Conference on Computer Supported Cooperative Work, pp. 321–330 (2011)
15. Gasparini, M., Ramponi, G., Brambilla, M., Ceri, S.: Assigning users to domains of interest based on content and network similarity with champion instances. In: Proceedings of the IEEE/ACM Conference on ASONAM, pp. 589–592 (2019)
16. Sabet, A.J.: Social media posts popularity prediction during long-running live events. a case study on fashion week (2019)
17. Kumar, R., Mahdian, M., McGlohon, M.: Dynamics of conversations. In: Proceedings of the 16th ACM SIGKDD, pp. 553–562 (2010)
18. Lai, L.S.L., To, W.M.: Content analysis of social media: a grounded theory approach. J. Electron. Commer. Res. **16**(2), 138 (2015)
19. Leskovec, J., Sosič, R.: Snap: a general-purpose network analysis and graph-mining library. ACM TIST **8**(1), 1–20 (2016)
20. Mcauley, J., Leskovec, J.: Discovering social circles in ego networks. ACM Trans. Knowl. Discovery Data (TKDD) **8**(1), 1–28 (2014)
21. Myers, S.A., Sharma, A., Gupta, P., Lin, J.: Information network or social network? the structure of the twitter follow graph. In: Proceedings of the 23rd International Conference on World Wide Web, pp. 493–498 (2014)
22. Ning, K., Li, N., Zhang, L.-J.: Using graph analysis approach to support question & answer on enterprise social network. In: IEEE APSCC (2012)
23. Qualman, E.: Socialnomics: How social media transforms the way we live and do business. Wiley (2012)
24. Rao , B., Mitra, A.: A new approach for detection of common communities in a social network using graph mining techniques. In: ICHPCA (2014)
25. Schreck, T., Keim, D.: Visual analysis of social media data. Computer **46**(5), 68–75 (2012)
26. Vasilescu, B., Serebrenik, A., Devanbu, P., Filkov, V.: How social q&a sites are changing knowledge sharing in open source software communities. In: Proceedings of the 17th ACM conference on CSCW, pp. 342–354 (2014)
27. Baoxun, X., Guo, X., Ye, Y., Cheng, J.: An improved random forest classifier for text categorization. JCP **7**(12), 2913–2920 (2012)
28. Yang, J., McAuley, J., Leskovec, J.: Community detection in networks with node attributes. In: 2013 IEEE 13th ICDM, pp. 1151–1156 (2013)
29. Zayats, V., Ostendorf, M.: Conversation modeling on reddit using a graph-structured LSTM. Trans. ACL **6**, 121–132 (2018)
30. Zhao, Z., Wei, F., Zhou, M., Ng, W.: Cold-start expert finding in community question answering via graph regularization. In: Renz, M., Shahabi, C., Zhou, X., Cheema, M.A. (eds.) DASFAA 2015. LNCS, vol. 9049, pp. 21–38. Springer, Cham (2015). https://doi.org/10.1007/978-3-319-18120-2_2

Web Modeling and Engineering

WTA: Towards a Web-Based Testbed Architecture

Valentin Siegert$^{(\boxtimes)}$ and Martin Gaedke

Distributed and Self-organizing Systems Group, Technische Universität Chemnitz,
Straße der Nationen 62, 09111 Chemnitz, Germany
{valentin.siegert,martin.gaedke}@informatik.tu-chemnitz.de

Abstract. Tests, evaluations, and solution comparisons in complex use cases are often realized by creating a testbed for a domain of use cases and solutions. Web-based testbeds add key advantages like results sharing, remote test execution, and collaboration. Focusing on their research objectives, creators see their testbeds as a means to that end. The resulting web-based testbeds are similar in structure and functionality, but there is no common architecture supporting their creation, introducing redundant design efforts. Therefore, we determine structural similarities based on insights into the architecture of current web-based testbeds, from which we derive a generic web-based testbed architecture. This framework of reference will help to develop future testbeds focusing on the testbed domain instead of reinventing general testbed functionality.

Keywords: Web · Testbeds · Software architecture

1 Introduction

Evaluations are an essential step for proving the capabilities of newly created solutions in developing software or publishing research findings. While limited feasibility and scalability can often be tested manually in the early stages with respective manual effort, comparing solutions in complex use cases is not possible. However, many conduct their evaluations in software development and research manually or within their environment to prove the initial step in the correct direction [15]. The need for evaluating solutions in complex use cases is emerging from the industry and the research community as first stage evaluations are limited by design. Proof of feasibility and scalability in bigger and more complex use cases as well as insights by comparing different solutions at such use cases establish the need for testbeds. These can support the evaluation and give those insights into complex constructs as they can be set up for different test runs in the same environmental conditions. Additionally, testbeds can also test a combination of known solutions on how they work together in exemplary use cases.

On the other hand, testbeds are often created out of the need for proof or insights. The testbeds' development process thus is not the main focus. Instead,

© Springer Nature Switzerland AG 2021
M. Brambilla et al. (Eds.): ICWE 2021, LNCS 12706, pp. 115–123, 2021.
https://doi.org/10.1007/978-3-030-74296-6_9

the potentially obtained knowledge out of the testbed's results is the motivation. With such focus, researchers tend to develop their testbeds well suited for their usage, which results in a limitation of testbeds and followingly more testbeds for slightly different motivations. For example, in the field of multi-agent trust management systems, Yu et al. [15] describe that researchers tend to design their evaluation environments, which are often also own testbeds.

In the past years, more and more web-based testbeds were presented and developed. The web-based architecture adds to testbeds key advantages like results sharing, remote test execution, and collaboration. They exist in different domains like Web Applications, Internet of Things (IoT), Semantic Web, Deep Web, and many more and are conceived from small-sized testbeds on one machine to globally distributed ones like PlanetLab [11], a testbed for network services. As web-based testbeds are not restricted to test things in a web-related domain, researchers of other domains make use of them as well. Some recent examples are microgrids [13], railways [10], or also underwater acoustic communication [16].

Even though the research domains are different, current web-based testbeds make use of similar concepts. Thus, most researchers seem to have a common understanding of how a web-based testbed needs to be implemented. Nevertheless, to the best of our knowledge, a general architecture for web-based testbeds does not exist. Cavalieri et al. [4] propose some principles, but they focused on industrial production systems and date back to the early 2000s. In other terms, researchers have to reinvent a web-based testbed for their own needs without being able to build upon a given architecture. Besides the manual reinvention effort, especially researchers from non-computer science domains might not exploit the full potential of a web-based testbed due to a lack of knowledge about the available functionalities and architectural choices. As testbeds are a means to achieve experimentation and evaluation objectives, their architecture and development are not of prime concern to most researchers and any reduction in the effort will allow them to focus more on their original research activities. A web-based testbed architecture can limit these several reinventions and in the best case also limit the reoccurring need for a new testbed due to better reusability.

With this work, we provide insights into relevant web-based testbeds and determine their structural similarities to create a web-based testbed architecture. Our approach can improve existing testbeds and give future needs of tests, evaluations, and comparisons of different solutions a chance to be done faster without having to reinvent what others already elaborated for their own needs. Our contributions are as follows: (1) We present a software architecture for web-based testbeds based on known principles and structural similarities in current testbeds. (2) The architecture integrates key advantages of the web like results sharing, remote test execution, and collaboration.

2   Recent Work: Web-Based Testbeds' Similarities

The most common conceptual similarity to realize a web-based testbed architecture in recent work is a concept with three actors: (1) the central node within the testbed, (2) an experimenter as a user of the testbed, and (3) the laboratory itself with its testbed environment capability to manage evaluations. The central node of a web-based testbed is often realized as a web server, which interacts as the interface between the experimenter and testbed. On the one side, it communicates with the experimenter via its web application. On the other side, the central node realizes the management of the testbed by preparation, execution, and clean-up of one evaluation [12]. The user interface is not necessarily a web UI [2], but in many cases it is. Such a UI supports thereby the users' work with the testbed by visualizations and maybe some wizard alike guides.

The Experimenter may only have central access via the web application on the testbed, but some indicate their testbed environment elements also as directly accessible. Such direct access can be distinguished into access to the environment elements with organizational relation [1] or to the ones required for the evaluation execution itself [14]. It is often realized via ssh and indicates the distribution of the testbed's actors on different machines.

The testbed's actual feasibility is delivered by the testbed environment and its elements, which represent the testbed's domain-specific motivation. In general it exists to set up the initial situation for each evaluation, to execute, and later collect all required results measured during execution. The environment elements interact therefore according to a description created by the experimenter. Some approaches highlight for this description also how to schedule it and call the elements of such procedures job, trace or observation [5,12,14].

Several approaches work on not only single but multi-tier architectures within all described technical actors. Multi-tier approaches appear e.g. at the web application which is developed in a multi-site fashion [6] or at the testbed environment, which can be organized in several tiers by domain [8], by evaluation need [2] or by testbed management need [1,12]. Besides, some also present how to create the central node in a multi-tier fashion [6,8,9].

The literature supposes also access points for different testbeds, e.g. model-based testbed creation [3] or an EaaS architecture [9]. These approaches add a meta management layer, such that the original organization elements of the environment and central node of one testbed are also dynamically created by the experimenters' description.

3   Web-Based Testbed Architecture (WTA)

To achieve a good web-based testbed architecture, several goals emerge from the identified conceptual similarities and the principles by Cavalieri et al. [4]. One architectural goal is to have a central node that serves as the interface between experimenters and testbed. It hereby should serve a web UI for the experimenters, independent of which device they use for access. We call this central node *Testbed Server*, which should contain besides the web application for the experimenter the laboratory management, which we call *Testbed Director*.

The web UI for the experimenters should be more than only the access point but deliver certain usability features to the experimenters. Thus, it should support all experimenters, also the rather inexperienced ones with a clear evaluation process and how to use the testbed. Wizard-like support with visual and textual help would be one way to realize this. Further, the UI needs to use a standardized representation according to the testbed's domain in visual and textual descriptions of any testbed artifacts, like measurements, use cases, evaluation descriptions, or results. As a testbed serves the need for testing, the experimenter should be able to get creative with combinations of possible solutions or use cases. Therefore, the web UI requires a playground for experimenters to change preferences of an evaluation, a set of pre-created artifacts like measurements or use cases, and a possibility to upload own created elements, like features to test or own created artifacts. The web UI should also contain a visualization of used schedulers within the testbed, if its domain requires such as in [5,12,14].

To have the possibility of choosing pre-created artifacts for evaluation preferences, web-based testbeds require a place to store its artifacts in a central place. We call this place the Testbed Library, originating from the library component in Cavalieri et al. [4]. The provided use cases are better if they are more complex, meaning not only many actors or events, but also include unforeseen events.

As a web-based approach, key advantages of the web like sharing, remote execution, and collaborative work should be included in the architectural design. Hereby, especially the Testbed Library and the web UI require to enable the user to share stored artifacts, to work collaboratively on artifacts, and to start a remote evaluation. The testbed server thus requires to proxy any experimenter for the evaluation run and has to ensure that one evaluation finishes when it is started or gives feedback to the experimenter on why it stopped intermediately. Combining direct access of elements with the named web's key advantages, any element of a web-based testbed should be accessible via the web.

The Testbed Director should be the experimenter's proxy accordingly and do everything to manage one evaluation execution. Therefore, it needs to set up the initial evaluation situation in the Testbed Environment, start the execution, gather all required results, and insure following evaluations with a releasing of preserved testbed performance for an evaluation execution.

A *Testbed Environment* is required to serve the actual testbeds functionality of evaluations. Depending on the testbed's domain and motivation of creation its environment has to be designed. Mostly it is a distributed system of different actors simulating a situation for one use case. It can thereby involve devices and simulated or virtualized elements. A separation of organizational and executional elements in the Testbed Environment will improve the evaluations' execution [4]. Not only environment elements should be separated into these two categories, but also artifacts and communication channels.

A clear hierarchy supports the future adaptability of a testbed. The testbed server is hereby the root, follows with organizational elements first, and ends with executional elements. To set up the distributed testbed faster, a bottom-up registration supports the process of dynamic ordered evaluations. Any element besides artifacts and used communication channels can be organized in a multi-tier fashion if required for the testbed's domain. While the organizational elements of the testbed are mostly described by the testbed's creator, the executional ones can also be configured by the experimenters according to their evaluations. EaaS infrastructures form the exceptions where also organizational elements are partially described by the experimenters.

A web-based testbed serves degrees of freedom in a 2-dimensional space. One is the freedom of experimenter interactions and one is the freedom of the testbed environment elements. In both dimensions, the creators require to identify the sweet spot and design the testbed accordingly. In terms of experimenter interactions it is a dimension with three possible values: (1) a testbed can be a strict demo without any possibility for an experimenter to choose anything, (2) a testbed with limited available possible use cases and solutions to choose of, and (3) a full creative playground where the experimenters can live out their creativity to create their preferred evaluation with many possibilities to choose and change individually. The dimension of the testbed environment elements' freedom is a scale between two extremes, where both are hindering a valuable evaluation execution. One is the full control of the testbed organizational elements over the executional ones, and the other is the opposite, so no control of the organizational elements over the executional ones.

Web-based testbeds should also be open for future changes in their architecture. Therefore a core of components should be given, but similar to an onion architecture [7], the creators should include interfaces for future changes according to newly discovered technology. A testbed can thereby serve more similar needs. Followingly the number of testbeds in one domain can decrease.

3.1 WTA Elements

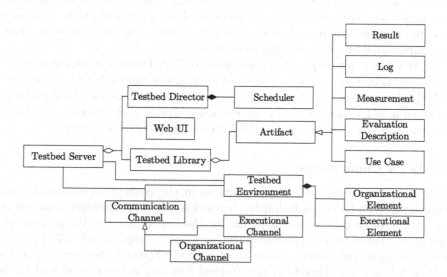

Fig. 1. Web-based testbed architecture elements.

The testbed server is the root of all involved elements and includes a Web UI, the Testbed Director, and the Testbed Library. Together with the testbed environment, they build the WTA components, which will be described in the following subsection with their interactions. Besides the WTA components, WTA includes elements like Scheduler, Artifact, and Communication Channel. Schedulers either order events into a sequence or schedule them on a timestamp if an evaluation description contains events or interactions to happen during the evaluation. Offering in a testbed several schedulers to choose from can be necessary because new insights into the testbed's domain could lead to new scheduling approaches in according evaluations. In WTA the schedulers relate to the events occurring in the testbed's domain and should be choosable by the experimenters for each evaluation if more than one is implemented.

Every web-based testbed has due to its distribution at least one communication channel to the experimenters' user agents. WTA-based testbeds need to communicate in the purpose of evaluation organization and maybe also within an executed use case between executional testbed environment elements. The organizational communication channels require thereby to be separated from the executional ones, such that they do not interfere with running evaluations. While the organizational channels mainly stick to web technology, executionals are influenced by the testbed's domain.

The artifacts of a WTA testbed are all the data within the testbed's process being stored, consumed, or both. Besides the evaluation results, which are the output artifacts, also input artifacts like standardized measurements, (real-world) use cases, or evaluation descriptions of experimenters exist in WTA. An instance of a WTA should also have measurements and use cases available to choose from in the Testbed Library. Additionally, some domains and their use cases might produce intermediate artifacts like logs, which need to be communicated to other environmental elements within the use case or serve an intermediate contemplation of an ongoing evaluation.

All WTA elements require to be accessible online. Thereby, experimenters can have potentially direct access to them and easily share especially the artifacts of a testbed. Maintaining a testbed and its executions is conducted in the distributed system of a WTA testbed with more efficiency due to such online accessibility. Therefore, all elements require a valid URL to be queried via the web.

3.2   WTA Components

WTA splits into three main components as in the conceptual similarities and includes the Web UI (1) such that the testbed server communicates with several user agents and serves as access points for the experimenters. We propose the implementation of the components in the component diagram in Fig. 2. The Web UI is then connected to two other components: the Testbed Director (2) and the Testbed Library (3). Therefore, the Testbed Director is the second half of the conceptual similarities' central node, and thus manages the Testbed Environment (4). It organizes the execution of a given evaluation description and later gathers all results from the environment.

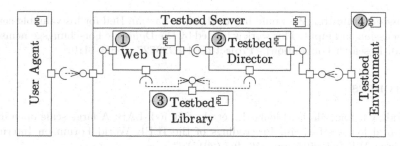

Fig. 2. Web-based testbed architecture components.

The Testbed Library offers an interface for Web UI and Testbed Director and saves all central artifacts of the testbed. Hereby, it saves the results of evaluations, real-world use cases, measurements, and other in advance created setup instructions for the testbed environment. All experimenters can access the library via the UI to either checkout results of passed evaluations or to create their next evaluation on the testbed. With such a library the ease of all experimenters is supported, such that they can focus on their main motivation of tests and evaluations and do not have to create everything from scratch.

The Testbed Environment is the most crucial aspect of the testbed as it realizes the required functionality. Thereby, its structure is highly dependent on the testbed's domain. It could be structured as in recent work from single-tier to multi-tier in as many layers as required for the testbed's domain. Also, additional layers to manage the correct testbed execution could be realized within.

The given architecture can by all components besides the User Agent be realized in a single- or multi-tier architecture. Figure 2 is hereby showing a single-tier version. Recent work proposes, that some domains or usages of a testbed might require such multi-tier testbed not only in executional elements but also in components like the Testbed Director or the Testbed Library.

4 Conclusion

In this work, we identified the recurrent innovation of web-based testbeds in different domains without a common architecture. To close the gap of especially testbed creators inexperienced in computer science towards full exploitation of the web-based testbed advantages, we identified conceptual similarities of recent web-based testbeds. Consequently, we presented a web-based testbed architecture (WTA) with emerging architectural goals out of the identified conceptual similarities and the principles initially proposed by Cavalieri et al. [4] which are still crucial. It conflates the common understanding and key advantages of the web. In the future, we need to support this first approach with a precise method supporting any testbed developer in his work, which will help especially researchers from non-computer science domains.

Acknowledgements. We would like to thank Sebastian Heil for his valuable conceptual discussion and input. This work is funded by the Deutsche Forschungsgemeinschaft (German Research Foundation) - Project-ID 416228727 - SFB 1410.

References

1. Adjih, C., Baccelli, E., Fleury, E., et al.: FIT loT-LAB: A large scale open experimental loT testbed. In: Proceedings of the IEEE World Forum on Internet of Things, WF-IoT 2015, pp. 459–464 (2015)
2. Akyildiz, I.F., Melodia, T., Chowdhury, K.R.: Wireless multimedia sensor networks: applications and testbeds. Proc. IEEE **96**(10), 1588–1605 (2008)
3. Bertolino, A., De Angelis, G., Frantzen, L., Polini, A.: Model-based generation of testbeds for web services. In: Suzuki, K., Higashino, T., Ulrich, A., Hasegawa, T. (eds.) FATES/TestCom-2008. LNCS, vol. 5047, pp. 266–282. Springer, Heidelberg (2008). https://doi.org/10.1007/978-3-540-68524-1_19
4. Cavalieri, S., Macchi, M., Valckenaers, P.: Benchmarking the performance of manufacturing control systems: design principles for a web-based simulated testbed. J. Intell. Manuf. **14**(1), 43–58 (2003)
5. Cecchet, E., Udayabhanu, V., Wood, T., Shenoy, P.: BenchLab: an open testbed for realistic benchmarking of web applications. In: The 2nd USENIX Conference on Web Application Development, pp. 37–48 (2011)
6. Gao, Y., Zhang, J., Guan, G., Dong, W.: LinkLab: a scalable and heterogeneous testbed for remotely developing and experimenting iot applications. In: 2020 IEEE/ACM 5th International Conference on Internet-of-Things Design and Implementation, pp. 176–188 (2020)
7. Khalil, M.E., Ghani, K., Khalil, W.: Onion architecture: a new approach for XaaS (every-thing-as-a service) based virtual collaborations. In: 2016 13th Learning and Technology Conference (LT), pp. 1–7 (2016)
8. Kouřil, D., Rebok, T., Jirsík, T., et al.: Cloud-based testbed for simulation of cyber attacks. In: 2014 IEEE Network Operations and Management Symposium (NOMS) (2014)
9. Lanza, J., Sánchez, L., Santana, J.R., et al.: Experimentation as a service over semantically interoperable internet of things testbeds. IEEE Access **6**, 51607–51725 (2018)
10. Neema, H., Koutsoukos, X., Potteiger, B., Tang, C.Y., Stouffer, K.: Simulation testbed for railway infrastructure security and resilience evaluation. In: 7th Symposium on Hot Topics in the Science of Security (2020)
11. Peterson, L., Roscoe, T.: The design principles of PlanetLab. ACM SIGOPS Oper. Syst. Rev. **40**(1), 11–16 (2006)
12. Siegert, V., Noura, M., Gaedke, M.: aTLAS: a testbed to examine trust for a redecentralized web. In: Proceedings of The 2020 IEEE/WIC/ACM International Joint Conference on Web Intelligence and Intelligent Agent Technology (2020, to be published)
13. Vargas-Salgado, C., Aguila-Leon, J., Chiñas-Palacios, C., Hurtado-Perez, E.: Low-cost web-based supervisory control and data acquisition system for a microgrid testbed: a case study in design and implementation for academic and research applications. Heliyon **5**(9), e02474 (2019)
14. Werner-Allen, G., Swieskowski, P., Welsh, M.: MoteLab: a wireless sensor network testbed. In: 4th International Symposium on Information Processing in Sensor Networks, pp. 483–488. IEEE (2005)

15. Yu, H., Shen, Z., Leung, C., Miao, C., Lesser, V.R.: A survey of multi-agent trust management systems. IEEE Access **1**, 35–50 (2013)
16. Zia, M.Y.I., Otero, P., Siddiqui, A., Poncela, J.: Design of a web based underwater acoustic communication testbed and simulation platform. Wirel. Pers. Commun. **116**, 1171–1193 (2020)

Towards Large-Scale Empirical Assessment of Web APIs Evolution

Fabio Di Lauro(✉) ⓘ, Souhaila Serbout ⓘ, and Cesare Pautasso ⓘ

Software Institute, USI, Lugano, Switzerland
{fabio.di.lauro,souhaila.serbout}@usi.ch, c.pautasso@ieee.org

Abstract. Web Application Programming Interfaces (APIs) decouple the internal implementation of a service from its consumers which can reuse and compose them to rapidly build new applications. Many Web APIs are described with the OpenAPI Specification (OAS). The goal of our research is to check the feasibility of using API descriptions found in public open source repositories to study how APIs evolve over time. To do so, we collected a large dataset of OAS documents by crawling open source repositories, we parsed the corresponding metadata and measured the API size in order to extract a simple model to track the lifecycle of API artifacts and observe common evolution behaviors. Our preliminary results indicate that only a subset of the APIs changes, but as opposed to the expectation that APIs should only grow to maintain backward compatibility we also detected a number of APIs with a more variable history. We also study the stability of API artifacts over time and whether APIs are more or less likely to change as they age.

Keywords: Web API · API evolution · OpenAPI

1 Introduction

Web Application Programming Interfaces (APIs) are used to remotely access software services over the HTTP protocol [16]. They make it possible to build complex applications rapidly by accessing third-party data sources and by reusing software delivered as a service, written in many programming languages [5]. APIs can evolve during their lifetime for different reasons [12,18]. These changes could have a minor impact or severely damage or break clients depending on whether, for example, API features are added, updated, or removed [13]. To mitigate this, service providers can guarantee the stability of their offerings, reveal a preview of new experimental versions to selected clients and support one or more versions of an API at the same time [14].

In this paper, we assume that the interface of a Web API is described using OpenAPI [1], an emerging standard specification language which supports versioning metadata embedded in the API description. Throughout the API evolution life cycle [15], the API documentation is also continuously changing [17]. These changes to the API description artifacts themselves are tracked via version control systems.

The original version of this chapter was revised: the term "paths" has been corrected to "operations" in several places of the paper. The correction to this chapter is available at https://doi.org/10.1007/978-3-030-74296-6_49

© Springer Nature Switzerland AG 2021, corrected publication 2021
M. Brambilla et al. (Eds.): ICWE 2021, LNCS 12706, pp. 124–138, 2021.
https://doi.org/10.1007/978-3-030-74296-6_10

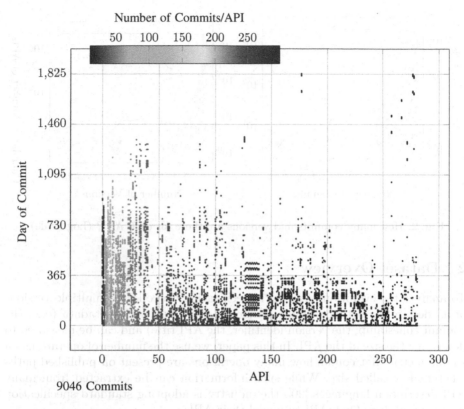

Fig. 1. Dataset Overview: Commit History of APIs with more than 10 commits, sorted by number of commits

Our goal is to assess the feasibility of using API descriptions collected from open-source repositories to study how Web APIs evolve over long periods of time. To do so, we collected on GitHub the change histories of 4,682 OpenAPI Specification (OAS) files.

Can these be used to trace, measure, and classify changes on APIs structures during their lifetime? What kind of changes can be detected by analyzing basic artifacts metadata? How stable are API artifacts over time? Do APIs tend to grow or shrink over time? How much is the frequency of change of an API dependent on its age? These are the research questions we aim to answer in this paper.

The rest of this paper is structured as follows. Section 2 presents an overview of collected API artifacts. Section 3 outlines the results that we obtained and shows selected Web API evolution cases. We discuss the results in Sect. 4. Section 5 summarizes the related work before we conclude in Sect. 6.

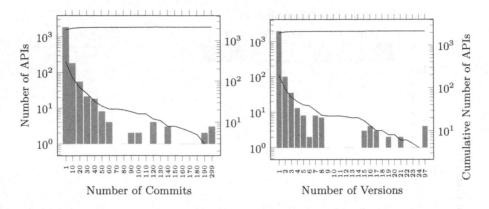

Fig. 2. How many commits and versions are there for each API? (Log Scale)

2 Dataset Overview

To analyze the evolution of an API specification we collected multiple versions of its description artifacts. Each artifact is associated with metadata (e.g., the commit timestamp, the version identifier, the API title) and can be measured to determine the size of the API. In this paper, we use the number of operations - a simple metric that counts how many operations are present on published paths - hereinafter called size. While such information can be extracted from many API description languages [20], the industry is adopting standard specification languages such as OpenAPI to model their APIs.

By crawling GitHub during December 2020, we collected 4,682 open-source API descriptions, written in both Swagger 2.0 and OpenAPI 3.0, with a total number of 34,638 commits, where 55% of the APIs have more than 1 commit. We downloaded all files and metadata in each commit and checked their compliance with the OpenAPI standard using **Prance** [2], configured with the validator **open-api-spec-validator** [3]. As a result, we obtained 13,786 commits labeled as *valid*, which we include in this analysis.

We visualize the entire dataset in Fig. 1, where each dot represents a commit. Its horizontal position shows which API changed, while the vertical position represents when the change occurred, relative to the time of the initial commit for the corresponding API. Its color highlights how many commits have been found in each API. We can see that for some APIs there are commits spanning across more than four years and that there are 280 APIs which have more than 10 commits.

3 Results

3.1 Change Granularity: Commits and Versions

Figure 2 shows how many commits and how many distinct version identifiers have been found for each API. All APIs have less than 300 commits and 44% of

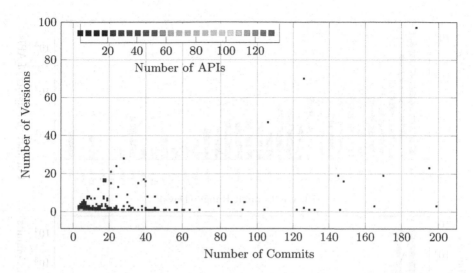

Fig. 3. Commits and versions (APIs with more than 2 commits)

them have only 1. We can also observe in Fig. 3 the relationship between changes that impact the versioning metadata embedded in the API description and the changes which only touch the artifact as tracked by the versioning system. It is clear that the number of versions is bound by the number of commits since every observable change of the version identifier requires a new commit to store the updated API specification. This chart helps to select a dozen of APIs which not only have many fine-grained changes over a long period of time but also have been explicitly annotated with different version identifiers by their developers.

3.2 API Age and Change Frequency

We define the *age* of the API as the time interval between the last and first commit of its history. The distribution of the age of the APIs in our collection is shown in Fig. 4 (top). While -again- most APIs have only 1 commit (thus, they have age 0), our collection also includes APIs whose history spans up to 5 years, which make them potential subjects for further study.

How often do API descriptions change? We measure the *change interval* as the duration of the time interval between two consecutive commits within an API history. As shown in Fig. 4 (bottom), most APIs change within the same day (change interval < 1) while there are some commits which occurred after leaving the API specification untouched for more than 3 years. It is interesting to note that, in many APIs, OAS files are committed and pushed only once, and afterward, they are no longer touched.

Does the age of the API impact its likelihood of changing? If we estimate the likelihood of change based on the time interval between commits, as shown in Fig. 5, we can observe that as APIs get older they still tend to change rather often.

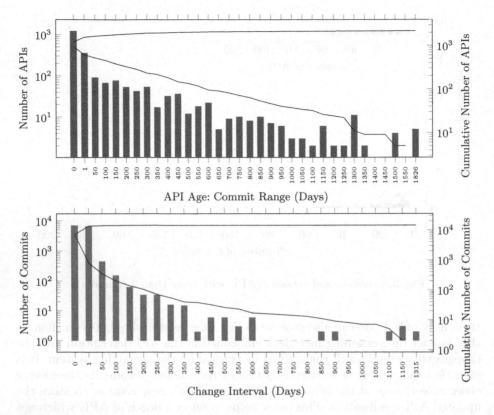

Fig. 4. API Age and Change Interval (Log Scale): How old are the APIs and how often do they change?

3.3 API Growth

While it is straightforward to observe the time of the commits, detecting actual change occurring to an API is more challenging. API descriptions are complex documents, which – in the case of OpenAPI specifications – enumerate the resource paths exposed by the API, define the corresponding resource representations, and prescribe which HTTP methods can be invoked on each path, using which parameters and which status codes can be expected as part of the responses.

To simplify the analysis while keeping the possibility to detect some changes, in this paper we abstract the content of the API specification with one metric: its *size*, measured as the number of operations. While there are many changes that can be made to an API specification document that does not impact the number of paths, we are interested in studying how many commits during the history of an API actually do so. This would already allow us to determine if the hypothesis that APIs tend to grow over time can be confirmed.

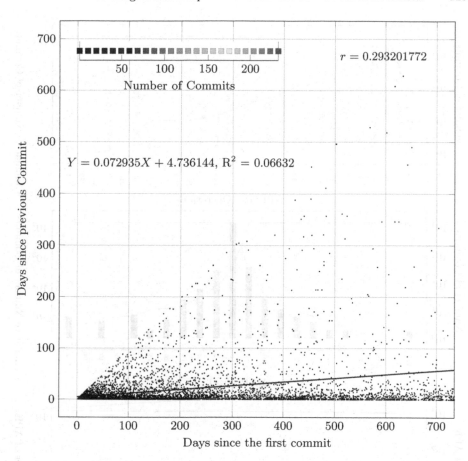

Fig. 5. Likelihood of change: Do APIs change less as they age?

In Fig. 6 (top) we report the API size distribution for every commit. While a few hundred commits do not contain any paths, the size follows an exponential distribution with a tail that reaches up to 357 operations.

Regarding how the size of API changes, we report the variance of the number of operations across we report the variance of the number of paths across the commit history of every API in Fig. 6 (bottom). Here we can see that 30% of APIs have a size variance of 0 over their commit history.

We have also computed the variation of the API size at every commit by comparing the size of the new version against the size of the previous one (Fig. 6, middle). While, in this case, the vast majority of commits do not change the size, we can also measure how much APIs grow or shrink after each commit.

In Fig. 7 we can observe absolute APIs size variations related to the time between the corresponding commits. There is no correlation between the amount of API size changes and the time needed to apply them.

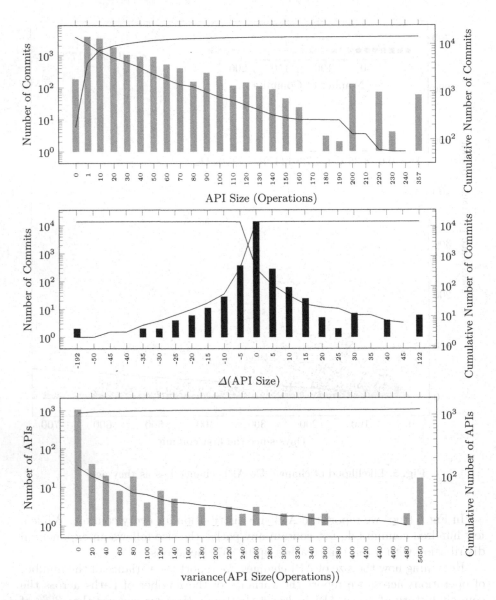

Fig. 6. Do changing APIs always grow larger? API Size, Size variation of every commit and Size variance of every API (Log Scale)

Measuring the size variation per unit of time represents the *API growth speed*: a negative speed value indicates how much an API has been shrinking (some operations were removed) and conversely, a positive speed value indicates a tendency to grow the number of operations. We measured this speed at every commit (Fig. 8) as well as aggregated it over the history of each API (Fig. 9).

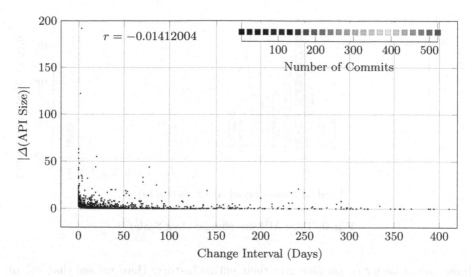

Fig. 7. Speed of change: How much time does it take to grow or shrink the API?

Given the fast-slow dynamics of APIs, which may remain unchanged for months and then go through a development iteration with multiple commits during the same day, we have chosen to measure the speed in terms of operations/day. The high values shown in the tails of the distribution are due to changes in the API size which have been amplified by the short change interval between the commits in which they were introduced.

We also computed the total size variation of APIs (Fig. 9), measured by comparing the size of the last commit and the first commit of its history. If we classify APIs in terms of whether they grow, shrink, or simply do not change, we obtain the groups shown in Table 1. The first table (a) counts how many APIs

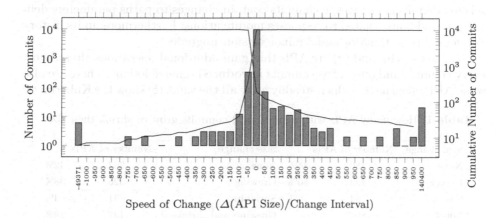

Fig. 8. Speed of change distribution: operations/day (Log Scale)

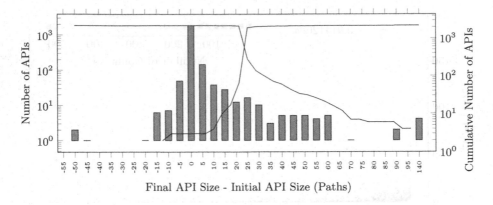

Final API Size - Initial API Size (Paths)

Fig. 9. Total API size change (Log Scale)

have grown larger or smaller over their entire history. Here we see that 6% of the APIs shrink, while 50% grow. If we also consider changes occurring at every commit (b), we see that 42% of the APIs keep a constant size in all the commits in their history. This leaves 17 APIs which change their intermediate size but end up with the same size as the initial one. Moreover, 16% of the APIs have a history with some commits increasing their size, and others reducing their size.

3.4   Web API Evolution Case Studies

Out of the large number of APIs we collected, we selected a set of APIs cases showing different evolution histories in Fig. 10 and 11 (a) is an example of an API which has 40 commits corresponding to 16 different versions. However, we can notice that its size, measured as the number of operations, remains the same during the whole evolution period. This case is an example where a more detailed metric is required to detect changes. In fact, 23 commits of its history contain schema definition changes, 6 commits contain changes to paths parameters definitions, and 2 are related to responses modifications; Furthermore, in its history developers push 6 major and 8 minor version upgrades.

Unlike (a), (b), and (d) are APIs that gain additional operations after almost every commit, and only a few commits introduced some deletions. There are also some APIs, such as (e), which steadily grow all the time. (f) show the Kubermatic

Table 1. How many APIs with more than 2 commits grow or shrink their size?

Size change	Number of APIs		Size change	Number of APIs	
None	380	44%	None	363	42%
Larger	423	50%	Growing	326	38%
Smaller	54	6%	Shrinking	31	4%
Total	857		Growing and shrinking	137	16%
(a) Total API change (Fig. 9)			(b) Commit Δ(API size) (Fig. 6 middle)		

API, which both grows and shrinks over its history of 199 commits over more than 2 years, eventually more than tripling its initial size. It grows rapidly with an average speed of 1.77 operations/day.

Another particular change-history example is the API depicted in (c), which has a commit where 192 operations were deleted at once. Then it started slowly growing during the next 254 days adding 85 operations more. On the day 394, there was a commit that inserted 122 operations to the API and, after that, we can observe minimal variations in its size with a variation of 5 operations from day 394 to 574. Also, while during the first half of its history there is no change in versioning metadata, it undergoes 23 different versions from day 279 onwards.

4 Discussion

Is it possible to find – by crawling open source repositories – enough machine-readable API descriptions suitable to study how Web APIs evolve over large periods of time? In this paper, we have shown that thanks to the growing adoption of the OpenAPI specification language, a sample of 875 APIs with a history of more than 2 commits can be found on GitHub.

We could also find many more API description artifacts (1322) without a commit history of significant length. While these are still interesting to analyze for synchronic studies, it remains to be seen whether developers pushed only a single commit because their APIs were committed only when stable, or we have crawled repositories of projects which never went beyond the first commit.

By analyzing basic artifact metadata (such as commit timestamps and version identifiers) we have begun to trace, measure and classify changes on APIs during their lifetime. For example, we have shown that the frequency of change of APIs is not dependent on the age of the API.

Likewise, different API developers follow different versioning practices, ranging from version identifiers incremented every other commit (like in the Open-Storage SDK shown in Fig. 10b) to API histories with only a few explicitly identified versions over hundreds of commits. We also found examples in which the title of the API itself would change, although the OAS document used to describe it would remain the same.

Regarding the evolution of the API content, in this paper, we have focused on one possible API size metric, which has allowed us to detect changes for more than half of the APIs in the collection. We certainly need a more in-depth analysis of API artifacts to detect and measure changes beyond the length of the resource operations, not only to distinguish whether existing operations are renamed but also to spot changes in parameters, responses and schema definitions. Still, by only looking at the size we could show that the majority of the APIs in our sample, which changed their size, have a tendency to grow larger over time.

4.1 Threats to Validity

One of the challenges faced when performing a study using datasets collected from open-source repositories is the quality of the retrieved data. In our case,

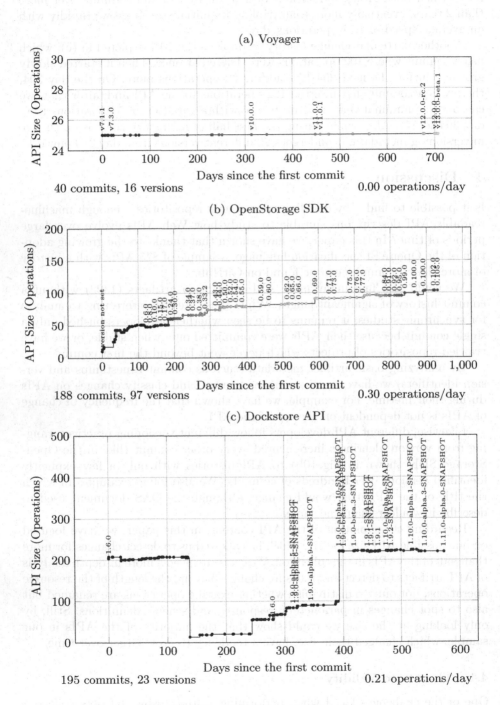

Fig. 10. API evolution histories examples

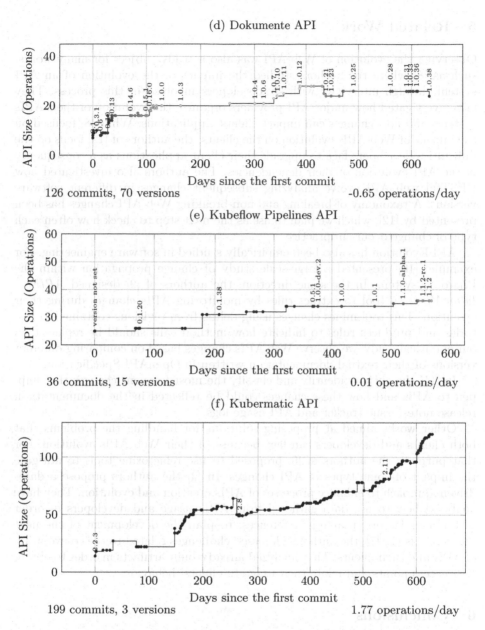

Fig. 11. API evolution histories examples (continued)

we are interested in observing the evolution of distinct real world Web API through their OAS description. Another threat to our sample validity could be represented by the fact that not all APIs are really implemented in up and running services. This fact could void the assumption that commits introduce always tested modifications as usually happen in productive environments.

5   Related Work

Observing the evolution of Web API was also a study subject for many works, such as [8] where the authors studied the impact of the evolution of an API system through interviews with six developers involved in this process. They also investigated how major API providers organize the evolution of their APIs systems and how changes can impact clients' applications. While [8] focused on the impact of Web APIs evolution on the clients, the authors of [19] focus on the difficulties developers face to upgrade their client applications as a consequence of the API evolution of their dependencies. The authors also investigated how RESTful web API evolve analyzing subsequent changes in different software versions. A taxonomy of breaking and non-breaking Web API changes has been presented by [12], which we plan to use as the next step to check how often each type of change occurs in practice.

API Evolution has also been empirically studied in software engineering. For example, [10] presented a large-scale study of change propagation within the Pharo ecosystem. In the same direction, the authors of [9] designed *APIEvolutionMiner*: a tool to extract rules by monitoring APIs changes during their evolution. This tool mines changes using deltas from revisions contained in histories and produces rules to indicate how method calls should be replaced. In our empirical study, we observe Web APIs changes based on comparing different versions of their textual documentation written in OpenAPI Specification.

In [11] the authors identify and classify the most frequent changes that happen to APIs and how these changes could be reflected in the documentation, release notes, issue tracker and API usage logs.

Other works aimed at proposing solutions for handling the problems that both clients and developers can face because of their Web APIs evolution. For that purpose, the authors of [6] proposed to use refactoring tools to mitigate the impact of some types of API changes. In [4] the authors propose a data-driven approach to enhance processes of APIs creation and evolution. They have analyzed how to use data gathered from APIs usage and developers in order to build indicators, usable as references, to plan the development of the next releases. Also in [7], the authors addressed challenges related to the co-evolution of APIs and their clients. They analyzed already-built artifacts in order to obtain API access points and relate their usage to clients' behavior.

6   Conclusions

To observe the evolution of Web APIs over time, we performed an empirical study over a dataset of 4,682 APIs. Our quantitative approach consists of extracting Web APIs changes from their textual documentation written in the OpenAPI Specification language, using the change histories from Github. Based on this meta-data, we have measured different change granularities, from fine-grained commits to coarse-grained version identifier changes. While most APIs have only a few commits and a single version, we were able to spot potentially interesting outliers worthy of further study with hundreds of commits and up to 97 different versions. We also analyzed temporal aspects of commit histories, attempting to correlate the age of APIs with their change frequency. To observe the impact of change on the API content, we used a simple size metric defined as the number of operations listed in the corresponding OAS specification. This allowed us to observe that if the APIs change size, they mostly do so by growing over time. We have also visualized the commit history of six representative examples of different types of Web API evolution.

As future work, we plan to define heuristics for classifying the changes occurring on the different files through the commits, using more metrics, such as HTTP methods, paths, and query parameters and properties of response objects. We also plan to establish a non-linear, partial order relationship between the artifacts which may undergo forks and merges across different repositories. Moreover, platforms such as GitHub allow forking repositories and their reuse, which means that the retrieved OAS cannot be treated as files with a linear, separate history but we have to track their provenance considering that they can be forked by other users and then extended or modified in different repositories. Thus, we will also trace changes occurring across forks.

Acknowledgements. This work is funded by the SNSF, with the API-ACE project nr. 184692.

References

1. OpenAPI Initiative. https://www.openapis.org/. Accessed 30 Dec 2020
2. Prance. https://pypi.org/project/prance/. Accessed 28 Dec 2020
3. open-api-spec-validator.   https://github.com/p1c2u/openapi-spec-validator. Accessed 29 Dec 2020
4. Abelló, A., Ayala, C.P., Farré, C., Gómez, C., Oriol, M., Romero, O.: A data-driven approach to improve the process of data-intensive API creation and evolution. In: Proceedings of the Forum and Doctoral Consortium Papers Presented at CAiSE, vol. 1848, pp. 1–8. CEUR-WS.org (2017)
5. Antonio, G.D., Pablo, F., Ruiz-Cortés, A.: An analysis of RESTful APIs offerings in the industry. In: Proceedings of the International Conference on Service-Oriented Computing (ICSOC), pp. 589–604 (2017)
6. Dig, D., Johnson, R.: How do APIs evolve? A story of refactoring. J. Softw. Maint. Evol. Res. Pract. **18**(2), 83–107 (2006)
7. Eilertsen, A.M., Bagge, A.H.: Exploring API/client co-evolution. In: 2nd IEEE/ACM International Workshop on API Usage and Evolution (WAPI@ICSE), pp. 10–13 (2018)
8. Espinha, T., Zaidman, A., Gross, H.G.: Web API growing pains: stories from client developers and their code. In: Proceedings of the IEEE Conference on Software Maintenance, Reengineering, and Reverse Engineering (CSMR-WCRE). IEEE (2014)
9. Hora, A., Etien, A., Anquetil, N., Ducasse, S., Valente, M.T.: APIEvolutionMiner: keeping API evolution under control. In: Proceedings of the IEEE Conference on Software Maintenance, Reengineering, and Reverse Engineering (CSMR-WCRE), pp. 420–424 (2014)

10. Hora, A., Robbes, R., Valente, M.T., Anquetil, N., Etien, A., Ducasse, S.: How do developers react to API evolution? A large-scale empirical study. Softw. Qual. J. **26**(1), 161–191 (2018)
11. Koçi, R., Franch, X., Jovanovic, P., Abelló, A.: Classification of changes in API evolution. In: Proceedings of the 23rd International Enterprise Distributed Object Computing Conference (EDOC), pp. 243–249 (2019)
12. Lauret, A.: The Design of Web APIs. Manning (2019)
13. Li, J., Xiong, Y., Liu, X., Zhang, L.: How does web service API evolution affect clients? In: Proceedings of the 20th International Conference on Web Services (ICWS) (2013)
14. Lübke, D., Zimmermann, O., Pautasso, C., Zdun, U., Stocker, M.: Interface evolution patterns—balancing compatibility and flexibility across microservices lifecycles. In: Proceedings of the 24th European Conference on Pattern Languages of Programs, EuroPLoP 2019. ACM (2019)
15. Murer, S., Bonati, B., Furrer, F.: Managed Evolution - A Strategy for Very Large Information Systems. Springer, Heidelberg (2010). https://doi.org/10.1007/978-3-642-01633-2
16. Pautasso, C., Zimmermann, O.: The Web as a software connector: Integration resting on linked resources. IEEE Softw. **35**, 93–98 (2018)
17. Shi, L., Zhong, H., Xie, T., Li, M.: An empirical study on evolution of API documentation. In: Proceedings of the 14th International Conference on Fundamental Approaches to Software Engineering: Part of the Joint European Conferences on Theory and Practice of Software, FASE 2011/ETAPS 2011, pp. 416–431 (2011)
18. Sohan, S.M., Anslow, C., Maurer, F.: A case study of Web API evolution. In: Proceedings of the IEEE World Congress on Services, pp. 245–252 (2015)
19. Wang, S., Keivanloo, I., Zou, Y.: How do developers react to RESTful API evolution? In: Franch, X., Ghose, A.K., Lewis, G.A., Bhiri, S. (eds.) ICSOC 2014. LNCS, vol. 8831, pp. 245–259. Springer, Heidelberg (2014). https://doi.org/10.1007/978-3-662-45391-9_17
20. Yang, J., Wittern, E., Ying, A.T.T., Dolby, J., Tan, L.: Towards extracting web API specifications from documentation. In: 2018 IEEE/ACM 15th International Conference on Mining Software Repositories (MSR), pp. 454–464 (2018)

Stability Metrics for Continuous Integration of Service-Oriented Systems

Dionysis Athanasopoulos[(✉)] and Daniel Keenan

School of Electronics, Electrical Engineering, Computer Science Queen's University Belfast, Northern Ireland, UK
{D.Athanasopoulos,dkeenan21}@qub.ac.uk

Abstract. One of the key principles of the service orientation is the standardised service contract. However, the assumption that the service contract is kept unmodified during the whole life-cycle of a system is not always held. Evolution changes on the service APIs have an impact on the maintainability of their programming clients within the system making difficult the continuous integration of the services. The metrics that have currently been applied for the service maintainability assess the service coupling, cohesion, complexity, and granularity. Software stability can further contribute in assessing the maintainability of systems. However, it is challenging to measure the stability of service APIs without having evolved their programming clients, because it should be measured by considering the types of the evolution changes in APIs that have direct impact on the programming clients. To address this challenge, we define a set of mappings between evolved service APIs based on which the stability changes can be determined. We further specify a generic algorithm that recognises the evolution changes required on the programming clients of the evolved APIs. We finally define an initial version of a suite of metrics that estimate the stability of a service system without assuming the existence of the evolved programming clients.

Keywords: Software stability · Service API · Evolution · Continuous integration

1 Introduction

Organizations have already migrated or developed from scratch the architecture of their software systems into service-oriented architecture (SOA) [1]. Service-orientation views systems as a composition of reusable services. Microservices currently are an increasingly popular SOA style due to the advantages microservices provide [2]. Microservices are highly cohesive and reusable services [3]. A key principle of the service orientation is the standardised service contract that consists of a set of service descriptions [1]. Each description specifies a (micro-) service from a different aspect, e.g., syntactic, semantic, behavioral, or QoS aspect [4]. The syntactic aspect specifies the syntax and the structure of the

© Springer Nature Switzerland AG 2021
M. Brambilla et al. (Eds.): ICWE 2021, LNCS 12706, pp. 139–147, 2021.
https://doi.org/10.1007/978-3-030-74296-6_11

public (micro-)service API (e.g., OpenAPI[1]). We use the term API to refer to the interface of a (micro-)service.

The core implication of the principle of the standardised service contract is that if the service contract is kept unmodified, then the code of the programming clients of the service will not be affected. The term of the programming client refers to the lines of code of the SOA system that invokes a (micro-)service API. However, the assumption that the service contracts are kept unmodified during the whole life-cycle of a SOA system does not always hold. Intuitively, changes in service contracts can be frequent in the case of microservices due to the low granularity and the high number of microservices that exist in a single large-scale SOA system.

To confirm our intuition, we did a preliminary assessment of the stability of the service APIs in open-source microservice systems [5] and we observed that most of the evolution changes were made in the operations of the microservice APIs. The evolution changes in the microservice APIs are significant because they have a direct impact on the programming clients of the microservices. In other words, evolution changes in the (micro-)service APIs increase the maintenance cost of SOA systems, i.e., the number of changes required in the programming clients of APIs. As an example, a change in a parameter data-type of an operation of a microservice API may trigger updates in tens of code lines that invoke the reusable operation. However, there may exist evolution changes in the (micro-)service APIs that do not affect the programming clients of the (micro-)services. For instance, a data-type modification from the `int` data-type of an input parameter of an API operation to a more general `double` data-type does not require changes on the programming client of the API. In this case, the programming client remains stable with respect to this specific evolution change in the used API.

The source code of the microservice systems that we checked is held within repositories of a collaborative development platform (e.g., GitLab[2]). We checked the evolution changes in the microservice APIs over the many pushed commits of the systems to the repositories. Collaborative platforms usually provide a level of automation in setting up and triggering continuous-integration pipelines[3]. A pipeline contains a sequence of steps (e.g., building, testing) that will be automatically executed when commits are pushed to a central repository. The continuous integration is one of the collaborative development practices followed to reduce the development and the maintenance times of software systems [6]. However, if the programming clients of an evolved API have not been updated before the API is pushed to a repository, then the execution of the continuous-integration pipeline will be broken. This frequently happens because separate (micro-)services are usually developed/maintained by separate engineers' teams.

To avoid to break a continuous-integration pipeline, developers should measure how much stable a SOA system can be before pushing the API evolution

---

[1] https://swagger.io/specification.

[2] https://gitlab.com.

[3] https://docs.gitlab.com/ee/topics/autodevops/.

changes to a repository. However, it is challenging to calculate the system stability because it is not clear how data-type evolution changes affect the system
stability. Evolution changes at the data-type level can be quite various and of a
high number because API operations take as input/return as output XML/JSON
schemas that generally consist of many and various data-types. On top of that,
the actual value of the system stability cannot be calculated at the API evolution
time because the programming clients of the evolved APIs have not been evolved
yet. Thus, the following research question is raised: "How can the stability of
a SOA system be estimated without having evolved the programming clients of
service APIs?"

To answer this question, we searched in the literature for stability metrics.
Software stability is a quality attribute that contributes to the maintainability
of systems [7]. The stability of a system is defined as its resistance to the ampli-
fication of its changes (additions, modifications, deletions) [8]. To the best of our
knowledge, there is no maintainability metric that assesses (micro-)service stability. Significant research has been carried out on stability in the object-oriented
domain at the level of classes [9] and more recently at the lesser-explored level of
packages [10]. Conceptually, the object-oriented inter-package stability is close
to (micro-)service stability because a (micro-)service can be considered as a set
of packages that expose a public API used by many programming clients of other
(micro-)services. In other words, we do not consider the intra-package stability
because it deals with the changes made in all the classes/packages of a (micro-
)service that do not necessarily affect the other (micro-)services of a system.
However, the package-level stability metrics proposed in [10] are coarse-grained
because these metrics do not consider the kind of the data-type changes in the
public APIs of packages. Given the evolution of programming clients depend
on the data-type changes, the above metrics do not suffice to assess the SOA
stability.

To cover this literature gap, we contribute an initial study of the API changes
that affect the stability of SOA systems. We also define a set of mappings between
evolved (micro-)service APIs based on which the stability changes can be determined. We further specify a generic algorithm that recognises (guided by the
API mappings) the evolution changes required on the programming clients of
the evolved APIs. We finally define an initial version of a suite of metrics that
estimate the stability of a SOA system without assuming the existence of the
evolved programming clients. The metrics use the API mappings and follow the
steps of the client-evolution algorithm. The metrics can be used for both services and microservices. Thus, we use the term of the service in the remainder
of the paper to refer to both services and microservices. We finally discuss the
employment of our stability metrics on a real-world microservice system [5].

The rest of the paper is structured as follows. Section 2 presents the related
state-of-the-art approaches and highlights the literature gaps. Section 3 defines
the concepts of SOA system, (micro-)service API, and API programming client.
Section 4 defines the mapping between evolved (micro-)service APIs. Section 5
defines the evolution changes on (micro-)service APIs and the evolution algo-

rithm of programming clients. Section 6 defines our proposed suite of stability metrics. Section 7 summarizes our contribution and discusses its future directions.

2   Related Work

The existing quality metrics for (micro-)services focus on the service cohesion, coupling, complexity, and granularity [11,12]. Further quality metrics specific for microservices have been proposed in the area of the microservice extraction from legacy systems. An example is the quality evaluation performed on extracted microservices in [13]. The authors describe a quality criterion called "functional independence", which focuses on cohesion and coupling.

[14] highlights that the microservice quality attributes of modularity, scalability, independence, and maintainability, have been frequently discussed in the literature, without though proposing specific quality metrics. The industrial research in [15] reveals that source code quality was the primary target of tools and metrics in industry, but this is missing at the level of (micro-)service architecture. [16] developed a tool which accepts microservice system source code as input, performs static analysis on the code, and computes metrics on the microservices. [17] proposes SOA maintainability metrics in terms of microservice coupling, cohesion, and complexity.

However, there is no stability metric for SOA systems. Software stability has been well explored in the domain of object-oriented software. This has resulted in metrics such as class stability metrics [7], class implementation instability [9], and more recently a suite of package metrics [10]. However, the package-level stability metrics proposed in [10] are coarse-grained because these metrics do not consider the kind of the data-type changes in the public APIs of packages. In particular, the metrics just increase by one the number of the evolution changes if a data-type has been changed, independently of the type of the change made to the data-type. Concluding, what is still missing in the literature are *inter-service stability metrics that take into account the fine-grained data-type evolution changes in the service APIs.*

3   Service API and SOA System

We define the concepts of service API, API client, and SOA system in a generic way, independently of the underlying specification language (e.g., Java, WSDL, OpenAPI).

Definition 1 (Service API). *Service API is modelled by a name and a set of operations.*

$$api := \Big(name, \{op_i\} \Big)$$

Definition 2 (API Operation). *An API operation is modelled by a name and (potentially empty) input and output messages, $op := (name, msg_{in}, msg_{out})$.*

Definition 3 (Operation Message). *The input/output message of an operation consists of a set of elements, $msg := \{e_i\}$.*

We define the operation message in this paper based on the leaf elements of the hierarchical structure of an XML/JSON schema, leaving as future work the consideration of the complete hierarchical structure.

Definition 4 (Message Element). *An element of a message is modelled by a tuple that consists of the name, the data-type, the min occurrence number, and the max occurrence number of the element, $e := (name, type, min, max)$.*

Given that the number of the instances of a leaf element appear in a schema instance equals the product of the numbers of the instances of the elements that belong to the path from the schema root to the leaf, the min/max occurrence numbers are calculated by the product of the min/max occurrence numbers of the elements of the path [18].

Definition 5 (API Programming Client). *An API programming client instantiates (assigning data values to) a number of (a part or all of) the leaf elements of the (input/output) message of an operation of a service API and finally invokes the operation.*

$$pc := \Big(api, \; op, \; \big\{(name, \; type, \; num, \; \{value_i\})\big\}\Big)$$

Definition 6 (SOA System). *A SOA system consists of a set of service APIs. Each API is associated with the set of its programming clients, $sys :=$*
$\Big\{\big(api, \; \{pc_i\}\big)\Big\}.$

4 Service API Mappings

We formally define the concept of the API mapping and we leave as future work the specification of an algorithm that technically identifies these mappings (e.g., by adapting existing schema/API mapping tool [19]). The API mapping definition considers a source API (old API version) is mapped to a target API (new API version). API mappings are hierarchically structured following the hierarchical structure of service APIs.

Definition 7 (API Mapping). *An API mapping consists of the source and the target APIs, along with a set of their $1 - 1$ operation mappings, $m_{api} :=$*
$\Big(api_s, \; api_t, \; \{m_{op}\}\Big).$

Definition 8 (Operation Mapping). *An operation mapping consists of the source and the target operations and their $1 - 1$ message mappings, $m_{op} :=$*
$\Big(op_s, \; op_t, \; \{m_{msg}\}\Big).$

Definition 9 (Message Mapping). *A message mapping consists of the source and the target messages, along with the* $1-1$ *mappings between their leaf elements.*

$$m_{msg} := \Big(msg_s, \ msg_t, \ \{m_e\}\Big)$$

Definition 10 (Element Mapping). *An element mapping consists of the source and the target elements, the absolute differences in their min/max occurrence numbers, and the amount of the information loss due to the translation of the value of the source element to conform to the data-type of the target element,* $m_e := (e_s, \ e_t, \ \Delta min, \ \Delta max, \ loss)$.

The concept of the information loss is specified in Sect. 5.

5   API Evolution Changes and Evolution Algorithm for API Clients

According to [20], there are the following types of evolution changes that can occur on the syntactic aspect of service APIs: i. add parameter; ii. remove parameter; iii. rename parameter; iv. change data-type of parameter; v. change min/max occurrence numbers of parameter; vi. change data-type of return value; vii. delete operation; viii. add operation; ix. rename operation; x. combine operations; xi. split operation. We focus in this paper on the first nine types of evolution changes, leaving as future work the last two types of changes. Even if there are empirical studies on how developers react to API evolution [21], these studies do not model the algorithmic steps of the client evolution. To cover this gap, we specify in Algorithm 1 an initial version of the evolution algorithm for API client, taking into account the above nine types of the API evolution changes.

Algorithm 1. Evolution of a programming client of an evolved service API

Input: op_s, op_t, m_{api}, pc;

1: **if** $m_{op} = \Big(op_s, \ op_t, \ \{m_{msg}\}\Big) \notin m_{api}$ **then** return -1;

2: **else**

3:      **if** $op_s.name \neq op_t.name$ **then** pc.op.name := op_t.name;

4:      **for** $pc.name \notin m_{msg}.m_e$ **do** pc := pc - (name, type, num);

5:      **for** $pc.name \in m_{msg}.m_e$ **do**

6:          **if** $pc.name \neq m_{msg}.m_e.e_t.name$ **then** pc.name := $m_{msg}.m_e.e_t$.name;

7:          **if** $pc.type \neq m_{msg}.m_e.e_t.type$ **then**

8:              **for** $pc.type.value_i$ **do** pc.type.$value_i$:= ($m_{msg}.m_e.e_t.type$) pc.type.$value_i$;

9:              **if** $pc.num > m_{msg}.m_e.e_t.max$ **then** removeValues (pc);

10:             **if** $pc.num < m_{msg}.m_e.e_t.max$ **then** addValues (pc);

Algorithm 1 accept as input the mappings between a source API and a target API, along with a programming client of the source API. Algorithm 1 first retrieves the mapping of the source operation to the target operation. If the source operation has been deleted, then Algorithm 1 aborts without success (Algorithm 1 (Step 1)). If the source operation has been renamed, then Algorithm 1 renames the source operation name to the target operation name (Algorithm 1 (Step 3)). Following, Algorithm 1 continues with the element mappings of the messages. For each source element, Algorithm 1 executes the following steps: if the source element has been deleted, then Algorithm 1 deletes the element instances from the programming client (Algorithm 1 (Step 4)). If the source element has been renamed, then Algorithm 1 renames the source element name to the target element name (Algorithm 1 (Step 6)). If the data-type of the source element has been changed, then Algorithm 1 casts the data value of the element parameter to conform to the data-type of the target element (Algorithm 1 (Step 8)). If the max (min) occurrence numbers of the source element is lower (resp. higher) than the instances number of the element, then Algorithm 1 removes (resp. add) the extra data values of the element (Algorithm 1 (Step 9 (resp. Step 10))). We assume the removal and the additional of data values are manually performed by developers.

The information loss that can happen in the casting of values of built-in data-types (e.g., converting a `double` value to an `int` value) has been quantified in [22].

6 Stability Metrics for SOA System

We define the stability metrics by using the API mappings and taking into account the steps of the client-evolution algorithm. The values of each metric belong to the interval $[0, 1]$ (the 1 value corresponds to the max stability value).

Definition 11 (System Stability). *The stability of a SOA system equals the average stability of the mapped operations of all the programming clients of the service APIs of the system,* $s_{sys} := \frac{\sum_{i=1}^{|sys.\{pc_i\}|} s_{op}(m_{op}) \mid pc_i.op \in m_{op}}{|sys.\{pc_i\}|}$.

Definition 12 (Operation Stability). *The operation stability equals the average stability of the mapped input/output operation messages,* $s_{op} := \frac{s_{msg}(m_{msg_{in}}) + s_{msg}(m_{msg_{out}})}{2}$.

Definition 13 (Message Stability). *The stability of a source message equals the average stability of the mapped message elements divided by the max number of the element between the source message and the target message,* $s_{msg} := \frac{\sum_{i=1}^{|\{m_e\}|} s_e(m_e)}{max(|msg_s|,|msg_t|)}$.

Definition 14 (Element Stability). *The element stability equals the product of the percentages of the differences in the min/max occurrence numbers and of the information loss,* $s_e := \frac{\Delta min}{max(e_s.min, e_t.min)} * \frac{\Delta max}{max(e_s.max, e_t.max)} * loss$.

Please note we use the product operator in Definition 14 because we consider that all the terms in the calculation of the element stability are equally important.

Illustrative example. We employed our stability metrics on an open-source microservice system which is available here [5]. We indicatively chose the real-world microservice system, Apollo[4], which contains three microservices and the mean number of API operations per microservice is 65. We focused on one of those microservices, `adminservice`, and especially, on the evolution of its API across various versions of the system. Through our inspection, we observed that most of the evolution changes on the API were additions/removals of parameters and changes in the data-types of the parameters. These cases of evolution changes are taken into account by our metrics as follows. The parameter additions/removals are considered by Definition 13 because there is no mapping between the source elements and the newly added target elements, while the denominator of the message stability value equals to the max number of the elements between a source message and a target message. Finally, the data-type changes are taken into account by Definition 14 because the differences in min/max multiplicities, along with the amount of the information loss, are considered.

7 Conclusions and Future Work

To address the challenge of measuring the stability of service APIs without having first evolved their programming clients, we defined a set of mappings between evolved service APIs based on which the stability changes can be determined. We further specified a generic algorithm that recognises the evolution changes required on the programming clients of the evolved APIs. We finally defined an initial version of a suite of metrics that estimate the stability of a service system without assuming the existence of the evolved programming clients.

We introduced in this work an early version of an automated approach for measuring service stability. The road ahead includes the definition of stability metrics that consider not only the leaf elements of the hierarchical structure of an XML/JSON schema, but the complete hierarchical structure. Moreover, all the evolution changes in the interface of APIs should be taken into account, including the combination and the split of operations. Finally, a research prototype of the approach is needed that can identify the mappings and calculate the values of the stability metrics to evaluate the effectiveness of our approach on real-world (micro-)service systems.

References

1. Erl, T.: Service-Oriented Architecture: Analysis and Design for Services and Microservices, 2nd edn. Prentice Hall (2016)
2. Newman, S.: Building Microservices, 1st edn. O'Reilly Media Inc. (2015)

---

[4] https://github.com/davidetaibi/Microservices_Project_List.

3. Taibi, D., Systä, K.: A decomposition and metric-based evaluation framework for microservices. CoRR, abs/1908.08513 (2019)
4. Andrikopoulos, V., Benbernou, S., Papazoglou, M.P.: On the evolution of services. IEEE Trans. Softw. Eng. **38**(3), 609–628 (2012)
5. Rahman, M.I., Panichella, S., Taibi, D.: A curated dataset of microservices-based systems. CoRR, abs/1909.03249 (2019)
6. Zhu, L., Bass, L., Champlin-Scharff, G.: Devops and its practices. IEEE Softw. **33**(3), 32–34 (2016)
7. Bogner, J., Wagner, S., Zimmermann, A.: Towards a practical maintainability quality model for service-and microservice-based systems. In: European Conference on Software Architecture, pp. 195–198. ACM (2017)
8. Soong, N.L.: A program stability measure. In: ACM Annual Conference, pp. 163–173 (1977)
9. Li, W., Etzkorn, L.H., Davis, C.G., Talburt, J.R.: An empirical study of object-oriented system evolution. Inf. Softw. Technol. **42**(6), 373–381 (2000)
10. Baig, J.J.A., Mahmood, S., Alshayeb, M., Niazi, M.: Package-level stability evaluation of object-oriented systems. Inf. Softw. Technol. **116**, 106172 (2019)
11. Perepletchikov, M., Ryan, C., Frampton, K.: Cohesion metrics for predicting maintainability of service-oriented software. In: International Conference on Quality Software, pp. 328–335. IEEE Computer Society (2007)
12. Perepletchikov, M., Ryan, C., Frampton, K., Tari, Z.: Coupling metrics for predicting maintainability in service-oriented designs. In: Australian Software Engineering Conference, pp. 329–340. IEEE Computer Society (2007)
13. Jin, W., Liu, T., Zheng, Q., Cui, D., Cai, Y.: Functionality-oriented microservice extraction based on execution trace clustering. In: International Conference on Web Services, pp. 211–218. IEEE (2018)
14. Alshuqayran, N., Ali, N., Evans, R.: A systematic mapping study in microservice architecture. In: International Conference on Service-Oriented Computing and Applications, pp. 44–51. IEEE Computer Society (2016)
15. Bogner, J., Fritzsch, J., Wagner, S., Zimmermann, A.: Assuring the evolvability of microservices: insights into industry practices and challenges. In: International Conference on Software Maintenance and Evolution, pp. 546–556. IEEE (2019)
16. Asik, T., Selçuk, Y.E.: Policy enforcement upon software based on microservice architecture. In: International Conference on Software Engineering Research, pp. 283–287. IEEE (2017)
17. Cardarelli, M., Iovino, L., Di Francesco, P., Di Salle, A., Malavolta, I., Lago, P.: An extensible data-driven approach for evaluating the quality of microservice architectures. In: Symposium on Applied Computing, pp. 1225–1234. ACM (2019)
18. Jiang, H., Ho, H., Popa, L., Han, W.-S.: Mapping-driven xml transformation. In: International Conference on World Wide Web, pp. 1063–1072 (2007)
19. Athanasopoulos, D., Zarras, A.V., Vassiliadis, P., Issarny, V.: Mining service abstractions. In: International Conference on Software Engineering, pp. 944–947. ACM (2011)
20. Li, J., Xiong, Y., Liu, X., Zhang, L.: How does web service API evolution affect clients? In: International Conference on Web Services, pp. 300–307. IEEE Computer Society (2013)
21. Hora, A., Robbes, R., Valente, M.T., Anquetil, N., Etien, A., Ducasse, S.: How do developers react to API evolution? A large-scale empirical study. Softw. Qual. J. **26**(1), 161–191 (2016). https://doi.org/10.1007/s11219-016-9344-4
22. Stroulia, E., Wang, Y.: Structural and semantic matching for assessing web-service similarity. Int. J. Coop. Inf. Syst. **14**, 407–438 (2005)

Web Big Data and Data Analytics

Attentive Hybrid Collaborative Filtering for Rating Conversion in Recommender Systems

Phannakan Tengkiattrakul[1,3]([✉]) [iD], Saranya Maneeroj[2],
and Atsuhiro Takasu[1,3] [iD]

[1] The Graduate University for Advanced Studies, SOKENDAI, Tokyo, Japan
[2] Department of Mathematics and Computer Science, Faculty of Science,
Chulalongkorn University, Bangkok, Thailand
`saranya.m@chula.ac.th`
[3] National Institute of Informatics, Tokyo, Japan
`{phannakan,takasu}@nii.ac.jp`

Abstract. Recommendation models that use collaborative filtering consider the influence of friends and neighbors when recommending suitable items for a target user. Most of these neighborhood-based models use the actual ratings from neighbors to predict the ratings of the target user toward target items, which often leads to a low accuracy prediction caused by the *improper rating-range* problem. Recently, rating conversion methods have been proposed to address this issue. Because each friend/neighbor can have a different level of influence on the target user, we propose a *friend* module, which converts their ratings to match the target user's perspective and assigns different weight to each user before modeling latent relations and predictions. In rating conversion, ratings that involve explicit feedback are important. Instead of the traditional approach to user embedding, we propose a novel approach that uses explicit feedback. This can express user features better than traditional methods and can then be used to convert ratings to match the target user's perspective. For better representation and recommendation, we also learn latent relations between each user and item by adopting *knowledge graph* ideas, which leads to more accurate results. The FilmTrust and MovieLens datasets are used in experiments comparing the proposed method with existing methods. This evaluation showed that our model is more accurate than existing methods.

Keywords: Recommender systems · Collaborative filtering · Rating conversion · Neural networks

1 Introduction

Following the rapid growth of online information in recent years, it has become difficult for users to choose items that would best suit them from among the

© Springer Nature Switzerland AG 2021
M. Brambilla et al. (Eds.): ICWE 2021, LNCS 12706, pp. 151–165, 2021.
https://doi.org/10.1007/978-3-030-74296-6_12

abundant choices. Recommender systems (RSs) have been developed during this time and have become a key approach to addressing this information overload problem. RSs are tools to find and suggest appropriate items to users, based on the users' individual preferences and tastes.

There are many approaches in RSs. The collaborative filtering (CF) approach is the most popular technique for recommending items to the *target user* (the user to whom recommendations are targeted) based on the similarity of users or items to previous interactions. In the real world, neighbors and friends can have an influence on the target user when making choices about items. Based on this real-world assumption, RSs, particularly CF-based systems, utilize the opinions of neighbors, friends, and others in predicting how much the target user would like an item. The opinion can be in the form of both explicit and implicit feedback.

To predict the rating score of the user toward a target item, an RS aims to identify the set of friends or neighbors, called *raters*, who have rated the target item in the past. The actual scores of raters are then used to calculate the predicted rating score for the target user toward the target item. However, using the actual ratings from raters often leads to low-accuracy predictions because of the *improper rating-range problem* [2].

This problem can be explained as follows. Because each user has an individual rating pattern, a rating score needs to be interpreted. Even though two users might rate the same item with the same score, it does not mean they like this item to the same extent. Therefore, using the actual ratings from users who rate items within different ranges to predict the rating score is improper and can lead to low recommendation accuracy. This problem has led some researchers [2,11,13] to adjust the ratings from different ranges to fit a common range.

In addition to this improper rating-range problem, another problem is that each friend is likely to have a different influence on the target user. All friends are not equal, with user A having more or less influence on the target user than user B. Therefore, we propose a *friend* module that modifies each friend's rating score to match the target user's perspective and then assigns an individual weight to each user.

For such rating conversions, ratings that involve explicit feedback are the most important input. For RSs, there are two popular approaches to evaluating the performance of the model, namely *rating prediction* and *item ranking*. Recently, *item ranking* has become more popular because some datasets involve implicit feedback and most recent work focuses on implicit feedback [9,18]. Implicit feedback is the interaction between a user and an item that has no rating score. Some methods consider explicit feedback as implicit feedback and input them into their model [9,18]. Explicit feedback or ratings are more powerful and more expressive than implicit feedback because each rating score can have a different meaning. In fact, just because a user rates an item, it does not mean that the user likes that item. For example, using a score of 1 in a 1–5 scoring range probably means that the user does not like that item. We therefore propose a novel approach to incorporating explicit ratings into an end-to-end item-ranking-based model. To replace traditional user embeddings, we introduce a *user representation matrix*, which can integrate explicit feedback into the model. In addition, we introduce a *user perspective unit matrix*, which can capture user preferences more richly by using several rating scores. This matrix aims to help the model convert a friend's rating scores to best match the target user's perspective.

In this work, we also adopt the idea of the knowledge graph (KG) embedding technique [1], aiming to learn the latent relation vector between user–item pairs instead of trying to assign a user–item pair to the same point in a vector space by minimizing the distance between each user–item interaction, as in collaborative metric learning (CML) [10]. Latent relational metric learning (LRML) [18] adopts the scoring function of TransE [1], which is the simplest KG embedding technique, to learn the latent relation between a user–item pair. It was found that this approach can help to ease the potential geometric inflexibility of CML. Another reason for introducing the KG embedding technique is that we believe the latent relation vector can help the model to learn better user and item embedding, which can lead to better recommendations. Because a vector value often has more expressive power than a scalar value, we can expect to obtain more effective embedding.

The main contributions of this paper are as follows.

- We propose an end-to-end KG-based attentive hybrid CF neural network (NN) for rating conversion in RSs and ranking using explicit feedback.
- We propose a *friend* module that can convert each friend's rating to match the target user's perspective and then assigns a different weight for each friend. For rating conversion, we propose a novel input representation that incorporates explicit feedback (ratings) into the model.
- We have conducted experiments using three datasets to evaluate our proposal. The experimental results demonstrate that our proposed method outperforms existing methods.

2 Related Work

2.1 Recommender Systems

RSs aim to suggest and recommend items to an individual user, with the hope that the user would be satisfied by the recommended item [16]. RS techniques are categorized into three main approaches: the CF approach, the content-based approach, and the hybrid approach.

The CF approach is the most popular and widely used technique. It recommends items to individual users based on their neighbors. Typically, CF is further divided into the *neighborhood-based* approach and the *model-based* approach. The neighborhood-based approach is memory-based in that user–item ratings are stored in the system and used directly to predict ratings for new items. The main advantages of the neighborhood-based approach are simplicity, justifiability, and stability [5].

Although the neighborhood-based approach is straightforward and works reasonably well in practice, there is a heavy computation cost involving both time and space complexity and it can also suffer from sparsity problems. Therefore, the model-based approach, which uses the user–item ratings to learn a predictive model, is now becoming more popular. Its main advantages over the model-based approach are scalability, prediction speed, and avoidance of overfitting. Therefore, most recent CF models adopt the model-based approach. In this work, we combine the advantages of both the neighborhood-based approach and the model-based approach in proposing a hybrid CF network for RSs.

2.2 Deep Learning and the Attention Mechanism in RSs

In recent years, NNs and deep learning have been applied to many research fields. Deep learning is now becoming the most popular technique for information retrieval and RSs [23].

Matrix factorization (MF) [12] is a standard baseline technique for CF that models the relationship between user and item via their inner product, with several implementations of deep learning models now being based on MF [7,9]. One such approach is neural MF (NeuMF) [9], a recent state-of-the-art deep learning model that combines MF with a multilayer perceptron (MLP).

The *attention mechanism* is widely used and is successful for learning a weighted representation across multiple samples. Inspired by human visual attention, the goal of the attention mechanism is to reduce noise and select more informative features for the final prediction. The attention mechanism has recently become popular in the fields of computer vision, natural language processing, and RSs [3,4,14,18].

Despite many advanced models emerging each year, with several types of NN and deep-learning techniques being applied to RSs, RSs still suffer from several challenges, such as data sparsity and cold start problems.

2.3 KG Embedding Techniques in RSs

KG embedding involves embedding the components of KG such as entities and relations into a continuous vector space. Many KG embedding techniques have recently been proposed and are rapidly gaining attention [21].

Researchers have applied KG embedding techniques to RSs for which the RS problem is defined as link prediction in a KG comprising users and items as the entities and ratings as the relations [8]. These techniques are being applied to RSs to mitigate the challenges mentioned above, such as data sparsity and cold start problems. Several approaches integrate *side information* into the RSs and treat the resultant data as a KG, aiming to address these issues.

Inspired by RotatE [17], Sun et al. proposed KG-embedding based CF [24]. Here, the RSs problem is defined as link prediction in a KG for which the users and items are the entities, and the interactions (implicit feedback) between user–item pairs form the relations.

LRML [18] is an attention-based memory-augmented neural architecture that uses a latent relation vector to model the relationship between user–item pairs in metric space. LRML tries to mitigate the problems with CML [10], whose scoring function is geometrically restrictive because the objective function of CML aims to minimize the distance between each user–item pair in a vector space. LRML adopts the scoring function from TransE [1] to model the latent relation vector of a user–item pair, instead of assigning them to the same spot, as does CML. TransE [1], as proposed by Bordes et al., is both the simplest and the most representative translation-based KG embedding technique. It represents both entities and relations as vectors in the same vector space. Our work is inspired by the ideas of LRML and TransE to enable learning an appropriate representation of users, items, and latent relations. However, our proposed model obtains the latent relation vector differently from LRML. We introduce *friends* to the model and propose using a module that converts friends' ratings into ratings that match the target user's perspective and then assigns an appropriate weight to each friend.

2.4   Rating Conversion Methods

Although many RSs have been proposed in recent years, most of them did not consider the improper rating-range problem. This problem occurs because different users may have different rating patterns. Suppose that in a 1–5 rating system, user A always rates items within a range of 1–4, whereas user B always rates items within a range of 2–5. In this case, a rating 4 by user A would then be considered as "most liked" whereas "most liked" of user B would be represented by a rating of 5. Thus, using the actual rating score from users who rate items within different ranges to calculate the predicted score of the item for the target user is considered *improper* and can leads to low accuracy in recommendations.

Therefore, *rating conversion* methods have been proposed to address this problem. Some approaches try to adjust the rating scores from different ranges to a common range. One such adjusting method is *normalization* [11], which converts rating scores to a specific range, usually between 0 and 1, to represent "most disliked" and "most liked", respectively.

However, normalization is insufficient because the conversion is based on data from the original user only. In an attempt to overcome this problem, several other rating conversion techniques have been proposed [2,13], most of which deal with rating scores in scalar form.

SAMN [4] is an attention-based memory network that constructs a user–friend relation vector. It contains a friend-level attention component to adaptively measure the social influence among each user's friends. However, this method did not consider the different ranges of rating for different users.

In a previous paper [19], we aimed to address the improper rating-range problem via a translation-based embedding model. However, it had the drawback of requiring many steps to complete a recommendation task. Recently, *end-to-end learning* has become popular for deep-learning applications, because it tends to achieve improved accuracy. Therefore, in this work, we propose an end-to-end NN architecture that includes both rating conversion and translation-based embedding ideas.

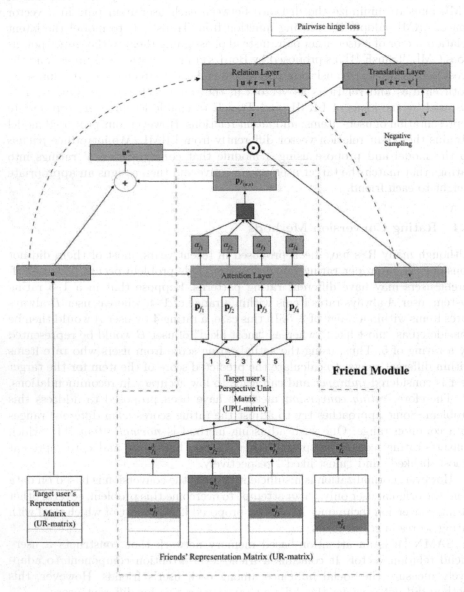

Fig. 1. Schematic illustration of our proposed architecture as an end-to-end NN. This example assumes a user–item pair $\langle u, v \rangle$, with the user's four friends $\{f_1, f_2, f_3, f_4\}$ rating item v with rating scores $\{3, 1, 3, 4\}$, respectively.

3   Proposed Method

In this section, we introduce our novel deep-learning recommendation architecture, which can be categorized as a hybrid CF based on the idea of KG embedding. Figure 1 shows the overall architecture of this model. Features of the proposed model are as follows.

- Users are converted to a dense matrix and items are converted to vector representations. Note that we introduce a dense matrix to represent a user unlike many recommendation systems that use a single vector for this purpose (see Sect. 3.1).
- For each target user and target item, we input the set of friends (users who have rated the target item in the past) into the Friend Module. This step generates a summation of the weighted projected vectors of the target user's friends, effectively realizing both rating conversion and weight assignment (see Sect. 3.2).
- The model aggregates the target user representation matrix into a single vector and combines it with the projected vectors of the target user's friends obtained in the previous step. It then calculates the latent relation vector $\mathbf{r}$, which is dependent on both user and item (see Sect. 3.3).
- Finally, the model uses pairwise hinge loss and negative sampling to optimize $\|\mathbf{u} + \mathbf{r} - \mathbf{v}\| \approx 0$ (see Sect. 3.4).

3.1   User and Item Representation

In most RSs, users and items are usually represented by embedding vectors. However, a single vector is unsuitable for our purpose because it cannot store rating patterns for each user. To realize the rating conversion requirement, we use a matrix to represent each user, called the user representation matrix (UR-matrix). We propose to store each user's rating information (explicit feedback) in their matrix representation and this is then available for rating conversion purposes.

For a user u, the UR-matrix is represented by $\mathbf{U} \in \mathbb{R}^{z \times d}$, where d is the dimensionality of user embeddings and z is number of rating scores. The s-th row of $\mathbf{U}_u$ corresponds to a rating score s and represents an embedding vector of u for s (e.g., the first row of the matrix represents score 1). Suppose that the RS accepts rating scores of $\{1, 2, 3, 4, 5\}$, then the UR-matrix comprises five rows and each row represents each rating score in $\{1, 2, 3, 4, 5\}$. In this way, the UR-matrix represents how each user rates items.

$\mathbf{U} \in \mathbb{R}^{m \times z \times d}$ and $\mathbf{V} \in \mathbb{R}^{n \times d}$ are embedding matrices that store user and item embeddings, respectively, where m and n are the total numbers of users and items, respectively. d denotes the dimensionality of the user and item embeddings. z is the number of rating values when the RS accepts rating scores such as $\{1, 2, \ldots, z\}$.

Note that this work focuses on rating conversion for users, for which we propose the UR-matrix. Our item embeddings are represented in the traditional way.

3.2   The Friend Module

In this subsection, we describe the details of the Friend Module, which aims to convert the target user's friend vector to match the target user's perspective. The output of this module is a summation of the weighted projected vectors of the target user's friends. To convert friend vectors, we introduce a user-perspective unit matrix (UPU-matrix) to the model.

Because users have their own individual perspective on items, they will have their own rating patterns. In [15], a *local context unit* is learned in addition to word embedding to utilize the word-specific influences of each word on its context words. Inspired by [15], our aim is to convert friend vectors to match the target user's perspective. We therefore introduce a UPU-matrix in addition to the UR-matrix. The matrix represents each user's individual perspective. Specifically, each column of the matrix captures a rich range of user preferences. It captures not only the user's overall preference but also preferences for specific rating scores. This matrix enables the model to convert friend vectors to match the target user's perspective. The UPU-matrix for user u is represented by $\mathbf{K} \in \mathbb{R}^{d \times z}$.

Consider the set of friends with respect to item v, denoted as F_v. Let $f \in F_v$ be a friend in a user–item pair $\langle u, v \rangle$. Suppose this friend has rated the target item v with a score s. If $\mathbf{u}_f^s \in U_f$ is the s-th row of friend f's UR-matrix and $\mathbf{k}_u^s \in \mathbf{K}_u$ is the s-th column of target user u's UPU-matrix, the projected vector of friend f with respect to target user u is calculated by

$$\mathbf{p}_f = \mathbf{k}_u^s \odot \mathbf{u}_f^s, \tag{1}$$

where $\odot$ is the Hadamard product (i.e., element-wise multiplication).

This equation converts each friend's vector so as to match the target user's perspective. In this step, the model calculates the projected vector $\mathbf{p}_f$ for each friend in F_v. The set of friends' projected vectors with respect to the target user's perspective is then input into the Attention Layer for weight assignment.

The Attention Layer (see Fig. 1). Because the importance of all friends is not the same, they should have different influence levels with respect to the target user, and so any weighting (to represent relative importance) should also vary. The function of the Attention Layer is to apply nonuniform weights for each friend, varying the weight for users interacting with different items. We therefore adopt an *attention mechanism* [20] that has been widely used in many fields and is successful for assigning nonuniform weights. According to its protocol, a two-layer network is applied to compute the attention score α_f, using the current user u, current item v, and projected friend vector $\mathbf{p}_f$ as inputs. The scoring function is then defined as

$$\beta_f = \mathbf{h}^T ReLU(W_1\mathbf{u} + W_2\mathbf{p}_f + W_3\mathbf{v}), \tag{2}$$

where $h \in \mathbb{R}^a, W_1, W_2, W_3 \in \mathbb{R}^{d \times a}$ are model parameters, a denotes the dimensionality of the Attention Layer, and $ReLU$ is a nonlinear activation function.

The final weight for each friend is then obtained by normalizing the attention weights using the softmax function, as is the common practice for neural attention networks. The attention score can then be calculated as

$$\alpha_f = \frac{exp(\beta_f)}{\sum_{j \in F_v} exp(\beta_j)},$$ (3)

where F_v is all friends of user u on the view of item v.

After obtaining the attention weight for each friend, the output of the Attention Layer represents the summation of the projected vector of friends $\mathbf{p}_{F_{(u,v)}}$. This summation vector represents all friends' vectors from the target user's perspective, with each friend having an individual weight representing importance to the target user. It can be calculated as

$$\mathbf{p}_{F_{(u,v)}} = \sum_{f \in F_v} \alpha_f \mathbf{p}_f.$$ (4)

3.3   Generating Latent Relations

After the summation of friends' weighted projected vectors $\mathbf{p}_{F_{(u,v)}}$ is obtained, we combine it with aggregated target-user representation vector $\mathbf{u} \in \mathbb{R}^d$. This vector is calculated as the means of each column of the UR-matrix.

The combination of the aggregated target-user representation and the summation of friends' weighted projected vectors can be calculated as

$$\mathbf{u}^* = \mathbf{u} + \mathbf{p}_{F_{(u,v)}}.$$ (5)

Finally, the Friend Module generates a latent relation vector $\mathbf{r}$ for each user–item pair by multiplying combined user $\mathbf{u}^*$ and the item $\mathbf{v}$ as

$$\mathbf{r} = \mathbf{u}^* \odot \mathbf{v}.$$ (6)

3.4   Optimization and Learning

This subsection explains details of the final layer of this model. Our model is an end-to-end NN. Inspired by LRML [18], it learns latent relation vectors for user–item pairs by adopting an idea from TransE [1]. This mitigates the geometric inflexibility of CML [10], whose objective function aims to place user–item pairs at the same point by minimizing the distance between each user–item interaction. Therefore, we learn the latent relation vector between a user–item pair as follows. **The Relation Modeling Layer (see Fig. 1).** For each pair comprising a user u and an item v, the scoring function $s(u, v)$ is defined as

$$s(u, v) = \|\mathbf{u} + \mathbf{r} - \mathbf{v}\|^2,$$ (7)

where r is the latent relation vector obtained from Eq. (6) and $\|\cdot\|^2$ is the L2 norm of the vector $\mathbf{u} + \mathbf{r} - \mathbf{v}$. This equation is adopted from TransE [1] because TransE is the simplest and most understandable KG embedding technique.

Objective Function. Like TransE [1], we also use pairwise ranking loss or *hinge loss* for optimization. For each positive (observed) user–item pair $\langle u, v \rangle$, we perform negative sampling by sampling a corrupted user–item pair denoted as $\langle u', v' \rangle$. The corrupted user–item pair goes through the same user–item embedding layer in the Translation Layer (see Fig. 1). The pairwise hinge loss is then defined as

$$L = \sum_{(u,v) \in \Delta} \sum_{(u',v') \notin \Delta} max(0, s(u,v) + \lambda - s(u',v')), \qquad (8)$$

where Δ is the set of all positive user–item pairs and λ is the margin that separates the observed pairs and the corrupted samples.

4 Experimental Evaluation

In this section, we present details of our experiments. Our experimental evaluation is designed to answer several research questions (**RQs**).

- **RQ1:** Is the proposed model more accurate than existing state-of-the-art methods for collaborative ranking?
- **RQ2:** Does the UR-matrix improve the model's accuracy?
- **RQ3:** Does the Friend Module affect the model's performance?

4.1 Datasets

We evaluated the method using three real datasets, namely FilmTrust[1] and two datasets from MovieLens[2]. FilmTrust is a recommendation dataset extracted from the entire FilmTrust website. MovieLens is a widely adopted benchmark dataset for CF in the application domain of recommending movies to users. In this work, we use two configurations of MovieLens, namely MovieLens100k and MovieLens1M. The numbers of users and items in each dataset are listed in Table 1.

Table 1. Datasets

Dataset	#Users	#Items	#Ratings
FilmTrust	1,508	2,071	35,497
MovieLens100K	943	1,682	100,000
MovieLens1M	6,040	3,706	1,000,209

---

[1] https://www.librec.net/datasets.html.
[2] https://grouplens.org/datasets/movielens.

4.2   Existing Systems

For each of the three datasets, we conducted experiments that compared our proposed model with the following existing methods.

- **LRML** [18]: an end-to-end attention-based memory-augmented neural architecture that models the relationship between users and items in metric space using latent relation vectors. To test the ability of the proposed UR-matrix against the original version, we experimented using two settings:

- The original LRML model.
- The LRML model using our proposed UR-matrix. (Instead of the original user embeddings, we used our UR-matrix as the input to the LRML model.)

- Generalized matrix factorization **(GMF)** [9]: an implementation of MF [12], a standard baseline for CF that models the relationship between users and items using inner products.
- **NeuMF** [9]: a state-of-the-art unified framework combining MF with an MLP.

In addition to comparison with these existing systems, we also conducted the experiments using our proposed model minus the Fried Module to test the module's relevance. This is denoted the **Simple Model**.

4.3   Implementation and Parameter Settings

In this work, we modified the source code of DeepRec, an open-source toolkit for deep-learning-based Recommendation systems [22], which includes several algorithms expressed in Python and Tensorflow[3]. DeepRec also includes the LRML, GMF, and NeuMF models.

All models were trained until convergence. We optimized the models by using AdaGrad [6], a stochastic optimization method that adapts the learning rate to the parameters. For all models, the dimension d was tuned amongst $\{50, 100, 200\}$, the learning rate was tuned amongst $\{0.1, 0.01, 0.001\}$, and the batch size is tuned amongst $\{256, 512, 1024\}$. For models that minimized the hinge loss, the margin γ was tuned amongst $\{0.1, 0.2, 0.5, 1.0\}$. For our proposed model, the attention size a was tuned amongst $\{50, 100, 200\}$. For the LRML model, we set the number of memory slices to 20, as recommended in [18]. Note that we did not use pretrained models in the NeuMF model to enable a fair comparison. For simplicity, each training instance was paired with only a single negative sample. All embeddings and parameters were initialized with a standard deviation of 0.01.

---

[3] https://www.tensorflow.org.

4.4   Evaluation Protocol and Metrics

Each dataset was separated into two parts: 80% for training and the remaining 20% for testing. In the training phrase, we sampled a single negative sampling for each user–item pair. After training the models, we performed the ranking recommendation task on the test set. Given a user–item pair $\langle u, v \rangle$, the negative samplings were all $\langle u, v' \rangle$, where v' is the set of items that had no interaction with the target user u. We used all the ranking-based metrics implemented in DeepRec [22], namely precision@n (P@10), recall@n (Re@10), mean average precision (MAP), mean reciprocal rank (MRR), and normalized discounted cumulative gain (NDCG).

4.5   Experimental Results

We compared the performance of our proposed model with the existing methods listed above. We separated the experiments into two sets: using our UR-matrix and using the original user embeddings. Because our optimization and learning techniques were similar to those for LRML, we also tested the use of our UR-matrix in LRML. Table 2 shows the empirical results for our proposed model and the existing methods for the three benchmark datasets. The results show that our proposed model was the best-performing model for most metrics and datasets. This answers **RQ1** in the affirmative (i.e., our proposed model can offer better accuracy in for collaborative ranking than existing systems).

For the FilmTrust dataset, our proposed model was the most accurate with respect to Re@10, MAP, MRR, and NDCG, but the GMF model performed best with respect to P@10. For the MovieLens100K and MovieLens1M datasets, our proposed model was the best-performing model for all evaluation metrics.

5   Discussion

In the previous section, we showed that our proposed model can provide the most accurate ranking recommendations for all datasets tested.

5.1   Performance of the Proposed UR-Matrix

We have proposed UR-matrix, a novel input representation for incorporating explicit feedback in the model. This matrix stores user rating information and expresses how each user rates items. Table 2 gives the comparative results for the original LRML method and the LRML method using the proposed UR-matrix as an input. These provide an answer to **RQ2**, namely that using the proposed UR-matrix leads to more accurate ranking recommendations for all metrics and all datasets tested. This is because a matrix can express more meaningful user features than can a single vector. In particular, a matrix in which each row is related to the user's rating information can store more relevant characteristics of the user than can a single vector. Moreover, it is better suited and directly applicable to rating conversion, unlike the traditional approach to user embedding.

Table 2. Evaluation results for experiments comparing with different methods

Dataset	Metrics	Our UR-matrix			Original user embedding		
		Our proposed model	Simple model	LRML	Original LRML	NeuMF	GMF
FilmTrust	P@10	0.3129	0.3090	0.3097	0.3022	0.3121	**0.3196**
	Re@10	**0.6021**	0.5968	0.5975	0.5751	0.5580	0.5834
	MAP	**0.4446**	0.4371	0.4312	0.4293	0.4258	0.4403
	MRR	**0.5719**	0.5622	0.5427	0.5500	0.5322	0.5571
	NDCG	**0.6232**	0.6158	0.6109	0.6105	0.6020	0.6143
ML100K	P@10	**0.3177**	0.2996	0.2965	0.2858	0.2507	0.1856
	Re@10	**0.2095**	0.1994	0.1977	0.1907	0.1461	0.0883
	MAP	**0.2493**	0.2417	0.2380	0.2276	0.1810	0.1325
	MRR	**0.6047**	0.5999	0.5864	0.5658	0.4985	0.4342
	NDCG	**0.5878**	0.5814	0.5776	0.5684	0.5196	0.4639
ML1M	P@10	**0.3310**	0.3129	0.2295	0.2295	0.2016	0.1841
	Re@10	**0.1371**	0.1357	0.0946	0.0937	0.0763	0.0662
	MAP	**0.2151**	0.2050	0.1388	0.1376	0.1290	0.0997
	MRR	**0.5963**	0.5821	0.4705	0.4767	0.4413	0.3768
	NDCG	**0.5755**	0.5643	0.5028	0.5020	0.4825	0.4521

5.2 Performance of the Friend Module

We make three assumptions: 1) friends' opinions affect the target user's decision to choose items, 2) each user has their own rating patterns, and 3) friends can be more or less important to the target user. These assumptions are all implemented in the Friend Module (see Sect. 3.2). The comparison between our proposed model and the Simple model (i.e., without the Friend Module) has shown that the Friend Module can help provide better recommendations. This provides an answer to **RQ3**, namely that the Friend Module enhances the model's performance.

There are three reasons for the Friend Module having a positive effect. First, our UR-matrix integrates explicit feedback (ratings) into each friend-representation matrix, thereby expressing how each user rates items and capturing this richer information in a way that a single vector cannot. Second, we propose the UPU-matrix, which aims to convert each friend's specific ratings to match the target user's perspective and thereby mitigate the improper rating-range problem. Finally, we assign a nonuniform weight to each user to indicate the relative importance of each user to the target user.

6 Conclusion

In this paper, we propose an end-to-end KG-based attentive hybrid CF NN architecture for rating conversion in RSs and ranking recommendations, using explicit feedback. Our proposed model includes a Friend Module that first converts friends' ratings to match the target user's perspective, and then assigns a nonuniform individual weight to each user. We also propose a novel input representation to enable the incorporation of explicit feedback (ratings) into the model. Our experimental results show that the proposed model can provide more accurate results than existing methods.

One future direction for research is the introduction of multiple types of relations to the model. There may be other useful side information available, in addition to the rating score. The properties of KG suggest that integrating multiple types of relations might help RSs to better model user and item representations, thereby leading to better recommendations.

References

1. Bordes, A., Usunier, N., Garcia-Durán, A., Weston, J., Yakhnenko, O.: Translating embeddings for modeling multi-relational data. In: Proceedings of the 26th International Conference on Neural Information Processing Systems, NIPS 2013, vol. 2, pp. 2787–2795. Curran Associates Inc., USA (2013). http://dl.acm.org/citation.cfm?id=2999792.2999923
2. Chalermpornpong, W., Maneeroj, S., Atsuhiro, T.: Rating pattern formation for better recommendation. In: 2013 24th International Workshop on Database and Expert Systems Applications, pp. 146–151 (August 2013). https://doi.org/10.1109/DEXA.2013.23
3. Chen, C., Zhang, M., Liu, Y., Ma, S.: Neural attentional rating regression with review-level explanations. In: Proceedings of the 2018 World Wide Web Conference, WWW 2018, pp. 1583–1592. International World Wide Web Conferences Steering Committee, Republic and Canton of Geneva, CHE (2018). https://doi.org/10.1145/3178876.3186070
4. Chen, C., Zhang, M., Liu, Y., Ma, S.: Social attentional memory network: modeling aspect- and friend-level differences in recommendation. In: Proceedings of the 12th ACM International Conference on Web Search and Data Mining, WSDM 2019, pp. 177–185. Association for Computing Machinery, New York, NY, USA (2019). https://doi.org/10.1145/3289600.3290982
5. Desrosiers, C., Karypis, G.: A comprehensive survey of neighborhood-based recommendation methods. In: Ricci, F., Rokach, L., Shapira, B., Kantor, P.B. (eds.) Recommender Systems Handbook, pp. 107–144. Springer, Boston, MA (2011). https://doi.org/10.1007/978-0-387-85820-3_4
6. Duchi, J., Hazan, E., Singer, Y.: Adaptive subgradient methods for online learning and stochastic optimization. J. Mach. Learn. Res. **12**, 2121–2159 (2011)
7. Dziugaite, G.K., Roy, D.M.: Neural network matrix factorization. CoRR abs/1511.06443 (2015). http://arxiv.org/abs/1511.06443
8. Guo, Q., et al.: A survey on knowledge graph-based recommender systems. arXiv abs/2003.00911 (2020)
9. He, X., Liao, L., Zhang, H., Nie, L., Hu, X., Chua, T.S.: Neural collaborative filtering. In: Proceedings of the 26th International Conference on World Wide Web, WWW 2017, pp. 173–182. International World Wide Web Conferences Steering Committee, Republic and Canton of Geneva, CHE (2017). https://doi.org/10.1145/3038912.3052569
10. Hsieh, C.K., Yang, L., Cui, Y., Lin, T.Y., Belongie, S., Estrin, D.: Collaborative metric learning. In: Proceedings of the 26th International Conference on World Wide Web, WWW 2017, pp. 193–201. International World Wide Web Conferences Steering Committee, Republic and Canton of Geneva, CHE (2017). https://doi.org/10.1145/3038912.3052639

11. Jin, R., Si, L.: A study of methods for normalizing user ratings in collaborative filtering. In: Proceedings of the 27th Annual International ACM SIGIR Conference on Research and Development in Information Retrieval, SIGIR 2004, pp. 568–569. ACM, New York (2004). https://doi.org/10.1145/1008992.1009124
12. Koren, Y., Bell, R., Volinsky, C.: Matrix factorization techniques for recommender systems. Computer **42**(8), 30–37 (2009). https://doi.org/10.1109/MC.2009.263
13. Lathia, N., Hailes, S., Capra, L.: Trust-based collaborative filtering. In: Karabulut, Y., Mitchell, J., Herrmann, P., Jensen, C.D. (eds.) Trust Management II, pp. 119–134. Springer, Boston (2008). https://doi.org/10.1007/978-0-387-09428-1_8
14. Li, M., Tei, K., Fukazawa, Y.: An efficient co-attention neural network for social recommendation. In: IEEE/WIC/ACM International Conference on Web Intelligence, WI 2019, pp. 34–42. Association for Computing Machinery, New York (2019). https://doi.org/10.1145/3350546.3352498
15. Qiao, C., et al.: A new method of region embedding for text classification. In: International Conference on Learning Representations (2018). https://openreview.net/forum?id=BkSDMA36Z
16. Ricci, F., Rokach, L., Shapira, B., Kantor, P.B.: Recommender Systems Handbook, 1st edn. Springer, Heidelberg (2010). https://doi.org/10.1007/978-0-387-85820-3
17. Sun, Z., Deng, Z., Nie, J., Tang, J.: RotatE: Knowledge graph embedding by relational rotation in complex space. CoRR abs/1902.10197 (2019). http://arxiv.org/abs/1902.10197
18. Tay, Y., Anh Tuan, L., Hui, S.C.: Latent relational metric learning via memory-based attention for collaborative ranking. In: Proceedings of the 2018 World Wide Web Conference, WWW 2018, pp. 729–739. International World Wide Web Conferences Steering Committee, Republic and Canton of Geneva, CHE (2018). https://doi.org/10.1145/3178876.3186154
19. Tengkiattrakul, P., Maneeroj, S., Takasu, A.: Translation-based embedding model for rating conversion in recommender systems. In: IEEE/WIC/ACM International Conference on Web Intelligence, WI 2019, pp. 217–224. Association for Computing Machinery, New York (2019). https://doi.org/10.1145/3350546.3352521
20. Vaswani, A., et al.: Attention is all you need. CoRR abs/1706.03762 (2017). http://arxiv.org/abs/1706.03762
21. Wang, Q., Mao, Z., Wang, B., Guo, L.: Knowledge graph embedding: a survey of approaches and applications. IEEE Trans. Knowl. Data Eng. **29**(12), 2724–2743 (2017). https://doi.org/10.1109/TKDE.2017.2754499
22. Zhang, S., Tay, Y., Yao, L., Wu, B., Sun, A.: DeepRec: an open-source toolkit for deep learning based recommendation. CoRR abs/1905.10536 (2019). http://arxiv.org/abs/1905.10536
23. Zhang, S., Yao, L., Sun, A., Tay, Y.: Deep learning based recommender system: a survey and new perspectives. ACM Comput. Surv. **52**(1), 38 (2019). https://doi.org/10.1145/3285029
24. Zhang, Y., Wang, J., Luo, J.: Knowledge graph embedding based collaborative filtering. IEEE Access **8**, 134553–134562 (2020). https://doi.org/10.1109/ACCESS.2020.3011105

Sentence Dependent-Aware Network for Aspect-Category Sentiment Analysis

Lianwei Li, Ying Yang, Shimeng Zhan, and Bin Wu[✉]

Beijing University of Posts and Telecommunications, Beijing, China
{llw,regulus,zhanshimeng,wubin}@bupt.edu.cn

Abstract. The purpose of Aspect-Category Sentiment Analysis is to predict sentiment polarities of given aspect categories in sentences. Most previous methods used attention-based neural network models to Establish connections between aspect categories and sentiment words and generate aspect-specific sentence representations. However, these models may mismatch sentiment words with aspect categories due to the complexity of sentence structures. To solve this problem, we reconstruct the dependency tree into an ACSA-oriented dependency tree, which builds a direct or indirect semantic connection between sentiment words and corresponding aspect categories, and avoid introducing redundant information from the original dependency tree. On this basis, we propose a Sentence Dependent-Aware Network (SDAN) to encode the tree effectively. The experimental results of applying SDAN to three public datasets demonstrate its effectiveness.

Keywords: Aspect-category sentiment analysis · Multi-task learning · Graph attention networks

1 Introduction

Aspect-based sentiment analysis is a fine-grained sentiment analysis task [8,9]. Specifically, its purpose is to determine the sentiment polarities of aspects included in a sentence. Aspect-based sentiment analysis has multiple subtasks, two of which are Aspect-Category Detection (ACD) and Aspect-Category Sentiment Analysis (ACSA). ACD is used to detect aspect categories mentioned in a sentence and ACSA predicts the sentiment polarities of the detected aspect categories. Aspect categories come from some predefined categories and may not appear explicitly in a sentence. Figure 1 is an example. *Sushi* indicates the aspect category *food*, and *waiters* indicates the aspect category *service*. We call these words that indicate aspect categories as indicator words. In this paper, we

This work is supported by the National Key Research and Development Program of China (2018YFC0831500), the National Natural Science Foundation of China under Grant No.61972047, the NSFC-General Technology Basic Research Joint Funds under Grant U1936220 and the Fundamental Research Funds for the Central Universities (2019XD-D01).

M. Brambilla et al. (Eds.): ICWE 2021, LNCS 12706, pp. 166–174, 2021.
https://doi.org/10.1007/978-3-030-74296-6_13

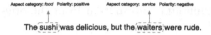

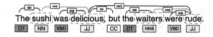

Fig. 1. An example of ACD and ACSA.   **Fig. 2.** An example of a dependency tree.

mainly focus on ACSA, ACD is an auxiliary task to find indicator words in a sentence. Since a sentence may contain several aspect categories with disparate sentiment polarities, the key to this task is accurately associating each aspect category with its respective sentiment words. It is a very intuitive idea to use the attention mechanism to establish this association. [1,14,17] used the attention mechanism to assign appropriate sentiment words to a given aspect category and achieved good results. However, due to the complexity of the sentence structure and the language itself, methods that rely solely on the attention mechanism may cause mismatch problems. Generally, we find that a dependency tree effectively shortens the distance between indicator words and sentiment words in a sentence and establishes a direct or indirect dependency path between indicator words and sentiment words. This allows the sentence representation learned by neural network models along the dependency path to avoid mismatching to a certain extent. Figure 2 is an example of a dependency tree.

Although a dependency tree can capture the semantic relationship characteristics between words, it is not appropriate to directly use an original dependency tree. Through observation, we find that using a complete dependency tree may introduce redundant or even wrong information. At this time, we need to prune and reconstruct the original dependency tree to preserve important relations, we call the reconstructed dependency tree the ACSA-oriented dependency tree.

In this paper, we put forward a Sentence Dependent-Aware Network (SDAN) for ACSA that can effectively use the dependency tree. SDAN mainly includes three modules: ACD task module, ACSA-oriented dependency tree module, and ACSA task module. Specifically, it first finds the indicator words of the aspect category through the ACD task module, then it builds ACSA-oriented dependency tree based on the indicator words, retaining the nodes and relations useful for predicting the aspect category's sentiment polarity. Finally, in the ACSA module, the node representations learned by grammar graph attention networks (G-GAT) is applied to predict the sentiment polarity of the aspect category. G-GAT that we proposed is an improved version of graph attention networks (GAT) [15] obtained by expanding the original GAT attention heads. It can encode graphs with additional information (part-of-speech information) and labeled edges (dependency relation type labels). We summarized our main contributions as follows:

- We put forward a Sentence Dependent-Aware Network, which can effectively use the dependency tree for Aspect-Category Sentiment Analysis.
- Specifically, we design an algorithm to build ACSA-oriented dependency tree, while establishing the semantic connection between indicator words and

sentiment words, it avoids introducing redundant information from the original dependency tree.
- We propose G-GAT model, which can learn a better node representation with some additional information.

2   Related Work

Many neural network models have been developed to solve the ACSA task. Wang et al. [17] first proposed aspect category embedding and used an attention-based LSTM to implicitly associate the aspect categories with the corresponding sentiment words for the aspect category sentiment analysis. Then some new attention-based models [1,4,14] optimize the process of assigning sentiment words to aspect categories and have led to promising progress. The pre-trained language model BERT [2] achieved success in a lot of tasks, including ACSA. Sun et al. [13] constructed auxiliary sentences and converted ACSA to a sentence-pair classification task. Several joint models [12,18,20] have been proposed that address both ACD and ACSA. Li et al. [7] introduced Multi-Instance Multi-Label learning, it first predicts the sentiments of the instances and finds the key instances for the aspect categories, then it obtains the sentiment polarities of the aspect categories by aggregating polarities of the key instance. Recently, the use of graph neural networks in ACSA has been explored. Li et al. [6] used the graph attention networks and sentence constituency parse trees to solve ACSA task.

3   Method

In this section, we describe how to build ACSA-oriented dependency tree and apply the ACSA-oriented dependency tree to the aspect category sentiment analysis task.

Problem Formulation. We first formulate the problem. There are N predefined aspect categories $C = \{c_1, c_2, \ldots, c_N\}$ and a predefined set of sentiment polarities $P = \{Neg, Neu, Pos\}$ (i.e., Negative, Neutral and Positive respectively). Given a sentence, denoted by $S = \{w_1, w_2, \ldots, w_n\}$, which contains K aspect categories $C^s = \{c_1^s, c_2^s, \ldots, c_K^s\}$, $C^s \subset C$, the ACSA task is to predict the sentiment polarity distributions of the K aspect categories, $P = \{P_1, P_2, \ldots, P_K\}$, where $P_k = \{p_{k_{Neg}}, p_{k_{Neu}}, p_{k_{Pos}}\}$.

ACSA-Oriented Dependency Tree Module. Given S, c_i^s, indicator words $I = \{I_1, I_2, \ldots, I_M\}(M < 4)$ of c_i^s and original dependency tree T, we use the indicator words to build the ACSA-oriented dependency tree $\hat{T}$: ① We set the aspect category c_i^s as the root node R of $\hat{T}$ (R is a node that does not exist originally), and then connect I to the R node. Here, we add the dir_con dependency type between I and R node to represent the indicator words and the

R node direct connection. ② Then, the words and dependency relations that have a direct dependency with the indicator words in T are added to $\hat{T}$. ③ Because the dependency parser cannot always generate the correct dependency, in order to increase the robustness of $\hat{T}$, we connect I and the words whose relative distance to the I is less than d in the sentence S, and set a new relationship n_con. The remaining nodes and relations in the original dependency tree T will be discarded. Figure 3 is an example of ACSA-oriented dependency tree. The idea is partially inspired by [16].

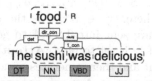

Fig. 3. The ACSA-oriented dependency tree is builded according to the *food*'s indicator word *sushi*, *food* is the root node R, the red line represents the *dir_con* relation, the green line is the relation retained from the original dependency tree, and the gray line is the n_con relation, because the distance between *was* and *sushi* is 1, so it is 1_*con*. (Color figure online)

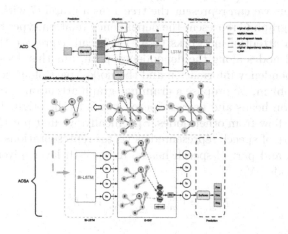

Fig. 4. Overall architecture of the proposed method.

Overall Processing. Our model mainly includes the ACD task module, ACSA-oriented dependency tree module, and the ACSA task module. Given S and c_i^s, Aspect-Category Detection (ACD) is used as an auxiliary task, its attention layer is used to get the weight of words in the sentence S. The weight indicates the probability that these words become indicator words for c_i^s. When selecting indicator words in ACD, we only select words with a weight greater than 0.3, making the number of indicator words at most 3 and at least 1 (When there is no word with a weight greater than 0.3, we do not reconstruct the dependency tree. Because when the weight of the words in the sentence are relatively evenly distributed, we think that the ACD task cannot provide good indicator words.). Then ACSA-oriented dependency tree module reconstructs the original dependency tree according to the indicator words to form an ACSA-oriented dependency tree. The ACSA task module predicts the sentiment polarity of c_i^s based on the ACSA-oriented dependency tree. The architecture diagram of the model is shown in the Fig. 4.

The ACD module includes four components: **Embedding layer**, this layer converts the input sentence $S = \{w_1, w_2, \ldots, w_n\}$ into a sequence of vector $V^D = \{v_1^D, v_2^D, \ldots, v_n^D\}$, where, $v_i^D \in R^d$, d is the dimension. **LSTM layer**, the word embeddings V^D are sent into LSTM to get the hidden states $H = \{h_1, h_2, \ldots, h_n\}$. The size of h_i is set to be d. **Attention layer**, this layer takes the hidden states H as input and then generates an attention [21] weight vector for each predefined aspect category. **Aspect category prediction layer**, we use the weighted hidden state as the sentence representation for ACD prediction.

The ACSA module also includes four components: **Embedding layer**, this layer's input is the nodes in the tree $\hat{T}$, the tree nodes are transformed into a sequence of vectors $V^{\hat{T}} = \{v_1^{\hat{T}}, v_2^{\hat{T}}, \ldots, v_m^{\hat{T}}\}$. Where $v_i^{\hat{T}} \in R^d$, d is the embedding dimension. **Bi-LSTM layer**, $V^{\hat{T}}$ is fed into a Bidirectional LSTM [3], and outputs hidden states $H = \{h_1, h_2, \ldots, h_m\}$. The size of the hidden state is set to be d. **G-GAT layer**, we can represent the tree $\hat{T}$ as a graph G with m nodes, and the edges of the graph G represent the dependency relation types between nodes. Using the graph attention networks (GAT) [15] can aggregate the information of neighborhood nodes along the dependency path, but this does not explicitly consider the dependency information and the nodes' part-of-speech information. To solve this problem, we propose a grammar graph attention network (G-GAT) by adding relation heads and part-of-speech heads to the original GAT to regulate information flow from other nodes. Specifically, we first put the dependency relations and part-of-speech represented as vector representations, then calculate relational heads and part-of-speech heads, in the l-th layer, given a node i, its neighborhood nodes $\mathcal{N}_i$:

$$h_{rel_i}^{l+1} = ||_{m=1}^M \sum_{j \in \mathcal{N}_i} \beta_{ij}^{lm} W_m^l h_j^l \tag{1}$$

$$h_{pos_i}^{l+1} = ||_{u=1}^U \sum_{j \in \mathcal{N}_i} \gamma_{ij}^{lu} W_u^l h_j^l \tag{2}$$

where $h_{rel_i}^{l+1}$ and $h_{pos_i}^{l+1}$ are the representation of the node i aggregated by the relational heads and part-of-speech heads at the l layer, $||$ represents vector concatenation, β_{ij}^{lm} and γ_{ij}^{lu} are normalized attention coefficient at layer l. W_m^l and W_u^l are linear transformation matrices. G-GAT has U part of speech heads, M relation heads and K attention heads. Finally update the node i through:

$$h_i^{l+1} = relu(W_{l+1}(h_{att_i}^{l+1} || h_{rel_i}^{l+1} || h_{pos_i}^{l+1}) + b_{l+1}) \tag{3}$$

where $h_{att_i}^{l+1}$ is the representation of the node i aggregated by the original attention heads at the l layer, W_{l+1}, b_{l+1} are learnable parameters. **Aspect category sentiment prediction layer**, since the information is propagated iteratively on the graph, we finally only need to use the representation of the root node R (It is the aspect category c_i^s) in the last layer of G-GAT to calculate the sentiment polarity distribution. We add up the loss functions of ACD and ACSA to jointly train the two tasks:

$$L(\theta) = L_{ACSA}(\theta_{ACSA}) + L_{ACD}(\theta_{ACD}) \qquad (4)$$

where θ contains all the trainable parameters.

4 Experiments

4.1 Datasets

Rest14: Rest14 dataset [11] has five predefined aspect categories, and each aspect category has four sentiment polarities (positive, negative, neutral, conflict) that can be assigned. Following previous works [4,14,17], we removed samples with conflicting polarities. **Rest14-hard:** Rest14-hard dataset is provided by Li et al. [7], the difference between Rest14-hard and Rest14 is that its test set is a subset of Rest14's test set. **MAMS-ACSA:** MAMS-ACSA is provided by Jiang et al. [5], all sentences in MAMS-ACSA contain several aspect categories, and these aspect categories have different sentiment polarities.

4.2 Experimental Setup

Some recent methods for aspect-category sentiment analysis have been compared. **non-BERT models:** GCAE [19], As-capsule [18], CapsNet [5], SCAN [6] and AC-MIMLLN [7]. **BERT based models:** BERT [5], BERT-pair-QA-B [13], SCAN-BERT [6], CapsNet-BERT [5] and AC-MIMLLN-BERT [7]. **Our models:** SDAN,SDAN-BERT (the embedding layer and the Bi-LSTM in SDAN have been replaced with pre-trained BERT). **Ablation models:** SDAN -w/o rel - w/o pos, remove the relation heads and the part-of-speech heads, degenerate into primitive GAT. SDAN -w/o rel, only remove the relation heads and keep the part-of-speech heads. SDAN -w/o pos, only remove the part-of-speech heads, keep the relation heads.

For SDAN, we use 300-dimensional word vectors trained by GloVe [10], the batch size is set to 32, the model is optimized using adam optimizer, and the learning rate is set to 0.001. We set the number of G-GAT layers to 2, and the dropout rate is set to 0.6. The batch size for SDAN-BERT model is set to 16, and use the last hidden states of the pre-trained BERT for word representations and fine-tune them on our task. It uses adam optimizer, and the learning rate is set to 0.00002, the number of G-GAT layers is set to 2, and the dropout rate is set to 0.2. We run all models for 10 times and report the average results on the test datasets.

Table 1. Results of the ACSA task in terms of accuracy (%).

Methods	Rest14	Rest14-hard	MAMS-ACSA
GCAE	81.593	58.372	72.174
CapsNet	81.772	54.061	73.150
As-capsule	82.479	61.844	75.308
SCAN	80.612	63.513	72.923
AC-MIMLLN	82.315	62.857	74.446
SDAN	**84.892**	**65.722**	**76.164**
BERT	87.441	70.545	77.202
CapsNet-BERT	86.768	53.304	78.438
AC-MIMLLN-BERT	87.751	73.829	80.129
SCAN-BERT	86.095	71.721	79.462
BERT-pair-QA-B	**88.375**	74.846	80.476
SDAN-BERT	87.872	**75.122**	**81.097**
SDAN-model -w/o rel -w/o pos	82.413	61.729	73.816
SDAN-model -w/o rel	84.573	64.701	75.485
SDAN-model -w/o pos	83.430	63.643	74.259

4.3 Results and Discussion

Table 1 lists the performance results. From the results, we can draw the following conclusions. In the non-BERT model, SDAN outperforms all other models on the three datasets, indicating that our model captures important syntactic structures and effectively connects aspect category words with corresponding sentiment words. Second, after combining BERT, SDAN has significantly improved performance. It has achieved the best results on the Rest14-hard and MAMS-ACSA datasets, but the accuracy on the rest14 dataset is 0.503% worse than BERT-pair-QA-B. The possible reason is that BERT's pre-training task (next sentence prediction) allows it to handle the relationship between sentences better, and BERT-pair-QA-B makes good use of this (processing the ACSA task in sentence pairs), and many sentences in the rest14 dataset have only one aspect category is not conducive to exploit the strengths of SDAN-BERT. By conducting ablation experiments on G-GAT, we find that adding relation heads or part-of-speech heads to the original GAT can improve the performance of the model. Separately comparing the functions of the part-of-speech heads and the relational heads, we can find that the part-of-speech heads have a greater impact on the performance of the model.

5 Conclusion

In this paper, we have proposed a Sentence Dependent-Aware Network for Aspect-Category Sentiment Analysis (SDAN). SDAN makes full use of the dependency tree to extenuate the mismatch problem. Experimental results on three public datasets prove the advantage of SDAN. In future work, we will focus on the sequence2graph method to generate dependencies instead of based on algorithm rules.

References

1. Cheng, J., Zhao, S., Zhang, J., King, I., Zhang, X., Wang, H.: Aspect-level sentiment classification with heat (hierarchical attention) network. In: CIKM, pp. 97–106 (2017)
2. Devlin, J., Chang, M.W., Lee, K., Toutanova, K.: BERT: Pre-training of deep bidirectional transformers for language understanding. In: NAACL-HLT, pp. 4171–4186 (2019)
3. Hochreiter, S., Schmidhuber, J.: Long short-term memory. Neural Comput. 9(8), 1735–1780 (1997)
4. Hu, M., et al.: CAN: Constrained attention networks for multi-aspect sentiment analysis. In: EMNLP-IJCNLP, pp. 4601–4610 (2019)
5. Jiang, Q., Chen, L., Xu, R., Ao, X., Yang, M.: A challenge dataset and effective models for aspect-based sentiment analysis. In: EMNLP-IJCNLP, pp. 6279–6284 (2019)
6. Li, Y., Yin, C., Zhong, S.: Sentence constituent-aware aspect-category sentiment analysis with graph attention networks. In: NLPCC, pp. 815–827 (2020)
7. Li, Y., Yin, C., Zhong, S., Pan, X.: Multi-instance multi-label learning networks for aspect-category sentiment analysis. In: EMNLP, pp. 3550–3560 (2020)
8. Liu, B.: Sentiment analysis and opinion mining. Synth. Lect. Hum. Lang. Technol. 5(1), 1–167 (2012)
9. Pang, B., Lee, L., et al.: Opinion mining and sentiment analysis. Found. Trends® Inf. Retrieval 2(1–2), 1–135 (2008)
10. Pennington, J., Socher, R., Manning, C.D.: Glove: Global vectors for word representation. In: EMNLP, pp. 1532–1543 (2014)
11. Pontiki, M., Galanis, D., Pavlopoulos, J., Papageorgiou, H., Androutsopoulos, I., Manandhar, S.: Semeval-2014 task 4: aspect based sentiment analysis. In: SemEval@COLING, pp. 27–35 (2014)
12. Schmitt, M., Steinheber, S., Schreiber, K., Roth, B.: Joint aspect and polarity classification for aspect-based sentiment analysis with end-to-end neural networks. In: EMNLP, pp. 1109–1114 (2018)
13. Sun, C., Huang, L., Qiu, X.: Utilizing BERT for aspect-based sentiment analysis via constructing auxiliary sentence. In: NAACL-HLT, pp. 380–385 (2019)
14. Tay, Y., Tuan, L.A., Hui, S.C.: Learning to attend via word-aspect associative fusion for aspect-based sentiment analysis. In: AAAI, pp. 5956–5963 (2018)
15. Velickovic, P., Cucurull, G., Casanova, A., Romero, A., Liò, P., Bengio, Y.: Graph attention networks. CoRR abs/1710.10903 (2017)
16. Wang, K., Shen, W., Yang, Y., Quan, X., Wang, R.: Relational graph attention network for aspect-based sentiment analysis. In: ACL, pp. 3229–3238 (2020)
17. Wang, Y., Huang, M., Zhao, L.: Attention-based lstm for aspect-level sentiment classification. In: EMNLP, pp. 606–615 (2016)
18. Wang, Y., Sun, A., Huang, M., Zhu, X.: Aspect-level sentiment analysis using as-capsules. In: WWW, pp. 2033–2044 (2019)

19. Xue, W., Li, T.: Aspect based sentiment analysis with gated convolutional networks. In: EMNLP, pp. 2514–2523 (2018)
20. Yang, Y., Wu, B., Li, L., Wang, S.: A joint model for aspect-category sentiment analysis with TextGCN and Bi-GRU. In: IEEE DSC, pp. 156–163 (2020)
21. Yang, Z., Yang, D., Dyer, C., He, X., Smola, A., Hovy, E.: Hierarchical attention networks for document classification. In: NAACL-HLT, pp. 1480–1489 (2016)

A Probabilistic Approach to Personalize Type-Based Facet Ranking for POI Suggestion

Esraa Ali[1(✉)] [iD], Annalina Caputo[2(✉)] [iD], Séamus Lawless[1] [iD],
and Owen Conlan[1] [iD]

[1] ADAPT Centre, School of Computer Science and Statistics, Trinity College Dublin,
Dublin, Ireland
{esraa.ali,seamus.lawless,owen.conlan}@adaptcentre.ie
[2] ADAPT Centre, School of Computing, Dublin City University, Dublin, Ireland
annalina.caputo@adaptcentre.ie

Abstract. Faceted Search Systems (FSS) have become one of the main
search interfaces used in vertical search systems, offering users meaningful facets to refine their search query and narrow down the results quickly
to find the intended search target. This work focuses on the problem of
ranking type-based facets. In a structured information space, type-based
facets (t-facets) indicate the category to which each object belongs. When
they belong to a large multi-level taxonomy, it is desirable to rank them
separately before ranking other facet groups. This helps the searcher in
filtering the results according to their type first. This also makes it easier to rank the rest of the facets once the type of the intended search
target is selected. Existing research employs the same ranking methods
for different facet groups. In this research, we propose a two-step approach to personalize t-facet ranking. The first step assigns a relevance
score to each individual leaf-node t-facet. The score is generated using
probabilistic models and it reflects t-facet relevance to the query and
the user profile. In the second step, this score is used to re-order and
select the sub-tree to present to the user. We investigate the usefulness
of the proposed method to a Point Of Interest (POI) suggestion task. Our
evaluation aims at capturing the user effort required to fulfil her search
needs by using the ranked facets. The proposed approach achieved better
results than other existing personalized baselines.

Keywords: Type-based Facets · Faceted search · Personalization

1 Introduction

In Faceted Search Systems (FSS), users explore the information space through
facets, which are attributes or meta-data that describe the underlying content of
the collection. As the magnitude of data in a collection increases, the number of
facets and their values becomes impractical to display on a single page. Providing
users with too many facets has been shown to overwhelm and distract them [6].

© Springer Nature Switzerland AG 2021
M. Brambilla et al. (Eds.): ICWE 2021, LNCS 12706, pp. 175–182, 2021.
https://doi.org/10.1007/978-3-030-74296-6_14

Faceted browsers overcome this problem by either displaying a small number of facets and making the rest accessible through a "more" button, or by displaying only the facet titles without the values: if the user is interested in a facet they can click on the title to view its values. In either case, ranking the top facets is required as it assists the searcher in narrowing down the information space and locate the target document with minimum effort.

In an information space that is structured, facets are either extracted from the edges or relationships between objects, in which case they are called *property-based facets (p-facets)*, or they are extracted from the types of the objects, in which case they are called *type-based facets (t-facets)* (e.g. values of subClassOf or isA relationships). Systems vary in their use of facets, some use a single type of facets, others mix the two types. Usually, this is done by presenting t-facets first, followed by the p-facets [10]. In FSS, which exploit multiple types of resources[1], it is important to prioritize and focus on the relevant t-facets. This is especially true when the types of resources come from a large multilevel hierarchy. This will encourage the user to filter the results by their type first and make it easier to rank the p-facets. Multilevel hierarchical types are derived from ontologies by exploiting the subClassOf relationships.

In this work, we focus on analysing the role of personalization in t-facet ranking in isolation from other FSS aspects. Existing facet ranking methods rely on attribute frequencies, navigation cost models, textual queries or click logs to order the facets [10]. Neither the special case of t-facet ranking nor the fact that t-facets relevance can be user dependant are addressed by these approaches. This experiment aims at answering the following research question: *RQ: Does personalizing the t-facet ranking using probabilistic scoring models minimize users effort to fulfil their search needs?*

This study contributes to the research in this area by introducing a novel ranking algorithm for type-based facets. The algorithm exploits the user's past preferences to build a user profile for ranking type-based facets. The proposed approach functions over two consecutive steps. The first step generates personalized relevance score for each t-facet at the end level of the taxonomy. Then, the second stage aggregates this score to re-arrange the ancestor t-facet nodes and re-build the final t-facet tree to be rendered to the user. To the best of our knowledge, this is the first approach that focuses on the special case of t-facet ranking. It investigates using topic-based user profiles to improve the ranking process. In addition to that, it provides an effective strategy to rank different t-facet levels and decide the final tree to be portrayed to the searcher. The approach operates on t-facets, which have a well structured tree-like hierarchical taxonomy.

The implemented approach is evaluated using the TREC Contextual Suggestion (TREC-CS) track dataset [5]. TREC-CS is a personalized Point-Of-Interest (POI) recommendation task, in which participants develop systems to give a ranked list of suggestions related to a given user profile and a context. We solve

---

[1] In the scope of this paper, we refer to resources (or information objects) being searched as venues or POIs.

the POI suggestion problem by ranking the types of venues as t-facets. In our evaluation, we measure the extent to which this ranked tree minimizes the user effort to reach the first relevant POI.

2   Facet Ranking Related Research

Several approaches have been proposed in the literature to solve the problem of personalized facet ranking that make use of individual user models, collaborative filtering (CF), or a mixture between the two. Factic is a FSS that personalizes by building models from semantic usage logs. Several layers of user adaption are implemented and integrated with different weights to enhance the facet relevance model [9]. Koren et al. [6] suggested a CF approach by leveraging explicit user feedback about the facets, which is used to build a facet relevance model for individuals. They also use the aggregated facet ratings to build a collaborative model for the new users in order to provide initial good facets in absence of a user profile. The Adaptive Twitter search system generates user models from Twitter to personalize facet-values ordering [1]. The user model contains entities extracted from the user's tweets. The facet-values are weighted higher if they exist in the user profile. Le et al. [7] also collects user profile from social networks. The profile is learned from user activities and preferences using a tf-idf feature vector model. Important facets are then highlighted through a matching with the model. A personalized ranking based on CF features was suggested by Chantamunee et al. [4].

They used user ratings and Matrix Factorization via SVM to learn facet ranks. All the discussed approaches in this section use the same strategy to rank p-facets and t-facets. They do not provide means to order the hierarchy of t-facets. We believe it is important to distinguish between the two types of facets during the ranking process as they each support the user in different ways in finding their intended target. Our approach exploits topic-based user profiles, which employs users' historical ratings to infer their preferred t-facet, an area which was not explored by earlier research in facet ranking.

3   Proposed Approach

Our method works in the context of personalized venue search. When a user submits a query, the underlying search engine retrieves a relevant set of venues for it[2]. Our method works on this set by collecting the t-facets associated with the retrieved venues. We assume that this set of retrieved venues is relevant for the query and can be considered as the input for the t-facet ranking algorithm.

The proposed t-facet ranking approach consists of two steps. Assuming that the t-facets are organized in a taxonomy, the first step assigns a relevance score to each t-facet leaf node. The input to this step is the retrieved venues with their relevancy score, the t-facets to which they belong, as well as the user profile.

---

[2] How the venue ranking is performed is outside scope of this research.

The second step constructs the final t-facet tree to be displayed to the user. The input to this step is both the score for each t-facet (generated at the first step) and the original hierarchical taxonomy from which we derived the t-facets. The output of the t-facet ranking is a sub-tree which contains the ordered set of relevant t-facets. The following sub-sections provide the details of each step.

3.1   Step 1: Scoring Using T-Facet Probabilistic Models

In this step, probabilistic models are developed to estimate a t-facet relevance score given a query and a user profile. The models are based on the well-known probabilistic models introduced by Sontag et al. for personalized web search [8]. They personalized the search results using topic-based user profiles collected from users' historical interactions with the system. Their approach re-weights the original document level search results according to topic relevancy to the user and query. In this work, we utilize the topic re-weighting factor to derive the t-facets score. The generated score reflects t-facet relevance to both the user and the input query. Below we re-define those models in the context of our t-facet scoring task. To generate the t-facet score, two models are proposed; **Model-1** assumes no background data available, it is calculated using the following formula:

$$score(f_i) = \sum_{f_u} P(f_u|q, \theta_u) \times P(cov(f_u, f_i)|f_u, f_i) \tag{1}$$

Where f_i is the current t-facet to be ranked, f_u are t-facets rated before by the user, θ_u is the user profile, and $P(cov(f_u, f_i)|f_u, f_i)$ is the probability that t-facet f_u is *covered* by the t-facet f_i. We estimate this probability using two methods, the first is the **exact** match, in which the probability equals to 1 if $f_u = f_i$, 0 otherwise. The second estimate (**cosine**) uses a function of distance between f_u and f_i. In our case, we employ the cosine similarity between BERT vectors generated for the input t-facet labels, using a pre-trained generic BERT model. Details about the probability $P(f_u|q, \theta_u)$ are provided later in this section.

Model-2 uses background data to estimate the score:

$$score(f_i) = \frac{\sum_{f_u} P(f_u|q, \theta_u) \times P(cov(f_u, f_i)|f_u, f_i)}{\sum_f P_r(f|q) \times P(cov(f, f_i)|f, f_i)} \tag{2}$$

The numerator is the same as Model-1. In the denominator, the background distribution $P_r(f|q)$ (where r denotes a random or generic user) is calculated by averaging the relevance score for the top N search results belonging to this t-facet when the query q is submitted to search engine. It can be obtained using the following equation:

$$P_r(f|q) = \frac{1}{N} \times \sum_{m=1}^{N} P(rel(d_m, q) = 1|q) \times P(f_d|d_m) \tag{3}$$

Note that in our case $P(f_d|d) = 1$, since the venues' types are assigned by their owners, i.e. the type of the venue is not estimated it is given, and hence can be dropped from (3). Details of the derivation of the models can be found in [8].

To model the user's preferences, we estimate $P(f_u|q, \theta_u)$, for which we use users historical ratings by assuming that users prefer t-facets of the venues they rated positively in the past. We use the generative model suggested in [8] to estimate this value by employing the Bayesian rule:

$$P(f_u|q, \theta_u) = \frac{P(f_u|\theta_u) \times P(q|f_u)}{\sum_{f'} P(f'|\theta_u) \times P(q|f')} \tag{4}$$

$P(f_u|\theta_u)$ is estimated by dividing how many times the user rated documents belong to f_u positively, divided by total number of documents rated by the user. The probability $P(q|f)$ is estimated by inverting $P(f|q)$ (see Eq. 3):

$$P(q|f) = c\frac{P_r(f|q)}{P_r(f)} \tag{5}$$

where c is a constant and $P_r(f)$ is the probability that a random user rates this facet positively obtained by counting how many times this t-facet's documents were rated positively by all users divided by the total number of rated documents.

3.2   Step 2: T-Facet Tree Building

The tree construction algorithm re-orders the original taxonomy tree by using the generated scores from the previous step. It follows a bottom-up approach where the t-facets at the lower level in the taxonomy are sorted first, then it proceeds by sorting all the ancestors of those t-facets, and so on up to the root of the hierarchy. At each level, the scores from the previous level are employed to induce the ranks of the current level. This step also decides which top t-facets sub-tree will appear to the user in the first result page. Remaining facets will be available to the user by clicking 'More' link.[3]

To build a final t-facet tree with v levels, we adopted a **fixed level** strategy that follows a bottom-up approach. The strategy respects the original taxonomy hierarchy and uses a predefined fixed page size for each t-facet level. The strategy starts by grouping t-facets at level-v by their parent. Then, it sorts the (parent) nodes at level-$(v - 1)$ by aggregating the scores of their top k children, the children are ordered by their relevance score generated in step 1, and so on up to level-1. Several aggregation functions can be used, in our experiments we used average (Avg) and maximum (Max) functions. Figure 1 shows an example for this process, categories (Cat.) correspond to level-1 t-facets and sub-categories correspond to level-2 t-facets. In the case where a level-1 facet has additional relevant t-facet children that are not displayed in first page, they will be available to the user through the "+ More Cat ...". Each following t-facet page will be sorted in the same way. The final output provides the user a more organized and readable t-facet tree.

---

[3] Although we acknowledge that other HCI factors may influence the decision of what portion of the tree should be displayed to the users, in this work we focus on studying how the tree building approach affects the user from a pure metric perspective.

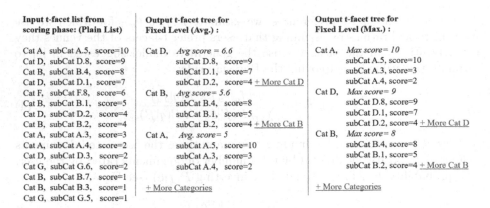

Fig. 1. Example output t-facet tree for a 2 level taxonomy using two aggregations: average and max, level-1 t-facet page size=3, level-2 t-facet page size=3.

4   Experimental Results

Experimental Setup. Our approach is evaluated on TREC-CS 2016 dataset [5]. The t-facet taxonomy is derived from the Foursquare venue category hierarchy[4]. Hence, having as much Foursquare venues linked to TREC-CS POIs as possible is paramount. For this reason, we complement the original data with three Foursquare supplementary datasets from [2,3] and our own crawled POIs. The final dataset has 58 requests and an average of 208 t-facets per request to be ranked. We consider the first two levels of the taxonomy, they contain 10 level-1 and 429 level-2 t-facets. The document search engine implements BM25 with NDCG value of 0.4023, the query is formed by combining user weighed tags by their most common rating.

The existence of relevance judgments makes it possible to evaluate our approach against a well established ground-truth. We follow the evaluation approach used in Faceted Search task of INEX 2011 Data-Centric Track [11].

We report two metrics suggested by task organizers. The number of actions (#Actions) metric counts how many clicks the user has to perform on the ranked facets list in order to reach the first relevant document in the top 5 results. The faceted scan (F-Scan) metric measures the user's effort to scan facets and documents until they reach the same document. We focus on these two metrics as a proxy for user's effort, which will help in answering our research question.

We report the results for the no background model (Model-1) and the background model (Model-2), each experimented using two coverage probability estimators (exact) and (cosine). To show the effect of different tree building approaches on the evaluation metrics, we produce results using two strategies: 1) fixed level with average (Avg), 2) fixed level with maximum (Max). Both use 3 level-1 t-facets per page, with 3 level-2 t-facets each.

Preliminary Results. The overall results in Table 1 show that the no Model-1 consistently outperforms Model-2 across all metrics and regardless the used

---

[4] https://developer.foursquare.com/docs/resources/categories, version: 20180323.

Table 1. Results for probabilistic scoring and fixed level tree building strategy with max and avg aggregation functions.

Scoring method	Max		Avg.	
	F-Scan	#Actions	F-Scan	#Actions
Model-1 + exact	4.258	1.534	4.051	1.517
Model-1 + cosine	**3.413**	**1.327**	**3.482**	**1.396**
Model-2 + exact	4.534	1.706	4.327	1.706
Model-2 + cosine	4.844	1.758	4.879	1.810

coverage probability method. One possible explanation is the small number of training points available for the estimation of the background model. The dataset has only 26 users, each rated either 30 or 60 venues, and the same 60 venues are rated by all users. As a result, the profiles are limited to a small set of t-facets, which ultimately affected the probability distributions. Further in depth analysis of the relation between the number of user historical POIs and the performance of the scoring methods is needed.

The skewed t-facet probability distribution also explains why the *cosine* similarity implementation gave better results in Model-1. It aids the score generation for new unseen, t-facets, where the strict *exact* match approach fails to handle such cases, since it assigns 0 score if the user never rated that category before.

From Table 1 we can also observe that the evaluation metrics were affected by the used tree building strategy. For the best performing scorer (Model-1 + cosine), the Fixed Level-Max strategy produced better results. Two factors played a role here: 1) The strategy maintains the top scored level-2 facets at the top of the final tree; 2) In estimating $P_r(f|q)$ (see Eq. 3) we set $N = 1$ (for all models) to favor t-facets which will promote the first relevant result early to the user, which in turn effectively minimized the user effort as shown in the results. When experimenting with higher N values, all metrics were negatively impacted.

Table 2 compares our system performance against three personalized facet ranking approaches. Since none of the existing methods handle the hierarchical nature of the t-facets, we use them as scoring methods with the Fixed Level-Max strategy. We can see that our Model-1+cosine scoring

Table 2. Comparing our results against baselines using Fixed Level-Max

Scoring method	F-Scan	#Actions
Model-1 + cosine	3.413	**1.327**
MF-SVM [4]	3.741	1.431
Most prob. (Person) [6]	4.000	1.672
Most prob. (Collab) [6]	**3.327**	1.379

method achieved minimum #Actions. The Most Prob. (Collab) approach achieved competing results, with F-Scan slightly better than our model. A reason for this result is that by favouring popular t-facets, this method worked well given the skewed t-facet probability distribution. However, it has the disadvantage of not handling new unseen t-facets and failing for users with unpopular preferences. Our approach on the other hand, handles both cases effectively.

5   Conclusions

This work has introduced a novel t-facet ranking approach. The two-step approach considers the hierarchical nature of t-facets as well as user individual preferences. The first step assigns score to t-facets. The second step uses the score to re-arrange and build the final t-facet tree to the user. To personalize the scores, we explored several probabilistic models. They have shown promising results given the limited user profiles in the dataset. Our future plans include experimenting with more POI suggestion datasets and experimenting with complex taxonomies to better understand the behavior of the proposed methods. Our experiments have demonstrated that even the straight-forward tree building approaches can aid the ranking process. Developing more advanced strategies can introduce further improvement.

Acknowledgements. This research was conducted with the financial support of Science Foundation Ireland (SFI) under Grant Agreement No. 13/RC/2106 at the ADAPT SFI Research Centre at Trinity College Dublin. The ADAPT Centre for Digital Media Technology is funded by SFI through the SFI Research Centres Programme and is co-funded under the European Regional Development Fund (ERDF) Grant No. 13/RC/2106_P2.

References

1. Abel, F., Celik, I., Houben, G.-J., Siehndel, P.: Leveraging the semantics of tweets for adaptive faceted search on twitter. In: Aroyo, L., et al. (eds.) ISWC 2011. LNCS, vol. 7031, pp. 1–17. Springer, Heidelberg (2011). https://doi.org/10.1007/978-3-642-25073-6_1
2. Aliannejadi, M., Mele, I., Crestani, F.: A cross-platform collection for contextual suggestion. In: SIGIR. ACM (2017)
3. Bayomi, M., Lawless, S.: Adapt_tcd: an ontology-based context aware approach for contextual suggestion. In: TREC (2016)
4. Chantamunee, S., Wong, K.W., Fung, C.C.: Collaborative filtering for personalised facet selection. In: IAIT. ACM (2018)
5. Hashemi, S.H., Clarke, C.L., Kamps, J., Kiseleva, J., Voorhees, E.M.: Overview of the trec 2016 contextual suggestion track. In: TREC (2016)
6. Koren, J., Zhang, Y., Liu, X.: Personalized interactive faceted search. In: WWW. ACM (2008)
7. Le, T., Vo, B., Duong, T.H.: Personalized facets for semantic search using linked open data with social networks. In: IBICA (2012)
8. Sontag, D., Collins-Thompson, K., Bennett, P.N., White, R.W., Dumais, S., Billerbeck, B.: Probabilistic models for personalizing web search. In: WSDM. ACM (2012)
9. Tvarožek, M., Bieliková, M.: Factic: personalized exploratory search in the semantic web. In: Benatallah, B., Casati, F., Kappel, G., Rossi, G. (eds.) ICWE 2010. LNCS, vol. 6189, pp. 527–530. Springer, Heidelberg (2010). https://doi.org/10.1007/978-3-642-13911-6_44
10. Tzitzikas, Y., Manolis, N., Papadakos, P.: Faceted exploration of rdf/s datasets: a survey. J. Intell. Inf. Syst **48**, 329–364 (2017)
11. Wang, Q., Ramírez, G., Marx, M., Theobald, M., Kamps, J.: Overview of the INEX 2011 data-centric track. In: Geva, S., Kamps, J., Schenkel, R. (eds.) INEX 2011. LNCS, vol. 7424, pp. 118–137. Springer, Heidelberg (2012). https://doi.org/10.1007/978-3-642-35734-3_10

Web Mining and Knowledge Extraction

Web Table Classification Based on Visual Features

Babette Bühler[1] and Heiko Paulheim[2](✉) (iD)

[1] Hector Research Institute of Education Sciences and Psychology,
University of Tübingen, Tübingen, Germany
`babette.buehler@uni-tuebingen.de`
[2] Data and Web Science Group, University of Mannheim, Mannheim, Germany
`heiko@informatik.uni-mannheim.de`

Abstract. Tables on the web constitute a valuable data source for many applications, like factual search and knowledge base augmentation. However, as genuine tables containing relational knowledge only account for a small proportion of tables on the web, reliable genuine web table classification is a crucial first step of table extraction. Previous works usually rely on explicit feature construction from the HTML code. In contrast, we propose an approach for web table classification by exploiting the *full* visual appearance of a table, which works purely by applying a convolutional neural network on the rendered image of the web table. Since these visual features can be extracted automatically, our approach circumvents the need for explicit feature construction. A new hand labeled gold standard dataset containing HTML source code and images for 13,112 tables was generated for this task. Transfer learning techniques are applied to well known VGG16 and ResNet50 architectures. The evaluation of CNN image classification with fine tuned ResNet50 (F1 93.29%) shows that this approach achieves results comparable to previous solutions using explicitly defined HTML code based features. By combining visual and explicit features, an F-measure of 93.70% can be achieved by Random Forest classification, which beats current state of the art methods.

Keywords: Web table · Genuine table · Layout table · Image classification · Convolutional neural network

1 Introduction

The world wide web constitutes the worlds largest freely available source of information covering almost every topic area. Especially web tables are of interest in this respect, because they present knowledge in a structured and concise form. They have been successfully employed as a data source in areas such as factual search [26], entity augmentation [25] and knowledge base augmentation [17].

Before web tables can be employed as a powerful knowledge resource they have to be extracted. As web pages are built using the Hyper Text Markup Language (HTML), the intuitive approach to locate a table is via the `<table>`

© Springer Nature Switzerland AG 2021
M. Brambilla et al. (Eds.): ICWE 2021, LNCS 12706, pp. 185–200, 2021.
https://doi.org/10.1007/978-3-030-74296-6_15

tag. Crestan and Pantel [5] suggest that, based on their investigation of table type distribution on the web, an overwhelmingly large proportion of 88% of tables defined by the `<table>` tag are layout tables, used for navigation or formatting purposes. Consequently, the very first step in table processing is the identification of genuine web tables presenting relational knowledge.

Figures 1b and 1d show the usage of HTML table elements for layout purposes, i.e., for arranging logos in a grid, and for a navigation bar. In contrast, Figs. 1a and 1c show genuine tables, once as a relational table and once as a table of key/value pairs referring to the same entity.

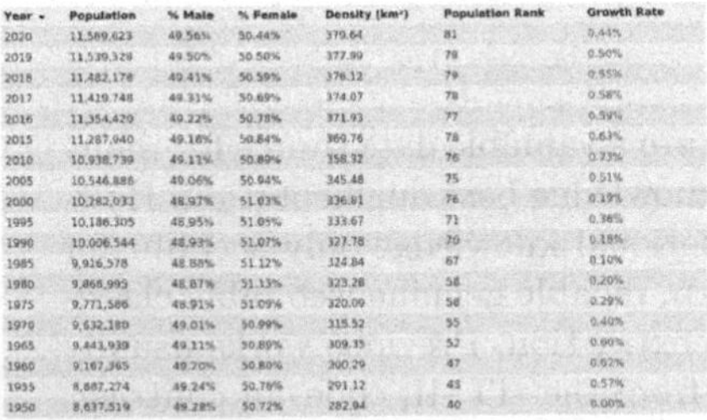

Year ▾	Population	% Male	% Female	Density (km²)	Population Rank	Growth Rate
2020	11,589,623	49.56%	50.44%	379.64	81	0.44%
2019	11,539,328	49.50%	50.50%	377.99	79	0.50%
2018	11,482,178	49.41%	50.59%	376.12	79	0.55%
2017	11,419,748	49.31%	50.69%	374.07	78	0.58%
2016	11,354,420	49.22%	50.78%	371.93	77	0.59%
2015	11,287,940	49.16%	50.84%	369.76	78	0.63%
2010	10,938,739	49.11%	50.89%	358.32	76	0.73%
2005	10,546,886	49.06%	50.94%	345.48	75	0.51%
2000	10,282,033	48.97%	51.03%	336.81	76	0.19%
1995	10,186,305	48.95%	51.05%	333.67	71	0.36%
1990	10,006,544	48.93%	51.07%	327.78	70	0.18%
1985	9,916,578	48.88%	51.12%	324.84	67	0.10%
1980	9,868,995	48.87%	51.13%	323.28	58	0.20%
1975	9,771,586	48.91%	51.09%	320.09	56	0.29%
1970	9,632,180	49.01%	50.99%	315.52	55	0.40%
1965	9,443,939	49.11%	50.89%	309.35	52	0.60%
1960	9,167,365	49.20%	50.80%	300.29	47	0.62%
1955	8,887,274	49.24%	50.76%	291.12	43	0.57%
1950	8,637,519	49.28%	50.72%	282.94	40	0.00%

(a) Example picture genuine table vertical listing

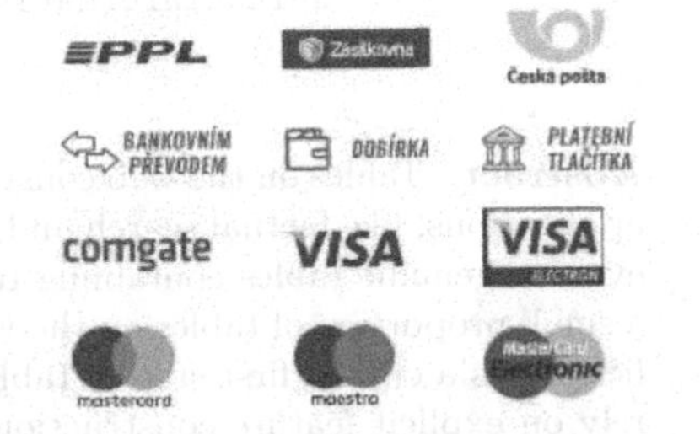

(b) Example picture layout table formatting

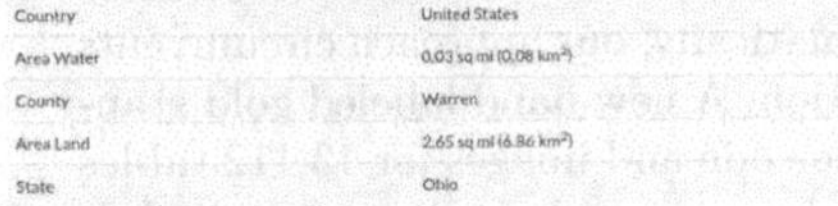

Country	United States
Area Water	0.03 sq mi (0.08 km²)
County	Warren
Area Land	2.65 sq mi (6.86 km²)
State	Ohio

(c) Example picture genuine table attribute/value

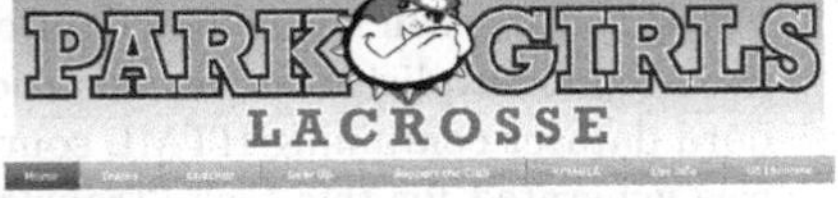

(d) Example picture layout table navigating

Fig. 1. Examples for layout and genuine tables

Previous research has worked on identifying genuine tables by applying extensive heuristic filter rules [2,21] and by using machine learning with explicitly defined features that describe the structure and genuine of a respective HTML table [1,7,24]. Most approaches extract those features from the HTML code. Exceptions are Cohen et al. [3] and Gatterbauer et al. [9] who employed quasi-rendered representations. However, the HTML code encodes the visual appearance of tables in the browser in a complex and indirect fashion. In contrast to this, it is in most cases intuitive for human viewers to distinguish layout from genuine tables in the rendered display of a website by their visual characteristics.

This paper proposes to automatically extract visual features by using convolutional neural networks from the rendered image representation of web tables. Two different strategies to the use of Convolutional Neural Networks (CNNs) for web table classification are presented. First, pre-trained and fine tuned CNNs are directly used to classify web tables, employing a dense classification layer. Further, pre-trained CNNs are used as standalone feature extractors and the extracted visual features, as well as their combination with explicitly defined features by Eberius et al. [7] are employed to train a Random Forest classifier. For each of the proposed approaches transfer learning and fine-tuning techniques for two well known deep learning architectures, VGG16 and ResNet50, with weights pre-trained on the ImageNet data, are tested.

The rest of this paper is structured as follows. Section 2 outlines related work. Section 3 introduces our approach, which is analyzed in a set of experiments in Sect. 4. We conclude with a summary and an outlook on future work.

2   Related Work

A range of research has been conducted in the area of discriminating genuine and layout tables on the web. The approaches can be roughly divided into three strands, i.e., heuristic rules, machine learning using HTML based features, and visual representation based features.

2.1   Heuristic Filter Rules

Chen et al. [2] propose a set of filter rules and the use of cell similarity measures to detect genuine tables. They filter tables containing less than two cells or containing too many hyperlinks, forms, and figures. For the remaining tables, the similarity of neighboring cells is considered to tell genuine and layout tables apart. On a test dataset of 3,218 tables, they report an F-measure of 86.5%.

In a similar approach, Penn et al. [21] propose a set of heuristics to distinguish genuine and layout tables. Following these heuristics, genuine tables do not contain other tables, lists, frames, forms, images, have multiple rows and columns, more than one non-text-level-formatting tags, or less than a minimum amount of words. On a dataset extracted from 75 news websites, the authors report 86.3% precision and 89.8% recall.

2.2   Machine Learning Using HTML Based Features

Wang and Hu [24] apply machine learning techniques for the genuine versus non-genuine table classification tasks. They propose a large set of layout and genuine type features, as well as a word group feature to train Decision Tree classifiers and Support Vector Machines (SVM). Layout features, e.g., the average number of rows or columns, were adopted to depict structural information, while genuine type features describe the type of the cells. On a test dataset consisting of 11,477 leaf tables they achieve a F-measure of 95.89% for SVM with a RBF kernel. Additionally, it was compared to the rule based system proposed by Penn et al. [21] which achieved a F-measure of 61.93% and a F-measure of 87.63% after ruling out the cell length threshold of four, on the same data.

Carafella et al. [1] employ a combination of heuristic filter rules and rule-based classifiers to distinguish between relational and non-relational tables. They filter out small tables, attribute/value tables, and tables embedded inside HTML forms and calendars, eliminating 89.4% of all tables. In order to train a classifier, they create seven features inspired by Wang and Hu [24]. While they do not propose novel approaches for web table detection, they are the first to apply the algorithms to a corpus at web scale, containing 14.1 billion HTML tables extracted from the google.com Web crawl. As they optimize for recall of relational tables, they report a F-measure of 73.1% on a labeled subsample of the data.

Crestan and Pantel [5] present a supervised framework to classify HTML tables into a more fine-grained table type taxonomy, consisting of nine types, constituting a more challenging classification task. Employing filter rules as a minimum of two rows and columns and no cell containing more than 100 characters about 80% of sampled tables were filtered out. A set of layout, genuine, and lexical features is proposed and used to train Gradient Boosted Tree classifier. On a dataset containing 5,000 randomly sampled tables, they report an F-measures of 68.3% for genuine and 89.3% for layout tables.

Son and Park [23] propose feature generation using the HTML document structure, incorporating the structure within a table as well as the structure appearing in the context of the table. In combination with the features proposed by Wang and Hu, they achieve an F-measure of 98.58% on their dataset [24].

Lehmberg et al. [17] conduct web table classification in order to create a large open corpus of relational HTML tables, i.e., the WebDataCommons HTML Tables Dataset[1] based on the 2012 version of the Common Crawl web corpus. They use heuristic filter rules eliminating tables containing nested tables as well as small tables, and employ a classifier using 16 layout, genuine type and word group features, similar to Wang and Hu [24]. On a manually labeled Gold Standard data set of 7,350 randomly sampled web sites, consisting of 77,630 tables, they report a precision of 58% and recall of 62%. Based on this, they created a web table corpus containing 35.7 million tables, which was later updated incorporating contributions by Eberius et al. [7].

Eberius et al. [7] address the distinction of layout and genuine tables, as well as a more fine-grained classification of the latter. They apply pre-selection Filters, eliminating small tables as well as tables that were invalid or could not be displayed correctly. They incorporated and extended features proposed by Wang and Hu [24] and Crestan and Pantel [5], differentiating between global features, considering the whole table, and local features only computed per row or column. The 29 most relevant features of the initial 127 created features were selected using correlation-based feature selection. The evaluation of different classifiers is performed on a manually labeled data set containing 1,022 tables. For the best performing classifier, the Random Forest a F-measure value of 95.2% is reported for the binary classification task. The proposed approach was used to create the Dresden Web Table Corpus[2] consisting of millions of web tables.

A similar method can be seen in all of those approaches: Typically, a two-step approach is used, which applies a rough pre-filter for non-genuine tables

---

[1] http://webdatacommons.org/webtables/.

[2] https://wwwdb.inf.tu-dresden.de/misc/dwtc/.

(usually based on the number of rows and columns and/or nested tables) as a first step. In a second step, a classifier is used to distinguish the remaining tables as genuine or non-genuine. This is done with the help of combinations of different features which can be divided into different groups [16]. Global features describe the table as a whole, while Local features that are similar to average cell length, which are created for rows or columns individually [5,7]. Another distinction is made between content type features and structural or layout features. The former describe for instance the frequency of certain types of content in cells as images, hyperlinks, forms, alphabetic or numeric characters or empty cells. The latter is for instance represented by the average, variance, minimum or maximum number of rows, columns or cell length [1,5,7,24].

2.3   Visual Representation Based Features

What unites all previous approaches is the approach to generate the features used for classification directly from the HTML source code of the tables. In contrast, only few approaches have been made to directly employ visual properties of web tables for table detection.

First, Cohen et al. [3] brought up the idea to include visual characteristics by "quasi-rendering" HTML source code and using the results to detect relational knowledge on the web. They presented a wrapper learning system, which employs multiple document representations. For the entailed table-based extraction, they define the table detection problem as a binary classification task for the <table> tag elements. Two classes of features are extracted, first those originating from the HTML representation of the table and second model based features that are extracted from an abstract rendering of the table in order to represent the two dimensional geometric structure of tables. This abstract rendering is achieved by a geometric table model inferred from processes considering how a HTML may be presented in the browser. On a labeled test sample of 339 tables, an F-measure of 95.9% is reported.

Another approach to identify and extract information from tables on the web, relying on visual features is taken by Gatterbauer et al. [9]. With the goal of domain independent information extraction from web tables they propose performing table extraction and interpretation on a variant of the CSS2 visual box model as rendered by a web browser, rather than on the source code tree structure (however, the actual style sheet information is not used). In contrast to all other literature considered, Gatterbauer et al. [9] do not use HTML <table> tag to identify the location of tables, arguing that tables as defined by representing relations reflected by certain visual properties and horizontal and vertical alignment of data in a grid structure become visible after a web page is rendered and are not necessarily defined by the corresponding HTML tag. For the task of table extraction on a data set of 493 web tables a recall 81% of and a precision of 68% are reported.

In a recent work, Kim and Hwang proposed a method for table detection in Web pages, which also exploits visual features derived from the image representation of the Web page [14]. The authors report an F1 score of 0.71 and 0.78 on two different test cases.

Although those approaches consider visual features of web tables for the detection of genuine tables, they both rely on rather coarse visual representations and do not use the actual image of the website. This implies that important signals that could be used for the detection (e.g., styling information such as lines or background colors and images, which are not defined in the DOM tree, but in an exterior CSS file) are, so far, not used by any approach. Hence, the approach pursued in this paper is the first approach to exploit the *full* visual appearance of a table, as it works on the rendered image as it would be presented to a human visitor of a web page.

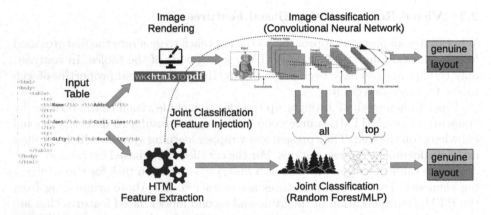

Fig. 2. Approach visualized. The upper part shows the purely visual approach. The dashed line and the lower part illustrate the joint approaches.

3   Approach

The key idea of our approach is that identifying genuine tables on web pages is rather straight forward for human beings, due to the fact that they have certain visual properties that characterize them and distinguish them from other website elements. Hence, it should be possible to also train a machine learning classifier to directly distinguish genuine and layout tables from the image of the rendered HTML table code. However, to obtain table images, only the part defined as a table by the <table> tags is rendered. When doing so, the already mentioned style information like CSS and style tags can be used to obtain the exact representation of the table on the website. Additionally, more complex tables structures, as nested tables, which are often filtered out during the filtering step, can be included in the analysis. The only filter rule applied before rendering the pictures is to eliminate obviously non-genuine tables with less than two rows or columns.

In the purely visual approach, the binary classification task is solved using solely a CNN classifier, including a fully connected classification layer. Furthermore, we propose two joint strategies for combining visual and HTML features: (1) injecting HTML as additional features in the fully connected classification layer of the CNN classifier, (2) and combining the features extracted by the CNN and the HTML features in a downstream classifier (here, we use a Random Forest and a MLP classifier). For the latter case, we experiment with extracting only the highest layer features, as well as features from all layers of the CNNs.

Additionally, CNNs are used to extract visual features from the web table images which are then used in a joint approach, using the original DWTC Random Forest classifier [7] combining HTML features and visual features.

Figure 2 shows the overall approach. The images are rendered in color employing the open source wkhtmltoimage package[3]. The rendered images then fed into a convolutional neural network for image classification, leading to a binary classification (*genuine* or *layout*).

3.1 Convolutional Neural Nets for Image Classification and Visual Feature Extraction

One of the most commonly used learning algorithms for image classification are Convolutional Neural Networks (CNNs). CNNs are hierarchical feed forward networks, implementing several convolution stages, which are often a combination of convolution layers, non-linear transformation and pooling layers [12, 15]. Convolution operations allow the network to extract relevant features from local correlated data points [13]. By the stacking of multiple of these feature extraction stages, more abstract representations of the image data are learned subsequently [27]. When used for classification, the convolution and pooling layers are connected to a classification module consisting of one or several dense layers, emitting classification predictions. Here, the convolutional and pooling layers can bee seen as automatic *feature extractors*, which create the features used by the downstream classifier.

Another way to leverage CNNs' ability to automatically learn representations of visual characteristics in images is to use it as a standalone feature extractor. After the weights have been trained on a certain image classification task, the fully connected layers of the network are removed. Thus, instead of a class prediction, the CNN outputs feature vectors that can be used in other downstream tasks. The use of such extracted visual feature vectors allows the combination with HTML-based features.

Since CNNs subsequently create higher level features, we inspected two different approaches: using only the most abstract representation (the approach depicted in Fig. 2 as *top*) and using features from all levels of abstractions (the approach depicted in Fig. 2 as *all*).

---

[3] https://github.com/wkhtmltopdf/wkhtmltopdf.

3.2   Transfer Learning with VGG16 and ResNet50

While in classic machine learning, a model for a given classification task is learned from scratch, using labeled examples for that task. In contrast, *transfer learning* refers to re-using a machine learning model trained for a different task, and adapting it for the task at hand [20]. In our case, we use re-use generic models for image classification and apply them to the task of table classification.

In our approach, we reuse pre-trained CNNs as a starting point. For adapting (i.e., *transferring*) them to the classification task at hand, we use new input data from our task. This can be accomplished either by freezing the pre-trained weights in the convolution part of the network and allowing only the dense classification layer to adjust weights (we refer to that approach as *frozen*), or by allowing all pre-trained weights in the network to adjust to the new task during training (we refer to that approach as *adapt*). Transfer learning increases efficiency compared to training the weights from scratch and has shown to produce good results. Some well established CNN architectures for the task of image classification are VGG16 and ResNet50 [13].

VGG16 is a deep convolutional neural network, built by stacking several convolutional layers while using small filters of size 3×3 [22]. The architecture consists of five convolutional blocks consisting of two to three convolution layers employing ReLu activation functions, followed by a max pooling layer. The output of the convolutions is flattened and send through two dense layers, followed by a classification layer on top. In total it entails 16 trainable layers, of which are 13 convolution layers and three dense layers. In this case of a binary classification task, a classification layer is replaced by a dense layer with one output node and sigmoid activation function is used. When used as feature extractor, global average pooling of the output of convolutional blocks is applied to obtain the feature vector.

ResNet50, short for *Residual Network*, is characterized by implementing a residual learning framework, where layers learn residual functions with regard to input layers, in order to facilitate training of very deep networks [11]. Besides implementing identity based skip connections to enable cross layer connectivity, it also incorporates batch normalization as regulating units. The model consists of a total of 50 layers. A first convolution block is followed by four stages of stacked convolution and identity blocks. Similar to the approach for VGG16, we refined the classification layer according to the binary classification task. When the model is used for feature extraction the output after applying global average pooling is used.

For both VGG16 and ResNet50, we use pre-trained models which were built on the ImageNet challenge dataset, an image classification training dataset of more than 1 million images and 1,000 classes.

4   Experiments

While most approaches discussed in Sect. 2 use datasets which are not publicly available, the only previous work using an open dataset is the work using the

Table 1. Gold standard dataset

	Layout	Genuine	Total
Training	3938	4454	8392
Validation	1018	1080	2098
Test	1267	1355	2622
Total	**6223**	**6889**	**13112**

Dresden Web Table Corpus (DWTC) [7]. However, that corpus does not contain the original CSS files and images from the Web pages; hence, a rendering of the Web page as it would look in a browser was not possible based on the dataset. Therefore, we manually annotated a new ground truth dataset.

4.1 Dataset

To collect the data used in this paper, the HTML code of roughly 1.25 million websites was sampled, by accessing 125 randomly chosen WARC files of the March 2020 common crawl[4]. From each of these websites one table, identified by the HTML <table> tag, was randomly selected if it contained one. Subsequently, a simple filter was applied, similar to Eberius et al. [7]. This filter eliminated all tables that had less than two columns or two rows. This simple filter rule alone led to an exclusion of about 65% the sampled tables. In addition, the language was restricted to English, using the langdetect[5] library in Python to ensure the interpretability of images during manual ground truthing.

Afterwards, the collected web tables present in the HTML were rendered to image files. To that end, linked images and CSS files were retrieved based on their URL (since they are often not contained in the Common Crawl). To handle cases where the style files were no longer accessible, we tried using the Wayback machine[6] to download historic snapshots instead, however, this lead to no improvements. Furthermore, we discarded tables that could not be rendered (e.g., due to invalid HTML code). However, the share of discarded tables in that step is only about .01%.

To label the tables consistently, a precise definition of layout and genuine tables must be established. The tables labeled as genuine tables largely correspond to those defined as relational tables by Crestan and Pantel [4]. These include vertical and horizontal lists, matrix and attribute/value tables and enumerations. Two examplary genuine tables can be seen in Figs. 1a and 1c. Only forms such as log in elements or address forms were not defined as genuine tables in this data generation. Although they are to be interpreted as relational tables according to Crestan and Pantel [4], they do not contain knowledge to be extracted but, as is the inherent characteristic of a form, blanks. Consequently,

---

[4] https://commoncrawl.org/2020/04/.

[5] https://github.com/shuyo/language-detection.

[6] https://archive.org/web/.

they do not serve the purpose of information extraction. Tables classified as layout tables are, for example, formatting tables used to visually arrange contents, as in Fig. 1b, or navigational tables used to navigate the website as in Fig. 1d.

The resulting gold standard dataset used to develop the classification models presented in this paper contains 13,112 tables, of which 6,889 were labeled as genuine and 6,223 as layout tables, as shown in Table 1. For these, the original HTML code as well as an image version is present. For model development the data is split into a training set of 80% and a test set of 20%, containing 2,622 tables. A 20% validation set was again split off from the resulting training set, resulting in a validation set of 2,098 tables and a training set of 8,392 tables.[7]

4.2   Experimental Setup

In order to evaluate our approach, we compare different settings to the state of the art classifier used to build the Dresden Web Table Corpus.

Baselines. As a baseline for this work, we use the approach presented by Eberius et al. [7] using a combination of content and layout features extracted from tables' HTML code. The best performing model was implemented in the extraction of the Dresden Web Table Corpus (DWTC), referenced earlier. The DWTC-Extractor[8], containing the full code used for the extraction is available on GitHub. Single elements of this extractor, namely the creation of HTML features and the trained WEKA Random Forest classifier for the classification of genuine and layout tables, can be accessed to apply the approach to the newly generated Gold Standard test data. On their own data, Eberius et al. [7] reported a weighted F1 score of 9.52%. In addition to applying the model trained on the original dataset, we also retrained the Random Forest classifier on our training dataset.

The DWTC extractor additionally filters nested tables before generating the features. Therefore, for the nested tables contained in our Gold Standard, a default layout classification was applied. Regarding the labels of these nested tables reveals that the vast majority indeed are layout tables.

The hyperparameters of the default DWTC classifier are the standard settings of the Weka Random Forest classifier, i.e., growing 10 trees and no other restrictions for the Random Forest. For the retrained Random Forest, trained with scikit-learn[9] in Python, randomized grid search was employed for hyperparameter tuning, using the described validation set. The best resulting hyperparameter setting was growing 1,600 trees, with a maximal depth of 80, a minimum of 4 samples per leaf, and a minimal number of samples per split of 2.

---

[7] The code and data used in this paper are available at https://github.com/babettebue/web-table-classification.

[8] https://github.com/JulianEberius/dwtc-extractor/.

[9] https://scikit-learn.org/stable/.

CNN Approaches. The CNN based approaches are implemented using Tensor-flow[10] in Python. The built in functional models of VGG16 and ResNet50, with an option to load weights pre-trained on the ImageNet dataset, were used and adapted. In order to adapt these networks, which are designed for classification on the ImageNet dataset containing 10 image classes, to the binary classification problem. The classification layer was replaced by a dense layer with one output node and a sigmoid activation function.

Before feeding the images into the CNN, they have to be resized and normal-ized. The latter is realized by implementing a rescaling layer into the network, rescaling all images to 224×224. First, the models were trained only employing the weights pretrained on the ImageNet dataset. This was achieved by setting all layers but the last dense layer used for classification to non-trainable. This setting is referred to as *frozen*. In a second configuration, the ImageNet weights were used as initialization weights, which could be fine tuned during the training for our binary classification task. This setting is referred to as *adapt*.

The models were trained for 100 epochs, using the Adam optimizer, binary crossentropy loss and the standard learning rate of .001 for the models with frozen ImageNet weights. The models allowed to fine-tune weights were trained with a smaller learning rate of .0001. A callback with a patience of 20, for frozen weight models and 50 for fine-tuned models, in case of steady validation accuracy was employed to prevent over-fitting. Training of VGG16 frozen was stopped after 36 epochs, training of VGG16 adapt after 58 epochs. The frozen ResNet50 was trained for 36 epochs and the fine-tuned ResNet allowed to adapt weights for 69 epochs.

Joint Approaches. For the combined architectures, we used both the extracted HTML features from the feature-based classification approach, as well as the latent features extracted by the CNNs. To extract features generated by the convolutional blocks of the networks, VGG16 and ResNet50 architectures are used without the top dense layers. For the VGG16 a GlobalAveragePooling layer is stacked on top of the convolutional network in order to obtain a one dimen-sional feature vector with reduced dimensionality [27]. The VGG16 outputs 512 visual features. The ResNet50 model already implements a GlobalAveragePool-ing layer after the last convolution, which outputs feature vector of length 2,048. For both architectures, models with the ImageNet weights, as well as the mod-els fine-tuned for the binary classification problem at hand, are used for feature extraction.

Additionally, for both models features of all levels of abstractions, referred to as *all*, are extracted, GlobalAveragePooling is applied and followed by a simple concatenation of the feature vectors. For VGG16 this results in a feature set containing 1,472 visual features and for ResNet50 in a set of 3,903 features.

---

[10] https://www.tensorflow.org/.

4.3   Results

The recall, precision, and F1 score both on the layout and genuine table class, as well as the weighted average of those, are shown in Table 2.

We can observe that while the original DWTC classifier does not perform optimally on the dataset at hand, retraining the classifier works a lot better. The results of the retrained classifier slightly outperform the results reported in the original paper, where a weighted average F1 score of .906 was reported [7].

Applying the *frozen* VGG16 and ResNet50 architectures without weight adaption yields results below the baseline. On the other hand, allowing fine-tuning of weights in the *adapt* setting, the results are in a similar range as the retrained DWTC classifier, with ResNet50 even outperforming those results by a small margin. The best joint approaches combining both the DWTC and the CNN features again perform a little better than the purely visual and the DWTC approach alone.

McNemar's non parametric test [8] was conducted to compare the best performing classifiers from each approach, as recommended by Dietterich et al. [6] if evaluation is performed on a single test set. The results reveal that there is *no* significant difference between the retrained DWTC classifier, the best performing CNN classifier. Hence, our conclusion is that both the visual approach and the approach based on explicit feature engineering work equally well.

While the results are very different in terms of overall performance, they reveal striking difference when looking at the mistakes they make. Figure 3 shows a few typical mistakes. More complex tables like the one shown in (a) are often misclassified by the DWTC approach, but handled correctly by the CNN-based classifiers. On the other hand, (b) and (c) show two typical mistakes made by the CNN-based classifiers: they tend to misclassify tables for layouting input forms as genuine tables, and often do not recognize tables without lines as genuine tables. This shows that vertical and horizontal lines are features which have a very strong importance for the CNN-based classifiers.

Another interesting observation is that when using the CNN architectures alone, the approaches based on adapting weights outperform those without, and ResNet50 outperforms VGG16. On the other hand, in the joint approaches, the trend is reversed: adapted approaches work worse, and the best results are achieved with VGG16. One possible explanation is that when fine-tuning the weights to the task of table classification, the features that are learned by the CNN become more similar to the explicitly created ones, and therefore, the information gain by combining the extracted features with the explicitly created ones is smaller. Moreover, being a smaller model, VGG16 might have a tendency to extract more coarse grained features which are less overlapping with the HTML based features.

Table 2. Results with baselines, visual classification approaches (upper part), and joint approaches based on feature injection, RandomForest (RF), and MLP classifiers (lower part)

Approach	Layout			Genuine			Weighted avg.		
	P	R	F1	P	R	F1	P	R	F1
DWTC original	.894	.916	.889	.917	.865	.890	.891	.890	.890
DWTC retrained	.934	.924	.929	**.930**	.939	.934	.932	.932	.932
VGG16 frozen	.901	.824	.861	.848	.916	.880	.873	.871	.871
VGG16 adapt	.915	.925	.920	.929	.920	.924	.922	.922	.922
ResNet50 frozen	.914	.875	.894	.887	.923	.905	.900	.900	.900
ResNet50 adapt	**.937**	**.929**	**.930**	.929	**.942**	**.936**	**.933**	**.933**	**.933**
Injection VGG16 frozen	.892	.921	.906	.924	.895	.909	.908	.908	.908
Injection VGG16 adapt	.878	.913	.895	.916	.881	.898	.897	.897	.897
Injection ResNet50 frozen	.821	.853	.837	.857	.826	.841	.840	.839	.839
Injection ResNet50 adapt	.854	.766	.807	.800	.877	.837	.826	.823	.823
RF VGG16 frozen (top)	.945	.923	.933	.930	.949	.939	.936	.936	.936
RF VGG16 frozen (all)	.943	.925	.934	.931	.949	**.940**	**.937**	**.937**	**.937**
RF VGG16 adapt (top)	.938	.913	.925	.921	.943	.932	.929	.929	.929
RF VGG16 adapt (all)	.931	.918	.925	.924	.937	.930	.928	.928	.928
RF ResNet50 frozen (top)	.938	.922	.930	.928	.943	.937	.933	.933	.933
RF ResNet50 frozen (all)	.937	.926	**.937**	.931	.942	.937	.934	.934	.934
RF ResNet50 adapt (top)	.930	.916	.923	.923	.936	.929	.926	.926	.926
RF ResNet50 adapt (all)	.927	.920	.923	.925	.932	.929	.926	.926	.926
MLP Joint VGG16 frozen (top)	.911	.927	.919	.931	.915	.923	.921	.921	.921
MLP Joint VGG16 frozen (all)	.922	.891	.906	.901	.929	.915	.911	.911	.911
MLP Joint VGG16 adapt (top)	.875	**.935**	.904	**.935**	.875	.904	.906	.904	.904
MLP Joint VGG16 adapt (all)	.907	.912	.909	.917	.912	.915	.912	.912	.912
MLP Joint ResNet50 frozen (top)	.914	.900	.907	.908	.921	.914	.911	.911	.911
MLP Joint ResNet50 frozen (all)	.910	.931	.920	.934	.914	.924	.922	.922	.922
MLP Joint ResNet50 adapt (top)	**.949**	.509	.663	.680	**.974**	.801	.810	.749	.734
MLP Joint ResNet50 adapt (all)	.918	.595	.722	.715	.951	.816	.813	.779	.771

(a) Nested table   (b) Form   (c) Table without lines

Fig. 3. Examples for misclassified tables

5   Conclusion and Outlook

In this paper, we have introduced a visual classification approach for distinguishing tables on the Web, in particular, genuine and layout tables. The results show that the purely visual approach yields results which are of the same quality as the current state of the art, which is based on extracting explicit features from the HTML code. We conclude that purely visual approaches are a suitable alternative to the state of the art, since they are also more versatile, as they can handle information defined in style sheets, dynamically built Web pages, etc.

An in-depth inspection of the results has revealed that the mistakes made by the approach based on HTML features and the visual approaches are different. This raises the assumption that joint approaches could yield even better results, however, our results so far did not show a significant improvement. Moreover, using other pre-trained image models more tailored to the task, like *TableNet* [19], might improve the results.

So far, we have only considered one task, i.e., the distinction of layout and genuine tables. While the approach could be transferred to other tasks, such as a finer-grained distinction of different table types [5,7], experimental results are still outstanding.

Web table classification is not the only task in Web information extraction where visual signals can be exploited. In the future, we plan to evaluate whether visual approaches can also be used for detecting certain content elements on a Web page which have a common visual appeal, such as addresses or opening hours. Since such elements are often marked up with Microdata or Microformat annotations, training data for such approaches could easily be sourced [18]. Here, visual approaches could also help in building information extraction systems which work on HTML data.

Another interesting field is the classification of entire Web pages. Since we assume that news pages, e-commerce pages, discussion pages etc. can also be identified based on certain visual signals, visual approaches could also be of interest here. Current works is usually based on images on the Web page, but not rendered images of HTML content [10].

Acknowledgements. We would like to thank Julius Gonsior and Maik Thiele at TU Dresden for their assistance in accessing the DWTC dataset and classifier for the experiments.

References

1. Cafarella, M.J., Wu, E.: Uncovering the relational web. In: 11th International Workshop on the Web and Databases (2008)
2. Chen, H.H., Tsai, S.C., Tsai, J.H.: Mining tables from large scale HTML texts. In: 18th Conference on Computational linguistics (COLING 2000), pp. 166–172 (2000)
3. Cohen, W.W., Hurst, M., Jensen, L.S.: A flexible learning system for wrapping tables and lists in HTML documents. In: 11th International Conference on World Wide Web, pp. 232–241 (2002)

4. Crestan, E., Pantel, P.: A fine-grained taxonomy of tables on the web. In: International Conference on Information and Knowledge Management, pp. 1405–1408 (2010)
5. Crestan, E., Pantel, P.: Web-scale table census and classification. In: 4th ACM International Conference on Web Search and Data Mining (WSDM), pp. 545–554 (2011)
6. Dietterich, T.G.: Approximate statistical tests for comparing supervised classification learning algorithms. Neural Comput. 10(7), 1895–1923 (1998)
7. Eberius, J., Braunschweig, K., Hentsch, M., Thiele, M., Ahmadov, A., Lehner, W.: Building the dresden web table corpus: a classification approach. In: 2nd International Symposium on Big Data Computing (BDC), pp. 41–50 (2015)
8. Everitt, B.S.: The Analysis of Contingency Tables. Chapman and Hall, London (1977). ISBN: 9781489929273
9. Gatterbauer, W., Bohunsky, P., Herzog, M., Krüpl, B., Pollak, B.: Towards domain-independent information extraction from web tables. In: 16th International Conference on World Wide Web, p. 71 (2007)
10. Hashemi, M.: Web page classification: a survey of perspectives, gaps, and future directions. Multimedia Tools Appl. 79, 1–25 (2020)
11. He, K., Zhang, X., Ren, S., Sun, J.: Deep Residual Learning for Image Recognition. arXiv:1512.03385 [cs] (2015)
12. Jarrett, K., Kavukcuoglu, K., Ranzato, M., LeCun, Y.: What is the best multi-stage architecture for object recognition? In: 12th International Conference on Computer Vision, pp. 2146–2153 (2009)
13. Khan, A., Sohail, A., Zahoora, U., Qureshi, A.S.: A survey of the recent architectures of deep convolutional neural networks. Artif. Intell. Rev 53(8), 5455–5516 (2020). https://doi.org/10.1007/s10462-020-09825-6
14. Kim, J., Hwang, H.: A rule-based method for table detection in website images. IEEE Access 8, 81022–81033 (2020)
15. LeCun, Y., Kavukcuoglu, K., Farabet, C.: Convolutional networks and applications in vision. In: International Symposium on Circuits and Systems, pp. 253–256 (2010)
16. Lehmberg, O.: Web table integration and profiling for knowledge base augmentation. Dissertation, University of Mannheim, Mannheim (2019)
17. Lehmberg, O., Ritze, D., Ristoski, P., Meusel, R., Paulheim, H., Bizer, C.: The Mannheim search join engine. J. Web Semant. 35, 159–166 (2015)
18. Meusel, R., Petrovski, P., Bizer, C.: The webdatacommons microdata, RDFa and microformat dataset series. In: Mika, P., et al. (eds.) ISWC 2014. LNCS, vol. 8796, pp. 277–292. Springer, Cham (2014). https://doi.org/10.1007/978-3-319-11964-9_18
19. Paliwal, S.S., Vishwanath, D., Rahul, R., Sharma, M., Vig, L.: Tablenet: deep learning model for end-to-end table detection and tabular data extraction from scanned document images. In: International Conference on Document Analysis and Recognition (ICDAR), pp. 128–133 (2019)
20. Pan, S.J., Yang, Q.: A survey on transfer learning. IEEE Trans. Knowl. Data Eng. 22(10), 1345–1359 (2009)
21. Penn, G., Hu, J., Luo, H., McDonald, R.: Flexible Web document analysis for delivery to narrow-bandwidth devices. In: 6th International Conference on Document Analysis and Recognition, pp. 1074–1078 (2001)
22. Simonyan, K., Zisserman, A.: Very deep convolutional networks for large-scale image recognition. arXiv:1409.1556 [cs] (2015)
23. Son, J.W., Park, S.B.: Web table discrimination with composition of rich structural and content information. Appl. Soft Comput. 13(1), 47–57 (2013)

24. Wang, Y., Hu, J.: A machine learning based approach for table detection on the web. In: 11th International Conference on World Wide Web, pp. 242–250 (2002)
25. Yakout, M., Ganjam, K., Chakrabarti, K., Chaudhuri, S.: InfoGather: entity augmentation and attribute discovery by holistic matching with web tables. In: ACM SIGMOD International Conference on Management of Data, pp. 97–108 (2012)
26. Yin, X., Tan, W., Liu, C.: FACTO: a fact lookup engine based on web tables. In: 20th International Conference on World wide web, pp. 507–516 (2011)
27. Zheng, L., Zhao, Y., Wang, S., Wang, J., Tian, Q.: Good Practice in CNN Feature Transfer. arXiv:1604.00133 [cs] (2016)

Automated Essay Scoring
via Example-Based Learning

Yupin Yang⑩ and Jiang Zhong(✉)

Chongqing University, Chongqing 400044, China
{yyp,zhongjiang}@cqu.edu.cn

Abstract. Automated essay scoring (AES) is the task of assigning grades to essays. It can be applied for quality assessment as well as pricing on User Generated Content. Previous works mainly consider using the prompt information for scoring. However, some prompts are highly abstract, making it hard to score the essay only based on the relevance between the essay and the prompt. To solve the problem, we design an auxiliary task, where a dynamic semantic matching block is introduced to capture the hidden features with example-based learning. Besides, we provide a hierarchical model that can extract semantic features at both sentence-level and document-level. The weighted combination of the scores is obtained from the features above to get holistic scoring. Experimental results show that our model achieves higher Quadratic Weighted Kappa (QWK) scores on five of the eight prompts compared with previous methods on the ASAP dataset, which demonstrate the effectiveness of our model.

Keywords: Automated essay scoring · Natural language processing · Example-based learning

1 Introduction

Automated essay scoring (AES) is the task of employing computer programs to assign grades to essays based on their content, grammar, and structure. It has become an important educational application of natural language processing (NLP). For example, Educational Testing Service (ETS) uses AES systems to evaluate the writing ability of students. Such systems can also be applied for quality assessment as well as pricing on User Generated Content. Typically, AES systems regard the task as a regression problem based on handcrafted features (e.g., length-based features and lexical features) and most of them have achieved good results [1,10,16]. However, such systems require feature engineering, which costs lots of time and effort. Therefore, a large number of researchers focus on neural networks that are capable of modeling complex patterns without human assistance [3,6,11,14].

Previous works mainly focus on the text itself [6,13,14], ignoring to investigate the topic information of the essays with prompts. Prompts indicate the requirements and topics for students' writing. As is observed, essays off the prompt always receive low scores while high score essays are relevant to the prompt. Chen and Li [2] extracted the similarity of the essay with the topic on document-level for scoring and achieved good performance. But only using document-level features for scoring may lose some information in detail. To learn how each part of the essay sticks to the prompt more accurately, Zhang and Litman [17] proposed the Co-Attention Based Neural Network to model the similarity of essays at sentence level. However, some prompts are highly abstract, making it hard to score the essay only based on the similarity between the essay and the prompt. Thus, we introduce the example-based learning as auxiliary task to capture the hidden features.

Our main contributions are as follows:

- We design a dynamic semantic matching block to capture the hidden features with example-based learning, which is an auxiliary task for AES.
- We provide a hierarchical model that can extract semantic features at both sentence-level and document-level, which are useful for evaluating coherence and relevance in the essays.
- Experimental results show that our model achieves higher Quadratic Weighted Kappa (QWK) scores on five of the eight prompts compared with previous methods on the ASAP dataset.

2   Related Work

Automated Essay Scoring (AES) systems have been deployed for assigning grades to essays since decades ago. The first AES system created in 1996 is Project Essay Grade which uses linguistic surface features [12]. Recent works mainly use neural networks for automated essay scoring. Dong and Zhang [5] employed a two-layer CNN model to learn sentence representations and essay representations. Differently, Taghipour and Ng [14] used LSTM in their model which effectively learned features for scoring. However, these works only focus on the essay itself, despite the relatedness of the essay to the topic.

High score essays always keep to the prompt closely. Some researchers consider the relevance of the essay to the given prompt for scoring since an essay cannot get a high score if it is not relevant to the prompt. There are many ways to compute the relevance of an essay to the prompt. Higgins et al. [8] extracted sentence features based on semantic similarity measures and the discourse structure, to capture breakdowns in coherence. Chen et al. [2] proposed hierarchical neural networks and used the similarity between the essay and topic as auxiliary information for scoring. All of them take prompt relevance into account as it is an important part of the guidelines. However, it is hard to do semantic matching with the prompt because the prompt is composed of abstract and general sentences. In our approach, we generate relevance features by performing semantic matching with the high score essays. The relevance features are used as auxiliary features for prediction.

3   Model

In this section, we describe the proposed hierarchical structured model named AES-SE, which contains three parts: 1) coherence modeling block, 2) relevance modeling block, 3) dynamic semantic matching block (Fig. 1).

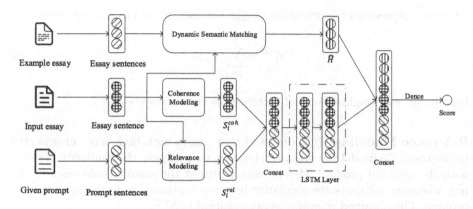

Fig. 1. An overview of our model. There are three parts: coherence modeling block, relevance modeling block and dynamic semantic matching block. All the extracted features are concatenated and sent to a dense layer for the final score.

3.1   Coherence and Relevance Modeling

For semantic coherence within a document and the relevance to the prompt, we apply the coherence modeling block and the relevance modeling block. It is not enough only considering features within cliques [7,9]. Instead, we use the self-attention mechanism to capture semantic changes within the whole document.

Sentence Representation. To capture lexical-semantic relations among words, we use pre-trained BERT [4] to get the sentence representation S_i.

$$S_i = BERT(W_e) \tag{1}$$

where W_e are the words of each sentence in the essay.

Coherence Modeling. To extract the coherence feature of the essay, we use self-attention mechanism to compute the similarity between sentences:

$$score(S_i, S_j) = S_i^{\mathrm{T}} W_a S_j \tag{2}$$

where S_i and S_j are sentences from the essay $\{S_1, S_2, S_3, ..., S_n\}$, W_a is the weight matrix to be learnt and the score function $score(S_i, S_j)$ tells how much similar the two sentences are.

$$\alpha_{ij} = \frac{exp(score(S_i, S_j))}{\sum_{k=1}^{n} exp(score(S_i, S_k))} \tag{3}$$

where α_{ij} represents the attention weight between S_i and other sentences.

$$S_i^{coh} = \sum_{j=1}^{n} \alpha_{ij} S_j \tag{4}$$

Finally, we use weighted sum of sentences as the coherence S_i^{coh}.

Relevance Modeling. It is observed that essays with high score always stick to the topic. To model the prompt relevance, we compute the similarity of essays with the assigned prompt. This process is almost the same as coherence modeling, where we compute the similarity between sentences from the essay and its prompt. The obtained relevance representation is S_i^{rel}.

3.2   Example-Based Learning

There are some consistent features that high-scoring essays usually have. Therefore, we design a dynamic semantic matching block to capture the hidden feature from high score essays as auxiliary information for holistic scoring.

Example Selection. To select typical examples, we use the k-means algorithm. We pick out full mark compositions, and use BERT to encode the sentences. Then, we take the averaged sentence vector of each essay as the input of k-means. Finally, we select essays that are closest to the cluster centers as examples.

Dynamic Semantic Matching. According to psychological researches, it is hard for people to pay close attention to too many things at the same time [15]. While understanding a text deeply, our focus may dynamically change to different sentences. With the aim to focus on the significant sentences with the consideration of learned information at each step, the dynamic semantic matching block is designed. To get the document representation of the essay. We utilize attention mechanism to integrate the sentences:

$$T_i = V_c tanh(W_c S_i + b) \tag{5}$$

$$\gamma_i = \frac{exp(T_i)}{\sum_{k=1}^{n} exp(T_k)} \tag{6}$$

where γ_i is the attention weight. V_c, W_c, and b are parameters to be trained. The document representation h_e is weighted sum of sentence vector S.

$$h_e = \sum_{i=1}^{n} \gamma_i S_i \tag{7}$$

The same is done on the example essay to get the document representation h_s. The inputs of the dynamic semantic matching block are sentence vectors from input essay $T_e = \{S_1, S_2, S_3, ..., S_n\}$ and the example essay $\{S_1', S_2', S_3', ..., S_m'\}$. For each step, an important sentence will be chosen for current input of an LSTM using attention mechanism. The choosing function $F_c(T_e, \hat{h_{t-1}}, h_s)$ is formulated as follows:

$$Z_i = V_d^T tanh(W_d S_i + U_d \hat{h_{t-1}} + M_d h_s) \tag{8}$$

$$\delta_i = \frac{exp(Z_i)}{\sum_{k=1}^{n} exp(Z_k)} \tag{9}$$

$$\hat{a_t} = \sum_{i=1}^{n} \delta_i S_i \tag{10}$$

where V_d, W_d, U_d and M_d are parameters to be trained. h_s is the document representation of the example essay and $\hat{h_{t-1}}$ is the last step of the LSTM as follows:

$$\hat{h_t} = LSTM(\hat{a_t}, \hat{h_{t-1}}) \tag{11}$$

We can get the last output $\hat{h_e}$ from the LSTM where we compare the essay with the example. To compare the example to the essay, we can also get $\hat{h_s}$. Then, we send them to multi-layer perceptron (MLP) to calculate the relation probability R:

$$R = MLP(\hat{h_e}, \hat{h_s}, \hat{h_e} \odot \hat{h_s}, \hat{h_e} - \hat{h_s}) \tag{12}$$

where $\odot$ means element-wise product. To each of the example essays, we repeat this process and get the averaged features $\hat{H}$:

$$\hat{H} = \frac{1}{q} \sum_{i=1}^{q} R_i \tag{13}$$

where q is the number of the example essays.

3.3   Scoring

After obtaining coherence features S^{coh} and relevance features S^{rel}, for each sentence, we concatenate the features together and send them to a BI-LSTM for modeling the document. After that, all the hidden states are fed into a mean-over-time layer. The function is defined as follows, where n denotes the num of sentences in an essay and h_t is the hidden state of the BI-LSTM at time t.

$$h_t = BI\text{-}LSTM(h_{t-1}, [S_t^{coh}; S_t^{rel}]) \tag{14}$$

$$H = \frac{1}{n} \sum_{t=1}^{n} h_t \tag{15}$$

Finally, we use the sigmoid function to compute the final score.

$$y = \sigma(W_y[H; \hat{H}] + b_y) \tag{16}$$

where W_y and b_y indicate the weight matrix and bias. H is the semantic representation of the essay. $\hat{H}$ is the semantic matching feature.

As for loss function, we use mean squared error (MSE) [6]. MSE is used to compute the average value of squared error between the predicted scores and golden ones, as follows:

$$mse(y, y^*) = \frac{1}{N} \sum_{i=1}^{N} (y_i - y_i^*)^2 \tag{17}$$

where y is the predicted score and y^* is the true value.

4   Experiments

In this section, we introduce the dataset and evaluation metric we use and the experimental results.

4.1   Dataset

We use the ASAP (Automated Student Assessment Prize) dataset[1] as it has been widely used to evaluate the performance of AES systems. There are 12976 essays written by students with 8 prompts of different genres. The students were from Grade 7 to Grade 10 and 2 human graders scored the essays.

4.2   Evaluation Metric

Quadratic Weighted Kappa (QWK) is the official evaluation metric in the ASAP competition, which measures the agreement between ratings assigned by humans and ratings predicted by AES systems. As the ASAP dataset is used in this paper for evaluation, we adapt QWK as our evaluation metric.

4.3   Experimental Results

In this section, we test the performance of AES-SE and the baselines on the ASAP dataset. The results in Table 1 are the QWK scores on the eight prompts from the ASAP dataset, where the best results are bold. The baselines include RNN, GRU, LSTM, CNN, EASE, SKIPFLOW LSTM, and HISK+BOSWE+

---

[1] https://www.kaggle.com/c/asap-aes/data.

Table 1. Comparison with state-of-the-art methods on the ASAP dataset

Models	Prompt1	Prompt2	Prompt3	Prompt4	Prompt5	Prompt6	Prompt7	Prompt8	Average
RNN	0.687	0.633	0.552	0.744	0.744	0.757	0.743	0.553	0.675
GRU	0.616	0.591	0.668	0.787	0.795	0.800	0.752	0.573	0.698
EASE(SVR)	0.781	0.621	0.630	0.749	0.782	0.771	0.727	0.534	0.699
EASE(BLRR)	0.761	0.606	0.621	0.742	0.784	0.775	0.730	0.617	0.705
CNN	0.774	0.662	0.639	0.753	0.748	0.766	0.751	0.626	0.714
LSTM	0.780	0.697	0.683	0.787	0.795	0.767	0.758	0.651	0.740
SKIPFLOW LSTM	0.832	0.684	0.695	0.788	0.815	0.810	0.800	0.697	0.765
HISK+BOSWE and ν-SVR	0.845	**0.729**	0.684	**0.829**	0.833	0.830	0.804	**0.729**	0.785
AES-SE	**0.864**	0.727	**0.717**	0.823	**0.838**	**0.835**	**0.812**	0.694	**0.788**

ν-SVR, which achieved state-of-the-art performance on the ASAP dataset. Compared with HISK+BOSWE+ ν-SVR [3], AES-SE achieves higher QWK scores on five of the eight prompts and the average QWK score of AES-SE is also higher. As shown in Table 1, AES-SE achieves new state-of-the-art performance on five of the eight prompts and the averaged QWK score. On average of the eight prompts, our AES-SE achieves 0.788, which is 0.3% higher than HISK+BOSWE+ ν-SVR [3].

5 Conclusion

In this paper, we conduct a hierarchical structure named AES-SE with an auxiliary task for automated essay scoring. We use BERT to encode sentences capturing lexical-semantic relations among words. We simultaneously consider coherence features and relevance features to evaluate cohesion and task achievement. Moreover, with dynamic semantic matching block, the similarity of an essay with high score essays is computed as auxiliary information for scoring. Finally, we concatenate all the extracted features and compute the final score. Experimental results show that our model outperforms the current state-of-the-art methods with the improvement of the QWK score by 0.3%. In addition, we also achieve a significant 11.7% improvement over feature engineering baselines. For future work, we will explore using domain adaptation in our model.

Acknowledgment. This research was partially supported by the National Key Research and Development Program of China (2017YFB1402400 and 2017YFB1402401), the Key Research Program of Chongqing Science and Technology Bureau (cstc2020jscx-msxmX0149), the Key Research Program of Chongqing Science and Technology Bureau (cstc2019jscx-mbdxX0012), and the Key Research Program of Chongqing Science and Technology Bureau (cstc2019jscx-fxyd0142).

References

1. Attali, Y., Burstein, J.: Automated essay scoring with e-rater® v.2. J. Technol. Learn. Assess. **4**(3) (2006)

2. Chen, M., Li, X.: Relevance-based automated essay scoring via hierarchical recurrent model. In: 2018 International Conference on Asian Language Processing (IALP), pp. 378–383. IEEE (2018)
3. Cozma, M., Butnaru, A.M., Ionescu, R.T.: Automated essay scoring with string kernels and word embeddings. In: ACL, no. 2, pp. 503–509 (2018). https://aclanthology.info/papers/P18-2080/p18-2080
4. Devlin, J., Chang, M.W., Lee, K., Toutanova, K.: BERT: pre-training of deep bidirectional transformers for language understanding. In: Proceedings of the 2019 Conference of the North American Chapter of the Association for Computational Linguistics: Human Language Technologies, vol. 1 (Long and Short Papers), pp. 4171–4186. Association for Computational Linguistics, Minneapolis (2019). https://doi.org/10.18653/v1/N19-1423, https://www.aclweb.org/anthology/N19-1423
5. Dong, F., Zhang, Y.: Automatic features for essay scoring-an empirical study. In: Proceedings of the 2016 Conference on Empirical Methods in Natural Language Processing, pp. 1072–1077 (2016)
6. Dong, F., Zhang, Y., Yang, J.: Attention-based recurrent convolutional neural network for automatic essay scoring. In: Proceedings of the 21st Conference on Computational Natural Language Learning (CoNLL 2017), pp. 153–162 (2017)
7. Farag, Y., Yannakoudakis, H., Briscoe, T.: Neural automated essay scoring and coherence modeling for adversarially crafted input. arXiv preprint arXiv:1804.06898 (2018)
8. Higgins, D., Burstein, J., Marcu, D., Gentile, C.: Evaluating multiple aspects of coherence in student essays. In: Proceedings of the Human Language Technology Conference of the North American Chapter of the Association for Computational Linguistics: HLT-NAACL, vol. 2004, pp. 185–192 (2004)
9. Li, J., Hovy, E.: A model of coherence based on distributed sentence representation. In: Proceedings of the 2014 Conference on Empirical Methods in Natural Language Processing (EMNLP), pp. 2039–2048 (2014)
10. Liu, J., Xu, Y., Zhu, Y.: Automated essay scoring based on two-stage learning. arXiv preprint arXiv:1901.07744 (2019)
11. Mesgar, M., Strube, M.: A neural local coherence model for text quality assessment. In: Proceedings of the 2018 Conference on Empirical Methods in Natural Language Processing, pp. 4328–4339 (2018)
12. Page, E.B.: The use of the computer in analyzing student essays. Int. Rev. Educ. **14**, 210–225 (1968)
13. Süzen, N., Gorban, A.N., Levesley, J., Mirkes, E.M.: Automatic short answer grading and feedback using text mining methods. Procedia Comput. Sci. **169**, 726–743 (2020)
14. Taghipour, K., Ng, H.T.: A neural approach to automated essay scoring. In: Proceedings of the 2016 Conference on Empirical Methods in Natural Language Processing, pp. 1882–1891 (2016)
15. Wang, J., Chen, H.C., Radach, R., Inhoff, A.: Reading Chinese Script: A Cognitive Analysis. Psychology Press, London (1999)
16. Zesch, T., Wojatzki, M., Scholten-Akoun, D.: Task-independent features for automated essay grading. In: Proceedings of the Tenth Workshop on Innovative Use of NLP for Building Educational Applications, pp. 224–232 (2015)
17. Zhang, H., Litman, D.: Co-attention based neural network for source-dependent essay scoring. arXiv preprint arXiv:1908.01993 (2019)

Conversation and Recommendation: Knowledge-Enhanced Personalized Dialog System

Ming He[1(✉)], Tong Shen[1], and Ruihai Dong[2]

[1] Beijing University of Technology, Beijing 100124, China
heming@bjut.edu.cn
[2] University College Dublin, Dublin, Ireland
ruihai.dong@insight-centre.org

Abstract. Traditional recommender systems are usually single-shot systems, lacking real-time dialog with customers. Using dialog as an interactive method can more accurately capture user preferences and enhance system transparency. However, building such a goal-oriented dialog system suffered many challenges as the system itself needs to collaborate with various sub-tasks, such as collecting user needs through interaction, recommending appropriate products to users. Most existing work of dialog systems does not comprehensively consider this scenario and the challenges caused. In this paper, we propose a novel memory network framework for conversational recommendation, which harness dialog historical information to endows our model with adaptability in different dialog scenarios, and leverage the knowledge base and user profiles to reweight candidates, to reduce the ambiguity during interactions and improve the quality of conversational recommender systems. Through the experiments on the personalized bAbI dialog dataset and restaurant recommendation application, we demonstrate that the proposed method can achieve state-of-the-art performance in a few classical tasks, such as options display and information provision, etc.

Keywords: Recommender systems · Dialog systems · Memory network · Knowledge base

1 Introduction

Recommender systems [8,30] integrate query and recommendation techniques with dialog systems, which enable users to ask questions about the recommendations and to provide feedback. Due to its potential in fields such as e-commerce websites, the interest in conversational recommender systems has significantly increased in the past few years. However, they also pose challenges to researchers from different perspectives, Fig. 1 illustrates these challenges described below with an example.

© Springer Nature Switzerland AG 2021
M. Brambilla et al. (Eds.): ICWE 2021, LNCS 12706, pp. 209–224, 2021.
https://doi.org/10.1007/978-3-030-74296-6_17

Fig. 1. Illustration of a conversational recommender system for restaurant reservation. (Color figure online)

First, current end-to-end models usually do not consider a situation in which the dialogue scenario can be divided into interaction or recommendation at each turn in conversation. For instance, as shown in Fig. 1, when a user requests a restaurant reservation, after interacting with the user and according to the user's "Dietary" and "Favorite", an Italian restaurant is recommended by our personalized model. This suggests, conversational recommendation usually includes interaction turns (blue box in Fig. 1) and recommendation turns (green box in Fig. 1). Interaction turns gather information from users and predict responses, while recommendation turns apply to rank the candidates. Therefore, the system is necessary to take the strategy correctly at each turn. In this way, it can more precisely capture user preference and will help to improve recommendation performance in the long run.

Second, the ambiguities in user requests are difficult to handle. For example, when a user Daniel requests for "direction" to the restaurant, this word can be interpreted into "parking" or "public transport" directions information in the knowledge base. Instead of selecting one randomly, the system handles this ambiguity based on the learned fact that driving is suitable for high priced restaurants while public transportation is more suitable for a lower price.

The third major issue of current recommendation methods is usually limited to the performance due to the irrelevant information in conversation. As an example, when a user Daniel sends a restaurant request to the system, the recommendation model will identify his intentions from the recommendation request that contains two keywords: "reservation" and "four people". Also, when Daniel queries some information about the restaurant, the "Restaurant" is also a keyword of dialog history. However, if the model pays more attention to irrelevant information in conversation might lead to poor conversational performance. Hence, it is necessary to apply a more effective way to extract keywords from user utterances during the conversation.

Considering the above challenges in the conversational recommendation and inspired by the wide success of leverage knowledge base, in this paper, we propose an innovative knowledge base (KB) enhanced model based on the end-to-end memory network (MEMN2N) framework named KB-enhanced MEMN2N. First, we employ a fully connected layer to learn the dialog state, which is able to help take an appropriate dialog strategy at each turn given the current user query and dialog history. Second, we capture user preferences over the knowledge base to solve the problem of ambiguity in user requests. Third, to avoid unrelated information extraction in dialog, we apply multi-head attention mechanism to perform keywords extraction automatically, which can provide more relevant information.

Experiments on personalized bAbI dialog dataset verified the effectiveness of our approach. In particular, our model shows significantly better performance compared with baselines for making restaurant recommendations and handling ambiguity in user requests by leveraging the knowledge base.

The key contributions of this paper are summarized as the following:

- To help improve recommendation accuracy, we consider the cases where the interaction turns and the recommendation turns in conversation for taking strategy correctly, we also propose a method to calculate user preference scores for recommendation ranking based on the knowledge base.
- We design an information inference method to handle ambiguities in user requests by modeling user preferences over the knowledge base. Unlike previous studies, this method takes advantage of both user profile and item attributes, which can better capture user preferences.
- We apply multi-head attention mechanism to conduct efficient keywords extraction from user queries, and the learned query representations can alleviate the irrelevant information in user utterances and dialog history.
- Based on the personalized bAbI dialog dataset, we have conducted extensive experiments to evaluate the effectiveness of our framework. The results reveal that our approaches significantly outperformed the baseline methods on two commendation tasks including option display and information provision.

2   Related Work

In the past few years, there is a trend to develop fully data-driven dialog systems by using deep neural networks, which directly map user input to agent output [7]. According to the purpose, the dialog system is expected to solve these kinds of problems: (1) question answering [7] and (2) task completion [14] and (3) social chat [2,12], and the first two categories can be framed as task-oriented system [25].

2.1   Task-Oriented System

Most of the existing works adopt the pipeline or end-to-end method. The typical structure of a pipeline dialog system contains natural language understanding

(NLU), dialog state tracker (DST), dialog policy learning (DPL), and natural language generation (NLG) four parts [18]. [3] proposes a conversational product search model based on negative user feedback. [11] proposes a new conversational recommender system framework that consists of three stages to better converse with users. But these pipeline models usually require some fixed slots and a rather complicated processing pipeline of many stages. [31] first presents an end-to-end reinforcement learning model to optimize the system actions more robustly, but the user can only do the binary answer of yes/no. [10] introduces an open dataset and applies memory network to the field of dialog systems, which shows that an end-to-end dialog system can reach a promising performance, and there are many subsequent dialog systems based on memory networks [6,15,21, 21]. *The major difference between these methods and ours is that KB-enhanced MEMN2N focuses on the personalization of a goal-oriented conversation and models user preferences over knowledge base by leveraging both user profile and item attributes.*

2.2 Personalization in Dialog

Research on personalization in the field of dialog systems has not been short. Considerable works have been done on chatbot [19,23,26,27] and many other task-oriented dialog systems, such as personal assistant systems [20,28,29], they both achieve remarkable performance on personalization. [1] proposes a multi-task learning method for integrating user characteristics into the conversation model through user-related data, which reflects the problem of too much lack of personalized conversation data in the current research. [10] presents a new dataset of goal-oriented dialogs and modified the architecture of the memory network, which makes task-oriented dialog systems that can be explored in terms of personalization. [16] modifies the memory network architecture and adds multiple modules to better mine the personalized information and combine it with the knowledge base. One of the major factors affecting personalized end-to-end models is the lack of consideration of dialog state when predicting response. *To the best of our knowledge, this paper is the first end-to-end model that decides which dialog strategy is appropriate to take given the current dialog state in conversational recommendation.*

3 Preliminaries

In this section, we give some preliminary knowledge about leveraging structural information in a knowledge base to improve the quality of conversational recommendation.

The knowledge base provides the details of the items. As shown in Table 1, each row denotes an item and each column denotes one of their corresponding attributes. However, a knowledge base typically only available in a closed domain, and the relationships among the items suffer from sparsity (i.e., limited relationships among items). Therefore, it's difficult to learn a low-dimensional

Table 1. Example of knowledge base facts.

Restaurant	Price	Location	Speciality	Phone
Restaurant1	Cheap	Madrid	Pizza	Phone_No1
Restaurant2	Moderate	Madrid	Pasta	Phone_No2
Restaurant3	Expensive	Madrid	Pie	Phone_No3
...	...	...	...	...

representation vector for each item and relation by representation learning [13,24]. To address this issue, existing methods often store the knowledge base triple (i.e., $subject - relation - object$) as a word sequence in the memory. However, since the information is far less structured, it is harder to retrieve relationships directly from word sequences than knowledge base triples. For example, it is not easy for memory networks to learn the relation between **McDonald** and **Cheeseburger** directly with a word sequence "McDonald speciality Cheeseburger". To effectively integrate recommendation with the knowledge base, we take inspiration from the work of [5,9,17], which found that key-value structural information can effectively utilize external knowledge. In KB-enhanced MEMN2N, we only retain the item and value of a knowledge base triple and combine them into a key-value pair. Then, we can switch the n attributes of an item into $\{(k^j, v_1^j), \ldots, (k^j, v_n^j)\}$, where all the k^j denote the same item and each v_i^j denotes one of the attributes.

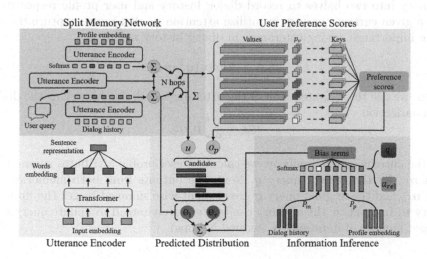

Fig. 2. The framework of KB-enhanced MEMN2N.

4   Methodology

Figure 2 illustrates the framework of the proposed model. Our model is built upon split memory network, and we develop two key components: **User Preference Scores Method** and **Information Inference Method**, which will be detailed the process in the following subsections.

4.1   Utterance and Profile Encoder

At any given time step t, the model takes the dialog history $\mathcal{X} = \{x_1, \ldots, x_{t-1}\}$ and the n attributes of user profile $\mathcal{A} = \{a_1, \ldots, a_n\}$ and the current step user query x_t as input. Each utterance or user profile attribute can be seen as a sequence of words $(w_1, w_2, \ldots, w_T)$. We map each word to its d-dimensional vector representation (initialized randomly and trained with back-propagation) and then we employ a transformer encoder [22] to model the dependencies of words in a sequence. Next, the words embedding are summed to get the sentence representation. Later, we will use this encoder to encode item attributes and the candidates.

4.2   Split Memory Network

Memory Network [4] can store historical dialogs and short-term context to predict the reasonable response by writing and then iteratively reading from a memory component. We extend the work from Joshi et al. [10] to divide the memory into two halves to record dialog history and user profile respectively. For a given current query q, we utilize attention mechanism to capture the relative importance among utterances in dialog history m:

$$p_i = \text{Softmax}\left(q^T m_i\right) \tag{1}$$

Then, we use the weighted sum of the utterances in dialog history as the dialog summarization

$$m_h = \sum_i p_i m_i \tag{2}$$

for the current query. Similarly, we calculate user profile attributes summarization m_p for the current query q. Next, the outputs from both memories m_h and m_p and the original query q are element-wise summed to get the updated query u. In practice, the memory can be iteratively reread to update query with a fixed number of iterations N (termed N hops).

4.3   Conversation or Recommendation?

If the system can take favorable strategy in corresponding dialog scenario, such as recommendation or interaction, it can reduce the candidate space greatly. Based on this assumption, we harness the dialog state to generate the probability of subsequent actions by applying a fully connected layer to learn the query q and dialog summarization m_h followed by a **Softmax** layer:

$$[\theta_i; \theta_r] = \text{Softmax}(W_\theta[q; m_h] + b_\theta) \tag{3}$$

where the concatenation of current query and the dialog summarization are interpreted as the dialog state. Then, θ_i denotes the probability of interaction, and θ_r denotes the probability of recommendations. We use θ_i and θ_r to weight interaction candidates and recommendation candidates respectively later.

4.4 User Preference Scores Method

In this subsection, we calculate user preference scores for recommendation candidates based on user profile and item knowledge base. As mentioned in Sect. 3, we integrate recommendation with the knowledge base by switching the n attributes of an item into a set of attributes $\{v_1^j, \dots, v_n^j\}$ and letting $k^j \in \mathbb{R}^{1 \times d}$ denotes the item. And then, we get the vector representations of the item and each of its attributes via the utterance encoder. To model the user preference over the items, we take a sum of the inner product of user profile m_p and each attribute i of the item j followed by a **Relu** activation as the match scores:

$$o_v^j = \text{Relu}\left(\sum_i^n m_p^T v_i^j\right) \tag{4}$$

Assume that there are totally J items in the knowledge base facts, we can obtain a set of match scores $\{o_v^1, \dots, o_v^J\}$. Next, we use the scores to calculate the probabilities $\{p_v^1, \dots, p_v^J\}$ of the items via a **Softmax** layer. Then, the user preference over the items can be aggregated by the probabilities as follows:

$$o_p = \sum_j^J p_v^j k^j \tag{5}$$

Subsequently, we get the candidates (all bot utterances in the dataset) vector representation $r \in \mathbb{R}^{w \times d}$ via the utterance encoder, where w is the number of the candidates. Note that the candidates that mention at least one item are used as recommendation candidates, and the others are used as interaction candidates. Thus, all candidates can be divided into interaction set r_i and recommendation set r_r. To obtain the two different sets, we create two duplicates for each candidate, and pad the unrelated candidates with zero according to different scenarios.

For recommendation, we combine the user profile m_p and the preference o_p to model the comprehensive user preference by calculating the inner product between the user preference and the recommendation set followed by a **Relu** activation:

$$s_r = \text{Relu}\left((m_p + o_p)^T r_r\right) \tag{6}$$

And then, we consider the dialog historical information and user profile for bot utterance prediction (i.e., interaction). The result can be calculated by taking the inner product between the updated query u and interaction set r_i:

$$s_i = u^\top r_i \tag{7}$$

In this way, s_i can pay attention to specific utterance and s_r captures better user preference. Next, the two parameters θ_i and θ_r can learn to implicitly track dialog state (never given explicitly) and control the cooperation of the above two scores.

Finally, the predicted response distribution is calculated as:

$$\hat{r} = \mathrm{Softmax}\left(s_i * \theta_i + s_r * \theta_r\right) \tag{8}$$

4.5   Information Inference Method

As we mentioned in Sect. 1, there may have more than one attributes are available when the users ask for specific information of an item. In this subsection, we investigate how to solve the ambiguity in the user requests. Since the user preference have decisive influence on the prediction, the user profile is applied to model the user preference on totally l different attributes as:

$$v_p = \mathrm{Relu}(m_p P_p) \tag{9}$$

where $P_p \in \mathbb{R}^{d \times l}$ is a parameter matrix.

It differs from Luo et al. [16] that does only use user preference, our method considers both user preference and the attributes of the item. Since the selected item is a choice made by the user during the dialog, we obtain tendency weights of each attribute by learning the dialog history:

$$v_h = \mathrm{Relu}(m_h P_h) \tag{10}$$

where $P_h \in \mathbb{R}^{d \times l}$ is a parameter matrix. Subsequently, we model a comprehensive preference by combining v_p and v_h. To pick out the relevant attribute for current query, we estimate the relevance between the attribute (phone, parking information, etc.) $a_{rel} \in \mathbb{R}^{l \times d}$ and query as:

$$\alpha_r = \mathrm{Softmax}(q^\top a_{rel}) \tag{11}$$

Therefore, we can intelligently select the most relevant attribute of the current query and obtain the comprehensive preference over the attributes by a dot product as:

$$v = \alpha_r \cdot (v_p + v_m) \tag{12}$$

As a result, v learns the user preference and the influence of the selected item. Next, we use these preference values as the bias term for the candidates. To establish the connection between the attributes and their corresponding values, we set up a feedback matrix to record the attributes that appear in each candidate. The matrix $\lambda \in \mathbb{R}^{w \times l}$ is constructed as the following rules. If the w-th candidate mentions a value a_n, which belongs to attribute n, then the corresponding element $\lambda_{w,n}=1$, otherwise the element is 0,

$$\lambda(w,n) = \begin{cases} 1, \text{ if entity } a_{m,n} \text{ is mentioned in candidate } w \\ 0, \text{ otherwise} \end{cases} \quad (13)$$

where the value 1 in matrix λ represents the corresponding bias term is valid. Then we obtain the bias term as follows:

$$b = v^\top \lambda \quad (14)$$

Finally, we can update the Eq. 8 to

$$\hat{r} = \text{Softmax}\left(s_i * \theta_i + s_r * \theta_r + b\right) \quad (15)$$

4.6   The Unified Model

With all the methods introduced previously, we can propose our final integrated framework to promote the recommendation performance by generating the user preference scores for the candidates and address the ambiguity by modeling user preference on the item attributes. Intuitively, we train the model by maximizing a standard cross-entropy loss between $\hat{r}$ and the true label r_{true}, and adopt stochastic gradient descent (SGD) for model training. In each turn, the model generates the response by selecting the candidate of the highest probability.

5   Experiments

In this section, we evaluate our proposed framework on the personalized bAbI dialog dataset for three separate tasks in a restaurant reservation scenario. The experimental results demonstrate evidence of significant improvement over many competitive baselines.

5.1   Dataset and Evaluation Metrics

We evaluate our model on the personalized bAbI dialog dataset [10], which is a multi-turn dialog corpus in a restaurant reservation scenario. This dataset builds upon the bAbI dialog dataset [10], it provides the profile information (gender, age, dietary preference, and favorite food item) of the current user before the first turn of dialog. In terms of task definitions, (1) **Displaying Options** gives a user request, and the knowledge base facts will be added to the dialog history. Then the bot must use a reasonable heuristic method based on the user preferences to sort the restaurants in the results. (2) **Providing Information** assumes that the user has selected a restaurant, then the user will ask for various information, the bot must learn to retrieve the correct knowledge base facts, tailored for the user. (3) **Full Dialog** conducts a complete dialog to verify all the above tasks.

The dataset provides two variations for each task: a full dataset with around 6000 dialogs, and a small sample dataset with 1000 dialogs.

Next, we report the accuracy of each response for all models and tasks in Table 2. This accuracy is the percentage of responses in which the correct candidate is chosen out of all possible ones.

M. He et al.

5.2 Baselines

To evaluate the performance of our whole framework, we compare our ultimate model against the following baselines:

- **Memory Network** [4] is a model that takes query and conversation history as input, and the history are appended to the memory, then the memory can be iteratively reread to look for additional pertinent information to update the query, finally outputs the prediction results.
- **Split Memory Network** [10] is a model that divides the memory of the model into two halves: profile attributes and conversation history. Both the two memories operate the same as the MEMN2N, and the outputs from both memories are summed to get the final response.
- **Personalized MEMN2N** [16] is a model based on MEMN2N that learns user personalities with distributed profile representation, and learns user preferences among ambiguous candidates by building a connection between the user profile and the knowledge base, which is a state-of-the-art method in this domain.

5.3 Experimental Setup

For the proposed **KB-enhanced MEMN2N**, we set the learning rate to 0.001, the regularization parameter to 0.001, the dimension of utterances to 20. Models are trained with a batch size of 32, gradients are clipped to avoid gradient explosion with a threshold of 15. For the part of memory network, we set the maximum context memory to 250 and fill it with zeros if the number of utterances in memory is less than 250. The above settings are for fair consideration. Other parameters in the baselines are set as default.

Table 2. Evaluation results of the models on the personalized bAbI dialog dataset.

Models	Displaying options	Providing information	Full dialog
Memory network	58.94(58.71)	57.17(57.17)	85.10(77.74)
Split memory network	68.60(68.56)	57.17(57.11)	87.28(78.10)
Personalized MEMN2N	71.43(71.52)	81.56(80.79)	95.33(88.07)
KB-enhanced MEMN2N	**74.70(74.73)**	**90.27(89.63)**	**96.43(90.14)**

5.4 Results

For the evaluation of response prediction, we compare each predicted response with the true label and calculate the correct percentage. The results of all models are presented in Table 2. In each cell, the first number represents the accuracy on the full set, and the number in parentheses represents the accuracy on a smaller set with 1000 dialogs. From which we have the following observations:

Table 3. Example of conversation.

Time	Locutor	Dialog history	Hop1	Hop2
1	User	good morning	0	0
2	Bot	greetings sir what may i assist you with today	0.65	0.37
3	User	can you book table for four in paris with italian cuisine	0.29	0.02
4	Bot	excellent sir i will start request now	0	0.51
5	User	SILENCE	0	0
6*	Bot	may i know your prefered price range	0	0
6	Bot	is this one cool:resto_rome_expensive_indian_8stars_2	0	0
7	User	in expensive price range please	0	0
8	Bot	excellent sir please give me moment	0.06	0.10
9	User	SILENCE	0	0
10	Bot	may i suggest this: resto_paris_expensive_italian_8stars_1	0	0

Time 6* is the correct answer and Time 6 is a wrong prediction.

- Since we consider the cases where the interaction turns and the recommendation turns in conversation, the user preference scores method based on the knowledge base can determine an appropriate timing to push recommendations according to the dialog state, and the user preference scores also can contribute to the recommendation so that KB-enhanced MEMN2N performs best on **Displaying Options**.
- As argued in [10], memory networks cannot effectively use knowledge base facts in the dialog. Personalized MEMN2N and our model predict the user preference according to the knowledge base, and achieve superior performance on **Providing Information**. Since we further consider the attributes of the restaurant mentioned in the dialog and balance the relative importance of multiple attributes, our performance is even better.
- **Full Dialog** comprehensively tests all of the previous tasks. Since our model has significantly improved on **Displaying Options** and **Providing Information**, it also leads to better performance on **Full Dialog**.

5.5 Analysis of User Preference Method

We briefly report the performance of the user preference scores method in this subsection. To show all the situations that may happen, we implement a variant of our model which divides all the candidates into two sets r_i and r_r as mentioned in Sect. 4.4, and do not add the user preference scores. Besides, we present a visualization of the predictions, and highlight the attention weights for the memory at 10-th turn over two iterations (called hops). As shown in the right two columns of Table 3, the model attends primarily to the utterance from the bot. It is possible that the model tends to focus on the existing bot utterance to maintain a consistent speech style, but this will lead to a lack of attention to the user intention. Furthermore, we can see that the bot makes a correct prediction at 10-th turn since the model take the strategy to recommend a restaurant that match the user preferences. But the bot mistakenly recommends a restaurant for the user at 6-th turn, since the model pays more attention to the candidate restaurants.

To validate our thoughts, we perform extensive ablation studies on **User Preference Scores Method (UPSM)**. Table 4 reports the accuracy on **Displaying Options** and the contribution of recommendation turns to the overall accuracy. We implement three simplified variants of the proposed method:

- UPSM-1, which does not divide the candidates.
- UPSM-2, which only apply s_i and divides the candidates.
- UPSM-3, which removes the weight coefficients θ_i and θ_r.

The results in Table 4 suggest that our approach indeed improves the recommendation accuracy by capturing user preferences through the knowledge base and narrowing down candidates for different dialog scenario, but putting too much focus on recommendation may weaken the performance of the interaction turns. So, this highlights the importance of our method that the weight coefficients θ_i and θ_r is needed to learn the dialog state and balance the importance of the two scores. We attribute the superiority of UPSM to its two properties: 1) UPSM learns dialog state to consider a strategy decision, which can determine an appropriate timing to push recommendation; 2) UPSM leverages the knowledge base to apply user preference scores, which better matches users preference and attributes of restaurants. Therefore, we improve the overall quality of the responses of conversational recommendation by promoting the accuracy of the recommendation turns.

Table 4. Ablation study of user preference scores method.

Method	Accuracy	Rec. contribution
UPSM-1	71.20	0
UPSM-2	66.92	4.13
UPSM-3	74.18	2.98

5.6   Analysis of Ambiguity

In this subsection, we investigate the performance of our information inference method. Specifically, we further consider the mutual influences among the restaurant attributes, which is different from the previous method [16] that only leverages user profile.

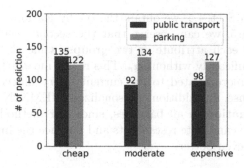

Fig. 3. Price range impact on restaurant directions information system flow diagram.

As we mentioned in Sect. 1, the probability of choosing "parking" or "public transport" should be affected by the price range of the recommended restaurant. The statistics of the predictions on this instance is depicted in Fig. 3, when the user has selected a restaurant in the moderate or expensive price range, the bot prefers to provide parking information. On the other hand, the bot tends to return the public transport information if the restaurant is cheap. The above results confirm our hypothesis that the existence of the inherent relationships among the attributes and our model does learn the mutual influences among the attributes base on the knowledge base.

Subsequently, we are curious about whether the weight coefficient α_r is helpful to balance the importance of the attributes. Table 5 shows the prediction accuracy of different attributes with and without the weight coefficient α_r. And these attributes can be grouped into two categories:

- *Phone* and *social media* both belong to contact information. The model can predict the responses just by learning the relationship between user profile and restaurant attributes. As expected, the problem is solved perfectly.
- *Parking* and *public transport* both belong to directions information. The model should learn the dialog history to find the selected restaurant and generate tendency weights through certain attributes of the restaurant, which requires a more complex process and the accuracy is relatively low.

Table 5. Accuracy of different types in different cases.

Type	Without α_r	With α_r
Phone	79.75%	100%
Social media	66.79%	100%
Parking	47.05%	54.83%
Public transport	32.62%	47.87%

As mentioned in Sect. 4.5, we obtain the α_r by learning queries and dialog history. From Table 5, we can observe that the second case with α_r achieves higher accuracy on each attribute in two groups, while the accuracy on each attribute drops significantly without α_r. This result means that picking out the attribute which is more related to the current query indeed helps to provide a reasonable response. In addition, personalized MEMN2N performs best on **Providing Information** in all baselines, since our method further considers the attributes of the candidate restaurants and balance the importance of them, our performance is even better.

5.7 Analysis of Information Extraction

To evaluate the contribution of multi-head attention in information extraction, we focus on the probability vector over the memory within the memory network. We use multi-head attention to process the query and the memory separately, and the results are used as input of our model. Then we can obtain the probability over the memory with and without multi-head attention in the memory network, respectively. As shown in Fig. 4, the probability enables us to visualize the weighted importance of memory for queries of each turn. The darker the color of the corresponding grid, the higher attention is paid to the memory. From Fig. 4(a) and Fig. 4(b), we can find that they have roughly the same distribution of the attention scores across the entire memory. Moreover, the attention distribution in Fig. 4(b) is more concentrated, while the attentions are spread evenly over the memory in Fig. 4(a). The difference in the probability over the memory also affects the final predicted results that the model with multi-head attention shows better results in the prediction. This means that the more efficient keywords are extracted from utterances, the more precise responses are predicted.

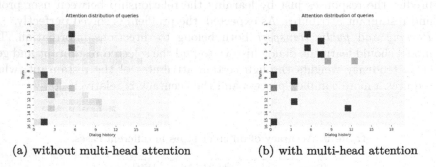

(a) without multi-head attention   (b) with multi-head attention

Fig. 4. Attention distribution over the memory for each query.

6 Conclusion and Future Work

In this work, we propose a KB-enhanced conversational recommendation framework based on the end-to-end memory network. Different from previous methods, our method can effectively take advantage of the knowledge base to extract the structural information. We then consider a strategy decision approach and apply user preference scores method into our framework in order to capture more precise user preferences and improve prediction accuracy. Through extensive experiments on the personalize bAbI dialog dataset, we validate the effectiveness of our framework. In the future, we will consider exploring the effectiveness of involving knowledge graphs and logic rules into our framework.

Acknowledgment. This work is supported by the Beijing Natural Science Foundation under grant 4192008, and the Science Foundation Ireland (SFI) under Grant Number 12/RC/2289_P2.

References

1. Multi-Task Learning for Speaker-Role Adaptation in Neural Conversation Models. In: IJCNLP, pp. 605–614 (2017)
2. Banchs, R., Li, H.: IRIS: a chat-oriented dialogue system based on the vector space model. In: ACL. pp. 37–42 (2012)
3. Bi, K., Ai, Q., Zhang, Y., Bruce Croft, W.: Conversational product search based on negative feedback. In: CIKM, pp. 359–368 (2019)
4. Bordes, A., Lan Boureau, Y., Weston, J.: Learning end-to-end goal-oriented dialog. In: ICLR, pp. 1–15 (2017)
5. Eric, M., Krishnan, L., Charette, F., Manning, C.D.: Key-value retrieval networks for task-oriented dialogue. In: SIGDIAL, pp. 37–49 (2017)
6. Gangi Reddy, R., Contractor, D., Raghu, D., Joshi, S.: Multi-level memory for task oriented dialogs. In: ACL, pp. 3744–3754 (2019)
7. Gao, J., Galley, M., Li, L.: Neural approaches to conversational AI. In: ACL, pp. 2–7 (2018)
8. He, X., Deng, K., Wang, X., Li, Y., Zhang, Y.D., Wang, M.: LightGCN: simplifying and powering graph convolution network for recommendation. In: SIGIR, pp. 639–648 (2020)
9. Huang, J., Zhao, W.X., Dou, H., Wen, J.R., Chang, E.Y.: Improving sequential recommendation with knowledge-enhanced memory networks. In: SIGIR, pp. 505–514 (2018)
10. Joshi, C.K., Mi, F., Faltings, B.: Personalization in goal-oriented dialog. In: NIPS, pp. 2440–2448 (2017)
11. Lei, W., et al.: Estimation-action-reflection: towards deep interaction between conversational and recommender systems. In: WSDM, pp. 304–312 (2020)
12. Li, J., Monroe, W., Ritter, A., Galley, M., Gao, J., Jurafsky, D.: Deep reinforcement learning for dialogue generation. In: EMNLP, pp. 1192–1202 (2016)
13. Lin, Y., Liu, Z., Sun, M., Liu, Y., Zhu, X.: Learning entity and relation embeddings for knowledge graph completion. In: AAAI, pp. 2181–2187 (2015)
14. Lipton, Z., Li, X., Gao, J., Li, L., Ahmed, F., Deng, L.: BBQ-networks: efficient exploration in deep reinforcement learning for task-oriented dialogue systems. In: AAAI, pp. 5237–5244 (2018)
15. Liu, F., Perez, J.: Gated end-to-end memory networks. In: EACL, pp. 1–10 (2017)
16. Luo, L., Huang, W., Zeng, Q., Nie, Z., Sun, X.: Learning personalized end-to-end goal-oriented dialog. In: AAAI, pp. 6794–6801 (2019)

17. Miller, A.H., Fisch, A., Dodge, J., Karimi, A.H., Bordes, A., Weston, J.: Key-value memory networks for directly reading documents. EMNLP **2016**, 1400–1409 (2016)
18. Sarnobat, A., Kalola, D.: A survey on recommender systems. In: IJSRP, p. 9356 (2019)
19. Su, F.G., Hsu, A.R., Tuan, Y.L., Lee, H.Y.: Personalized dialogue response generation learned from monologues. In: INTERSPEECH, pp. 4160–4164 (2019)
20. Sun, Y., Yuan, N.J., Wang, Y., Xie, X., McDonald, K., Zhang, R.: Contextual intent tracking for personal assistants. In: SIGKDD, pp. 273–282 (2016)
21. Tsumita, D., Takagi, T.: Dialogue based recommender system that flexibly mixes utterances and recommendations. In: WI, pp. 51–58 (2019)
22. Vaswani, A., et al.: Attention is all you need. In: NIPS, pp. 5998–6008 (2017)
23. Wang, D., Jojic, N., Brockett, C., Nyberg, E.: Steering output style and topic in neural response generation. In: EMNLP, pp. 2140–2150 (2017)
24. Wang, Z., Zhang, J., Feng, J., Chen, Z.: Knowledge graph embedding by translating on hyperplanes. In: AAAI, pp. 1112–1119 (2014)
25. Wen, T.H., et al.: A network-based end-to-end trainable task-oriented dialogue system. In: EACL, pp. 438–449 (2017)
26. Wu, Y., Wei, F., Huang, S., Wang, Y., Li, Z., Zhou, M.: Response generation by context-aware prototype editing. In: AAAI, pp. 7281–7288 (2019)
27. Xing, C., et al.: Topic aware neural response generation. In: AAAI, pp. 3351–3357 (2017)
28. Yang, L., et al.: A hybrid retrieval-generation neural conversation model. In: CIKM, pp. 1341–1350 (2019)
29. Yang, L., et al.: Response ranking with deep matching networks and external knowledge in information-seeking conversation systems. In: SIGIR, pp. 245–254 (2018)
30. Zhang, Y., Chen, X., Ai, Q., Yang, L., Bruce Croft, W.: Towards conversational search and recommendation: system ask, user respond. In: CIKM, pp. 177–186 (2018)
31. Zhao, T., Eskenazi, M.: Towards end-to-end learning for dialog state tracking and management using deep reinforcement learning. In: SIGDIAL, pp. 1–10 (2016)

MPIA: Multiple Preferences with Item Attributes for Graph Convolutional Collaborative Filtering

Ming He[(✉)], Zekun Huang, and Han Wen

Faculty of Information Technology, Beijing University of Technology, Beijing, China
heming@bjut.edu.cn, {huangzekun,wenhan}@emails.bjut.edu.cn

Abstract. Personalized recommender systems are playing an increasingly critical role in a variety of online applications. In recent years, advancements in graph-structured deep neural networks have attracted considerable interest and achieved state-of-the-art performance on recommender system benchmarks. However, existing graph-based recommendation methods generally characterize each user with just one representation vector, which is insufficient to convey diverse preferences of users. To address this issue, in this paper, we approach the learning of user representations from a different perspective, by modeling users based on multiple representation embeddings. We propose a Multiple Preferences with Item Attributes for Graph Convolutional Collaborative Filtering (MPIA) framework built upon the message-aggregation concept of graph neural networks, which can generate preference-specific user representations to better model the diverse preferences of users. By taking advantage of graph representation learning techniques, MPIA learns preference-specific embeddings for users and attribute-specific embeddings for items. Moreover, we utilize shared embeddings for user and item representations to obtain the commonalities in multiple networks. Specifically, we construct a user-item bipartite graph for each preference, and enrich the representation of each node with the topological structure and features of its neighbors. We also design a preference-attribute fusion method to acquire more accurate item retrievals for every aspect of interest. Extensive experiments conducted on three real-world datasets demonstrate the effectiveness of the proposed MPIA framework.

Keywords: Recommender systems · Graph convolution networks · Graph neural network · Collaborative filtering

1 Introduction

With the exponential growth of information on the Internet, recommender systems have been successfully applied in online service scenarios such as e-commerce, advertising, and social media. Collaborative filtering (CF) is one of the most commonly used techniques for building recommender systems, which

© Springer Nature Switzerland AG 2021
M. Brambilla et al. (Eds.): ICWE 2021, LNCS 12706, pp. 225–239, 2021.
https://doi.org/10.1007/978-3-030-74296-6_18

models user preferences based on similarities in the interaction data of users or items. Essentially, user-item interactions can be naturally modeled as bipartite graph edges between users and items. Thereby, CF can be transformed into an edge prediction problem in the graph.

Graph Convolutional Networks (GCNs) have achieved considerable success and are widely utilized in graph learning tasks as they can extract abundant information from graph data. Recently, the introduction of GCNs into CF for modeling more complex user-item interactions has attracted the attention of researchers. Motivated by the strength of GCNs, some recent efforts, including Neural graph collaborative filtering (NGCF) [20], and Graph convolutional matrix completion (GC-MC) [2], use GCNs to model higher-layer collaborative signals by adapting GCNs to a user-item interactions graph, in which CF signals can be captured in high-hop neighbors for making recommendations. These GCN-based CF models achieve state-of-the art performance. Despite their enormous success, they suffer from two limitations:

First, most current models do not model multiple user preferences. In the real world, users usually have diverse preferences for items, which correspond to varied attributes of items. In online shopping scenarios, people are attribute-sensitive when choosing which products to buy. For example, some users are interested in a product with the attributes *"appearance"* and *"performance"*, whereas others may prefer products that emphasize *"price"* and *"performance"* . Failing to identify the diverse interests of users can limit the recommendation performance. As a consequence, it is crucial to design a novel method that can extract user's diverse interests, and capture fine-grained user preferences. Despite the design of a new type of multi-component learner reported in Multi-Component graph convolutional Collaborative Filtering (MCCF) [21], which can capture fine-grained user preferences, and generates user representation by combining multiple latent components of users, we argue that it ignores the commonality of the node shared by multiple networks and fails to distinguish multiple features better.

Second, existing methods typically focus on the aggregation of a user's multiple preferences to generate a final embedding of the user, with little attention paid to the combination of these preferences and item attributes. Cen et al. [3] applies a multi-preference extraction module to generate multiple user interests, and then uses an aggregation module to obtain the overall top-N items. Wei et al. [23] models user preferences hierarchy for multiple dimensions and arbitrary depth. Although both approaches successfully build a multi-preference framework, they ignore the combination of these preferences with item attributes. Thus, they directly generate a unified user/item embedding for the final recommendation, which can lead to the inferior usage of this fine-grained information. Therefore, it is necessary to fuse the diverse preferences of users with item attributes for improving recommendations.

Considering the above mentioned factors and inspired by the wide success associated with the leveraging of GCNs, in this paper, we propose a novel model for generating personalized recommendation tasks, namely the Multiple

Preferences with Item Attributes for Graph Convolutional Collaborative Filtering (MPIA). With users/items represented as nodes and different types of preferences represented as multiple types of edges in the graph model, MPIA constructs a user-item bipartite graph for each kind of preference. To capture the commonality of a user shared by all preferences and the characteristic of a particular preference for each bipartite graph, we apply shared and preference-specific embeddings to represent the multiple preferences of users. Specifically, we leverage an attention-based method to extract user preferences by aggregating the corresponding attributes (e.g., *price*) of items that have interacted. Meanwhile, we boost the representation of an item with its user group. Then, we design a key component in the MPIA, named preference-attribute fusion layer, to fuse the user's multiple preferences with item specific attributes, which can better utilize the fine-grained preference/attribute information. To demonstrate the effectiveness of our method, we validated the MPIA framework on three publicly accessible datasets: Yelp, Amazon, and MovieLens. The experimental results show that our model can yield promising performance.

The contributions of this paper are summarized as follows:

- We design a preference-level attention method for extracting the diverse interests of users, which better captures the commonality of the node shared by multiple networks and the characteristic of a particular preference.
- We propose MPIA, a novel collaborative filtering framework based on graph neural networks, which leverages a preference-attribute fusion layer to combine multiple user preferences with specific item attributes.
- Based on three real-word datasets, we have conducted extensive experiments to evaluate the effectiveness of our framework. The results reveal that our method significantly outperforms baseline methods.

2   Related Work

2.1   Collaborative Filtering

Collaborative filtering (CF) [17] methods, which have proven to be successful in real-world recommender systems, find similar users and items and make recommendations on this basis. Early approaches to CF considered the user–item rating matrix and predicted ratings via user-based [9] or item-based [12,16] CF methods. With the development of dimension reduction methods, latent factor models such as matrix factorization have been widely adopted in recommender systems. Koren et al. [10] and Rendle et al. [15] project the ID of a user (or an item) into an embedding vector. Recently, deep learning and neural models have further extended CF. Neural recommender models like Neural graph collaborative filtering (NCF) [20] uses the same embedding component, while enhancing the interaction modeling with neural networks. Lately researchers have realized that historical items make different contributions to the shaping of personal interests. To this end, attention mechanisms, such as Attentive collaborative filtering (ACF) [4] and Neural attentive item similarity model for recommendation

(NAIS) [6], have been introduced to capture varying contributions, whereby the importance of each historical item is automatically learned. *Our model differs significantly from these works, because most of these approaches presume that user-item interactions can be uniformly represented by the edges in the user-item bipartite graph, which fail to recognize multiple preferences. In this paper, we adopt an attention-based method that captures multiple preferences of users and common characteristic of the node across all networks.*

2.2 Graph Methods for Recommendation

Very recently, Graph Neural Networks(GNNs) have been proven to be capable of learning on graph structure data [8]. In the task of recommender systems, the user-item interaction contains item ratings by users, which is a typical graph data. Therefore, GNNs have been proposed to solve recommendation problems [2]. GC-MC [2] treats recommender systems as the view of link prediction on graphs and proposes a graph auto-encoder framework based on message passing on the bipartite interaction graph. Ying et al. [24] develops and deploys a large-scale deep recommendation engine at Pinterest for image recommendation. Zheng et al. [25] considers the category and price of items as nodes in the graph, builds a graph consisting of four types of nodes, and then applies GCN for the price-aware recommendation. Monti et al. [14] adopts GNNs to extract graph embeddings for users and items, and then combines them with recurrent neural networks to perform a diffusion process. *Different from existing works that do not consider combinations of user preferences and item attributes, we propose a preference-attribute fusion layer to address this gap.*

3   Method

Figure 1 shows the architecture of our proposed method, in which the model takes the user–item bipartite graph as input and predicts user ratings for items. Our framework consists of two important components: 1) an aggregation layer that learns the characteristics of each node from interaction data; 2) a preference-attribute fusion layer that fuses the multiple preferences of users with attributes of items. Finally, the MLP layers are applied to the learned embeddings to output the rating r.

3.1   Preference-Aware User-Item Graphs

We aim to generate multi-preference representations to perform the recommendation for the target user. To do so, we treat each preference individually. The input interaction data is represented by an undirected graph $G = (V, E, R)$, where the nodes are represented by V, and consist of user nodes $u \in U$ and item nodes $i \in I$. The edges in E contain the different user-item interaction edges, which correspond different preferences of users, where an edge $e_{ui} = 1$ indicates an observed interaction between user u and item i; otherwise $e_{ui} = 0$. The rating

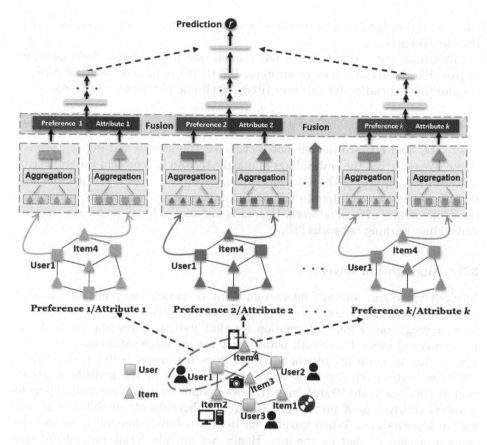

Fig. 1. Illustration of the proposed framework, where the node User 1 is the target user and Item 4 is the target item. A user-item bipartite graph is constructed for each preference to capture the preference-specific user representation.

set $\mathbf{R}$ comprises the rating scores of users for the items $\{1, ..., 5\}$. The aggregation part aggregates the interacted item/user features to learn the user/item embeddings. The preference-attribute fusion layer considers the diverse interests separately in the matching stage. To accurately capture the particular preference of users, we split the bipartite graph $\mathbf{G}_k$ from $\mathbf{G}$ by keeping the features in preference k solely, with different subgraph indicating different preference subspace.

3.2 Embedding Layer

Let $\mathbf{U}_0$ denote the shared embedding set for users, $\mathbf{I}_0$ denote the shared embedding set for items, and the embedding vectors $e_l^u \in R^d$, $e_j^i \in R^d$, be denoted as follows:

$$\mathbf{U}_0 = (e_1^u, ..., e_n^u), \quad \mathbf{I}_0 = (e_1^i, ..., e_m^i), \tag{1}$$

where n and m indicate the numbers of users and items respectively, and d is the embedding size.

To ensure the extensibility of our model, one hot vector is used as input to describe the ID of a user or an item. We then use matrix multiplication to acquire the embedding for this user (item) with one hot vector as follows:

$$e_l^u = \mathbf{U}_0 \cdot \mathbf{ID}_l^U, \quad e_j^i = \mathbf{I}_0 \cdot \mathbf{ID}_j^I, \tag{2}$$

where $\mathbf{ID}_l^U$ and $\mathbf{ID}_j^I$ are the one hot vectors for the user u_l and item i_j, respectively. We note that the embeddings in matrix $\mathbf{U}_0$ and $\mathbf{I}_0$ represent the respective initialization features of the users and items, which can be seen as the input features for each user and item in the GNN framework [8]. Specifically, to capture the commonality of each network, $\mathbf{U}_0$ and $\mathbf{I}_0$ are shared by all preference-specific embedding learning networks [22].

3.3 Aggregation Layer

Intuitively, we can leverage interaction data to enrich the representations of users and items. To be more specific, the historical interactions of a user, which is an aggregation of item information for that user, can describe the multiple preferences of users. It is worth noting that for the aggregation operation, the aggregation of more neighborhood nodes does not mean better performance, which we verify in the experimental section. Inspired by the multi-head attention mechanism in the Transformer [18], we assume that the user-item bipartite graph $\mathbf{G}$ is driven by K preferences. Different subgraphs obtain different preference representations. When learning an item attribute embedding, we use the same procedure as that for the user. Hence, we provide details only of the user preference embedding process.

User preference and item attribute embedding vectors can be expressed by embedding matrices $\mathbf{U}_P^k$ and $\mathbf{I}_A^k$ respectively, as follows:

$$\mathbf{U}_P^k = (u_1^k, ..., u_n^k), \quad \mathbf{I}_A^k = (i_1^k, ..., i_m^k), \tag{3}$$

where k is the tag of the k_{th} preference/attribute of user/item.

Preference-Level Attention. The Graph Attention Networks [19] leverages an attention mechanism to consider the different weights of neighboring nodes, and enables the model to filter out noise and focus on important adjacent nodes. Inspired by this approach, we use preference-level attention for users to obtain preference-specific attention weights from the item attribute set $\mathbf{I}_A^k$, as follows:

$$f_{lj} = \mathcal{Z}(\mathbf{W}_k u_l^k, \mathbf{W}_k i_j^k), \tag{4}$$

where $\mathbf{W}_k \in R^{d \times d}$ is shared by every user/item under preference k/attribute k, and f_{lj} indicates the contribution of item i_j's k_{th} attribute to user u_l's k_{th}

preference. To better compare the coefficients of different nodes, we normalize them for all choices of j using the softmax function:

$$\alpha_{lj} = softmax(f_{lj}) = \frac{exp(f_{lj})}{\sum_{j \in N_l} exp(f_{lj})}, \tag{5}$$

where N_l is a subset of adjacent nodes for user u_l. We set $\mathcal{Z}$ as a neural network, parameterized by a weight vector $\vec{a} \in R^{2d \times 2d}$ and apply $Relu$ as a nonlinear activation function. The coefficients computed by the attention mechanism are represented as follows:

$$\alpha_{lj} = softmax(f_{lj}) = \frac{exp\left[Relu\left(\vec{a}^T(\mathbf{W}_k u_l^k || \mathbf{W}_k i_j^k)\right)\right]}{\sum_{j \in N_l} exp\left[Relu\left(\vec{a}^T(\mathbf{W}_k u_l^k || \mathbf{W}_k i_j^k)\right)\right]}, \tag{6}$$

where T is the transposition and $||$ is the concatenation operation.

Preference-Specific Embedding. After obtaining the normalized attention coefficients, we compute a weighted summation with nonlinear transformation σ for the attributes of items, which serve as preference-specific embedding for user u_l:

$$p_l^k = \sigma\left(\sum_{j \in N_l} \alpha_{lj} \mathbf{W}_k i_j^k\right), \tag{7}$$

where p_l^k indicates the k_{th} preference-specific embedding of user u_l, which contains information about the k_{th} attribute of some rated items. To better capture distinct features, we apply disagreement regularization [11] to maximize the cosine distance between the preference-specific embeddings:

$$D = \frac{-1}{K^2} \sum_{i=1}^{K} \sum_{j=1}^{K} \frac{p_l^i \cdot p_l^j}{||p_l^i|| \cdot ||p_l^j||}. \tag{8}$$

Concatenation Combination. In multi-preference recommendation scenarios, users may interact with an item for some but not all preferences, which demonstrates the commonality and specificity of user preferences in their decisions. For every node in a preference network, we concatenate the preference-specific embedding and the shared embedding to generate the final embedding of the user u_l as follows:

$$z_l^k = p_l^k || e_l^u. \tag{9}$$

In this way, the shared embedding and a preference-specific embedding are combined for the later procedure. Because the shared embedding and preference-specific embedding only capture partial node characteristic, they are combined to obtain a complete embedding.

3.4 Preference-Attribute Fusion Layer

Existing approaches (e.g., MCCF [21], DHAN [23]) generally compress all the information about multiple features of users into a single vector. We argue that representing the diverse preferences of users by a unified representation vector can be an obstacle to the leveraging of multiple user preferences. When all the information related to the multiple interests of users is mixed together, this causes the inaccurate matching of user preferences with item attributes. Instead, we adopt multiple channels to separately fuse multiple preferences of user u_l with corresponding attributes of item i_j, which process the learned features of different subgraphs respectively. In this way, the diverse interests of users are considered respectively in the matching stage, which enables more accurate item retrieval for every aspect of interest:

$$h_1 = z_l^1||v_j^1, \cdots, h_K = z_l^K||v_j^K, \tag{10}$$

where $h_1, \cdots, h_K$ are the final K fusion results, and v_j^k represent the k_{th} attribute-specific embedding of item i_j. Inspired by previous work [1], we adopt the idea of the coordinated approach, and project h_k into the latent space which is the same as the user ID u_{id}:

$$y_k = Relu(\mathbf{W}^\gamma h_k) + u_{id}, \tag{11}$$

where $\mathbf{W}^\gamma \in R_{n\times d}$ is a weight matrix.

3.5 Rating Prediction

In this subsection, we design recommendation tasks to learn the model parameters. There are various recommendation tasks, including item ranking and rating prediction. In this work, we apply our proposed MPIA model to the recommendation task of rating prediction. First, we feed all fusion information into the MLP to obtain a rating prediction, as follows:

$$g_1^1 = \sigma(\mathbf{W}_1^1 y_1 + b_1^1), \cdots, g_1^K = \sigma(\mathbf{W}_1^K y_K + b_1^K),$$

$$\vdots \tag{12}$$

$$g_t^1 = \sigma(\mathbf{W}_t^1 g_{t-1}^1 + b_t^1), \cdots, g_t^K = \sigma(\mathbf{W}_t^K g_{t-1}^K + b_t^K),$$

$$r_{lj} = g_t^1 + g_t^2 + \cdots + g_t^K.$$

We then sum the K matching results to obtain the final predicted rating r_{lj} of user u_l for item i_j, and t represents the index of a hidden layer.

3.6 Optimization

For model training, we specify an objective function to achieve optimization. As our task in this work is rating prediction, a widely used objective function is formulated as:

$$\mathscr{L} = \frac{1}{2|\mathcal{O}|}\left(\sum_{(l,j)\in\mathcal{O}}(r_{lj} - r_0)^2\right) + \lambda||\Theta||_2^2, \tag{13}$$

where r_0 is the ground truth rating assigned by the user u_l to item i_j; and λ, $|\mathcal{O}|$, and Θ represent the regularization weight, number of observed ratings, and the parameters of the model, respectively.

4 Experiments

4.1 Experimental Settings

Datasets. To evaluate the performance of our model, we conducted experiments on three real-world datasets: Yelp[1], Amazon[2], and MovieLens[3], which provide large amounts of rating information. Yelp is an online location-based social network, in which users make friends with others and express their experiences through reviews and ratings. For our recommendation task experiment, we adopted Yelp's rating data. Amazon is an open dataset collected from Amazon e-commerce activity, which comprises large corpora of product ratings crawled from Amazon.com. MovieLens is a widely used movie ratings dataset for evaluating CF algorithms. We used the MovieLens version (MovieLens-1M) that includes 100,000 user ratings. Each user provides ratings in the range [1, 5]. Besides, we randomly split the dataset into training and testing sets with 8:2 ratios. The statistics of these three datasets are presented in Table 1.

Table 1. Basic statistics for the three datasets.

Dataset	Yelp	Amazon	MovieLens
# of Users	1286	1000	943
# of Items	2614	1000	1682
# of Ratings	30838	65170	100000
# Density	0.917%	6.517%	6.304%

Baselines. To demonstrate the effectiveness of our MPIA model, we compare it with several state-of-the-art methods. These baseline methods are mainly classified into matrix factorization (MF) and GCN-based methods:

- **PMF** [13]: This model leverages a user-item rating matrix only and models the latent factors of users and items by Gaussian distributions.
- **FISM** [7]: A general model that indirectly obtains user representations by factorizing an item-to-item similarity matrix. The original implementation was for top-N recommendation task, and we adjusted its loss to the squared loss for rating prediction.

---

[1] https://www.yelp.com/dataset/challenge/.
[2] http://jmcauley.ucsd.edu/data/amazon/.
[3] https://grouplens.org/datasets/movielens/1M/.

- **BiasMF** [10]: This method is a classical MF-based model that factorizes the user-item interaction matrix to optimize the embeddings of users and items by introducing a new bias term.
- **GraphSAGE** [5]: A general inductive framework that utilizes node features to update node representations for previously unseen data. Specifically, it considers structural information as well as the distribution of node features in the neighborhood.
- **MCCF** [21]: This model is a state-of-the-art recommender model with GNN architecture. It introduces two attention modules to extract the various purchasing motivations of a user.
- **GC-MC** [2]: This method is a GCN-based collaborative filtering model, that utilizes a user-item bipartite graph and the associated features of users and items to generate recommendations. Each user embedding is convolved in an aggregation of the embeddings of rated items, and each item embedding is convolved in an aggregation of rated user embeddings.

Evaluation Metrics and Hyper-parameter Setting. To verify the performance of our recommendation model, we used the mean absolute error (MAE) and root mean squared error (RMSE), whereby smaller MAE and RMSE values indicate better predictive accuracy. We implemented our proposed method using Pytorch, a popular framework for neural networks. For all the weight parameters, we initialized latent vectors with small random values. In the model learning process, we used the Adam optimization method for all networks that rely on gradient back-propagation method. We used the early stopping strategy and the batch size was searched in $\{8, 16, 64, 128, 256, 512\}$. In our proposed MPIA model, we applied the regularization parameter α in the range $\{0.0001, 0.001, 0.01, 0.1, 1\}$, and found $\alpha = 0.001$ to realize the best performance. The $L2$ normalization coefficient was tuned in $\{0, 0.00001, 0.0001, 0.001, 0.01, 0.1, 0.15\}$. In addition, we used the node dropout technique in our model and the GCN-based models, in which the ratio is searched in $\{0, 0.1, ..., 0.8\}$. The number of user preferences K changed in the range $\{1, 2, 3, 4, 5\}$. The parameters for the baseline methods were initialized as reported in corresponding papers, and were then carefully tuned to achieve optimal performance.

4.2 Results

Comparison with Baselines. In this subsection, first, we compare the recommendation performance of our proposed MPIA with those of the other baselines. Table 2 presents the results obtained on the three datasets by all the recommendation methods, based on the overall RMSE and MAE rating orediction error. It's worth noting that, MPIA-1, MPIA-2 and MPIA-3 correspond to three variants of our MPIA model: MPIA-1 eliminates the shared embeddings of U_0 and I_0, MPIA-2 eliminates the preference-level attention, and MPIA-3 removes the preference-attribute fusion layer. The best result in each row is bolded, and the second best is underlined.

We can see that compared with all the baseline methods, our MPIA method achieved the best performance on all three datasets, which clearly demonstrates the superiority of our proposed model. When comparing our results on the Yelp dataset, we find almost no difference between the MPIA and its two variants: MPIA-1 and MPIA-3, because we set the hyper-parameter number of preference $K = 1$. Hence, we trained only one network in this dataset, which fails to show the effect of shared embedding or the fusion of multiple user preferences with item attributes. In the Amazon and MovieLens datasets, we set the hyper-parameter K to be larger than 1, which demonstrates the effectiveness of these two modules. We note that MPIA-2, in which the preference-level attention was removed, performed poorly on all datasets. The reason for this may be due to the fact that multiple preference networks that do not implement attention mechanism can't capture key information effectively and adds redundant information.

Table 2. Recommendation performances of different models.

Dataset	Yelp		Amazon		MovieLens	
Metrics	RMSE	MAE	RMSE	MAE	RMSE	MAE
PMF	0.3967	0.1571	0.9339	0.7113	0.9638	0.7559
BiasMF	0.3902	0.1616	0.9028	0.6759	0.9257	0.7258
FISM	0.3852	0.1235	0.9056	0.6728	0.9259	0.7294
GCMC	0.3850	0.1354	0.8946	0.6619	0.9145	0.7165
MCCF	0.3806	0.1029	0.8876	0.6428	0.9070	0.7050
GraphSAGE	0.3759	0.1128	0.8894	0.6379	0.9108	0.7082
MPIA-1	0.3695	0.0891	0.8847	0.6385	0.9052	0.7054
MPIA-2	0.3955	0.1342	0.9067	0.6658	0.9294	0.7241
MPIA-3	0.3684	0.0885	0.8939	0.6472	0.9165	0.7094
MPIA	**0.3684**	**0.0885**	**0.8741**	**0.6294**	**0.8948**	**0.6953**

The GNN-based models basically outperformed the MF-based models on all three datasets. These results are attributed to the graph convolution layers, which fuse the information of neighboring users (items) into their embeddings, thereby enhancing the effectiveness of the representation learning. It also proves that GNNs are powerful in the representation learning of graph data, as they naturally integrate node information as well as the topological structure.

In the comparison of the MCCF, GC-MC, and GraphSAGE methods, we find that considering multi-preference in user representations improves performance. Our proposed model outperforms MCCF, which shows the effectiveness of the preference-attribute fusion process in the final matching stage. Therefore, it is necessary to fuse the different preferences of users with the corresponding item attributes in multi-preference recommendations.

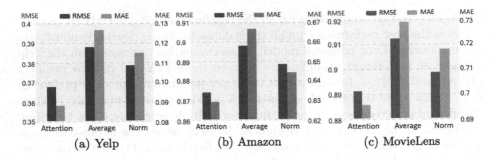

Fig. 2. Impact of using preference-level attention on three datasets.

Impact of Preference-Level Attention. To explore the effect of preference-level attention, we compare the results obtained when using different aggregation methods on the three datasets, as shown in Fig. 2. We used three types of aggregation methods: attention-based, average-based, and the graph Laplacian norm $1/\sqrt{|N_u||N_i|}$, where N_u and N_i denote the neighbors of user u and item i. For a fair comparison, we used the same number of aggregation neighbors in the three methods. The results show that using the attention mechanism achieved the best result, which demonstrate the superiority of the attention mechanism in multi-graph networks embedding learning. We can also see that the average-based method performed poorly on all three datasets, which may be because this method incorrectly assumes that different neighbors make the same contributions to the node representation in this situation. The results further demonstrate that not all the interacting items of one user contribute equally to the user preference representations, and not all interacting users have the same degree of importance for learning item attributes.

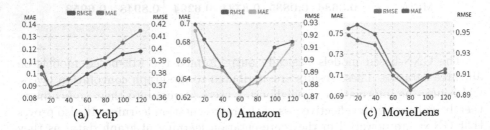

Fig. 3. Impact of sample numbers on three datasets.

Impact of Sample Numbers. In this subsection, we describe the experiments we conducted to study the impact of the number of neighborhood samples on the recommendation performance. For all three datasets, we specified the same number of neighborhood samples for both the users and items. Therefore, if the number of neighbors for a node was more than the specified threshold x, we selected only x neighbors. Conversely, we selected all neighbors when the number of neighbors was less than x. In accordance with the ratings, the principle for selecting neighborhood nodes was from large to small, as items with high ratings better reflect the preferences of users. Accordingly, the characteristics of the users also reflect the item attributes.

Figure 3 shows a comparison of the experimental results, in which we find that only approximately twenty neighbors must be sampled for both users and items to achieve good performance in the Yelp dataset. However, for the Amazon and MovieLens datasets, more neighborhood samples are needed. A possible reason for this is that, the density of both the Amazon and MovieLens datasets is much higher than that of Yelp, as shown in Table 1. Because high density means more abundant feature information, more neighborhood nodes are needed to capture multiple features. It's obvious that for all datasets, too much or too little neighborhood sampling leads to performance degradation, which is likely because a small amount of neighborhood information is insufficient for capturing complex features, whereas excessive sampling can introduce too much noise.

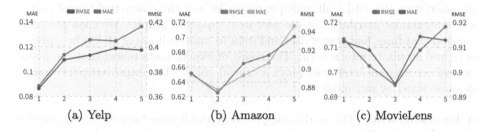

(a) Yelp   (b) Amazon   (c) MovieLens

Fig. 4. Impact of preference number K on three datasets..

Impact of Preference Number K. To determine the effectiveness of multiple user preferences, we designed experiments in which we changed the number K to determine its effect. As shown in Fig. 4, the optimal value of K increases with the density of the datasets. Datasets like Amazon and MovieLens, which are denser and in which the ratings are more evenly distributed, benefit from using the multiple preferences mechanism. However, if the number of preferences is too great, the complexity of our model significantly increases. This is likely because the extraction of too many features introduces a lot of noisy information, which can lead to greater model complexity and performance degradation. Therefore, we must set the appropriate hyper-parameters to achieve trade-off between performance and complexity. This issue further demonstrates that user preference representations are closely related to the content of item attributes, and the same considerations apply to items.

Impact of Preference-Attribute Fusion. As we can see in Table 2, the MPIA-3 method without the preference-attribute fusion layer exhibits inferior performance. Although the use of multi-preference representations allows the model to jointly consider information from different representation subspaces, simply compressing all the information about the multiple features of users into a single vector does not make full use of all kinds of information obtained. In addition, the aim of using multiple preferences, is to learn independent information in different representation subspaces, but there is no mechanism that guarantees that different attention modules capture absolutely independent features [11]. The extracted features are not completely unrelated, so direct mixing will inevitably result in information redundancy. Therefore, we use multiple channels to fuse preferences of user with corresponding item attributes, whereby some features that are not completely irrelevant can be leveraged respectively.

5   Conclusion

In this work, we propose a Graph Neural Network framework (MPIA) to model recommendation for rating prediction. Specifically, this method constructs a user-item bipartite graph for each preference, to capture the commonality of the user/item shared by all multiple networks and the characteristics of particular preferences/attributes in the user-item bipartite graphs. We then present a method that fuses features of user and item to make full use of all kinds of preference and attribute information. The result of experiments reveal that the fusion of preferences and attributes plays a crucial role in the improved performance demonstrated by our model.

Acknowledgments. This work is supported by the Beijing Natural Science Foundation under grant 4192008.

References

1. Baltrušaitis, T., Ahuja, C., Morency, L.P.: Multimodal machine learning: a survey and taxonomy. IEEE Trans. Pattern Anal. Mach. Intell. **41**(2), 423–443 (2018)
2. Berg, R.V.d., Kipf, T.N., Welling, M.: Graph convolutional matrix completion. arXiv preprint arXiv:1706.02263 (2017)
3. Cen, Y., Zhang, J., Zou, X., Zhou, C., Yang, H., Tang, J.: Controllable multi-interest framework for recommendation. arXiv preprint arXiv:2005.09347 (2020)
4. Chen, J., Zhang, H., He, X., Nie, L., Liu, W., Chua, T.S.: Attentive collaborative filtering: multimedia recommendation with item-and component-level attention. In: Proceedings of the 40th International ACM SIGIR Conference on Research and Development in Information Retrieval, pp. 335–344. ACM (2017)
5. Hamilton, W.L., Ying, R., Leskovec, J.: Inductive representation learning on large graphs. arXiv preprint arXiv:1706.02216 (2017)
6. He, X., He, Z., Song, J., Liu, Z., Jiang, Y.G., Chua, T.S.: NAIS: neural attentive item similarity model for recommendation. IEEE Trans. Knowl. Data Eng. **30**, 2354–2366 (2018)
7. Kabbur, S., Ning, X., Karypis, G.: Fism: factored item similarity models for top-n recommender systems. In: Proceedings of the 19th ACM SIGKDD international conference on Knowledge discovery and data mining, pp. 659–667. ACM (2013)

8. Kipf, T.N., Welling, M.: Semi-supervised classification with graph convolutional networks. arXiv preprint arXiv:1609.02907 (2016)
9. Konstan, J.A., Miller, B.N., Maltz, D., Herlocker, J.L., Gordon, L.R., Riedl, J.: GroupLens: applying collaborative filtering to Usenet news. Commun. ACM **40**, 77–87 (1997)
10. Koren, Y., Bell, R., Volinsky, C.: Matrix factorization techniques for recommender systems. Computer **42**(8), 30–37 (2009)
11. Li, J., Tu, Z., Yang, B., Lyu, M.R., Zhang, T.: Multi-head attention with disagreement regularization. arXiv preprint arXiv:1810.10183 (2018)
12. Linden, G., Smith, B., York, J.: Amazon. com recommendations: item-to-item collaborative filtering. IEEE Internet Comput. **7**(1), 76–80 (2003)
13. Mnih, A., Salakhutdinov, R.R.: Probabilistic matrix factorization. Adv. Neural. Inf. Process. Syst. **20**, 1257–1264 (2007)
14. Monti, F., Bronstein, M.M., Bresson, X.: Geometric matrix completion with recurrent multi-graph neural networks. arXiv preprint arXiv:1704.06803 (2017)
15. Rendle, S., Freudenthaler, C., Gantner, Z., Schmidt-Thieme, L.: BPR: Bayesian personalized ranking from implicit feedback. arXiv preprint arXiv:1205.2618 (2012)
16. Sarwar, B., Karypis, G., Konstan, J., Riedl, J.: Item-based collaborative filtering recommendation algorithms. In: Proceedings of the 10th International Conference on World Wide Web, pp. 285–295. ACM (2001)
17. Schafer, J.B., Frankowski, D., Herlocker, J., Sen, S.: Collaborative filtering recommender systems. In: Brusilovsky, P., Kobsa, A., Nejdl, W. (eds.) The Adaptive Web. LNCS, vol. 4321, pp. 291–324. Springer, Heidelberg (2007). https://doi.org/10.1007/978-3-540-72079-9_9
18. Vaswani, A., et al.: Attention is all you need. arXiv preprint arXiv:1706.03762 (2017)
19. Veličković, P., Cucurull, G., Casanova, A., Romero, A., Lio, P., Bengio, Y.: Graph attention networks. arXiv preprint arXiv:1710.10903 (2017)
20. Wang, X., He, X., Wang, M., Feng, F., Chua, T.S.: Neural graph collaborative filtering. In: Proceedings of the 42nd International ACM SIGIR Conference on Research and Development in Information Retrieval, pp. 165–174. ACM (2019)
21. Wang, X., Wang, R., Shi, C., Song, G., Li, Q.: Multi-component graph convolutional collaborative filtering. In: Proceedings of the AAAI Conference on Artificial Intelligence, pp. 6267–6274. ACM (2020)
22. Xu, L., Wei, X., Cao, J., Yu, P.S.: Multi-task network embedding. Int. J. Data Sci. Anal. **8**(2), 183–198 (2018). https://doi.org/10.1007/s41060-018-0166-2
23. Xu, W., He, H., Tan, M., Li, Y., Lang, J., Guo, D.: Deep interest with hierarchical attention network for click-through rate prediction. In: Proceedings of the 43rd International ACM SIGIR Conference on Research and Development in Information Retrieval, pp. 1905–1908. ACM (2020)
24. Ying, R., He, R., Chen, K., Eksombatchai, P., Hamilton, W.L., Leskovec, J.: Graph convolutional neural networks for web-scale recommender systems. In: Proceedings of the 24th ACM SIGKDD International Conference on Knowledge Discovery and Data Mining, pp. 974–983. ACM (2018)
25. Zheng, Y., Gao, C., He, X., Li, Y., Jin, D.: Price-aware recommendation with graph convolutional networks. In: 2020 IEEE 36th International Conference on Data Engineering (ICDE), pp. 133–144. IEEE (2020)

Better Call the Plumber: Orchestrating Dynamic Information Extraction Pipelines

Mohamad Yaser Jaradeh[1]([⊠])(iD), Kuldeep Singh[2](iD), Markus Stocker[3](iD),
Andreas Both[4](iD), and Sören Auer[3](iD)

[1] L3S Research Center, Leibniz University Hannover, Hanover, Germany
jaradeh@l3s.de
[2] Zerotha-Research and Cerence GmbH, Aachen, Germany
kuldeep.singh1@cerence.com
[3] TIB Leibniz Information Centre for Science and Technology, Hanover, Germany
{markus.stocker,auer}@tib.eu
[4] Anhalt University of Applied Sciences, Bernburg, Germany
andreas.both@hs-anhalt.de

Abstract. We propose PLUMBER, the first framework that brings together the research community's disjoint information extraction (IE) efforts. The PLUMBER architecture comprises 33 reusable components for various Knowledge Graphs (KG) information extraction subtasks, such as coreference resolution, entity linking, and relation extraction. Using these components, PLUMBER dynamically generates suitable information extraction pipelines and offers overall 264 distinct pipelines. We study the optimization problem of choosing suitable pipelines based on input sentences. To do so, we train a transformer-based classification model that extracts contextual embeddings from the input and finds an appropriate pipeline. We study the efficacy of PLUMBER for extracting the KG triples using standard datasets over two KGs: DBpedia, and Open Research Knowledge Graph (ORKG). Our results demonstrate the effectiveness of PLUMBER in dynamically generating KG information extraction pipelines, outperforming all baselines agnostics of the underlying KG. Furthermore, we provide an analysis of collective failure cases, study the similarities and synergies among integrated components, and discuss their limitations.

Keywords: Information extraction · NLP pipelines · Software reusability · Semantic search · Semantic Web

1 Introduction and Motivation

In last one decade, publicly available KGs (DBpedia [2] and Wikidata [42]) have become rich sources of structured content used in various applications, including Question Answering (QA), relation extraction, and dialog systems [4,39].

© Springer Nature Switzerland AG 2021
M. Brambilla et al. (Eds.): ICWE 2021, LNCS 12706, pp. 240–254, 2021.
https://doi.org/10.1007/978-3-030-74296-6_19

The research community developed numerous approaches to extract triple statements [44], keywords/topics [9], tables [22,23,45], or entities [35,36] from unstructured text to complement KGs. Despite extensive research, public KGs are not exhaustive and require continuous effort to align newly emerging unstructured information to the concepts of the KGs.

Research Problem: This work was motivated by an observation of recent approaches [14,35,45] that automatically align unstructured text to structured data on the Web. Such approaches are not viable in practice for extracting and structuring information because they only address very specific subtasks of the overall KG information extraction problem. If we consider the exemplary sentence *Rembrandt painted The Storm on the Sea of Galilee. It was painted in 1633.* (cf. Fig. 1). To extract statements aligned with the DBpedia KG from the given sentences, a system must first recognize the entities and relation surface forms in the first sentence. The second sentence requires an additional step of the coreference resolution, where *It* must be mapped to the correct entity surface form (namely, *The Storm on the Sea of Galilee*). The last step requires the mapping of entity and relation surface forms to the respective DBpedia entities and predicates. There has been extensive research in aligning concepts in unstructured text to KG, including entity linking [14,17], relation linking [4,36,38], and triple classification [13]. However, these efforts are disjoint, and little has been done to align unstructured text to the complete KG triples (i.e., represented as subject, predicate, object) [25]. Furthermore, many entity and relation linking tools have been reused in pipelines of QA systems [26,39]. The literature suggests that once different approaches put forward by the research community are combined, the resulting pipeline-oriented integrated systems can outperform monolithic end-to-end systems [27]. The motivation of our work is also shared with this similar integrative effort in the software architecture community [19] For the KG information extraction task, however, to the best of our knowledge, approaches aiming at dynamically integrating and orchestrating various existing components do not exist.

Objective and Contributions: Based on these observations, we build a framework that enables the integration of previously disjoint efforts on the KG-IE task under a single umbrella. We present the PLUMBER framework (cf. Fig. 2) for creating Information Extraction pipelines. PLUMBER integrates 33 reusable components released by the research community for the subtasks entity linking (EL), relation linking (RL), text triple extraction (TE) (subject, predicate, object), and coreference resolution (CR). Overall, there are 264 different composable KG information extraction pipelines (generated by the possible combination of the available 33 components, i.e., for DBpedia 3 CRs, 8 TEs, 10 EL/RLs gives $3*8*10 = 240$, and $4*3*2 = 24$ for the ORKG. Hence, $240 + 24 = 264$ pipelines). PLUMBER implements a transformer-based classification algorithm that intelligently chooses a suitable pipeline based on the unstructured input text.

We perform an exhaustive evaluation of PLUMBER on the two large-scale KGs DBpedia, and Open Research Knowledge Graph (ORKG) [24] to investigate the efficacy of PLUMBER in creating KG triples from unstructured text. We demonstrate that independent of the underlying KG; PLUMBER can find and assemble different extraction components to produce better suited KG triple extraction pipelines, significantly outperforming existing baselines. In summary, we provide the following novel contributions: i) The PLUMBER framework is the first of its kind for dynamically assembling and evaluating information extraction pipelines based on sequence classification techniques and for a given input text. PLUMBER is easily extensible and configurable, thus enabling the rapid creation and adjustment of new information extraction components and pipelines. Researchers can also use the framework for running IE components independently for specific subtasks such as triple extraction and entity linking. ii) A collection of 33 reusable IE components that can be combined to create 264 distinct IE pipelines. iii) The exhaustive evaluation and our detailed ablation study of the integrated components and composed pipelines on various input text will guide future research for collaborative KG information extraction.

We motivate our work with a running example; the sentence *Rembrandt painted The Storm on the Sea of Galilee. It was painted in 1633.* Multiple steps are required to extract these formally represented statements from the given text. First, the pronoun *it* in the second sentence should be replaced by *The Storm on the Sea of Galilee* using a coreference resolver. Next, a triple extractor should extract the correct text triples from the natural language text, i.e., <Rembrandt, painted, The Storm on the Sea of Galilee>, and <The Storm on the Sea of Galilee, painted in, 1633>. In the next step, the entity and relation linking component aligns the entity and relation surface forms extracted in the previous step to the DBpedia entities: dbr:Rembrandt for *Rembrandt van Rijn*, and dbr:The_Storm_on_the_Sea_of_Galilee for *The Storm on the Sea of Galilee*, and for relations: dbo:Artist for *painted*, and dbp:year for *painted in*. Figure 1 illustrates our running example and shows three PLUMBER IE pipelines with different results. In Pipeline 1, the coreference resolver is unable to map the pronoun *it* to the respective entity in the previous sentence. Moreover,

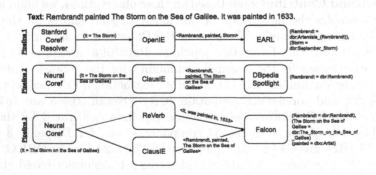

Fig. 1. Three example information extraction pipelines showing different results for the same text snippet. Each pipeline consists of coreference resolution, triple extractors, and entity/relation linking components.

the triple extractor generates incomplete triples, which also hinders the task of the entity and relation linker in the last step. Pipeline 2 uses a different set of components, and its output differs from the first pipeline. Here, the coreference resolution component is able to correctly co-relate the pronoun *it* to *The Storm on the Sea of Galilee*, and extract the text triple correctly. However, the overall result is only partially correct because the second triple is not extracted. Also, the linking component is not able to spot the second entity. Pipeline 3 correctly extracts both triples. This pipeline employs the same component as the second pipeline for coreference resolution but also includes an additional information extraction component (i.e., ReVerb [15]) and a joint entity and relation linking component, namely Falcon [35]. With this combination of components, the text triple extractors were able to compensate for the loss of information in the second pipeline by adding one more component. Using the extracted text triples, the last component of the pipeline, a joint entity and relation linking tool, can map both triple components correctly to the corresponding KG entities.

The reminder of this article is organized as follows. Related work is reviewed in Sect. 2. Section 3 presents PLUMBER, which is extensively evaluated in Sect. 4. Section 5 discusses the results, and Sect. 6 concludes and outlines directions for future research and work.

2 Related Work

In the last decade, many open source tools have been released by the research community to tackle IE tasks for KGs. These IE components are not only used for end-to-end KG triple extraction but also for various other tasks, such as:

Text Triple Extraction: The task of open information extraction is a well studied researched task in the NLP community [1]. It relies on NER (Named Entity Recognition) and RE (Relation Extraction). SalIE [33] uses MinIE [21] in combination with PageRank and clustering to find facts in the input text. Furthermore, OpenIE [1] leverages linguistic structures to extract self-contained clauses from the text. A comprehensive survey by Niklaus et al. [32] provides detailed about such techniques.

Entity and Relation Linking: Entity and relation linking is a widely studied researched topic in the NLP, Web, and Information Retrieval research communities [3,4,11]. Often, entity and relation linking is performed independently. DBpedia Spotlight [10] is one of the first approaches for entity recognition and disambiguation over DBpedia. TagMe [17] links entities to DBpedia using in-link matching to disambiguate candidates entities. Others tools such as RelMatch [38] do not perform entity linking and only focus on linking the relation in the text to the corresponding KG relation. Recon [4] uses graph neural networks to map relations between the entities with the assumption that entities are already linked in the text. EARL [14] is a joint linking tool over DBpedia and models the task as a generalized traveling salesperson problem. Sakor et al. [35] proposed Falcon, a linguistic rules based tool for joint entity and relation linking over DBpedia.

Coreference Resolution: This task is used in conjunction with other tasks in NLP pipelines to disambiguate text and resolve syntactic complexities. The Stanford Coreference Resolver [34] uses a multi pass sieve of deterministic coreference models. Clark and Manning [8] use reinforcement learning to fine-tune a neural mention-ranking model for coreference resolution. And more recently [37].

Frameworks and Dynamic Pipelines: There have been few attempts in various domains aiming to consolidate the disjoint efforts of the research community under a single umbrella for solving a particular task. The Gerbil platform [41] provides an easy-to-use web-based platform for the agile comparison of entity linking tools using multiple datasets and uniform measuring approaches. OKBQA [26] is a community effort for the development of multilingual open knowledge base and QA systems. Frankenstein integrates 24 QA components to build QA systems collaboratively on-top of the Qanary integration framework [6]. Other ETL pipelines system exists such as Apache NiFi. Semantic Web Pipes [31] and LarKC [16] are other prominent examples.

End-to-End Extraction Systems: More recently, end-to-end systems are gaining more attention due to the boom of deep learning techniques. Such systems draw on the strengths of deep models and transformers [29]. Kertkeidkachorn and Ichise [25] present an end-to-end system to extract triples and link them to DBpedia. Other attempts such as KG-Bert [44] leverage deep transformers [29] for the triple classification task, given the entity and relation descriptions of a triple. KG-Bert does not attempt end-to-end alignment of KG triples from a given input text. Liu et al. [28] design an encoder-decoder framework with an attention mechanism to extract and align triples to a KG.

3   Dynamic Information Extraction Pipelining Framework

PLUMBER has a modular design (see Fig. 2) where each component is integrated as a microservice. To ensure a consistent data exchange between components, the framework maps the output of each component to a homogeneous data representation using the Qanary [6] methodology. PLUMBER follows three design principles of i) *Isolation*, ii) *Reusability*, and iii) *Extensibility* inspired by [39,41].

Dynamic Pipeline Selection: PLUMBER uses a RoBERTa [29] based classifier that given a text and a set of requirements, PLUMBER predicts a good pipeline to extract KG triples. Rather than handcrafting features to train models on, we let the RoBERTa model acts as intermediary that classifies the contextual embeddings extracted from the input text into a class which represents one of the possible pipelines. Regarding RoBERTa's training, we run each input sequence on all possible pipelines and compute the evaluation metrics F1-score (i.e., estimated performance). RoBERTa is fed with the sentence and the sentence-level performance with the best value among all pipelines as the target class. Hence, in practice, the user points PLUMBER to a piece of text and internally it uses RoBERTa to classify the text to a class (i.e., the pipeline) to execute against the input text. We choose a transformer-based architecture due to its ability to

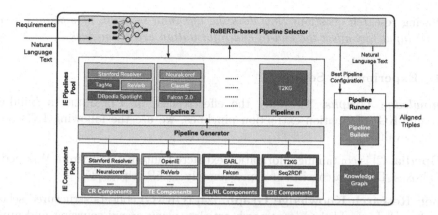

Fig. 2. Overview of PLUMBER's architecture highlighting the components for pipeline generation, selection, and execution. PLUMBER receives an input sentence and requirement (underlying KG) from the user. The framework intelligently selects a suitable pipeline based on the contextual features captured from the input sentence.

encode the contextual knowledge from the input text, providing more accurate classification.

Architecture: PLUMBER includes the following modules: **i) IE Components Pool:** All information extraction components that are integrated within the framework are parts of the pool. The components are divided based on their respective tasks, i.e., coreference resolution, text triple extraction, as well as entity and relation linking. These components have different input requirements and output formats; thus, PLUMBER provides standard interfaces to facilitate the interaction between pipeline components. **ii) Pipeline Generator:** This module creates possible pipelines depending on the requirements of the components (i.e., the underlying KG). Users can manually select the underlying KG and, using the metadata associated with each component, PLUMBER aggregates the components for the concerned KG. **iii) IE Pipelines Pool:** PLUMBER stores the configurations of the possible pipelines in the pool of pipelines for faster retrieval and easier interaction with other modules. **iv) Pipeline Selector:** Based on the requirements (i.e., underlying KG) and the input text, a RoBERTa based model extracts contextual embeddings from the text and classifies the input into one of the possible classes. Each class corresponds to one pipeline configuration that is held in the IE pipelines pool. **v) Pipeline Runner:** Given the input text, and the generated pipeline configuration, the module executes the pipeline and produce the final KG triples.

4   Evaluation

In this section, we detail the empirical evaluation of the framework in comparison to baselines on different datasets and knowledge graphs. As such, we study the following research question: *How does the dynamic selection of pipelines based on the input text affect the end-to-end information extraction task?*

4.1 Experimental Setup

Knowledge Graphs. To study the effectiveness of PLUMBER in building dynamic KG information extraction pipelines, we use the following KGs during our evaluation:

DBpedia. [2] is containing information extracted automatically from Wikipedia info boxes. DBpedia consists of approximately 11.5B triples [35].

Open Research Knowledge Graph. [24] (ORKG) collects structured scholarly knowledge published in research articles, using crowd sourcing and automated techniques. In total, ORKG consists of approximately 984K triples.

Datasets. Throughout our evaluation, we employed a set of existing and newly created datasets for structured triple extraction and alignment to knowledge graphs: the WebNLG [20] dataset for DBpedia, and COV-triples for ORKG.

WebNLG. is the Web Natural Language Generation Challenge. The challenge introduced the task of aligning unstructured text to DBpedia. In total, the dataset contains 46K triples with 9K triples in the testing and 37K in the training set.

COV-Triples. Is a handcrafted dataset that focuses on COVID-19 related scholarly articles. The COV-triples dataset consists of 21 abstracts from peer-reviewed articles and aligns the natural language text to the corresponding KG triples into the ORKG. Three Semantic Web researchers verified annotation quality, and triples approved by all three researchers are part of the dataset. The dataset contains only 75 triples. Hence, we use the WebNLG dataset for training, and 75 triples are used as a test set.

Components and Implementation. The PLUMBER framework integrates 33 components, the components span different IE tasks from Triple Extraction, Entity and Relation Linking, and Coreference Resolution. Most of the components used are open-sourced and they have been evaluated and used by the community in their respective publications. PLUMBER's code and all related resources are publicly available online at https://github.com/YaserJaradeh/ThePlumber.

Baselines. We include the following baselines:

T2KG. [25] is an end-to-end static system aligns a given natural language text to DBpedia KG triples.

Frankenstein. [39] dynamically composes Question Answering pipelines over the DBpedia KG. It employs logistic regression based classifiers for each component for predicting the accuracy and greedily composes a dynamic pipeline of the best components per task. We adapted Frankenstein for the KG information extraction over DBpedia.

4.2   Experiments

The section summarizes a variety of experiments to compare the PLUMBER framework against other baselines. Note, that evaluating the performance of individual components or their combination is out of this evaluation's scope, since they were already used, benchmarked, and evaluated in the respective publications. We report values of the standard metrics Precision (P), Recall (R), and F1 score (F1). In all experiments, end-to-end components (e.g., T2KG) are not part of PLUMBER.

Performance of Static Pipelines. In this experiment, we report results of the static pipelines, i.e., no dynamic selection of a pipeline based on the input text is considered. We ran all 264 pipelines and Table 2 (T2KG & Static noted rows) reports the performance of the best PLUMBER pipeline against the baselines. PLUMBER static pipeline for DBpedia comprises of NeuralCoref [8] for coreference resolution, OpenIE [1] for text triple extraction, TagMe [17] for EL, and Falcon [35] for RL tasks. Also, in case of Frankenstein, we choose its best performing static pipeline. Results illustrated in the Table 2 confirm that the static pipeline composed by the components integrated in PLUMBER outperforms all baselines on DBpedia. We observe that the performance of pipeline approaches is better than an end-to-end monolithic information extraction approaches. Although the PLUMBER pipeline outperforms the baselines, the overall performance is relatively low. All our components have been trained on distinct corpora in their respective publications and our aim was to put them together to understand their collective strengths and weaknesses. Note, Frankenstein addresses the QA pipeline problem and not all components are comparable and can be applied in the context of information extraction. Thus, we integrated NeuralCoref coreference resolution component and OpenIE triple extraction component used in PLUMBER static pipeline into Frankenstein for providing the same experimental settings.

Static Pipeline for Scholarly KG. In order to assess how PLUMBER performs on domain-specific use cases, we evaluate the static pipelines' performance on a scholarly knowledge graph. We use the COV-triples dataset for ORKG. To the best of our knowledge, no baseline exists on information extractions of research contribution descriptions over ORKG. Hence, we execute all static pipelines in PLUMBER tailored to ORKG to select the best one as shown in Table 2 (COV-triples rows). PLUMBER pipelines over ORKG extract statements determining the reproductive number estimates for the COVID-19 infectious disease from scientific articles as shown below.

```
@prefix orkg: <http://orkg.org/orkg/resource/>.
@prefix orkgp: <http://orkg.org/orkg/property/>.

orkg:R48100    orkgp:P16022    "2.68" .
```

In this example, *orkg:R48100* refers to the city of Wuhan in China in the ORKG and *orkgp:P16022* is the property "has R0 estimate (average)". The number "2.68" is the reproductive number estimate. Although COV-triples is a small and manually annotated dataset, we believe that it sheds some light on how

Table 1. 10-fold CV of pipeline selection classifiers wrt. Precision, Recall, and F1 score.

Pipeline selection approach	Dataset	Knowledge graph	Classification		
			P	R	F1
Frankenstein [39]	WebNLG	DBpedia	0.732	0.751	0.741
	COV-triples	ORKG	0.832	0.858	0.845
PLUMBER	WebNLG	DBpedia	**0.877**	**0.900**	**0.888**
	COV-triples	ORKG	**0.901**	**0.917**	**0.909**

PLUMBER will perform on different domains and datasets. Furthermore, it is the first step in creating such a scholarly dataset for IE tasks.

Comparison of the Classification Approaches for Dynamic Pipeline Selection. In this experiment, we study the effect of the transformer-based pipeline selection approach implemented in PLUMBER against the pipeline selection approach of Frankenstein. For a comparable experimental setting, we re-use Frankenstein's classification approach in PLUMBER, keeping the underlying components precisely the same. We perform a 10-fold cross-validation for the classification performance of the employed approach. Table 1 indicates that the PLUMBER pipeline selection significantly outperforms baselines across the board.

Performance Comparison for KG Information Extraction Task. Our third experiment focuses on comparing the performance of PLUMBER against previous baselines for an end-to-end information extraction task. The results in Table 2 illustrate that the dynamic pipelines built using PLUMBER for KG information extraction outperform the best static pipelines of PLUMBER as well as the dynamically selected pipelines by Frankenstein (rows noted with dynamic). The end-to-end baselines, such as Kertkeidka-chorn and Ichise [25]. We also observe that in cross-domain experiments for COV-triples datasets, dynamically selected pipelines perform better than the static pipeline. In the cross-domain experiment, the static and dynamic PLUMBER pipelines are relatively better performing than the other two KGs. Unlike components for DBpedia, components integrated into PLUMBER for ORKG are customized for KG triple extraction. We conclude that when components are integrated into a framework such as PLUMBER aiming for the KG information extraction task, it is crucial to select the pipeline based on the input text dynamically. The superior performance of PLUMBER shows that the dynamic pipeline selection has a positive impact agnostic of the underlying KG and dataset. This also answers our overall research question.

4.3 Ablation Studies

PLUMBER and baselines render relatively low performance on all the employed datasets. Hence, in the ablation studies our aim is to provide a holistic picture of underlying errors, collective success, and failures of the integrated components.

In the first study, we calculate the proportion of errors in PLUMBER. The modular architecture of the proposed framework allows us to benchmark each component independently. We consider the erroneous cases of PLUMBER on the test set of the WebNLG dataset. We calculate the performance (F1 score) of the PLUMBER dynamic pipeline (cf. Table 2) at each step in the pipeline. The results show that the coreference resolution components caused 21.54% of the errors, 33.71% are caused by text triple extractors, 18.17% by the entity linking components, and 26.58% are caused by the relation linking components.

We conclude that the text triple extractor components contribute to the largest chunk of the errors over DBpedia. One possible reason for their limited performance is that open-domain information extracting components were not initially released for the KG information extraction task. Also, these components do not incorporate any schema or prior knowledge to guide the extraction. We observe that the errors mainly occur when the sentence is complex (with more than one entity and predicate), or relations are not explicitly mentioned in the sentence. We further analyze the text triple extractor errors. The error analysis at the level of the triple subject, predicate, and object showed that most errors are in predicates (40.17%) followed by objects (35.98%) and subjects (23.85%).

Further Analysis. Aiming to understand why IE pipelines perform with low accuracy, we conduct a more in-depth analysis per IE task. In the first analysis, we evaluated each component independently on the WebNLG dataset. Researchers [12,40] proposed several criterion for micro-benchmarking tools/components for KG tasks (entity linking, relation linking, etc.) based on the linguistic features of a sentence. We motivate our analysis based on the following:

I) *Text Triple Extraction:* We consider the number of words (wc) in the input sentence (a sentence is termed by "simple" with average word length of 7.41 [39]. Sentences with higher number of words than seven are complex sentences). Furthermore, having a comma in a sentence (sub-clause) to separate clauses is another factor. Atomic sentences (e.g., *"cats have tails"*) are a type of

Table 2. Overall performance comparison of static and dynamic pipelines for the KG information extraction task.

System	Dataset	Knowledge graph	Performance		
			P	R	F1
T2KG [25]	WebNLG	DBpedia	0.133	0.140	0.135
Frankenstein (Static) [39]	WebNLG	DBpedia	0.177	0.189	0.181
PLUMBER (Static)	WebNLG	DBpedia	0.210	0.225	0.215
	COV-triples	ORKG	0.403	0.423	0.413
Frankenstein (Dynamic) [39]	WebNLG	DBpedia	0.199	0.208	0.203
	COV-triples	ORKG	0.403	0.424	0.413
PLUMBER (Dynamic)	WebNLG	DBpedia	**0.287**	**0.307**	**0.297**
	COV-triples	ORKG	**0.411**	**0.437**	**0.424**

sentence that also affects triples extractors' behavior. Moreover, nominal relation as in *"Durin, son of Thorin"* is another impacting factor on the performance. Uppercase and lowercase mentions of the words (i.e., correct capitalization of the first character and not the entire word) in a sentence are standard errors for entity linking components. We consider this as a micro-benchmarking criteria.

II) *Coreference Resolution:* We focus on the length of the coreference chain (i.e., the number of aliases for a single mention). Additionally, the number of clusters is another criterion in the analysis. A cluster refers to the groups of mentions that require disambiguation (e.g., *"mother bought a new phone, she is so happy about it"* where the first cluster is *mother → she* and the second is *phone → it*). The presence of proper nouns in the sentence is studied as well as acronyms. Furthermore, the demonstrative nature of the sentence is also observed as a factor. Demonstrative sentences are the ones that contain demonstrative pronouns (this, that, etc.).

III) *Entity Linking:* The number of entities in a sentence ($e = 1,2$) is a crucial observation for the entity linking task. Capitalization of the surface form is another criterion for micro-benchmarking entity linking tools. An entity is termed as an explicit entity when the entity's surface form in a sentence matches the KG label. An entity is implicit when there is a vocabulary mismatch. For example, in the sentence *"The wife of Obama is Michelle Obama."*, the surface form *Obama* is expected to be linked to dbr:Barack_Obama and considered as an implicit entity [40]. The last linguistic feature is the number of words (w) in an entity label (e.g., *The Storm on the Sea of Galilee* has seven words).

IV) *Relation Linking:* Similar to the entity linking criteria, we focus on the number of relations in a sentence ($rel = 1,2$). The type of relation (i.e., explicit, or implicit) is another parameter. Covered relation (sentences without a predicate surface form) is also used as a feature for micro-benchmarking: *"Which companies have launched a rocket from Cape Canaveral Air Force station?"* where the dbo:manufacturing relation is not mentioned in the sentence. Covered relations highly depend on common sense knowledge (i.e., reasoning) and the structure of the KG [40]. Lastly, the number of words ($w <= N$) in a predicate surface form is also considered.

Figure 3 illustrates micro-benchmarking of various PLUMBER components per task. We observe that across IE tasks, the F1 score of the components varies significantly based on the sentence's linguistic features. In fact, there exist no single component which performs equally well on all the micro-benchmarking criteria. This observation further validates our hypothesis to design PLUMBER for building dynamic information extraction pipelines based on the strengths and weaknesses of the integrated components. We also note in Fig. 3 that all the CR components report limited performance for the demonstrative sentences (*demonstratives*). When there is more than one coreference cluster in a sentence, all other CR components observe a discernible drop in F1 score. The Neural-Coref [8] component performs best for *proper nouns*, whereas PyCobalt [18] performs best for the *acronyms* feature (almost being tied by NeuralCoref). In the TE task, Graphene [7] shows the most stable performance across all categories.

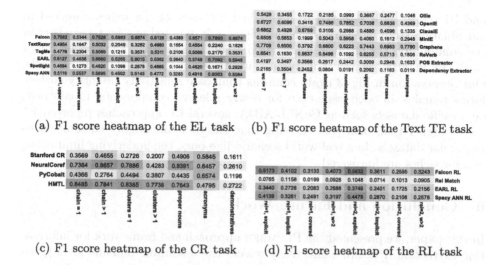

(a) F1 score heatmap of the EL task

(b) F1 score heatmap of the Text TE task

(c) F1 score heatmap of the CR task

(d) F1 score heatmap of the RL task

Fig. 3. Comparison of F1 scores per component for different IE tasks based on the various linguistic features of an input sentence (number of entities, word count in a sentence, implicit vs. explicit relation, etc.). Darker colors indicate a higher F1 score.

However, the performance of all components (except Dependency Parser) drops significantly when the number of words in a sentence exceeds seven (wc > 7). Case sensitivity also affects the performance and all components observe a noticeable drop in F1 score for lowercase entity mentions in the sentence. Similar behavior is observed for entity linking components where case sensitivity is a significant cause of poor performance. When the sentence has one entity and it is implicit (e = 1, implicit); all entity linking components face challenges in correctly linking the entities to the underlying KG. Relation linking components also report lower performance for implicit relations.

5 Discussion

Even though the dynamic pipelines of PLUMBER outperforms static pipelines, the overall performance of PLUMBER and baselines for the KG information extraction task remains low. Our detailed and exhaustive ablation studies suggest that when individual components are plugged together, their individual performance is a major error source. However, this behavior is expected, considering earlier research works in other domains also observe a similar trend. As in 2015 Gerbil framework [41] and in 2018 Frankenstein [39]. Within two years, the community has released several components dedicated to solving entity linking and relation linking [14,30,35], which were two loopholes identified by [39] for the QA task.

We observe that state of the art components for information extraction still have much potential to improve their performance (both in terms of runtime and F1 score). It is essential to highlight that some of the issues observed in our ablation study are very basic and repeatedly pointed out by researchers in the community. For instance, Derczynski et al. [12] in 2015, followed by Singh et al. [39] in 2018, showed that case sensitivity is a main challenge for EL tools. Our observation in Fig. 3 again confirms that case sensitivity of entity surface forms remains an open issue even for newly released components. In contrast, on specific datasets such as CoNLL-AIDA, several EL approaches reported F1 scores higher than 0.90 [43], showing that EL tools are highly customized to particular datasets. In a real-world scenario like ours, the underlying limitations of approaches are uncovered.

6   Conclusion and Future Work

In this paper, we presented the PLUMBER approach and framework for information extraction. PLUMBER effectively selects the a suitable pipeline for a given input sentence using the sentential contextual features and a state-of-the-art transformer-based classification model. PLUMBER has a service-oriented architecture which is scalable, extensible, reusable, and agnostic of the underlying KG. The core idea of PLUMBER is to combine the strengths of already existing disjoint research for KG information extraction and build a foundation for a platform to promote reusability for the construction of large-scale and semantically structured KGs. Our empirical results suggest that the performance of the individual components directly impacts the end-to-end information extraction accuracy.

This article does not focus on internal system architecture or employed algorithms in a particular IE component to analyze the failures. The focus of the ablation studies is to holistically study the collective success and failure cases for the various tasks. Our studies provide the research community with insightful results over two knowledge graphs, 33 components, 264 pipelines. Our work is a step in the larger research agenda of offering the research community an effective way for synergistically combining and orchestrating various focused IE approaches balancing their strengths and weaknesses taking different application domains into account. We plan to extend our work in the following directions: i) extending PLUMBER to other KGs such as UMLS [5] and Wikidata [42]. ii) addressing multilinguality with PLUMBER, and iii) creating high performing RL components.

Acknowledgements. This work was co-funded by the European Research Council for the project ScienceGRAPH (Grant agreement ID: 819536) and the TIB Leibniz Information Centre for Science and Technology.

References

1. Angeli, G., Premkumar, M.J.J., Manning, C.D.: Leveraging linguistic structure for open domain information extraction, pp. 344–354. ACL (2015)

2. Auer, S., Bizer, C., Kobilarov, G., Lehmann, J., Cyganiak, R., Ives, Z.: DBpedia: a nucleus for a web of open data. In: Aberer, K., et al. (eds.) ASWC/ISWC-2007. LNCS, vol. 4825, pp. 722–735. Springer, Heidelberg (2007). https://doi.org/10.1007/978-3-540-76298-0_52

3. Balog, K.: Entity linking. Entity-Oriented Search. TIRS, vol. 39, pp. 147–188. Springer, Cham (2018). https://doi.org/10.1007/978-3-319-93935-3_5

4. Bastos, A., et al.: RECON: relation extraction using knowledge graph context in a graph neural network. In: Proceedings of The Web Conference (WWW) (2021)

5. Bodenreider, O.: The unified medical language system (UMLS): integrating biomedical terminology. Nucleic Acids Res. **32**, D267–D270 (2004)

6. Both, A., Diefenbach, D., Singh, K., Shekarpour, S., Cherix, D., Lange, C.: Qanary - A methodology for vocabulary-driven open question answering systems, vol. 9678, pp. 625–641 (2016)

7. Cetto, M., Niklaus, C., Freitas, A., Handschuh, S.: Graphene: semantically-linked propositions in open information extraction. In: Proceedings of the 27th COLING, pp. 2300–2311 (2018)

8. Clark, K., Manning, C.D.: Deep reinforcement learning for mention-ranking coreference models. In: Proceedings of the 2016 EMNLP, pp. 2256–2262 (2016)

9. Cui, W., Liu, S., Wu, Z., Wei, H.: How hierarchical topics evolve in large text corpora. IEEE TVCG **20**(12), 2281–2290 (2014)

10. Daiber, J., Jakob, M., Hokamp, C., Mendes, P.N.: Improving efficiency and accuracy in multilingual entity extraction. In: Proceedings of the 9th I-Semantics (2013)

11. Delpeuch, A.: OpenTapioca: lightweight entity linking for Wikidata (2019)

12. Derczynski, L., et al.: Analysis of named entity recognition and linking for tweets. Inf. Process. Manage. **51**, 32–49 (2015)

13. Dong, T., Wang, Z., Li, J., Bauckhage, C., Cremers, A.B.: Triple classification using regions and fine-grained entity typing. In: Proceedings of the AAAI Conference on Artificial Intelligence, vol. 33, pp. 77–85 (2019)

14. Dubey, M., Banerjee, D., Chaudhuri, D., Lehmann, J.: EARL: joint entity and relation linking for question answering over knowledge graphs. In: Vrandečić, D., et al. (eds.) ISWC 2018. LNCS, vol. 11136, pp. 108–126. Springer, Cham (2018). https://doi.org/10.1007/978-3-030-00671-6_7

15. Fader, A., Soderland, S., Etzioni, O.: Identifying relations for open information extraction. In: Proceedings of the 2011 EMNLP, pp. 1535–1545, July 2011

16. Fensel, D., et al.: Towards LarKC: a platform for web-scale reasoning. In: IEEE ICSC, pp. 524–529 (2008)

17. Ferragina, P., Scaiella, U.: TAGME: on-the-fly annotation of short text fragments (by wikipedia entities), pp. 1625–1628 (2010)

18. Freitas, A., Bermeitinger, B., Handschuh, S.: Lambda-3/pycobalt: coreference resolution in python. https://github.com/Lambda-3/PyCobalt

19. Garcia, J., et al.: Constructing a shared infrastructure for software architecture analysis and maintenance. In: ICSA (2021)

20. Gardent, C., Shimorina, A., Narayan, S., Perez-Beltrachini, L.: Creating training corpora for NLG micro-planners, pp. 179–188 (2017)

21. Gashteovski, K., Gemulla, R., del Corro, L.: MinIE: minimizing facts in open information extraction. In: Proceedings of the 2017 EMNLP, pp. 2630–2640 (2017)

22. Hou, Y., Jochim, C., Gleize, M., Bonin, F., Ganguly, D.: Identification of tasks, datasets, evaluation metrics, and numeric scores for scientific leaderboards construction. In: Proceedings of the 57th ACL, pp. 5203–5213 (2019)

23. Ibrahim, Y., Riedewald, M., Weikum, G., Zeinalipour-Yazti, D.: Bridging quantities in tables and text. In: 2019 IEEE 35th ICDE, pp. 1010–1021 (2019)

24. Jaradeh, M.Y., et al.: Open Research Knowledge Graph: Next Generation Infrastructure for Semantic Scholarly Knowledge. Marina Del K-CAP19 (2019)
25. Kertkeidkachorn, N., Ichise, R.: T2kg: an end-to-end system for creating knowledge graph from unstructured text. In: AAAI Workshops, vol. WS-17 (2017)
26. Kim, J.D., et al.: OKBQA framework for collaboration on developing natural language question answering systems (2017)
27. Liang, S., Stockinger, K., de Farias, T.M., Anisimova, M., Gil, M.: Querying knowledge graphs in natural language (2020)
28. Liu, Y., Zhang, T., Liang, Z., Ji, H., McGuinness, D.: Seq2rdf: an end-to-end application for deriving triples from natural language text (2018)
29. Liu, Y., et al.: RoBERTa: a robustly optimized BERT pretraining approach (2019)
30. Mihindukulasooriya, N., et al.: Leveraging semantic parsing for relation linking over knowledge bases. ISWC (2020)
31. Morbidoni, C., Polleres, A., Tummarello, G., Le-Phuoc, D.: Semantic web pipes (2007)
32. Niklaus, C., Cetto, M., Freitas, A., Handschuh, S.: A survey on open information extraction. In: Proceedings of the 27th COLING, pp. 3866–3878 (2018)
33. Ponza, M., Del Corro, L., Weikum, G.: Facts that matter. In: Proceedings of the 2018 EMNLP, pp. 1043–1048. ACL (2018)
34. Raghunathan, K., et al.: A multi-pass sieve for coreference resolution. In: EMNLP (2010)
35. Sakor, A., et al.: Old is gold: linguistic driven approach for entity and relation linking of short text, pp. 2336–2346. ACL (2019)
36. Sakor, A., Singh, K., Patel, A., Vidal, M.E.: Falcon 2.0: an entity and relation linking tool over wikidata. In: CIKM (2020)
37. Sanh, V., Wolf, T., Ruder, S.: A hierarchical multi-task approach for learning embeddings from semantic tasks. In: Proceedings of the AAAI, vol. 33, pp. 6949–6956 (2019)
38. Singh, K., et al.: Capturing knowledge in semantically-typed relational patterns to enhance relation linking. In: Proceedings of the Knowledge Capture Conference, K-CAP 2017, 4–6 December 2017, Austin, TX, USA, pp. 31:1–31:8 (2017)
39. Singh, K., et al.: Why reinvent the wheel: let's build question answering systems together, pp. 1247–1256. WWW 2018 (2018)
40. Singh, K., et al.: QaldGen: towards microbench marking of question answering systems over knowledge graphs. In: ISWC, pp. 277–292 (2019)
41. Usbeck, R., Röder, M., et al., N.N.: GERBIL: general entity annotator benchmarking framework. In: Proceedings of the 24th WWW, pp. 1133–1143 (2015)
42. Vrandečić, D., Krötzsch, M.: Wikidata: a free collaborative knowledgebase. Commun. ACM **57**(10), 78–85 (2014)
43. Yang, X., et al.: Learning dynamic context augmentation for global entity linking. In: EMNLP-IJCNLP, pp. 271–281 (2019)
44. Yao, L., Mao, C., Luo, Y.: KG-BERT: BERT for knowledge graph completion (2019)
45. Yu, W., Li, Z., Zeng, Q., Jiang, M.: Tablepedia: automating pdf table reading in an experimental evidence exploration and analytic system. WWW 2019, pp. 3615–3619 (2019)

Preprocessing Techniques for End-To-End Trainable RNN-Based Conversational System

Hussein Maziad[1], Julie-Ann Rammouz[1], Boulos El Asmar[2], and Joe Tekli[1(✉)]

[1] E.C.E. Department, Lebanese American University, Byblos 36, Lebanon
{hussein.maziad,julieann.rammouz}@lau.edu, joe.tekli@lau.edu.lb
[2] Logistics Robotics, BMW Group, 80788 Munich, Germany
boulos.el-asmar@bmw.de

Abstract. Spoken dialogue system interfaces are gaining increasing attention, with examples including Apple's Siri, Amazon's Alexa, and numerous other products. Yet most existing solutions remain heavily data-driven, and face limitations in integrating and handling data semantics. They mainly rely on statistical co-occurrences in the training dataset and lack a more profound knowledge integration model with semantically structured information such as knowledge graphs. This paper evaluates the impact of performing knowledge base integration (KBI) to regulate the dialogue output of a deep learning conversational system. More specifically, it evaluates whether integrating dependencies between the data, obtained from the semantic linking of an external knowledge base (KB), would help improve conversational quality. To do so, we compare three approaches of conversation preprocessing methods: i) no KBI: considering conversational data with no external knowledge integration, ii) All Predicates KBI: considering conversational data where all dialogue pairs are augmented with their linked predicates from the domain KB, and iii) Intersecting Predicates KBI: considering conversational data where dialogue pairs are augmented only with their intersecting predicates (to filter-out potentially useless or redundant knowledge). We vary the amount of history considered in the conversational data, ranging from 0% (considering the last dialogue pair only) to 100% (considering all dialogue pairs, from the beginning of the dialogue). To our knowledge, this is the first study to evaluate knowledge integration in the preprocessing phase of conversational systems. Results are promising and show that knowledge integration – with an amount of history ranging between 10% and 75%, generally improves conversational quality.

Keywords: Conversational dialogue systems · Data semantics · Knowledge base · Knowledge integration · Conversational data preprocessing

1 Introduction

Spoken dialogue system interfaces are gaining increasing attention, with examples including Apple's Siri, Google Assistant, Microsoft's Cortana, Amazon's Alexa, and numerous other products. Most existing solutions utilize deep learning, where recurrent neural networks (RNNs) have been successfully adapted to dialogue systems through

© Springer Nature Switzerland AG 2021
M. Brambilla et al. (Eds.): ICWE 2021, LNCS 12706, pp. 255–270, 2021.
https://doi.org/10.1007/978-3-030-74296-6_20

encoder-decoder architectures [31]. While the main advantage of deep (RNN) learning is its reduced feature engineering, it often requires large amounts of labeled data (which are not always available), and purely data-driven learning can lead to unexpected results (depending on the quality of the training data) [20, 29]. In this context, recent works in language representation and processing, e.g., [1, 5, 12, 16], have investigated the integration of external domain knowledge to augment the training of deep learners. Yet their applications and related data preprocessing do not target conversational dialogue systems.

The development of an RNN-based dialogue system consists of four main steps: i) preprocessing the conversational dataset at hand to use as the training data, ii) building the RNN responsible for inferring dialogue policies from the conversational data, iii) training the model with and without testing and eventually preprocessing external knowledge, and iv) representing the external knowledge alongside the conversational data to compare the obtained results. In this context, data preprocessing techniques for end-to-end RNN-based conversational systems seem to lack common grounds and comparative evaluations. Results in [24] show that data representation plays a crucial role in the performance of a neural network. In other words, the initial preprocessing step, including input data and context representation, is of central importance in building an end-to-end RNN-based dialogue system, and needs to be properly designed and fine-tuned before diving deeper into external knowledge integration and processing.

This paper evaluates the impact of performing knowledge base integration (KBI) to regulate the dialogue output of a deep learning conversational system. More specifically, it evaluates whether integrating dependencies between the data, obtained from the semantic linking of an external knowledge base (KB), would help improve conversational quality. In contrast with most existing solutions (cf. Section 2), where the authors rely solely on the quality of the training data to improve conversational quality, this study aims at evaluating whether integrating additional dependencies between the data, obtained from the semantic linking of an external KB, would help improve conversational quality. To do so, we evaluate and compare three approaches of conversation preprocessing methods: i) *No KBI*: considering conversational data with no external knowledge integration, ii) *All Predicates KBI*: considering conversational data where all dialogue pairs are augmented with their linked predicates from the domain KB, and iii) *Intersecting Predicates KBI*: considering conversational data where dialogue pairs are augmented only with their intersecting (common) predicates (in order to reduce and filter-out potentially useless or redundant knowledge). For each of the mentioned approaches, we vary the amount of history considered in the conversational data, ranging from 0% (considering the last dialogue pair only) to 100% (considering all dialogue pairs, from the beginning of the dialogue). To our knowledge, this is the first study to evaluate knowledge integration in the preprocessing phase of conversational systems. Results are promising and show that knowledge integration – with an amount of history ranging between 10% and 75%, generally improves conversational quality.

The remainder of this paper is organized as follows. Section 2 briefly reviews the related works. Section 3 describes our proposal and the suggested conversation preprocessing methods. Section 4 describes our experimental evaluation and results, before concluding with future work in Sect. 5.

2   Related Works

2.1   Conversational Systems

The main functionality of a spoken dialogue system consists in decoding text utterances to extract semantic information through spoken language understanding techniques [34]. The semantic representation of every utterance is then processed by a dialogue state tracker, which estimates the dialogue state in order to decide what action to take, according to a pre-defined dialogue policy. Such modular architectures depend to a large extent on a series of hierarchical handcrafted rules to adapt the dialogue policy according to the detected entities and to the utterance intent. This may work, with much effort, for restricted domains where the number of intents is generally limited. However, the extraction of semantic information becomes much more intricate when shifting to a more general domain environment, or when the dialogue is required to cover more features during the conversation. Providing an exhaustive list of references for such traditional dialogue systems is out of the scope of the current work. However, recent advances in end-to-end training of neural networks, along with the availability of large-scale conversation datasets [23] has permitted to directly infer dialogue policy from conversational data. Notably, recurrent neural networks (RNNs) have been successfully adapted to dialogue systems through encoder-decoder architectures [31]. While the main advantage of (deep) RNN learning is its reduced feature engineering, yet it often requires large amounts of labeled data (which are not always available), and the purely data-driven learning can lead to unexpected results (depending on the quality of the training data) [20, 29]. However, integrating domain knowledge, in the form of an external knowledge base (KB) semantic linking approach – which we refer to as KB Integration (KBI) – has many advantages, including: i) resolving ambiguity in language, ii) performing semantic-aware data integration, and iii) linking conversations with relevant documents and meta-data through semantic search and semantic similarity evaluation. KBI does introduce an increase in training time and computation, which might not be a major concern since the training is done offline, prior to system run-time.

2.2   Generative Sequence-to-Sequence Deep Learning Models

Generative sequence-to-sequence (seq2seq) models follow the line initiated by Ritter et al. [22] who treats the generation of conversational dialogue as a statistical machine translation problem. Seq2seq models have recently shown promising results, mapping complicated structures together. This has direct applications in natural language understanding [28], and in dialogue response generation by mapping queries with responses [26], such as in recent works [25, 26] where RNNs have been used to model dialogue in short conversations. Seq2seq models have also been used for neural machine translation [2, 15, 28], and have achieved remarkable results in syntactic constituency parsing [30], and in image captioning [32]. As it is the case for most deep learning models, seq2seq requires little feature engineering and domain specificity whilst matching or surpassing state-of-the-art results. However, these models, being based on recurrent neural networks (RNNs), suffer from the vanishing gradient problem, that's why variants of Long Short-Term Memory (LSTM) RNNs [11] are mostly used. Yet it is often very hard to control the output of such models, primarily determined by statistical co-occurrences in the used training data with limited synthesis of additional external knowledge (cf. Section 2.3). Furthermore, such approaches are still unable to generate coherent responses [17] which remains a major drawback for conversational dialogue applications.

2.3 Deep Neural Models with External Knowledge

Incorporating external knowledge within deep neural models has been of increasing interest recently, promising to enhance generalization, increase interpretability, and control network output. Recent works in [12, 13], have focused on transferring logical knowledge into diverse neural network architectures by imposing posterior constraints on the network. Also, the authors in [5] have used a structured label relation graph to improve object classification. Other approaches integrate domain knowledge on training time, consist in integrating first order logic with Bayesian models [6], or deriving probabilistic graphical models for Markov logic networks from a set of rules. Also, in [1] a novel neural knowledge language model was developed, bringing symbolic knowledge from a knowledge graph into the expressive power of RNN language models. In a related study, the authors in [17] improve generative models by learning external knowledge, represented as distributed embeddings, and refined during training time to increase model consistency and infer speaker-specific characteristics. External knowledge integration approaches have also been investigated with neural networks using external memory [4, 14, 27], where a long-term memory structure acts as a (dynamic) knowledge base. However, the latter approaches focus on learning attention models over unstructured data, whereas we aim to link to entities using a structured knowledge base (KB).

3   Proposal: Preprocessing Techniques for Conversational RNN

We process the dialogue as a seq2seq learning problem within a neural encoder-decoder architecture. The overall architecture of our approach is shown in Fig. 1.

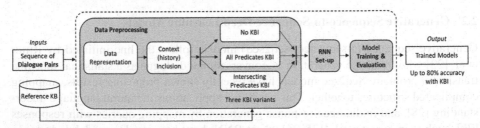

Fig. 1. Simplified activity diagram describing our approach

3.1   Data Representation

We adopt a typical data representation model where dialogue utterances are represented as a sequence of user requests u and system responses s: (u1, s1), (u2, s2), ..., (uk, sk), and k represents the number of turns in the dialogue [33]. More specifically, we first parse the raw text, split it into conversations, and then split every conversation into turns, where every turn consists of a pair of user utterance and the corresponding system response. In order to easily process the dialogue within a seq2seq learning problem, we represent each word in every utterance and reply as a one-hot vector[1]. Additionally, we use a unique index per word to represent the input and targets of the network.

Note that the different preprocessing techniques considered in this study will produce different variations of the above-mentioned data representation, which we present and discussion in the following sections.

3.2 Context and History

We define the context of a dialogue training pair (u_i, s_i) as $([u_1, u_2,..., u_{i-1}, u_i], s_i)$, where the network is fed: a concatenation of all previous user utterances (i.e., the user request history) up until the current one u_i, as well as the current system response s_i. Accordingly, we define the history of a dialogue as the context of the dialogue starting from the present utterance, by specifying the percentage of the previous utterance that will be included in the following one. For instance, $([u_1^{50\%}, u_2^{50\%},..., u_{i-1}^{50\%}, u_i], s_i)$ represents 50% of (u_i, s_i)'s dialogue history where $u_{i-1}^{50\%}$ represents half of u_{i-1}'s textual tokens, and so forth. Similarly, $([u_1^{100\%}, u_2^{100\%},..., u_{i-1}^{100\%}, u_i], s_i)$ represents 100% of the dialogue history, and is equivalent to the complete context of training pair (u_i, s_i), i.e., $([u_1, u_2,..., u_{i-1}, u_i], s_i)$.

3.3 RNN Set-up

We utilize a typical seq2seq network where two RNNs work together in order to transform one sequence into another. The first network, i.e., the encoder, reads the input sequence and condenses it into a vector using typical one-hot-encoding. The decoder network reads the vector and its context and transforms it into an output sequence. More specifically, the decoder network accepts as input the context vector which includes the history of the entire sequence. At every decoding stage, the decoder is given an input token and a hidden state where the context vector serves as an initial hidden state. A problem with typical decoders is that they process the complete context vectors which carry the dialogue's entire sequence (100% history). For this reason, and in order to improve our model, we add an attention mechanism which teaches the decoder to focus on a particular part of the input sequence. To do so, we compute a set of attention weights, and multiply them by the encoder output vectors to create a weighted combination which contains information about the specific part of the input sequence that helps the decoder produce the right output sequence. The attention weights are calculated using an additional feed-forward layer, which accepts as input the decoder's input and hidden states and produces the weights accordingly.

---

[1] It is called one-hot because only one bit is "hot" or TRUE at any time. For example, a 3-bit one-hot encoding would have three states: $001, 010$, and 100, compared with 2^3 binary combinations obtained with binary encoding. Note that other encodings such as word2vec and GloVe vetor representations can be used.

3.4 Knowledge Representation

We represent domain knowledge in the form of a machine readable knowledge base (KB), consisting of nodes and edges, where nodes represent groups of words/expressions and edges represent the semantic links connecting the nodes (synonymy, hyponymy (Is-A), meronymy (Part-Of), etc. [19]). The latter can also be represented as sets of triplets: *concept₁-relationship-concept₂*, or as more commonly known: *subject-predicate-object* triplets [10] (cf. Fig. 2).

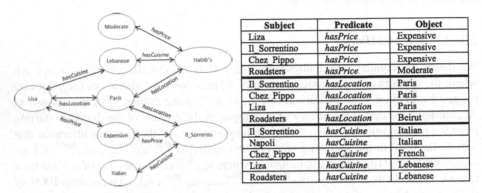

Subject	Predicate	Object
Liza	*hasPrice*	Expensive
Il Sorrentino	*hasPrice*	Expensive
Chez Pippo	*hasPrice*	Expensive
Roadsters	*hasPrice*	Moderate
Il Sorrentino	*hasLocation*	Paris
Chez Pippo	*hasLocation*	Paris
Liza	*hasLocation*	Paris
Roadsters	*hasLocation*	Beirut
Il Sorrentino	*hasCuisine*	Italian
Napoli	*hasCuisine*	Italian
Chez Pippo	*hasCuisine*	French
Liza	*hasCuisine*	Lebanese
Roadsters	*hasCuisine*	Lebanese

Fig. 2. Sample KB tailored base on DSRC2 [7]

In the following, we evaluate the impact of performing KB integration (KBI) at the data preprocessing stage, to regulate the dialogue output of a conversational system.

3.5 Data Preprocessing Techniques

As motivated previously, data preprocessing in conversational systems is of central importance in building an end-to-end RNN approach. For this reason, we propose and evaluate three methods for KBI at the input and output of the encoder and decoder networks: i) *No KBI*, ii) *All Predicates KBI*, and iii) *Intersecting Predicates KBI*. These methods can be applied to preprocess the training, the validation, and the testing data sets.

3.5.1 No Knowledge Base Integration (no KBI)

This is the elementary approach where the dialogue exchange is represented in its most basic form: $(u_1, s_1), (u_2, s_2),\ldots (u_k, s_k)$, i.e., as a sequence of pairs of user utterance u and system reply s tokens. We do not consider any external knowledge here and vary dialogue history to include more or less of the previous user utterances following our context model: $([u_1, u_2,\ldots, u_i], s_i)$ where the system is fed an amount of previous user utterances following user-specified history percentage (cf. Sect. 3.2).

Consider for instance the examples in Table 1: 0% history in considered in Table 1.a where no previous user utterances are included in the training pairs, 50% history is considered in Table 1.b where the first half of the previous user utterances is included in the training pair, and 100% history is considered in Table 1.c where all the previous user utterances are included in the training pair. By observing this representation, one can notice that the size of the training data increases significantly with the increase in the percentage of history. This will impact both training speed and quality as we will observe in the experimental evaluation section.

Table 1. Sample examples for *No KBI* preprocessing approach

Text in red represents the additions from previous user utterance history

a. 0% history

Pair	User Utterance	System Response
1	Hello	Hi, how can I help you?
2	I would like to book a reservation at an expensive restaurant in Paris	Sure, I will look one up
3	<Silence>	Do you have a cuisine in mind?
4	Italian would be great	Okay, how about Il Sorrentino?

b. 50% history

Pair	User Utterance	System Response
1	Hello	Hi, how can I help you?
2	I would like to book a reservation at an expensive restaurant in Paris	Sure, I will look one up
3	<Silence> I would like to book	Do you have a cuisine in mind?
4	Italian would be great <Silence> I would	Okay, how about Il Sorrentino?

c. 100% history No KBI

Pair	User Utterance	System Response
1	Hello	Hi, how can I help you?
2	I would like to book a reservation at an expensive restaurant in Paris Hello	Sure, I will look one up
3	<Silence> I would like to book a reservation at an expensive restaurant in Paris Hello	Do you have a cuisine in mind?
4	Italian would be great <Silence> I would like to book a reservation at an expensive restaurant in Paris Hello	Okay, how about Il Sorrentino?

All examples presented in the paper are prepared based on the real dialogues from the restaurant reservation system dataset: DSTC2 [9], using the dataset's reference KB (cf. Fig. 2).

3.5.2 All Predicates KBI

Our ambition is to integrate knowledge at the level of the preprocessing step. As such, we introduce the *All predicates KBI* representation, which scans each word token in the current user utterance to identify matching objects in the reference KB. Then, it intersects the subjects connected with the matching object predicates and appends them to the user utterance. It also allows appending a varying amount of dialogue history to include more or less of the previous user utterances with their augmented KB subjects.

Consider in Table 2 an extension of the examples from Table 1: 10% history in Table 1a where no previous user utterances are included in the training pairs, 50% history in

Table 1b where the first half of the previous user utterances is included in the training pair, and 100% history in Table 1c where all the previous user utterances are included in the training pair.

Table 2. Sample examples extended from Table 1, to represent *All Predicates KBI* preprocessing approach

Text in red represents the additions from previous user utterance history
Text in blue represents the additions of subject tokens from the knowledge base
Test underlined represents a matching user utterance with an object from the knowledge base

a. 0% history

Pair	User Utterance	System Response
1	Hello	Hi, how can I help you?
2	I would like to book a reservation at an <u>expensive</u> restaurant in <u>Paris</u> Liza Chez_Pippo il_Sorrentino	Sure, I will look one up
3	<Silence>	Do you have a cuisine in mind?
4	<u>Italian</u> would be great Il_Sorrentino Napoli	Okay, how about Il_Sorrentino?

b. 50% history

Pair	User Utterance	System Response
1	Hello	Hi, how can I help you?
2	I would like to book a reservation at an <u>expensive</u> restaurant in <u>Paris</u> Liza Chez_Pippo il_Sorrentino	Sure, I will look one up
3	<Silence> I would like to book a reservation at an	Do you have a cuisine in mind?
4	<u>Italian</u> would be great Il_Sorrentino Napoli <Silence> I would like to	Okay, how about Il_Sorrentino?

c. 100% history

Pair	User Utterance	System Response
1	Hello	Hi, how can I help you?
2	I would like to book a reservation at an <u>expensive</u> restaurant in <u>Paris</u> Liza Chez_Pippo il_Sorrentino Hello	Sure, I will look one up
3	<Silence> I would like to book a reservation at an expensive restaurant in Paris Liza Chez_Pippo il_Sorrentino Hello	Do you have a cuisine in mind?
4	<u>Italian</u> would be great Il_Sorrentino Napoli <Silence> I would like to book a reservation at an expensive restaurant in Paris Liza Chez_Pippo il_Sorrentino Hello	Okay, how about Il_Sorrentino?

While the *All Predicates KBI* approach seems promising, it presents a major drawback: for every single matching object token between a training pair and the reference KB, this approach will retrieve all matching subjects whose number might be significantly large, depending on the size of the KB. Consider for instance the example in Table 3, where certain pairs contain hundreds of matching entries, while other pairs contain only a few. This makes the dialogue unbalanced in terms of the number of terms per sequence. While Table 3 presents a case for 0% history, the problem will be further exacerbated when including more of the conversation history, as shown in Table 4.

Note that in the last pair of Table 4, we have thousands of entries, which will probably make the training model overfitted, and will thus reflect badly on the results. In other words, a single training pair with only one matching object token might end up encompassing a huge number of subject tokens, resulting in crowded (oversized) training pairs which would negatively affect both training time and quality (including potentially noisy data entries).

Table 3. Crowded data example for *All Predicates KBI* with 0% history

Pair	User Utterance	System Response
1	Hello	Hi, how can I help you?
2	I would like to book a reservation at an <u>expensive</u> restaurant in <u>Paris</u> Liza Chez_Pippo il_Sorrentino	Sure, I will look one up
3	<Silence>	Do you have a cuisine in mind?
4	<u>Italian</u> would be great (250 italian restaurants augmented here…)	Okay, how about Il_Sorrentino?
5	I think I will go for <u>Lebanese</u> instead (250 Lebanese restaurants augmented here…)	Sure, I have found ten in Paris
6	<Silence>	Anything else?
7	I would rather have them in <u>madrid</u> (300 restaurants in madrid augmented here…)	I will look for restaurants in madrid
8	Please make sure the restaurants are in a <u>moderate</u> price range (1500 moderately priced restaurants augmented here…)	I will have them ready in no time

Table 4. Crowded data example for *All Predicates KBI* with 100% history

Pair	User Utterance	System Response
1	Hello	Hi, how can I help you?
2	I would like to book a reservation at an <u>expensive</u> restaurant in <u>Paris</u> Liza Chez_Pippo il_Sorrentino Hello	Sure, I will look one up
3	<Silence> I would like to book a reservation at an expensive restaurant in Paris Liza Chez_Pippo il_Sorrentino Hello	Do you have a cuisine in mind?
4	<u>Italian</u> would be great (250 Italian restaurants augmented here…) + (18 terms from pair 3)	Okay, how about Il_Sorrentino?
5	I think I will go for <u>Lebanese</u> instead (250 Lebanese restaurants augmented here…) + (~250 from pair 4)	Sure, I have found ten in Paris
6	<Silence> + (~500 from pair 5)	Anything else?
7	I would rather have them in <u>madrid</u> (300 restaurants in madrid augmented here…) + (~500 from pair 6)	I will look for restaurants in madrid
8	Please make sure they are in <u>moderate</u> price range (1500 moderately priced restaurants augmented here…) + (~800 from pair 5)	I will have them ready in no time

3.5.3 Intersecting Predicates KBI

By closely analyzing the example in Table 4, one can realize that the *All Predicates KBI* approach does not accumulate the user's choices on every new request. For instance, if the user asks for "Italian" in pair #3, and then "expensive" in pair #4, we would expect to have in pair #4 restaurants that intersect both descriptions, i.e., "expensive Italian" restaurants, instead of retrieving restaurants of each description separately. To solve this problem, as well as the data crowding issue discussed in the previous sub-section, we introduce a dedicated data structure that maps two entries: one storing keys as the KB predicates, and the other storing values as the KB objects. The contents of this map are updated with new values as the system iterates over each user-system pair. At each pair, we return the intersection of the subjects corresponding to these predicates if the pair contains a predicate itself. We refer to this enhanced approach as the *Intersection Predicated KBI* solution.

Table 5. Applying *Intersecting Predicates KBI* on the example from Tables 3 and 4.

a. 0% history

Pair	User Utterance	Map	System Response
1	Hello	{ **hasPrice**: "", **hasLocation**: "", **hasCuisine** : "" }	Hi, how can I help you?
2	I would like to book a reservation at an <u>expensive</u> restaurant in <u>Paris</u> Liza Chez_Pippo il_Sorrentino	{ **hasPrice**: "expensive", **hasLocation**: "Paris", **hasCuisine** : "" }	Sure, I will look one up
3	\<Silence\>	{ **Price**: "expensive", **hasLocation**: "Paris", **hasCuisine** : "" }	Do you have a cuisine in mind?
4	<u>Italian</u> would be great Il_Sorrentino	{ **hasPrice**: "expensive", **hasLocation**: "Paris", **hasCuisine** : "Italian" }	Okay, how about Il_Sorrentino?

b. 50% history

Pair	User Utterance	Map	System Response
1	Hello	{ **hasPrice**: "", **hasLocation**: "", **hasCuisine** : "" }	Hi, how can I help you?
2	I would like to book a reservation at an <u>expensive</u> restaurant in <u>Paris</u> Liza Chez_Pippo il_Sorrentino	{ **hasPrice**: "expensive", **hasLocation**: "Paris", **hasCuisine** : "" }	Sure, I will look one up
3	\<Silence\> Liza Chez_Pippo	{ **hasPrice**: "expensive", **hasLocation**: "Paris", **hasCuisine** : "" }	Do you have a cuisine in mind?
4	<u>Italian</u> would be great Il_Sorrentino	{ **hasPrice**: "expensive", **hasLocation**: "Paris", **hasCuisine** : "Italian" }	Okay, how about Il_Sorrentino?

c. 100% history

Pair	User Utterance	Map	System Utterance
1	Hello	{ **hasPrice**: "", **hasLocation**: "", **hasCuisine** : "" }	Hi, how can I help you?
2	I would like to book a reservation at an <u>expensive</u> restaurant in <u>Paris</u> Liza Chez_Pippo il_Sorrentino	{ **hasPrice**: "expensive", **hasLocation**: "Paris", **hasCuisine** : "" }	Sure, I will look one up
3	\<Silence\> Liza Chez_Pippo Sorrentino	{ **hasPrice**: "expensive", **hasLocation**: "Paris", **hasCuisine** : "" }	Do you have a cuisine in mind?
4	<u>Italian</u> would be great Il_Sorrentino	{ **hasPrice**: "expensive", **hasLocation**: "Paris", **hasCuisine** : "Italian" }	Okay, how about Il_Sorrentino?

Using the same examples from Tables 3 and 4, we showcase the following three samples using the *Intersecting Predicates KBI* approach. In Table 5b (50% history), we update the map at each pair with the new objects, and then insert the intersection of the corresponding subjects at the end of the same pair. If the pair does not contain an object, then we insert 50% of the previous objects. The same goes for Table 5c (100% history).

One can realize that *Intersecting Predicates KBI* allows to gradually converge toward the subject tokens that match the user's evolving requests, and thus significantly reduces the amount of knowledge added to the individual training pairs, compared with *All Predicates KBI* described previously.

4 Experimental Evaluation

4.1 Experimental Data

To evaluate our approach, we utilize the Dialogue State Tracking Challenge 2 (DSTC2) dataset [9] consisting of restaurant reservation user-system conversation pairs. These dialogues are derived from a real-world system rendering the data raw and real, while training a task-oriented dialogue system. The dialogs come from 6 conditions consisting of the combinations of 3 dialog managers and 2 speech recognizers. There are roughly 500 dialogs in each condition, of average length 7.88 turns from 184 unique users. In our current study, we use the raw version of dataset from [3] which only includes user and system utterances[2]. We also utilize DSTC2's underlying KB[3] (cf. Fig. 2) as the reference source of knowledge when performing KBI. It consists of 8400 subject-predicate-object triplets where subjects represent restaurant names, predicates represent semantic relationships, e.g., *hasPrice*, *hasLocation*, or *hasCuisine*, and objects represent relationship properties, e.g., price could be *cheap*, *moderate*, or *expensive*. For better visualization and understanding of the results, data is pre-processed and cleaned such that all API calls are removed before using the data in any further steps.

4.2 Experimental Results

The evaluation of conversational dialogue systems remains an open problem. With the lack of structure in the dialogues, it remains unclear which attributes of the conversation are relevant to measure the response's quality. Evaluations can be of two types: i) coarse-grained, which focus on the appropriateness (accuracy) of a response, and ii) fine-grained, which focus on the specific behaviors a dialogue system should manifest (such as perceived human likeness) [6]. In this study, we adopt the former approach (coarse-grained) and utilize k-fold cross validation applied on each of the three preprocessing variations: *No KBI*, *All Predicates KBI*, and *Intersecting Predicates KBI*. For each variation, we vary the amount of conversational history from 0%, 10%, 25%, 50%, 75%, to 100%. Also, for each amount of history, we perform two degrees of k-fold: k

---

[2] Available online at: https://github.com/HLTCHKUST/Mem2Seq/tree/master/data/dialog-bAbI-tasks

[3] https://github.com/HLTCHKUST/Mem2Seq/blob/master/data/dialog-bAbI-tasks/dialog-babi-kb-all.txt

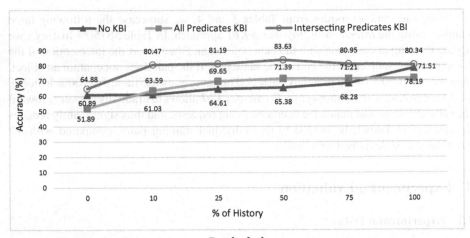

a. Results for k=5

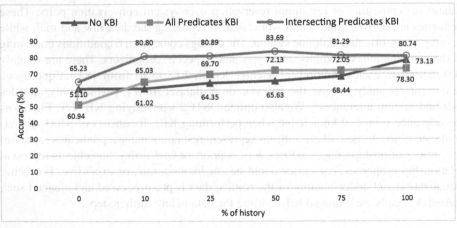

b. Results for k=10

Fig. 3. Accuracy of conversation results applied on DSTC2 dataset, using k-fold cross validation with k = 5 and k = 10.

= 5 and k = 10. This brings the total number of trained models to 3*6*(5 + 10) = 270, requiring a total number of 2,845 h to train. For every trained model, we compare the generated system response with the expected response obtained from the reference dataset, and then compute the number of matching responses (i.e., hits). We then evaluate accuracy as the sum of all the matching responses (hits) over the total number of compared responses. Fig. 3 shows the average accuracy levels for the different iterations of each k-fold degree.

Comparing No KBI with All Predicates KBI: we notice that performing KBI generally improves overall accuracy, except at the boundaries: with 0% and 100% history. This is probably due to the following: i) at 100% history, many subject tokens are added to every training pair which leads to overfitting; ii) at 0% history, some user-system pairs contain thousands of subjects from the KB while other pairs contain only a few or none at all, which renders the training data unbalanced and unpredictable; hence iii) an amount of history between the boundaries allows the training data to become more balanced which generally produces better results.

Comparing Intersecting Predicates KBI with alternatives: This approach yields the highest accuracy levels for every history %. This is because it keeps the dataset balanced while making most of the KB by converging to a handful of useful subject tokens as the dialogue evolves. One important observation is that the accuracy of Intersecting Predicates KBI peaks almost in the middle of the history % (at around 50%). This concurs with the observations made in the previous paragraph regarding the need for a balanced training set to improve training quality.

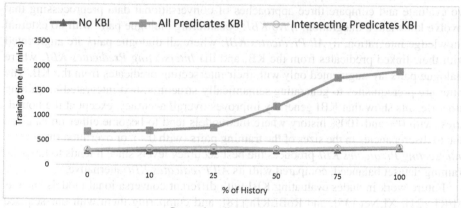

a. Comparing all three approaches

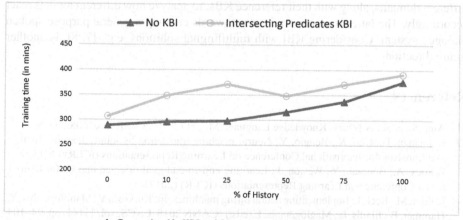

b. Comparing *No KBI* and *Interescting Predicates KBI* only

Fig. 4. Training time of conversation results applied on DSTC2 dataset, using k-fold cross validation with k = 5 (similar results are obtained for k = 10, with an average 5% increate in time)

Concerning training time, results in Fig. 4 show that the *All Predicates KBI* approach introduces a significant increase in training time compared with its counterparts. This is due to the substantial increase in training data with the inclusion of all matching predicates in every training pair, resulting in oversized training pairs which require more time to process and train. While the *Intersection Predicates KBI* approach requires more training time than its *No KBI* counterpart (cf. Fig. 4b), yet the two approaches are almost undiscernible compared with *All Predicated KBI* (cf. Fig. 4a).

5 Conclusion

Knowledge base integration (KBI) in the training of sequence-to-sequence (seq2seq) generative conversational approaches has not been widely explored so far. In this work, we evaluate and compare three approaches of conversational data preprocessing that involve knowledge integration: i) *No KBI*: considering dialogue pairs with no external knowledge integration, ii) *All Predicates KBI*: where all dialogue pairs are augmented with their linked predicates from the KB, and iii) *Intersecting Predicates KBI*: where dialogue pairs are augmented only with their intersecting predicates from the KB. The latter are prerequisites to generating semantically structured text integrated at training time. Results show that KBI generally improves overall accuracy, except at the boundaries: with 0% and 100% history where the models tend to become either unbalanced due to discrepancies in the sizes of the training pairs (with 0%), or overfitted (at 100%). *Intersecting Predicates KBI* produces the best accuracy levels since it tends to keep the training dataset balanced, compared with its *All Predicates KBI* alternative.

Future work includes evaluating KBI with different conversational models such as BERT [21], XLNet [35], and RoBERTa [18], and comparing them with our seq2seq RNN-based solution. This also requires combining multiple conversational datasets from different domains, along with their reference KBs, to analyze how different models react accordingly. The latter is an important step towards creating a general purpose spoken dialogue system. Considering KBI with multilingual solutions, e.g., [7, 8], is another future direction.

References

1. Ahn, S., et al.: A Neural Knowledge Language Model (2016). CoRR abs/1608.00318
2. Bahdanau, D., Cho, K., Bengio, Y.: Neural machine translation by jointly learning to align and translate. In: International Conference on Learning Representations (ICLR) (2015)
3. Bordes, A., Boureau, Y., Weston, J.: Learning end-to-end goal-oriented dialog. In: International Conference on Learning Representations (ICLR) (2017)
4. Collier, M., Beel, J.: Implementing neural turing machines. In: Kůrková, V., Manolopoulos, Y., Hammer, B., Iliadis, L., Maglogiannis, I. (eds.) ICANN 2018. LNCS, vol. 11141, pp. 94–104. Springer, Cham (2018). https://doi.org/10.1007/978-3-030-01424-7_10
5. Deng, J., et al.: Large-scale object classification using label relation graphs. In: Fleet, D., Pajdla, T., Schiele, B., Tuytelaars, T. (eds.) ECCV 2014. LNCS, vol. 8689, pp. 48–64. Springer, Cham (2014). https://doi.org/10.1007/978-3-319-10590-1_4
6. Deriu, J., et al.: Survey on Evaluation Methods for Dialogue Systems (2019). CoRR abs/1905.04071

7. Haraty, R., El Ariss, O.: Lebanese colloquial arabic speech recognition. In: ISCA International Conference on Computer Applications in Industry and Engineering (CAINE), pp. 285–291 (2005)
8. Haraty, R., Nasrallah, R.: Indexing arabic texts using association rule data mining. Libr. Hi Tech **37**(1), 101–117 (2019)
9. Henderson, M., Williams, J., Thomson, B.: The second dialog state tracking challenge. In: SIGDIAL Conference, pp. 263–272 (2014)
10. Ticona-Herrera, R., Tekli, J., Chbeir, R., Laborie, S., Dongo, I., Guzman, R.: Toward RDF normalization. In: Johannesson, P., Lee, M.L., Liddle, S.W., Opdahl, A.L., López, Ó.P. (eds.) Conceptual Modeling, pp. 261–275. Springer International Publishing, Cham (2015). https://doi.org/10.1007/978-3-319-25264-3_19
11. Hochreiter, S., Schmidhuber, J.: Long short-term memory. Neural Comput. **9**(8), 1735–1780 (1997)
12. Hu, Z., et al.: Harnessing deep neural networks with logic rules. In: Annual Meeting of the Association for Computational Linguistics (ACL) (2016)
13. Hu, Z., et al.: Deep neural networks with massive learned knowledge. In: Conference on Empirical Methods in Natural Language Processing (EMNLP), pp. 1670–1679 (2016)
14. Jafari, R., Razvarz, S., Gegov, A.: End-to-end memory networks: a survey. In: Arai, K., Kapoor, S., Bhatia, R. (eds.) SAI 2020. AISC, vol. 1229, pp. 291–300. Springer, Cham (2020). https://doi.org/10.1007/978-3-030-52246-9_20
15. Kalchbrenner, N., Blunsom, P.: Recurrent continuous translation models. In: Conference on Empirical Methods in Natural Language Processing (EMNLP), pp. 1700–1709 (2013)
16. Karaletsos, T., Belongie, S.J., Rätsch, G.: When crowds hold privileges: bayesian unsupervised representation learning with oracle constraints. In: International Conference on Learning Representations (ICLR) (2016)
17. Li, J., et al.: A persona-based neural conversation model. In: Annual Meeting of the Association for Computational Linguistics (ACL) (2016)
18. Liu, Y., et al.: RoBERTa: A Robustly Optimized BERT Pretraining Approach (2019). CoRR abs/1907.11692
19. Miller, G.A., Fellbaum, C.: WordNet then and now. Lang. Resour. Eval. **41**(2), 209–214 (2007)
20. Nguyen, A., Yosinski, J., Clune J.: Deep neural networks are easily fooled: high confidence predictions for unrecognizable images. In: Proceedings of the IEEE Conference on Computer Vision and Pattern Recognition, pp. 427–436 (2015)
21. Qu, C., et al.: BERT with history answer embedding for conversational question answering. In: Proceedings of the 42nd International ACM SIGIR Conference on Research and Development in Information Retrieval, pp. 1133–1136 (2019)
22. Ritter, A., Cherry, C., Dolan, W.: Data-driven response generation in social media. In: Conference on Empirical Methods in Natural Language Processing (EMNLP), pp. 583–593 (2011)
23. Serban, J., Lowe, R., et al.: A survey of available corpora for building data-driven dialogue systems: the journal version. Dial. Discourse **9**(1), 1–49 (2018)
24. Shaik, R., et al.: The analysis of data representation techniques for early prediction of breast cancer. Int. J. Pure Appl. Math., 1311–8080 (2017)
25. Shang, L., Lu, Z., Li, H.: Neural responding machine for short-text conversation. In: Annual Meeting of the Association for Computer Linguistics (ACL), pp. 1577–1586 (2015)
26. Sordoni, A., et al.: A neural network approach to context-sensitive generation of conversational responses. In: North American Chapter of the Association for Computational Linguistics (NAACL), pp. 196–205 (2015)
27. Sukhbaatar, S., et al.: End-to-end memory networks. In: Neural Information Processing Systems (NeurIPS), pp. 2440–2448 (2015)

28. Sutskever, I., Vinyals, O., Le, Q.V.: Sequence to sequence learning with neural networks. In: Neural Information Processing Systems (NeurIPS), pp. 3104–3112 (2014)

29. Szegedy, C., et al.: Intriguing properties of neural networks. In: International Conference on Learning Representations (ICLR) (2013)

30. Vinyals, O., et al.: Grammar as a foreign language. In: Neural Information Processing Systems (NeurIPS), pp. 2773–2781 (2015)

31. Vinyals, O., Le, Q.: A Neural Conversational Model (2015). CoRR abs/1506.05869

32. Vinyals, O., et al.: Show and tell: a neural image caption generator. In: Computer Vision and Pattern Recognition (CVPR), pp. 3156–3164 (2015)

33. Wen, T., et al.: A network-based end-to-end trainable task-oriented dialogue system. In: Conference of the European Chapter of the Association for Computational Linguistics (EACL), pp. 438–449 (2017)

34. Williams, J., Raux, A., Henderson, M.: The dialog state tracking challenge series: a review. Dial. Discourse 7(3), 4–33 (2016)

35. Yang, Z., et al.: XLNET: generalized autoregressive pretraining for language understanding. In: Advances in Neural Information Processing Systems, pp. 5753–5763 (2019)

Effective Seed-Guided Topic Labeling for Dataless Hierarchical Short Text Classification

Yi Yang[1,3] , Hongan Wang[1,3], Jiaqi Zhu[1,2,3(✉)] , Wandong Shi[1,3],
Wenli Guo[1], and Jiawen Zhang[1,3]

[1] SKLCS, Institute of Software, Chinese Academy of Sciences, Beijing, China
{yangyi2012,hongan}@iscas.ac.cn, zhujq@ios.ac.cn
[2] Zhejiang Lab, Hangzhou, Zhejiang, China
[3] University of Chinese Academy of Sciences, Beijing, China
{shiwandong18,guowenli17,zhangjiawen181}@mails.ucas.edu.cn

Abstract. Hierarchical text classification has a wide application prospect on the Internet, which aims to classify texts into a given hierarchy. Supervised methods require a large amount of labeled data and are thus costly. For this purpose, the task of dataless hierarchical text classification has attracted more and more attention of researchers in recent years, which only requires a few relevant seed words for given categories. However, existing approaches mainly focus on long texts without considering the characteristics of short texts, so are not suitable in many scenarios. In this paper, we tackle dataless hierarchical short text classification for the first time, and propose an innovative model named Hierarchical Seeded Biterm Topic Model (HierSeedBTM), which effectively leverages seed words in Biterm Topic Model (BTM) to guide the hierarchical topic labeling. Specifically, our model introduces iterative distribution propagation mechanism among topic models in different levels to incorporate the hierarchical structure information. Experiments on two public datasets show that the proposed model is more effective than the state-of-the-art methods of dataless hierarchical text classification designed for long texts.

Keywords: Hierarchical text classification · Topic model · Seed word

1 Introduction

With the rapid development of social media, short texts are increasing and widespread on the internet, when people obtain and exchange information through tweets, reviews, and queries. It is important to acquire interesting information from these huge number of short texts with text classification. In many

This work is supported by National Key Research and Development Program of China (2018YFC0116703), Strategic Priority Research Program of Chinese Academy of Sciences (XDC02060500), and Zhejiang Lab (2020NF0AC02).

M. Brambilla et al. (Eds.): ICWE 2021, LNCS 12706, pp. 271–285, 2021.
https://doi.org/10.1007/978-3-030-74296-6_21

scenarios, the category labels of short texts are often organized in a hierarchical structure. Hierarchical text classification (HTC) aim to classify text into a given hierarchy, has a wide variety of applications such as search result classification [2], review classification [20] and sentiment classification [24]. Comparing with flat text classification, HTC leverages the interrelationships among hierarchical structure, and acquires more accurate classification results.

Some models [7,9] adopt a greedy strategy: a local classifier is trained for each category node, and then the classification results are propagated to the next level in a top-down manner. However, the greedy strategy may lead to classification error propagation along the hierarchy. Other models [1] employ the down-up backpropagation strategy: the leaf level is classified at first, and the results are propagated to the top level. Although the models above are widespread used, the lack of plentiful labeled data for training the classifiers limits the application scenario of these models, since carefully-labeled documents require domain expertise and are thus costly.

For this purpose, many researchers focused on dataless hierarchical text classification task as it can successfully reduce the effort in labeling documents. Xiao et al. [26] proposed a generative framework to leverage the hierarchical structural information and compute path-generated probability to classify documents. Meng et al. [18] utilizes a class distribution to generate pseudo documents for training local classifiers and then iteratively refine the global hierarchical model. However, these seed-guided dataless hierarchical text classification methods are designed for long texts without considering the characters of short texts, which are extremely sparse so that only limited features are available to train a classifier. Hence, these models get unsatisfactory performance for classifying short texts.

Recently, some dataless short text classification approaches [11,28] are proposed in a generative framework and achieve significant improvement, which guides the topic labeling process based on a short text topic model to alleviate the data sparsity. Inspired by these studies, we tackle the dataless hierarchical short text classification task for the first time and propose a model named HierSeedBTM. Specifically, we at first calculate the semantic similarity between document words (biterms) and categories as prior knowledge in each level separately, through integrating the seed words along the path from the current category node to the root node in the category hierarchy. That directly guides the generative process of BTM-like topic model for hierarchical topic labeling and inference. Then, an iterative distribution propagation mechanism among topic models in different levels is introduced to incorporate the hierarchical and structural information to make up for the limited data.

In summary, the main contributions of this paper include:

(1) A model HierSeedBTM is presented to solve the task of dataless hierarchical short text classification with seed words, by combining word co-occurrence information and category-word semantic similarity based on word embeddings. To the best of our knowledge, it is the first successful work to tackle the task of dataless hierarchical short text classification.

(2) To effectively utilize the hierarchical structure, a novel iterative propagation mechanism is put forward during the topic sampling process of the topic model. Topic distribution and topic-word distribution are propagated in a top-down manner respectively in each sampling iteration.

(3) Informative experiments are conducted on two hierarchical short text datasets to show that our model outperforms the state-of-the-art baseline methods designed for long texts, especially when the documents are very short.

The remainder of the paper is organized as follows. In Sect. 2, we review recent related work. In Sect. 3, we formalize the problem to be tackled. Section 4 introduces our model in detail. In Sect. 5, the experimental results on hierarchical short text datasets are shown. Section 6 concludes this paper and discusses future work.

2 Related Work

2.1 Dataless Text Classification

Dataless text classification attracts much attention as it only needs a few user-provided seed words for classification, which can successfully reduce the effort in labeling documents. Some researchers studied the methods to generate pseudo-labels or pseudo-documents utilizing seed words for constructing training dataset, and then classify texts with a supervised classification model [6,15]. In particular, Mekala et al. [16] proposed a contextualized weak supervision framework (ConWea) for text classification. The model generates the pseudo-label of documents based on the frequency of seed words, and leverages contextualized representations of words to iteratively train the classifier and expand seed words. Meng et al. [17] proposed a novel weakly-supervised text classification model (WeSTClass). It constructs a semantic space to generate pseudo-documents to train a neural classifier, then fits unlabeled data through bootstrapping.

Another group of researchers studied topic-based models [11,12], in which the generative process is guided by seed words to form category-aware topics. Li et al. [13] proposed Seed-Guided Topic Model (STM), assuming that each document is associated with a single category-aware topic and a mixture of general topics. Yang et al. [28] proposed Seeded Biterm Topic Model (SeedBTM) for dataless short text classification, which leverages both word co-occurrence information from BTM and category-word semantic similarity from word embeddings to classify short texts. All the methods above are designed for flat text classification.

2.2 Dataless Hierarchical Text Classification

As hierarchical text classification can obtain more accurate classification results by leveraging the interrelated structure of categories in different levels, some dataless hierarchical text classification models are studied. Song et al. [23] proposed a dataless hierarchical text classification framework, which firstly represents the document semantics with three kinds of methods, then calculates the semantic similarity between documents and categories as local classification results, and finally adopts a standard hierarchical classification strategy to classify documents. Meng et al. [18] leveraged seed words to model the category semantics as a mixture of von Mises Fisher distributions, and generated meaningful pseudo-documents with LSTM-based language model. Then, the local classifiers are trained and the global hierarchical model is refined iteratively. Xiao et al. [26] proposed a generative framework for weakly hierarchical text classification. It puts a path-dependent score to the cost-sensitive learning algorithm and makes the classification consistent with the category hierarchy during the inference process. However, None of the above models consider the characteristics of short texts.

2.3   Topic Models for Short Texts

Many researchers proposed short text topic models to alleviate the problem of data sparsity. Some studies adopt aggregation strategy [22,25] to generate long documents by aggregating short texts. Others are based on the assumption that each document has only a single latent topic [29,30]. In another direction, Yan et al. [27] proposed BTM, which models the word co-occurrence explicitly and aggregates patterns in the whole corpus for learning topics. Many researches extended BTM with additional information [3,14] or aggregating strategy [8] to make up for the limited data. Our approach selects BTM as the base model, since the model is more flexible for different scenarios and can easily be extended.

3   Preliminaries

In dataless hierarchical short text classification, the class categories constitute a hierarchy τ. It is a tree structure of depth H, and the node in depth 0 is defined as ROOT. The categories of τ are distributed from depth 1 to H. Following the definition in [26], all leaf nodes are in depth H, which can always be satisfied by giving the shallower leaf node a child node until the node reaches depth H.

The categories at each level are denoted as $C_1, C_2, ..., C_H$, with sizes $M_1, M_2, ..., M_H$, respectively. The category $c_{h,k} \in C_h$ means the category k in the level h, and its representative seed word set is $S_{h,k} = \{s_{h,k,1}, s_{h,k,2}, ..., s_{h,k,l}\}$.

Given an unlabeled document set $D = \{D_1, D_2, ..., D_N\}$, a category hierarchy tree τ and the corresponding seed word sets S, the task of dataless hierarchical short text classification is to assign the most likely category $c_{h,k}$ for each level h to each document D_i. Table 1 summarizes the main notations used in this paper.

4   Proposed Models

In this section, we at first present the overview of our approach and then elaborate the key steps. The first step is estimating category-path-biterm similarity and the second is inferring modified biterm-topic distributions based on topic model for calculating document categories (Fig. 1).

Table 1. Notation in this paper.

Symbol	Description
w	Word
b	Word pair
h	The level in the hierarchy
N	The number of biterm set
B	Biterm set
H	The number of levels in the hierarchy
z_h	The topic in level h
M_h	The number of topics in level h
θ'_h	The modified prior topic distribution in level h
θ^b_h	The modified topic distribution from the dot product of θ_h and $\zeta_{b,h}$
$\zeta^p_{b,h}$	The similarity vector between b and topics in level h
$\phi_{h,z}$	The topic-word distribution of topic z in level h
α_h, β	Hyper-parameter

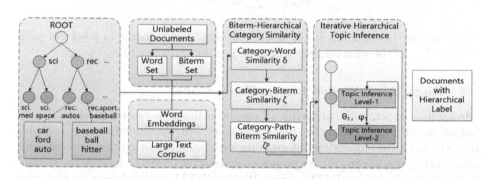

Fig. 1. Overview of the dataless hierarchical short text classification approach.

4.1 Estimating Category-Path-Biterm Similarity

In BTM, a biterm $b_{i,j}$ consists of two words w_i and w_j, which are co-occurring in the same short text regardless of the order. Given a biterm set B, a category hierarchy τ as well as the corresponding seed word set S, our purpose is to calculate semantic similarity between each biterm and each category for guiding the topic labeling.

We at first calculate the semantic similarity between each corpus word w and each seed word s in $c_{h,k}$ through external word embeddings, as it is easy accessible, less time consuming, and can provide external similarity information to alleviate the data sparsity [28]. Obviously, the similarity calculation method can be easily replaced by other methods [18,23] based on different scenarios. We get the word vectors v_s and v_w of a corpus word w and a seed word s respectively, and then calculate the semantic similarity $sim(s, w)$ as follows:

$$sim(s, w) = \max(\cos(v_s, v_w), \epsilon) \qquad (1)$$

The threshold $\epsilon > 0$ is the lower bound of $sim(s, w)$ to make it positive. Then, we calculate the category-word similarity $\delta_{h,k,w}$, which is the maximal similarity between each seed word in $S_{h,k} = \{s_{h,k,1}, s_{h,k,2}, ..., s_{h,k,n}\}$ and the document word w:

$$\delta_{h,k,w} = \max_i (sim(s_{h,k,i}, w)) \qquad (2)$$

Next, we calculate the category-biterm similarity for each biterm b_{w_1,w_2} as the mean value of δ_{h,k,w_1} and δ_{h,k,w_2}:

$$\zeta_{b,h,k} = (\delta_{h,k,w_1} + \delta_{h,k,w_2})/2 \qquad (3)$$

To leverage the hierarchical and structural information, the path from ROOT to the leaf node $c_{h,k}$ is denoted as $p_{h,k}$ (abbreviated as p when there is no ambiguity for the leaf node), and our model propagates the semantic similarity along p to obtain the category-path-biterm similarity $\zeta^p_{b,h,k}$ as follows:

$$\zeta^p_{b,h,k} = \sum_{i=1}^{h} \zeta_{b,i,u(k,p,i)} \qquad (4)$$

where $u(k, p, i)$ is denoted as the upper category of category k in level i of path p, and $\zeta^p_{b,h,k}$ is the sum similarity of path p from $c_{1,u(k,p,1)}$ to $c_{h,u(k,p,h)}$.

4.2   Hierarchical Seeded Biterm Topic Model

Obviously, the semantic similarity ζ^p can be utilized as biterm-category distribution directly to calculate the document label, but the similarity only contains the external word embedding information without considering the co-occurrence information. Similar to [26], we propose a generative model to modify the semantic similarity based on BTM, named HierSeedBTM, which leverages the prior similarity information and hierarchical structure information to guide the topic labeling.

In HierSeedBTM, the generative process of a topic z_h is influenced by both prior category-path-biterm similarity ζ^p and the topic-word distribution ϕ_z, which guides the model to induce category-aware topics. Moreover, in order to leverage the hierarchical and structural information, the topic distribution θ_h and topic-word distribution ϕ_h are propagated along the path as prior parameters to influence the generative process of the lower level. Notice that the topic number in each level of τ is different, so we define α_h with different dimensions to represent the hyper-parameter of prior topic distribution in each level.

The graphical representation of HierSeedBTM is described in Fig. 2, and the generative process of HierSeedBTM is as follows:

1. Modify the prior topic probability $\theta'_{h,k} \leftarrow \theta_{h-1,u(k,p,h-1)}$
2. Draw a topic-word distribution $\theta_h \sim Dir(\alpha_h + \theta'_h)$
3. For each topic $k = 1, ..., M_h$ in level h
   (a) Draw a topic-word distribution $\phi_h \sim Dir(\beta + \phi_{h-1})$

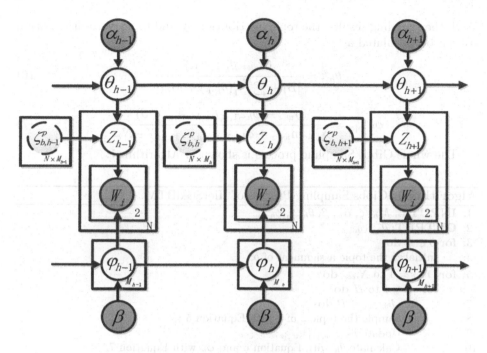

Fig. 2. Graphical representation of HierSeedBTM.

4. For each biterm b in the biterm set B
   (a) Modify the topic distribution $\theta_h^b \propto \zeta_{b,h}^p \cdot \theta_h$
   (b) Draw a topic $z_h \sim Multi(\theta_h^b)$
   (c) Draw two words to form b: $w_i, w_j \sim Multi(\phi_{h,z_h})$

As the category number of level h is different from that of level $h-1$, we assign the topic probability $\theta_{h-1,u(k,p,h-1)}$ in level $h-1$ to the prior topic probability $\theta_{h,k}$ in level h along all paths.

Inference via Gibbs Sampling. Similar to BTM, as the model is intractable, we utilize the Gibbs Sampling to perform the approximate inference. After random initialization on the Markov chain, we iteratively calculate the conditional distribution $P(z_b = z|\mathbf{z}_{\neg b}, B, \zeta, h, \theta_{h-1}, \phi_{h-1})$ for each biterm in each level.

$$P(z_b = z|\mathbf{z}_{\neg b}, B, \zeta, h, \theta_{h-1}, \phi_{h-1}) \propto \zeta_{b,z}^p \cdot (n_z + \theta'_{h,z} + \alpha)$$
$$\cdot \frac{(n_{w_j|z} + \phi_{h-1,u(k,p,h-1),w_j} + \beta)(n_{w_i|z} + \phi_{h-1,u(k,p,h-1),w_i} + \beta)}{\sum_w(\sum_w n_{w|z} + \phi_{h-1,u(k,p,h-1),w_j} + M\beta)(n_{w|z} + 1 + \phi_{h-1,u(k,p,h-1),w_i} + M\beta)} \quad (5)$$

where $z_{\neg b}$ is denoted the topic assignments for all biterms except b, n_z is the number of biterms assigned to the topic z, and $n_{w|z}$ is the number of times when the word w is assigned to the topic z. When sampling on level 1, the parent node is ROOT, so the $\theta_{h-1,u(k,p,h-1)}$ and $\phi_{h-1,u(k,p,h-1)}$ are all zero.

With the sampling results, the topic distribution θ_h and topic-word distribution ϕ_h can be calculated as:

$$\theta_{h,z} = \frac{(n_z + \theta'_{h,z} + \alpha)}{|B| + \sum_{k=1}^{M_h}(\theta'_{h,k}) + M_h\alpha} \tag{6}$$

$$\phi_{h,w|z} = \frac{(n_{w|z} + \phi_{h-1,u(k,p,h-1),w} + \beta)}{\sum_{w'}(n_{w'|z} + \phi_{h-1,u(k,p,h-1),w'}) + N\beta} \tag{7}$$

The whole Gibbs Sampling process is shown in Algorithm 1:

Algorithm 1. Gibbs Sampling Process of HierSeedBTM

1: **INPUT**:B, M_h, ζ, α_h, β, θ_{h-1}, ϕ_{h-1}
2: **OUTPUT**: θ_h, ϕ_h
3: **for** $b \in B$ **do**
4:     Initialize the topic assignment of b;
5: **for** $iter = 1$ to N_{iter} **do**
6:     **for** $h = 1$ to H **do**
7:         **for** $b_{w_i,w_j} \in B$ **do**
8:             Sample the topic z of b with Equation 5 ;
9:             Update $n_z, n_{w_i|z}, n_{w_j|z}$;
10:            Calculate θ_h with Equation 6 and ϕ_h with Equation 7;

Predicting Document Category. The classification results of our model are obtained from the leaf level, and the probabilities of inner categories are calculated by summing up the probabilities of their child categories. Specifically, we treat the expectation of the topic proportions of biterms in a document as the topic proportions of the document [27], as shown below:

$$P(z_{h,k}|d,h) = \sum_b P(z_{h,k,b}|b,h)P(b|d) \tag{8}$$

where $P(z_{h,k,b}|b,h)$ can be calculated by Eq. 5 and $P(b|d)$ is estimated based on the relative frequency of b in d. Finally, for document d, the category label z_d can be predicted as the topic with the highest probability:

$$z_{d,h} = \arg\max_k P(z_{h,k}|d,h) \tag{9}$$

5   Experiments

5.1   Datasets

We use two hierarchical short text datasets to evaluate the effectiveness of our model. For both datasets, we at first lower and lemmatize all corpus words and remove stop words, and then filter out the documents that contain only one word or more than 50 words to obtain the short text datasets. The statistics of the two datasets are shown in Table 2.

Table 2. Statistics of datasets.

Dataset	Categories (Level 1 + Level 2)	Documents	Average document length
20NG	7 + 20	10493	23
HuffPost	3 + 9	37054	3.8

- The 20 Newsgroups(20NG)[1] [10] : 20 Newsgoups is a widely used dataset for the text classification task, including flat text classification and hierarchical text classification. It contains about 20,000 newsgroups messages from 20 newsgroups. After filtering long documents, we retain about 10,000 messages as short text datasets. As the categories are close to each other, 20NG can be categorized into a hierarchical structure with two levels. The upper level contains 7 inner categories, and the leaf level contains 20 categories [26].
- HuffPost[2] [19] : It is obtained from HuffPost and contains around 200K news headlines from 2012 to 2018. There are totally 42 categories, and many of them are overlapping, from which we select 9 leaf categories with 3 upper categories. The categories and their statistics are shown in Table 3.

Table 3. Categories and their statistics of the HuffPost dataset.

Category in level 1	Categories in level 2
Family (5)	WEDDINGS (1488), HOME & LIVING (3271), PARENTING(5437),PARENTS (3443), DIVORCE (1418)
Healthy (2)	HOME & LIVING (3271), WELLNESS (10655)
Food (2)	FOOD & DRINK (3890), TASTE (1862)

The number in the first column indicates the respective child category number, and the number in the second column indicates the document number of each category.

5.2 Baselines

We evaluate our model with six baseline models, all of which can leverage seed words to deal with the task of dataless text classification. The first four methods aim at dataless hierarchical classification for general texts, and the last two are dataless short text classification models.

---

[1] http://qwone.com/jason/20Newsgroups/.
[2] https://www.kaggle.com/rmisra/news-category-dataset.

- Hier-Dataless[3] [23]: it introduces three ways to calculate the semantic similarity between document and category with seed words as document-category probabilities. To be fair, we choose the same word embedding as the semantic representation to calculate semantic similarity.
- WeSHClass[4] [18]: it is a successful weakly-supervised hierarchical text classification model, which leverages seed words to generate pseudo-labeled documents, and then iteratively refines the global hierarchical classifier with supervised methods.
- PCNB[5] [26]: it is a state-of-the-art weakly-supervised hierarchical text classification model within a generative framework. The model adopts the initial semantic similarity calculation method of Hier-Dataless, and constructs a path-cost sensitive Bayes classifier.
- PCEM [26]: it improves the path-cost sensitive classifier and adopts EM technique for semi-supervised hierarchical text classification.
- SeedBTM [28]: it is a state-of-the-art dataless short text classification approach. This model leverages both word co-occurrence information and prior category-word similarity to classify short texts, utilizing seed words to calculate category-word similarity to guide the topic-word distributions of BTM.
- SeedBTM* : it is a variant of SeedBTM with category-biterm similarity ζ to guide the generative process rather than category-word similarity.

For all baseline models, we adopt their implementation codes and parameter settings directly.

5.3 Experiment Settings

For seed words of 20NG, we adopt the setting of Hier-Dataless [23], and for HuffPost, we use descriptive LDA (DescLDA)[4] to select 3~9 representative words for each category as seed words, as shown in Table 4.

For all datasets, we set the topic number $K_h' = M_h$ (category number in each level), $\alpha = 50/K_h'$, $\beta = 0.3$ and $\epsilon = 0.0001$. We set the number of iterations to 8 as our model achieves competitive performance since then. For word embeddings, we employ the widely used GloVe Common Crawl[6] [21], which contains 840B tokens, 2.2M vocab and 300d vectors. It is also used in baseline models Hier-Dataless, PCNB, PCEM, SeedBTM, and SeedBTM*. WeSHClass adopts the self-training word embeddings based on the unlabeled documents.

---

[3] https://github.com/CogComp/cogcomp-nlp/tree/master/dataless-classifier.
[4] https://github.com/yumeng5/WeSHClass.
[5] https://github.com/HKUST-KnowComp/PathPredictionForTextClassification.
[6] http://nlp.stanford.edu/data/glove.840B.300d.zip.

Table 4. Seed words of the HuffPost dataset.

Category	Seed words
FAMILY	Family adorable divorce daughter parent
HEALTH	Health weight yoga mental drug cancer disease doctor
FOOD	Food sweet cake chocolate cheese
HOME & LIVING	Home house room
DIVORCE	Divorce child parent relationship kid couple split
PARENTS	Mom kid parent baby dad girl
WEDDINGS	Wedding marriage couple bride love bridal
PARENTING	Kid child parent mom teach study learn life
HEALTHY LIVING	Health life cancer mental care
WELLNESS	Wellness cancer drug heart weight stress
FOOD & DRINK	Food cook taste wine cake chocolate
TASTE	Taste cook dinner ice breakfast wine meal delicious sweet

5.4 Experimental Results

We evaluate the classification performances of HierSeedBTM using Macro-F1 and Micro-F1. For each model, we calculate the F1 scores for Level-1 and Level-2 based on the hierarchy, and then get the F1 scores for all categories of Level-All in general. We run 10 times on each dataset to get the average values, as shown in Table 5 and Table 6.

Table 5. Macro-F1 (%) of HierSeedBTM and baselines on all datasets.

Dataset	20NG			HuffPost		
	Level-1	Level-2	Level-all	Level-1	Level-2	Level-all
HierSeedBTM	53.5	**48.1**	**49.5**	**71.2**	**41**	**48.5**
WeSHClass	**54.7**	37.7	41.2	61.7	30.7	38.9
PCNB	35.8	22	25.5	66.2	34.8	42.7
PCEM	47.9	30.9	35.3	67.6	40.3	47.1
Hier-Dataless	46.2	34.4	37.5	65.3	34.7	42.4
SeedBTM	38.9	25.8	29.2	65	38.6	45.2
SeedBTM*	42	34	36.1	65.1	38.4	45.1

The best results in the table are highlighted in bold, and we can observe that HierSeedBTM performs better than almost all baseline models in both datasets.

For Macro-F1 in Table 5, on the 20NG dataset, HierSeedBTM increases 8.3 than the second WeSHClass and increases 12 than PCEM in level-all.

That certifies our model can make better use of hierarchical structures to improve the classification accuracy of leaf nodes. The small deficiency against WeSHClass in level-1 can be attributed to the reduced difficulty of classifying texts with moderate length in an abstract level. On the HuffPost dataset, HierSeedBTM improves 1.4 than PCEM and 9.6 than WeSHClass in level-all. For Micro-F1 in Table 6, HierSeedBTM is in line with WeSHClass on the 20NG dataset, but increases 5.8 than WeSHClass on the HuffPost dataset in level-all.

Table 6. Micro-F1 (%) of HierSeedBTM and baselines on all datasets.

Dataset	20NG			HuffPost		
	Level-1	Level-2	Level-all	Level-1	Level-2	Level-all
HierSeedBTM	65.6	**49.4**	**57.5**	**70.8**	**37.6**	**54.2**
WeSHClass	**73.8**	41.1	**57.5**	62.8	32.7	48.4
PCNB	52.5	27.8	40.1	66.7	35.4	51
PCEM	63.2	39.7	51.5	67.7	38.4	53.1
Hier-Dataless	55.4	36.0	45.8	65.2	34.0	49.6
SeedBTM	54	24.7	32.9	66.1	35.7	51.1
SeedBTM*	57.4	31.2	36.2	66	35.3	50.8

For WeSHClass, the pseudo-labeled documents are relatively noisy and the trained classifier cannot well distinguish short texts due to the sparse feature, so WeSHClass gets poorer performance in HuffPost than the generative models. For PCEM, only category-word similarities are propagated along paths, but our model further propagates the distributions among each iteration and gets better performance. The results indicate that the propagation mechanism and generative framework for short texts make our model more effective to leverage the hierarchical structure information and alleviate the data sparsity of short texts. Moreover, the performances of baseline models fluctuate among datasets with different lengths, while HierSeedBTM behaves more stable.

Compared with SeedBTM and the variant model SeedBTM*, HierSeedBTM increases 3.3~12 in Macro-F1 and 3.1~21.4 in Micro-F1 respectively, which explains that our propagation strategy based on the hierarchical structure can integrate more evidences from different abstraction levels to classify short texts accurately.

5.5   Parameter Study

In this section, we study the impact of different parameter settings on the classification performance of HierSeedBTM. When paying attention to one parameter, other parameters are fixed to the default values given in Sect. 5.3.

The Impact of Iteration Number. Iteration number is an important parameter to our model, because the smaller of this number means the more efficient of our model. We change the value in the range of [1,20], and its Macro-F1 and Micro-F1 results are shown in Fig. 3.

When the number of iterations is 6, HierSeedBTM can achieve good classification performance, and F1-score is almost stable after this point. Therefore, we set the iteration number to 8 in our model. The fast convergence should give credit to the regulating effect of information propagation mechanism among the hierarchical structure and the prior knowledge from word embeddings.

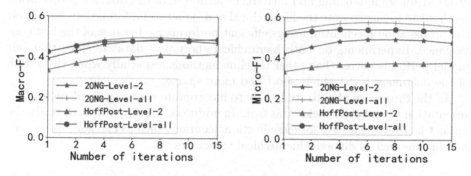

Fig. 3. F1 values of level-2 and level-all with different iterations.

The Impact of β. β is the hyper-parameter of the topic model, which affects the topic word distribution ϕ. We vary the value in the range of [0.01, 0.6] to evaluate its impact, and the results are shown in Fig. 4.

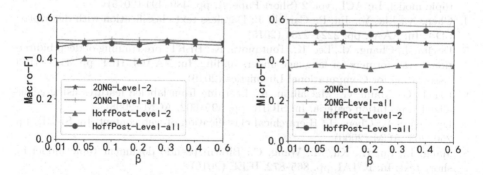

Fig. 4. F1 values of level-2 and level-all with different β values.

The flat lines of the 20NG dataset indicates that the dataset with a longer text length is relatively insensitive to β. But for the shorter HuffPost, the results fluctuate and arrive at the best performance in the range of [0.3, 0.4], so we set β to 0.3 in our model.

For the other hyper-parameter α, $\alpha = 50/K'_h$ is a widely used parameter setting of topic models [13,27], and the experimental results also indicate that the classification accuracy of our model is insensitive to α. Hence, the detailed comparison is omitted here due to the page limit.

6   Conclusion

In this paper, we propose an effective model for dataless hierarchical short text classification. Our model leverages seed words to guide the generative process of BTM for topic labeling and introduces an iterative distribution propagation mechanism to incorporate the hierarchical and structural information. Moreover, the propagation mechanism brings efficient performance because of the fast convergence. Experiments on both hierarchical short text datasets show that our model performs better than other baseline methods, especially when the length of the document is extremely short and more sparse.

In the future, we plan to study how to incorporate contextualized vector representation [5] to better tackle this task. In addition, it is important to study the impact factors of datasets for classification accuracy, such as category imbalance and bias as well as different hierarchical structures.

References

1. Bennett, P., Nguyen, N.: Refined experts: improving classification in large taxonomies. In: SIGIR, pp. 11–18. ACM (2009)
2. Chen, H., Dumais, S.T.: Bringing order to the web: automatically categorizing search results. In: CHI, pp. 145–152. ACM (2000)
3. Chen, W., Wang, J., Zhang, Y., Yan, H., Li, X.: User based aggregation for biterm topic model. In: ACL, vol. 2 (Short Papers), pp. 489–494 (2015)
4. Chen, X., Xia, Y., Jin, P., Carroll, J.: Dataless text classification with descriptive LDA. In: AAAI, pp. 2224–2231 (2015)
5. Devlin, J., Chang, M., Lee, K., Toutanova, K.: BERT: pre-training of deep bidirectional transformers for language understanding. In: NAACL-HLT, pp. 4171–4186. Association for Computational Linguistics (2019)
6. Druck, G., Mann, G., McCallum, A.: Learning from labeled features using generalized expectation criteria. In: SIGIR, pp. 595–602. ACM (2008)
7. Dumais, S.T., Chen, H.: Hierarchical classification of web content. In: SIGIR, pp. 256–263. ACM (2000)
8. Jiang, L., Lu, H., Xu, M., Wang, C.: Biterm pseudo document topic model for short text. In: ICTAI, pp. 865–872. IEEE (2016)
9. Koller, D., Sahami, M.: Hierarchically classifying documents using very few words. In: ICML, pp. 170–178. Morgan Kaufmann (1997)
10. Lang, K.: Newsweeder: learning to filter netnews. In: ICML, pp. 331–339. Morgan Kaufmann (1995)
11. Li, C., Chen, S., Qi, Y.: Filtering and classifying relevant short text with a few seed words. Data Inf. Manag. 3(3), 165–186 (2019)
12. Li, C., Chen, S., Xing, J., Sun, A., Ma, Z.: Seed-guided topic model for document filtering and classification. ACM Trans. Inf. Syst. 37(1), 9:1–9:37 (2019)

13. Li, C., Xing, J., Sun, A., Ma, Z.: Effective document labeling with very few seed words: a topic model approach. In: CIKM, pp. 85–94. ACM (2016)
14. Li, X., Zhang, A., Li, C., Guo, L., Wang, W., Ouyang, J.: Relational biterm topic model: short-text topic modeling using word embeddings. Comput. J. **62**(3), 359–372 (2018)
15. Liu, B., Li, X., Lee, W.S., Yu, P.S.: Text classification by labeling words. In: AAAI, vol. 4, pp. 425–430 (2004)
16. Mekala, D., Shang, J.: Contextualized weak supervision for text classification. In: ACL, pp. 323–333. Association for Computational Linguistics (2020)
17. Meng, Y., Shen, J., Zhang, C., Han, J.: Weakly-supervised neural text classification. In: CIKM, pp. 983–992. ACM (2018)
18. Meng, Y., Shen, J., Zhang, C., Han, J.: Weakly-supervised hierarchical text classification, vol. 33, no. 01, pp. 6826–6833 (2019)
19. Misra, R.: News category dataset (2018). https://doi.org/10.13140/RG.2.2.20331.18729
20. Pang, B., Lee, L., Vaithyanathan, S.: Thumbs up? sentiment classification using machine learning techniques. In: EMNLP, pp. 79–86 (2002)
21. Pennington, J., Socher, R., Manning, C.: Glove: global vectors for word representation. In: EMNLP, pp. 1532–1543. Association for Computational Linguistics (2014)
22. Quan, X., Kit, C., Ge, Y., Pan, S.J.: Short and sparse text topic modeling via self-aggregation. In: IJCAI, pp. 2270–2276 (2015)
23. Song, Y., Roth, D.: On dataless hierarchical text classification. In: AAAI, pp. 1579–1585. AAAI Press (2014)
24. Tang, D., Qin, B., Liu, T.: EMNLP, pp. 1422–1432. The Association for Computational Linguistics (2015)
25. Weng, J., Lim, E.P., Jiang, J., He, Q.: Twitterrank: finding topic-sensitive influential Twitterers. In: WSDM, pp. 261–270. ACM (2010)
26. Xiao, H., Liu, X., Song, Y.: Efficient path prediction for semi-supervised and weakly supervised hierarchical text classification. In: WWW, pp. 3370–3376. ACM (2019)
27. Yan, X., Guo, J., Lan, Y., Cheng, X.: A biterm topic model for short texts. In: WWW, pp. 1445–1456. ACM (2013)
28. Yang, Y., et al.: Dataless short text classification based on biterm topic model and word embeddings. In: Bessiere, C. (ed.) International Joint Conferences on Artificial Intelligence Organization, IJCAI, pp. 3969–3975 (2020)
29. Yin, J., Wang, J.: A Dirichlet multinomial mixture model-based approach for short text clustering. In: SIGKDD, pp. 233–242. ACM (2014)
30. Zhao, W.X., et al.: Comparing twitter and traditional media using topic models. In: Clough, P., et al. (eds.) ECIR 2011. LNCS, vol. 6611, pp. 338–349. Springer, Heidelberg (2011). https://doi.org/10.1007/978-3-642-20161-5_34

PrivaSeer: A Privacy Policy
Search Engine

Mukund Srinath[(⊠)], Soundarya Nurani Sundareswara, C. Lee Giles,
and Shomir Wilson

Pennsylvania State University, University Park, State College, PA, USA
{mukund,sxn5310,clg20,shomir}@psu.edu

Abstract. Web privacy policies are used by organisations to disclose
their privacy practices to users on the web. However, users often do
not read privacy policies because they are too long, time consuming, or
too complicated. Attempts to simplify privacy policies using natural language processing have achieved some success, but they face limitations of
scalability and generalization. While this puts an onus on researchers and
policy regulators to protect users against unfair privacy practices, they
often lack a large-scale collection of policies to study the state of internet privacy. To remedy this bottleneck, we present PrivaSeer, the first
privacy policy search engine. PrivaSeer has been indexed on 1,400,318
English language website privacy policies and can be used to search privacy policies based on text queries and several search facets. Results can
be ranked by PageRank, query-based document relevance, and the probability that a document is a privacy policy. Results also can be filtered
by readability, vagueness, industry, and mentions of tracking technology,
self-regulatory bodies, or regulations and cross-border agreements in the
policy text. PrivaSeer allows legal experts, researchers, and policy regulators to discover privacy trends and policy anomalies in privacy policies
at scale. In this paper we present the search interface, ranking technique,
and filtering techniques for PrivaSeer. We create two indexes of privacy
policies: one including supplementary non-policy content present in privacy policy web pages and one without. We evaluate the functionality of
PrivaSeer by comparing ranking techniques on these two indexes.

Keywords: Privacy · Search engine · Ranking

1 Introduction

A privacy policy is a legal document that an organisation uses to disclose how it
collects, uses, shares and secures its customers' personal data. Laws around the
world such as the General Data Protection Regulation (GDPR) and the Califor-
nia Consumer Privacy Act (CCPA) require organisations to make their privacy
policies readily available to their users. These laws assume that users will read
the privacy policy of an organisation and either accept the practices or abstain
from using the offered services. However, a number of studies have shown that

© Springer Nature Switzerland AG 2021
M. Brambilla et al. (Eds.): ICWE 2021, LNCS 12706, pp. 286–301, 2021.
https://doi.org/10.1007/978-3-030-74296-6_22

although average internet users have a basic interest in online privacy [19], they rarely read privacy policies as they are either too long [15] or too complicated to understand [7]. Additionally, suggestions to improve the comprehensibility of privacy policies [10] have not been adopted by most organisations.

Natural Language Processing (NLP) techniques to simplify privacy policies tested on small corpora of privacy policies [24,26,27] have shown promising results. However, they face issues of accuracy, scalability and generalization due to their small datasets, often consisting of fewer than 10K policies. This paucity of large datasets leads to a lack of robust techniques which could be used to easily understand the wide range of privacy policies on the web. Without automated tools, regulators in some jurisdictions (such as the European Union) rely on user complaints to investigate privacy practices [23] while others (such as the United States) rely on organisations to self-certify their compliance[1] and only investigate when a privacy policy is at odds with real world privacy practices.

To remedy the lack of a publicly accessible large-scale privacy policy resource, we present PrivaSeer[2], a privacy policy search engine that currently indexes 1,400,318 privacy policies collected from the web. PrivaSeer can be used to find policies based on policy text using facets such as sector of commerce, policy vagueness, policy readability, tracking technology mentioned, regulatory bodies mentioned and regulations or cross-border agreements mentioned in the policy text. Search results can be ranked by popularity of the website of the policy, relevance based on the query and the probability that a document is a privacy policy. To the best of our knowledge, PrivaSeer is the first search engine specifically designed to support privacy research.

PrivaSeer gives researchers the ability to quantify and examine sets of policies based on key features, enabling them to discover trends in privacy practices online. Similarly, policy regulators and legal experts can use PrivaSeer to find anomalies in policies, thereby empowering them to protect users from privacy-eroding practices. The simple and intuitive search interface allows privacy concerned web users to find features of particular privacy policies and search for privacy-friendly alternatives for everyday services.

2 Related Work

The related work can be categorised into two areas: collections of privacy policies and methods to simplify privacy policy documents.

To the best of our knowledge, PrivaSeer is the first privacy policy search engine, but a few prior attempts have focused on making privacy policies more accessible to the public. The Usable Privacy Policy Project made available a collection of 115 privacy policies with fine grained human annotation of privacy practices in policies [24]. These policies can be accessed through the website and filtered based on the URL[3]. They display the sector of activity, readability

---

[1] https://www.privacyshield.gov/Program-Overview.
[2] https://privaseer.ist.psu.edu/.
[3] https://explore.usableprivacy.org/.

and popularity of the website from which the policy was originally obtained. In addition, they also created a collection of seven thousand privacy polices which contain machine annotated privacy practices which can be filtered by URL. Similarly, Polisis[4] is a collection of about 31,000 privacy policies which generates automatic summaries of privacy policies based on various data practices. While the privacy policies can be filtered based on their URL, they cannot be searched based on user queries [9]. More recently, Amos et al. [1] released a longitudinal corpus of privacy policies collected from around 130,000 websites.

Privacy policies have been simplified using various machine learning approaches. PrivacyCheck is a an application that automatically summarizes privacy policies online and answers ten basic questions on any privacy policy [26]. Similarly, Privee uses both rule-based and machine learning methods to classify privacy policies based on predefined categories of privacy practices [27]. Question answering techniques to simplify privacy policies have achieved some success. The PrivacyQA corpus was introduced to promote question answering in the privacy domain [16]. Opt-Out Easy is a web browser extension designed to present available opt-out choices to users as they browse the web [3]. Additionally, Apple has begun displaying privacy labels in its MacOS and iOS app stores having collected the information from App developers; however, they are available exclusively for apps in the Apple ecosystem.

While all the above techniques are geared towards simplifying privacy policies for everyday internet users, there is a lack of tools to aid privacy researchers and help regulators manage the vast number of privacy policies online. PrivaSeer has the capacity to help researchers and regulators analyse privacy policies based on required features and enforce regulations at scale.

3 Data Collection

The privacy policies for the PrivaSeer search engine come from the PrivaSeer Corpus[5] [21,22]. Srinath et al. built the PrivaSeer Corpus using two separate crawls of the web. The first crawl occurred in July 2019 with seed URLs from Common Crawl[6], a non-profit organisation which has been releasing large monthly archives of the internet since 2008. The URLs in the Common Crawl archive were first filtered based on a selection criteria that took advantage of the fact that most privacy policy URLs either have the word 'privacy' or the words 'data' and 'protection' in them. The candidate URLs were then re-crawled. The crawled documents were put though a filtering pipeline which included language detection, document classification, duplicate and near-duplicate removal, URL re-verification and non-policy content removal.

The second crawl, in February 2020, used seed URLs from the Free Company Dataset[7]. Candidate documents were filtered using the crawl pipeline after which

---

[4] https://pribot.org/polisis.

[5] We refer to the corpus as PrivaSeer Corpus and the search engine as simply PrivaSeer.

[6] https://commoncrawl.org/.

[7] https://docs.peopledatalabs.com/docs/free-company-dataset.

duplicates between the first and second crawls were resolved. The Free Company Dataset provided additional website metadata such as year founded, industry, size range, country, and employee estimate. The final set in the PrivaSeer Corpus consists of around 1.4 million English language website privacy policies.

4   Search Interface

The user interface of PrivaSeer resembles a standard search engine, in order to keep the system familiar and easy to use. A user enters a query in the search text box on the landing page and can opt to search either the privacy policy URLs or the policy text by selecting a radio button. Figure 1 shows a screenshot of the landing page. Clicking *Search* takes the user to the results page.

Fig. 1. Snapshot of landing page

By default, the privacy policies in the results page are ordered based on a custom ranking function discussed in Sect. 6. The result page displays the top ten results with options to go to the next page. Each result has the title of the webpage, the URL, the date it was crawled and snippets of text in the document with words matching the query words highlighted. The user can re-filter the results based on search facets on either side of the page. Figure 2 shows a screenshot of the results page for the query 'address', a common personal information type mentioned in privacy policies.

5   Indexing

We created two separate indexes: one for privacy policy web pages with non-policy content included and one without. Non-policy content refers to content in a privacy policy web page such as header, footer and navigation menus which are irrelevant to the privacy policy as a legal text. We used Elasticsearch [8] to create an inverted index and divided the documents into the title, URL, and body for indexing. We tokenized the body and title of the privacy policy using grammar based tokenization that works based on the Unicode text segmentation algorithm [5] and tokenized the URL based on a regex tokenizer.

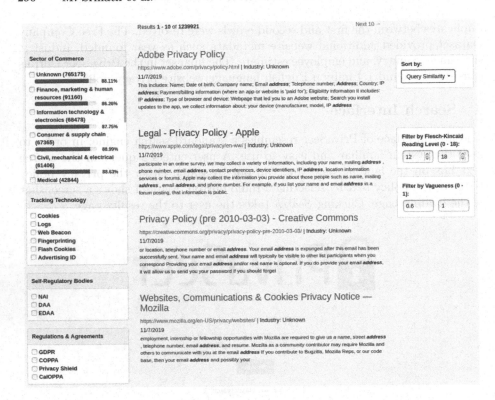

Fig. 2. Snapshot of results page

6   Ranking

The results in PrivaSeer are ranked based on PageRank, query based document relevance and the probability of the document being a privacy policy.

PrivaSeer uses the bag-of-words based Okapi BM25 [17] ranking function to estimate the relevance of a document given a search query. Given a search query Q with terms q_i where $i = i...n$, the score of a document D is given by the following function.

$$\sum_1^n idf(q_i) \times \frac{(k_1 + 1).tf(q_i, D)}{tf(q_i, D) + k_1(1 - b + b.|D|/dl_{avg})} \tag{1}$$

Where, $idf(q_i)$ is given by the following equation.

$$idf(q_i) = log\frac{N - n(q_i) + 0.5}{n(q_i) + 0.5} \tag{2}$$

In the equations, N is the total number of documents in the collection, $n(q_i)$ is the number of documents containing q_i, $tf(q_i, D)$ is the term frequency of q_i

in document D, k_1 and b are tuned constants, $|D|$ is the number of words in document D and dl_{avg} is the average document length in the collection.

We extracted the PageRanks of the domains in the corpus Common Crawl's web graph. Common Crawl use the Gauss-Seidel algorithm [2] to calculate the PageRanks in the web graph. Only a few domains have a high PageRank suggesting that ranking based only on PageRank might limit the discovery of privacy policies from the domains that are not very popular. The custom ranking function combines the scores derived from query based document relevance with PageRank and the probability of the document being a privacy policy. The final score of a document D given query Q is given by the following function.

$$P(D) \times Relevance(D, Q) \times log_{10}(D_{pr}) \tag{3}$$

In the equation, $P(D)$ is the probability that the document is a privacy policy, $Relevance(D, Q)$ is defined in Eq. 1, and D_{pr} is the PageRank of the website from which the document was crawled.

The PrivaSeer Corpus was created by training a random forest model to classify whether a document is a privacy policy. Srinath et al. [21] labeled 1000 crawled documents as either a privacy policy or not. We used the labeled data to train a machine learning model and obtained the probability of a document being a privacy policy. We used 100 documents as the validation set to tune hyperparameters and divided the rest of the documents into train and test sets in the ratio 4:1. We then tokenized and removed stop words before using term-frequency inverse-document-frequency features extracted from the URL and document. The average precision and recall score after 5-fold cross validation were 0.96 and 0.97 respectively.

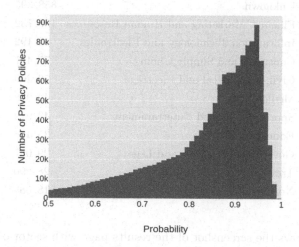

Fig. 3. Distribution of probabilities of documents (being a privacy policy) in the PrivaSeer Corpus

Figure 3 shows the distribution of the probabilities of documents classified as a privacy policy for all the documents in the PrivaSeer Corpus. The horizontal axis begins at 0.5 since the binary classification cutoff probability was 0.5, with 1 being the label for a privacy policy and 0 being the label for its negation. The figure shows that most of the documents are classified with high confidence with only a few documents having a probability less than 0.7.

7   Filtering and Observations on the Document Set

7.1   Sectors of Commerce

The Free Company Dataset, which was used to obtain seed URLs for the PrivaSeer Corpus, maps website URLs to a set of 148 unique industries. Two researchers worked independently and arrived at a consensus to consolidate the industries into 11 sectors of commerce. Table 1 shows the distribution of privacy policies across different sectors of commerce in the PrivaSeer Corpus. *Unknown* consists of extracted privacy policies whose sector of commerce information could not be found on the Free Company Dataset. Expected norms for privacy practices differ based upon sectors of commerce. For example, privacy policies in the medical sector are more likely to address users' health information, which has its own privacy laws (i.e., HIPAA in the US). Thus, we provide sector of commerce as a filter facet to enable policy regulators to compare and find anomalies between privacy policies of the same sector.

Table 1. Distribution of privacy policies across different sectors of commerce

Sector of commerce	Number
Unknown	858, 395
Finance, Marketing and Human Resources	106, 732
Information Technology and Electronics	82, 192
Consumer and Supply Chain	77, 477
Civil, Mechanical and Electrical	70, 209
Medical	49, 918
Sports, Media and Entertainment	43, 912
Education	35, 468
Government, Defense and Legal	29, 037
Travel, Food and Hospitality	28, 290
Non-Profit	18, 688

Figure 2 shows the screenshot of the results page with sector of commerce as a filter facet. For a given query, the number of privacy policies in each sector is specified next to sector name. The progress bar and percentage value for each sector indicate the number of privacy policies retrieved for the query out of the total number of privacy policies for that sector in PrivaSeer Corpus.

7.2   Readability

Readability of a text can be defined as *the ease of understanding or compre-hension due to the style of writing* [12]. One of the main critiques of privacy policies is that they are too complicated to read and understand. Studies have found that privacy policies are difficult to read and require a college-level reading ability [6,7]. The online privacy paradigm follows the *Notice and Choice* frame-work. *Notice* is a presentation of terms by an organisation, usually in the form of a privacy policy and *choice* is an action by a user signifying the acceptance of terms [20]. When privacy policies are difficult to understand, the notice and choice framework breaks down. To assess readability, we calculate the Flesch-Kincaid Grade Level (FKG) [11] for all the policies in the corpus and include it as a facet to filter privacy policies. FKG gives the United States school grade level an average user would need to be in order to understand the text. Srinath et al. show the distribution of readability scores in the PrivaSeer Corpus based on a number of readability techniques [21].

7.3   Tracking Technology

Tracking technologies are used by organisations to keep track of web users' brows-ing habits. We selected six different types of tracking technologies and extracted their mentions in all the policies in the PrivaSeer Corpus. Table 2 shows the dis-tribution of these mentions, extracted using regex queries in an approach similar to Amos et al. [1]. To study the effectiveness of the regex technique, we manually sampled 10 privacy policies from each category of the facet and found no false positives for any category. Intuitively, privacy policies rarely mention tracking technologies which they do not use. While there is a possibility that mentions of some tracking technologies were not captured by the regex technique, thereby leading to false negatives, we believe that the regex expressions captured the common terms for all tracking technology thereby minimizing false negatives.

Studies have found a misalignment between the use and mentions of various tracking technology in privacy policies [1]. While tracking technologies are com-mon in practice, they may not always be mentioned in the privacy policy. Thus, to enable further investigation of discrepancies and trends in the use of tracking technology we include tracking technologies as a facet.

Table 2. Distribution of tracking technology

Tracking technology	Number of policies	% of total
Cookies	1,179,351	84.2%
Logs	249,901	17.8%
Web Beacon	236,099	16.9%
Fingerprinting	73,969	5.3%
Flash Cookies	39,199	2.8%
Advertising ID	15,366	1.1%

7.4   Self-regulatory Bodies

Some jurisdictions rely on organisations to self-certify their privacy regulation compliance. Organisations therefore work with self-regulatory bodies to provide them with privacy seals and certificates verifying the organization's adherence to certain specified privacy standards [18]. Amos et al. presented a longitudinal analysis of self-regulatory compliance by examining the mentions of self-regulatory bodies in privacy policies [1]. We applied the same method of using regex queries to extract mentions of nine self-regulatory bodies in privacy policies of the PrivaSeer Corpus. Similar to the regex technique applied to extracting tracking technologies, we sampled ten random privacy policies for each item in the facet and found no false positives.

Table 3. Distribution of self-regulatory bodies

Self-regulatory bodies	Number	% of total
NAI	88,964	6.35%
DAA	72,754	5.19%
EDAA	22,874	1.63%
BBBOnLine	3,190	
TrustArc	2,300	
CNIL	1,767	<1%
ePrivacy	899	
VeraSafe	180	
Evidon	109	

Table 3 shows the percentage of privacy policies mentioning each of the self-regulatory organizations in the PrivaSeer Corpus. Only initiatives such as Network Advertising Initiative (NAI), Digital Advertising Alliance (DAA) and European Interactive Digital Advertising Alliance (EDAA) that develop self-regulatory standards for online or digital advertising, have significant number of mentions (present in over 1% of privacy policies in the corpus). Therefore, we only provide these as filterable items in PrivaSeer.

7.5   Regulations and Agreements

While some jurisdiction rely on organisations to self-certify their privacy compliance, others rely on concrete regulations and cross-border agreements. Similar to self-regulatory bodies, we extracted mentions of eight regulations and cross-border agreements in privacy policies of the PrivaSeer Corpus. We also included a sector-specific government regulation, the Health Insurance Portability and Accountability Act (HIPAA). Table 4 shows the percentage of privacy policies mentioning different regulations and agreements in the PrivaSeer Corpus. GDPR and Privacy Shield have the highest number of mentions among regulations and cross-border agreements respectively. We include regulations and agreements as a filter facet in PrivaSeer to enable users to identify privacy policies that refer to these regulations.

Table 4. Distribution of regulations & agreements

Regulations & agreements	Number	% of total
GDPR	228, 726	16.33%
COPPA	73, 745	5.27%
Privacy shield	62, 778	4.48%
CalOPPA	57, 819	4.13%
CCPA	13, 215	
SCC	6, 834	
HIPAA	3, 713	<1%
BCR	2, 105	

7.6   Vague Language

A term is regarded as *vague* if it admits borderline cases, where speakers are reluctant to say either the term definitely applies or does not apply [4]. Vagueness in privacy policies is a pervasive problem [13], limiting the ability of readers to precisely interpret their contents. Uncertainly in future needs prompts organisations to resort to using vague language to describe their privacy practices [4]. This diminishes the effectiveness of policies making them unclear to users, thereby reducing trust and causing potential user privacy issues. Thus, we calculate the vagueness scores of all policies in the PrivaSeer Corpus and make them available as a search facet, for regulators and researchers to study at scale.

We use the corpus on vagueness in privacy policies made available by Lebanoff and Liu [13] to calculate the vagueness of policies in PrivaSeer. To create their corpus, Lebanoff and Liu first extracted sentences from 100 privacy policies that contain 40 cue words for vagueness [4]. Each sentence was considered separately and the vague words/phrases in it were identified and annotated. Since the sentence context was not considered, co-referential words were annotated as vague. For example, in the sentence *You can find out more about this on the anonymous edits page*, the word 'this' was annotated as vague. Since our aim was to find the vagueness of the privacy policy as a whole, we ignored annotations on words that were only annotated as vague due to co-reference issues. We ignored the annotations on the following words when they were annotated as vague: *it, this they, them, that, these, here, there, you, us, we,* and *following.* We also ignored annotations on the following phrases when they were annotated as vague: *personal information, personally identifiable information,* and *third party (parties)* as they might have been defined in the privacy policy prior to usage.

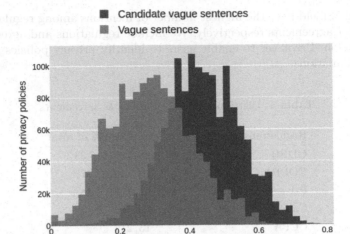

Fig. 4. Distribution of vague sentences

We treated the problem as a token classification problem where each word in a sentence would be predicted as either vague or not. We fine-tuned a pre-trained transformer based model, namely Roberta [14], using the Roberta token classification head from Huggingface [25]. We divided the corpus into train, development, and test sets in the ratio 3:1:1. We used the development set for hyper-parameter tuning. Table 5 shows the results for vague word prediction. While Lebanoff and Liu achieve better precision and recall scores, the corpus that we report on is a modified version due to the removed co-references.

For predicting vagueness of all the policies in the corpus, we extracted sentences form the corpus that had any one of the 40 cue words [4] similar to Lebanoff and Liu [13]. We call these *candidate vague sentences*. Following the candidate sentence extraction, if any word in a sentence was found to be vague by the Roberta model, we considered the sentence to be vague. We then normalised the number of vague sentences with the total number of sentences in the privacy policy to obtain a vagueness score for each policy.

Table 5. Vague word prediction results

Model	Precision	Recall	F1
Lebanoff and Liu	68.4	53.8	60.08
Roberta	65.1	52.6	58.3

The distribution of candidates and vague sentences is shown in Fig. 4. From the figure we can see that on average around 50% of the sentences in a privacy policy are candidates for vague sentences, while about 30% are actually vague. There appears to be a long tail with some privacy policies having almost no vague sentences and some with almost all vague sentences. Manual evaluation of the policies in tail shows that most of them are very short with at most three or four sentences. Figure 2 shows the filter facet for vagueness based on a measure of the ratio of vague sentences to the total number of sentences in the policy. Users can filter results by entering a range between 0 and 1 to select the proportion of vague sentences they would like to see in policies.

8   Ranking Evaluation and Discussion

We perform an exploratory evaluation, since no prior work exists on evaluating a privacy policy search engine. Precision at k or $P@k$ measures the number of relevant results among the top k returned results. We report precision at 10 and precision at 5 scores for two indexes of privacy policies as discussed in Sect. 5, one with the context provided by non-policy content and one without.

Prior research identified ten categories of privacy practices that lawyers expect privacy policies to contain [24]. To evaluate PrivaSeer, we created three themes for queries based on the ten categories in prior work. These themes comprise of *personal information type (PI)*, *security information (S)*, and *privacy practice type (PP)*. The queries were designed and evaluated so that even if a returned result for a query was a privacy policy with the query words, it was deemed irrelevant if it did not fall in the expected category. For example, The query 'health information' is from the category *personal information type*. If a returned result for the query was a privacy policy from a hospital which did not mention how users' health information would be collected or managed, then the query was deemed irrelevant.

Table 6. Queries and their categories

Category	Queries
Personal information type	Payment information, health information, social security number, phone number, photos, private messages, microphone
Security	Firewall, encryption, SSL, data breach, deletion
Privacy practice type	Opt-out, retention period, change notification, do not track, European audience

The categories of queries and each query that was used for evaluation are shown in Table 6. Table 7 shows the comparison of P@5 and P@10 results between three ranking schemes over the different type of query categories and indexes. The results suggest that the custom ranking technique works best followed by PageRank and finally the simple query-document matching.

Table 7. PrivaSeer evaluation results

	Non-policy content Excluded						Non-policy content Included					
	PI		S		PP		PI		S		PP	
	@5	@10	@5	@10	@5	@10	@5	@10	@5	@10	@5	@10
Relevance	0.54	0.48	0.28	0.38	0.66	0.63	0.37	0.31	0.48	0.44	0.6	0.62
PageRank	0.6	0.56	0.6	0.62	0.48	0.5	0.51	0.41	0.56	0.6	0.72	0.7
Custom	**0.88**	**0.9**	**0.92**	**0.92**	**1**	**0.9**	**0.83**	**0.76**	**0.76**	**0.78**	**0.9**	**0.9**

We tested a version of the custom ranking technique without document probability scores and found that the results were slightly better than either PageRank or query based document relevance individually. Although this technique was able to leverage PageRank and query based document relevance scores together, we found that it performed poorly in cases where false positive privacy policies came from domains with a high PageRank. It was only able to perform well when both PageRank and query based document relevance scores presented reasonable results on their own. The use of document probabilities significantly improved ranking performance. The document probability scores suppress documents with a high PageRank or high query based document relevance scores but which might not be a privacy policy in reality.

Performance of all the techniques deteriorated on the index with non-policy content, across all the categories. This suggests that content in the header, footer or navigation menu do not provide much context while ranking queries related to privacy practices. It is likely that non-policy content would improve ranking in cases where users would like to filter results based on a specific industry. While the 'sector of commerce' facet allows users to filter results based on course grained industry categories, queries which include industry specific words on an index with non-policy content might serve as a stronger filter.

The custom ranking technique outperforms the PageRank and query based document relevance techniques and also has a higher variability in the returned results when compared to the PageRank technique. The PageRank technique usually returns the same set of documents for most queries. We hypothesize that this behaviour is because most popular websites have a comprehensive coverage of privacy practices.

9   Conclusion

We present PrivaSeer, the first privacy policy search engine. PrivaSeer is a necessary tool that is the first of its kind and is helpful to several distinct groups with goals in furthering user privacy. Documents can be ranked by query based document relevance scores, PageRank values, and document probabilities. They also can be filtered based on sector of commerce, policy vagueness, policy readability, tracking technology mentioned, regulatory bodies mentioned, and regulations/cross-border agreements mentioned in the policy text.

On average about 30% of the sentences in a privacy policy were found to have at least one vague word in them. This suggests that vagueness in privacy policy documents is a pervasive problem. We used regex text matching to extract details about tracking technology, regulatory bodies, and regulations/cross-border agreements and found non instances of false positives. We believe this is because privacy policies only record elements of privacy that they use/comply while rarely mentioning other elements/alternatives that exist.

An exploratory evaluation of PrivaSeer based on PageRank, query based relevance, and our custom ranking technique found that the custom ranking technique outperformed the others in all categories. We found that our custom technique had higher variability in returned results and was able to overcome limitations caused by the presence of false positive privacy policies in the results. Future work could concentrate on adding a temporal component to the collection of privacy policies and explore alternative ranking methods.

Acknowledgements. This work was partly supported by a seed grant from the College of Information Sciences and Technology at the Pennsylvania State University. We also acknowledge Adam McMillen for technical support and Ellen Poplavska for providing feedback.

References

1. Amos, R., Acar, G., Lucherini, E., Kshirsagar, M., Narayanan, A., Mayer, J.: Privacy policies over time: curation andanalysis of a million-document dataset. arXiv preprint arXiv:2008.09159 (2020)
2. Arasu, A., Novak, J., Tomkins, A., Tomlin, J.: Pagerank computation and the structure of the web: experiments and algorithms. In: Proceedings of the Eleventh International World Wide Web Conference, Poster Track, pp. 107–117 (2002)
3. Bannihatti Kumar, V., et al.: Finding a choice in a haystack: automatic extraction of opt-out statements from privacy policy text. In: Proceedings of The Web Conference, vol. 2020, pp. 1943–1954 (2020). https://doi.org/10.1145/3366423.3380262
4. Bhatia, J., Breaux, T.D., Reidenberg, J.R., Norton, T.B.: A theory of vagueness and privacy risk perception. In: 2016 IEEE 24th International Requirements Engineering Conference (RE), pp. 26–35. IEEE (2016). https://doi.org/10.1109/RE.2016.20
5. Davis, M., Iancu, L.: Unicode text segmentation. Unicode Stand. Annex **29**, 1–30 (2012)
6. Ermakova, T., Fabian, B., Babina, E.: Readability of privacy policies of healthcare websites. Wirtschaftsinformatik **15**, 1–15 (2015)
7. Fabian, B., Ermakova, T., Lentz, T.: Large-scale readability analysis of privacy policies. In: Proceedings of the International Conference on Web Intelligence, pp. 18–25 (2017). https://doi.org/10.1145/3106426.3106427
8. Gormley, C., Tong, Z.: Elasticsearch: The Definitive Guide: A Distributed Real-Time Search and Analytics Engine. O'Reilly Media, Inc., Newton (2015)
9. Harkous, H., Fawaz, K., Lebret, R., Schaub, F., Shin, K.G., Aberer, K.: Polisis: automated analysis and presentation of privacy policies using deep learning. In: 27th USENIX Security Symposium, pp. 531–548 (2018)

10. Kelley, P.G., Cesca, L., Bresee, J., Cranor, L.F.: Standardizing privacy notices: an online study of the nutrition label approach. In: Proceedings of the SIGCHI Conference on Human factors in Computing Systems, pp. 1573–1582 (2010). https://doi.org/10.1145/1753326.1753561
11. Kincaid, J.P., Fishburne Jr, R.P., Rogers, R.L., Chissom, B.S.: Derivation of new readability formulas (automated readability index, fog count and flesch reading ease formula) for navy enlisted personnel (1975). https://doi.org/10.21236/ada006655
12. Klare, G.R., et al.: Measurement of readability (1963). https://doi.org/10.1177/002194366400100207
13. Lebanoff, L., Liu, F.: Automatic detection of vague words and sentences in privacy policies. In: Proceedings of the 2018 Conference on Empirical Methods in Natural Language Processing, pp. 3508–3517 (2018). https://doi.org/10.18653/v1/D18-1387
14. Liu, Y., et al.: Roberta: a robustly optimized bert pretraining approach. arXiv preprint arXiv:1907.11692 (2019)
15. McDonald, A.M., Cranor, L.F.: The cost of reading privacy policies. Isjlp **4**, 543 (2008)
16. Ravichander, A., Black, A.W., Wilson, S., Norton, T., Sadeh, N.: Question answering for privacy policies: combining computational and legal perspectives. In: Proceedings of the 2019 Conference on Empirical Methods in Natural Language Processing and the 9th International Joint Conference on Natural Language Processing (EMNLP-IJCNLP), pp. 4949–4959 (2019). https://doi.org/10.18653/v1/D19-1500
17. Robertson, S.E., Walker, S., Beaulieu, M., Willett, P.: Okapi at TREC-7: automatic ad hoc, filtering, VLC and interactive track. Nist Spec. Publ. SP **500**, 253–264 (1999)
18. Rodrigues, R., Wright, D., Wadhwa, K.: Developing a privacy seal scheme (that works). Int. Data Priv. Law **3**(2), 100–116 (2013). https://doi.org/10.1093/idpl/ips037
19. Rudolph, M., Feth, D., Polst, S.: Why users ignore privacy policies – a survey and intention model for explaining user privacy behavior. In: Kurosu, M. (ed.) HCI 2018. LNCS, vol. 10901, pp. 587–598. Springer, Cham (2018). https://doi.org/10.1007/978-3-319-91238-7_45
20. Sloan, R.H., Warner, R.: Beyond notice and choice: privacy, norms, and consent. J. High Tech. L. **14**, 370 (2014). https://doi.org/10.2139/SSRN.2239099
21. Srinath, M., Wilson, S., Giles, C.L.: Privacy at scale: introducing the privaseer corpus of web privacy policies. arXiv preprint arXiv:2004.11131 (2020)
22. Sundareswara, S.N., Wilson, S., Srinath, M., Giles, C.L.: Privacy not found: a study of the availability of privacy policies on the web. In: Sixteenth Symposium on Usable Privacy and Security (SOUPS 2020). USENIX Association (2020)
23. Supervisor, F.E.D.P.: What to expect when we inspect (2018)
24. Wilson, S., et al.: The creation and analysis of a website privacy policy corpus. In: Proceedings of the 54th Annual Meeting of the Association for Computational Linguistics, pp. 1330–1340 (2016). https://doi.org/10.18653/v1/P16-1126
25. Wolf, T., et al.: Transformers: state-of-the-art natural language processing. In: Proceedings of the 2020 Conference on Empirical Methods in Natural Language Processing: System Demonstrations, pp. 38–45 (2020). https://doi.org/10.18653/v1/2020.emnlp-demos.6

26. Zaeem, R.N., German, R.L., Barber, K.S.: Privacycheck: automatic summarization of privacy policies using data mining. ACM Trans. Internet Technol. (TOIT) **18**(4), 1–18 (2018). https://doi.org/10.1145/3127519
27. Zimmeck, S., Bellovin, S.M.: Privee: an architecture for automatically analyzing web privacy policies. In: 23rd USENIX Security Symposium, pp. 1–16 (2014)

Web of Things

Knowledge-Driven Architecture Composition: Assisting the System Integrator to Reuse Integration Knowledge

Fabian Burzlaff[✉][iD] and Christian Bartelt[iD]

Institute for Enterprise Systems (InES), University of Mannheim,
68131 Mannheim, Germany
{burzlaff,bartelt}@es.uni-mannheim.de

Abstract. Semantic interoperability for web services is still a problem. Although decentralized solutions such as describing the integration context with a formal mapping language or using a web service description language exist, practitioners rely on implementing software adapters manually. For IoT and Web of Things systems, current scientific solutions fall short as changing them, once defined, requires strenuous effort. However, devices and thus, their interfaces change often in this class of system. This paper tackles the barrier of high formalization effort for mappings between required and provided interfaces. Therefore, we apply and evaluate a novel integration method for web service choreography. Our empirical experiment shows that this method lowers the integration time and number of errors by assisting the system integrator to reuse integration knowledge from previous integration cases.

Keywords: Knowledge-driven architecture composition · Web service integration · Reuse

1 Introduction

In the universe of IoT, there will not exist one distinct standard for each use-case [1]. The agreement process and keeping standards up-to-date is not feasible for dynamically changing IoT systems. Hence, system integrators are currently forced to implement software adapters. What's bad about this is not the manual implementation effort but the circumstance that the same integration knowledge is repeatedly implemented in these software adapters.

Bottom-up approaches that do not rely on a predefined standard try to automate service integration by describing each integration context based on service

This work has been developed in the project BIoTope (Research Grant Number 01lS18079C) and is funded by the German Ministry of Education and Research (BMBF).

descriptions and interface mappings. These integration contexts are defined with a closed-wold assumption in mind and relate to the concept of service choreography. However, if an unforeseen integration case comes up, no automated service integration occurs as the composition model is assumed to be complete. In dynamically changing IoT environments, this results in a high formalization effort that does not yield the desired benefits as structural and behavioral interface mappings are assumed to be stable once they are defined. High formalization effort such as adapting interface service descriptions, adjusting the underlying ontology or resolving reasoning errors rather increases than decreases integration effort over time. Furthermore, formalizing possible integration contexts ahead to put them into inventory increases the specification effort even more as they may not be used [2].

Within this gap, a novel integration method called knowledge-driven architecture composition (KDAC) has been suggested [3]. This method does not aim at a stable composition model of the desired domain. In contrast to existing bottom-up solution proposals, it refrains from formalizing integration contexts in a big-bang manner at system design time. Instead, the approach explicitly allows for interface mappings that are formalized incrementally and are thus incomplete. Interface mappings are only written in a machine-understandable way if a concrete integration case is present.

In this paper, we evaluate this so far conceptual method for web service composition. Therefore, we design an empirical experiment and build up the necessary tooling infrastructure. The method and tooling may assist the system integrator in reusing existing integration knowledge and lowering the required implementation effort. However, it is unclear if formalizing integration knowledge and implementing a software adapter in the beginning results in lower integration effort due to integration knowledge reuse over time.

2   Background for Applied Approach

The goal of KDAC is to assist the system integrator in generating software adapters automatically. The leverage of the method is to make integration knowledge reusable and reason about interface mappings [3]. Therefore, interface mappings must be stored in a machine-understandable way and made publicly available. These mappings must respect the semantic interoperability of services (e.g., REST). Semantic interoperability ensures that data exchanges between a provided and a required service make sense – that the requester and provider have a common understanding of the meaning of services and data [7]. Semantic interoperability in distributed systems is mainly achieved by establishing semantic correspondences (i.e., mappings) between vocabularies of different sources [1, 14].

From an engineering perspective, software adaptability (e.g., service choreography) can be achieved by engineering principles (i.e., explicitly planned component configurations), emergent properties (i.e., implicitly derived from cooperation patterns of the participants), or evolutionary mechanisms (i.e., replacing components) [15]. KDAC tackles engineering principles, emergent properties and evolutionary mechanisms in the following way:

Engineering: At the core, KDAC is a software engineering method that tries to minimize the mapping formalization effort by relying on concrete integration cases instead of using predefined composition models (e.g., as known from component-based software engineering). We can integrate KDAC into current software engineering methods such as agile development or other incremental development modes. In addition to implementing an imperative software adapter, mappings are only formalized if a concrete integration case occurs (i.e., bottom-up). These mappings are stored incrementally using a declarative language. A declarative language allows for applying reasoning principles. In contrast to top-down methods (e.g., integration based on standards) and other knowledge-based bottom-up methods (e.g., describing an integration context using ontologies), KDAC explicitly allows for incomplete integration knowledge at all times.

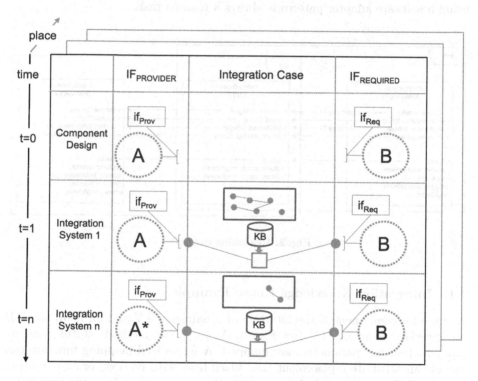

Fig. 1. Knowledge-driven architecture composition [adapted from [3]]

Evolution: In the beginning, the human-in-the-loop principle applies as the underlying knowledge base is empty (see KB in Fig. 1). Over time, integration knowledge is added to the knowledge base when new devices are integrated (see dots and lines at t = 1 in Fig. 1). Hence, in the beginning, more formalization effort takes place. The declarative formalization allows for knowledge reuse from previous integration cases independent of the service model and service description syntax. Finally, the formalization effort is reduced by reusing mappings and reasoning principles (see dots and lines at t = n in Fig. 1).

Emergent: Although integration knowledge is incomplete, automated integration is possible over time so that the system integrator fades out of the loop. Instead of integrating each device with one central domain model in a star-like manner (i.e., the domain model acts similar to a 'translator-in-the-middle'), we can build up complex mapping chains. This structure allows for applying two reasoning principles which are transitive relationships and inverse mappings. Moreover, we can integrate unforeseen component replacements without human anticipation.

In contrast, detecting semantic interoperability for ad-hoc integration cases using a software adapter pattern is always a manual task.

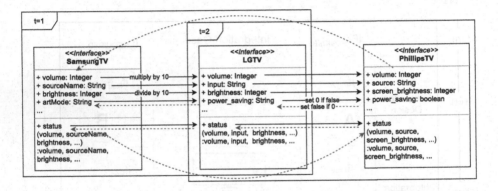

Fig. 2. Reasoning example

2.1   Integration Knowledge Reuse Example

Assume for component A the interface of a Samsung TV and for component B the interface of an LG TV (see Fig. 2). At t = 1, the method "status" and its input and output parameters are mapped. A formalized mapping function can include an attribute replacement (i.e., black lines with no text) or an operation (i.e., black lines with text). As we can retrieve no mappings from the knowledge base for the Samsung and LG interface, all mappings have to be created manually by the system integrator. At t = n, these mapping functions can be reused for the same integration case or for the inverse integration case (i.e., LG TV is substituted by the Samsung TV). Furthermore, we can also reuse formalized mappings for extensions of already seen interfaces (i.e., indicated by component A* in Fig. 1).

For a transitive mapping chain, assume another integration from LG TV to a Philips TV at t = 2 (see Fig. 2). Now, we can deduce the integration case from Samsung TV to Philips TV. Furthermore, the inverse integration case from Philips to Samsung may also be covered if there exists an inverse function for each formalized mapping function within the chain Philips TV ↔ LG TV ↔ Samsung TV. Hence, as soon as the system integrator selects the required and provided interfaces based on the available components, a software adapter can be (partially) generated.

However, integration knowledge is always incomplete, as not all methods offered by all available devices and their possible combinations are formalized or can be derived.

3   Evaluation Design and Results

In this experiment, we illustrate and test the end-to-end application of the proposed method for web services. The participants have to work in two environments. This also allows for editing mappings within the mapping and coding environment. The central evaluation goal is to compare implementing software adapters, generating software adapters without reasoning principles, and generating software adapters with reasoning principles. Thereby we allow reusing mapping functions between attributes and methods (see Fig. 2). As an effort indicator, we measure the integration time and the number of mapping errors and discuss problems during software adapter implementation.

3.1   Evaluation Setup

Challenge: It is unclear how KDAC can assist the system integrator during software adapter (SA) implementation. Especially, the additional time to formalize mappings should result in a working software adapter.

Experiment Design: We empirically compare the software adapter implementation method against KDAC applying a within-subject design [12,17]. SA represents implementing a software adapter. KDAC is split up in generating software adapter without any mappings stored in the knowledge base (variant 1 – no reasoning) and with mappings stored in the knowledge (variant 2 – reasoning). Hence, we can compare the mapping time and errors made by the system integrator and, if any, made by the reasoning algorithms. Thereby we focus on creating correct mappings according to their semantic interoperability.

Therefore, three to five integration cases have been assigned to four students each week (i.e., 16th October 2020 until 16th December 2020).

Participants: The students study Informatics at the Bachelor (two students) or the Master (two students) level. All students did not have working experience in implementing software adapters in the given programming language.

Experiment Scope: As we are interested in the method's performance and not in the underlying technology, we chose a technology stack that can be utilized by both methods (i.e., SA and KDAC). Regarding the underyling KDCA method, we focus on empty knowledge-bases and high formalization effort in the beginning (i.e., $t = 0$ and $t = 1$ within Fig. 1). We do not evaluate how reasoning principles and the underlying method perform on a large knowledge base (i.e., $t = 0$ in Fig. 1).

Success Indicator: An integration task is finished if the request to a required service is successfully transformed to the request of a provided service instance and vice versa for the respective response. There is a test criterion for each integration task that tells the students whether their mapping is correct or not. In essence, the test criterion contains all attributes as defined for the required operation and the values as produced by the provided operations. This test criterion is checked every time the student runs the software adapter. If the test fails, a snapshot of the software adapter is stored. This allows for a qualitative evaluation of the code.

Metrics: The quantitative implementation effort is measured in integration time and component interaction correctness. Integration time is measured from starting the integration task until the students finished the mapping in the KDAC tool in minutes. Component interaction correctness is measured by the number of retries needed when the test criterion is not met.

Hypothesis: The independent variable is the engineering method. The dependent variables are integration time and component interaction correctness. We suspect that the component interaction correctness and integration time is highest using the KDAC method (see Fig. 1).

Technology Stack: We rely on the HTTP/JSON component model using POST and GET service calls. For specifying mapping functions in a declarative way, we use JSONata [9], and for implementing the software adapter, we use the Visual Studio Code Web IDE. For implementing the software adapter, we choose NodeJS. A project setup script is provided so that the participants can resolve all necessary dependencies by issuing one command line statement within the Web IDE.

All HTTP/JSON endpoints have been designed based on publicly available endpoints from the OpenAPI repositories (e.g., https://rapidapi.com/) or Smart Home Adapter repositories (e.g., https://www.openhab.org/addons/). Here, OpenAPI refers to a syntactical description of service instances (i.e., device abstraction) that does not support any relationship to a machine-readable or machine-understandable domain standard (e.g., URL links to an ontology). Then, service instances from the OpenAPI specifications have been mocked.

3.2 Evaluation Execution Process

The leitmotif for the students is that a client requests a required server interface (e.g. POST Samsung), but only a semantically identical provided interface instance (e.g. POST LG) is available. This means that the needed software adapter translates one interface to precisely one other interface. Thus, all request parameters from the provided interface must be present in the required request,

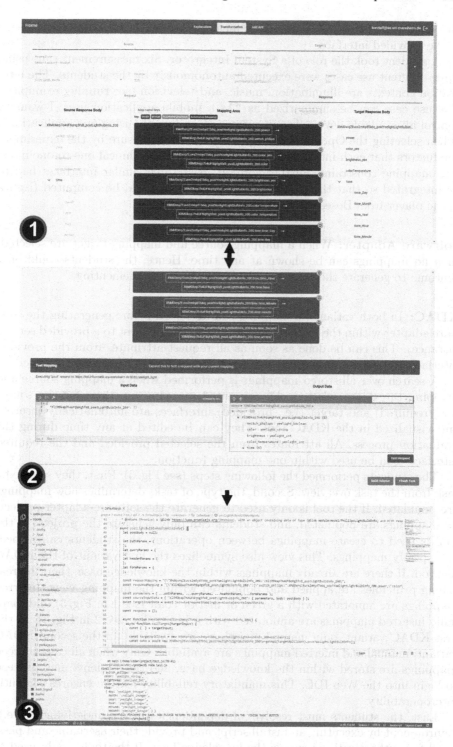

Fig. 3. Evaluation steps

and all required response parameters must be present in the response message of the provided interface.

A student took the role of a System Integrator. Six measurement runs using three different use cases were executed autonomously by the students. The integration contexts are illumination, music, and television (see running example). The use case can be summarized as "As a mobile application user, I want to control all available devices in my current room by only using one application". When selecting the OpenAPI descriptions, it was made sure by the experiment conductors that each integration context fulfilled the technical one-to-one interface mapping constraint. Furthermore, at least three similar interfaces had to be integrated so that the transitive mapping chain could be computed (e.g., a music player from Bose, Sony, and Sonos).

Software Adapter: When a mapping source and mapping target are selected, then no mappings can be shown at any time. Hence, the students could only continue to generate the software adapter and start implementing.

KDAC: In both variants, a mapping can be tested before generating the software adapter within the KDAC tool (i.e., perform a request to a provided service instance). This can be done as soon as all request attributes from the provided interface and all response attributes from the required interface are mapped.

A search over all stored mappings is performed when a mapping source and mapping target are selected. All computed mapping functions for the source (i.e., required) and target (i.e., provided) interfaces are automatically inserted and visualized in the KDAC tool. They can be edited at any time during the evaluation process. All attributes from the selected provided and the required interfaces can be used within one mapping function.

The students performed the following steps (see Fig. 3): First, they selected a task from the task overview. Second, the type of tasks determines how mappings are populated. If the tool is only used to generate the software adapter project, no mappings are populated, and students can only generate the project. If the tool is used to create mappings between operations, the students can inspect and specify mappings. This view also symbolizes the first variant of the KDAC method. If there are already mappings within the knowledge base, then the reasoning principles are applied and populated within the mapping view. Inferred mappings are annotated with a green or merlot color (see 1 in Fig. 3) and manually inserted mappings are annotated with a blue color (see 2 in Fig. 3). In the first KDAC variant, only manual mappings are available. In the second KDAC variant, manual and inferred mappings are available. Only when all calls succeed mappings are stored within the knowledge base, and the students may proceed to login into the Web IDE. This mandatory reliability feature ensures semantic interoperability.

Last, the students must resolve all dependencies in the underlying Node.js environment by executing an install script and provide their username and password for authentication towards the knowledge base. If the tool is only used to generate the adapter skeleton, then the method that should contain the actual transformations had to be implemented. Suppose the tool was used to formalize mappings or mappings have been computed based on the reasoning principles. In that case, these mappings are inserted into the software adapter code that had to be implemented (see 3 in Fig. 3).

Finally, the students can check anytime by executing a test script if their operationalized mappings are correct according to the test criterion (see 3 Fig. 3). If this is the case, then a corresponding message is printed on the terminal, and the students end the task by switching back to the KDAC tool and click the finish task button (see 2 in Fig. 3).

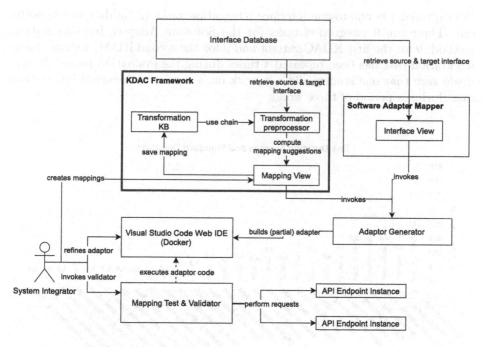

Fig. 4. High-level system architecture for evaluation setup

3.3   Implementation

The overall KDAC framework is built up of three parts responsible for generating interface mappings. In addition, a generic *Mapping Test & Validator* for testing the created mappings was implemented (see Fig. 4). Depending on the task type, a preprocessor might be applied. Their duty is to populate the *Mapping View* with automatically created suggestions of mapping functions. In the case of the first variant of the KDAC method (i.e., no reasoning), the web-tool only provides a graphical user interface for specifying mappings with JSNOata. The web-tool is used to generate the software adapter project skeleton so that both approaches are as similar as possible. Hence, the first and second variant only differentiate in whether existing mappings are evaluated or not. In the case of the second variant of the KDAC method, the *Transformation preprocessor* is invoked. It first tries to find a transitive mapping chain between the selected source and target interface using a breadth-first search on the *Transformation KB*. Once such a chain is identified, the preprocessor recursively applies the mappings stored in JSONata to each other, producing a final mapping from the source to the target interface (i.e., POST Samsung → POST LG). This is done for both, request and response data.

3.4   Results

We captured 108 one-to-one interface integration tasks to validate our hypothesis. There are 9 integration tasks for the Software Adapter Implementation method, 9 for the first KDAC variant and 9 for the second KDAC variant. Each integration task has been repeated 4 times during the evaluation period. It was made sure that one student did not work on a similar or identical integration task during a period of three weeks.

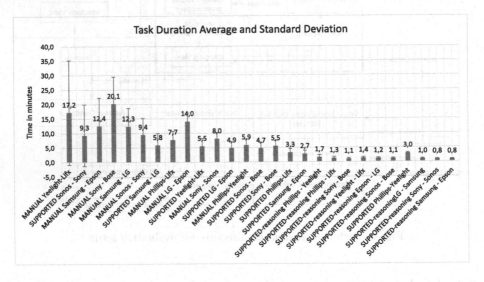

Fig. 5. Average and standard deviation for all integration tasks

Figure 5 outlines the duration average for all integration tasks. An integration task involved ten to 16 attributes that had to be mapped. The integration time is measured in minutes, and the description of each task involves the integration task type. Here, "MANUAL" corresponds to only using the tool (see Fig. 3) as a software adapter generation environment where all mapping logic has to be implemented in the generated adapter project. "SUPPORTED" relates to the first variant of the KDAC method, where mappings between interfaces are defined using JSONata. Last, "SUPPORTED-reasoning" is the second variant of the KDAC method with reasoning and integration knowledge reuse. The devices from Sony, Bose, and Sonos are speakers, Yeelight, Lifx, and Philips are lamps, and Epson, LG, and Samsung are TVs.

Overall, the average time needed for constructing a working software adapter is the highest for implementing software adapters and the lowest when mappings can be reused. Furthermore, the manual task's standard deviation is higher compared to the second variant of the KDAC method. This is mainly because of the presence or absence of errors during code writing. The number of attributes does not seem to directly affect the average integration time as the highest value of 20.1 min had 13 attributes to be mapped. The first integration task with 16 attributes scored an average duration of 14 min.

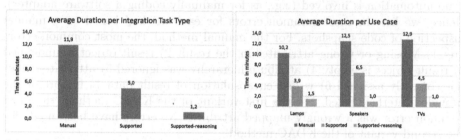

(a) Average Integration Duration per Method

(b) Average Integration Duration per Use Case

Fig. 6. Metric integration time

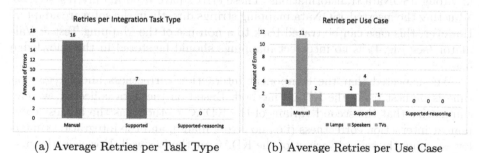

(a) Average Retries per Task Type

(b) Average Retries per Use Case

Fig. 7. Metric errors

Figure 6a illustrates the average integration time per engineering method and Fig. 6b the average integration time per use case. On average, the participants need 11.9 min to implement a software adapter, 5.0 min to create mappings in the tool and then generate a software adapter, and 1.2 min when mappings could be reused. For all integration tasks type, the same number of attributes had to be mapped (i.e., 117 attributes in total). For the three use cases, this equality does not apply. However, this does not necessarily result in higher average integration times. Concerning the traditional software adapter implementation method, the use case with lamps (90 attributes in total) lasted 10.2 min, speakers (117 attributes in total) lasted 12.5 min, and TVs (141 attributes in total) lasted 12.9 min. The average integration times are highest for the manual integration task types and lowest for the second variant of the KDAC method.

Figure 7a and Fig. 7b illustrate the amount of retries from the viewpoints of integration task types and use cases. Naturally, the sum of retries per use case equals the number of retries per integration task type. It can be stated the errors made is highest for the manual software adapter implementation method and lowest for the second variant of the KDAC method. This circumstance is straight forward as the number of errors possibly made by the students' increases if no automation is involved (e.g., as for manually coding a software adapter). Hence, we list the most common errors for each method based on a manual inspection of code snapshots. For the manual method, the most common errors are: 1) Missing or wrong attributes in the result 2) result object is undefined 3) result object is empty 4) attribute hierarchy was ignored 5) attribute values not correctly assigned 6) wrong encapsulation of result data 7) import of the provided interface failed. For the first variant of the KDAC method, the most common error was a wrongly mapped attribute. No errors have been made for the second variant of the KDAC method.

Error resolving strategies for all methods include the usage of logging functionality offered by the IDE. Regarding the manual method, this allowed for identifying attributes with different semantics as the retrieved values from the provided interfaces did not match the specified test criterion. Regarding the KDAC method's first variant, errors made in mapping from within the tool resulted in wrong JSONata transformations. These errors have been mainly resolved by adjusting the inserted JSONata mapping strings directly in the software adapter. However, this case can be traced back to a non-use of the Mapping Test & Validator (see Fig. 4) as no incorrect mappings should be stored in the knowledge base.

We suspected that the component interaction correctness and integration time is highest using the KDAC method. Based on the data collected, we can summarize that the second variant of the KDAC method has the highest component interaction correctness (i.e., no errors made), and the integration time is lowest using the second variant of the KDAC method as well. However, the first variant of the KDAC method involved some errors. Nevertheless, a low number of the student population and the applicability of reasoning principles allow for improvement.

3.5   Threats to Validity

Apparently, implementing interface mappings in a textual programming language and implementing interface mappings in a graphical web-tool poses a different challenge for novices. Therefore, we ensured that the students working on software adapter implementation tasks also could rely on the NodeJS project skeleton generation service. Furthermore, we measure the results for using the graphical tool without reuse and reasoning functionality (i.e., KDAC variant 1). Consequently, we can identify the time saved by switching from the textual to the graphical syntax for mapping creation. Although we can see that the second variant of KDAC is the fastest, we can only approximate the point where using KDAC in addition to implementing the software adapter pays off. This is mainly due to the challenge of collecting realistic engineering data over time.

Overall, the presented evaluation design favors internal over external validity. Hence, we eliminated the confounding factors for the independent variable engineering method as much as possible. Tasks are randomly assigned to the students, but it is made sure that no student works on the same integration task in subsequent measurement runs.

Nevertheless, we can only discuss generalized statements based on this experiment within the following frame: There may be a selection bias as only four students were serving as study population members. The representativeness of use cases is ensured by using OpenAPI specifications from external product vendors. However, it is made sure during OpenAPI interface description selection that mappings could be chained early in the experiment. This may not hold in practice. Furthermore, it may not always be the case that there is a one-to-one mapping between a set of interfaces. However, the tool also supports one-to-many mappings. Nevertheless, manual mappings are inevitable if there are multiple paths from a source to a target interface within the knowledge base.

The evaluation focuses on the engineering method. Hence, different technologies might have produced other results. We assume that more complex interface descriptions (e.g. using stateful services) would slow our approach down.

Last, there exists a learning curve by the students for all use cases. The first integration contexts worked on (i.e., lamps) have a higher standard variation than the later use case (i.e., TVs). This learning curve applied to all students and all task types as they had no prior experience in implementing software adapters or using the KDAC. Here, no experience can be measured more precisely than some experience.

4 Related Work

There are four different research streams that deal with semantic service interoperability for various system classes (e.g., web services, interactive systems, or embedded systems) based on interface mappings [4]. These are symbolic artificial intelligence [11], component-based software development [5], software architecture [2,16], and web services [6,8] .

For web service composition approaches with an explicit semantic layer, the following approaches are related to KDAC. Bennaceur et al. [2] present a fully automatable approach that achieves interoperability through semantics-based technologies. Their approach uses a domain-specific ontology, already annotated services based in SAWSDL, and model-checking techniques to generate correct-by-construction mediators automatically. They target the run time phase and minimize additional specification effort by using reasoning principles.

Khodadadi et al. [10] suggest a framework for service definition and discovery. This framework relies on ontologies paired with JSON-LD and is a prime example for bottom-up service integration as services are annotated incrementally.

Kovatsch et al. [13] introduce a practical approach to semantics for the IoT regarding physical states and device mashups. Their approach calculates an execution plan based on RESTdesc service descriptions to facilitate service composition. They note that calculating an execution plan took longer than expected and is a potential obstacle to applying their approach out-of-the-box.

Like KDAC, all approaches describe the integration context, such as in our example (see Sect. 2.1) in a decentralized manner. Hence, no global standard is used by any of the approaches. However, Kovatsch et al. [13] and Bennaceur et al. [2] assume that their decentralized integration context is complete (i.e., contains also all needed interface mappings for future cases). If a change occurs, updating these mappings requires substantial effort. Here, KDAC allows for incomplete mappings that can be easily edited. Khodadadi et al. [10] also support incompleteness by incrementally annotating data JSON data. However, they provide no leverage to support mapping creation as they only focus on creating interface descriptions. This means that only identical integration contexts can be solved. Here, KDAC offers reasoning principles to integrate also unseen integration cases.

5   Conclusion

Semantic interoperability for web services is still a problem for IoT and Web of Things systems. In this paper, we lower the formalization effort for web services and their integration context by applying and evaluating an integration method that makes use-case specific integration knowledge reusable. Therefore, we performed an empirical experiment that compares manual software adapter implementation with the knowledge-driven integration method. Our results suggest that, over time, reusing incrementally formalized integration knowledge is indeed faster than implementing software adapters manually without any integration knowledge reuse. In the future, we plan to extend the mapping language used to cover other domains that do not only rely on the HATEOAS principle for web services (e.g., cyber-physical systems).

References

1. Barnaghi, P., Wang, W., Henson, C., Taylor, K.: Semantics for the internet of things: early progress and back to the future. Int. J. Semant. Web Inf. Syst (IJSWIS) 8(1), 1–21 (2012)
2. Bennaceur, A., Issarny, V.: Automated synthesis of mediators to support component interoperability. IEEE Trans. Softw. Eng 41(3), 221–240 (2015). https://doi.org/10.1109/TSE.2014.2364844

3. Burzlaff, F., Bartelt, C.: Knowledge-driven architecture composition: Case-based formalization of integration knowledge to enable automated component coupling. In: 2017 IEEE International Conference on Software Architecture Workshops (ICSAW), pp. 108–111. IEEE (2017)
4. Burzlaff, F., Wilken, N., Bartelt, C., Stuckenschmidt, H.: Semantic interoperability methods for smart service systems: a survey. IEEE Trans. Eng. Manag., 1–15 (2019). https://doi.org/10.1109/TEM.2019.2922103
5. Chang, H., Mariani, L., Pezze, M.: In-field healing of integration problems with COTS components. In: 2009 IEEE 31st International Conference on Software Engineering, pp. 166–176. IEEE (2009)
6. Garriga, M., Mateos, C., Flores, A., Cechich, A., Zunino, A.: RESTful service composition at a glance: a survey. J. Netw. Comput. Appl **60**, 32–53 (2016)
7. Heiler, S.: Semantic interoperability. ACM Comput. Surv. (CSUR) **27**(2), 271–273 (1995)
8. Jara, A.J., Olivieri, A.C., Bocchi, Y., Jung, M., Kastner, W., Skarmeta, A.F.: Semantic web of things: an analysis of the application semantics for the IoT moving towards the IoT convergence. Int. J. Web Grid Serv. **10**(2–3), 244–272 (2014)
9. JSONata: Json query and transformation language. https://jsonata.org/, Accessed 29 Oct 2020
10. Khodadadi, F., Sinnott, R.O.: A semantic-aware framework for service definition and discovery in the internet of things using coap. Procedia Comput. Sci. **113**, 146–153 (2017)
11. Klusch, M., Kapahnke, P., Zinnikus, I.: SAWSDL-MX2: a machine-learning approach for integrating semantic web service matchmaking variants. In: 2009 IEEE International Conference on Web Services, pp. 335–342 (2009). https://doi.org/10.1109/ICWS.2009.76
12. Ko, A.J., LaToza, T.D., Burnett, M.M.: A practical guide to controlled experiments of software engineering tools with human participants. Empirical Softw. Eng. **20**(1), 110–141 (2013). https://doi.org/10.1007/s10664-013-9279-3
13. Kovatsch, M., Hassan, Y.N., Mayer, S.: Practical semantics for the internet of things: physical states, device mashups, and open questions. In: 2015 5th International Conference on the Internet of Things (IOT), pp. 54–61. IEEE (2015)
14. Noy, N.F., Doan, A., Halevy, A.Y.: Semantic integration. AI Mag. **26**(1), 7–7 (2005)
15. Rausch, A., Bartelt, C., Herold, S., Klus, H., Niebuhr, D.: From software systems to complex software ecosystems: model- and constraint-based engineering of ecosystems. In: Münch, J., Schmid, K. (eds.) Perspectives on the Future of Software Engineering: Essays in Honor of Dieter Rombach, pp. 61–80. Springer, Heidelberg (2013). https://doi.org/10.1007/978-3-642-37395-4_5
16. Spalazzese, R., Inverardi, P.: Mediating connector patterns for components interoperability. In: Babar, M.A., Gorton, I. (eds.) ECSA 2010. LNCS, vol. 6285, pp. 335–343. Springer, Heidelberg (2010). https://doi.org/10.1007/978-3-642-15114-9_26
17. Wohlin, C., Runeson, P., Höst, M., Ohlsson, M.C., Regnell, B., Wesslén, A.: Experimentation in Software Engineering. Springer, Heidelberg (2012). https://doi.org/10.1007/978-3-642-29044-2

A-MaGe: Atomic Mashup Generator
for the Web of Things

Ege Korkan[1]($\boxtimes$) iD, Fady Salama[1] iD, Sebastian Kaebisch[2] iD,
and Sebastian Steinhorst[1] iD

[1] Technical University of Munich, Munich, Germany
{ege.korkan,fady.salama,sebastian.steinhorst}@tum.de
[2] Siemens AG, Munich, Germany
sebastian.kaebisch@siemens.com

Abstract. Individually, Internet of Things (IoT) devices are often not able to achieve complex functionalities and, therefore, need to be composed together into useful mashups. However, given the current fragmentation of the IoT domain, designing a mashup is still a manual task that is time-consuming and error-prone. The introduction of the Thing Description (TD) from the World Wide Web Consortium (W3C) is meant to facilitate the interoperability between IoT devices and platforms by providing a standardized format to describe the network interfacing of entities, called Things, participating in the Web of Things (WoT). Furthermore, the System Description (SD) extension introduces the notion of Atomic Mashups (AMs), small mashup building blocks that are easier to design. However, designing AMs remains a manual task and, given the rising complexity of IoT devices, manually exploring the resulting design space is infeasible. In this paper, we introduce A-MaGe: a method and its open-source implementation that takes the TDs as an input and uses predefined templates, user-configurable rules, semantic annotation filtering and natural language processing to automatically explore and reduce the design space. SD-compliant UML Sequence Diagrams of the resulting mashups are presented to the human agent for further selection to generate the SD of the mashup as well as implementation code based on the W3C WoT Scripting API. We show that the generation process is fast, allowing multiple iterations by the human agent to increase reduction and we evaluate the filtering power of different filters and constraints. Thus, in combination with the TD standard, our method ensures easy composition of services in heterogeneous environments.

Keywords: Web of Things · Mashup composition

1 Introduction

The domain of Internet of Things (IoT) has been rapidly growing, with the number of connected devices projected to increase to 50 billion devices by 2030 [1].

M. Brambilla et al. (Eds.): ICWE 2021, LNCS 12706, pp. 320–327, 2021.
https://doi.org/10.1007/978-3-030-74296-6_24

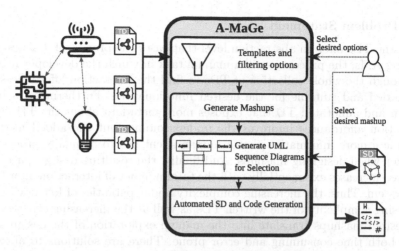

Fig. 1. A-MaGe takes Thing Descriptions (TDs) and based on constraints and filters, Atomic Mashups are generated and presented to the human agent in form of UML Sequence Diagrams. The human agent can then choose to generate the System Description (SD) and the code for the selected mashup.

With this vast increase comes the challenge of connecting devices from different vendors. To facilitate it, vendors offer IoT platforms, software that handles the communication of different devices and exposes the functionalities. However, there are currently over 620 different IoT platforms on the market [2] and this causes a high fragmentation in the IoT domain as well as a difficulty in developing applications that leverage functionalities from the resulting silos.

To address this problem, the World Wide Web Consortium (W3C) proposed the Web of Things (WoT) architecture as a standardized means to allow the interoperability of different IoT platforms [3]. The main building block of the WoT architecture is the Thing Description (TD) [4], which is a JSON-Linked Data (JSON-LD) document [5] that is both machine- and human-readable and describes the network-interfacing of the interaction affordances offered by any IoT entity, called a *Thing* in the context of this paper.

However, TDs have no means to describe how a system of *Things* interacts together to offer some functionality. To this end, the System Description (SD) was proposed [6], a superset of the TD that offers additional keywords for describing such systems, called mashups in the context of this paper. The SD also specifies a second representation format for mashups using a subset of the Unified Modeling Language (UML) Sequence Diagrams, as well as an algorithm for converting one representation to the other. To describe complex functionalities, the SD uses a sequence of building blocks that together form an execution sequence called a Path. The smallest building block of a Path is an Atomic Mashup (AM), in which a mashup controller performs a specific number of interactions, waits asynchronously for the results of these interactions and, based on these inputs, performs a series of asynchronous output interactions.

1.1   Problem Statement

While the TDs offer an abstraction level that eases the process of designing and creating AMs, the process is still a manual task in which the developer needs to go through the whole collection of TDs to find the interaction affordances that are needed and suitable for the desired functionalities. Furthermore, a better written and annotated TD that exposes more metadata about the TD and its interaction affordances improves the understanding, but the added metadata introduces more information that a human agent has to manually process and consider when designing mashups. And finally, the resulting design space to be explored increases exponentially with the total number of interaction affordances in a system. Thus, the increasing complexity and capabilities of IoT devices, the increasing complexity of the written TDs as well as the increasing complexity of the desired mashups translate into the manual exploration of the design space, being both time-consuming and error prone. There are solutions to automate the generation of mashups which are discussed in Sect. 4, but to the best of our knowledge, none are centered around the TD standard without extending its standardized core vocabulary. Hence, the generation of mashups using the core TD vocabulary remains unexplored.

1.2   Contributions

In this paper we introduce A-MaGe, a method and a corresponding implementation as a solution for system designers to automatically reduce the design space that needs to be explored manually as well as automate the creation of AMs as illustrated in Fig. 1. In particular, we make the following contributions:

- We introduce a method that takes TDs as an input and generates AMs that conform to predefined templates as well as user-defined constraints and filters leading to a reduction in the design space, introduced in Sect. 2.
- We propose a tool that uses the above-mentioned method to generate SD-compliant UML Sequence diagrams, allowing further selection of the AMs for automatic SD and code generation based on SD-algorithms.
- We show that the above-mentioned method achieves a design space reduction of several orders of magnitude, while being sufficiently fast for a human agent to allow multiple iterations of filtering to further reduce the design space, explained in Sect. 3.

Section 4 explores other approaches and related work for mashup composition and Sect. 5 concludes this paper.

2   A-MaGe Methodology

A-MaGe: an Atomic Mashup Generator is a method that is able to automatically explore and reduce the possible design space of Atomic Mashups (AM) given a set of TDs as an input with minimal direct intervention from a human agent. It relies on the AM abstraction defined in the SD which we describe in the following paragraph.

Atomic Mashup: A unique building block defined by the SD is the AM, which describes an undividable execution sequence that performs a specific functionality, similar to atomic operations in programming. An AM is defined as an unordered sequence of interactions performed by a mashup controller, called receive/input interactions (*readproperty, observeproperty, subscribeevent* or *invokeaction*), followed by an unordered sequence of interactions performed called send/output interactions (*writeproperty* or *invokeaction*). This makes it possible to describe synchronous and asynchronous sensing-actuating behaviors of a system and can then be combined using the aforementioned building blocks such as loops and conditional execution to achieve any desired system behaviour.

Given a system of *Things*, we can define the set all interaction affordances that can be considered as inputs as In_{tot} and similarly Out_{tot} for output interactions. For AMs with a specific input length l_{in} and specific output length l_{out}, we can calculate the resulting design space using the following equation:

$$C(|In_{tot}|, l_{in}) \cdot C(|Out_{tot}|, l_{out}) = \frac{|In_{tot}|!|Out_{tot}|!}{l_{in}!l_{out}!(|In_{tot}| - l_{in})!(|Out_{tot}| - l_{out})!} \quad (1)$$

with $C(a, b)$ denoting the combination formula.

On the other hand, the design space of mashups in general can be used with the permutations function:

$$P(n, k) = \frac{|A|!}{(|A| - k)!} \quad (2)$$

with $|A|$ denoting the number of interaction affordances in a system and k the mashup length respectively.

Looking at an example of a system with four *Things* exposing five input and five output interactions each and a desired mashup with two input and two output interactions, meaning that $|A| = 40$, $|In_{tot}| = |Out_{tot}| = 20$, $k = 4$, $l_{in} = l_{out} = 2$. Using these parameters, we can calculate using Eq. 1 that the maximum number of AMs that can be generated is 36100, in contrast to 2193360 mashups in total as per Eq. 2, which means that in this case there is a 98.35% reduction in the design space that needs to be explored manually.

2.1 Design Space Reduction Using Templates and Constraints

A human agent designing a mashup may have some prior expectations and constraints on how the mashup should operate or such constraints may arise during the design phase, which can be added incrementally. A computer can take advantage of these constraints and expectations to further reduce the design space and generate mashups that adhere to them, making it easier for a human agent to review and evaluate the results. With A-MaGe, we propose:

1. Filtering the considered mashup space by limiting the number of Things or interactions considered for input or output
2. Matching input and output interactions who use the same vocabulary
3. Semantic context matching of input and output interactions, meaning only interactions with annotations from the same vocabulary are considered.

4. Data type based filters to match input and output interactions based on their Data Schemas or to filter out an interaction based on its type
5. Template rules to choose how the controller receives its inputs in order to limit the *InputTypes*
    - **Subscription-driven template**: The mashup controller starts by subscribing to events or observing properties from input *Things* and waits asynchronously for the data pushes.
    - **Read-driven template**: The mashup controller starts by reading a set of properties from input *Things*.
    - **Action-driven template**: The mashup controller starts by invoking a set of actions in input *Things* and receives the interactions' outputs.
    - Allowing mashups that mix the above-mentioned templates or not. Mixed template mashups include multiple input interaction types.
6. matching input and output interactions filters using Natural Language Processing (NLP) based on the similarity of their names using a similarity score Word2Vec model [7] and based on the similarity of their descriptions by augmenting the Word2Vec approach using Word Mover's Distance algorithm [8].
7. filtering mashups based on specific semantic annotations and/or interactions, which can be described using Linear Temporal Logic (LTL) formulas $\mathbf{F}\phi$ and $\mathbf{G}\neg\phi$ respectively. Our method proposes three path variables ϕ:
    (a) ϕ_1: An interaction from a TD, that was annotated on the top-level with a specific semantic annotation, was performed.
    (b) ϕ_2: An interaction with a specified semantic annotation was performed.
    (c) ϕ_3: A specific interaction was performed.
    To allow a granular selection, these constraints can be specified individually to input, output, and input/output *Things* in case of ϕ_1 as well as to each type of input and output interactions in case of ϕ_2 and ϕ_3, respectively.

Based on the AM concept, the filters and constraints provided by the human agent, our method generates all the possible mashups. These are then presented to the human agent in the form of an SD-compliant UML Sequence Diagram. The human agent can view them and further adjust the filters and constraints. When the desired mashup is found, the human agent can then choose to generate the equivalent SD. The Sequence Diagram is then converted to an SD document using the SD conversion algorithm and the human agent can then automatically generate executable code according to the WoT Scripting API [9].

3   Evaluation

To evaluate A-MaGe, we implemented our proposed method in the **W**oT **A**PI **D**evelopment **E**nviroment (WADE)[1] [10]. However, our method does not rely on any specific programming language or framework to function. We evaluate the viability of our approach by looking at the execution time of our method

---

[1] https://github.com/tum-esi/wade.

and explore the filtering power of different user-defined constraints. Therefore, we perform two different tests[2], which are described in detail in this section.

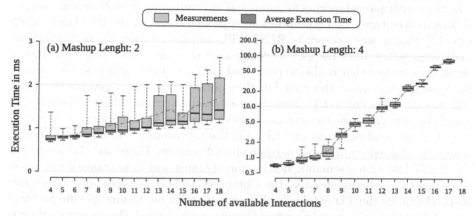

Fig. 2. We perform a number of measurements for mashups with the lengths two, four, six, eight and for interaction pools with sizes between the size of the mashup and 20 interactions. Note: The y-axis of Figure b is in logarithmic scale.

Testing Execution Time: In this test, we estimate the upper bound of execution time needed to generate all mashups given a specific mashup length and number of available interactions. Hence, we run A-MaGe with all templates enabled, as well as allowing mixed template mashups, but without any further constraints or filters to be able to generate the maximum number of mashups. We perform test runs for mashups with the lengths two, four, six, eight and for interaction pools with sizes between the size of the mashup and 20 interactions. The execution time for each specific test is measured 20 times to account for execution time fluctuations and the results of measurements for the mashups length of two and four can be viewed in Fig. 2.

Given that intended scope is small AMs and given these findings, we conclude that our method is viable and is able to generate an exhaustive list of all mashups conforming to certain constraints with acceptable speeds. The process of the human agent further adjusting the filters and constraints and re-running the code takes at most a few seconds, allowing for multiple iterations of filtering and generation in a small span of time.

Testing Filtering Power: We also perform a set of measurements to test the filtering power of different filters and constraints in different scenarios. We selected a number of filters on three different systems from three different domains: smart agriculture, smart home and smart industry. Each system differs in the devices used as well as the variety in the input and output interactions or multiplicity of Things. For each of these setups, we apply a selected number of filters and constraints one at a time and record the number of generated mashups. The results of this experiment can be viewed in Fig. 3.

---

[2] Both tests are done using a computer with an Intel© Core™ i7-8750H Processor, 8 GB of DDR4-2666 memory, Windows 10 Home 64-bit operating system.

4   Related Work

There are multiple approaches for semi- and fully automated (web) service compositions in literature. [11,12] proposes an approach based on the RESTdesc ontology [13], that is able to describe REST APIs and the relationship between them. Both approaches allow the user to define a set of goals to be achieved and use a semantic reasoner that is able to parse and logically chain APIs based on semantic reasoning to achieve this goal, but they differ in how they represent the goals. [12] uses goals similar to LTL formulas used in our method, where a specific API should be performed and the reasoner finds the chain of APIs that can be connected together that lead to the desired API. On the other hand, [11] allows the user to define the desired state that a mashup should achieve. Therefore, [11] augments the RESTdesc with a semantic description of states and state transition to allow for semantic reasoning about states. Compared to both of these approaches, our method utilizes the TD ontology, which is not restricted to any specific protocol or architecture, as long as the protocol bindings are defined. Hence, our method is more universally applicable. Thus, to the best of our knowledge, no other method was proposed that leverages the TD and the AM abstraction for mashup design space exploration and automatic mashup composition.

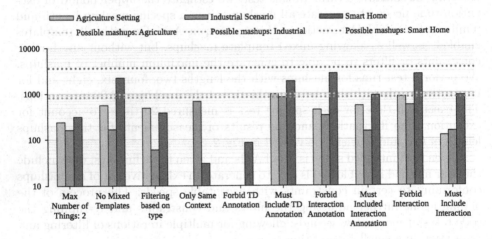

Fig. 3. We evaluate the filtering power of different filters and constraints in different scenarios. The results show that coarse forbidding using annotations is more powerful than granularly forbidding specific interactions, but the opposite is true for enforcing an annotation or interactions to be included.

5   Conclusion

In this paper, we proposed A-MaGe, a method that takes a set of TDs, as well as multiple filters and constraints as an input, and is able to automatically generate an exhaustive list of all possible Atomic Mashups (AMs) that adhere to the specified constraints. We started by formally defining the design space of mashups in general and showed that by focusing on AMs, we decrease the design space by several orders of magnitude. Subsequently, we introduced our method that uses a set of pre-defined templates, as well as filters and constraints that allow a human agent to further decrease the design space. We showed that our method is capable of generating AMs in maximum a few seconds and that filtering power of different filters and constraints work in different application domains. Both evaluations show that our method a viable approach while being universally applicable to all WoT devices.

References

1. Mercer, D.: Global Connected and IoT Device Forecast Update (2019). https://www.strategyanalytics.com/access-services/devices/connected-home/consumer-electronics/reports/report-detail/global-connected-and-iot-device-forecast-update, Accessed 26 Nov 2020
2. Lueth, K.L.: IoT Platform Companies Landscape 2019/2020: 620 IoT Platforms globally (2019). https://iot-analytics.com/iot-platform-companies-landscape-2020/, Accessed 27 Nov 2020
3. Kovatsch, M., Matsukura, R., Lagally, M., Kawaguchi, T., Toumura, K., Kajimoto, K.: Web of Things (WoT) Architecture. Technical report (2020) https://www.w3.org/TR/2020/REC-wot-architecture-20200409/
4. Kaebisch, S., Kamiya, T., McCool, M., Charpenay, V., Kovatsch, M.: Web of Things (WoT) Thing Description. Technical report (2020). https://www.w3.org/TR/2020/REC-wot-thing-description-20200409/
5. Sporny, M., Longley, D., Kellogg, G., Lanthaler, M., Champin, P.A., Lindström, N.: JSON-LD 1.1 (2020). https://www.w3.org/TR/2020/REC-json-ld11-20200716/
6. Kast, A., Korkan, E., Käbisch, S., Steinhorst, S.: Web of things system description for representation of mashups. In: 2020 COINS, pp. 1–8 (2020). https://doi.org/10.1109/COINS49042.2020.9191677
7. Mikolov, T., Chen, K., Corrado, G., Dean, J.: Efficient estimation of word representations in vector space. arXiv preprint arXiv:1301.3781 (2013)
8. Kusner, M.J., Sun, Y., Kolkin, N.I., Weinberger, K.Q.: From word embeddings to document distances. In: ICML2015, vol. 37, pp. 957–966. JMLR.org (2015)
9. Kis, Z., Peintner, D., Aguzzi, C., Hund, J., Nimura, K.: Web of Things (WoT) Scripting API (2020). https://www.w3.org/TR/2020/NOTE-wot-scripting-api-20201124/
10. Schlott, V.E., Korkan, E., Kaebisch, S., Steinhorst, S.: W-ADE: timing performance benchmarking in web of things. In: Bielikova, M., Mikkonen, T., Pautasso, C. (eds.) ICWE 2020. LNCS, vol. 12128, pp. 70–86. Springer, Cham (2020). https://doi.org/10.1007/978-3-030-50578-3_6
11. Mayer, S., Verborgh, R., Kovatsch, M., Mattern, F.: Smart configuration of smart environments. IEEE Trans. Autom. Sci. Eng 13(3), 1247–1255 (2016). https://doi.org/10.1109/TASE.2016.2533321
12. Ventura, D., Verborgh, R., Catania, V., Mannens, E.: Autonomous composition and execution of REST APIs for smart sensors. In: CEUR Workshop Proceedings, vol. 1488, pp. 1–12 (2015). http://ceur-ws.org/Vol-1488/paper-02.pdf
13. Verborgh, R., et al.: RESTdesc–a functionality-centered approach to semantic service description and composition. In: Proceedings of the 9th ESWC, Crete, Greece, pp. 27–31 (2012)

WebAssembly Modules as Lightweight Containers for Liquid IoT Applications

Niko Mäkitalo[1]([⊠]), Tommi Mikkonen[1], Cesare Pautasso[2], Victor Bankowski[1], Paulius Daubaris[1], Risto Mikkola[1], and Oleg Beletski[3]

[1] University of Helsinki, Helsinki, Finland
{niko.makitalo,tommi.mikkonen,victor.bankowski,
paulius.daubaris,risto.mikkola}@helsinki.fi
[2] University of Lugano, Lugano, Switzerland
cesare.pautasso@usi.ch
[3] Huawei Technologies, Helsinki, Finland
oleg.beletski@huawei.com

Abstract. Going all the way to IoT with web technologies opens up the door to isomorphic IoT system architectures, which deliver flexible deployment and live migration of code between any device in the overall system. In this vision paper, we propose using WebAssembly to implement lightweight containers and deliver the required portability. Our long-term vision is to use the technology to support developers of liquid IoT applications offering seamless, hassle-free use of multiple devices.

Keywords: Light-weight containers · Internet of Things · IoT · Liquid software · Containers · WebAssemly · Web of Things · WoT

1 Introduction

Today, in the context of Internet of Things (IoT), web APIs are commonly used, but actual devices and applications in them are often implemented with native technologies. However, going all the way to IoT with web technologies would open up the door to *isomorphic* IoT system architectures. In such architectures, devices, gateways, and the cloud can run the same software components and services, unaltered. This will allow flexible migration of code between any element in the overall system. Practical isomorphic application scenarios include virtual assistants and other ubiquitous applications for messaging, gaming, reading, writing, listening to music/podcasts/news, or watching video.

Unfortunately, today's container techniques are often too heavy-weight for that, especially when considering devices with limited resources or direct access to hardware [5,21]. A recent taxonomy of IoT client architectures [25] distinguishes bare metal RTOS systems, systems with a language runtime, and systems with full OS. Besides, some propose containers as a solution for IoT systems, where requirements regarding resources are relaxed. However, the taxonomy overlooks other architecture options than that the containers are built on top of an OS.

© Springer Nature Switzerland AG 2021
M. Brambilla et al. (Eds.): ICWE 2021, LNCS 12706, pp. 328–336, 2021.
https://doi.org/10.1007/978-3-030-74296-6_25

In this paper, we propose using the language runtime approach – the simplest option to enable 3rd party application code [25] – as the basis for lightweight containers. As the concrete implementation environment, we use WebAssembly (WASM). WASM was initially conceived to enable near-native execution speed [10] inside the browser. Following the same path of JavaScript runtimes which left the browser many years ago, today there are WASM implementations that can be run outside the browser as well [3].

Our long-term vision is to use WASM to implement the concept of liquid software [20] – user-centric, hassle-free use of multiple computers with software which can dynamically flow between them – in the context of the IoT. In essence, building liquid web applications needs two facilities, (i) ability to relocate code freely across different computing environments; and (ii) ability to synchronize the state of the application across all devices running the code. In our previous work, we have used the DOM [26] and Web Components with Polymer [7] as the underlying technology. However, both technologies are closely tied to the browser, and target at the UI layer of web applications. In particular, the unit of deployment in both approaches has been a web page, which is not optimal for embedded device, especially those that have no screen. WASM's characteristics – small footprint, near-native performance, advanced security, support for modules, and in-built support for isomorphic use – make it an attractive candidate for considering to use the Web as a platform for IoT applications.

2 Background and Related Work

This work is based on and related to the following relatively distinct technologies:

Web of Things. Web of Things (WoT) describes a set of standards by the W3C for solving the interoperability issues of different Internet of Things (IoT) platforms and application domains[1]. In essence, WoT is about making each 'thing' part of the Web by giving it an URI that can be used for communicating with it. The communication with each thing should be supported with a common data model and a uniform interface that is recognized by every thing[2].

Assuming such Web API for things deployed widely, programming IoT could be simplified to a large degree. Then, every device would provide this API and its features for programs that want to address its properties. Given a powerful enough API – in the context of this work, powerful enough to allow offloading of software on the fly – the promise of the Programmable Web [19] could be extended to cover the programmable world concept [27], using the Web as the underlying standard, interoperable technology platform [18].

WebAssembly. WASM [29] is a fast, safe and portable binary instruction format which can be executed on a stack-based virtual machine that can leverage

---

[1] https://www.w3.org/TR/wot-architecture/Overview.html, accessed Oct. 21, 2020.
[2] https://iot.mozilla.org/wot/, accessed Oct. 21, 2020.

contemporary hardware [3, 12]. WASM code is validated and run in a sandboxed environment; there is no ambient access to the computing environment in which code is being run except through explicit permission. Actual programs have compact representation, so they are small to transmit, especially in comparison to text or native code. Programs can be written by a variety of programming languages and then compiled to WASM for execution.

WASM programs are organized into modules, which are the unit of deployment, loading, and compilation [10]. Each module can contain definitions for types, functions, tables, memory areas, and global variables. These definitions may be imported or exported. To support rapid startup and dynamic configurations, WASM offers facilities for execution time dynamic linking.

Each WASM module executes within a sandboxed environment separated from the host runtime using fault isolation techniques. Hence, applications execute independently, and only specific features can be accessed by providing explicit permissions to APIs. Moreover, the security policies of its embedding are applied to the module. Within a web browser, this means the same-origin policy. On a non-web platform, no uniform model exists yet. So far, domain-specific and capability-based security models have been proposed.

The original design goals of WASM were to make it compatible with the web browser [29]. To this end, WASM applications can call into and out of the JavaScript context and access browser functionality through the same Web APIs accessible from JavaScript. For web pages and browser applications, which have already become overly complex [4], embedding WASM to JavaScript is an option that does not add many memory or performance related constraints.

Despite the increasing computing capacity of chips, it is still expected that the future networks include memory and performance-related challenges as many devices have limited memory. Moreover, in the context of IoT systems, computers, in general, have diverging performance capabilities, ranging from almost bare metal in sensors to cloud systems where everything is virtualized [22].

Lightweight WASM Containers for IoT. There are numerous WASM virtual machines that can be run outside the browser. The exact features of these systems vary[3], with some targeted for smallest devices, with the simplest possible interpretation, and others supporting sophisticated features such as streaming and ahead-of-time compilation[4]. Thus, small memory footprint and near-native performance make it an attractive alternative for building IoT systems [28].

Some work on the performance of WASM has already been composed, but the results seem inconclusive. The reasons are many, and include the fact that there are multiple runtimes for WASM, with varying performance and resource consumption[5]. For instance, [13] claim that in many of their benchmark

---

[3] https://github.com/appcypher/awesome-wasm-runtimes, accessed Jan. 6, 2020.

[4] https://github.com/wasm3/wasm3/blob/master/docs/Performance.md, accessed Jan. 5, 2020.

[5] https://medium.com/wasmer/benchmarking-webassembly-runtimes-18497ce0d76e, accessed Oct. 21, 2020.

applications, WASM was slower than native by a factor of 1.5. The work was conducted inside the browser, not using a runtime only, which may have affected the results. At the same time, [28] claim that the Wasmachine runtime is up to 11% faster than Linux for common IoT and fog applications.

With the above facilities, we seek to build lightweight IoT containers, using the WASM language runtime as the basis for the implementation. Such systems can support third-party application development and dynamic changes, and it is possible to update the device software (or parts thereof) dynamically without having to reflash the entire firmware. Basically, applications run in a sandbox that provides only limited access to the underlying platform features – something that WASM immediately provides us at the level of modules.

Despite the idea's attractiveness, it seems that the idea has not received much attention in research. A recent thesis that includes a literature review points out that little research has been invested in considering the use of WASM modules as lightweight containers [23]. The study also points out that there are issues with memory usage at runtime when comparing WASM to Docker containers. What the study overlooks, however, is the fact that WASM module images are smaller than corresponding Docker images (or even smaller than compiled C/C++ modules), where facilities related to the infrastructure are included. Furthermore, while some WASM virtual machines can be run in various micro-controllers[6] and play the role of an operating system [28] – even bare-metal implementation is proposed[7].

Finally, to complement the ability to use WASM runtimes and modules as lightweight containers for IoT devices, WASM has also been used for serverless computing [11,24]. Hence, the same technology has been demonstrated to be feasible across all the elements needed to build IoT applications.

3   Our Vision

Our prime motivation of this work is to rely on Web technologies all the way to IoT. Figure 1 represents how our goal is to push the boundaries of the development up to a point we reach *isomorphic* computations, where no constraints regarding the underlying architecture or platform are placed on applications, but they can be run everywhere, taking the context and its computational resources into account. In this deployment, using the Web as the underlying platform liberates developers from the restrictions of mainstream containers that rely on virtualizing a full operating system. This, in turn, results in more fine-grained deployment. Moreover, it is possible to consider hardware-related aspects by discovering the features available in this particular computing unit. Hence, the deployment loads modules on-demand basis only when necessary and customizes which module gets loaded, depending on the device. Such dynamic self-configuration is difficult to achieve with static images, which are commonly used

---

[6] https://github.com/bytecodealliance/wasm-micro-runtime, accessed Oct. 21, 2020.
[7] https://github.com/lastmjs/wasm-metal, accessed Oct. 21, 2020.

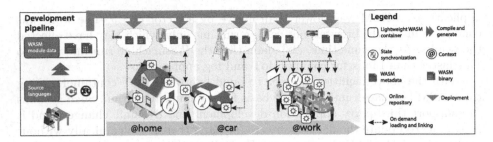

Fig. 1. Liquid IoT application lifecycle.

by mainstream containers. Finally, since the device configurations and availability can change over time, the running software's deployment configuration needs to adapt dynamically. In other words, we want to go past dynamic deployment only and reach the full liquid web software vision [20], where software can flow and adapt to multiple devices. In essence, the solution must be able to migrate the execution's code and state so that the execution can continue one computer from the same program execution state it had on the previous computer [6].

WebAssembly's characteristics – small footprint, near-native performance, advanced security, support for modules, availability of language runtimes for different hardware devices – lead to potential support for isomorphic IoT applications. Using WebAssembly, one can relocate application code in a fine-grained fashion to different computing units commonly used in IoT systems. To this end, an approach similar to Apple's Handoff API [9] where applications can roam from device to device can be constructed, or one can rely on mobile agents for IoT like in [14], for instance.

In addition to simply deploying WebAssembly modules, it is also possible to support self-configuration by allowing the application to determine its environment, and dynamically load the necessary modules on the fly. Then, the initial deployment can be rapid – only a bootloader that is able to determine its functions at a particular location is needed. With the isomorphic nature of WebAssembly, actual application code can be the same despite its eventual location in the IoT architecture. This turns WebAssembly modules into lightweight containers that can easily be relocated.

Relocating and adapting code is only half of the liquid web application vision; also, application state and data should be transferred [20]. As WebAssembly relies on binary formats, techniques proposed in previous work, relying on browser facilities, cannot transform the application state. However, serialization techniques proposed in, e.g., [2] can be used to transfer the state of the applications when a WebAssembly module is relocated somewhere else in the IoT system. For the data part, techniques proposed in our previous work will be enough [7].

4   Proof of Concept Design

Currently, WebAssembly virtual machines outside of the browser do not support dynamic linking. Instead, all parts of an application must be present to run it. This essentially predefines task allocation at startup, and does not leverage full benefits of isomorphic architectures. To support more liberal configurations, we have implemented an execution time dynamic linking system, where modules can be loaded on the need basis [17]. With this facility, the application can adapt to the role of the bigger context. The implementation uses execution time shared-everything linking approach, meaning that modules can use each other's functions and resources once they have been loaded. A video of these loading capabilities is available for demonstration purposes on YouTube[8].

Based on its context, the application can decide what modules to load. Modules can be loaded from the local disk or from an online repository, which in turn can contain parts of the code that can be freely allocated in the IoT network. At present, the implementation still lacks support for migrating live applications. Here, we plan to follow the approach of [14], where the developer defines the migration with a special API, at least initially.

5   Way Forward to the Vision

While the research done for this paper has been promising, there are numerous issues that still require practical solutions. Some key issues are listed below.

State Synchronization. As already mentioned, our proof-of-concept implementation lacks support for application state migration. The main design decision documented in the design space [8] concerns whether developers need to explicitly annotate the state to be migrated and synchronized or whether the underlying runtime transparently takes care of it. In particular, reflection will be a topic of further investigation to help automate the migration.

Dynamic Orchestration. Migrating applications from one computer to another cannot happen randomly, but it needs orchestration. This facility is to some degree a novel avenue to us, although it has received some attention in the context of stream processing [1]. In addition to an API that assumes full control, as in [1], we also plan to consider techniques used for self-organization [16].

Generalized API for Hardware Access. To truly enable isomorphic software architectures, also the environment where the software is run should be similar. In our present implementation, we have introduced adaptability mechanisms for taking the environment into account, but for large-scale use, such requirement can be a burden. Instead, a generalized API for hardware access would be a

---

[8] https://youtu.be/gZj3M31ZfuI, accessed Dec. 28, 2020.

better solution. At the moment, WebAssembly offers WASI[9], a modular system interface for WebAssembly applications, but it is not generic enough for arbitrary IoT devices. However, it can act as a starting point for designing a uniform hardware access API across IoT architectures. Finally, even with a generalized hardware API, mechanisms are needed to discover what hardware modules are present at runtime, where the situation may change over time.

Fine-Grained Security Model. While WebAssembly provides a sandboxing mechanism for applications at runtime level, something more comprehensive is needed at the scale of full liquid applications, their adaptive configurations, and migration. Here, our plan is to seek inspiration from mobile agents [15]. However, to truly address this aspect in detail, more specific use cases need to be considered, whereas here we have focused on technological factors only.

Benchmarking. As already mentioned, there is no conclusive data on the performance of WebAssembly applications in comparison to native ones. Performing systematic tests in the context of IoT and containers is therefore in our interests when our prototype implementation is more mature. Moreover, issues related to migration and liquid features also require benchmarking in the context of IoT to better understand the feasibility of the approach.

6 Conclusion

Going all the way with web in IoT development will help iron out numerous device and technology specific complications. In this paper, we propose using WebAssembly as a mechanism for building lightweight containers, which are capable of assuming different roles, depending on their location and roles in an IoT application. We demonstrated the use of the technology with a proof-of-concept implementation, and provided links to solutions that can be used to fill in the missing pieces needed for migrating full-fledged live applications.

References

1. Babazadeh, M., Pautasso, C.: A restful api for controlling dynamic streaming topologies. In: Proceedings of the 23rd International Conference on World Wide Web, pp. 965–970 (2014)
2. Bellucci, F., Ghiani, G., Paternò, F., Santoro, C.: Engineering javascript state persistence of web applications migrating across multiple devices. In: Proceedings of the 3rd ACM SIGCHI Symposium on Engineering Interactive Computing Systems, pp. 105–110 (2011)
3. Bryant, D.: Webassembly outside the browser: a new foundation for pervasive computing. In: Keynote at ICWE 2020, Helsinki, Finland, 9–12 June 2020 (2020)

---

[9] https://wasi.dev/, accessed Oct. 21, 2020.

4. Butkiewicz, M., Madhyastha, H.V., Sekar, V.: Characterizing web page complexity and its impact. IEEE/ACM Trans. Netw. **22**(3), 943–956 (2013)
5. Celesti, A., Mulfari, D., Fazio, M., Villari, M., Puliafito, A.: Exploring container virtualization in iot clouds. In: 2016 IEEE International Conference on Smart Computing (SMARTCOMP), pp. 1–6. IEEE (2016)
6. Fuggetta, A., Picco, G.P., Vigna, G.: Understanding code mobility. IEEE Trans. Softw. Eng. **24**(5), 342–361 (1998)
7. Gallidabino, A., Pautasso, C.: The liquid.js framework for migrating and cloning stateful web components across multiple devices. In: Proceedings of the 25th International Conference Companion on World Wide Web, pp. 183–186 (2016)
8. Gallidabino, A., Pautasso, C., Mikkonen, T., Systä, K., Voutilainen, J.P., Taivalsaari, A.: Architecting liquid software. J. Web Eng. **16**(5&6), 433–470 (2017)
9. Gruman, G.: Apple's handoff: What works, and what doesn't. InfoWorld (2014)
10. Haas, A., et al.: Bringing the web up to speed with webassembly. In: Proceedings of the 38th ACM SIGPLAN Conference on Programming Language Design and Implementation, pp. 185–200 (2017)
11. Hall, A., Ramachandran, U.: An execution model for serverless functions at the edge. In: Proceedings of the International Conference on Internet of Things Design and Implementation, pp. 225–236 (2019)
12. Jacobsson, M., Willén, J.: Virtual machine execution for wearables based on webassembly. In: Sugimoto, C., Farhadi, H., Hämäläinen, M. (eds.) BODYNETS 2018. EICC, pp. 381–389. Springer, Cham (2020). https://doi.org/10.1007/978-3-030-29897-5_33
13. Jangda, A., Powers, B., Berger, E.D., Guha, A.: Not so fast: analyzing the performance of webassembly vs. native code. In: 2019 USENIX Annual Technical Conference, pp. 107–120 (2019)
14. Järvenpää, L., Lintinen, M., Mattila, A.L., Mikkonen, T., Systä, K., Voutilainen, J.P.: Mobile agents for the internet of things. In: 2013 17th International Conference on System Theory, Control and Computing, pp. 763–767. IEEE (2013)
15. Kumar, S.A., et al.: Classification and review of security schemes in mobile computing. Wirel. Sensor Netw. **2**(06), 419–440 (2010)
16. Kurzyniec, D., Wrzosek, T., Drzewiecki, D., Sunderam, V.: Towards self-organizing distributed computing frameworks: the H2O approach. Parallel Process. Lett. **13**(02), 273–290 (2003)
17. Mäkitalo, N., Bankowski, V., Daubaris, P., Mikkola, R., Beletski, O., Mikkonen, T.: Bringing webassembly up to speed with dynamic linking. Accepted to SAC 2021 (2021)
18. Mäkitalo, N., Nocera, F., Mongiello, M., Bistarelli, S.: Architecting the web of things for the fog computing era. IET Softw. **12**(5), 381–389 (2018)
19. Maximilien, E.M., Ranabahu, A.: The programmable web: agile, social, and grassroot computing. In: International Conference on Semantic Computing (ICSC 2007), pp. 477–481. IEEE (2007)
20. Mikkonen, T., Systä, K., Pautasso, C.: Towards liquid web applications. In: Cimiano, P., Frasincar, F., Houben, G.-J., Schwabe, D. (eds.) ICWE 2015. LNCS, vol. 9114, pp. 134–143. Springer, Cham (2015). https://doi.org/10.1007/978-3-319-19890-3_10
21. Morabito, R.: A performance evaluation of container technologies on internet of things devices. In: 2016 IEEE Conference on Computer Communications Workshops (INFOCOM WKSHPS), pp. 999–1000. IEEE (2016)
22. Morabito, R., Cozzolino, V., Ding, A.Y., Beijar, N., Ott, J.: Consolidate IoT edge computing with lightweight virtualization. IEEE Netw. **32**(1), 102–111 (2018)

23. Napieralla, J.: Considering webassembly containers for edge computing on hardware-constrained IoT devices. Master's thesis, Blekinge Institute of Technology, Karlskrona, Sweden (2020)
24. Shillaker, S., Pietzuch, P.: Faasm: Lightweight isolation for efficient stateful serverless computing. arXiv preprint arXiv:2002.09344 (2020)
25. Taivalsaari, A., Mikkonen, T.: A taxonomy of IoT client architectures. IEEE Softw. **35**(3), 83–88 (2018)
26. Voutilainen, J.-P., Mikkonen, T., Systä, K.: Synchronizing application state using virtual DOM trees. In: Casteleyn, S., Dolog, P., Pautasso, C. (eds.) ICWE 2016. LNCS, vol. 9881, pp. 142–154. Springer, Cham (2016). https://doi.org/10.1007/978-3-319-46963-8_12
27. Wasik, B.: In the programmable world, all our objects will act as one. Wired (2013). http://www.wired.com/2013/05/internet-of-things-2/, Accessed 13 Oct 2020
28. Wen, E., Weber, G.: Wasmachine: bring IoT up to speed with a webassembly OS. In: 2020 IEEE International Conference on Pervasive Computing and Communications Workshops (PerCom Workshops), pp. 1–4. IEEE (2020)
29. World Wide Web Consortium: WebAssembly Core Specification (2019). https://www.w3.org/TR/wasm-core-1/, https://webassembly.github.io/spec/core/_download/WebAssembly.pdf

Leveraging Web of Things W3C Recommendations for Knowledge Graphs Generation

Dylan Van Assche$^{(\boxtimes)}$ ⓘ, Gerald Haesendonckⓘ, Gertjan De Mulderⓘ,
Thomas Delvaⓘ, Pieter Heyvaertⓘ, Ben De Meesterⓘ,
and Anastasia Dimou$^{(\boxtimes)}$ ⓘ

IDLab, Department of Electronics and Information Systems,
Ghent University – imec, Technologiepark-Zwijnaarde 122, 9052 Ghent, Belgium
{dylan.vanassche,gerald.haesendonck,gertjan.demulder,thomas.delva,
pieter.heyvaert,ben.demeester,anastasia.dimou}@ugent.be

Abstract. Constructing a knowledge graph with mapping languages,
such as RML or SPARQL-Generate, allows seamlessly integrating heterogeneous data by defining access-specific definitions for e.g., databases or
files. However, such mapping languages have limited support for describing Web APIs and no support for describing data with varying velocities, as needed for e.g., streams, neither for the input data nor for the
output RDF. This hampers the smooth and reproducible generation of
knowledge graphs from heterogeneous data and their continuous integration for consumption since each implementation provides its own extensions. Recently, the Web of Things (WoT) Working Group released a
set of recommendations to provide a machine-readable description of
metadata and network-facing interfaces for Web APIs and streams. In
this paper, we investigated (i) how mapping languages can be aligned
with the newly specified recommendations to describe and handle heterogeneous data with varying velocities and Web APIs, and (ii) how
such descriptions can be used to indicate how the generated knowledge
graph should be exported. We extended RML's Logical Source to support
WoT descriptions of Web APIs and streams, and introduced RML's Logical Target to describe the generated knowledge graph reusing the same
descriptions. We implemented these extensions in the RMLMapper and
RMLStreamer, and validated our approach in two use cases. Mapping
languages are now able to use the same descriptions to define the input
data but also the output RDF. This way, our work paves the way towards
more reproducible workflows for knowledge graph generation.

1 Introduction

Mapping languages, such as the RDF Mapping Language (RML) [6], allow defining mapping rules to describe how to generate a knowledge graph from heterogeneous data. This is achieved by aligning the mapping rules with access-specific

---

The original version of this chapter was revised: the email addresses of some
authors have been corrected. The correction to this chapter is available at
https://doi.org/10.1007/978-3-030-74296-6_49

definitions for e.g., databases or files, to integrate data from heterogeneous formats, e.g., CSV, XML, JSON. However, we observe that: (i) data velocity is not well supported in mapping languages and corresponding processors, compared to data variety and volume [8,18,20]; and, (ii) the characteristics and destination of the generated knowledge graph remain unexplored.

Mapping languages declaratively describe how to integrate heterogeneous data without considering their data velocity, e.g., when new data is available for retrieval. Consequently, processors cannot generate knowledge graphs from data sources with varying data velocities, such as streams, as they lack the descriptions that determine their execution. This results in non-reproducible knowledge graph generation, because processors have each their own (use case-depending) approach to deal with data sources with varying data velocities.

Mapping languages only partly align with Web APIs and streams descriptions. When they do, they are limited to a set of protocols and do not describe how authentication against Web APIs and streams should be performed. Existing approaches describe access Web APIs, but only for a subset of the HTTP protocol, to retrieve data from Web APIs, while other protocols, e.g., MQTT or CoAP, and use cases of Web APIs are not considered. Because of this, additional steps outside the processor are needed to use other protocols. If authentication is needed, data cannot be retrieved from Web APIs, as the processors do not know how to handle authentication from the access description in mapping rules.

Last, mapping languages only define how a knowledge graph should be generated from heterogeneous data, but not how a knowledge graph should be exported and handled afterwards. Each processor has its own approach to retrieve this information, using e.g. a configuration file or command line arguments as this information is not declaratively described in the mappings. Furthermore, the velocity of the input data, also influences the output velocity when exporting knowledge graphs. Thus, it is necessary to consider the data velocity when retrieving the input data as well when exporting a knowledge graph.

We address the aforementioned issues by leveraging the recent W3C recommendations of the Web of Things (WoT) Working Group [2,10,13]. On one hand, we adapt the data source descriptions to describe how processors can *access and process Web APIs and streams with the WoT W3C recommendations*. On the other hand, we introduce a *target description* which declaratively describes how a knowledge graph should be exported. The target description defines in which format and where the knowledge graph is exported. Since the target description reuses same access descriptions as the input data sources, the generated knowledge graph can be exported in various ways, e.g., file dumps or triple stores.

We apply our proposed approach to the RDF Mapping Language (RML) [6]. Our contributions are: (i) **RML's Logical Source adaptation to the new WoT W3C recommendations** to support more data structures, data velocity and authentication; (ii) **RML's Logical Target introduction** to define how the knowledge graph should be handled and exported; (iii) **Implementation of**

our proposed approach in the RMLMapper[1] and RMLStreamer[2]; and (iv) **Validation of our approach** in two use cases: ESSENCE and DAIQUIRI.

Lack of access to data with different velocities and knowledge graph's characteristics' descriptions hampers the knowledge graphs' *reproducible generation* from heterogeneous data. It also hampers their *continuous integration for consumption* as additional steps are needed to retrieve the data and transform these in an appropriate format. Our proposed approach shows how mapping languages can use same descriptions for input data and output knowledge graph. This reduces the processor's implementation costs, as the same descriptions are reused for both input and output and all processors follow the same descriptions, resulting in more reproducible knowledge graph generation.

Section 2 describes the state of the art and Sect. 3 our motivating use cases and issues encountered in our use cases. Section 4 explains how we aligned the WoT W3C recommendations with RML and how we implemented our approach in the RMLMapper and RMLStreamer. We validate our approach in Sect. 5 with two real-life use cases. In Sect. 6, we discuss conclusions and future work.

2   State of the Art

In this Section, we describe our related work (Sect. 2.1), and introduce the Web of Things W3C recommendations and RML (Sect. 2.2).

2.1   Related Work

We outline vocabularies (Table 1) to describe Web APIs and streams, and investigate how current approaches use these vocabularies to access Web APIs, deal with streams' varying velocities and export the generated knowledge graph.

Vocabularies for Web APIs and Streams. Data sources on the Web come in various forms and protocols while sharing common practices for identifying resources or authentication schemes. Various vocabularies exist to describe access to Web APIs and streams, e.g., Hydra, DCAT, HTTP, VoCaLS, and OWL-S.

The Hydra vocabulary [14] is proposed by the Hydra W3C Community Group to describe Web APIs but it is not a W3C recommendation. The Hydra vocabulary describes Web APIs but does not describe how a processor must perform authentication against Web APIs or use protocol-specific features.

DCAT [16] is a W3C recommendation to describe data catalogs on the Web. DCAT only describes datasets in a DCAT data catalog without covering protocol-specific features or authentication.

The HTTP W3C vocabulary [11] describes the HTTP protocol and can be used to describe HTTP Web APIs. However, the HTTP W3C vocabulary is limited to a single protocol, namely HTTP, does not describe how processors must perform authentication against Web APIs, nor does it describe streams.

---

[1] https://github.com/RMLio/rmlmapper-java.
[2] https://github.com/RMLio/rmlstreamer.

OWL-S is a W3C member submission to semantically describe Web services [17] such as Web APIs and streams. OWL-S consists of Service Profiles to describe what the service does, Service Models to specify how it works, and Service Grounding which describes how to access the service. OWL-S' Service Grounding leverages the Web Services Description Language [4] to describe access to Web services. Although, OWL-S can describe access to Web services, it does not cover authentication and never became a W3C recommendation.

VoCaLS [22] is a vocabulary and catalog description for data streams. It extends the DCAT W3C recommendation to describe streams without being limited to a specific stream protocol. VoCaLS can be used to describe access to data streams, but not other Web APIs.

The Web of Things (WoT) W3C Working Group recently released recommendations for describing IoT devices on the Web [2,10,13] by providing an abstract layer to access Internet of Things (IoT) devices. WoT uses a similar approach as OWL-S by applying binding templates to bind this layer to an underlying protocol used by an IoT device. New protocols can be added by defining a new binding template without influencing the access abstraction layer [13]. We leverage the WoT W3C recommendations to showcase how processors can access Web APIs and streams without depending on a specific protocol.

Table 1. Existing vocabularies for describing access to Web APIs and streams.

Vocabulary	Protocol independent	Authentication	Web APIs	Streams	W3C recommendation
Hydra	✓	✗	✓	✗	✗
DCAT	✗	✗	✓	✗	✓
HTTP W3C	✓	✗	✓	✗	✓
OWL-S	✗	✗	✓	✓	✗
VoCaLS	✓	✗	✗	✓	✗
WoT W3C	✓	✓	✓	✓	✓

Mapping Languages. Existing mapping languages share same principles for describing input data sources by defining iterators and access descriptions for the data sources and leave the characteristics of exporting generated knowledge graphs up to the implementation. Most mapping languages, e.g., RML and SPARQL-Generate, reuse existing specifications e.g. R2RML and SPARQL respectively, to define a mapping language for generating knowledge graphs from heterogeneous data sources. RML [6] broadens the scope of R2RML [5] from relational databases to heterogeneous data sources using RML's Logical Source, while still being backwards compatible. SPARQL-Generate [15] extends SPARQL [9] instead of R2RML to integrate heterogeneous data sources into knowledge graphs with iterators to access and iterate over the data sources.

Such mapping languages describe how processors should access various heterogeneous data sources except for Web APIs and streams. RML leverages the Hydra vocabulary to provide access to Web APIs [7], SPARQL-Generate and xR2RML define each their own approach to accomplish this [15,19]. However, they can only perform HTTP GET requests without authentication to retrieve data from the Web. D2RML argues it is needed to describe access to Web APIs in more detail [3] but D2RML can only describe HTTP requests using the W3C HTTP vocabulary, other protocols are not supported.

Data Velocity. In recent years, there has been an increasing interest in generating knowledge graphs from data with different velocities than static data, such as data streams. Several approaches were introduced, for example: TripleWave [18], RDF-Gen [20], SPARQL-Generate [15], and Chimera [21]. However, these approaches do not declaratively describe how different data velocities must be handled during the knowledge graph generation.

TripleWave uses R2RML mappings for specifying the subject, predicate and object of the generated RDF triples, but handles the data velocity problem in its processor through a wrapper. This wrapper is mostly use case specific and not reusable for other use cases. SPARQL-Generate provides access to data streams, but delegates the processing and handling of the different data velocities to the underlying SPARQL engine. RDF-Gen claims it can access and process data streams but does not mention how different data velocities are handled. CARML³ also access streams by extending RML with its own extension, a single access description for streams (`carml:Stream`) but only describes the name of the stream to use. Recently, a data transformation framework Chimera was proposed [21] which allows to uplift data into a knowledge graph using RML and lower this knowledge graph later on in various data formats through Apache Velocity templates and SPARQL queries [21]. Chimera leverages Apache Camel's Routes [21] for constructing its data processing pipelines. Because of this, Chimera can have multiple input and output channels and access data sources included in the Apache Camel framework, such as Web APIs or streams. However, no declarative access description is available to describe Web APIs and streams; instead, the `rml:source` property in RML's Logical Source refers to a generic InputStream, an extension of RML used in Chimera, which only specifies the name of the InputStream to use as data source.

RDF Output. Mapping languages has not yet determined how the serialisation, storage or velocity of the generated knowledge graph (output) should be handled, exported, and described. Each processor of a mapping language has its own way to handle the knowledge graph after its generation. Processors mainly use command line arguments (e.g., RMLMapper, RMLStreamer, SPARQL-Generate), or configuration files (e.g., RMLMapper, SPARQL-Generate, Chimera) to specify a single target such as a local file, access configuration of the SPARQL endpoint containing the knowledge graph, or Kafka stream.

Exporting knowledge graphs to multiple output targets is not considered by mapping languages, nor is generating a knowledge graph as a stream. While processors such as SPARQL-Generate [15], RDF-Gen [20], and TripleWave [18] can export their knowledge graphs as a stream during generation, these processors

---

³ https://github.com/carml/carml.

do not enrich existing knowledge graphs but recreate the knowledge graph from scratch when new data is retrieved. R2RML-Parser [12] avoids the former, but it only focuses on relational databases. In case multiple sets of targets are needed, the same mapping rules need to be executed multiple times, one set for each target. Since there is no declarative way for specifying where the output must be directed, processors cannot send parts of a knowledge graph to different or multiple output targets. Furthermore, these existing approaches lack the ability to describe if compression should be applied when exporting a knowledge graph.

2.2 Preliminaries

W3C Web of Things. A set of W3C recommendations were published by the W3C Web of Things Working Group for describing IoT devices and their capabilities such as interfaces, security, or protocols [2,10,13]. This way, machines can retrieve metadata about IoT devices (Listing 1.1 lines 3–4), understand how to interact with them (lines 8–10). The WoT W3C recommendations also describe which security practices must be applied when interacting with the IoT device (lines 5–6). These recommendations do not enforce a certain protocol, instead, they provide an abstraction layer that describes the protocol that must be used to interact with the device. External vocabularies, such as the W3C HTTP vocabulary [11], are leveraged to describe protocol-specific options. This way, new protocols can be added without changing the recommendation.

Listing 1.1. WoT Thing Description in JSON-LD for an MQTT illumance sensor

```
1   {
2     "@context": "https://www.w3.org/2019/wot/td/v1",
3     "title": "MyIlluminanceSensor",
4     "id": "urn:dev:ops:32473-WoTIlluminanceSensor-1234",
5     "securityDefinitions": {"nosec_sc": {"scheme": "nosec"}},
6     "security": ["nosec_sc"],
7     "events": {  "illuminance": { "data":{"type": "integer"},
8       "forms": [ {
9         "href": "mqtt://example.com/illuminance", "contentType" : "text/plain",
10        "op" : "subscribeevent" } ] } }
11  }
```

RDF Mapping Language (RML). RML [6] broadens R2RML's scope and covers mapping rules from data in different (semi-)structured formats, e.g., CSV, XML, JSON which define how heterogeneous data is transformed in RDF.

Listing 1.2. RML mapping definitions

```
1   <#Mapping> rml:logicalSource <#InputX> ;
2     rr:subjectMap [ rr:template "http://ex.com/{ID}"; rr:class foaf:Person ];
3     rr:predicateObjectMap [ rr:predicateMap [ rr:constant foaf:knows ];
4       rr:objectMap [ rr:parentTriplesMap <#Acquaintance> ] ].
5   <#Acquaintance> rml:logicalSource <#InputY> ;
6     rr:subjectMap [ rml:reference "acquaintance"; rr:termType rr:IRI;
7       rr:class foaf:Person ] .
```

The main building blocks of RML are Triples Maps (Listing 1.2: line 1). A Triples Map defines how triples of the form subject, predicate, and object, will be generated. A Triples Map consists of three main parts: the Logical Source, the Subject Map, and zero or more Predicate-Object Maps. The Subject Map (line 2, 6) defines how unique identifiers (URIs) are generated for the mapped resources and is used as the subject of all RDF triples generated from this Triples Map. A Predicate-Object Map (line 3) consists of Predicate Maps, which define the rule that generates the triple's predicate (line 3) and Object Maps or Referencing Object Maps (line 4), which define how the triple's object is generated. The Subject Map, the Predicate Map, and the Object Map are Term Maps, namely rules that generate an RDF term (an IRI, a blank node or a literal). A Term Map can be a constant-valued term map (`rr:constant`, line 3) that always generates the same RDF term, or a reference-valued term map (`rml:reference`, line 6) that is the data value of a referenced data fragment in a given Logical Source, or a template-valued term map (`rr:template`, line 2) that is a valid string template that can contain referenced data fragments of a given Logical Source.

3   Motivation

In this Section, we introduce our motivating use cases, ESSENCE and DAIQUIRI (Sect. 3.1), and derive open issues (Sect. 3.2) with existing mapping languages which we encountered while trying to address these use cases.

3.1   Motivating Use Cases: ESSENCE and DAIQUIRI

We describe here our motivating use cases, ESSENCE and DAIQUIRI.

In ESSENCE[4], we had requirements related to data access, authentication and knowledge graph export during knowledge graph generation. ESSENCE focuses on data storytelling in smart cities with IoT sensors. These IoT sensors provides information about the weather or traffic in the city and their measurements are available through multiple Web APIs. We need to generate knowledge graphs from measurements of these sensors[5], such as rain sensors, water flow meters, and vehicle counters[6], and the generated knowledge graphs are published in a triple store. The measurements are available through various Web APIs, each with their own way of authentication. The generated knowledge graphs are exported to a triple store to be consumed by other partners, and are also stored locally to create backups.

In DAIQUIRI[7], we found requirements for data access, data velocity and exporting knowledge graph to various targets. DAIQUIRI is also a use case on data storytelling but for sports games, such as cycling or hockey. Athletes are

---

[4] https://www.imec-int.com/en/what-we-offer/research-portfolio/essence
[5] https://open-livedata.antwerpen.be/#/org/digipolis/api/weerobservatiecutler-actu elewaarden/v1/documentation.
[6] https://telraam-api.net/.
[7] https://www.imec-int.com/en/what-we-offer/research-portfolio/daiquiri.

tracked through sensors to provide sport analysts interesting facts in real time about the game. We integrate several sport tracking sensors into knowledge graphs and export these graphs for consumption. Data from these sensors are available from multiple infinite streams such as movement speed or heart rate. Multiple types of tracking sensors are used. Consequently, each sensor has its own data velocity. While in ESSENCE, we exported the graphs to a triple store, in DAIQUIRI we export the generated knowledge graphs as an stream and create local backups on disk. The generated knowledge graph is continuously enriched.

3.2   Open Issues

In this Section, we describe open issues we encountered in our motivating use cases (Sect. 3.1). While these issues are inspired by our use cases, we generalize them in this Section aiming to tackle them with generic solutions. The Knowledge Graph Construction (KGC) Community Group also has a list of unsolved challenges for mapping languages. Several issues we encounter in our use cases were also highlighted by other researchers and companies[8]

Open Issue 1. Streams. Since mapping languages do not describe access to data with different velocities, processors implemented their own extensions, even for the same mapping language, e.g., RML[9]. We encountered this issue in our use cases when retrieving sensor measurements through Web APIs and streams which required a use case specific preprocessing step to overcome this obstacle. This issue is encountered and acknowledged by the KGC Community Group as well in their mapping challenges[10], verifying that this issue goes beyond our use cases. Mapping languages need to describe access to data with different velocities and indicate to processors how to handle data with different data velocities.

Open Issue 2. Web APIs. While mapping languages have preliminary support for Web APIs [7,15,19], they do not consider defining authentication, or protocol-specific features such as custom HTTP headers or other HTTP methods besides HTTP GET. As mentioned in Sect. 3.1, we encountered this issue when accessing Web APIs in our ESSENCE use case. These Web APIs required authentication with a custom HTTP header. We had to create a use case specific preprocessing step to authenticate with the Web APIs and retrieve the data. Mapping languages need to describe in detail how Web APIs must be accessed by processors to avoid such preprocessing steps.

---

[8] https://github.com/kg-construct/mapping-challenges/issues.

[9] CARML's Stream: https://github.com/carml/carml
RMLStreamer's RML extension: https://github.com/RMLio/rmlstreamer
Chimera's InputStream: https://github.com/cefriel/chimera.

[10] https://github.com/kg-construct/mapping-challenges/issues/7.

Open Issue 3. Description of the Generated Knowledge Graph. Mapping languages do not describe how a processor must export a knowledge graph. In both ESSENCE and DAIQUIRI, we had to store and publish the generated knowledge graph of sensor measurements. Thus, processors cannot determine from the mapping rules the serialization of a graph or where it must be exported. Therefore, we created a postprocessing step in our use cases to export the generated knowledge graph. There is a need for mapping languages to describe the characteristics of exporting a knowledge graph as RDF.

4 Approach

In this Section, we describe how we leveraged WoT W3C recommendations to extend RML's Logical Source (Sect. 4.1) and introduce RML's Logical Target (Sect. 4.2) to solve the open issues we discussed in Sect. 3.2.

4.1 WoT W3C Recommendations as Data Access Description

We leverage the WoT W3C recommendations as data source description in RML to describe how processors access Web APIs and streams and perform authentication, if needed (Open Issues 1 & 2). The access description of the Web API or stream is described as `td:PropertyAffordance` (Listing 1.3: lines 3–9, 18–23) which consists of an abstraction layer and protocol bindings. The abstraction layer specifies the location of the resource (Listing 1.3: lines 4, 19), the content type of the data (Listing 1.3: lines 5, 20), and if the property can be read (Listing 1.3: lines 6, 21). A `td:PropertyAffordance` can be combined with other protocol-specific vocabularies through binding templates [13], e.g. the HTTP W3C vocabulary [11] (Listing 1.3: lines 7–9, 23). This way, we describe common information, e.g., resource location, content-type, etc. in a generic way and describe protocol-specific features in the mapping rules.

Listing 1.3. WoT based access description for performing an HTTP GET request with authentication through an API key in a custom HTTP header and subscribing to an MQTT stream with authentication embedded in the message body

```
1   <#WoTWebAPISecurity> a wotsec:APISecurityScheme;
2     wotsec:in "header"; wotsec:name "apikey".
3   <#WoTWebAPISource> a td:PropertyAffordance;
4     td:hasForm [ hctl:hasTarget "http://example.com/data.json";
5       hctl:forContentType "application/json";
6       hctl:hasOperationType td:readproperty;
7       htv:headers ([ htv:fieldName "User-Agent";
8         htv:fieldValue "Mapping language processor"; ]);
9       htv:methodName "GET"; ].
10  <#WoTWebAPI> a td:Thing ;
11    td:hasSecurityConfiguration <#WoTWebAPISecurity>;
12    td:hasPropertyAffordance <#WoTWebAPISource>.
13  <#LogicalSource1> a rml:logicalSource;
14    rml:source <#WoTWebAPISource>;
15    rml:referenceFormulation ql:JSONPath; rml:iterator "$".
16  <#WoTMQTTSecurity> a wotsec:BasicSecurityScheme;
17    wotsec:in "body".
18  <#WoTMQTTSource> a td:PropertyAffordance;
19    td:hasForm [ hctl:hasTarget "mqtt://example.com/mqtt";
20      hctl:forContentType "application/json";
21      hctl:hasOperationType td:readproperty ;
22      mqv:controlPacketValue "SUBSCRIBE"; ].
23  <#WoTMQTT> a td:Thing ;
24    td:hasSecurityConfiguration <#WoTMQTTSecurity>;
25    td:hasPropertyAffordance <#WoTMQTTSource>.
26  <#LogicalSource2> a rml:logicalSource;
27    rml:source <#WoT_MQTT_source>;
28    rml:referenceFormulation ql:JSONPath; rml:iterator "$".
```

We also use the WoT W3C recommendations to describe the authentication of Web APIs and streams. Processors use this information to know how they must authenticate against the Web API or stream to retrieve the data. The WoT W3C recommendations provide several common authentication descriptions such as `wotsec:APISecurityScheme` (Listing 1.3: lines 1–2) for token based authentication or `wotsec:BasicSecurityScheme` (Listing 1.3: lines 16–17) for authenticating with an username and password. These descriptions not only describe the type of authentication (Listing 1.3: lines 1, 16) but also how the credentials must be provided to the Web API or streams (Listing 1.3: lines 2, 17). This way, we declaratively describe the authentication of Web APIs and streams in the mapping rules. However, the WoT W3C recommendations do not describe the actual credentials such as token, username or password, needed to authenticate with the Web API or stream to avoid leaking the credentials in the WoT descriptions. To overcome this problem, existing vocabularies such as the International Data Spaces Information Model[11] can be used to specify credentials. This way, we declaratively describe the credentials for processors and avoid to leak them by keeping them separated from the mapping rules.

---

[11] https://w3id.org/idsa/core.

4.2   Introducing RML's Logical Target

We introduce the Logical Target[12] in RML which describes the characteristics of the generated knowledge graph, e.g., serialization format, and target destination of the generated knowledge graph, e.g., storage location (Open Issue 3).

While a Logical Source is part of a Triples Map, a Logical Target is a part of a Term Map specified by `rmlt:logicalTarget` (Listing 1.4: lines 12, 15) which expects a RML Logical Target description. This way, we have fine-grained control over where each triple is exported to (Listing 1.4: lines 12, 15).

We follow the same approach for the output description as RML does for the input description to specify how a target must be accessed and where the knowledge graph must be exported to. We consider the same vocabularies, e.g., VoID [1], SD [23] or WoT, to describe the access to the target destination of the generated knowledge graph as to specify the access to a data source.

A Logical Target describes how a processor accesses a target and the location where the knowledge graph must be exported to with the `rmlt:target`[13] property (Listing 1.4: line 7). This way, we reuse the data source access descriptions used in RML's Logical Source to specify RML's Logical Target. For instance, we use a `void:Dataset` description as data target (Listing 1.4: lines 4–5) in a Logical Target to export the generated knowledge graph to the local disk or a `sd:Service` description to export to a triple store using SPARQL UPDATE queries (Listing 1.4: lines 1–3).

A Logical Target also contains an optional `rmlt:serialization`[14] property (Listing 1.4: line 8) to specify which serialization format must be used to export the generated knowledge graph. The `rmlt:serialization` property reuses the existing W3C `formats` namespace[15] as declarative description of the output RDF format. If no format is specified, the serialization format is N-Quads by default.

We also added an optional `rmlt:compression`[16] property to the domain of RML's Logical Target to describe which compression algorithm is used to save network bandwidth and storage when exporting a knowledge graph (Listing 1.4: line 9). `rmlt:compression` requires an object from the Compression (`comp`) namespace[17]. By specifying the compression algorithm through the `comp` namespace, we declaratively describe the compression algorithms. When the property is not specified, no compression is applied when exporting the knowledge graph.

---

[12] https://rml.io/specs/rml-target.
[13] http://semweb.mmlab.be/ns/rml-target#.
[14] http://semweb.mmlab.be/ns/rml-target#.
[15] https://www.w3.org/ns/formats/.
[16] http://semweb.mmlab.be/ns/rml-target#.
[17] http://semweb.mmlab.be/ns/rml-compression#.

Listing 1.4. RML Logical Target to export a knowledge graph to local disk as N-Triples with GZip compression & SPARQL endpoint with SPARQL UPDATE.

```
1   @prefix sd: <http://www.w3.org/ns/sparql-service-description#> .
2   <#SPARQLUPDATE> a sd:Service;
3     sd:endpoint  <http://example.com/sparql-update>;
4     sd:supportedLanguage sd:SPARQL11Update.
5   <#FileDump> a void:Dataset;
6     void:dataDump <file:///home/dylan/out.nq>.
7   <#LogicalTarget1> a rmlt:LogicalTarget;
8     rmlt:target <#FileDump>;
9     rmlt:serialization formats:N-Triples;
10    rmlt:compression comp:GZip.
11  <#TriplesMap> a rr:TriplesMap;
12    rr:subjectMap [ rr:template "http://example.com/{name}";
13      rmlt:logicalTarget <#LogicalTarget1> ];
14    rr:predicateObjectMap [ rr:predicate foaf:name;
15    rr:objectMap [ rml:reference "name";
16      rml:logicalTarget [ a rml:LogicalTarget; rml:target <#SPARQLUPDATE> ];
17    ];
18  ].
```

5   Validation

In this Section, we explain how we implemented our approach (Sect. 5.1) in the RMLMapper and RMLStreamer, and how we applied our approach to two use cases: ESSENCE (Sect. 5.2) and DAIQUIRI (Sect. 5.3).

5.1   Implementation

We implemented our approach in two RML processors, the RMLMapper[18] and RMLStreamer[19], to show that our approach can be applied to any implementation following the RML specification. The RMLMapper follows a mapping-driven approach by executing each Triples Map one by one to generate a single knowledge graph. To the contrary, the RMLStreamer uses a data-driven approach by executing the Triples Maps based on the retrieved data records. The knowledge graph is generated continuously as a data stream.

5.2   ESSENCE Use Case

Initial Pipeline. We created an initial pipeline (Fig. 1) consisting of several scripts and mapping rules to retrieve the measurement data, authenticate against Web APIs, generate knowledge graphs, and export the generated knowledge graphs to multiple targets. The mapping rules describe only how the retrieved data need to be integrated into a knowledge graph. The authentication against the Web API, the data retrieval, and export of the generated knowledge graphs are not declaratively described. Instead, they are handled by the use case specific scripts. Each script was especially written for the ESSENCE use case, and cannot be reused for our other use cases.

---

[18] https://github.com/RMLio/rmlmapper-java.
[19] https://github.com/RMLio/rmlstreamer.

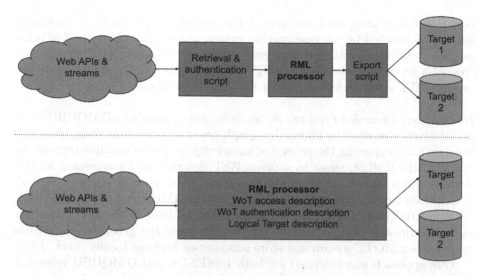

Fig. 1. Above, the initial use case specific pipeline with use case specific scripts to retrieve the data and export the generated knowledge graph. Below, our approach which declaratively describes how the data should be retrieved and how the generated knowledge graph should be exported.

Declaratively Described Pipeline. In our approach[20], we not only declaratively describe how the data must be integrated into a knowledge graph, but also how processors must authenticate against Web APIs, retrieve the data from Web APIs and how processors must export the generated knowledge graphs to multiple targets. This way, the mapping rules not only describe how the data is integrated, but also how the data is accessed and how the knowledge graphs are exported. We replaced our retrieval and authentication script with Web of Things Web API access and authentication descriptions (Sect. 4.1, Fig. 1). This way, the RMLMapper can authenticate to the Web APIs and retrieve the necessary data. Since these descriptions are reusable in other use cases, our approach provides a generic solution for Open Issue 2. Afterward, we replaced the export script as well with Logical Target descriptions (Sect. 4.2, Fig. 1). Consequently, the RMLMapper can export its generated knowledge graph directly to a triple store and local disk for backups. The local backups are also compressed during the export to save disk space (Sect. 4.2).

5.3 DAIQUIRI Use Case

Initial Pipeline. As in ESSENCE, we first created an initial pipeline (Fig. 1) consisting of several scripts and mapping rules to retrieve the data from the MQTT stream, integrate the data into knowledge graphs, and export the generated knowledge graphs to multiple targets. The mapping rules only describe

---

[20] https://github.com/RMLio/web-of-things-icwe2021.

how the data is integrated, the actual data retrieval and export of knowledge graphs are handled by use case specific scripts which cannot be reused in other use cases. Since the RMLStreamer only supports Kafka and TCP streams, we created a script to transform the MQTT stream into a Kafka stream and back to an MQTT stream when exporting the knowledge graph.

Declaratively Described Pipeline. By applying our approach to DAIQUIRI[21], we declaratively describe the knowledge graph generation pipeline from retrieving the data until exporting the generated knowledge graphs to multiple targets. We extended the RMLStreamer to support WoT descriptions for accessing MQTT streams which allowed us to remove our initial data retrieval script. The WoT descriptions contain sufficient information for the RMLStreamer to retrieve the data directly (Sect. 4.1, Fig. 1) which solves Open Issue 1. We also reused the same descriptions in a Logical Target for exporting the generated knowledge graphs as an MQTT stream and store compressed backups locally (Sect. 4.2).

Our approach was validated for both ESSENCE and DAIQUIRI regarding to exporting a knowledge graph by using the same access descriptions for heterogeneous data sources in RML (Open Issue 3).

6   Conclusion

In this paper, we investigated how mapping languages can describe the characteristics of (i) accessing data streams and Web APIs, and (ii) exporting a knowledge graph. We validated our approach with two real-life use cases which showcases that our approach can be used for accessing Web APIs and streams and exporting knowledge graphs. This shows that our approach improves the reproducibility of knowledge graph generation as we not only declaratively describe how the knowledge graph should be generated, but also how the Web APIs and streams should be accessed, and the generated knowledge graph exported. WoT W3C recommendations enable mapping languages to access Web APIs and streams without depending on a specific protocol. More, access descriptions can be leveraged for describing how generated knowledge graphs must be exported.

Only a limited amount of protocol bindings are standardized so far. The WoT Working Group released several recommendations, which are used in this paper, but some parts of the recommendations are still in development such as the protocol bindings. These protocol bindings provide descriptions for protocol-specific options and need to be provided for each protocol separately. However, if no protocol-specific options are needed, the abstraction layer of the WoT W3C recommendations covers the necessary parts to access a Web API or stream.

Further research should be undertaken to investigate how pagination in Web APIs can be handled as our work only covers access of Web APIs in mapping languages. Furthermore, more investigation must be applied to determine that our work covers all possible Web API use cases.

---

[21] https://github.com/RMLio/web-of-things-icwe2021.

References

1. Alexander, K., Cyganiak, R., Hausenblas, M., Zhao, J.: Describing Linked Datasets with the VoID Vocabulary. Interest group note, World Wide Web Consortium (W3C) (2011). https://www.w3.org/TR/void/
2. Charpenay, V., Lefrançois, M., Poveda Villalón, M., Käbisch, S.: Thing Description (TD) Ontology. Working group editor's draft, World Wide Web Consortium (W3C) (2020). https://www.w3.org/2019/wot/td
3. Chortaras, A., Stamou, G.: Mapping diverse data to RDF in practice. In: Vrandečić, D., et al. (eds.) ISWC 2018. LNCS, vol. 11136, pp. 441–457. Springer, Cham (2018). https://doi.org/10.1007/978-3-030-00671-6_26
4. Christensen, E., Curbera, F., Meredith, G., Weerawarana, S.: Web ServicesDescription Language (WSDL) 1.0 (2000)
5. Das, S., Sundara, S., Cyganiak, R.: R2RML: RDB to RDF Mapping Language. Working group recommendation, World Wide Web Consortium (W3C) (2012). http://www.w3.org/TR/r2rml/
6. Dimou, A., Sande, M.V., Colpaert, P., Verborgh, R., Mannens, E., Van de Walle, R.: RML: a generic language for integrated RDF mappings of heterogeneous data. In: Proceedings of the 7th Workshop on Linked Data on the Web. CEUR Workshop Proceedings, vol. 1184. CEUR-WS.org (2014)
7. Dimou, A., Verborgh, R., Sande, M.V., Mannens, E., de Walle, R.V.: Machine-interpretable dataset and service descriptions for heterogeneous data access and retrieval. In: Proceedings of the 11th International Conference on Semantic Systems - SEMANTICS 2015. ACM Press (2015)
8. Haesendonck, G., Maroy, W., Heyvaert, P., Verborgh, R., Dimou, A.: Parallel RDF generation from heterogeneous big data. In: Proceedings of the International Workshop on Semantic Big Data - SBD 2019. ACM Press, Amsterdam, Netherlands (2019)
9. Harris, S., Seaborne, A.: SPARQL 1.1 Query Language. Recommendation, World Wide Web Consortium (W3C) (2013). https://www.w3.org/TR/sparql11-query/
10. Kaebisch, S., Kamiya, T., McCool, M., Charpenay, V., Kovatsch, M.: Web of Things (WoT) Thing Description. Working group recommendation, World Wide Web Consortium (W3C) (2020). http://www.w3.org/TR/wot-thing-description/
11. Koch, J., Valesco, C.A., Ackermann, P.: HTTP Vocabulary in RDF 1.0. Working group note, World Wide Web Consortium (W3C) (2017). http://www.w3.org/TR/HTTP-in-RDF10/
12. Konstantinou, N., Spanos, D.E., Houssos, N., Mitrou, N.: Exposing scholarlyinformation as Linked Open Data: RDFizing DSpace contents. The ElectronicLibrary (2014)
13. Koster, M., Korkan, E.: Web of Things (WoT) Binding Templates. Working group note, World Wide Web Consortium (W3C) (2020). http://www.w3.org/TR/wot-binding-templates/
14. Lanthaler, M.: Hydra Core Vocabulary: A Vocabulary for Hypermedia-Driven Web APIs. Unofficial draft, World Wide Web Consortium (W3C) (2019). http://www.hydra-cg.com/spec/latest/core/
15. Lefrançois, M., Zimmermann, A., Bakerally, N.: A SPARQL extension for generating RDF from heterogeneous formats. In: Blomqvist, E., Maynard, D., Gangemi, A., Hoekstra, R., Hitzler, P., Hartig, O. (eds.) ESWC 2017. LNCS, vol. 10249, pp. 35–50. Springer, Cham (2017). https://doi.org/10.1007/978-3-319-58068-5_3

16. Maali, F., Erickson, J.: Data Catalog Vocabulary (DCAT). Recommendation, World Wide Web Consortium (W3C) (2014). https://www.w3.org/TR/vocab-dcat/

17. Martin, D., et al.: OWL-S: Semantic Markup for Web Services. Member submission, World Wide Web Consortium (W3C) (2004). http://www.w3.org/Submission/OWL-S/

18. Mauri, A., et al.: TripleWave: spreading RDF streams on the web. In: Groth, P., et al. (eds.) ISWC 2016. LNCS, vol. 9982, pp. 140–149. Springer, Cham (2016). https://doi.org/10.1007/978-3-319-46547-0_15

19. Michel, F., Djimenou, L., Faron-Zucker, C., Montagnat, J.: Translation of heterogeneous databases into RDF, and application to the construction of a SKOS taxonomical reference. In: Monfort, V., Krempels, K.-H., Majchrzak, T.A., Turk, Ž. (eds.) WEBIST 2015. LNBIP, vol. 246, pp. 275–296. Springer, Cham (2016). https://doi.org/10.1007/978-3-319-30996-5_14

20. Santipantakis, G.M., Kotis, K.I., Vouros, G.A., Doulkeridis, C.: RDF-Gen: generating RDF from streaming and archival data. In: Proceedings of the 8th International Conference on Web Intelligence, Mining and Semantics (2018)

21. Scrocca, M., Comerio, M., Carenini, A., Celino, I.: Turning transport data to comply with EU standards while enabling a multimodal transport knowledge graph. In: Pan, J.Z., et al. (eds.) ISWC 2020. LNCS, vol. 12507, pp. 411–429. Springer, Cham (2020). https://doi.org/10.1007/978-3-030-62466-8_26

22. Tommasini, R., et al.: VoCaLS: vocabulary and catalog of linked streams. In: Vrandečić, D., et al. (eds.) ISWC 2018. LNCS, vol. 11137, pp. 256–272. Springer, Cham (2018). https://doi.org/10.1007/978-3-030-00668-6_16

23. Williams, G.: SPARQL 1.1 Service Description. Recommendation, World Wide Web Consortium (W3C) (2013). https://www.w3.org/TR/sparql11-service-description/

A Standalone WebAssembly Development Environment for the Internet of Things

István Koren[✉][ID]

Chair of Process and Data Science, RWTH Aachen University, Aachen, Germany
koren@pads.rwth-aachen.de

Abstract. In Industry 4.0, there is a growing demand to perform high-performance and latency-sensitive computations at the edge. Increasingly, machine data is not only collected but also processed and translated into actionable decisions influencing production parameters in real-time. However, heterogeneous hardware in the Internet of Things prevents the adoption of consistent development and deployment structures as known from service containers. WebAssembly is a recent hardware-agnostic bytecode format that is capable of running not only in the browser, but also on microcontrollers and in cloud environments. In this article, we argue that this web technology can have a real impact by leveraging tools and programming languages that web engineers are familiar with. As a first step, we present a proof-of-concept integrated development and deployment environment to execute WebAssembly modules on microcontrollers. Its key feature is a built-in web server that provides a self-contained browser-based IDE to directly develop, compile and flash AssemblyScript code to a device. In this sense, the Web of Things will unfold a streamlined development and deployment context for the agile and low-latency operationalization of adjustable data streaming and action-oriented process adaptations for industrial devices.

Keywords: WebAssembly · Internet of Things · Industry 4.0

1 Introduction

Digitalization of industrial assets comes with many promises like higher productivity, less rejects and smaller lot sizes. For instance, recent developments in the application of machine learning in the production context allow for data-driven decisions like parameter tuning in order to obtain a desired quality in the manufactured part. However, there are a number of challenges towards a fully connected smart production. First, the asset-heavy manufacturing industry is characterized by long-term investments with many legacy devices on the shop floor; while state-of-the-art industrial assets are able to push data over protocols like OPC-UA, many legacy machines only feature serial communication ports. Even programmable logic controllers are often restricted to a proprietary programming language that only specialized developers can work with. Furthermore,

© Springer Nature Switzerland AG 2021
M. Brambilla et al. (Eds.): ICWE 2021, LNCS 12706, pp. 353–360, 2021.
https://doi.org/10.1007/978-3-030-74296-6_27

many industrial processes are time-critical, thus parameter adaptions need to be carried out within a narrow window. For instance, compensations for disruptions in steel production must be made within a few milliseconds.

The concept of *Retrofitting* [10] refers to augmenting industrial assets with computational equipment able to forward data from serial interfaces via modern Internet of Things (IoT) protocols. It can be achieved by using microcontrollers, industrial-grade versions of boards like Raspberry Pi, or specialized edge cloud hardware. By bringing computation close to the devices, Retrofitting is therefore also useful for addressing latency issues. Overall, in the highly heterogeneous system landscape of the shop floor, different computational hardware like proprietary programmable logic controllers prevail together with custom modules. Yet, following the idea of agile manufacturing, software on the edge underlies frequent incremental changes [9]. To tackle this highly complex environment, a development and deployment structure is required that can handle this heterogeneity, i.e. produces service components that run on microcontrollers, on edge devices as well as in the cloud.

Over the last decade, containerization of microservices through technologies like Docker achieved low coupling of heterogeneous technologies with clearly cut functionalities. However, these containers are not lightweight enough to be run on low-powered IoT devices. To this end, WebAssembly (WASM) is a recent web standard. Originally, it was conceived for computationally intensive tasks within browser clients that need near-native performance, of that the interpreted JavaScript environment is not capable of, like image processing. Initiatives like WASI (WebAssembly Systems Interface) aim to make system calls available to WASM modules, making them a suitable platform to tackle the above challenges on the shop floor. In this article, we present a proof-of-concept that allows to run the same code on different hardware platforms. It features a built-in web server that delivers a simple IDE to develop code, compile it to bytecode, and flash it to the device. After its initialization, the binary code is capable of accessing device in- and output pins, for instance, to forward data from the device, or to directly change control parameters as the result of stripped-down machine learning algorithms. While essentially powered by web technologies, this opens many use cases, e.g. for the low-latency operationalization of real-time decisions.

This article is organized as follows. Section 2 motivates WebAssembly usage in service-oriented architectures and discusses related work. Section 3 presents the conceptual design and implementation of our proof-of concept. Section 4 discusses our findings, experiences and limitations. Finally, Sect. 5 concludes the article with an outlook on future work.

2   Towards Code Mobility on the Web of Things

Microservices and the containerization paradigm introduced by technologies like Docker and Kubernetes changed development and deployment structures in the last decade. By running isolated software containers, processes are sandboxed from each other, i.e., services cannot access each other's memory. However, because of the large overhead of software containers, this approach is not feasible

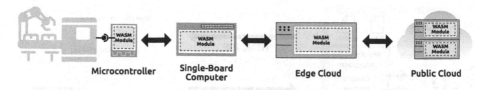

Fig. 1. Migration of unmodified WebAssembly modules from edge to cloud

for resource-constrained devices like single-board computers or even microcontrollers. Even though WebAssembly has only been introduced recently, there is already a vast adoption on frontend and backend as it harmonizes well with the serverless computing paradigm [3,6]. A curated list of use cases in the browser can be found on the list of *Awesome Wasm*[1]. Besides, open source and commercial offerings recognize the potential of WebAssembly for deploying functionalities on the backend. *Fastly Inc.*, one of the world's largest edge cloud providers, feature a dedicated WebAssembly runtime in their content delivery network. WebAssembly has an inherent sandbox based on design decisions such as linear memory management, ensuring that program code cannot break out its dedicated memory addresses. Its bytecode format can be cross-compiled from various programming languages and interpreted on platforms like IoT devices and the cloud. The format is governed by an open alliance of industry and research partners. For instance, AssemblyScript, a derivate of TypeScript, can be compiled into WASM bytecode. TypeScript, in turn, is very similar to JavaScript, opening access to a large number of web developers. It adds variable type declarations while staying syntactically close to JavaScript. The compiled WebAssembly modules can move freely between different hardware architectures. We argue, that it is therefore suited as code mobility [2] framework for small-scale functions in the Web of Things, adopting principles of *Liquid Web Applications* [5] on the backend. Our use case are deployments in the heterogeneous device landscape of industrial machines as illustrated in Fig. 1.

A number of researchers evaluated WebAssembly in serverless contexts outside the browser. Hall et al. run serverless functions and compare the execution as WebAssembly with Docker containers [3]. In their system, a node.js context executes WebAssembly modules. As primary advantage, they identify the absence of a large cold start penalty, as opposed to Docker. Tiwary et al. confirm that spawning WebAssembly modules in a containerized environment suffers from cold-start problems [11]. Murphy et al. compare the performance of different native runtimes and find executing in a pure node.js environment to be the fastest [6].

3   Proof-of-Concept WASM on the Edge

In this section, we discuss our proof-of-concept, by demonstrating the viability of WASM modules on microcontrollers.

---

[1] cf. https://github.com/mbasso/awesome-wasm.

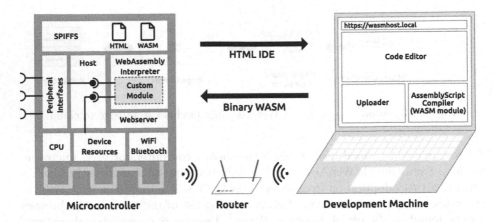

Fig. 2. Overall system architecture with microcontroller and development laptop

3.1 Conceptual Design

The main conceptual idea is to provide a code execution layer on top of the microcontroller firmware whose code is exchangeable. Our prototype consists of three parts: the host environment, the runtime, as well as the development environment. Figure 2 presents the basic architecture. On the left, the components of a microcontroller are shown. On its top, SPIFFS (Serial Peripheral Interface File System) is a lightweight system for storing files. Other peripheral interfaces connect to external hardware over serial connections. The host is the firmware that gets activated once the controller is booted. It connects to the WiFi network and ensures availability via Bluetooth, if needed. Then, if a WebAssembly module has been loaded, it gets instantiated and provided access to the device's in- and output pins. Any external dependency needs to be explicitly declared beforehand to be available from within the module.

The host features a built-in web server. It delivers a simple HTML page that has a code editor and a button. The HTML page references the external compiler. Once the button is clicked, the compiler gets called. If the code can be compiled without errors, the resulting binary WebAssembly module is uploaded to the host environment on the microcontroller. For this purpose, the same web server that provides the code editor also has an HTTP endpoint for accepting and storing the binary module. After deployment, the microcontroller reboots and executes the new module. In the next section, we discuss the implementation and present the libraries used.

3.2 Microcontroller Implementation

As microcontroller, we chose an ESP32 board. The successor of the ESP8266 is extremely popular for tiny IoT projects, and comes with a dual-core processor, as well as WiFi and Bluetooth connectivity. Most of the development boards come with 4 MB of flash size. We specifically used modules from TTGO

Listing 1.1. AssemblyScript Code Passing Sensor Value Every Third Time

```
 1  // the pass function is imported from the host
 2  declare function pass(data: f32): void;
 3
 4  // a global variable to store the number of cycles
 5  let cycle:f32 = 0;
 6
 7  // the process function gets called from the host
 8  export function process(a: f32): f32 {
 9    cycle++;
10    if (cycle == 3) { // only send value upstream on every third cycle
11      pass(a);
12      cycle = 0;
13    }
14    return a;
15  }
16
17  export function _start(): void {
18    while (true) { // keep module active
19    }
20  }
```

and the DEVKIT V1, which are in a price range between 4–9 Euros. The host firmware is developed using the Arduino framework that is compatible to the native ESP development kit. As WebAssembly interpreter, we decided to use the open source Wasm3 library[2]. The web server is available via a Multicast DNS hostname over the local WiFi network. It is powered by the ESPAsyncWeb-Server library[3]. The WebAssembly module is developed with AssemblyScript[4]. It is a variant of TypeScript that is popular in the web development community. The compiler that translates AssemblyScript into the binary bytecode format is available as WebAssembly module itself, it can thus be called from within an HTML5 application context. We load it from the *unpkg.com* CDN to free as much memory as possible for the application code. After its compilation, the WASM file is uploaded via a HTTP multi-part form upload to the microcontroller. On the microcontroller, it is saved within the flash that is formatted as SPI file system.

Listing 1.1 shows an example AssemblyScript code. It is a very basic module with a **process** function, that forwards every third call to the **pass** method. With **declare** (line 2) we import functions of the host into the module. In the other direction, functions that are called from the host are marked with **export** (line 8 and 17). The **_start** function is called for initializing resources; it is also responsible for keeping the module active (cf. the **loop()** function in Arduino code). Due to the sandbox, it is not possible to call other environment functions from within the developed module. Consequently, all external functions must be declared at compile time. WebAssembly is using a linear memory management with allocated memory locations. In our demo code, we import and export for

---

[2] cf. https://github.com/wasm3/wasm3.

[3] cf. https://github.com/me-no-dev/ESPAsyncWebServer.

[4] cf. https://www.assemblyscript.org/.

now only integer and float types, as the management of elaborate types involving strings and objects is more complicated and error-prone.

4   Applicability of WebAssembly on Microcontrollers

Our proof-of-concept allows to run user-contributed code on microcontrollers and to exchange it during runtime. It brings advantages known from container-based deployments to the Internet of Things with its resource-constrained devices and variety of architectures. Our approach allows for the fast exchange of code, but promises a certain level of security that is achieved through sandboxing. At the same time, the standardized bytecode format allows to leverage various programming languages. We are convinced that these characteristics make WASM applicable for realizing the potential of the Web of Things in the industrial area.

Running replaceable user-contributed code on the edge, both in the browser and as in our case on IoT devices, opens a number of security issues. Attack vectors of running code in web browsers are discussed by Papadopoulos et al. [7]. The authors analyze the use of service workers for leveraging the processing power of client devices, for instance to mine cryptocurrencies. Service workers can execute code in the background, even if the user is not actively using the originating website. WebAssembly adds a controllable sandbox. However, through the bytecode format, it is much harder to anticipate what code is running. Security measures therefore need to be undertaken, and access to the outer world needs to be limited to the absolutely necessary.

4.1   Preliminary Evaluation

The firmware size of our host, including the WASM and server libraries is around 1.1 MB. On a typical ESP32 chip, this leaves around 2.9 MB of flash that has to be shared with RAM and the SPI file system. The AssemblyScript compiler has a size of around 1 MB; to save SPIFFS space, we load it as external dependency. To compare the performance of our WebAssembly framework with running code natively on the microcontroller, we ran evaluations that confirmed the performance penalty described in Sect. 2. For instance, Jangda et al. calculated an average decrease between 1.5x and 2x [4]. The authors note that WebAssembly is still a rather new technology that is constantly optimized. The range of possible functionalities in the module versus natively on the host, however, is not limited, as it depends on what device resources are linked into the module.

4.2   Limitations of the Prototype

Conceptually, our proof-of-concept shares limitations with WebAssembly. For instance, it does not support threads, even though the ESP32 has a dual-core processor. WebAssembly does not allow for hardware-specific abstractions [3] like graphics card based matrix multiplication for machine learning algorithms. This could be a limiting factor when running (even light-weight) machine learning models. Moreover, researchers have highlighted issues inherent to WebAssembly, like decreased memory safety when compiling from other languages [1].

Our built-in IDE currently only supports AssemblyScript. We are planning to add further languages, like Python or Rust, depending on the availability of compilers that can be executed in a browser context. Besides, modules can already be written in various languages, as described in Sect. 2. For this, the modules need to import and export the specified methods. Regarding data exchange with the underlying host, we only support integer and float types. Also, no security, like access control, is part of our firmware. We are evaluating different mechanisms, like private-key signatures and identification via OpenID Connect to overcome this. Specific to the ESP32, we experienced a challenge with processor interrupts caused by timeouts. To overcome this, we regularly call Arduino's `delay()` function. In this regard, we do also not handle errors besides catching exceptions and closing the module gracefully. To overcome this, we are planning to introduce a fallback firmware. However, broken AssemblyScript modules are detected at compile-time and thus cannot be flashed onto the device.

5 Conclusion and Outlook

Data-driven insights are currently driving the fourth industrial revolution. Industrial assets are equipped with sensors that are able to provide fine-grained properties in a high frequency. However, there are many challenges towards agile software development structures in this highly complex area. Heterogeneous hardware architectures on the edge, from Arduino-driven microcontrollers up to specialized edge hardware make it hard to uniformly develop functionalities. Also, updating code is cumbersome and varies across boards. Following the ideas of agile manufacturing [9], frequent updates are part of the approach.

Our proposal is to introduce a common development methodology and framework powered by web technologies, that can run on edge-deployed hardware as well as in the cloud. For this, WebAssembly is an ideal candidate. In this article, we introduced a working proof-of-concept. It features a web server that delivers a complete IDE to develop, compile and deploy new firmware modules within a browser. In the future, we plan to support a peer-to-peer firmware propagation between modules. On the ESP platform, we can use built-in functionalities that build a mesh via Bluetooth or WiFi. Similarly, we want to enable a dynamic context-dependent code mobility from IoT device to edge, cloud and vice versa. For instance, if the processor load becomes to high, the device should be able to move its module to a near-by edge device. Both peer-to-peer deployment and context adaptation require higher security measures. This can be achieved by a security layer, e.g., by signing flashed modules.

We are currently equipping industrial laboratories of the engineering department at our university to trial industrial use cases. As described, agile updates of developed modules can be leveraged not only for data collection, but also for the operationalization of, e.g., business processes. We are convinced that faster development and deployment methodologies can finally enable the age of the

Internet of Production [8], where data collection powers artificial intelligence algorithms that in turn achieve action-oriented data insights.

Acknowledgement. Funded by the Deutsche Forschungsgemeinschaft (DFG, German Research Foundation) under Germany's Excellence Strategy - EXC-2023 Internet of Production - 390621612.

References

1. Disselkoen, C., Renner, J., Watt, C., Garfinkel, T., Levy, A., Stefan, D.: position paper: progressive memory safety for WebAssembly. In: Proceedings of the 8th International Workshop on Hardware and Architectural Support for Security and Privacy, pp. 1–8. ACM, New York (2019). https://doi.org/10.1145/3337167.3337171
2. Fuggetta, A., Picco, G.P., Vigna, G.: Understanding code mobility. IEEE Trans. Software Eng. **24**(5), 342–361 (1998). https://doi.org/10.1109/32.685258
3. Hall, A., Ramachandran, U.: An execution model for serverless functions at the edge. In: Landsiedel, O., Nahrstedt, K. (eds.) Proceedings of the International Conference on Internet of Things Design and Implementation, pp. 225–236. ACM, New York (2019). https://doi.org/10.1145/3302505.3310084
4. Jangda, A., Powers, B., Berger, E.D., Guha, A.: Not so fast: analyzing the performance of WebAssembly vs. Native Code. In: 2019 USENIX Annual Technical Conference (USENIX ATC 19), pp. 107–120. USENIX Association, Renton (2019). https://www.usenix.org/conference/atc19/presentation/jangda
5. Mikkonen, T., Systä, K., Pautasso, C.: Towards liquid web applications. In: Cimiano, P., Frasincar, F., Houben, G.-J., Schwabe, D. (eds.) ICWE 2015. LNCS, vol. 9114, pp. 134–143. Springer, Cham (2015). https://doi.org/10.1007/978-3-319-19890-3_10
6. Murphy, S., Persaud, L., Martini, W., Bosshard, B.: On the use of web assembly in a serverless context. In: Paasivaara, M., Kruchten, P. (eds.) XP 2020. LNBIP, vol. 396, pp. 141–145. Springer, Cham (2020). https://doi.org/10.1007/978-3-030-58858-8_15
7. Papadopoulos, P., Ilia, P., Polychronakis, M., Markatos, E.P., Ioannidis, S., Vasiliadis, G.: Master of Web Puppets: Abusing Web Browsers for Persistent and Stealthy Computation. http://arxiv.org/pdf/1810.00464v1
8. Pennekamp, J., et al.: Towards an infrastructure enabling the internet of production. In: 2019 IEEE International Conference on Industrial Cyber Physical Systems (ICPS), pp. 31–37. IEEE (06052019–09052019). https://doi.org/10.1109/ICPHYS.2019.8780276
9. Schuh, G., Reuter, C., Prote, J.P., Brambring, F., Ays, J.: Increasing data integrity for improving decision making in production planning and control. CIRP Ann. **66**(1), 425–428 (2017). https://doi.org/10.1016/j.cirp.2017.04.003
10. Stock, T., Seliger, G.: Opportunities of Sustainable Manufacturing in Industry 4.0. Procedia CIRP 40, 536–541 (2016). https://doi.org/10.1016/j.procir.2016.01.129
11. Tiwary, M., Mishra, P., Jain, S., Puthal, D.: Data aware web-assembly function placement. In: Seghrouchni, A.E.F., Sukthankar, G., Liu, T.Y., van Steen, M. (eds.) Companion Proceedings of the Web Conference 2020, pp. 4–5. ACM, New York (2020). https://doi.org/10.1145/3366424.3382670

Web Programming

Full Stack Is Not What It Used to Be

Antero Taivalsaari[1,4], Tommi Mikkonen[2(✉)], Cesare Pautasso[3],
and Kari Systä[4]

[1] Nokia Bell Labs, Tampere, Finland
antero.taivalsaari@nokia-bell-labs.com
[2] University of Helsinki, Helsinki, Finland
tommi.mikkonen@helsinki.fi
[3] USI, Lugano, Switzerland
cesare.pautasso@usi.ch
[4] Tampere University, Tampere, Finland
kari.systa@tuni.fi

Abstract. The traditional definition of *full stack development* refers to
a skill set that is required for writing software both for the frontend and
backend of a web application or site. In recent years, the scope of full
stack development has expanded significantly, though. Today, a full stack
software developer is assumed to master various additional areas especially related to cloud infrastructure and deployment, message brokers
and data analytics technologies. In addition, the emergence of Internet
of Things (IoT) and the rapidly spreading use of AI/ML technologies are
introducing additional skill set requirements. In this paper, we discuss
the expectations for a modern full stack developer based on our industry
observations, and argue that these expectations have significant implications for software and web engineering education.

Keywords: Education · Software engineering · Web engineering ·
Software architecture · Cloud · Internet of Things · IoT ·
Programmable world

1 Introduction

According to the traditional definition, the term *full stack developer* refers to
a web engineer or developer who works with both the frontend and backend
of a website or a web application. This means that a full stack developer is
typically expected to participate in projects that involve not only the user facing
features of web applications, but also databases and other server-side components
that are used for storing and delivering the contents of a web site. Full stack
software developers are commonly also expected to work with customers during
the planning and design phases of projects.

The "classic" skill set of a full stack developer includes the following [12]:

- HTML, CSS and JavaScript,
- one or more popular web frameworks such as Angular, React or Vue,

© Springer Nature Switzerland AG 2021
M. Brambilla et al. (Eds.): ICWE 2021, LNCS 12706, pp. 363–371, 2021.
https://doi.org/10.1007/978-3-030-74296-6_28

- experience with databases,
- experience with version control systems (at least Git),
- knowledge of web design, visual design and user experience best practices,
- knowledge of web security challenges and security best practices,
- experience with web server installation, configuration and web traffic log analytics, and
- some knowledge of additional programming languages that are commonly used in web backend development such as Python, PHP and Ruby (more recently also Go and Scala).

In general, full stack web developer job listings typically include a mix of frontend and backend skills, covering just about everything that it takes to compose a running application or a web site.

In recent years, the scope of full stack development has expanded considerably, though. In this short paper we present our observations based on various industry projects as well as discussions with our students and colleagues both in the academia and in the industry. We argue that the requirements presented by employers for full stack web engineers have grown significantly in recent years, and that these expanded expectations are not yet really taken into account in software engineering and web engineering education.

2   Software as a Service and the Disappearance of the IT Department

> "Dear Recruiters, That's not a Full Stack Developer. That's an IT Department."
>
> – Attributed to *Giulio Carrara*

The widespread adoption of the World Wide Web has fundamentally changed the landscape of software development. In the past 10–15 years, the Web has become the *de facto* deployment environment for new software systems and applications. Today, the majority of new software applications used on desktop computers or laptops are written for the Web, instead of conventional computing architectures, specific types of CPUs or operating systems.

From its relatively humble origins at Salesforce.com and later at Amazon.com, Software as a Service evolved into the dominant form of computing, effectively displacing traditional, locally installed software applications and conventional binary "shrink wrap" software [16]. As a side effect, the centralization of software onto externally hosted cloud platforms and virtual machines gradually killed the IT departments that nearly all major companies used to have. Nowadays, based on our observations and discussions with various companies, even in relatively large organizations there may be just one person who is responsible for all aspects related to system management, including deployment and operation of a large number of virtual machines rented from external providers.

As a result of this transition, many of the tasks that were traditionally handled by IT departments are now expected to be part of the job description of software developers themselves. The disappearance of the IT department was amplified by the *DevOps* movement [5] that shifted the majority of software deployment tasks from the IT department to the developers. In recent years, the transition towards *cloud native software* [3] and *serverless computing* [1]) has accelerated the trend towards externally hosted web applications. In these systems, the allocation and maintenance of physical servers is handled by external cloud providers, which significantly reduces the need for traditional IT tasks.

IaaS Platforms. The disappearance of the IT department has had a notable impact on the skill set that web developers are expected to possess. Nowadays, developers are assumed to master the basics of *Infrastructure as a Service (IaaS) platforms* such as AWS, Azure or Google Cloud, including the use of various services that are available in their management consoles. Many employers require an AWS certification or Azure Developer Associate certification.

Web Servers and Backend Development Frameworks. Developers not only have to be familiar with *web servers* (e.g., Apache, NGINX, Node.js) but also with how to set up the necessary *reverse proxies and security perimeters* (e.g., with NGINX). In addition, they are nowadays commonly assumed to master various *backend development frameworks* (typically written in either JavaScript/Node.js or Python). The developers are also assumed to be familiar with *cloud automation/scripting languages* such as Ansible.

Service Scaling, Monitoring, Logging and Fault Tolerance and Backup Services. In addition, developers are commonly expected to master the delivery of *scalable services with high availability*. They need to understand how to architect software that can benefit from load balancing, fault tolerance and automated switchover in case of VM or server domain failure, utilizing the services offered by IaaS platforms. Good understanding of *data storage and backup services* such as AWS Simple Storage Service (S3) and Glacier is also a common expectation, as well as system monitoring and logging technologies including Grafana, Kibana or CloudWatch.

Continuous Integration, Delivery and Deployment. Developers are also expected to adopt processes enabling *continuous integration and deployment* [2]. They have to set up GitLab CI/CD pipelines for automatically building, testing and deploying their latest software versions to staging and production environments. This also requires them to use the appropriate testing techniques across the frontend and backend.

Containerization and Container Management. More recently, it is taken for granted that the developers can perform the *containerization/dockerization* of their software (packaging of their software into Docker containers), as well as define the necessary Helm charts to enable their software to run in a Kubernetes cluster or some other popular *management and orchestration platform for containerized applications*. Note that Kubernetes is a huge toolset; however, a developer does not necessarily need Kubernetes to implement and deploy containers, so there are different levels of complexity also in this area.

Serverless Computing. It should be remarked that if serverless computing [1] becomes mainstream, the need for service management and IaaS platform related tasks may reduce but yet another – often vendor-specific – approach to architect and deploy applications needs to be learned. Details vary greatly between the Function-as-a-Service providers.

In any case, the skill set is so broad that universities struggle to include all the areas in their curricula, especially since a lot of the technologies are vendor-specific and tightly coupled with particular commercial offerings. The breadth of the expected skill set has led to a number of jokes, including the "dear recruiters" quote at the beginning of this section.

3   The Implications of Microservice Architectures

Another major occurrence has been the *emergence of microservice architectures* [10]. Originally, a key motivation behind microservice architectures was the idea of *polyglot programming* [4]: as different microservices are implemented and maintained by different subteams, each team could independently choose and use the most suitable technologies to support the task while also matching the existing competencies of each team. However, just as with deployment topics, it is an increasingly common expectation that full stack developers will be able to design and implement a broad variety of microservices and their APIs which would typically communicate with each other using synchronous calls, or asynchronous message brokers.

Message Brokers. Orchestration and internal communication to "glue" different microservices together to a larger functional entity is typically performed using a message broker [14]. Basically, in addition to adopting the HTTP protocol following the REST architectural style [13], developers are expected to have at least basic knowledge of popular *message brokers* such as ActiveMQ, RabbitMQ and/or Kafka.

Database Technologies Beyond SQL. In addition to traditional relational (SQL) database skills, developers are also assumed to be familiar with popular *noSQL databases* (such as Cassandra, Neo4j, Redis, or MongoDB) and in many cases *time-series databases* such as InfluxDB or Riak. The use of time-series databases is especially important in building microservices that deal with data acquisition from a large number of devices. *In-memory database systems* such as Apache Ignite are also a popular option in implementing microservices. Common additional skill expectations in the storage and database query area include technologies such as ElasticSearch, GraphQL and Hive.

Node.js and/or Python Backend Development Frameworks. The microservices themselves are commonly written either in JavaScript or Python, leveraging the massive number of frameworks and components available in

Node.js NPM and Python PyPI ecosystems. The selection of applicable components can be a daunting task, as discussed in papers focusing on *opportunistic design* [8].

Web API Design. Along with knowledge about backend development frameworks, developers are generally expected to be familiar with Web API design principles and best practices, including RESTful API design [9], and the corresponding API description languages such as OpenAPI, while keeping track of emerging alternatives such as GraphQL or gRPC.

4   Emerging Expectations

Data Analytics. About ten years ago, *data analytics* became an important topic and one of the hottest and highest paying technical professions in the IT industry. Nowadays, even regular developers are expected to be familiar with at least some of the popular data analytics technologies. Depending on the needs of the particular project, focus may be more on *real-time analytics* or *offline analytics technologies*. Popular real-time analytics platforms include Apache Storm and Spark. For offline analytics, HADOOP (along with its distributed file system HDFS) is a common choice. More recently, managed technologies such as Snowflake and BigQuery have become popular. In the context of data analytics, knowledge of query languages such as GraphQL and data visualization libraries such as D3.js or Vis.js is also a common expectation. For fancier visualizations, WebGL knowledge (and knowledge of accompanying 3D convenience libraries such as Plotly.js or Three.js) is a plus.

AI/ML Technologies. Turning raw data into valuable information requires full stack developers to skillfully apply popular AI/ML technologies such as Apache Mahout, Caffe, TensorFlow or Torch. While regular developers might not be expected to be able to build/train AI models, they *are* expected to be able to set up AI/ML pipelines to perform tasks such as object detection, face recognition or voice/phrase recognition using available technologies (e.g. [15]). While such tasks would have been considered very advanced or even impossible in the early days of Web engineering, they are now considered "basic" tasks in many contexts and applications. The availability of inexpensive AI/ML hardware is raising the expectations further (see the edge intelligence discussion below).

Internet of Things and the Programmable World. The Internet of Things (IoT) and the Web of Things (WoT) represent the next significant step in the evolution of the Internet and software development. Advances in hardware development and the general availability of powerful but very inexpensive integrated chips will make it possible to embed connectivity and full-fledged virtual machines and dynamic language runtimes virtually everywhere. The future potential of this *Programmable World* disruption will be as significant as the mobile application revolution that was sparked when similar technological advances made it possible to open up mobile phones for third-party application developers in the early 2000s [17,18].

Factors that this disruption builds upon include (i) multidevice programming, (ii) heterogeneity and diversity of devices, (iii) intermittent, potentially highly unreliable connectivity, (iv) the distributed, highly dynamic, and potentially migratory nature of software (between devices/cloud/fog/edge), (v) the reactive, continuous, always-on nature of the overall system, and (vi) the general need to write software in a highly fault-tolerant and defensive manner. Furthermore, IoT is bringing back the need for embedded software development skills and the ability to build software which can run on slow processors, with limited memory and consuming little energy [11].

Streaming Data Systems. As devices themselves are becoming more data intensive as their sensing capabilities (e.g., audio, video, LIDAR) become more advanced, AI/ML capabilities benefit vastly when raw data *streams* from the devices are made available in the cloud [7]. Developers must thus know how to implement cloud backend capable of ingesting continuously streaming data from a potentially very large numbers of devices – even millions of them.

Edge Computing and Edge Intelligence. Classic web sites and cloud computing systems were highly centralized – nearly all of the computation apart from web page rendering was performed in the backend. While centralized computing has significant benefits, it can also be very costly in terms of communication and power consumption. For instance, if an IoT system consists of a large collection of devices that are in close proximity of each other, it may be inefficient to transmit all the data from those devices to a faraway data center for processing, and then transmit actuation requests back from the remote data center to the individual devices. In an IoT deployment with tight latency requirements, latency overhead alone can make such solutions impractical.

In recent years, the emergence of inexpensive but computationally powerful hardware solutions has made edge computing practical. This has made it feasible to perform data analytics or at least initial data filtering and processing in the IoT devices and gateways themselves, without having to send all the raw measurement data to data centers for processing. Furthermore, growing privacy concerns and the availability of inexpensive AI/ML hardware such as, for example, NVIDIA's Jetson or Arduino Nano 33 BLE devices have made it both necessary and possible to bring AI/ML capabilities (e.g., object detection and face recognition) to the edge with very little development effort. Consequently, it is rapidly becoming an expectation than an average full stack developer must master at least the basic use of these technologies.

5   The New Full Stack – Implications for Software and Web Engineering Education

Most university curriculums aim at a balance between theory and practice [6]. To complement teaching of theoretical aspects, universities commonly include practical projects and hands-on exercises. However, the wide range of concepts and technology choices in the new full stack poses challenges for this approach – there are simply too many topics and technologies to cover. Furthermore, many of the relevant technologies tend to be rather vendor-specific. At the same time, students graduating from the universities are clearly in a better position with respect to their employment opportunities if they possess hands-on skills on the entire spectrum of full stack technologies.

It is important to note that full stack does not mean "all" technologies. To us, it seems that we must first define which "core" technologies the students absolutely must master in order to be well versed for basic development tasks. Beyond the core topics, the needs for specific technologies will be to at least some extent dependent on use cases and roles, e.g., whether the developer is focusing on "AI full stack" vs. "analytics full stack" vs. "IoT full stack". At the moment, no comprehensive taxonomy of core and advanced full stack technologies exists. We see this as an interesting avenue for further research.

In the short term, one solution to this dilemma is to build extensive, industry-grade systems around the aforementioned core full stack, where use case specific modules can be added as subsystems, thus decomposing the projects to different courses. Furthermore, as almost all modern full stack technologies have online courses, e.g., in the form of Massive Open Online Courses (MOOCs) or online tutorials and exercises, those can be used as educational material. As an example of this model, the University of Helsinki has introduced *Fullstack Challenge*[1] in which students work with modern web technologies and tools on practical projects in collaboration with companies. At USI, practical *ateliers* scheduled in the afternoons complement and integrate the theoretical morning lectures.

No matter which approach is taken, given the increasing complexity and breadth of expected functionality, in most software systems it is no longer realistic to implement everything from scratch, even if parts of the system were built over time in different classes. Instead, the new full stack development is characterized by plentiful use of public-domain software components from repositories such as NPM and PyPI. Instead of using a fixed set of technologies or blindly following recommendations in a cargo-cult fashion, the students should still learn to think for themselves and carefully consider the implications of the selections that they make. At the same time, every developer needs a "full stack Swiss army knife" as the starting point.

In summary, the increased scope of full stack development challenges the universities to recognize, formulate, conceptualize, and teach the new general principles that provide long-term competencies. Students should learn how to recognize fundamental problems so that they can solve them with the appropriate conceptual tools using the corresponding technology of the day. This requires research on effective technical paradigms, understanding of how to anticipate practical needs of the companies, and also knowledge of the modern technologies and their associated online courses.

---

[1] https://fullstackopen.com/en/.

6   Conclusions

In this paper we have presented our observations on the rapidly growing requirements for a full stack web developer. While the classic full stack was concerned
primarily with the basic frontend and backend split and technologies required
for developing web sites and applications, the expectations for a modern full
stack developer are far more comprehensive. Effectively, expected skills cover
a spectrum of areas that would have been the responsibility of an entire IT
department in the earlier days. Moreover, we foresee further technologies emerging and broadening the expected skill set even more in the coming years. This
evolution will force us to reconsider the role of university degrees, technology
certificates and lifelong learning efforts together with new tools such as MOOCs
in the software and web engineering education.

References

1. Baldini, I., et al.: Serverless computing: current trends and open problems. In:
   Chaudhary, S., Somani, G., Buyya, R. (eds.) Research Advances in Cloud Computing, pp. 1–20. Springer, Singapore (2017). https://doi.org/10.1007/978-981-10-
   5026-8_1
2. Fitzgerald, B., Klaas-Jan, S.: Continuous software engineering: a roadmap and
   agenda. J. Syst. Softw. **123**, 176–189 (2017)
3. Gannon, D., Barga, R., Sundaresan, N.: Cloud-native applications. IEEE Cloud
   Comput. **4**(5), 16–21 (2017)
4. Harmanen, J., Mikkonen, T.: On Polyglot programming in the web. In: Modern
   Software Engineering Methodologies for Mobile and Cloud Environments, pp. 102–
   119. IGI Global (2016)
5. Hüttermann, M.: DevOps for Developers. Apress (2012)
6. Jazayeri, M.: The education of a software engineer. In: Proceedings of the 19th
   International Conference on Automated Software Engineering (2004)
7. Maier, D., Chandramouli, B. (eds.): Special Issue on Next-Generation Stream Processing. Bulletin of the Technical Committee on Data Engineering, vol. 38, no. 4
   (2015)
8. Mäkitalo, N., Taivalsaari, A., Kiviluoto, A., Mikkonen, T., Capilla, R.: On opportunistic software reuse. Computing **102**(11), 2385–2408 (2020)
9. Masse, M.: REST API Design Rulebook: Designing Consistent RESTful Web Service Interfaces. O'Reilly Media Inc. (2011)
10. Newman, S.: Building Microservices: Designing Fine-Grained Systems. O'Reilly,
    Newton (2015)
11. Noble, J., Weir, C.: Small Memory Software: Patterns for Systems with Limited
    Memory. Addison-Wesley Longman Publishing Co., Inc. (2001)
12. Northwood, C.: The Full Stack Developer. Your Essential Guide to the Everyday
    Skills Expected of a Modern Full Stack Web Developer. Apress, Berkeley (2018).
    https://doi.org/10.1007/978-1-4842-4152-3
13. Pautasso, C., Zimmermann, O.: The web as a software connector: integration rest-
    ing on linked resources. IEEE Softw. **35**(1), 93–98 (2018)
14. Pautasso, C., Zimmermann, O., Amundsen, M., Lewis, J., Josuttis, N.: Microser-
    vices in practice, part 2: service integration and sustainability. IEEE Softw. **2**,
    97–104 (2017)

15. Ravulavaru, A.: Google Cloud AI Services Quick Start Guide: Build Intelligent Applications with Google Cloud AI Services. Packt Publishing Ltd. (2018)
16. Szyperski, C.: Objectively: components versus web services. In: Magnusson, B. (ed.) ECOOP 2002. LNCS, vol. 2374, p. 256. Springer, Heidelberg (2002). https://doi.org/10.1007/3-540-47993-7_11
17. Taivalsaari, A., Mikkonen, T., et al.: A roadmap to the programmable world: software challenges in the IoT era. IEEE Softw. **34**(1), 72–80 (2017)
18. Wasik, B.: In the Programmable World, All Our Objects Will Act as One. http://www.wired.com/2013/05/internet-of-things-2/. Accessed 13 Oct 2020

An Improving Approach for DOM-Based Web Test Suite Repair

Wei Chen[1,2], Hanyang Cao[1,2], and Xavier Blanc[1(✉)]

[1] University of Bordeaux, LaBRI, UMR 5800, 33400 Talence, France
[2] Beihang University, Beijing, China

Abstract. Developers increasingly rely on end-to-end (E2E) testing to test the web applications they develop and check whether there are no bugs from the end user's perspective. An E2E test simulates the actions performed by the user using a browser and checks whether the web application returns the expected output. It considers web applications as a black box and only knows what user actions are and what their expected output is. However, once some evolutions are implemented on a web application, user actions may change (a button has been added, deleted, or just moved to another location), which may break the E2E test. Rebuilding new test suites takes a lot of time, especially for large web applications. Therefore, E2E testing needs to evolve with the development of web applications. To help the developers who face this situation, we present an approach, named WebTestSuiteRepair (WTSR), that aims to generate and compare test suite graphs to identify candidates for broken actions, hence helps to automatically and efficiently repair the E2E tests for web applications.

Keywords: Web test repair · Test suite · Web test evolution · Test case · Automated E2E test

1 Introduction

Nowadays, web applications have to evolve frequently to satisfy their user's needs. For example, there are 228 different releases of web app Joomla[1] from July 27, 2011, to our searched day on April 18, 2019, which means 28.5 releases are submitted every year. A total of 325 releases of Moodle[2] are updated from August 19, 2002, to April 18, 2019, which means 19.1 releases are submitted every year. Each new release will improve the quality of service in a web application or update its appearance and style. To ensure a high level of quality, the developers should test the new web application release and make sure that there are no bugs [17]. To this extent, developers can choose automated end-to-end testing (automated E2E testing) [15].

---

[1] https://github.com/joomla/joomla-cms.
[2] https://github.com/moodle/moodle.

© Springer Nature Switzerland AG 2021
M. Brambilla et al. (Eds.): ICWE 2021, LNCS 12706, pp. 372–387, 2021.
https://doi.org/10.1007/978-3-030-74296-6_29

An *automated E2E test* is a test case that aims to validate a user scenario [6]. A set of test cases constitute a test suite. Several well-known E2E test frameworks exist and help developers to design and run E2E tests (i.e., Puppeteer[3], Selenium[4], Nightwatch[5], etc.).

However, the evolution performed on the web application may change its graphical interface (a button has been deleted or just moved to another location), which may interrupt the test case [13]. The broken E2E test is a testcase that cannot be played because at least one of its user actions cannot be performed. Such action is called broken action [14]. Structural and logical changes are the main causes of damage to test cases [12], and Hammoudi [8] provided more detailed reasons for breaking web testing.

Developers that face the broken test have to handle two problems. First, they have to identify the broken action and the changes in the web application that cause the E2E test to break. Second, once they identified the cause, they have to fix the E2E test and make it supporting the performed evolution. These two steps are time-consuming and error-prone. In some situations, the developers even trash their broken E2E tests and rebuild new ones [4].

For these two problems, only a few DOM-based technologies have been proposed in the web domain to automatically repair broken tests of web applications, such as Water [4] and Waterfall [7]. However, it is challenging for these DOM-based technologies because the breakages do not always occur at the same location where the test execution breaks [8]. Moreover, in many situations, there is more than one breakage in a web test case.

In addition to the web domain, there are other GUI test repair techniques, such as Sitar [5]. Sitar is one of existing automated GUI test repair techniques. However, these technologies have some difficulties in the web domain. First, it is difficult to traverse the entire website to make an event flow graph (EFG) if a web application has a large number of web pages [5]. Second, unlike desktop software, some web applications avoid overloading their websites with many requests like a robot. So the repair tool is prohibited from requesting too many web pages. Third, performing certain actions of the web test case will cause web navigation [3], which takes one to several seconds. Compared to other GUI applications, this navigation is another challenge in repairing test cases in the web domain.

In this article, we try to focus on web domains other than other GUI apps to repair DOM-based test cases. We build Test Suite Graphs (TSG) for different releases of a web application and compare these two TSGs to help developers repair their broken tests. To this extent, we propose an approach named WebTestSuiteRepair, which will compare TSGs to identify substitutes for broken actions, and hence that developers can utilize this approach to repair broken tests automatically. In this study, we make the following contributions:

– An approach to generate test suite graphs of web applications, which helps to repair web test cases.

---

[3] https://pptr.dev/.
[4] https://selenium.dev/.
[5] https://nightwatchjs.org/.

– An algorithm to automatically repair the DOM-based test suite by comparing TSGs of web applications.
– An implemented tool WTSR for testers to repair broken web test cases.
– An empirical evaluation of our approach to repair broken tests for three real web applications.

The rest of this article is structured as follows: Sect. 2 introduces the background of web test evolution. Section 3 proposes our approach to generate TSGs and determine substitutes for broken actions to repair web test cases. Section 4 presents the evaluation of our approach for repairing broken tests. Section 5 discusses related work, and Sect. 6 concludes.

2 Background and Motivation

This section gives some basic definitions for web applications and E2E tests. It then highlights how the evolution performed on a web application that may cause a test break due to broken action. To scope this article, we present the break type of DOM-based web test case that we are target to repair.

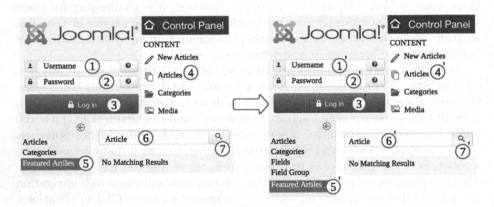

Fig. 1. Web application Joomla from release 3.6.0 (R1) to release 3.7.0 (R2).

2.1 Web Application and Evolution

Figure 1 presents the screen-shots of a real web application named Joomla[6]. This web application is a content management system (CMS), which allows its users to build websites and online applications. Figure 1 illustrates a simple evolution that changes elements of Joomla. For the sake of clarity, we will refer to these two releases of this web application as R1 and R2.

During the evolution of web application Joomla from R1 to R2, certain HTML elements have changed. The sub-menu named *Featured Articles*

---
[6] https://www.joomla.org/.

(tag ⑤ on the left of Fig. 1) in R1 has been moved to the position of tag ⑤'
in R2 (see Fig. 1). Moreover, in Fig. 1, the sub-menus named *Fields* and *Field
Groups* (above tag ⑤') are new features in R2. This is an evolution example of
web application Joomla by changing the layout in its new release.

2.2 E2E Test

To ensure web app quality, developers usually use a test suite for regression
testing. A test suite consists of a set of test cases. And each test case is an
automated E2E test. The definition of an automated E2E test is as follows.

Definition 1 (Automated E2E Test). *An automated E2E test is a test case
that composed of a sequence of **user actions** that simulate actions performed by
a user on its browser (open a page, click a button, etc.). In addition to that, the
automated E2E test is also composed of **an assertion** that checks the expected
output. A set of test cases constitute a test suite.*

```
1   puppeteer.page.type("input[name='username']", "admin")
2   puppeteer.page.type("input[name='password']", "123456")
3   puppeteer.page.click("#login")
4   puppeteer.page.click(".Articles")
5   puppeteer.page.click("#content > DIV:nth-child(3)")
6   puppeteer.page.type("input[name='search']", "Article")
7   puppeteer.page.click(".Search")
```

```
1   puppeteer.page.type("input[name='username']", "admin")
2   puppeteer.page.type("input[name='password']", "123456")
3   puppeteer.page.click("#login-button")
4   puppeteer.page.click(".Articles")
5   puppeteer.page.click("#content > DIV:nth-child(5)")
6   puppeteer.page.type("input[name='search']", "Article")
7   puppeteer.page.click(".Search")
```

Fig. 2. The test case in two releases of Joomla.

Figure 2 is a test case in two releases of Joomla. Developers write a suite of
test cases for R1 of Joomla (see a test case example at the top of Fig. 2). That
test case is consists of seven actions from line 1 to line 7. Each action corresponds
to one user's operation (see tags from ① to ⑦ in Fig. 1). From tag ① to tag ⑦,
these actions input **Username**, input **Password**, click **Login Button**, click
menu **Articles**, click sub-menu **Featured Articles**, input **Search Content**,
click **Search Button**. When this test case is executed, it will automatically
launch and run *Google Chrome* to simulate user actions on the website. Each
action in the test case can be described in JSON format[7].

---

[7] https://github.com/webautotester/scenario.

2.3 Broken Test and Action

Definition 2 (Broken E2E Test, Broken Action). *A broken E2E test is a test case that cannot be executed on a given release of a web application. A broken action is an action that cannot be performed in a broken E2E test.*

In addition, to make the scope of this study more clear, we should make a distinction between **breakage** and **error**. According to *Definition* 2, a breakage occurs that a test case T can be performed in web release R_n but break in the following web release R_{n+i} (i>0), which is caused by web evolution. Differently, an error is that a test case fails due to bugs in web applications. In this research, we focus on the breakages of test cases, not test errors. The problem of test error is in the future work plan.

In a recent study, some researchers have classified the reasons for the break of web tests [8]. They concluded that locator is the first major cause of breakage (73.62% of all causes of test breakages), and value is the second major cause of breakage (15.21% of all causes of test breakages). In this study, we focus on locator cause because it merits the greatest attention [8], and we do not target value reason because data of input is related to the backend database. For example, if the password value (see line 2 at the top of Fig. 2) is the cause of test case breakage, then repairing the test case is a huge challenge.

Further, the locator breakage can be divided into **non-selection** breakage and **mis-selection** breakage [8,10]. For non-selection breakage, a locator can target the DOM element in release R_n but is unable to select the target element in release R_{n+i} (i>0), which usually warnings that could not find the locator. For mis-selection breakage, a locator target a DOM element in release R_n but select a wrong element in release R_{n+i} (i>0), which causes the interruption of the following action or assertion.

3 WTSR: Web Test Suite Repair

This section presents our approach WebTestSuiteRepair (WTSR), which aims to repair the test suite for web applications. In this section, we first introduce an overview of WTSR and then detail all of its parts.

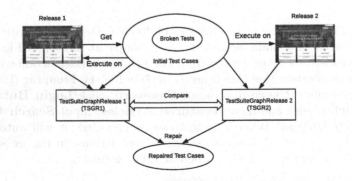

Fig. 3. The architecture of web test suite repair.

Algorithm 1. Algorithm to automatically repair web test suite

---

Require: Initial Test Suite (ITS_{set})   ▷ A set of Test Cases
Ensure: The Repaired Test Suite
1: **procedure** WEBTESTSUITEREPAIR:
2:     $TSGR1 \leftarrow CreateTSG(ITS_{set})$
3:     $TSGR2 \leftarrow CreateTSG(ITS_{set})$
4:     $TestRepair \leftarrow Compare(TSGR1, TSGR2)$
5: **end procedure**
6: **function** CREATETSG(ITS_{set})
7:     **for** $Each(action_i)$ in ITS_{set} **do**
8:         $WebPage \leftarrow browser.run(action_i)$
9:         **if** $WebPage.true$ **then**
10:             $TSG \leftarrow generateTSG(WebPage)$
11:         **else**
12:             $TSG.breakInfo \leftarrow getBreakInfo(WebPage)$
13:         **end if**
14:     **end for**
15: **end function**
16: **function** COMPARE($TSGR1, TSGR2$)
17:     $BrokenTestR2_{set} \leftarrow getBrokenTests(TSGR2)$
18:     **for** $Each(TestCase_i)$ in $BrokenTestR2_{set}$ **do**
19:         $breakLocation \leftarrow get(TestCase_i.breakLocation)$
20:         **for** $j \leftarrow 1$ to $breakLocation$ **do**
21:             $(R1CA_{set}, R2CA_{set}) \leftarrow getCA(action_i)$
22:             $CA_{set} \leftarrow compareCA(R1CA_{set}, R2CA_{set})$
23:             $OCA_{set} \leftarrow Order(CA_{set})$
24:             **for** $Each(CA_i)$ in OCA_{set} **do**
25:                 $CandiTestCase \leftarrow replace(breakAction, CA_i)$
26:                 $CandiResult \leftarrow play(CandiTestCase)$
27:             **end for**
28:         **end for**
29:     **end for**
30: **end function**

3.1 Overview

Figure 3 presents an overview of WTSR. We assume that testers capture the initial test cases from *Release* 1 of a web app. WTSR tries to execute the initial E2E tests on *Release* 1 to build the TSGR1. WTSR then runs these initial test cases on Release 2 to build the TSGR2. WTSR compares these two TSGs to repair the test suite. It repairs broken cases by utilizing a substitute to replace broken action in *Release* 2. The following subsections will present these steps in detail.

3.2 Create Test Suite Graph Release 1

In Algorithm 1, WTSR plays these initial test cases over the web application's *Release* 1 to create the TSGR1 (line 2). To create TSG, it will run each action of test case in ITS_{set} (from line 7 to line 14). In other words, it performs each action to interact with the web application. We use Puppeteer[8] to run each action and get the web page (line 8). It then generates TSGR1 in detail (line 10).

For this step to generate TSGR1 (line 10), it records the URL of each action and saves these URLs to MongoDB. It can extract the actions and links between actions from initial test cases. And, it crawls web pages to obtain DOM to extract web elements that are the parameters of the candidate actions. To generate candidate actions, we use the JS library[9] that were developed before. The test case and its running result will be saved to MongoDB (line 12). The TSG can be regarded as a 5-tuple structure <S, U, A, L, C>:

- S is a test suite that consists of a set of test cases representing all tests.
- U is a set of URLs representing all web pages of test cases.
- A is a set of actions representing object events in the URLs, and actions in different URLs are different.
- L ⊆ A × A is a set of links that may follow edges between different actions. (Ai, Aj) means Aj executes immediately after Ai.
- C is a set of candidate actions after each test action.

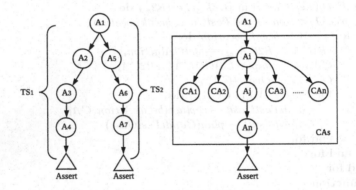

Fig. 4. The test suite graph release 1.

Now we use two similar test cases to explain 5-tuple <S, U, A, L, C> architecture of TSG. For example, TSGR1 in Fig. 4 keeps these two test cases in the mongo database. In Fig. 4, TS_1 includes A_1, A_2, A_3, A_4, and assertion. TS_2 includes A_1, A_5, A_6, A_7, and assertion. TSGR1 also keeps these actions and their links in the database. The URL of every action is stored in MongoDB. The link (A1, A2) means *Action* 2 is performed directly after *Action* 1. During the execution of the test case, WTSR crawls the candidate actions after each action and saves them in the database. For TSGR1, it is only a simple example in Fig. 4. TSGR1 is more complicated in an actual web application that contains more test cases and a lot of actions.

[8] https://github.com/puppeteer/puppeteer.
[9] https://github.com/webautotester/scenario.

3.3   Generate Test Suite Graph Release 2

In this step, we aim to generate TSGR2 by executing the test cases on web application release 2. This process for generating TSGR2 is the same as the process of creating TSGR1. In Algorithm 1, input test suite and use the same function to create TSGR2 (line 3). For all the test cases, run them on web app release 2 (from line 6 to line 15). The function to play each test case has been presented in detail in Sect. 3.2. And there appeared interruptions (lines 12) in some test cases during this process of creating TSGR2 because of the evolution of web application.

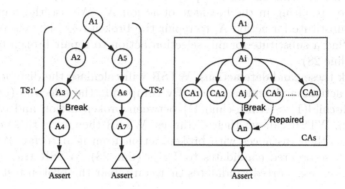

Fig. 5. The test suite graph release 2.

In Algorithm 1, after performing each action, WTSR will also crawl the web page to obtain DOM to extract web elements, which can be used to generate candidate actions. However, during the process of creating TSGR2, some test cases are broken due to web evolution. So WTSR needs to get the broken test cases and the stopped actions (lines 12). And it will repair these damaged cases in the next Sect. 3.4. For example, A_3 on the left side of Fig. 5 is a broken action that can not be performed. So TS_1' keeps the breaking information with A_3. Figure 5 presents an example of TSGR2 that needs to be replenished and updated in the next Sect. 3.4 by comparing TSGs.

3.4   Compare TSGs

After creating these two different TSGs, the next step is to compare them to repair test cases. In Algorithm 1, it compares the TSGs to find the broken tests (line 17). For these damaged tests, try to identify a substitute action from the candidate set as a replacement of broken action to repair the breaking test case (from line 18 to line 29). During the process of repairing the test case, WTSR gets the candidate action set (line 21). It then compares the candidates for different releases to get the candidate set(line 22). And WTSR orders these candidate actions (line 23) owing to that top-ranked action is more likely to be a substitute. This is because elements close to each other are more similar [9]. For instance, Action 4 is broken in Fig. 5, and we identify the substitute action CA3 from ordered candidates to repair the break test in Fig. 5.

In Algorithm 1, WTSR then tries to find the correct substitute to replace the broken path on the right side of Fig. 5. For this purpose, we present a loop in approach WTSR to try each candidate action to repair the broken test from line 24 to line 27 in Algorithm 1. And play the new case (line 26) to judge whether this replacement is correct. The function of RedoRepair is from line 19 to line 28. If we can not find the substitute action, there may be a mis-selection in previous actions. For example, the locator of action A_i in Fig. 5 does not change, but the corresponding element on the web page is different from R1. So action A_i is a mis-selection resulting in the breakage of action A_j. We use the same method to find a substitute for action A_i to repair the broken test. Therefore, we make a loop to find a substitute for mis-selection action to repair broken tests (from line 20 to line 28).

To rank these candidate actions, WTSR will calculate the distance between candidate actions and broken action. By comparing the selectors (i.e. #id-left > DIV:nth-child(1) > A:nth-child(1)) between broken action and each candidate action, WTSR can get their distances. WTSR then sorts these candidates according to their distances with broken action from near to far. WTSR then feedback these ordered candidates to TSGs (line 23). WTSR tries to identify correct action from sorted candidates that can repair the broken test (line 25).

4   Empirical Evaluation

To evaluate the feasibility and efficiency of our approach to evolving the test suite, we choose three research subjects and present a set of experiments with quantitative analysis. Then we present experimental results and threats to the validity of our approach. To evaluate the effectiveness of our approach WTSR in this study, we try to answer three research questions:

- RQ1: Is it possible to generate test suite graphs for two different releases of a web application?
- RQ2: Is it possible to automatically and efficiently repair these test cases for web applications by comparing their test suite graphs?
- RQ3: How effective is our test suite evolution method?

The experiment verification is based on three real web applications. For RQ1, we count the actions and links in each TSG. We count the candidates after each action in TSG. And we count broken tests in TSG. We also record the execution time that indicates how long it takes to create TSG. For RQ2, we count the number of repaired test cases. For RQ3, we record how long it takes to repair broken test cases.

4.1 E2E Test Subjects

Based on this research, we implemented a tool called WTSR. As shown in Table 1, we choose three web apps Joomla[10], Moodle[11], and Dolibarr[12] as our subjects of this experiment. They are real subjects that can contribute to evaluating the potential performance and efficiency of our framework in a real test environment.

Table 1. E2E test subjects of web applications

Web App	Releases	# Release 1	# Release 2
Joomla	228	3.6.0 (Jul 12, 2016)	3.7.0 (Apr 25, 2017)
Moodle	325	3.5.0 (May 16, 2018)	3.6.0 (Dec 2, 2018)
Dolibarr	112	5.0.0 (Feb 27, 2017)	6.0.0 (Aug 30, 2017)

To obtain different releases of the web applications, we checked their releases under each repository at Sourceforge and Github. They are sorted by release date, and we can get all the releases for each target web application. The second column in Table 1 presents the total release number of each web application (searched on April 18, 2019). From these releases, we randomly select two different major releases for each web application. For these two major releases, we assume that the lower is Release 1 (R1) and the higher is Release 2 (R2). In Table 1, the third column is Release 1 of each web app with its release date. The fourth column is Release 2 of each web app with its release date. Therefore, R1 and R2 of each web application are arbitrary to avoid prejudice.

4.2 Results

After obtaining two releases of each web application, we try to design the experimental process. We first committed to creating an original test suite (a set of test cases) for each web application. Then we run these test cases on two releases of each web application to build TSGs and use our approach to evolve the test suite by comparing TSGs. At last, we compare WTSR with Water [4] to validate the efficiency and correctness of our approach. After getting the results of this implementation, we then conduct a qualitative analysis in this subsection.

For RQ1: WTSR generates two TSGs for three real web apps, and the data of TSGs are shown in Table 2. The first column presents the name of web applications, such as Joomla, Moodle, and Dolibarr. The second column is the releases (Abbreviated as Re) of each web app subject. From the third column to the seventh column is the <S, U, A, L, C>. The third column is the test suite, which contains the number of test cases, including the number of broken test

---

[10] https://sourceforge.net/software/product/Joomla/.
[11] https://sourceforge.net/projects/moodle/.
[12] https://sourceforge.net/projects/dolibarr/.

Table 2. Test suite graphs of web applications

WebApp	Re	Suite(B/T)	URL(ge/up)	Action(ge/up)	Link(ge/up)	CA	Time(s)
Joomla	R1	96	50	214	205	94.8	986
	R2	38/96	28/51	142/209	145/211	97.73	845
Moodle	R1	39	27	72	77	45.47	393
	R2	36/39	5/29	10/73	7/80	35.86	201
Dolibarr	R1	47	57	130	131	29.58	423
	R2	27/47	35/55	63/132	63/134	29.57	352

cases and the total number of test cases. B represents the number of *Broken* test cases, and T represents the *Total* number of test cases in R2. For example, a total of 96 test cases have been written for Joomla R1. However, when executed on R2, 38 test cases were broken. The fourth column is the number of URLs. The same URL has been excluded, which means that the same URL can only be counted once. For example, a total of 96 test cases of Joomla executed on R1 have 50 different URLs. However, WTSR only *generates* (abbreviated as ge in Table 2) 28 URLs when performed on Joomla R2 because some URLs can not be recorded due to broken cases. When comparing TSGs, WTSR can explore more URLs by repairing broken tests. After the *update* (abbreviated as up in Table 2), there are 51 URLs of Joomla R2. The fifth column is the number of actions, and the sixth column is the number of links. The seventh column is the average number of candidate actions (CA) after each action. And the last column is the total cost time to generate TSG for each web app release. For instance, WTSR takes 986 s to create TSG for Joomla R1, including the navigation time between web pages.

The numbers of breakage for each app are different. As shown in Table 2, Joomla has 38 broken test cases over a total of 96 tests and the corresponding breaking percentage over the total number of tests is 39.58%. Moodle has a total of 39 test cases created from R1, and there are 36 breaks when they are running on R2. The breaking radio of Moodle is 92.31%. Dolibarr has 27 breaks over a total of 47 test cases and the percentage of test breakage is 57.45%. The test case was interrupted due to changes in the web application evolution, Hammoudi [8] has detailed the reasons for these breaks. The breakages show that not all the test cases are still usable for the next release when web applications evolve. This illustrates that test cases are fragile and not robust to overcome the problem of web application evolution. So it is necessary for testers to find an approach like our framework WTSR to overcome the evolution issue of test cases. Furthermore, the time cost of generating TSG is related to the number of test cases. More precisely, the time cost of generating TSG is related to the number of actions in test cases. As Table 2 depicts, the time has a linear relationship with the number of total actions. The more actions it runs, the more time it takes.

For RQ2 and RQ3: After comparing test cases and candidates in TSGs, WTSR evolves the test suite by repairing broken test cases. We count the number of

Table 3. Web application test suite repair results

WebApp	WTSR				Water			
	#(R/B)	ReRatio	Time(s)	AT(s)	#(R/B)	ReRatio	Time(s)	AT(s)
Joomla	33/38	86.84%	1182	35.81	25/38	65.79%	1073	42.92
Moodle	28/36	77.78%	674	24.07	19/36	52.78%	721	37.95
Dolibarr	22/27	81.48%	896	40.73	16/27	59.26%	834	52.13
Total	83/101	82.17%	2752	33.16	60/101	59.41%	2628	43.80

repaired tests and record the execution time. Table 3 indicates test suite repair results, including the repaired number of test cases, execution time, and repair ratios. The first column is the web app subjects. The second column shows the number (#) of test cases repaired (R) by WTSR from the broken (B) tests. The repair ratio (ReRatio) of each web app using WTSR is in the third column. The fourth column presents the total execution time for repairing broken test cases. And the fifth column is the average time (AT) to repair one test case. Table 3 also illustrates the running result of Water from column 6 to 9.

The repair time is related to the number of test cases that need to be repaired. When the number of these cases is larger, the execution time will be longer. For the repair ratio of each web app, the second column in Table 3 illustrated details. Joomla's repair ratio of broken tests is 86.84%. For web app Moodle, the ratio of repairing tests is 77.78%. And Dolibarr's percentage of test repair is 81.48%. For these three web apps, WTSR has repaired 83 cases of a total of 101 broken tests and the corresponding repair ratio is 82.17%. Water can repair 60 cases of 101 broken tests, the repair ratio is 59.41%. Water's execution time is less than WTSR, but the difference is small. Therefore, building TSGs is useful for the repair of test cases. Our approach can help testers repair broken tests effectively.

Table 4. Number of broken actions of each test case

WebApp	One	Two	Three	Four	Five	Six
Joomla	28	8	2	0	0	0
Moodle	11	13	5	6	0	1
Dolibarr	18	5	1	1	1	1
Total	57	26	8	7	1	2

Each test case may be interrupted in multiple places. Table 4 shows the number of broken actions in each test case. The second column indicates the number of test cases with one broken action. The third column is the number of test cases that have two broken actions. Take Joomla as an example, 28 test cases have one interrupted action in each test case. By observing the data in each row, the number of test cases is inversely proportional to the number of interrupts.

As the number of broken actions in each test case increase, the number of test cases decreases.

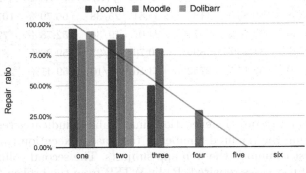

Fig. 6. The repair ratio of test case with multiple breaks.

Because there is sometimes more than one interruption in a test case, WTSR executes in a loop to fix more broken actions in the test case. Figure 6 presents the repair ratio of the test case with a different number of interrupts. The horizontal axis means the number of broken actions in each test case. And the vertical axis is the repair ratio. For example, Joomla has 28 test cases with one interrupt, 27 of which have been successfully repaired, and the repair ratio is 96.42% for the test case with one breakage. Figure 6 indicates that the repair ratio is inversely proportional to the number of broken actions. As the number of broken actions in each test case increases, the repair ratio will decrease. The test case with more than five broken actions can not be repaired anymore.

4.3   Threats to Validity

Now we discuss threats to the validity of our framework that need to be cautious about. One threat to validity is that the number of web applications and test cases is limited in the experiment. However, it is enough to prove the effectiveness of our approach in experiments, which can apply to general web test repair. Moreover, the test executions may be affected by the changes of external third-party components because some libraries are called in approach WTSR.

5   Related Work

In the past years, there are a lot of papers talking about the automatic web test. This section present the details of each related work to solve the problem of test breakage in the following.

Breakage Prevention: Leotta et al. [13] propose a voting algorithm to select the most robust DOM element locator from multi-locators to increase the robustness of the locators for web test cases. Bajaj et al. [1] improve this algorithm by generating locators from positive and negative examples of DOM elements for multiple DOM elements. Their preventive methods improve the robustness of test cases, but there are still some breakages that require the use of techniques such as WTSR to repair broken tests.

Visual-Based Web Test: Bajammal et al. [2] employ visual analysis to generate reusable web components from a mockup for web development. Stocco [16] uses a fast image-processing pipeline to analyze relevant visual pictures obtaining from test execution and suggest potential fixes of test breakages to testers. Leotta et al. [11] compare the robustness of the locators created by visual and DOM-based approaches, then compare their cost for test case maintenance during code evolution. The results of these articles show that DOM-based locators are generally more robust than visual ones, and DOM-based test cases can be developed from scratch and evolved at a lower cost. Besides, in some web evolution situations, the appearance of web pages is the same, but the corresponding selector in HTML has been changed. These broken tests still need DOM-based techniques to repair.

DOM-Based Web Test: Choudhary et al. [4] propose Water, a technique to record the changes in the two web application versions and the break reasons for broken test scripts, which can be applied to repair broken tests. By comparing these two executions of different web releases and analyzing broken reasons, it then recommends repair suggestions to users. Waterfall [7] focuses on repair broken tests of fine-grained versions between main releases of web apps, which is a supplement to Water. Water's technique is similar to our approach, it introduces mis-selection breakage in content, but it is not solved in their algorithm. Moreover, it only repairs the test case with one break, but a test case may break in multiple locations in some situations. To improve it, we generate TSGs to automatically repair tests that including mis-selection breakage, and repair the test with multiple break locations.

6 Conclusion

With the development of web applications, some damaged test cases need to be repaired. So test cases need to evolve according to the evolution of web applications. For this reason, we proposed a novel framework WTSR that efficiently evolves test cases by repairing broken tests. Our experiments show that: (1) the cost of time spent to build TSGs is related to the number of actions, and they have a positive linear correlation; (2) building TSGs is useful for the evolution of test cases; (3) the key issue in the evolution of web testing is to repair broken tests; (4) the more actions break in a test case, the harder it is to repair this case; (5) WTSR is effective to repair test case for web apps. Therefore, WTSR can evolve test cases corresponding to the evolution of web applications. We believe that our approach can apply to general web test evolution, which is helpful to developers to repair test cases.

In our future work, we plan to: (1) Collect user feedbacks on our technique to make our approach better for web test repair; (2) Experiment our approach to the web applications with bugs to study how do bugs affect the usefulness of this test repair approach; (3) Do a case study of all the web test repair tools by comparing their efficiency; (4) Update our algorithm to continuously improve the efficiency of test suites repair and try to deal with value-caused breakages.

References

1. Bajaj, K., Pattabiraman, K., Mesbah, A.: Synthesizing web element locators (t). In: 2015 30th IEEE/ACM International Conference on Automated Software Engineering (ASE), pp. 331–341. IEEE (2015)
2. Bajammal, M., Mazinanian, D., Mesbah, A.: Generating reusable web components from mockups. In: Proceedings of the 33rd ACM/IEEE International Conference on Automated Software Engineering, pp. 601–611 (2018)
3. Biagiola, M., Stocco, A., Mesbah, A., Ricca, F., Tonella, P.: Web test dependency detection. In: Proceedings of the 2019 27th ACM Joint Meeting on European Software Engineering Conference and Symposium on the Foundations of Software Engineering, pp. 154–164 (2019)
4. Choudhary, S.R., Zhao, D., Versee, H., Orso, A.: Water: Web application test repair. In: Proceedings of the First International Workshop on End-to-End Test Script Engineering, pp. 24–29. ACM (2011)
5. Gao, Z., Chen, Z., Zou, Y., Memon, A.M.: SITAR: GUI test script repair. IEEE Trans. Software Eng. **42**(2), 170–186 (2015)
6. Guarnieri, M., Tsankov, P., Buchs, T., Dashti, M.T., Basin, D.: Test execution checkpointing for web applications. In: Proceedings of the 26th ACM SIGSOFT International Symposium on Software Testing and Analysis, pp. 203–214. ACM (2017)
7. Hammoudi, M., Rothermel, G., Stocco, A.: WATERFALL: an incremental approach for repairing record-replay tests of web applications. In: Proceedings of the 2016 24th ACM SIGSOFT International Symposium on Foundations of Software Engineering, pp. 751–762. ACM (2016)
8. Hammoudi, M., Rothermel, G., Tonella, P.: Why do record/replay tests of web applications break? In: 2016 IEEE International Conference on Software Testing, Verification and Validation (ICST), pp. 180–190. IEEE (2016)
9. Heil, S., Bakaev, M., Gaedke, M.: Measuring and ensuring similarity of user interfaces: The impact of web layout. In: International Conference on Web Information Systems Engineering (2016)
10. Imtiaz, J., Sherin, S., Khan, M.U., Iqbal, M.Z.: A systematic literature review of test breakage prevention and repair techniques. Inf. Softw. Technol. **113**, 1–19 (2019)
11. Leotta, M., Clerissi, D., Ricca, F., Tonella, P.: Visual vs. DOM-based web locators: an empirical study. In: Casteleyn, S., Rossi, G., Winckler, M. (eds.) ICWE 2014. LNCS, vol. 8541, pp. 322–340. Springer, Cham (2014). https://doi.org/10.1007/978-3-319-08245-5_19

12. Leotta, M., Clerissi, D., Ricca, F., Tonella, P.: Approaches and tools for automated end-to-end web testing. In: Advances in Computers, vol. 101, pp. 193–237. Elsevier (2016)
13. Leotta, M., Stocco, A., Ricca, F., Tonella, P.: Using multi-locators to increase the robustness of web test cases. In: 2015 IEEE 8th International Conference on Software Testing, Verification and Validation (ICST), pp. 1–10. IEEE (2015)
14. Leotta, M., Stocco, A., Ricca, F., Tonella, P.: ROBULA+: an algorithm for generating robust Xpath locators for web testing. J. Softw. Evol. Process **28**(3), 177–204 (2016)
15. Stocco, A., Leotta, M., Ricca, F., Tonella, P.: APOGEN: automatic page object generator for web testing. Software Qual. J. **25**(3), 1007–1039 (2017)
16. Stocco, A., Yandrapally, R., Mesbah, A.: Visual web test repair. In: Proceedings of the 2018 26th ACM Joint Meeting on European Software Engineering Conference and Symposium on the Foundations of Software Engineering, pp. 503–514. ACM (2018)
17. Tonella, P., Ricca, F., Marchetto, A.: Recent advances in web testing. In: Advances in Computers, vol. 93, pp. 1–51. Elsevier (2014)

Communicating Web Vessels: Improving the Responsiveness of Mobile Web Apps with Adaptive Redistribution

Kijin An[(✉)] and Eli Tilevich

Software Innovations Lab, Virginia Tech, Blacksburg, USA
{ankijin,tilevich}@vt.edu

Abstract. In a mobile web app, a browser-based client communicates with a cloud-based server across the network. An app is statically divided into client and server functionalities, so the resulting division remains fixed at runtime. However, if such static division mismatches the current network conditions and the device's processing capacities, app responsiveness and energy efficiency can deteriorate rapidly. To address this problem, we present Communicating Web Vessels (CWV), an adaptive redistribution framework that improves the responsiveness of full-stack JavaScript mobile apps. Unlike standard computation offloading, in which client functionalities move to run on the server, CWV's redistribution is bidirectional. Without any preprocessing, CWV enables apps to move any functionality from the server to the client and vice versa at runtime, thus adapting to the ever-changing execution environment of the web. Having moved to the client, former server functionalities become regular local functions. By monitoring the network, CWV determines if a redistribution would improve app performance, and then analyzes, transforms, sandboxes, and moves functions and program state at runtime. An evaluation with third-party mobile web apps shows that CWV optimizes their performance for dissimilar network conditions and client devices. As compared to their original versions, CWV-powered web apps improve their performance (i.e., latency, energy consumption), particularly when executed over limited networks.

Keywords: Mobile web apps · Javascript · Dynamic adaptation · Program analysis & transformation · Web frameworks

1 Introduction

Mobile web apps are fundamentally distributed: browser-based clients communicate with cloud-based servers over the available networks. Distribution assigns an app component to run either on the client or on the server. Some distribution strategies are predefined; for example, user interfaces must display on the client. Other distribution strategies aim at improving performance; for example, a powerful cloud-based server can execute some functionality faster than can a mobile

© Springer Nature Switzerland AG 2021
M. Brambilla et al. (Eds.): ICWE 2021, LNCS 12706, pp. 388–403, 2021.
https://doi.org/10.1007/978-3-030-74296-6_30

device. Network communication significantly complicates the device/ cloud performance equation. For a client to execute a cloud-based functionality, it needs to pass parameters and receive results over the network. Transferring data across a network imposes latency and energy consumption costs. For low-latency, high-bandwidth networks, these costs are negligible. For limited networks, these costs can grow rapidly and unexpectedly. The overhead of network transfer can not only negate the performance benefits of remote cloud-based execution, but also strain the mobile device's energy budget. Operating over limited high-loss networks requires retransmission, which consumes additional battery power [17]. Hence, fixed distribution can hurt app responsiveness and energy efficiency.

Changing the locality of a software component can be non-trivial due to the differences in latency, concurrency, and failure modes between centralized and distributed executions [18]. Researchers and practitioners alike have thoroughly explored the task of rendering local components remote. *Cloud offloading* moves local functionalities to execute remotely in the cloud [4,9,15,19]. Nevertheless, standard offloading is *unidirectional*: it can only move a client functionality to run on a server. If mobile web apps are to flexibly adapt to the ever-changing execution environment of the web, client and server functionalities may need to adaptively switch places at runtime.

We address this problem by adaptively redistributing the client and server functionalities of already distributed applications to optimize their performance and energy efficiency. Our approach works with full-stack JavaScript apps, written entirely (i.e., client and server) in JavaScript. By dynamically instrumenting and monitoring app execution, our approach detects when network conditions deteriorate. In response, it moves the JavaScript code, program state, and SQL statements of a remote service to the client, so the service can be invoked as a regular local function. To prevent cross-site scripting (XSS) or SQL injection attacks, the moved code is sandboxed, creating a separate context with reduced privileges for safe execution in the mobile browser. Thus, the same functionality can be invoked locally or remotely as determined by the current execution environment. To the best of our knowledge, our approach is the first one to support *bidirectional dynamic redistribution of distributed mobile web apps*. Moreover, to take advantage of our approach, a mobile app needs not be written against any specific API or be pre-processed prior to execution.

We called the reference implementation of our approach—Communicating Web Vessels (CWV)—due to its reminiscence of *communicating vessels*, a physical phenomenon of connected vessels with dissimilar volumes of liquid reaching an equilibrium. CWV balances mobile execution by adaptively redistributing functionalities between the server and the client, thus optimizing app performance for the current execution environment. Our contribution is three-fold:

1. A novel bidirectional redistribution approach that dynamically adapts distributed mobile apps for the current execution environment.
2. A reference implementation of our approach, CWV, that works with increasingly popular full-stack JavaScript mobile apps. Requiring no pre-processing,

CWV dynamically adapts apps by redistributing their JavaScript code, program state, and SQL statements at runtime.
3. A comprehensive evaluation with 23 remote services of 8 real-world apps. To assess the effectiveness of CWV's adaptations, we report on their impact on execution latency and energy consumption.

The rest of this paper is structured as follows. Section 2 motivates and explains our approach. Section 3 describes the reference implementation of our approach. Section 4 presents our evaluation results. Section 5 compares our approach to the related state of the art. Section 6 presents concluding remarks.

2   Approach

We first present a motivating example, then give an overview of CWV, and finally discuss our performance model.

2.1   Motivating Example

Consider *Bookworm*, an e-reader app for reading books on mobile devices. The app also provides text analysis features that report various statistical facts about the read books. The app is distributed: the client hosts the user interface; the server hosts a repository of available books and a collection of text processing routines. The current architecture of *Bookworm* is well-optimized for a typical deployment environment: a resource-constrained mobile device and a powerful server, connected to each other over a reliable network. For limited networks, the performance equation can change drastically. Hence, to exhibit the best performance for all combinations of client and server devices and network connections, the app would have to be distributed in a variety of versions. Even if developers were willing to expend a high programming effort to produce and maintain all these versions, network conditions can change rapidly while the app is in operation, necessitating a different client/server decomposition. Clearly, achieving optimal performance under these conditions would require dynamic adaptation.

Our framework, CWV, can adapt *Bookworm*, so its remote text processing routines could migrate to the client at runtime for execution. CWV monitors the network conditions, migrating server-side functions to the client and reverting the execution back to the server, as determined by the network conditions. The app can start executing with all the text processing routines running on the server. Once the network connection deteriorates, a portion of these routines would be transferred over the network to the client, so they could execute locally. CWV's static and dynamic analyses determine the dependencies across server functions and their individual computational footprints. This information parameterizes CWV's performance model, which determines which part of server functionality needs to migrate to the client under the current network conditions.

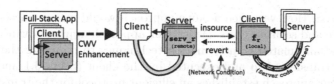

Fig. 1. Conceptual view of Communicating Web Vessels (CWV)

2.2   Approach: Communicating Web Vessels

To optimize the performance of mobile web apps for the current network conditions, CWV continuously applies the two operations depicted in Fig. 1:

1. $f_r = insource(/service\_r)$: The client requests that the server transfer the remote functionality($/service\_r$)'s partition f_r to the client.
2. $revert(f_r)$: The client stops locally invoking the insourced partition f_r, and starts remotely invoking its original server version $/service\_r$.

2.3   Reasoning About Responsiveness

Responsiveness is a subjective criteria: application is responsive if the user perceives the time taken to execute app functionalities as "short". For this reason, we define the responsiveness of a remote execution as the total execution time that elapses between the client invoking a remote functionality and the results presented to the user. We define the response time of a remote functionality f_r as $RT(f_r)$. The $RT(f_r)$ mainly depends on the "server speed" and "network speed" parameters. We simplify the responsiveness of f_r by means of the execution time f_r on the server $T_{server}(f_r)$ and the remaining remote execution overheads. The resulting Round Trip Time (RTT) is highly affected by the current network conditions. To estimate the network conditions, CWV utilizes the RTT^{net} metrics, detailed in Sect. 3.3.

$$RT(f_r) = \begin{cases} T_{server}(f_r) + RTT^{net} & \text{remote exec.,} \\ T_{client}(f_r) & \text{local exec.} \end{cases} \tag{1}$$

If f_r is executed locally, the responsiveness becomes the execution time f_r on the client $T_{client}(f_r)$.

3   Reference Implementation

To move a server-side functionality to the client at runtime, one has to migrate both the relevant source code and program state, which has to be captured and restored at the client. JavaScript has a powerful facility, the `eval` function, which executes a JavaScript program passed to it as a string argument. One could simply duplicate the entire server-side code and its state, passing them to a client-side eval. However, such a naïve approach would incur unacceptably high performance and security costs. Hence, our approach applies advanced program analysis and automated transformation techniques to minimize the amount of code to be transferred to and executed by the client (Sects. 3.1 and 3.2). Furthermore, our approach establishes an efficient protocol for the transformed app to switch between different execution modes (Sect. 3.3), transferring the relevant code correctly and safely (Sects. 3.4 and 3.5).

3.1 Analyzing Full-Stack JavaScript App

Server code comprises business logic and middleware libraries. The server-side business logic can include database access routines. The portion that needs to be insourced is business logic only. In other words, business logic must be reliably separated from all middleware-related functionality. To that end, CWV identifies the entry and exit statements of the business logic portion and then extracts all the code executed between these statements, converting that code to a new regular JavaScript function. All the dependent code of this new function is also extracted and transferred, thus producing a self-sufficient execution unit.

The specific steps are as follows. First, CWV normalizes the server code to facilitate the process of separating its business logic from middleware functionality. Then, CWV locates the statements that "unmarshal" the *client parameters* and "marshal" the *result* of executing the business logic. CWV automatically identifies these statements by capturing the client server HTTP traffic and instrumenting code at the server and at the client (Fig. 2-(a)). To that end, CWV uses Jalangi [14], a state-of-the-art dynamic analyzer for JavaScript. CWV modifies the built-in Jalangi's callback API calls to be able to detect the events that correspond to the "unmarshal/marshal" statements. By following these steps, CWV identifies the specific lines of code and variables that correspond to the entry and exit points of remote invocations, both at the server and the client.

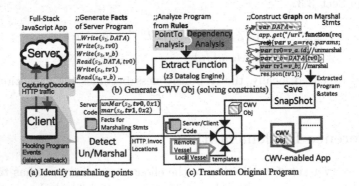

Fig. 2. Automated program transformation for enabling CWV

The statements executed between these points comprise the server-side business logic and its dependent program states that may need to be moved to the client at runtime. To identify a subset of statements that satisfies a pair of entry/exit statements, CWV follows a strategy similar to that of other declarative program analysis frameworks that analyze JavaScript code by means of a datalog engine [2,16]. CWV encodes the declarative facts that specify the behavior of JavaScript statements of server program: 1) declarations of variables/functions, 2) their read/writes operations, and 3) control flow graphs. The dependency analysis query constructs a dependency graph between statements. Then, CWV solves constraints describing these points with the z3 engine [5] and then extracts them into a CWV-specific object that is movable between vessels (Fig. 2-(b)).

Some server-side program statements use third-party APIs, whose libraries and frameworks are deployed only at the server. CWV provides domain-specific handling of the statements that interact with relational databases. In particular, some statements interacting with a server-side relational database cannot be directly migrated to the client. As a specific example, consider the statement `mysql_server.query(SQL_STATEMENT)`, which queries the server-side MySQL database engine. Mobile clients can also use relational databases, but of a different type, a browser-hosted SQL engine. Hence, the database-related statement above should be replaced with `a_mobile_engine(SQL_STATEMENT)`. To identify such database-related statements, CWV instruments all function invocations whose arguments are SQL commands by using callback API of Jalangi. Despite the fragility of relying on the usage of SQL commands, our approach presents a practical solution for supporting domain-specific server-to-client migrations. Finally, CWV transforms the identified entry/exit points at the client and server sides to insert the CWV functionality with the local and remote vessels respectively that we explain in the next section (Fig. 2-(c)).

3.2   Transforming Programs to Enable CWV

CWV enhances application source code to enable its transformation as follows.

Client Enhancements. CWV transforms the identified HTTP invocation in the client program to be able to CWV's functionality as follow. The CWV-enabled client can operate and switch between these two modes: *Original* and *Local.* In *Original* mode, the app operates the original remote execution and can switch to Local mode by means of *Insourcing.* The *Local* mode designates that the local version of the insourced remote functions is to be invoked and can revert to the original mode by means of *Reverting* (See Fig. 3). To switch to a mode, the client invokes `fuzzMode(mode)` that simply fuzzes a certain parameter of the HTTP command that invokes the original remote service name. For instance, the client can dynamically fuzz a remote service `"/a_service"` (Original Request) into `"/a_service?CWVmode=Local"` (Local). And the app initiates the movement of the relevant remote server code and execution states $rcwv$ to the client by fuzzing the original invocation into `"/a_service?CWVmode=Insourcing"` (Insourcing Request).

Insourcing. CWV moves a set of received server statements into a client's container, referred to as the *local vessel*. Initially, the local vessel is empty. When the client device determines to switch from the *Original* mode into the *Local* mode, the app issues the Insourcing Request and then invokes the `moveToLocalVessel (rcwv)` call, only then adding received server code and state to the local vessel. The client and server share all the referenced names for global entries added to the local vessels. To that end, CWV also adds a special-purpose global object for the client, $lcwv$. This object is used for storing functions and other JavaScript objects received from the server[1]. Finally, the app fuzzes the HTTP command into Local `"CWVmode=Local"` to change the current mode. After that, invoking the `rebalance()` function compares the local replica's execution time with that of its original remote version.

Reverting. If the local execution stops being advantageous, the app with *Local* mode reverts to *Original* mode and clears the local vessel with `clearLocalVessel()`, overriding the local vessel into the empty function again. And then, the app switches the mode by fuzzing HTTP command into the original mode.

Server Enhancements. In a CWV-enabled app, the server part can operate in one of three modes to respond the client's requests: *Original*, *Insourcing*, and *Local*. With the detected entry/exit points of a remote functionality, CWV transforms it to be able to detect the mode switching queries and switch to the client-requested modes. The *Original* mode refers to the original unmodified execution, with the exception for the profiling of the time taken to execute the program statements that implement business logic $T_{server}(f_r)$ of the Eq. (1). The client uses resulting performance profiles to ascertain the current network conditions RTT^{net} from the measured response time $RT(f_r)$. And $T_{server}(f_r)$ will be used to determine a threshold when to switch modes.

In the *Insourcing* mode, the server responds to the client's special insourcing query by serializing the relevant portions of a given remote functionality into a JSON string. To that end, CWV calls $saveSnapshot(f_r)$, whose invocation creates a snapshot of the remote functionality f_r. CWV adds to the server part a special-purpose global object, $rcwv$, which represents a *remote vessel*. This object's properties contain the extracted functions, $rcwv.main, rcwv.$ $ftns[0], \cdots, rcwv.ftns[k]$ and their corresponding saved states for global variables $rcwv.gvars[0], \cdots, rcwv.gvars[l]$. To migrate f_r with database dependent statements, CWV takes a snapshot of database's table in terms of SQL commands to enable restoration in the client $rcwv.sql[0], \cdots, rcwv.sql[m]$. To implement $saveSnapshot(f_r)$, CWV instruments 1) the declarations of global variables and 2) *Call Expressions* of embedded SQL statements extracted by the constraints solving phrase. Finally, in the *Local* mode, the server executes no

---

[1] The properties of $lcwv$ are the same as of the remote object $rcwv$.

business logic, but responds to periodic pings from the client. Based on the roundtrip time of these pings, the client monitors the network conditions to detect if the *Local* mode execution no longer provides any performance advantages and then switches the app to the *Original* mode.

3.3 Updating Modes and Cutoff Latency

The transition diagram in Fig. 3 shows how an app can transition between different modes. CWV-enabled client always starts in the Original mode. An insourcing request issued in the Original mode can be either fulfilled (i.e., switching to the Local mode) or declined (i.e., continuing to execute remotely in the Original mode), with the latter incurring a large performance overhead. To avoid this overhead, the system determines the optimal time window for issuing "Insourcing Request" as soon as the app is automatically initialized with a couple of original executions. The procedure that determines the window is as follows. First, the client profiles both $RT(f_r)$ and $T_{server}(f_r)$ by means of multiple "Original Requests" during the initialization (Sect. 3.2). After that, the procedure invokes the "Insourcing Request" and extrapolates how much time it would take to execute the same business logic locally $T_{client}(f_r)$.

Estimating Network Delay. CWV-enabled mobile clients continuously monitor the underlying network conditions. The client collects the RTT_{raw}^{net} metric that represents raw network delay. Specifically, the client is continuously monitoring the RTT_{raw}^{net} by subtracting $T(f_r)$ from $RT(f_r)$, which are obtained from the server. Since the raw roundtrip is subject to sudden spikes [8], CWV filters out such temporary fluctuations by applying an adaptive filter [11], which cal-

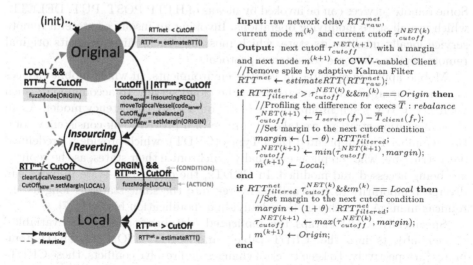

Fig. 3. Transition Diagram for CWV-enabled Client (left). Algorithm for updating cutoffs and modes (right).

culates the covariance matrices and noise values for RTT^{net}_{raw} and then estimates the RTT^{net} metric in Eq. (1).

Cutoff Network Latency. The resulting difference between the local and remote execution times is used as the threshold that determines when switching to the Local mode would become advantageous from the performance standpoint. In other words, the difference value is compared with the overhead of network communication, and when the latter starts exceeding the former, the app switches to the Local mode. We define this network condition as *cutoff network latency*, τ^{NET}_{cutoff}. Thus, a CWV-enabled app obtains this threshold as soon as it start executing, and then stays in the *Original* mode until reaching the *cutoff*. Then, it tries switching to the Local mode. Because this request is executed only upon reaching the *cutoff*, it is more likely to be fulfilled as offering better performance.

Since switching between modes incurs communication and processing costs, frequent switching in response to insignificant network changes should be prevented. To that end, the *margin* parameter expresses by how much the network conditions need to change and remain changed. The algorithm in Fig. 3 explains how the *margin* and the current cutoff latency $\tau^{NET(k)}_{cutoff}$ determine the next cutoff latency $\tau^{NET(k+1)}_{cutoff}$. The margin parameter θ prevents switching in response to insignificant $\tau^{NET(k)}_{cutoff}$ changes. After switching to the Local mode, the app periodically pings the network to determine if the current conditions are advantageous for reverting to the Original remote mode.

3.4 Synchronizing States

Some remote services can be invoked by means of HTTP POST, PUT, DELETE, which are all state-modifying operations. Invoking an insourced stateful remote service locally modifies its state, which must be synchronized with its original remote version via some consistency protocol.

Mobile apps are operated in volatile environments, in which mobile devices become temporarily disconnected from the cloud server. To accommodate such volatility, CWV's synchronization is based on a weak consistency model. As an implementation strategy, we take advantage of a proven weak consistency solution, Conflict-Free Replicated Data Types (CRDT), which provide a predefined data structure, whose replicas eventually synchronize their states, as the replicas are being accessed and modified. In CRDTs, the concurrent state updates can diverge temporarily to eventually converge into the same state, as long as the replicas manage to exchange their individual modification histories [7].

Specifically, CWV wraps the replicated 'database' and 'global variables' of *cwv* objects into the 'CRDT-Table', and 'CRDT-JSON' of CRDT templates[2], respectively. To keep track of changes and resolve conflicts, these CRDT-

---

[2] https://github.com/automerge/automerge.

structures provide the API calls `getChanges` and `applyChanges`. By continuously applying/transmitting the reported changes, the device-based clients and the cloud-based server maintain their individual modification histories and exchange them, thus eventually converging to the same state. To that end, the cloud server periodically sends its state changes on $rcwv$ to each client, while each client starts sending its state changes on $lcwv$ to the cloud server, as soon as this client reverts to executing remotely.

3.5 Sandboxing Insourced Code

Whenever code needs to be moved across hosts, the move can give rise to vulnerabilities unless special care is taken. The issue of insourcing JavaScript code from the server to the client is security sensitive. Server-side code has several privileges that cannot be provided by mobile browsers. In addition, as it is being transferred, the insourced code can be tempered with to inject attacks. Finally, the transferred segments of server-side database can be accessed by a malicious client-side actor. To mitigate these vulnerabilities, the insourced code is granted the least number of privileges required for it to carry out its functionality. To that end, we *sandbox* the insourced code. Specifically, CWV's sandboxing is applied to the entire local vessel. The insourced functionality has exactly one entry point through which it can be invoked. The sandbox guards the insourced execution from performing operations that require escalating privileges. Finally, because the insourced database data cannot be accessed directly, malicious parties would not be able to exfiltrate it.

As a specific sandboxing mechanism, we take advantage of *iframe*, which has become a standard feature of modern browsers. An iframe creates a new nested browser context, separate from the global scope. Operating in a separate context precludes any shared state between the insourced code and the original client-based code. In addition, HTML5 supports the `sandbox` attribute to further restrict what iframes are allowed to execute[3]. It protects the client from the vulnerability related to client XSS. For instance, a sandboxed iframe is prohibited from accessing `window.localStorage[..]`.

4 Evaluation

Our evaluation seeks answers to the following questions:

- **RQ1:—Redistribution Adaptivity for different Devices:** How beneficial is CWV's redistribution for different mobile devices?
- **RQ2:—Redistribution Adaptivity for Networks:** How beneficial is CWV's redistribution for different networks?
- **RQ3:—Energy Savings:** How does CWV's redistribution affect the energy consumption of mobile devices?
- **RQ4:—Overheads:** When integrated with mobile apps, what is the impact of CWV on their performance?

---

[3] https://developer.mozilla.org/en-US/docs/Web/HTML/Element/iframe.

4.1 Device Choice Impact

Dataset. Our evaluation subjects are 23 remote services of 8 full-stack applications, 5 real-world full-stack mobile JavaScript applications, and 3 JavaScript distributed system benchmarks [19]. These subject apps use different middleware frameworks to implement their client/server (*tier-1/-2*) communication and database (*tier-3*), with these frameworks being most popular in the JavaScript ecosystem.

To that end, we searched the results based on combinations of keywords for popular server and client HTTP middleware frameworks, curated by the community. For server-side keywords, we used 'Express', 'Restify', etc., while for client-side keywords we used 'Ajax', 'Angular', etc. Table 1 summarizes their names and the number of source files; 4 subject applications contain database-dependent code. To answer **RQ1**, we tested how the introduced network delays affect different devices. At launch time for each device, CWV automatically calculates the *cutoff network latency* and applies it when scheduling mode switches to minimize the switching overhead. For example, CWV determined the cutoff network latency for the remote service "/hbone" as 26ms for device 1 (D1) in Table 1, having profiled the execution time at the server ($T_{server}(\text{"/hbone"})$) and the client ($T_{client}^{D1}(\text{"/hbone"})$) as 14ms and 40ms, respectively. Device 1 is a Qualcomm Snapdragon 616 (8 × 1.5 GHz),

Table 1. Subject remote services

Subject # of files	Remote Services	τ_{cutoff}^{D1} (msec)	τ_{cutoff}^{D2} (msec)
Bookworm (*729 files*)	/ladypet	176ms	421ms
	/thedea	1120ms	2332ms
	/thered	158ms	424ms
	/thegift	97ms	120ms
	/bigtrip	146ms	224ms
	/offshore	619ms	1528ms
	/wallp	146ms	458ms
	/thecask	90ms	102ms
DonutShop (*4.9k files*)	/Donut	0.66ms	1.54ms
	/Donut:id	0.71ms	2.2ms
	/Empls	0.55ms	1.33ms
	/Empls:id	0.81ms	1.23ms
recipebook (*8k files*)	/recipe	0.7ms	1.66ms
	/recipe:id	0.68ms	1.1ms
	/ingts/:id	0.82ms	2.3ms
	/dirs/:id	0.75ms	2.1ms
pstgr-sql (*4k files*)	/user	1.33ms	2.71ms
	/user:id	1.72ms	2.92ms
chem-rules 2.8k files	/hbone	26ms	59ms
	/molec	131ms	202ms
Benchmark in [19] (*117 files*)			
str-fasta	/str-fasta	656ms	1424ms
fannk	/fannk	2576ms	4982ms
s-norm	/s-norm	1896ms	4873ms

and Device 2 is an A8-iphone 6 (2 × 1.4 GHz); Device 1 outperforms Device 2. The server is an Intel desktop (i7-7700 4 × 3.6 GHz). We natively build the subject web apps (JavaScript, html, and CSS) for iOS and Android by using Apache Cordova, a cross-platform development framework. Table 1 demonstrates that the *cutoff latency* of Device 2 (τ_{cutoff}^{D2}) is always larger than that of Device 1 (τ_{cutoff}^{D1}).

4.2 Network Latency Impact

To answer **RQ2**, we set up a test-bed for evaluating network latency impact (See Fig. 5-(a)). Even though, network latency can be changed by controlling RSSI levels, we change network conditions explicitly by means of an application-level network emulator[4]. Then, we examine how CWV reacts by redistributing the running applications. In these experiments, the server and the mobile device are connected with a wireless router. We establish a high-speed wireless link between the router and the device (–55dBm or better). By configuring the router to different delays, we simulate different network conditions in the increasing order of delay. Our test-bed has a minimum delay of about 100ms for the simulator's zero delay. Therefore, our starting point is 100ms, with the delays increased in the increments of 20m, 50ms, and 100ms, based on the amount of *cutoff network latency* for each subject. For each increment, we measure the average delay in the execution of our subject applications (response time or responsiveness of a functionality), run in two configurations: (1) the original unmodified version (**Before**), (2) dynamically redistributed with CWV version (**CWV**). Figure 4 shows the performance results.

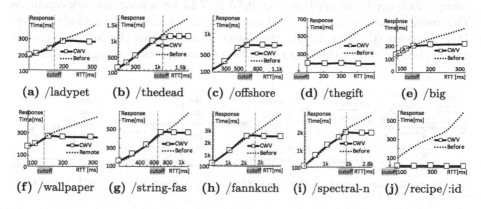

(a) /ladypet   (b) /thedead   (c) /offshore   (d) /thegift   (e) /big

(f) /wallpaper   (g) /string-fas   (h) /fannkuch   (i) /spectral-n   (j) /recipe/:id

Fig. 4. Client's responsiveness comparisons. Cutoff equals to τ^{D1}_{cutoff} in Table 1.

Across all experimental subjects, the CWV-enabled configuration consistently outperforms the original version, once the network latency surpasses the *cutoff network latency* mark. Once the network delay reaches the *cutoff network*, the difference in performance starts increasing by a large margin, as accessing any remote functionality becomes prohibitively expensive. Before reaching the *cutoff network* mark, the majority of CWV-enabled apps and their original version exhibit comparable performance since two versions are operated in remote execution. When operating over a high-speed network, CWV-enabled apps remain in the original mode due to the remote execution's performance advantages. Some subjects consistently exhibit better performance when executed locally. These subjects with their relatively low utilization of server resources are better off not making any remote invocations, as the overhead of network delays is not offset by the server's superior processing capacity.

---

[4] https://github.com/h2non/toxy.

4.3   Energy Consumption

Next, we evaluate how much energy is consumed by a mobile device executing CWV-enabled and original versions of the same subjects (**RQ3**). We profile the energy consumption of Android devices with a Qualcomm's Trepn-Profiler. We executed each subject 100 times and collected the profiled results for power (mW). Figure 5 shows the obtained samples of the power measurements over time. To test the consumed energy under a low speed network environment, we placed the Android client device far from the wireless router, so the signal strength level (RSSI) was -75dBm. The resulting energy profiles in Fig. 5 show that CWV always uses more power than the original version despite shortening the execution time. Remote execution consumes no device power for executing the business logic, even if it takes much longer for the client to receive the results. By removing the need to communicate with the server, our approach shortens the overall execution time. Compared to the original version, our approach improves energy efficiency by as much as from **9.7J** to **74J** for a poor network condition. This result is not unexpected, as a large RTT causes longer idle periods between TCP windows [6]. Even tough, the device switches into the low power mode during the idle states, the longer execution consumes more energy overall.

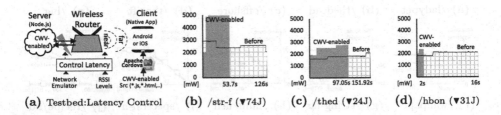

(a) Testbed:Latency Control   **(b)** /str-f (▼74J)   **(c)** /thed (▼24J)   **(d)** /hbon (▼31J)

Fig. 5. Testbed and consumed energy

4.4   Communication Overhead

To insource server execution, CWV serializes relevant code and state to transfer and reproduce at the client. To evaluate the resulting communicating overhead (**RQ4**), we compared the amount of network traffic during the regular remote execution for unmodified version (Tr_{reg}) vs. the additional traffic resulting from CWV insourcing server execution (Tr_{cwv}).

Among our subjects, the Bookworm app exhibits the largest of Tr_{orig}, as this app's remote services need to transfer not only the book content but also the statistical information extracted from that content. Whereas, the med-chem app shows the largest of Tr_{cwv}, as CWV needs to replicate all server-side DB entries. However, the transmitting overhead is occurred only once at initialization as these services are stateless. The resulting overall overhead ratio Tr_{cwv}/Tr_{reg} turned out to be **2.4** on

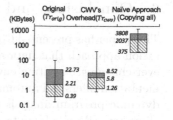

Fig. 6. CWV's overhead

average for our subjects (Fig. 6). To quantify the benefits of CWV's insourcing transferring only the necessary code and state, we also measured the overhead of the naïve approach, which transfers the entire server code and state to the client. The performance overhead of transferring everything is about two orders of magnitude slower than CWV, an unacceptable slowdown for any practical purposes (Fig. 6).

5   Related Work

Program Synthesis and Transformation: CWV automatically identifies a remote service's business functionality that satisfies the client's input and server's output constraints, akin to program synthesis systems, concerned with producing a program that satisfies a given set of input/output relationships. CodeCarbon-Reply [15] and Scalpel [4] support for programmer this functionality by means of manually annotating the code regions to integrate the transferred functionality. In contrast, CWV is both fully automated and dynamic, integrating program code and state at runtime. CanDoR [1] fixes the bug in the centralized variant version with existing tools, then CanDoR applies the resulting fixes to the original distributed app by using program transformation.

Adaptive Middleware: Several middleware-based approaches have been proposed to reduce the costs of invoking remote functionalities. APE [12] defers remote invocations until some other apps switch the device's state to network activation. DR-OSGi [10] enhances middleware mechanisms with resilience against network volatility. D-Goldilocks [3] adapts distributed web apps to adjust their distribution granularity to improve both performance and invocation costs. CWV is yet another middleware, albeit tailored for the realities of adapting mobile apps by transforming their code at runtime.

Executing Code in a Mobile Browser: Ours is not the only approach that moves server-side components and data to the client. Meteor [13] transparently replicates given parts of a server-side MongoDB at the client, so these parts can be used for offline operations. Browserify enables a browser to use modules in the same way as regular Node.js modules at the server.

6   Conclusions and Future Work

This paper has presented Communicating Web Vessles (CWV), a dynamic adaptation approach that improves the responsiveness of mobile web apps under the ever-changing execution environment of the web. The CWV's reference implementation offers full automation and a low performance overhead. By featuring dynamic program analysis and transformation to ensure both correctness and efficiency, CWV adapts to dissimilar execution conditions by moving app functionalities from the server to the client and vice versa at runtime. As a future work direction, we plan to apply our approach to address the resource constraints and execution volatility of edge computing applications.

Acknowledgments. This research is supported by the National Science Foundation through the Grant # 1717065.

References

1. An, K., Tilevich, E.: Catch & release: an approach to debugging distributed full-stack JavaScript applications. In: Web Engineering, pp. 459–473 (2019)
2. An, K., Tilevich, E.: Client insourcing: bringing ops in-house for seamless re-engineering of full-stack JavaScript Applications. Proc. Web Conf. **2020**, 179–189 (2020)
3. An, K., Tilevich, E.: D-goldilocks: Automatic redistribution of remote functionalities for performance and efficiency. In: Proceedings of the 27th IEEE International Conference on Software Analysis, Evolution and Reengineering(SANER) (2020)
4. Barr, E.T., Harman, M., Jia, Y., Marginean, A., Petke, J.: Automated software transplantation. In: Proceedings of the 2015 International Symposium on Software Testing and Analysis, pp. 257–269. ISSTA 2015 (2015)
5. de Moura, L., Bjørner, N.: Z3: an efficient SMT solver. In: Ramakrishnan, C.R., Rehof, J. (eds.) TACAS 2008. LNCS, vol. 4963, pp. 337–340. Springer, Heidelberg (2008). https://doi.org/10.1007/978-3-540-78800-3_24
6. Ding, N., Wagner, D., Chen, X., Pathak, A., Hu, Y.C., Rice, A.: Characterizing and modeling the impact of wireless signal strength on smartphone battery drain. In: ACM SIGMETRICS Performance Evaluation Review, pp. 29–40 (2013)
7. Gomes, V.B., Kleppmann, M., Mulligan, D.P., Beresford, A.R.: Verifying strong eventual consistency in distributed systems. In: Proceedings of the ACM on Programming Languages 1(OOPSLA), pp. 1–28 (2017)
8. Jacobsson, K., Hjalmarsson, H., Möller, N., Johansson, K.H.: Estimation of RTT and bandwidth for congestion control applications in communication networks. In: IEEE CDC, Paradise Island, Bahamas. IEEE (2004)
9. Kwon, Y.W., Tilevich, E.: Power-efficient and fault-tolerant distributed mobile execution. In: ICDCS 2013, IEEE (2013)
10. Kwon, Y.-W., Tilevich, E., Apiwattanapong, T.: *DR-OSGi*: hardening distributed components with network volatility resiliency. In: Bacon, J.M., Cooper, B.F. (eds.) Middleware 2009. LNCS, vol. 5896, pp. 373–392. Springer, Heidelberg (2009). https://doi.org/10.1007/978-3-642-10445-9_19
11. Marchthaler, R., Dingler, S.: Beispiel: Bias-Schätzung. Kalman-Filter, pp. 119–135. Springer, Wiesbaden (2017). https://doi.org/10.1007/978-3-658-16728-8_9

12. Nikzad, N., Chipara, O., Griswold, W.G.: APE: an annotation language and middleware for energy-efficient mobile application development. In: Proceedings of the 36th International Conference on Software Engineering, pp. 515–526. ACM (2014)
13. Robinson, J., Gray, A., Titarenco, D.: Getting started with meteor. Introducing Meteor, pp. 27–41. Apress, Berkeley (2015). https://doi.org/10.1007/978-1-4302-6835-2_2
14. Sen, K., Kalasapur, S., Brutch, T., Gibbs, S.: Jalangi: A selective record-replay and dynamic analysis framework for JavaScript. In: Proceedings of the 2013 9th Joint Meeting on Foundations of Software Engineering, pp. 488–498 (2013)
15. Sidiroglou-Douskos, S., Lahtinen, E., Eden, A., Long, F., Rinard, M.: CodeCarbonCopy. In: Proceedings of the 2017 11th Joint Meeting on Foundations of Software Engineering, pp. 95–105 (2017)
16. Sung, C., Kusano, M., Sinha, N., Wang, C.: Static DOM event dependency analysis for testing web applications. In: Proceedings of the 24th ACM SIGSOFT International Symposium on Foundations of Software Engineering, pp. 447–459 (2016)
17. Tsaoussidis, V., Badr, H., Ge, X., Pentikousis, K.: Energy/throughput tradeoffs of TCP error control strategies. In: Proceedings ISCC 2000. Fifth IEEE Symposium on Computers and Communications, pp. 106–112. IEEE (2000)
18. Waldo, J., Wyant, G., Wollrath, A., Kendall, S.: A note on distributed computing. In: Vitek, J., Tschudin, C. (eds.) MOS 1996. LNCS, vol. 1222, pp. 49–64. Springer, Heidelberg (1997). https://doi.org/10.1007/3-540-62852-5_6
19. Wang, X., Liu, X., Zhang, Y., Huang, G.: Migration and execution of JavaScript applications between mobile devices and cloud. In: Proceedings of the 3rd Annual Conference on Systems, Programming, and Applications: Software for Humanity, pp. 83–84 (2012)

Snapshot-Based Migration of ES6 JavaScript

Yong-Hwan Yoo$^{(\boxtimes)}$ (iD) and Soo-Mook Moon

Seoul National University, 1 Gwanak-ro, Gwanak-gu, Seoul, South Korea
{yyh729,smoon}@snu.ac.kr

Abstract. Recently, researches have proposed application (app) migration approaches for JavaScript programs to enable a non-breaking user experience across different devices. To migrate a stateful JavaScript app's runtime, past studies have proposed snapshot-based techniques in which the app's runtime state is profiled and serialized into a text form that can be restored back later. A common limitation of existing literature, however, is that they are based on old JavaScript specifications. Since major updates introduced by ECMASCript2015 (a.k.a. ES6), JavaScript supports various features that cannot be migrated correctly with existing methods. Some of these features are in fact heavily used in today's real-world apps and thus greatly reduces the scope of previous works.

In this paper, we analyze ES6 features such as block scopes, modules, and class syntax that were previously uncovered in app migration. We present an algorithm that enables migration of apps implemented with these new features. Based on the standards adopted in modern JavaScript engines, our approach serializes a running program into a scope tree and reorganizes it for snapshot code generation. We implement our idea on the open source V8 engine and experiment with complex benchmark programs of modern JavaScript. Results show that our approach correctly migrates 5 target programs between mobile devices. Our framework could migrate the most complex app of source code size 213 KB in less than 200 ms in a X86 laptop and 800 ms in an embedded ARM board.

Keywords: JavaScript · App migration · Serialization · Code generation

1 Introduction

JavaScript is undeniably one of the most pervasive programming languages that exist today. According to recent survey results from StackOverflow[1], its popularity remains unsurpassed for several consecutive years. An important factor for this popularity is its compatibility with web browsers which are available in most mobile devices by default. Moreover, adoption of JavaScript outside web browsers has given rise to server-side or desktop apps that run in popular

---

[1] https://insights.stackoverflow.com/survey/.

© Springer Nature Switzerland AG 2021
M. Brambilla et al. (Eds.): ICWE 2021, LNCS 12706, pp. 404–419, 2021.
https://doi.org/10.1007/978-3-030-74296-6_31

runtime environments such as Node.js or electron. Also, several smart device vendors support built-in web browers (e.g. Samsung Tizen, LG webOS), thus readily running web applications written in JavaScript.

The wide platform pool of JavaScript makes it suitable for a cross-device computing concept called *liquid software* [5,6,16] in which the workflow of interactions and services are continued across devices. While similar approaches were proposed for native mobile platforms [1], they lacked support for devices from different vendors. Yet, the high portability of web apps and freedom from predatory control of OS vendors exempt them from such issues.

Similarly, [3,13–15] proposed *app migration* frameworks for stateful web apps, in which browser sessions can be migrated across devices to provide a continuous user experience in web apps. Their main approach is to profile a running program's states, such as the objects in JavaScript heap, and saving them into a text-formatted file (i.e. snapshot). Generating a snapshot as a JavaScript code enables a low-overhead framework for continuous user experience across a heterogeneous device pool. Recent studies extended the techniques to IoT [8] and compute offload [7,11], suggesting novel use cases like multi-device web games and collaborative machine learning in browsers.

In implementing app migration for JavaScript apps, previous works addressed important challenges raised by the dynamic nature of JavaScript. [15] suggested solutions for saving variables hidden inside a function closure. [13] extended this and proposed a *scope tree* building algorithm to save complex scope hierarchy of function closures. However, JavaScript language, as well as its ecosystem, has evolved significantly and has continuously been refined on a yearly basis. Modern JavaScript engines support by default various features[2] used in real-world web apps (e.g. slack, ebay, duckduckgo). These apps make heavy use of new language features (e.g. block scoping, class, module and new built-in types) introduced in ECMAScript2015 standards[3]. This raise non-trivial issues to all prior works which, at their best, are based on the old ECMAScript5.1 standards.

In this paper, we tackle the problem of migrating runtime states of ES6 JavaScript programs. We analyze the major language features defined in ES6 specifications and discuss the main challenges in app migration. Our work expands *scope tree* building by [13] to support two new variable scopes introduced by block scoping and module system. Based on analyses of scope trees, we propose methods for restoring class syntax included in modern JavaScript programs together with new built-in types. We implement our work as a JavaScript module and tested our idea using 5 modern benchmark programs. Experimental results in two different mobile devices show that our approach correctly migrates all programs with minimal overhead, suggesting feasibility of in resource-constrained environments. In short, this paper following contributions:

– To the best of our knowledge, this is the first study on runtime migration of ES6 JavaScript. We analyze the challenges raised by new languages features and propose new ways to serialize and restore their states.

---

[2] https://kangax.github.io/compat-table/es6/.
[3] http://www.ecma-international.org/ecma-262/6.0/.

- We evaluate our work on complex benchmark programs written in ES6. Experiments in 2 different mobile devices show the app migration causes low time overhead and is thus feasible in resource-constrained devices.
- We show that the size of restoration code generated by our framework is comparable to previous state-of-the-art. We further analyze different ES6 programs based on the generated scope trees and snapshot codes.

2 Background and Related Works

2.1 Snapshot-Based JavaScript App Migration

Recent literature on JavaScript app migration have proposed capturing the application state at JavaScript level [3,8,13–15]. As JavaScript engines save variables of the global scope as the *global object*'s properties, their values can be accessed by enumerating these properties cleverly. After each element state is serialized at a source device, a snapshot code can be generated to restore their values at the target device. When this code is executed at the target device, original global scope state can be migrated with minimal overhead, allowing the user to resume execution of the app from the serialized state. Since this simplifies the process of restoring an app as opposed to native-level solutions [2,9], we follow the state-of-the-art approach proposed by [13] and incrementally build on this baseline study throughout the paper.

2.2 Function Closure and Scope Tree

At runtime, the JavaScript engine manages a call stack to save the context, a.k.a. the *execution context*, in which the code is executed. Each execution context consists of a *lexical environment* (LE) whose *environment record* saves the set of variables, functions, etc. bound to the LE. Another component of an LE is a reference to the outside LE, which is referred to as "outer", together defining the variable's scope.

When a JavaScript code makes a function call, the JavaScript engine dynamically creates a new execution context and a corresponding LE. Then, the function is dynamically bundled with its outer LE in which it is defined as a closure. These closures are discussed as a major challenge in previous works on JavaScript app migration. In fact, to preserve a function's state completely, we need to save and restore the "outer" LE accessed by the function's closure which is internally managed by JavaScript engines. To tackle this issue at JavaScript-level, [15] modified the JavaScript engine to gain direct access to the internal property 'Scope' to recursively obtain the chain of LEs, a.k.a. *scope chain*. This enables a function to be restored together with the original context.

As demonstrated in later works, however, migrating functions is more challenging when multiple closures share the same LEs. For example, Fig. 1 illustrates two functions `print` and `reset` that reference the same variable `msg` via their closures. In this case, simply saving the LE of each function will not restore the whole program correctly. If the relationship between two closures is not captured, restoring each scope chain will generate multiple copies of shared contexts. Thus, the whole scope hierarchy needs to be serialized in order to prevent unexpected breakdowns in mysterious cases.

```
1  function wrapper() {
2      var msg = 'closure!';
3      function print() { console.log(msg); }
4      function reset() { msg=''; }
5      return {print, reset};
6  }
7  var {print, reset} = wrapper();
```

(a) source code

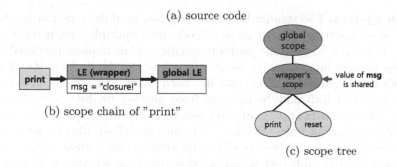

(b) scope chain of "print"

(c) scope tree

Fig. 1. Scope chain and scope tree example

To solve the above problem, [13] proposed combining all the scope chain information into a single data structure called *scope tree*. Figure 1c shows an example scope tree generated for Fig. 1. In this scope tree, "print" and "reset" become child nodes of the same node because they are defined inside the local scope of **wrapper**. Afterwards, traversing this tree in pre-order generates a restoration code for the original program state.

3   ES6 Features and Issues in App Migration

Although previous works incrementally addressed important issues in JavaScript app migration, modern JavaScript apps rely on newer complex features to which existing approaches do not provide solutions. We analyzed new specifications in ES6 standards not addressed in previous approaches, specifically focusing on 4 features prevalent in modern JavaScript apps and frameworks: block scoping, module system, class syntax, and new data types.

Block Scoping. Prior to ES6, a JavaScript variable was declared with keyword **var** and scoped to the innermost surrounding function (a.k.a. function-scoped).

This means variables were available anywhere within the function it is declared. On the other hand, ES6 introduced a new variable type called block-scoped variables as a core update. Declared with keywords `let` or `const`, these variables follow a more common convention of other languages and are scoped to any innermost block that surround them and cannot be accessed until their lexical bindings are evaluated.

Introduction of block-scoped variables in ES6 allow block statements other than function blocks to create nodes on a scope chain. For instance, if-statement and loops can form nodes on the scope chain that saves the block-scoped variable declared inside them. In order to preserve the original scope chain correctly, a block statement's scope (`BlockScope`) needs to be differentiated from a function's scope (`FunctionScope`).

Module System. ES6 standards introduced a new module system to JavaScript which allows splitting a large piece of code into multiple files using built-in syntax. This replaced previous platform-specific module implementations[4,5] and has been shipped into all major JavaScript engines as the de facto standard. A module's code is stored in a separate file, each containing a set of declarations and statements which may be accessed from another module as read-only. In practice, programmers specify an entry point module and explicitly load it, for example, via a ⟨script type="module"⟩ tag into an HTML file of a web app.

JavaScript engines execute modules differently from regular scripts, so the same code can have different semantics depending on whether it is loaded as a script or module. For example, calling `this` keyword at top-level will give different results in a script (*global object*) and module (*undefined*). Thus, ES6 app migration needs to preserve such semantics of modules.

util.js

```
1  var foo = 'util-foo';
2  export function bar(){
3      print(foo);
4  }
```

main.js

```
1  import {bar} from './util.js
       ';
2  var foo = 'main-foo';
3  bar();    // 'util-foo'
```

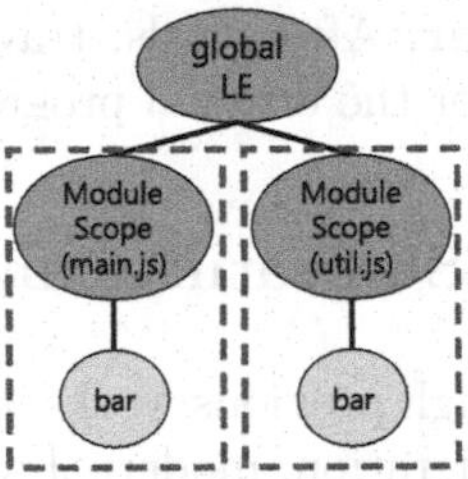

(b) scope tree of 2a

(a) source code

Fig. 2. ES6 module example

[4] http://www.commonjs.org/.
[5] https://github.com/amdjs/.

Internally, the JavaScript engine creates a new LE, a.k.a. ModuleScope whenever a new module's code is executed, thereby isolating each module's scope. In perspective of a scope tree, this means that each module's top-level bindings are saved in a separate node. The challenge here is that the scope tree alone cannot capture the order of each module's declaration (i.e. relationship between the modules). For example, Fig. 2b shows scope tree generated for the code of Fig. 2a. Both ModuleScope nodes save the same function bar, but we cannot identify in which module this function was first declared.

Class Syntax. ES6 also defined class definitions as a special function type while reserving several keywords to mimic syntax similar to class-based languages on top of JavaScript's object-based nature. A class's constructor function is differentiated from normal functions and is bound to a new BlockScope generated for that class. Subclassing in ES6 classes is done with the extends keyword, for which the JavaScript engine evaluates the parent class and dynamically links the child class's constructor and prototype to their parent class counterparts.

```
1   var Circle;
2   var Shape;
3   Shape = class {
4       constructor(x,y){
5           this.x = x
6           this.y = y
7       }
8   }
9   Circle = class extends Shape {
10      constructor(x,y,r) {
11          super (x,y)
12          this.r  = r
13      }
14  }
15  var c = new Circle();
```

(a) source code

```
1   var Circle = class
        extends Shape {
2       ...
3   } // syntax error
4   var Shape = class {
        ... }
5
6   var c = new Circle();
```

(b) wrong snapshot code

Fig. 3. Wrong restoration of class definitions

In order to save and restore class definitions for app migration, naively treating them as regular functions and capturing their states using a scope tree will not preserve the syntactic order between different classes. More specifically, the extends keyword used in class subclassing requires that a parent class's BlockScope is evaluated before executing a child class's BlockScope.

Due to JavaScript's dynamic nature, however, such order between subclassing classes are often not captured automatically. Figure 3a is a source code of two class variables whose declarations (line 1–2) and definitions (line 4–5) are in different order. If we restore this app like using a scope tree [13], identifier Circle will be restored before Shape. Because dependencies between the two identifiers are not explicit, a generated snapshot code (Fig. 3b) will raise a syntax error when it is executed (line 1). Identifying such dependencies becomes more challenging if classes are defined in different scopes (e.g. in different lexical blocks) or if parent classes are defined by arbitrary expressions. Thus, we need a new strategy that can generalize and account for such new syntax.

4 Proposed Approach

Figure 4 is a high-level overview of our framework. Given a target app, we save its module structure into a JSON file ("module_dep.json") with a lightweight static analysis (module profiler) which is loaded together for later use. The app user can trigger app migration by calling a global function ("SaveSnapshot") of our framework ("migrator.js") to generate a snapshot code ("snapshot.js"). The user can load this snapshot code at the target device and restore original app state in the source device so that app execution can continue seamlessly. We now explain details of each stage.

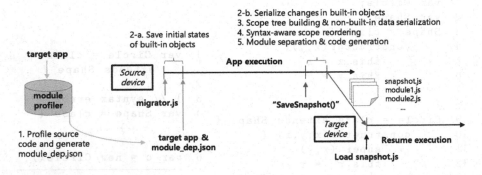

Fig. 4. High-level overview

4.1 Module Profiling

To address the challenge of restoring module structure in the target device, our framework statically analyzes the app source code and saves dependencies between different modules included in the app. This is because a static analysis can capture any complex relationship between ES6 modules that cannot be captured easily at runtime, such as two different JavaScript modules that have cyclic dependencies. As such, we add a module profiler stage in advance to app deployment. Given an app's source code and its entry module name, we generate a JSON file ("module_dep.json") that saves the dependency graph between modules. This dependency graph models each module as a node and variables imported to each module as an incoming edge. This file is later loaded with the target app to restore the relationship between different modules.

4.2   Migrating Modified Built-In Objects

In advance to target app loading, our framework saves the initial states of JavaScript's built-in objects such as Array, String, etc. This is an optimization to efficiently migrate JavaScript built-in objects based on the intuition that after a JavaScript engine initializes their properties, most built-in objects are rarely modified during program execution [11,12]. Inspired by this observation, we do not serialize the unmodified properties redundantly and instead restore them at the target device via default engine startup. To save the other modified portion and minimize our snapshot code size, our framework loads our app migration script before the actual app is loaded by the JavaScript engine and immediately save initial states of built-in objects (step 2-a). At the actual app migration, we traverse these built-in object once again to find the properties that are modified from their initial states during app execution (step 2-b) and generate a JavaScript code that restores these changes via assignment.

4.3   Scope Tree Building

Our framework saves global identifiers (e.g. variables, objects) that were created during app execution, together with their values and properties. If some object is found to be a function (LeafFunction), we traverse the scope chain and collect scope information (i.e. LEs) recursively up to the outermost scope (GlobalScope). At the end of each traversal, we update the scope tree with the collected information as in previous approaches [13] so that closure variables and their relationships are serialized. At the end of this stage, the resulting scope tree can be composed of 5 node types which we abbreviate as following:

- G = GlobalScope; global scope of a program.
- M = ModuleScope; top-level scope of a module.
- F = FunctionScope; scope introduced by a function.
- B = BlockScope; scope introduced by a block statement.
- L = LeafFunction; function that starts a scope chain.

4.4   Syntax-Aware Tree Re-ordering

After a scope tree is generated, we collect dependency information between tree nodes to address the issue raised by subclassing syntax in class definitions. More specifically, this dependency defines the order in which a parent class and a child class will be declared so that the extends clause (i.e. reference to the parent) in every class definition is evaluated without syntax error. By re-ordering the scope tree with respect to such dependency, we ensure that a parent class is present with the right values when evaluating the child.

The challenge in syntax-aware tree re-ordering is finding relationship between these class constructors, i.e. finding each class's parent. Here, we exploit the prototype-based inheritance model of ES6 classes and inspect the internal links between JavaScript classes to find each class's parent. Since every object in

JavaScript, including class definitions, has an internal property named 'Prototype', recursively following these links up to **null** give us its "prototype chain". Based on this principle, we first iterate all observable class constructors and their parent class and locate their least common ancestor node in our scope tree. We then rearrange the two child branches to which the classes are bound, so that a pre-order depth first search reaches the parent class's scope before the child's.

4.5 Tree Partitioning

Next, we restore the original partitioning of the source code so that each module's code can be generated separately. Since every module creates its own LE whose "outer" element points at the global LE, a ModuleScope node in our scope tree forms its own subtree as a direct child of GlobalScope node. Separating each module is straightforward: we iterate children of the root node to find all ModuleScope nodes and split their subtrees from the original scope tree.

To restore the relationship between module partitions, we examine the declarations saved in each module partition's root node (i.e. ModuleScope node) and recursively map each ModuleScope to a node in our previously saved dependency graph ("module_dep.json"), thus restoring the original relationship between them. Finally, generating a glue code (e.g. ⟨script type="module"⟩) to load the entry module into global scope restores the original module structure of the application. As an example, Fig. 5 shows tree partitions of a target app called **UniPoker**, originally composed of three code fragments.

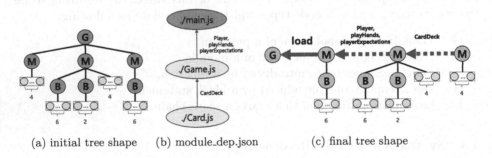

(a) initial tree shape   (b) module_dep.json   (c) final tree shape

Fig. 5. Tree partitioning example (UniPoker)

4.6 Snapshot Code Generation

After our scope tree is reordered and partitioned, we generate a snapshot code for each scope tree partition. The final result of this stage will be multiple JavaScript files, each corresponding to a tree partition. Code for a partition can be generated by traversing the partition's nodes in pre-order and applying an appropriate code generation scheme to each visited node. We implement function `generateScope` which generates code for a given node and recursively invokes itself until a leaf node is reached. In other words, invoking `generateScope` with some partition's root node as argument returns its snapshot code. We show pseudo code of the code generator in Fig. 6.

Algorithm 1: Code Generator

```
1   function generateScope(node):
2       switch node.type do
3           case BlockScope do
4               code += "{"
5               foreach variable ∈ node.LE do
6                   code += "let" + serialize(variable)
7               end
8               foreach childNode ∈ node.children do
9                   generateScope (childNode)
10              end
11              code += "}";
12          end
13          case FunctionScope do
14              code += "(function(){"
15              foreach variable ∈ node.LE do
16                  code += "var" + serialize(variable)
17              end
18              foreach childNode ∈ node.children do
19                  generateScope (childNode)
20              end
21              code += "})"
22          end
23          case LeafFunction do
24              if node.function.startsWith("class") then
25                  code += serializeClass(node.function)
26              else if node.function.prototype == undefined then
27                  code += serializeMethod(node.function)
28              end
29              else
30                  code += serializeFunction(node.function)
31              end
32          end
33      end
```

Fig. 6. Pseudo code for code generation

In line 2, we first check the type of the visited node to select an appropriate code generation scheme. If the node type is BlockScope (line 3) or a Function-Scope (line 13), we generate a wrapper code corresponding to the scope type, i.e. lexical block statement (line 4 & 11) or an immediately invoked function expression (line 14 & 21). Inside the wrapper code, we serialize the value of each closure variable and invoke `generateScope` for each child node in the scope tree. Note that variables are declared differently in each case so that they are bound to the correct LE type.

When we visit a leaf node during a pre-order traversal (line 23), our code generator first checks if the function is a class (line 24), a method (line 26) or neither of two types (line 29). A class constructor is distinguishable lexically at JavaScript level by its keyword "class" while a method function is unique in that it does not have a "prototype" property. We again serialize its scope chain (i.e. *node.function*), process it with respect to the syntax of the type, and concatenate the resulting code.

Our framework also adds supports for new data types introduced in ES6 which cannot be serialized with existing methods. For instance, we introduce an auxiliary array to migrate the new primitive type `symbol` since it can cause aliasing issues if serialized into strings directly like other primitive types. For migrating standard built-in objects (e.g. Map, Set, Typed Arrays), our code generator adds declaration for an empty prototype of the built-in object and copies each element of the target object in the original insertion order using the corresponding built-in methods (e.g. `Map.set("key", "value")`).

5   Evaluation

5.1   Implementation and Setup

We used the V8 JavaScript engine of the open-source chromium browser to implement and evaluate our work, as it is currently the most popular platform adopted by major browser (Google Chrome, Microsoft Edge) and non-browser platforms (Node.js, electron). We cloned the source code of a recent version chromium browser (version 82.0.4060.0, Feb 15, 2020) to add accesses to internal 'Scope' property of functions. Our *module profiler* extends an open source npm package[6] built on Esprima JavaScript parser[7]. The rest of the framework is implemented as a module named "migrator.js" so as to be easily plugged into other JavaScript apps for app migration support. "SaveSnapshot" function in the module is attached to a button click event to provide interactive interface.

We compiled our modified V8 engine to experiment in two environments: (1) a X86 laptop with Intel Core i7-7700 3.6 GHz CPU and 32 GB memory (2) ODROID-XU4 embedded board with ARM Cortex-A15 Quad 2 Ghz & Cortex-A7 Quad 1.3 GHz CPUs, and 2 GB of memory, to simulate resource-constrained scenarios. We then adapted several programs from JetStream2 benchmark (Table 1) that show various real-world usages of ES6 features. Original details of the benchmark can be found in [4]. Since we couldn't find any standard benchmark for testing ES6 modules, we additionally split source codes of two target programs (UniPoker and ML) into multiple modules.

---

[6] https://www.npmjs.com/package/es-dependency-graph.
[7] https://esprima.org/.

Table 1. Target programs for app migration

App	Description	ES6 features
UniPoker	5 card stud poker simulation using Unicode (U+1F0A1). 3 modules (Card.js, Game.js, main.js)	let/const, classes, new built-in types, module
Air	ES6 port of WebKit B3 JIT's allocateStack phase. Runs hot function bodies of popular benchmarks	let/const, classes, new built-in types
Basic	ES6 implementation of ECMA-55 BASIC standard. Runs several simple apps (e.g. find prime numbers)	let/const, classes, new built-in types
Babylon	JavaScript parser used in Babel transpiler. Parses 4 JavaScript sources with intensive string processing	let/const, classes, new built-in types
ML	Feedforward neural network for machine learning. Trains several networks with different activation functions and datasets. Refactored into 5 modules	let/const, classes, subclassing built-in types, module

We first downloaded source codes of the target apps, saved them in the source device, and adapted each app so that it imports our framework in advance of app loading. We loaded each app in our modified browser and executed app migration at 2 different execution points: (1) after a target app is fully loaded and (2) after program finished several iteration. A generated snapshot file ("snapshot.js") is then loaded into a new browser session in a target device.

To ensure correctness of app migration, we first checked the runtime behavior of each benchmark program by resuming their execution after app migration multiple times. We also inspected all global identifiers in the original and new session and made sure their all values are preserved. Lastly for the 2 benchmarks written using ES6 modules, we checked if each module is properly split from each other with the correct import/export statements. Our inspection results showed that our snapshot codes restored the original program correctly.

5.2 RQ1: How Do ES6 Features Affect the Scope Tree Results?

We summarized scope tree results of our benchmark programs in Table 2. Results of UniPoker and ML show that tree partitioning will yield 3 and 5 additional module partitions respectively, same as the original source codes. Compared to other programs, scope trees of Babylon and ML had relatively more complex structures (Fig. 7). For example, in the center of ML's result we can observe a branch of length 5 (G-M-B-F-B) shared by 180 different leaf function nodes. We observed that most of the LE nodes in these complex tree structures are BlockScope nodes. In fact, a large portion of these nodes are created by class definitions and thus their child nodes are subject to syntax-aware re-ordering.

Table 2. Scope tree details

| App | Tree height | # of LEs | | | | # of function |
		G	M	F	B	
UniPoker	3	1	3	0	3	31
Air	2	1	0	0	14	251
Basic	2	1	0	0	7	50
Babylon	3	1	0	1	30	290
ML	5	1	5	1	43	598

Table 3. Code size across migration

App	Source (KB)	Snapshot1 (KB)	Snapshot2 (KB)
UniPoker	16	24	26
Air	403	625	626
Basic	45	68	68
Babylon	238	514	622
ML	213	644	644

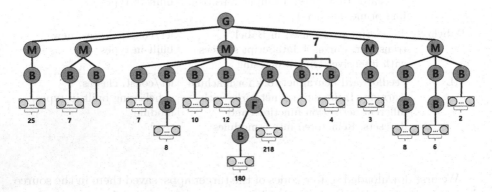

Fig. 7. Scope tree example (ML benchmark)

One of our framework's limitations lies in supporting asynchronous features in JavaScript (e.g. Promise API and generators) which is outside the scope of this paper. For now, we simply disable app migration when such features are detected and leave support for them as future research direction. Yet, it is worth mentioning that these features essentially do not add new scoping rules and thus will not break the semantics of our overall scope serialization process.

5.3   RQ2: Are Snapshot Codes Generated in Small Sizes?

In our framework, a small snapshot code size is desirable because it can reduce time to transmit the snapshot code between devices and shorten app loading time in the target device. Table 3 shows the source code and snapshot code size at the two execution points. Intuitively, size increase will be relatively larger for complex scope trees with more LEs, since we restore each LE by generating reference codes that is not present in the original source.

Unlike other benchmarks whose snapshot code sizes are mostly consistent across all execution points, noticeable increase exists between snapshot1 and snapshot2 in Babylon. This is because in between the two snapshot points, Babylon read 4 JavaScript source codes from external files and loads them into memory, thus greatly increasing program state size. Also,code size increase is unusually larger in ML compared to any other program. This is because ML's source code heavily uses the eval() function for code compression, which has long been deprecated. Even including such exceptional cases, the snapshot codes sizes are only 2.01X larger than the source code on average. This is comparable to previous state-of-the-art baseline result by [13], which reports 1.97X code size increase for the Octane benchmark 2.0 based on ES5 syntax. Considering the extra lines of code added to support ES6 features (e.g. glue codes for restoring dependencies in modules and classes), we conclude that the snapshot size is reasonably small even for resource-constrained devices.

5.4 RQ3: How Much Is the Framework's Time Overhead?

Loading the framework and serializing initial built-in object states was consistent across benchmarks: 93ms (std 1ms) in laptop and 346ms (std 2ms) in ARM board, i.e. initial steps take similar times regardless of target apps. Figure 8 shows additional time overhead imposed by each stage. Total time spent for snapshot generation is less than 200ms in laptop and 800ms in ARM board in the worst case (ML). This is considered small enough for continuous progression in multi-device experience [13] and even for single-device experience [10]. Thus, the time overhead is small enough to provide seamless experience across devices from a user-centric perspective, and feasible in resource-constrained environments.

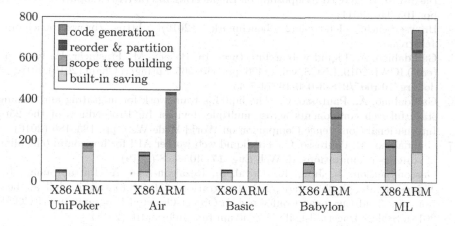

Fig. 8. Breakdown of our framework's time overhead (ms)

While built-in saving time is measured almost the same throughout all programs, the other 3 measurements are dependent on the source program itself and thus largely different by program. This is consistent to that of code sizes (i.e. the larger the snapshot size, the longer the framework took to generate it). Among the three items, time spent in reorder & partition was substantially lower than other stages in all cases, implying that extra steps for migrating ES6 features causes minimal extra overhead.

6   Conclusion

In this paper, we addressed challenges in snapshot-based app migration of ES6 JavaScript programs. We analyzed various features in ES6 standards and proposed methods to handle them efficiently, including manipulation of the scope tree and code generation for new scope types and data types. We implemented our proposal on the open-source V8 engine as an easily pluggable module. Evaluation on complex ES6-based benchmark programs shows that our framework can generate reasonable size snapshots with little time overhead in mobile devices.

Acknowledgement. This work was supported by the National Research Foundation of Korea (NRF) grant funded by the Korea government (MSIT) (No. 2020R1A2B5B02001845) and BK21 FOUR.

References

1. Apple: Handoff for developers (2018). https://developer.apple.com/handoff/
2. Barr, E.T., Marron, M., Maurer, E., Moseley, D., Seth, G.: Time-travel debugging for javascript/node.js. In: Proceedings of the 2016 24th ACM SIGSOFT International Symposium on Foundations of Software Engineering, pp. 1003–1007 (2016)
3. Bellucci, F., Ghiani, G., Paternò, F., Santoro, C.: Engineering javascript state persistence of web applications migrating across multiple devices. In: Proceedings of the 3rd ACM SIGCHI Symposium on Engineering Interactive Computing Systems, pp. 105–110 (2011)
4. Browserbench: Jetstream2 benchmark (2019). https://browserbench.org/JetStream/
5. Gallidabino, A.: Liquid web architectures. In: Bakaev, M., Frasincar, F., Ko, I.-Y. (eds.) ICWE 2019. LNCS, vol. 11496, pp. 560–565. Springer, Cham (2019). https://doi.org/10.1007/978-3-030-19274-7_45
6. Gallidabino, A., Pautasso, C.: The liquid.js framework for migrating and cloning state ful web components across multiple devices. In: Proceedings of the 25th International Conference Companion on World Wide Web, pp. 183–186 (2016)
7. Gallidabino, A., Pautasso, C.: The liquid web worker API for horizontal offloading of stateless computations. J. Web Eng. **17**, 405–448 (2019)
8. Gascon-Samson, J., Jung, K., Goyal, S., Rezaiean-Asel, A., Pattabiraman, K.: Thingsmigrate: platform-independent migration of stateful javascript IoT applications. In: 32nd European Conference on Object-Oriented Programming (ECOOP 2018), Schloss Dagstuhl-Leibniz-Zentrum fuer Informatik (2018)
9. Google: Custom startup snapshots. https://v8.dev/blog/custom-startup-snapshots
10. Google: Measure performance with the rail model (2020). http://web.dev/rail
11. Jeong, H.J., Shin, C.H., Shin, K.Y., Lee, H.J., Moon, S.M.: Seamless offloading of web app computations from mobile device to edge clouds via html5 web worker migration. In: Proceedings of the ACM Symposium on Cloud Computing, pp. 38–49 (2019)
12. Kwon, J., Lee, H.-J., Moon, S.-M.: WebDelta: lightweight migration of web applications with modified execution state. In: Bielikova, M., Mikkonen, T., Pautasso, C. (eds.) ICWE 2020. LNCS, vol. 12128, pp. 435–450. Springer, Cham (2020). https://doi.org/10.1007/978-3-030-50578-3_29

13. Kwon, J.W., Moon, S.M.: Web application migration with closure reconstruction. In: Proceedings of the 26th International Conference on World Wide Web, pp. 133–142 (2017)

14. Lo, J.T.K., Wohlstadter, E., Mesbah, A.: Imagen: Runtime migration of browser sessions for javascript web applications. In: Proceedings of the 22nd International Conference on World Wide Web, pp. 815–826 (2013)

15. Oh, J., Kwon, J.W., Park, H., Moon, S.M.: Migration of web applications with seamless execution. In: Proceedings of the 11th ACM SIGPLAN/SIGOPS International Conference on Virtual Execution Environments, pp. 173–185 (2015)

16. Taivalsaari, A., Mikkonen, T., Systä, K.: Liquid software manifesto: The era of multiple device ownership and its implications for software architecture. In: 2014 IEEE 38th Annual Computer Software and Applications Conference, pp. 338–343. IEEE (2014)

Web User Interfaces

Automated Repair of Layout Bugs
in Web Pages with Linear Programming

Stéphane Jacquet, Xavier Chamberland-Thibeault, and Sylvain Hallé[✉]

Laboratoire d'informatique formelle, Université du Québec à Chicoutimi,
Chicoutimi, Canada
{stephane.jacquet1,xavier.chamberland-thibeault1,shalle}@uqac.ca

Abstract. The paper addresses the issue of layout bugs, in which elements of a web page may overlap, become misaligned or protrude from their parent container for fortuitous reasons. It proposes a technique to apply corrections to a rendered page by formulating its current state and associated layout constraints into a Mixed Integer Linear Programming problem. An off-the-shelf numerical solver is used to generate a layout that satisfies the constraints, in such a way that disruptions to the original page are minimized. A probe then injects these corrections in the form of a temporary "hotfix". The approach has been implemented and tested on samples of real-world web pages; using techniques that aim to reduce the size of the optimization problem, a solution can often be computed in a few seconds on commodity hardware.

Keywords: Layout bugs · Declarative specifications · Linear programming

1   Introduction

The complex interaction of HTML, CSS and JavaScript inside a page may cause its elements to be displayed and behave in ways that are not always anticipated by the designer. A recent study of dozens of real-world web sites has shown that bugs related to the user interface of a web page are very frequent, and even occur in high-profile sites such as Facebook or YouTube [6]. Such bugs may have various causes, including cross-browser rendering inconsistencies [13], responsive web design complexities [2,20] and unforeseen internationalization side effects [14].

Several tools and approaches have been proposed over the past decade to automatically discover such bugs, and potentially identify the elements responsible for the problematic rendering [12,17,18,20]. A page under test may be compared to a reference page, or be evaluated against a set of declarative constraints that it is expected to fulfill. However, much fewer approaches take the problem to the next step, and actually attempt to *repair* the problems that are detected. Web designers are therefore left with the task of finding a suitable fix

© Springer Nature Switzerland AG 2021
M. Brambilla et al. (Eds.): ICWE 2021, LNCS 12706, pp. 423–439, 2021.
https://doi.org/10.1007/978-3-030-74296-6_32

by themselves. Existing solutions sometimes require many minutes before finding an appropriate fix [7,13], which makes them unsuitable for on-the-fly corrections.

This is precisely the problem addressed by the present paper, which focuses on a particular class of user interface disruptions called *layout bugs*. These bugs, which are geometrical in nature, occur when the elements of a page are incorrectly placed, have improper dimensions, are misaligned or overlap each other while they should not. Our approach tackles the issue by attempting to generate what we call a "hotfix" —a temporary patch to the properties of elements as they are displayed in the current page, which restores the satisfaction of declarative layout constraints given beforehand. The solution we propose is to convert the state of a page and its constraints into a Mixed Integer Linear Programming problem (MILP). This makes it possible to leverage the use of an industrial-level numerical solver to quickly compute a layout that satisfies the constraints.

This solution faces two key challenges. The first is to keep the size of the numerical model small, in order to produce a result in acceptable time for an end user (seconds rather than minutes). To this end, we introduce the concept of "zone of influence", which allows us to circumscribe in advance the set of elements that may need to be modified in a page, and drastically reduce the number of variables in the corresponding numerical problem. The second challenge is the actual application of the fix into the page; we describe a technique that is guaranteed to impose the given size and position to a given element, which avoids the need to test a candidate repair into an actual browser. We present a proof-of-concept implementation of this technique and report on experimental results; they confirm that our hotfix generation technique can correctly modify the elements of a page to solve a layout bug, in reasonable time for pages of size corresponding to real-world websites.

This paper is structured as follows. Section 2 describes three types of layout bugs with examples, and then covers related works on UI bug detection and repair. Section 3 explains how we handle the correction through a Mixed Integer Linear Program. Section 4 describes a proof-of-concept implementation that has been tested on both real-world and synthetic pages of large size. Section 5 ends the paper with a conclusion, with suggestions of future work.

2   State of the Art for Fixing Layout Bugs in Web Pages

Presentation bugs can routinely be found in web sites, ranging from subtle inconsistencies to more serious errors that may even break a page's functionality. Case in point, a recent study on UI bugs has found more than 100 issues in the pages of various web sites [6]. In this section, we first describe the particular types of layout bugs that are the focus of this work. We then briefly present the various approaches that have been proposed in the past to automatically detect and/or correct such bugs inside web pages.

2.1   Types of Layout Bugs

Among all bugs reported in previous works, we focus in this paper on bugs that
are related to a page's geometrical features, namely the size and positioning of
the various elements ("boxes") that compose the page; we call these bugs *layout
bugs*. In the GUI fault model developed by Lelli *et al.*, these bugs correspond to
sub-category GSA1 [11]. Following the terminology introduced by Walsh *et al.*
[20], the layout bugs we consider can be divided in three categories.

Overlapping Elements. Figure 1 shows an example of overlapping elements on
the login page for an installation of the Moodle[1] platform. The leftmost button,
labeled "Connexion", extends over the password recovery button that lies to its
right.

(a) French text   (b) English text

Fig. 1. Example of overlapping elements.

The effect produced by overlapping elements is often very easy to spot, yet
the causes of the presence of such overlapping elements are multiple. In the
example shown above, it appears that the position of the buttons is hard-coded
based on the size of the English version of their text. Case in point, Fig. 1b shows
the effect of changing the button's text to "Login", which restores an eye-pleasing
layout.

Misaligned Elements. Misaligned elements is a second common type of layout
bug, which can sometimes be subtle to detect. An example is shown in Fig. 2a,
which comes from the LinkedIn platform[2]; in this screenshot, the "Interests"
menu is placed one pixel lower than the other elements.

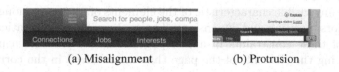

(a) Misalignment   (b) Protrusion

Fig. 2. Examples of misaligned and protruding elements.

---

[1]   https://moodle.org.
[2]   https://linkedin.com.

As with overlapping elements, the causes of misalignment are varied. In the previous example, one can observe by investigating the page's source code that the "Interests" menu is not clickable, contrary to the other elements of the bar. To this end, it is given a different CSS class than the rest of the menu items, which has a slightly different definition for its margins and padding.

Protruding Elements. The last type of bug occurs when an element extends beyond the boundaries of another element that should contain it completely. This is what Walsh *et al.* call *element protrusion* [20]. Figure 2b shows an example of such an issue, taken from the site AgentSolo[3]: one can see that the Search button extends beyond the region that is reserved for the menu bar of the page.

2.2 UI Bug Detection

Over the past decade, several approaches have been proposed for the automated detection of UI bugs in web applications. For example, WebDiff [18] identifies cross-browser layout issues in a web page. The tool harvests the DOM tree of a page on a reference browser multiple times in order to identify the variable elements that should not be considered. Then, it harvests the DOM tree of the same page on other browsers and compares it node by node, to identify mismatches in these nodes' properties and report them.

Walsh *et al.* [20] used Responsive Layout Graphs, which are constructed by querying the DOM tree of a web page under different viewport sizes, to compare a page to itself at various viewport size aiming to find relative layout issues. The DOM trees of each viewport are compared to identify elements that behave incorrectly and report them to the developers. The work by Ryou and Ryu [19] uses a crawler that interacts as much as possible with a web page, building graphs of the page's state along the way. These multiple graphs are then compared: discrepancies between nodes representing the same page element in two graphs are then identified.

All these works are based on the principle of comparison between multiple versions of a page, or between a page and a reference version that is considered correct. An alternate approach consists of asking the developer to write statements that describe the intended appearance of the page in advance. In this line of works, Cornipickle is a web testing tool that focuses on the detection of bugs related to the user interface of a web application [6]. It provides an expressive language in which declarative constraints can be expressed by a web developer, and refer to any visible characteristic of the elements of a page—among others its content, colors, position and dimensions. The tool can then automatically detect violations of these constraints in a web page, and also provides a mechanism for pinpointing the elements of the page that are involved in the corresponding violation.

Similarly, the Cassius framework works as a declarative browser used to verify web pages [17]. Rather than checking constraints on a single rendition of a

---

[3] https://www.agentsolo.com.

web page, the tool reasons symbolically over all possible viewports; therefore, if an assertion passes, this guarantees that no possible set of device size or user preferences can ever violate the assertion. In the opposite case, a counterexample layout is produced and an element violating the assertion is identified. Finally, although not a bug detection tool *per se*, we shall mention SeeSS [12], which is a tool that highlights the portions of a web page that are subject to visual modifications when a developer changes a CSS declaration and saves the file that contains it.

2.3 Automated Repair

While most of the aforementioned solutions can identify portions of a page that violate a given condition, none of them attempt to fix the issue. On the contrary, Hallé and Beroual [7] proposed a generic model for correcting abstract objects that do not satisfy a condition, based on the concept of *repair*. Formally, if φ is a condition that some object $o \in \mathcal{O}$ violates, and $\tau_1, \ldots, \tau_n$ are endomorphisms $\mathcal{O} \rightarrow \mathcal{O}$, a repair is any composition τ of some of the τ_i such that $\tau(o)$ satisfies φ. Intuitively, each τ_i applies a different modification to the object o, and the process of fixing o is reduced to the problem of searching for a combination of modifications that makes the "corrected" object satisfy the condition. Web page layout bugs are cited as one of the potential domains of application of this general theory.

However, the search for an appropriate repair is computationally very expensive, and ultimately amounts to a brute-force generate-and-test algorithm—which, as it turns out, has not been experimentally tested on web pages. Moreover, in this generic model, all potential repairs are seen as black boxes with an equal likelihood of fixing the input object. In the case of violations of layout constraints, which are intrinsically numerical, such a solution does not exploit the geometric nature of the problem to converge more quickly towards a possible fix.

The work closest to the problem we tackle here is an approach to make automated repairs on cross-browser rendering inconsistencies, implemented in a tool called X-Fix [13]. This is done by first comparing an incorrect page with a reference copy, to identify any elements with a different rendering. CSS properties of these elements that have an impact on the rendering discrepancy are identified for each of them. The tool then proceeds to a search for alternate values that could be given to these properties and that would fix the problem, called candidate fixes. The process loops until all bugs have been resolved, or if no improvement on an existing fix can be found.

The generation of candidate fixes is done by implementing a basic numerical solver within the tool, which performs small positive or negative increments to CSS properties of elements and watches for improvements in the value of a fitness score. However, each such candidate requires the page to be re-rendered and re-examined in the browser under test; consequently, experimental results report running times in the order of minutes to find a proper fix. Moreover, in the same way as most tools described in Sect. 2.2, it requires a correct rendering as a reference. In this respect, one could say that the tool already knows the proper positions and sizes that each element is supposed to have (from the reference page), and searches for appropriate CSS declarations that result in such positions and sizes.

2.4 Optimization-Based Techniques

Several methods using optimization-based techniques have been used in the context of GUIs. A survey has been conducted on using combinatorial optimization for GUI layouts [16]. Mixed Integer Linear Programming (MILP) have been developed in the past two decades to correct layout bugs in web pages. MILP are problems were the objective function and the constraints are described by linear functions. Cassowary[1] was an algorithm developed to solve problems of linear equality and inequality constraints, using a modified version of the simplex algorithm. However, the formulation of the problem initially did not contain an objective function; this means that it was not possible to orient the solver towards preferable solutions.

More recently, the GRIDS system [5] proposed layout management of GUIs using MILP with a multi-objective formulation. A drawback of having multiple functions to optimize is that the user has to chose between a large (theoretically infinite) number of solutions located on a curve called the "Pareto front". To help the user, GRIDS only provides a small sample of feasible pages on that front that are quite different one another. Among the objectives, we find the fact that the outer hull of the GUI is as rectangular as possible, that there are as few holes as possible, and that related elements are grouped together.

The same year, LaaS [10] handled this problem through a MILP while offering two possibilities as objective function. The first one is the selection time. The idea is to make sure that the most important elements take as little time as possible to be found. Typically, the most important items might become bigger than the others elements and closer to the top-left corner. The other one is "visual saliency". It describes basically how the elements catch the eyes of the user. Tests have been done on a single element of attention, which means that a single element of the page needed be found quickly using the time selection criteria or to be catchy using the visual saliency criteria.

3   Modelization of Layout Bugs as MILP

In this section, we describe our proposed approach to fix layout bugs in a web page. Given a page rendered by a browser, and constraints expressed on some of its elements (called alignment, inclusion and containment), violations of these constraints are automatically detected. The page's state and these constraints are converted into a linear optimization problem, which computes new positions and dimensions for the elements; a patch is then directly injected into the page, which restores the layout constraints.

This approach distinguishes itself from existing works in several aspects. First, we do not assume the presence of a reference page, but only declarative constraints that must hold for the specified elements; therefore, our proposed tool must find the proper layout by itself. Second, the goal is to produce a fix on-the-fly, as the user is viewing the page: therefore, the time required to produce a solution should be on the order of a few seconds at most. This is why our approach leverages the use of an external numerical constraint solver, and does not require the re-rendering of the page in order to test candidate fixes. Moreover, the proposed solution relies on a few key techniques that aim to keep the linear optimization problem small.

3.1   Layout Constraints

First, the DOM tree of a web page is modeled as a set of nested rectangles, corresponding to the various HTML elements of the page, from the top-level <body> all the way down to individual text leaves (CDATA). Each rectangle is defined by the (x, y) coordinates of its top-left corner, its height and its width (in displayed pixels). It follows that a complete web page, made of $n \in \mathbb{N}^*$ elements, is a set of quadruplets $(x^{(i)}, y^{(i)}, w^{(i)}, h^{(i)})$, $i \in \{1, \ldots, n\}$. A web page is described by the characteristics of each rectangle. The complete page is hence a vector of $4n$ components $(x^{(1)}, y^{(1)}, w^{(1)}, h^{(1)}, \ldots, x^{(n)}, y^{(n)}, w^{(n)}, h^{(n)})$.

Essentially, the layout constraints will be expressed on pairs of elements $A = (x^{(a)}, y^{(a)}, w^{(a)}, h^{(a)})$ and $B = (x^{(b)}, y^{(b)}, w^{(b)}, h^{(b)})$; in terms of their position in the DOM tree, these elements will typically be involved either in a parent-child relationship, or a sibling relationship. Each constraint will contribute to the addition of a number of linear equalities or inequalities between some of the variables of the model. We assume that the set of element pairs subject to each type of constraint is given, and known in advance.

Alignment Constraints. Alignment constraints are straightforward to handle by linear equalities. For example, if A and B are expected to be aligned vertically, the equality $x^{(a)} = x^{(b)}$ is added to the system. Similarly, the fact that A and B must be aligned horizontally is described by $y^{(a)} = y^{(b)}$. This means that each alignment constraint requires one linear constraint and no extra variables.

Inclusion Constraints. The case of inclusion constraints can be handled in a similar way. An element B is completely included within an element A if and only if these four inequalities hold. This means that each inclusion constraint requires four linear constraints and no extra variable.

$$x^{(a)} \leq x^{(b)} \qquad x^{(a)} + w^{(a)} \geq x^{(b)} + w^{(b)}$$
$$y^{(a)} \leq y^{(b)} \qquad y^{(a)} + h^{(a)} \geq y^{(b)} + h^{(b)}$$

Disjointedness Constraints. It is easy to see that A is disjoint from B if and only if at least one of these four inequalities hold:

$$x^{(a)} + w^{(a)} \leq x^{(b)} \qquad y^{(a)} + h^{(a)} \leq y^{(b)}$$
$$x^{(b)} + w^{(b)} \leq x^{(a)} \qquad y^{(b)} + h^{(b)} \leq y^{(a)}$$

However, such a simple modeling causes problems for linear solvers, which typically cannot directly handle the fact that it suffices that *one* of the constraints must be fulfilled. We therefore propose an alternate modelization, using additional constraints and auxiliary variables. Elements A and B are disjoint if and only if:

$$x^{(a)} + w^{(a)} \leq x^{(b)} + M(1 - z_1) \qquad y^{(b)} + h^{(b)} \leq y^{(a)} + M(1 - z_4)$$
$$x^{(b)} + w^{(b)} \leq x^{(a)} + M(1 - z_2) \qquad z_1 + z_2 + z_3 + z_4 \geq 1$$
$$y^{(a)} + h^{(a)} \leq y^{(b)} + M(1 - z_3) \qquad z_1, z_2, z_3, z_4 \in \{0, 1\}$$

where $M \in \mathbb{R}_+$ is a sufficiently large number. Intuitively, the z_i are "choice" variables: setting them to 0 or to 1 determines whether the constraint they are associated with must be fulfilled or not. An equivalent modelization can also be done by replacing the next-to-last equation by $z_1 + z_2 + z_3 + z_4 = 1$. In such a case, z_4 can be removed and replaced by $1 - (z_1 + z_2 + z_3)$, which creates a system with one fewer variable. This means that each disjointedness constraint implies 4 linear constraints and 3 extra binary variables.

Non-Decreasing Sizes. If no constraints on the sizes is given, then some boxes can become smaller. This can lead to some cases where it would be easier for the solver to have a box of length or width equal to 0. Such a thing should not be possible and could happen due to the fact that we lack information in our formulation. In order to avoid that, we add the constraints that the boxes cannot become smaller. Each non-decreasing size constraint adds one linear constraint and no extra variables.

3.2   Defining an Objective Function

Given a set of element pairs that are subject to either alignment, inclusion or disjointedness constraints, it is easy to define a system of inequalities that corresponds to these constraints. Given an input vector $(x^{(1)}, y^{(1)}, w^{(1)}, h^{(1)}, \ldots, x^{(n)}, y^{(n)}, w^{(n)}, h^{(n)})$, a constraint solver will produce an output vector that defines the position and dimensions of each element, such that all constraints are satisfied, if such a solution exists. Therefore, if the original page had a layout that violated one of the constraints, the modifications to the elements' properties describe a way to "fix them".

One could think that merely asking for a solution—any solution—to the solver is sufficient. However, without additional instructions, it is possible that the solver produces a version of the page that satisfies the constraints, but is drastically different from the original. For example, if a single element in a group is misaligned, a valid solution could be to move all elements to a new location in the page. This goes against the intuition that the expected correction would simply move the single misaligned element. Therefore, in order to guide the solver towards solutions that minimally disturb the original document, an *objective function f* must also be provided. A solver can hence be instructed to find solutions that satisfy the constraints, and such that the value of f is minimized.

In the present case, this function should represent the amount of changes made to the original vector. Given an initial page state $(x_0^{(1)}, y_0^{(1)}, w_0^{(1)}, h_0^{(1)}, \ldots, x_0^{(n)}, y_0^{(n)}, w_0^{(n)}, h_0^{(n)})$, the function f to minimize is defined as:

$$\sum_{i=1}^{n} |x^{(i)} - x_0^{(i)}| + |y^{(i)} - y_0^{(i)}| + w^{(i)} - w_0^{(i)} + h^{(i)} - h_0^{(i)}$$

One can see that each term of the sum computes the absolute difference between the initial and the final (x, y) position, and the variation of width and height of each element. Therefore, minimizing f under the layout-bug-free constraints means finding the layout-bug-free web page which is the most similar to the initial web page.

An advantage of this formulation is that the objective function is piecewise linear. Such functions can still be managed through MILP using a proper formulation [4]. One can also note that no absolute values are required for the width and height of the elements, assuming the non-decreasing sizes constraints are used. This allows us to avoid adding $2n$ constraints and $4n$ variables to get the MILP reformulation. Adding those would only lead to longer computation time to solve the MILP.

3.3 Reducing the Number of Constraints

Modeling the previous layout requirements may result in a large number of constraints, affecting an equally large number of elements inside a page. The size of the problem sent to a solver can quickly exceed the limits of what can be handled in reasonable time in terms of user experience. However, the number of variables and constraints can be reduced by taking advantage of the observation that many layout disruptions (and their associated corrections) are local in nature—that is, they have an impact on a limited part of the page, while most of the document typically remains unaffected (and consequently, does not need to be changed).

Fig. 3. Displacing an element, and its impact on elements surrounding it.

Let us first consider the case of a correction to an element that requires it to be displaced. For example, Fig. 3 shows that element B must be moved up. Doing so without any other change may result in a disjointedness constraint to be violated. Therefore, surrounding elements such as A and C can also have to be moved in order to make room for B at its new location. But this, in turn, can shift elements beyond the original size of their container, and potentially violate a protrusion constraint. In order to fix this issue, the size of the parent element may have to be enlarged to accommodate all elements in their new positions. The end result is the right-hand side of Fig. 3; it shows that, when an element needs to be moved, its siblings in the DOM tree may also move, and its parent in the DOM tree may need to be enlarged. A similar reasoning could be made in the case of an element that needs to be enlarged: again, the siblings of this element may need to move, while its parent container may need to be enlarged.

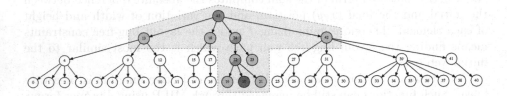

Fig. 4. An illustration of the concept of zone of influence. (Color figure online)

These changes cascade recursively through the document: if the parent of an element needs to be resized, then its siblings may need to be moved, and so on. Although this looks like modifications can potentially affect most of the elements, it turns out not to be the case. This is illustrated in Fig. 4, which shows an abstract DOM tree. We suppose that node 20, marked in red, needs to be either enlarged or displaced. As per the rules mentioned above, some of the other nodes related to node 20 may need to be displaced (marked in yellow), enlarged (marked in green) or both (marked in both colors). The set of all DOM nodes that are susceptible to either type of correction is called the *zone of influence* of a given element, identified by a gray area in the tree.

Note that a fair fraction of the tree actually stays as is: in our example, 34 of the 44 nodes are assured to require no modification. Consequently, these nodes and their associated constraints do not even need to be included in the model submitted to the solver. This would result, in this case, in a fourfold reduction in the number of variables and constraints.

3.4   Hotfix Application

The schematics of the hotfix generation system can be separated into two phases: the detection phase and the correction phase.

Detection Phase. A JavaScript probe P is first injected inside a web page. This probe traverses the DOM tree of the page in a depth-first fashion, and adds to each element a custom attribute called `eid`, whose value is an incrementing number. This procedure makes sure that every element of the page is given a unique numerical identifier. This traversal progressively builds the vector $(x_0^{(1)}, y_0^{(1)}, w_0^{(1)}, h_0^{(1)}, \ldots, x_0^{(n)}, y_0^{(n)}, w_0^{(n)}, h_0^{(n)})$, by recording for each element its displayed position and dimensions, as they are rendered by the browser.

This vector is returned to our Java program, which is also provided with a set of constraints C. In its current form, constraints are represented as triplets of the form (i, j, t), where i and j are numerical IDs representing individual elements of the page, and $t \in \{V, H, D, I\}$ indicates whether elements i and j should be respectively vertically aligned, horizontally aligned, disjoint, or if i should be included within j. The program uses these constraints to generate an input model S for a numerical constraint solver. The solution from the solver is a new vector v that stipulates the new position and size of each element in the "corrected" version of the page.

Correction Phase. It shall be noted that there is no back-and-forth interaction between the solver and the browser; contrary to some other approaches (notably X-Fix [20]), the candidate solutions examined by the solver do not need to be rendered in real to evaluate their actual effect. This, however, supposes that whatever position and size the solver assigns to elements are guaranteed to be the position and size the elements will indeed have in the corrected page.

It turns out that this task is less trivial than it seems. For example, to place an element e at a particular horizontal coordinate x, it does not suffice to issue a statement such as `e.style.left = x`. The positioning of the element's containing parent, its display properties, as well as additional attributes may lead to the element being placed at a different coordinate than x. In other words, there is a difference between the actual geometry of the element, and the values that must be applied to the element for it to assume the desired geometry.

Changing the width or the height of e is relatively straightforward. The probe starts by measuring the actual rendered properties of the selected element e in the browser, which are retrieved via the `getBoundingClientRect()` method. However, its padding and borders, which are recovered via the `window.getComputed-Style()` method, must first be subtracted from the prescribed dimensions, since both properties are included within the actual width of the element. This newly calculated value is then apply to the element's width or height.

Changing the element's position is more delicate. First, one must determine the reference coordinates of the element, which correspond to the top-left corner of the closest ancestor a whose position is `absolute`, or the document's <body> if no such element can be found. Once this ancestor has been found, its absolute positioning and margin sizes are retrieved using the two aforementioned methods. Both of these values must be subtracted from the coordinates returned by the solver, in order to get the position that must actually be applied to the specified element.[4] The `position` attribute of e is then set to `absolute`, and its `top` and `left` properties are set to the calculated values.

4   Experimental Evaluation

The correction scheme detailed in the previous section has been concretely implemented as a proof-of-concept hotfix generation system for web pages, whose goal is to evaluate the potential of the approach for fixing minor layout bugs. In this section, we describe this implementation and report on experimental results on samples of actual and synthetic web pages.

The system is implemented as a Java program, which uses the Selenium WebDriver[5] library to interact with a controllable instance of a web browser. The probe is a custom-made JavaScript piece of code that is injected inside the page by the Java program, and is instructed to extract the properties of elements with specific IDs, for which layout constraints are expected to apply. The Java program then generates an input model for the IBM CPLEX numerical solver [9]. Finally, the solution computed by CPLEX is retrieved by the Java program, and the corresponding JavaScript hotfix is re-injected back into the original page.

4.1   Real-World Bugs

In order to assess the feasibility of the proposed approach to correct actual bugs in a page, two sets of experiments have been conducted, which we describe below. In the first set of experiments, we tested the approach on a sample of real-world web pages presenting layout bugs, taken from a previous study [6]. The goal of these experiments is to determine whether, in an actual web page, the system can not only correctly catch and fix a layout constraint stipulated by the designer beforehand, but also avoid disturbing other (correct) parts of the page. In each of the sampled pages, the appropriate constraints (alignment, containment or disjointedness) on the faulty element and its neighbors were manually identified. The page, along with these constraints, was then sent to our hotfix generator, and the result of the hotfix application was then visually inspected.

(a) Moodle   (b) AgentSolo

Fig. 5. Examples of the application of a hotfix to an incorrect page.

---

[4] Except if p is the document's `<body>`, which behaves differently and where margins must be ignored.

[5] https://seleniumhq.org.

Figure 5a shows an example of the application of a hotfix, on the Moodle page already shown in Fig. 1a. One can observe that the two green buttons, which overlapped in the original page, are now placed exactly side by side. Although no constraint was expressed on the alignment of these two buttons, they remain horizontally aligned. This is due to the fact that the numerical solver is instructed to minimize the changes applied to the original document: moving any of the two buttons up or down would amount to a greater total change to the page than simply keeping them aligned. This also explains why the size of each button has been left unchanged.

We obtained similar results for the other pages we tested. For example, Fig. 5b shows the hotfix for the protruding button illustrated in Fig. 2b. Note how the red menu bar has been extended in width exactly enough to contain the search button. Although not visible in this screenshot, the rest of the page remained untouched.

4.2   Synthetic Pages

MILPs formulations are easy to formulate but they are NP-hard, implying that their worst case complexity is not polynomial [15]. Therefore, a second set of experiments aims to measure the scalability of the approach with respect to the number of elements in a page. To this end, we conducted a systematic stress test by running our hotfix tool on a sample of synthetic DOM trees, produced by a random page generator we implemented and called PageGen[6]. The experiments have been implemented in the form of a LabPal package [8] that is publicly available online[7].

The page generator works recursively as follows. First, for a given element p, a number of children c is randomly selected. For each of these children, a depth d is also randomly selected. If $d = 0$, an element b, of randomly selected width and height, is created and added as a child of p. Otherwise, b is recursively populated before being added to p's children. Once all the children of p have been created, the last step is to arrange them inside p, either following a horizontal or a vertical layout, separated by an equal margin. Once the elements are arranged, the dimensions of p are set to a rectangle that includes all the children. The end result is a tree of nested rectangles, which can be exported as an HTML document made of <div> elements, one for each box. Since the goal of our approach is to correct properties related to the position and size of arbitrary elements, the actual tag names and their content are irrelevant.

What is more, layout bugs can also be artificially injected when a page is generated. Once all elements are arranged within their parent (according to the horizontal or vertical layout), a coin is flipped for each to determine whether the element should be purposefully misaligned with respect to the others, moved to overlap with one of its siblings, or enlarged to extend beyond the dimensions of its parent. Using this generator, we produced a sample of 100 generated web

---

[6] https://github.com/sylvainhalle/pagegen.
[7] https://github.com/liflab/hotfix-lab.

pages, which includes trees ranging between 2 and 10450 elements. We shall mention that a recent empirical analysis of real-world web sites observed that 90% of pages had fewer than 2,000 nodes [3]. Therefore, we can safely conclude that our sample contains pages of size comparable to (and even larger than) sites that are actually present on the web.

For each of these pages, we measured the total time required to generate and apply a hotfix to the layout bug contained in the page. Since the goal is to generate fixes on-the-fly, the solver was given a very short time budget to produce a result (at most 2 s). The running times are shown in Fig. 6a, plotted in function of page size. One can see that, for most pages, solving time remains well under 1 s; only a few pages exceeded the timeout. These running times should be compared with those obtained by X-Fix [13], which reports a median solving time of 841 s on a sample of web sites containing an average of 425 DOM nodes each. Our faster running times, however, are crucial, since our goal is to produce a fix to a page on-the-fly, and not to find a more permanent way of correcting the issue at the CSS level.

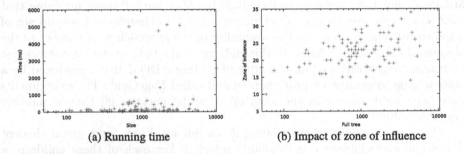

(a) Running time   (b) Impact of zone of influence

Fig. 6. Experimental results from our benchmark.

Figure 6b is a visualization of the impact that the use of zones of influence has on the analysis of a page. Each point in this plot represents a pair of trees: on the x-axis is the original size of the tree, and on the y-axis the size of the tree trimmed to retain only the zone of influence of the faulty elements. One can see the drastic reduction in the number of nodes that need to be modeled: pages of thousands of DOM nodes are reduced to a portion containing a few dozens at most. Without such a reduction, the MILP problem to solve would quickly become intractable.

5   Conclusion and Future Work

In this work, we proposed a technique for automatically generating repairs in the case where a web page violates conditions on the layout of its DOM elements. The problem has been modeled as a MILP problem, using an objective function that aims to minimize the disruptions introduced into the page to restore the conditions. The approach has been implemented as a proof-of-concept tool using a combination of the Selenium browser driver for page manipulation, and the IBM CPLEX software for solving numerical constraints. An experimental evaluation of this implementation has shown that our hotfix generation technique can correctly modify the elements of a page to solve a layout bug (§4.1); moreover, the introduction of the concept of zone of influence can reduce the optimization problem and produce results in reasonable time in terms of user experience (a few seconds), for pages of size corresponding to real-world websites (§4.2).

However, these conclusions rest on several hypotheses, which we discuss below. First, the proposed approach shares an issue that is common to all declarative systems based on assertions: in order for bugs to be detected and pages to be fixed, a page must be accompanied by appropriate constraints that should be followed by its elements. Moreover, these constraints must be *complete*, in the sense that any page that satisfies them should be considered valid. It turns out that the human eye makes many implicit assumptions over the expected size, position and alignment of elements which, in our approach, must be explicitly provided. For example, without further constraint, the fix shown in Fig. 5b will correctly enlarge the red menu area, but not the white parent element that contains this menu. To decrease the burden on the designer of writing such tedious conditions, a future work we consider is to automatically deduce such "obvious" layout conditions based on heuristics.

The hotfix generated by our approach may only modify the page in a subtle way visually, however it alters the structure of the page in a drastic way. Each element to which a patch is applied has its position property set to "absolute": this makes sure that changing its `top` and `left` attributes are guaranteed to move the element to the exact location stipulated by the solver. This avoids having to test a candidate fix to make sure it has the intended effect, as needs to be done in tools such as X-Fix. However, resizing the page after the application of the hotfix may result in the element being yet again incorrectly placed; an immediate workaround is to recompute a new hotfix when this happens. Absolute positioning also removes the element from the normal flow inside its parent container. For an element that is relatively positioned, an alternate fix, which involves modifying the element's margins, is currently being worked on.

We have also seen that the number of variables and constraints sent to the solver was kept to a manageable level thanks to the observation that only elements in a so-called "zone of influence" need to be modeled. However, this only works under the hypothesis that no element is ever reduced in size, because changes only propagate upwards through the DOM tree. In contrast, if an element can be made smaller, then this change propagates *downwards* to all its children, and in such a case, the zone of influence of an element becomes the whole document. Circumscribing the zone of influence in the case of element reductions is the subject of ongoing work, which shall be integrated in a future version of our system.

Finally, we plan to integrate this hotfix generation mechanism directly into the Cornipickle declarative testing tool, and extend it to other types of constraints beyond the three types of layout bugs addressed in this paper. Another step would be to test the tool on a larger sample of bugs and websites, and reenact the same tests on different browsers to ensure the complete validity of the tool, since all the present tests have been realized only on Chrome.

References

1. Badros, G.J., Borning, A., Stuckey, P.J.: The Cassowary linear arithmetic constraint solving algorithm. ACM Trans. Comput.-Hum. Interact. **8**(4), 267–306 (2001)
2. Beroual, O., Guérin, F., Hallé, S.: Detecting responsive web design bugs with declarative specifications. In: Bielikova, M., Mikkonen, T., Pautasso, C. (eds.) ICWE 2020. LNCS, vol. 12128, pp. 3–18. Springer, Cham (2020). https://doi.org/10.1007/978-3-030-50578-3_1
3. Chamberland-Thibeault, X., Hallé, S.: Structural profiling of web sites in the wild. In: Bielikova, M., Mikkonen, T., Pautasso, C. (eds.) ICWE 2020. LNCS, vol. 12128, pp. 27–34. Springer, Cham (2020). https://doi.org/10.1007/978-3-030-50578-3_3
4. Croxton, K., Gendron, B., Magnanti, T.: A comparison of mixed-integer programming models for non-convex piecewise linear cost minimization problems. Manage. Sci. **49**, 1268–1273 (2003)
5. Dayama, N.R., Todi, K., Saarelainen, T., Oulasvirta, A.: GRIDS: Interactive layout design with integer programming. In: CHI, pp. 1–13. ACM (2020)
6. Hallé, S., Bergeron, N., Guerin, F., Breton, G.L., Beroual, O.: Declarative layout constraints for testing web applications. J. Log. Algebraic Methods Program. **85**(5), 737–758 (2016)
7. Hallé, S., Beroual, O.: Fault localization in web applications via model finding. In: Gößler, G., Sokolsky, O. (eds.) CREST@ETAPS. EPTCS, vol. 224, pp. 55–67 (2016)
8. Hallé, S., Khoury, R., Awesso, M.: Streamlining the inclusion of computer experiments in a research paper. Computer **51**(11), 78–89 (2018)
9. IBM: IBM ILOG CPLEX optimization studio CPLEX user's manual, version 12 release 6 (2013). https://public.dhe.ibm.com/software/products/Decision_Optimization/docs/pdf/usrcplex.pdf
10. Laine, M., Nakajima, A., Dayama, N., Oulasvirta, A.: Layout as a service (LaaS): a service platform for self-optimizing web layouts. In: Bielikova, M., Mikkonen, T., Pautasso, C. (eds.) ICWE 2020. LNCS, vol. 12128, pp. 19–26. Springer, Cham (2020). https://doi.org/10.1007/978-3-030-50578-3_2
11. Lelli, V., Blouin, A., Baudry, B.: Classifying and qualifying GUI defects. In: ICST, pp. 1–10. IEEE Computer Society (2015)
12. Liang, H., Kuo, K., Lee, P., Chan, Y., Lin, Y., Chen, M.Y.: SeeSS: seeing what I broke - visualizing change impact of cascading style sheets (CSS). In: Izadi, S., Quigley, A.J., Poupyrev, I., Igarashi, T. (eds.) UIST, pp. 353–356. ACM (2013)
13. Mahajan, S., Alameer, A., McMinn, P., Halfond, W.G.J.: Automated repair of layout cross browser issues using search-based techniques. In: ISSTA, ISSTA 2017, pp. 249–260. ACM (2017)
14. Mahajan, S., Alameer, A., McMinn, P., Halfond, W.G.J.: Automated repair of internationalization presentation failures in web pages using style similarity clustering and search-based techniques. In: ICST, pp. 215–226. IEEE Computer Society (2018)

15. Morrison, D.R., Jacobson, S.H., Sauppe, J.J., Sewell, E.C.: Branch-and-bound algorithms: a survey of recent advances in searching, branching, and pruning. Discrete Optim. **19**, 79–102 (2016)
16. Oulasvirta, A., Dayama, N., Shiripour, M., John, M., Karrenbauer, A.: Combinatorial optimization of graphical user interface designs. In: Proceedings of the IEEE, pp. 1–31 (2020)
17. Panchekha, P., Torlak, E.: Automated reasoning for web page layout. In: Visser, E., Smaragdakis, Y. (eds.) OOPSLA, pp. 181–194. ACM (2016)
18. Roy Choudhary, S., Versee, H., Orso, A.: WEBDIFF: automated identification of cross-browser issues in web applications. In: ICSM, pp. 1–10. IEEE (2010)
19. Ryou, Y., Ryu, S.: Automatic detection of visibility faults by layout changes in HTML5 Web Pages. In: ICST, pp. 182–192. IEEE (2018)
20. Walsh, T.A., Kapfhammer, G.M., McMinn, P.: Automated layout failure detection for responsive web pages without an explicit oracle. In: Bultan, T., Sen, K. (eds.) ISSTA, pp. 192–202. ACM (2017)

A Model-Based Chatbot Generation Approach to Converse with Open Data Sources

Hamza Ed-douibi[1], Javier Luis Cánovas Izquierdo[1(✉)], Gwendal Daniel[1],
and Jordi Cabot[1,2]

[1] UOC., Barcelona, Spain
{hed-douibi,jcanovasi,gdaniel}@uoc.edu
[2] ICREA., Barcelona, Spain
jordi.cabot@icrea.cat

Abstract. The Open Data movement promotes the free distribution
of data. More and more companies and governmental organizations are
making their data available online following the Open Data philosophy,
resulting in a growing market of technologies and services to help publish
and consume data. One of the emergent ways to publish such data is via
Web APIs, which offer a powerful means to reuse this data and integrate it with other services. SOCRATA, CKAN or ODATA are examples
of popular specifications for publishing data via Web APIs. Nevertheless, querying and integrating these Web APIs is time-consuming and
requires technical skills that limit the benefits of Open Data movement
for the regular citizen. In other contexts, chatbot applications are being
increasingly adopted as a direct communication channel between companies and end-users. We believe the same could be true for Open Data
as a way to bridge the gap between citizens and Open Data sources.
This paper describes an approach to automatically derive full-fledged
chatbots from API-based Open Data sources. Our process relies on a
model-based intermediate representation (via UML class diagrams and
profiles) to facilitate the customization of the chatbot to be generated.

Keywords: Open data · UML · Chatbots · API · OpenAPI

1 Introduction

Open Data has emerged as a movement that promotes the free distribution of
data for everyone to consume and republish. Governmental organizations are
one of the significant sources of Open Data resources. They make their data
publicly available online to provide more transparency and enable the general
public to monitor and control the action of government bodies. For instance,
the Spanish Open Data portal registers more than 20,000 resources while the
European portal, which harvests the metadata of Public Sector Information

Work supported by the Spanish government (TIN2016-75944-R project).

available on public data portals across European countries, links to over 1 million already.

On the one hand, Open Data promotes public awareness and aims at boosting citizen participation but, still, regular citizens hardly benefit from them as consuming Open Data requires non-trivial technical skills. Indeed, more and more Open Data sources are released as "web-friendly" artifacts (e.g., Linked-Data, APIs or NoSQL databases) that facilitate their consumption by external software applications and not directly by end-users. In particular, some specific technologies to support the publication of Open Data in the Web have been widely adopted in the last years, namely: SOCRATA[1], CKAN[2] and ODATA[3]. Other organizations also rely on OPENAPI[4], an initiative to formally describe general-purpose REST APIs, to document their Open Data APIs. While all these Web APIs "standards" offer a powerful means for writing complex data queries, they require advanced technical knowledge that hampers their actual use by non-technical people.

On the other hand, chatbots are intelligent conversational agents typically embedded in websites and instant messaging platforms. Users can ask questions or send requests to the chatbot using natural language, with no need to learn any technical knowledge/language. Chatbots have proven useful in various contexts to automate tasks and improve the user experience, such as automated customer services [22], education [13], e-commerce and, basically, every single domain involving any type of user interaction, including technical domains such as database queries [1]. Thus, we believe chatbots are the ideal interface to access and query Open Data sources, thus allowing citizens to access the government/company data they need directly. Citizens would ask the questions in their own language, and the chatbot would be the one in charge of translating that question into the corresponding API request/s.

In this sense, we propose a model-based approach to generate chatbots tailored to the Open Data API technologies mentioned above. As input of our process, an API definition is analyzed and imported as a UML schema annotated with UML profiles, which address specific domain information for chatbot configuration and Web API query generation. This API model is then used to generate the corresponding chatbot to access and query the Open Data source. Via the chatbot, users can ask direct queries or follow one of the guided query paths that facilitate the Open Data exploration. To validate our approach, we provide a proof-of-concept Eclipse plugin that fully supports SOCRATA and allows the integration of other Open Data specifications (i.e., ODATA, CKAN) as well as generic Web APIs (via OPENAPI specification).

Note that we focus on chatbots to help citizens exploit and dialogue with the Open Data resource they are interested in, not on chatbots aimed to help citizens find the best candidate/s data source/s based on their search interests [14], which

---

[1] https://dev.socrata.com/.
[2] https://ckan.org/.
[3] https://www.odata.org/.
[4] https://www.openapis.org/.

is also useful but can be easily replaced with a proper keyword-based search interface. This is not the case for the approach we propose here as, even when citizens know which data sources to query, they typically lack the technical skills to do it on their own and therefore will benefit from our chatbot to act as an "interpreter" between them and the underlying API technology.

The rest of the paper is organized as follows. Section 2 introduces the background of our work. Section 3 briefly describes our approach while Sects. 4 and 5 describe its main phases, namely, Open Data Import and Bot Generation, respectively. Section 6 described the tool support and Sect. 7 presents the related work. Finally, Sect. 8 ends the paper and presents the future work.

2 Background

2.1 Open Data

The Open Data movement aims to make data free to use, reuse, and redistribute by anyone. In the last years, Open Data portals have evolved from offering data in text formats only (e.g., CSV, XML) towards web-based formats, such as LinkedData [2] and Web APIs, that facilitate the reuse and integration of Open Data sources by external Web applications. In this subsection, we briefly describe the most common Web API technologies for Open Data, based on their popularity in governmental Open Data portals.

SOCRATA. Promoted by Tyler Technologies, the SOCRATA data platform provides an integrated solution to create and publish Open Data catalogs. SOCRATA supports predefined web-based visualizations of the data, the exporting of datasets in text formats and data queries via its own API that provides rich query functionalities through a SQL-like language called SoQL. SOCRATA has been adopted by several governments around the world (e.g., Chicago[5] or Catalonia[6]).

CKAN. Created by the Open Knowledge Foundation, CKAN is an Open Source solution for creating Open Data portals and publishing datasets in them. As an example, the European Data Portal relies on CKAN. Similar to SOCRATA, CKAN allows viewing the data in Web pages, downloading it, and querying it using a Web API. The CKAN DataStore API can be used for reading, searching, and filtering data in a classical Web style using query parameters or by writing SQL statements directly in the URL.

ODATA. Initially created by Microsoft, ODATA is a protocol for creating data-oriented REST APIs with query and update capabilities. ODATA is now also an OASIS standard. It is especially adapted to expose and access information from a variety of data sources such as relational databases, file systems, and content management systems. ODATA allows creating resources that are defined

---

[5] https://data.cityofchicago.org.
[6] http://governobert.gencat.cat/en/dades_obertes/index.html.

according to a data model and can be queried by Web clients using a URL-based query language in a SQL-like style. Many service providers adopted and integrated ODATA in their solutions (e.g., SAP or IBM WEBSPHERE).

OPENAPI. Evolving from Swagger, the OPENAPI specification has become the *de facto* standard to describe REST APIs. Though not specific for Open Data, OPENAPI is commonly used to specify all kinds of Web APIs, including Open Data ones (e.g., Deutsche Bahn[7]).

In our approach, we target Open Data Web APIs described by any of the previous solutions. We rely on model-driven techniques to cope with the variety of data schema and operation representations, as described in the next sections.

2.2 Chatbots

Chatbots are conversational interfaces able to employ Natural Language Processing (NLP) techniques to "understand" user requests and reply accordingly, either by providing a textual answer and/or executing additional external/internal services as part of the fulfillment of the request.

NLP covers a broad range of techniques that may combine parsing, pattern matching strategies and/or Machine Learning (ML) to represent the chatbot knowledge base. The latter is the dominant one at the moment thanks to the popularization of libraries and Cloud-based services like DIALOGFLOW or IBM WATSON ASSISTANT, which rely on neural networks to match user intents.

However, chatbot applications are much more than raw language processing components [17]. Indeed, the conversational component of the application is usually the front-end of a larger system that involves data storage and service integration and execution as part of the chatbot reaction to the user intent. Thus, we define a chatbot as an application embedding a *recognition engine* to extract *intentions* from user inputs, and an *execution component* performing complex event processing represented as a set of *actions*.

Intentions are named entities that can be matched by the recognition engine. They are defined through a set of *training sentences*, which are input examples used by the recognition engine's ML/NLP framework to derive a number of potential ways the user could use to express the intention. Matched intentions usually carry *contextual information* computed by additional extraction rules (e.g., a typed attribute such as a city name, a date, etc.) available to the underlying application. In our approach, *Actions* are used to represent simple responses such as sending a message back to the user; as well as advanced features required by complex chatbots, like database querying or external service calling (e.g., API queries in this paper). As we will see, in this paper these actions will involve querying the API in charge of providing the Open Data information requested by the user. Finally, we define a *conversation path* as a particular sequence of received user *intentions* and associated *actions* (including non-messaging actions) that can be executed by the chatbot application.

---

[7] https://developer.deutschebahn.com/store.

3   Overview

In this section, we present an overview of our proposal, depicted in Fig. 1. Our proposal is split into two main phases, *Open Data Import* and *Bot Generation*.

During the import phase, an Open Data API model is injected (see OPEN-DATA *injector*) and refined (see *Model refinement*). The injector supports several input formats (i.e., SOCRATA, CKAN, ODATA and OPENAPI) and the result is a unified model representation of the API information (i.e., operations, parameters and data schemas).

Without loss of generality, this inferred API model is expressed as a UML class diagram to represent the API information plus two additional UML profiles. The first one, the OPENDATA profile, is used to keep track of technical information on the input source (e.g., to be used later on by the Bot to know which API endpoint to call and how). The second one is the BOT profile, proposed to annotate the model with bot-specific configuration options (e.g., synonyms or visibility filters) allowing for a more flexible chatbot generation. Once the injector finishes, the *Bot Designer* refines the obtained model using this second profile. During this step, elements of the API can be hidden, their type can be tuned, or synonyms can be provided (so that the chatbot knows better how to match requests to data elements).

The generation phase is in charge of creating the chatbot definition (see *Bot Generation*). This phase involves specifying both the bot intentions and its response actions. In our scenario, responses involve calling the right Open Data API operation/s, processing the answer, and presenting it back to the user.

As bot platform we use XATKIT [7], a flexible multi-platform (chat)bot development framework, though our proposal is generic enough to be adapted to work with other available chatbot frameworks. XATKIT comprises two main Domain-Specific Languages (DSLs) to define bots: INTENT DSL, which defines the user inputs through training sentences, and context parameter extraction rule (see *Intents*); and EXECUTION DSL, in charge of expressing how the bot should respond to the matched intents (see *Execution*). If preferred, XATKIT can also work with an internal Java-based DSL, that has the same semantics of the two (external) DSLs mentioned before but offering an alternative syntax (based on a chatbot fluent API), easier to adopt for programmers with Java knowledge.

XATKIT comes with a runtime to interpret and execute the bots' definitions. The execution engine includes several connectors to interact with external platforms (e.g., SLACK or GITHUB). In the context of this work, we implemented a new runtime in XATKIT to enable the communication with Web APIs.

The next sections describe each of these components in more detail. We will use the following running example to illustrate them. The example is based on an API provided by the Transparency Portal of Catalonia. In particular, the API that gives access to pollution data gathered by the surveillance network deployed within Catalonia. The data registers the air quality in Catalonia from 1991 until now, and it is updated daily. Besides the concentration of pollutants in the air, it is also possible to query the location and type of the measurement stations.

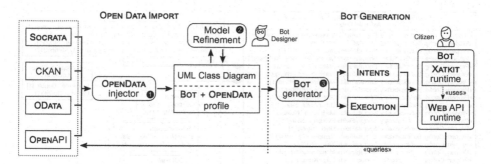

Fig. 1. Overview of our approach.

4 Importing Open Data APIs as Models

The import phase starts by analyzing the Open Data API description to inject a UML model representing its concepts, properties, and operations. This model is later refined by the bot designer. Next sections describe the main elements of this process. We will introduce first the modeling support required to represent Open Data APIs, then the injection step and finally the main tasks to tackle in the refinement step.

4.1 Modeling Open Data APIs

To model Open Data APIs, we propose employing UML class diagrams plus two UML profiles required to optimize and customize the bot generation.

Core Open Data Representation as a UML Class Diagram. Concepts, properties and operations of Open Data APIs are represented using standard elements of UML structural models (classes, properties and operations, respectively). Figure 2 shows an excerpt of the UML model for the running example[8]. As can be seen, the model includes the core concept of the API, called *AirQuality-Data*; plus two more classes to represent data structures (i.e., *Address* and *Location*). Note that the some elements include stereotypes that we will present later.

It is worth noting that most Open Data APIs focus around a single core data element composed of a rich set of properties which can be split (i.e., "normalized") into separate UML classes following good design practices, also facilitating the understanding of the model. This is what we have done for the UML diagram shown in Fig. 2.

The Bot Profile. To be able to generate more complete bots, in particular, to expand on aspects important for the quality of the conversation, the BOT profile adds a set of stereotypes for UML model elements that cover (1) what

---

[8] Full model available at http://hdl.handle.net/20.500.12004/1/C/ICWE/2021/232.

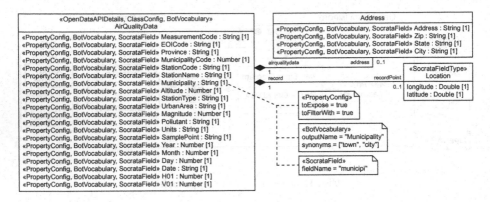

Fig. 2. UML model for the running example (our editor can show/hide the stereotypes to show a simplified representation of the diagram).

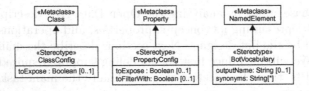

Fig. 3. BOT profile.

data the chatbot should expose, (2) how to refer to model elements (instead of the some obscure internal API identifiers), and (3) synonyms for model elements that citizens may employ when attempting to alternatively name the concept as part of a sentence.

Figure 3 shows the specification of the BOT profile. It comprises three stereotypes, namely, *ClassConfig*, *PropertyConfig* and *BotVocabulary*, extending the *Class*, *Property* and *NamedElement* UML metaclasses, respectively. The *ClassConfig* stereotype includes the *toExpose* property, in charge of defining if the annotated Class element has to be made visible to end-users via the chatbot. The *PropertyConfig* stereotype also includes the *toExpose* property, with the same purpose; plus the *toFilterWith* property, which indicates if the corresponding annotated property can be used to filter results as part of a conversation iteration. For instance, in our running example, pollution data could be filtered via date. Finally, the *BotVocabulary* stereotype can annotate almost any UML model element and allows specifying a more "readable" name to be used when printing concept information and a set of synonyms for the element.

In Fig. 2 we see the BOT profile applied on the running example. Note, for instance, how we define that *town* and *city* could be used as synonyms of *Municipality* and that this attribute can be used to filter *AirQuality* results.

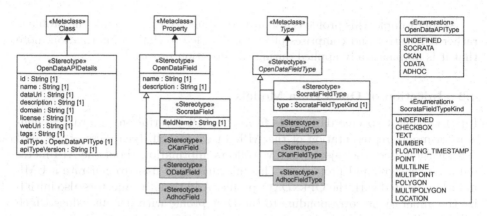

Fig. 4. OPENDATA profile.

The OpenData Profile. While the previous profile is more oriented towards improving the communication between the chatbot and the user, this OPENDATA profile is specially aimed at defining the technical details the chatbot needs to know in order to communicate with the Open Data API backend. The profile defines a set of stereotypes that cover how to access the information of the model elements via the Web API. The access method depends on the specification followed by the Open Data API, which can be SOCRATA, CKAN, ODATA or OPENAPI.

Figure 4 shows the OPENDATA profile. As can be seen, we have defined three stereotypes, namely, *OpenDataAPIDetails*, *OpenDataField* and *OpenDataField-Type*, which extend *Class*, *Property* and *Type* UML metaclasses, respectively. The *OpenDataAPIDetails* stereotype includes a set of properties to enable the API query of the annotated UML Class. For instance, it includes the *domain* and *webUri* to specify the host and route parameters to build the query. It also includes the *APIType* property, which sets the kind of Open Data API (see values of the *OpenDataAPIType* enumeration). The *OpenDataField* stereotype annotates properties with additional information depending on the type of Open Data API used. For instance, the *SocrataField* stereotype indicates the name of the field (see *fieldName*) that has to be queried to retrieve the annotated property. Finally, the *OpenDataFieldType* stereotype includes additional information regarding the types of the properties used by the Open Data APIs.

Figure 4 also includes stereotypes prefixed with *CKAN*, *OData* and *Adhoc* (in grey) to cover the information required for CKAN, ODATA and OPENAPI specifications. We do not fully detail them due to the lack of space but they are available online[9]. Besides, the *Adhoc* annotations also use the OPENAPI profile [8].

---

[9] http://hdl.handle.net/20.500.12004/1/C/ICWE/2021/411.

As an example, this profile is also used to annotate Fig. 2. While the profile is rather exhaustive and comprises plenty of detailed, technical information, note that it is automatically applied during the injection process.

4.2 Injection of Open Data Models

Injectors collect specific data items from the API descriptions in order to generate a model representation of the API. In a nutshell, regardless of the API specification used, the injector always collects information about the API metadata, its concepts and properties. This information is used to generate a UML model annotated with the OPENDATA profile. Additionally, injectors also initialize the annotations corresponding to the BOT profile with default values which will later be tuned during the refinement step (see next subsection).

In our running example, the injector takes as input the SOCRATA description of the data source[10] to create the UML model classes and stereotypes. To complement the definition of the data fields and their types, the injector also calls the VIEWS API[11], an API provided by SOCRATA to retrieve metainformation about the data fields of datasets.

4.3 Refinement of Open Data Models

Once the injection process creates a UML schema annotated with stereotypes, the bot designer can revise and complete it to generate a more effective chatbot. The main refinement tasks cover: (a) providing default names and synonyms for model elements, which enriches the way the chatbot (and the user) can refer to such elements; and (b) set the visibility of data elements, thus enabling the designer to hide some elements of the API in the conversation.

During the refinement step, the bot designer can also revise the OPENDATA profile values if the API description is not fully aligned with the actual API behavior, as sometimes the specification (input of the process) unfortunately is not completely up-to-date with the API implementation deployed (e.g., type mismatches).

5   Generating the Bot

The generation process takes the annotated model as input and derives the corresponding chatbot implementation. As our proposal relies on XATKIT, this process generates the main artifacts required by such platform, specifically: (1) *intents* definition, which describes the user intentions using training sentences (e.g., the intention to retrieve a specific data point from the data source, or to filter the results), contextual information extraction, and matching conditions; and (2) *execution* definition, which specifies the chatbot behavior as a set of

---

[10] https://analisi.transparenciacatalunya.cat/api/views/metadata/v1/tasf-thgu.json.
[11] https://analisi.transparenciacatalunya.cat/api/views.json?id=tasf-thgu.

bindings between user intentions and response actions (e.g., displaying a message to answer a question, or calling an API endpoint to retrieve data). A similar approach could be followed when targeting other chatbot platforms as they all require similar types of input artefact definitions in order to run bots.

The main challenge when generating the chatbot implementation is to provide effective support to drive the conversation. To this aim, it is crucial to identify both the topic/s of the conversation and the aim of the chatbot, which will enable the definition of the conversation path. In our scenario, the topic/s is set by the API domain model (i.e., the vocabulary information embedded in the UML model and the BOT profile annotations) while the aim is to query the API endpoints (relying on the information provided by the OPENDATA profile).

Our approach supports two conversation modes, which are implemented in the *intents* file. Table 1 lists the main intents generated for the conversation, which we will present while describing the conversation modes. For each intent, we also generate the corresponding set of training sentences, following a predefined set of patterns that are instantiated based on the conversation context and the API vocabulary.

Direct queries The most basic communication in a chatbot is when the user directly asks what is needed (e.g., *What was the pollution yesterday?*). To support this kind of query, we generate intents for each class and attribute in the model[12] enabling users to ask for that specific information. Moreover, we also generate filtering intents that help users choose a certain property as filter to cope with queries returning too many data. Table 1, row 1, shows an example of this type of direct intent generated and a possible user utterance (i.e., concrete user input query) corresponding to this intent kind.

Guided queries We call *guided queries* those interactions where there is an exchange of questions/requests between the chatbot and the user, simulating a more natural Open Data exploration approach. Their implementation requires a clear definition of the possible dialog paths driving the conversation. Table 1, rows 2–6, shows the intents generated for guided conversations, which are applied in order (starting with *GuidedSearch* and then adding filters using the rest of the intents). Figure 5a aims to summarize the possible conversation paths and the application order of the intents. The shown paths start once the user provides an exploratory query of a specific concept made available by the API (e.g., *Show me the list of X*). If the concept can be filtered, the chatbot will ask the user whether he wants to apply filters. If the answer is yes, the chatbot will provide buttons to help the user choose the parameters he wants to filter with (e.g., date, address) and the operations he wants to apply (e.g., before, equals). This step repeats while the user wants to apply more filters. Figure 5b shows an example of guided query for our running example.

---

[12] Note that this scales well as we do not actually create completely separate intents for each possible combination but use intent templates that can be instantiated at run-time over the list of elements in the model.

Table 1. Main intents generated.

Mode	Intent	Description	Example sentence
Direct	*DirectSearch*	Shows elements given a filter	`show me all the air quality data with municipality equals to"Barcelona"`
Guided	*GuidedSearch*	Shows elements in conversation	`show me the list of air quality data`
Guided	*AddFilter*	Chooses an attribute to filter	`date`
Guided	*ChooseOperator*	Chooses an operator	`equals`
Guided	*ProvideValue*	Sets a value	`yesterday`
Guided	*EndFilter*	Ends filter for results	`I don't want to add filters`
Both	*SelectField*	Select fields for results	`municipality`
Both	*ShowResult*	Ends field selection for results	`I don't want to add fields`
Both	*AddPostFilter*	Adds a filter in results	`add filter magnitude less than "14"`
Both	*SortOrderBy*	Sorts/Orders the result	`sort by name ASC` `order by date ASC`
Both	*NextPage*	Shows the next page of results	`show me next page`
Both	*AddPostFunction*	Calls function on results	`calculate FUN ATT`

As input assistance, both direct and guided modes include buttons as short-cuts in the conversation interface (see Fig. 5b). Once the chatbot collects the request (with the possible filters) from the user, the next step is to query the involved Open Data Web API, which relies on the information provided in the OPENDATA profile. The implementation of this step is specified in the *execution* file, where the steps to query, filter and retrieve the information from the API are generated.

The final step in every query performed by the chatbot involves present-ing and post-processing the results. In the presentation step, the user indicates the fields to show. Table 1, rows 7–8, shows the intents for setting the fields to present. Figure 5c shows an example of the result for our running example showing the fields *Municipality* and *Magnitude*. In the post-processing step, the user can apply additional filters, sort the results and paginate them. Table 1, rows 9–12, shows the intents for post-processing the results. Finally, note that our approach also incorporates aggregation functions (e.g., calculate the aver-age, minimum o maximum) as post-processing operators, and built-in pagination support to facilitate the navigation of large result sets.

6   Tool Support

Our approach has been implemented as a new plugin for the Eclipse platform[13]. We rely on the environment extensibility and modeling support provided by Eclipse to import and generate the chatbot definition, which is then eventually executed by XATKIT.

Figure 6 shows several screenshots of the development environment. It com-prises two wizards to perform the import and generation phases. During the

---

[13] https://github.com/opendata-for-all/open-data-chatbot-generator.

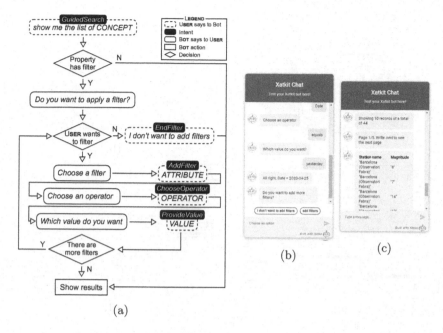

Fig. 5. (a) Conversation path in guided queries. (b) A guided conversation. (c) Showing the results.

import phase, the UML model is loaded (see wizard in Figs. 6a and 6b) visualized and refined using the PAPYRUS modeling IDE. Once completed, our generation wizard (see Figs. 6c and 6d) creates the definition of the chatbot.

7 Related Work

Facilitating the interaction with Open Data sources has been studied from different perspectives. For instance, the work by González-Mora *et al.* [12] aims to generate REST APIs for Open Data sources while the works by Cao *et al.* [3] and Ed-Douibi *et al.* [9] look to generate the specification of such REST APIs to simplify their consumption by client applications.

Nevertheless, the role of chatbots in Open Data has not been widely studied. Keyner *et al.* [14] proposed a chatbot to help users find data sources in an Open Data repository by relying on geo-entity annotations. However, the chatbot only suggests the data sources to explore. It does not provide querying capabilities to consult those data sources. The work by Neumaier *et al.* [16] is similar, also focusing on the suggestion of potential useful datasets. Instead, Porreca *et al.* [19] described a case study of using a chatbot for a concrete dataset. In all cases, chatbots are manually created.

A couple of works address the creation of chatbots to query Web APIs. Our own OPENAPI bot [11] helps developers understand what they could do with

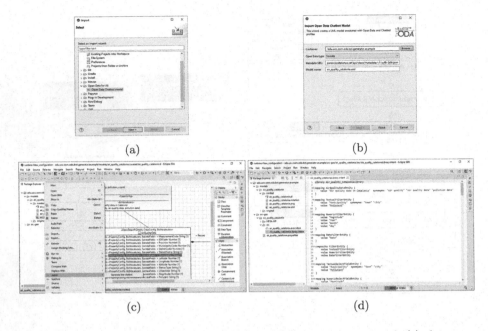

Fig. 6. Screenshots of the tool support: (a) and (b) the import wizard, (c) the generation wizard and (d) the generated bot.

an API if its OPENAPI definition is available, more than targeting the end-users. More similar to ours, the work by Vazir *et al.* [21] generates a chatbot to facilitate the execution of calls to the API itself. Nevertheless, they remain very implementation-oriented and focus on helping users learn how to query the API and assisting them in providing the right parameters for the call more than offering any abstraction mechanism to add further semantics, configuration and flexibility to the bot generation process, as we do.

Chatbot modeling and generation has also been proposed in some works (i.e., [4,5,18,20]) but none of these works proposes an end-to-end approach as ours, from the reverse engineering of the Open Data source to the generation of a chatbot actually able to directly call the initial source.

Therefore, to the best of our knowledge, ours is the first work aimed at automatically generating chatbots to directly interact with Open Data sources using a model-based approach.

8   Conclusion

In this paper, we have presented a model-based approach to generate chatbots as user-friendly interfaces to query Open Data sources published as Web APIs. The resulting chatbot accepts both direct queries and guided conversations, where the chatbot and the user interact to precise the final query to send to the API. We have implemented our approach as an Eclipse plugin that fully supports

SOCRATA and allows the integration of other Open Data specifications (i.e., ODATA, CKAN) as well as generic Web APIs (via OPENAPI specification); and generates chatbots using the XATKIT platform.

As further work, we plan to work on several extensions of this core framework:

Support for Advanced Queries. Our approach supports descriptive queries where users navigate the data. However, there are other types of interesting queries; for instance, we could have: (i) diagnostic queries, which focus on the analysis of potential reasons for a fact to happen; (ii) predictive queries, aimed at exploring how a fact may evolve in the future; and (iii) prescriptive ones, which study how to reproduce a fact. We plan to extend our query templates to provide initial support for these types of queries. Some of these queries (especially if detected at often ones) could even be an inspiration for an API extension to better match the API design with the actual information needs of the API users.

Composition of Several Open Data sources. Many times, the data needs of a citizen span several Web APIs. The chatbot should be able to query and combine those different sources, dealing with potential composition links among them. This composition is not trivial and involves the well-known challenges of any data integration scenario (e.g., entity matching) plus some others more API-specific like finding the optimal paths (even based on non-functional properties), as sometimes similar information can be obtained from different overlapping sources. Existing works on API composition [6,10,15] can be used here to present to the chatbot a single unified API to simplify this process.

Massive Chatbot Generation for Open Data Portals. Our approach works on either individual APIs or a set of interrelated ones (see the point above). We plan to extend our tool support with an automated pipeline able to retrieve and process all available APIs in a given open data portal.

Voice-Driven Chatbots. The growing adoption of smart assistants emphasizes the need to design chatbots supporting not only text-based conversations but also voice-based interactions. We believe that our chatbot could benefit from such a feature to improve the citizen's experience further when manipulating Open Data APIs. While XATKIT's modular architecture supports both textual and voice-based chatbots, additional research is required to translate raw data returned by the API into sentences that can be read by the bot.

Additional Types of Data Sources. We cover the most common choices in governmental Open Data portals, but they are not the only ones. For instance, LINKEDDATA sources, pure RDF files, GEOJSON collections, or database dumps, among others, are also used. We plan to develop additional import components that can target these technologies and integrate them into our framework.

References

1. Alghamdi, A., Owda, M.S., Crockett, K.A.: Natural language interface to relational database (NLI-RDB) through object relational mapping (ORM). In: Workshop on Computational Intelligence. Advances in Intelligent Systems and Computing, vol. 513, pp. 449–464 (2016)
2. Bizer, C., Heath, T., Berners-Lee, T.: Linked data: The story so far. In: Semantic Services, Interoperability and Web Applications: Emerging Concepts, pp. 205–227. IGI Global (2011)
3. Cao, H., Falleri, J.-R., Blanc, X.: Automated generation of REST API specification from plain HTML documentation. In: Maximilien, M., Vallecillo, A., Wang, J., Oriol, M. (eds.) ICSOC 2017. LNCS, vol. 10601, pp. 453–461. Springer, Cham (2017). https://doi.org/10.1007/978-3-319-69035-3_32
4. Castaldo, N., Daniel, F., Matera, M., Zaccaria, V.: Conversational data exploration. In: international conference on Web Engineering, pp. 490–497 (2019)
5. Chittò, P., Baez, M., Daniel, F., Benatallah, B.: Automatic generation of chatbots for conversational web browsing. In: Dobbie, G., Frank, U., Kappel, G., Liddle, S.W., Mayr, H.C. (eds.) ER 2020. LNCS, vol. 12400, pp. 239–249. Springer, Cham (2020). https://doi.org/10.1007/978-3-030-62522-1_17
6. Cremaschi, M., De Paoli, F.: Toward automatic semantic API descriptions to support services composition. In: De Paoli, F., Schulte, S., Broch Johnsen, E. (eds.) ESOCC 2017. LNCS, vol. 10465, pp. 159–167. Springer, Cham (2017). https://doi.org/10.1007/978-3-319-67262-5_12
7. Daniel, G., Cabot, J., Deruelle, L., Derras, M.: Xatkit: a multimodal low-code chatbot development framework. IEEE Access **8**, 15332–15346 (2020)
8. Ed-Douibi, H., Cánovas Izquierdo, J., Bordeleau, F., Cabot, J.: WAPIml: towards a modeling infrastructure for web APIs. In: International Conference on Model Driven Engineering Languages and Systems Companion, pp. 748–752 (2019)
9. Ed-douibi, H., Cánovas Izquierdo, J.L., Cabot, J.: Example-driven web API specification discovery. In: Anjorin, A., Espinoza, H. (eds.) ECMFA 2017. LNCS, vol. 10376, pp. 267–284. Springer, Cham (2017). https://doi.org/10.1007/978-3-319-61482-3_16
10. Ed-douibi, H., Cánovas Izquierdo, J.L., Cabot, J.: APIComposer: data-driven composition of REST APIs. In: Kritikos, K., Plebani, P., de Paoli, F. (eds.) ESOCC 2018. LNCS, vol. 11116, pp. 161–169. Springer, Cham (2018). https://doi.org/10.1007/978-3-319-99819-0_12
11. Ed-Douibi, H., Daniel, G., Cabot, J.: OpenAPI bot: a chatbot to help you understand REST APIs. In: Bielikova, M., Mikkonen, T., Pautasso, C. (eds.) ICWE 2020. LNCS, vol. 12128, pp. 538–542. Springer, Cham (2020). https://doi.org/10.1007/978-3-030-50578-3_40
12. González-Mora, C., Garrigós, I., Jacobo Zubcoff, J., Mazón, J.: Model-based generation of web application programming interfaces to access open data (In Prepress). J. Web Eng. **19**(7–8), 194–217 (2020)
13. Kerlyl, A., Hall, P., Bull, S.: Bringing chatbots into education: towards natural language negotiation of open learner models. In: International Conference on Applications and Innovations in Intelligent Systems, pp. 179–192 (2006)
14. Keyner, S., Savenkov, V., Vakulenko, S.: Open data chatbot. In: Satellite Events of The Semantic Web, pp. 111–115 (2019)
15. Musyaffa, F.A., Halilaj, L., Siebes, R., Orlandi, F., Auer, S.: Minimally invasive semantification of light weight service descriptions. In: International Conference on Web Services, pp. 672–677 (2016)

16. Neumaier, S., Savenkov, V., Vakulenko, S.: Talking open data. In: Satellite Events of The Semantic Web, pp. 132–136 (2017)
17. Pereira, J., Díaz, Ó.: Chatbot dimensions that matter: lessons from the trenches. In: International Conference on Web Engineering, pp. 129–135 (2018)
18. Pérez-Soler, S., Daniel, G., Cabot, J., Guerra, E., de Lara, J.: Towards automating the synthesis of chatbots for conversational model query. In: Nurcan, S., Reinhartz-Berger, I., Soffer, P., Zdravkovic, J. (eds.) BPMDS/EMMSAD -2020. LNBIP, vol. 387, pp. 257–265. Springer, Cham (2020). https://doi.org/10.1007/978-3-030-49418-6_17
19. Porreca, S., Leotta, F., Mecella, M., Vassos, S., Catarci, T.: Accessing government open data through chatbots. In: International Workshop on Current Trends in Web Engineering, pp. 156–165 (2017)
20. Sindhgatta, R., Barros, A., Nili, A.: Modeling conversational agents for service systems. In: On the Move to Meaningful Internet Systems, pp. 552–560 (2019)
21. Vaziri, M., Mandel, L., Shinnar, A., Siméon, J., Hirzel, M.: Generating chat bots from web API specifications. In: ACM SIGPLAN Onward!, pp. 44–57 (2017)
22. Xu, A., Liu, Z., Guo, Y., Sinha, V., Akkiraju, R.: A new chatbot for customer service on social media. In: Conference on Human Factors in Computing Systems, pp. 3506–3510 (2017)

Open Data Accessibility Based on Voice Commands

César González-Mora[1]([✉]), Irene Garrigós[1], Jose-Norberto Mazón[1],
Sven Casteleyn[2], and Sergio Firmenich[3]

[1] Web And Knowledge Research Group, Department of Software
and Computing Systems, University of Alicante, Alicante, Spain
{cgmora,igarrigos,jnmazon}@ua.es
[2] Geospatial Technologies Lab (GEOTEC), Institute of New Imaging
Technologies (INIT), University Jaime I, Castellón de la Plana, Spain
sven.casteleyn@uji.es
[3] LIFIA, Facultad de Informatica, UNLP and CONICET, La Plata, Argentina
sergio.firmenich@lifia.info.unlp.edu.ar

Abstract. Nowadays, the accessibility of open data on the Web is problematic, in particular for those data enthusiasts (non-technical users really interested in data) with visual disabilities. They generally experience accessibility barriers when browsing open data portals. Therefore, in order to improve accessibility and facilitate visually impaired users to obtain open data, we propose a Web Augmentation Framework for Accessibility for Open Data (WAFRA4OD). The proposed approach uses Web augmentation techniques and voice interaction to help users in finding relevant open data by offering them various useful comments, including a full fledged voice interaction interface. Thereby, WAFRA4OD enables visually impaired data enthusiasts to explore and interact with open data portals using voice commands, and thus improves the accessibility of open data. To show the feasibility of WAFRA4OD we demonstrate its use in a case study using the European Data Portal.

Keywords: Web accessibility · Web augmentation · Open data · Voice interaction

Dedication

With great sadness in our hearts, we dedicate this work to Florian Daniel, our friend and colleague who recently passed away, way too early. We know Florian for his brilliant mind and scientific work, we will remember him for his kind, warm and engaging personality, and for his optimistic spirit and catchy laugh.

1 Introduction

Open data portals aim to publish datasets equipped with metadata and organised as searchable catalogues. They are generally accessed by data enthusiasts [8], those users with no technical skills but willing to consume data to

© Springer Nature Switzerland AG 2021
M. Brambilla et al. (Eds.): ICWE 2021, LNCS 12706, pp. 456–463, 2021.
https://doi.org/10.1007/978-3-030-74296-6_34

answer domain-specific questions. Although governments and institutions that create open data portals generally adopt publishing guidelines (such as the Data Catalogue Vocabulary (DCAT) standard[1]), the accessibility of open data on these portals remains an issue [6,10], particularly for visually impaired users. For example, in most open data portals such as the European Data Portal[2], in order to search open data users must choose one of the available categories in the screen or enter a search term in a text box which may be difficult to find. Then, a list of datasets is shown, from which users can access to a specific dataset's webpage. Finally, in this dataset's page, a great deal of information and metadata is available, including the links to the dataset contents as external resources. Therefore, without any help, they find it hard to obtain data from these open data portals [5].

In order to allow visually impaired users to access websites, several approaches and tools have been proposed. Most popularly, screen readers [3] render textual and visual web content as audio output. These screen readers have been enhanced by annotation and/or voice interaction [1,2,12,13] to facilitate browsing in generic websites. However, there is still a gap between open data Web portals and users with disabilities because current solutions focus on day-to-day websites and they do not provide specific support for open data Web portals for data enthusiasts.

Therefore, in this paper we propose the Web Augmentation Framework for Accessibility for Open Data (WAFRA4OD), which takes into account the structure of open data portals through the use of DCAT standard. This approach can be used with different voice commands to perform speech synthesis operations. The main novelty of WAFRA4OD is the specific support for open data portals, considering portals structure, datasets' metadata and data contents.

This article is structured as follows. First, Sect. 2 gives more details about related works. Then, Sect. 3 presents our approach for Web accessibility in open data portals with a case study in Sect. 4 to better explain the voice operations, and finally, conclusions are drawn in Sect. 5.

2   Related Work

In order to improve Web accessibility, there are several related works. On the one hand, screen readers [3] are among the most used tools to facilitate the interaction with computer systems for users with disabilities, including the Web browser. Great examples of current screen readers are JAWS[3] and BrowseAloud[4]. However, these kind of solution are intended to read websites aloud but in a straightforward way, reading even metadata. Therefore, users - specially non-experienced users - may have a hard time to find what they are looking for on the Web [3]. To tackle screen readers' problems, different approaches

---

[1] https://www.w3.org/TR/vocab-dcat-2/.

[2] https://www.europeandataportal.eu/en.

[3] https://www.freedomscientific.com/products/software/jaws/.

[4] https://www.texthelp.com/en-gb/products/browsealoud/.

aim to improve websites so they can be easily accessed by screen readers. The Dante [13] approach semantically annotates Web objects with the Web Authoring for Accessibility (WAfA) ontology [9], using a tool or as part of the web engineering process [11], and then it transcodes the contents of the website to improve its accessibility. A conversational Web interaction system [2] has also been proposed in order to change the way users interact with a website. With this system, users are able to ask a chatbot to obtain specific contents in natural language, but the main focus is usability, not accessibility. Only adapting the original website by their authors, making it compliant with the proposed specification, could provide some accessibility support. The HearSay system [4] proposes an improvement for voice browsing, a similar approach to screen readers which do not provide filtering of Web content to eliminate "noise". This proposal presents a dialog interface, a voice interactive way of obtaining the information from websites. This approach is specifically committed to help only blind people to navigate Web contents. These solutions aim to improve accessibility in data-intensive websites but their application to open data portals is not sufficient, as the complex structure of open data portals based on metadata coming from DCAT standard is not provided. Moreover, they do not consider the access to external resources whose contents are not presented on the screen - such as datasets in open data portals.

Therefore, although there are approaches which deal with Web accessibility problems, a complete solution focused on open data portals is still needed for visually impaired data enthusiasts.

3   Web Augmentation Framework for Open Data Accessibility

In this section we present the Web Augmentation Framework for Accessibility for Open Data (WAFRA4OD), which aims to improve open data portals accessibility. The approach started with a previous version created by the authors [7] consisting of a voice-based interactive framework which aimed to improve the accessibility of data-intensive websites, such as Wikipedia. With WAFRA4OD, we now focus on the access of data enthusiasts with visual problems to open data from Web portals.

These data enthusiasts with visual disabilities are the main beneficiaries of our current approach (Fig. 1). These users are now impeded to access these data, because they need help to find relevant data within the open data catalogue and then read data contents. Therefore, in order to improve Web portals accessibility, WAFRA4OD proposes a predefined set of accessibility operations based on the Web Content Accessibility Guidelines[5]. Furthermore, these operations are aligned with the Data Catalogue Vocabulary (DCAT) in order to consider Web open data portals structure and thus better access open data. WAFRA4OD has been designed by using the European Data Portal as case study, but it can easily be applied to other portals if they are DCAT-compliant.

---

[5] https://www.w3.org/WAI/WCAG21/quickref/.

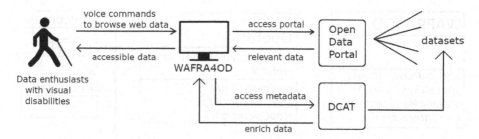

Fig. 1. Overview of WAFRA4OD

First of all, a set of operations are offered to help users find relevant data, dealing with lists of datasets and different filters to be applied. Then, operations that deal with dataset metadata are offered, similarly as a screen reader functions. However, in our case, we are considering the structure of the Web open data portal (through DCAT standard), and easily read aloud information that may be difficult to find on the screen. Finally, operations that deal with datasets' content help visually-impaired users to access tabular contents from open data sources. All these operations are explained in detail in the following Sect. 4.

3.1 Extending WAFRA4OD with New Operations

Apart from the existing operations, new accessibility operations can easily be added by users with programming skills as WAFRA4OD is a framework. The framework is based on a "WAFRA4OD" main class (Fig. 2). This class is responsible of speech recognition and synthesis, and includes a set of operations. These operations inherit from the "Operation" abstract class which includes different properties and methods. A default implementation of all these methods from this abstract class is provided, facilitating the task of creating new operations. Moreover, as the already existing operations follow this class inheritance structure, they can serve as example, or even as reusable components, for the implementation of new operations for WAFRA4OD.

3.2 Implementation Details

WAFRA4OD consists of a script developed in Javascript. Before installing it from Greasy Fork[6], the browser extension Tampermonkey[7] is required. Once installed, visually impaired users can start using the accessibility operations to access open data. WAFRA4OD implements speech recognition and synthesis in order to hear for operations and the apply them with the help of the Web Speech API[8] of JavaScript. Moreover, most of the operations offered by WAFRA4OD take into account the DCAT standard by using a CKAN API to access portals' metadata.

---

[6] https://greasyfork.org/es/scripts/419908-wafra4od.
[7] https://www.tampermonkey.net/.
[8] https://wicg.github.io/speech-api/.

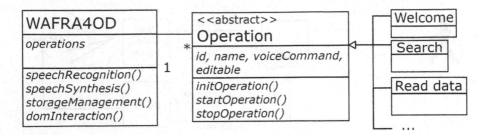

Fig. 2. WAFRA4OD framework structure overview.

The implementation of WAFRA4OD has been successfully tested on the European Open Data portal, which has a CKAN-based infrastructure (not pure CKAN, but DCAT-compliant). Importantly, WAFRA4OD can be easily applied to other pure CKAN open data portals, by adapting existing operations to different implementation of DCAT.

4   WAFRA4OD Case Study

Our case study is focus on a user interested in obtaining tabular data about street lighting in the Candem Council from the European Data Portal.

After installing Tampermonkey and our script, at the European Data Portal's main webpage the available operations are automatically read aloud by WAFRA4OD. At any moment, they can be read aloud again using the voice command "welcome". In this main page, the "search" voice command is available to search by text terms. In this case, the user is interested in searching datasets by filtering with the voice command "search" followed by the term "candem street lighting", as the dataset to find by the user is about street lighting in Candem.

After that, the user is redirected to the page with the list of datasets related to street lighting (Fig. 3). In this results page the user can take advantage of the same operations of the main page, but also there are different operations to apply (which are explained to the user when the page is loaded): "add filter" to know available filters and apply them, "results" to read aloud the list of datasets, and "choose" to access the specific page of a dataset and other accessibility operations. In this case study, the user wants to know the obtained results so the voice command "results" is the most suitable, making WAFRA4OD to read aloud the list of datasets. As the user is interested in tabular data, first the voice command "add filter" can be used to know available filters and then "add filter format csv" to apply the filter specified. Once the user has filtered the results, if the user considers one dataset interesting, the command "choose" followed by the dataset position in the list is used to access the dataset's page, in this case the dataset about street lighting in Candem Council[9] shown in Fig. 4.

---

[9] https://www.europeandataportal.eu/data/datasets/camden-street-lighting.

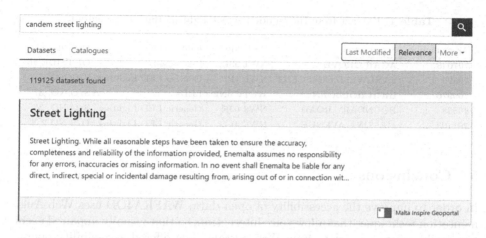

Fig. 3. Extract from the European data web portal results page.

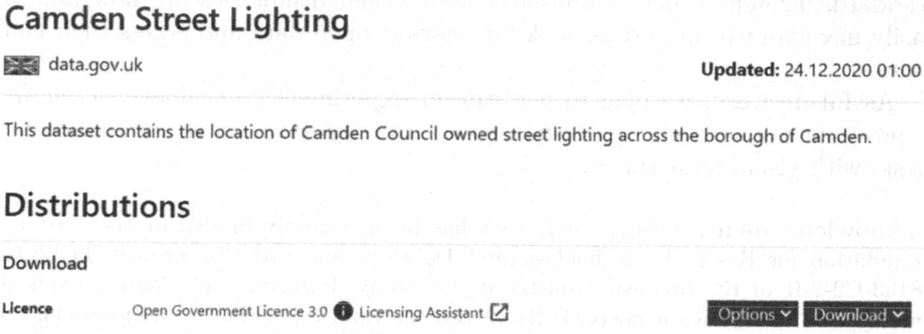

Camden Street Lighting

🏴 data.gov.uk   **Updated:** 24.12.2020 01:00

This dataset contains the location of Camden Council owned street lighting across the borough of Camden.

Distributions

Download

Licence   Open Government Licence 3.0 ⓘ Licensing Assistant ☑   Options ⌄ Download ⌄

Fig. 4. Extract from the European data web portal dataset's page.

Now, in the dataset's page, the user is able to ask for dataset metadata (already obtained with the "details" command) and also access dataset's contents. The user is first interested in knowing the columns of the dataset, so that the "read columns" command is available. Then, the user can use the following voice commands related to data contents: "read row" followed by the row number, "read rows" to read all the dataset's contents and "read rows from n to m" to read a range of rows. Finally, the user is able to download the dataset tabular resource using the "download" voice command. An extract of the dataset is presented in Table 1.

The complete case study to access open data in the European data portal is shown in a demo video[10] to better demonstrate how the user interacts with WAFRA4OD through voice operations.

---

[10] https://youtu.be/HvUw9o3IvDY.

Table 1. Extract from the camden street lighting dataset's content.

Asset number	Street name	Postcode	Lamp type	Description
707048	AGAR GROVE	NW1 9SL	Cosmopolis	OUTSIDE 15
70590	SANDWELL CRESCENT	NW6 1PB	Generic LED Lighting	S/O NO. 5
709976	HIGH HOLBORN	WC1V 6NP	LEDs	S/O NO. 37
70858	BOUNDARY ROAD	NW8 0JE	Generic LED Lighting	S/O NO. 35
701403	MESSINA AVENUE	NW6 4LD	Generic LED Lighting	O/S NO 2/4

5   Conclusions

In order to improve the accessibility of open data, WAFRA4OD uses Web Augmentation techniques that allow voice interaction, so that visually impaired users can easily access open data from Web portals. The offered accessibility operations by WAFRA4OD are tailored to open data portals based on the DCAT standard. Therefore, data enthusiasts with visual disabilities are now able to easily navigate within portals, look for relevant open data and access their contents.

As future work, we plan to perform an experiment to evaluate the actual improvement of accessibility of our approach in open data portals for data enthusiasts with visual impairment.

Acknowledgement. This research work has been partially funded by the National Foundation for Research, Technology and Development with the project TIN2016-78103-C2-2-R of the Spanish Ministry of Economy, Industry and Competitiveness; and by the DataTourism postCOVID-19 project funded by the "Consejo Social" of University of Alicante.

References

1. Ashok, V., Billah, S.M., Borodin, Y., Ramakrishnan, I.: Auto-suggesting browsing actions for personalized web screen reading. In: Proceedings of the 27th ACM Conference on User Modeling, Adaptation and Personalization, pp. 252–260 (2019)
2. Baez, M., Daniel, F., Casati, F.: Conversational web interaction: proposal of a dialog-based natural language interaction paradigm for the web. In: Proceedings of the Third International Workshop on Chatbot Research and Design (2019)
3. Borodin, Y., Bigham, J.P., Dausch, G., Ramakrishnan, I.V.: More than meets the eye: a survey of screen-reader browsing strategies. In: Proceedings of the International Cross Disciplinary Conference on Web Accessibility (W4A) (2010)
4. Borodin, Y., Mahmud, J., Ramakrishnan, I.V., Stent, A.: The HearSay non-visual web browser. In: Proceedings of the International Cross-Disciplinary Conference on Web Accessibility (W4A), W4A 2007, pp. 128–129 (2007)
5. Doush, I., Pontelli, E.: Non-visual navigation of spreadsheets. Univ. Access Inf. Soc. 12 (2012)
6. Ferati, M., Dalipi, F., Kastrati, Z.: Open government data through the lens of universal design. In: Universal Access in Human-Computer Interaction. Applications and Practice, pp. 331–340 (2020)

7. González-Mora, C., Garrigós, I., Casteleyn, S., Firmenich, S.: A web augmentation framework for accessibility based on voice interaction. In: ICWE, pp. 547–550 (2020)
8. Hanrahan, P.: Analytic database technologies for a new kind of user: The data enthusiast. In: Proceedings of the ACM SIGMOD International Conference on Management of Data, pp. 577–578 (2012)
9. Harper, S., Yesilada, Y.: Web authoring for accessibility (WAfA). J. Web Semant. 5(3), 175–179 (2007)
10. Manchova, R., Hub, M., Lnenicka, M.: Usability evaluation of open data portals evaluating data discoverability, accessibility, and reusability from a stakeholders' perspective. ASLIB. J. Inf. Manage. 70(3), 252–268 (2018)
11. Plessers, P., et al.: Accessibility: a web engineering approach. In: Proceedings of the 14th international conference on World Wide Web, pp. 353–362 (2005)
12. Ripa, G., Torre, M., Firmenich, S., Rossi, G.: End-user development of voice user interfaces based on web content. In: End-User Development, pp. 34–50 (2019)
13. Yesilada, Y., Stevens, R., Harper, S., Goble, C.: Evaluating DANTE: Semantic transcoding for visually disabled users. ACM Trans. Comput.-Hum. Interact. 14(3), 14-es (2007)

PWA vs the Others: A Comparative Study on the UI Energy-Efficiency of Progressive Web Apps

Stefan Huber[1]([✉]) [iD], Lukas Demetz[1] [iD], and Michael Felderer[2] [iD]

[1] University of Applied Sciences Kufstein, Kufstein, Austria
{stefan.huber,lukas.demetz}@fh-kufstein.ac.at
[2] Department of Computer Science, University of Innsbruck, Innsbruck, Austria
michael.felderer@uibk.ac.at

Abstract. Developing the same mobile app for multiple platforms is a prominent challenge for practitioners in mobile software development. When starting an app project, practitioners are faced with a plethora of development approaches to choose from. Progressive Web Apps (PWAs) are a novel and promising approach for mobile cross-platform development (MCPD). As mobile devices are limited regarding battery capacity, the energy footprint of a mobile app should be kept as low as possible. Thus, the aim of this study is to analyze the difference in energy consumption of PWAs and other mobile development approaches with a focus on UI rendering and interaction scenarios. For this, we implemented five versions of the same app with different development approaches and examined their energy footprint on two Android devices with four execution scenarios. The results show that the used development approach influences the energy footprint of a mobile app. Native development shows the lowest energy consumption. PWAs, albeit not the lowest energy consuming mobile development approach, are a viable alternative to other MCPD approaches. Moreover, the web-browser engine used to execute the PWA has a significant influence on the energy footprint of the app.

Keywords: Mobile cross-platform development · Mobile web engineering · Mobile app energy efficiency · Progressive web apps

1 Introduction

Mobile devices have seen a significant increase in terms of CPU and memory performance over the last years. Still, power supply and energy consumption are limiting factors of mobile devices [23]. Thus, practitioners must pay attention to the energy consumed by their implemented mobile apps, which is, a challenging task [22]. Furthermore, users are interested in energy efficient apps and are not reluctant to rate energy inefficient apps negatively [28].

© Springer Nature Switzerland AG 2021
M. Brambilla et al. (Eds.): ICWE 2021, LNCS 12706, pp. 464–479, 2021.
https://doi.org/10.1007/978-3-030-74296-6_35

When developing mobile apps, developers are presented with a myriad of development approaches. Progressive web apps (PWAs) are a rather novel approach to develop mobile apps that can be run on different mobile platforms (e.g., Apple iOS and Google Android). PWAs are websites with additional functionality, such as offline availability and the possibility to install the PWA on the user's home screen. As such, PWAs are an example of mobile cross-platform development (MCPD) approaches. The idea of such development approaches is to deploy mobile apps to multiple mobile platforms from a single code base. They allow writing code once and run it anywhere [8]. App market analytics[1] indicate that these development approaches are highly popular among developers. In contrast to MCPD approaches, mobile apps can be developed natively, in which dedicated mobile apps have to be implemented for each mobile platform. Currently, there are two leading mobile platforms, Google Android and Apple iOS. Developing mobile apps for multiple platforms is a prominent challenge for developers [13] as dedicated code bases need to be maintained for each supported mobile platform.

Previous research showed that apps developed with MCPD approaches consume more energy during execution than native apps [4,6]. As PWAs are websites with additional functionality, they seem to be more lightweight compared to mobile apps developed with other MCPD approaches. Thus, the goal of this present research is to investigate the energy consumption of PWAs compared to other mobile development approaches with a dedicated focus on UI rendering and interactions. In doing so, this paper strives to answer the following research questions:

RQ1: How do PWAs differ in terms of energy consumption to other mobile development approaches when executing typical UI rendering and interaction scenarios?

RQ2: How does the web-browser engine executing the PWA influence the energy consumption of the PWA?

To answer the research questions, we implemented five versions of a sample app. For each implementation, a different development approach was used. In the sample app, we implemented four common interaction scenarios typically found in mobile apps. We focus on UI interactions, as mobile apps are primarily interactive in nature [27]. To gather data, we developed and executed automated tests in which the interaction scenarios were executed repeatedly. For answering the research question, we then developed hypotheses and tested them using a statistical analysis.

The results show that the used development approach influences the energy footprint of a mobile app. PWAs, albeit not the lowest energy consuming mobile development approach, are a viable alternative to other MCPD approaches. Moreover, the web-browser engine used to execute the PWA has a significant influence on the energy footprint.

The main contributions of this study are: (1) an experimental comparison of the UI energy-efficiency of PWAs related to other mobile development

---

[1] https://appfigures.com/top-sdks/development/apps.

approaches; (2) an experimental comparison of the energy-efficiency of web-browser engines executing PWAs; (3) a discussion of the results from the perspective of mobile web developers; (4) a replication package containing all research artifacts.

The paper is structured as follows. Starting with Sect. 2, we lay out the background of this study, in which possible ways of developing a mobile app are described. Section 3 presents related work highlighting how our research differs from existing research. Section 4 outlines the applied research method. We start by detailing the interaction scenarios and by highlighting the details of the app implementations and the test procedure. Afterwards, we present the energy measurement and the test devices. We then describe our hypotheses and the data analysis. In Sect. 5, we present the results of this study. The results and limitation are discussed in Sect. 6. Finally, Sect. 7 concludes this paper and provides possible directions of future research.

2   Background

When developing apps for mobile platforms, a developer can choose between two possible approaches. The first option is to use a native development approach. When using this approach, a developer has to build and maintain unique code bases for each mobile platform on which the app should run. Currently, there are the two dominating mobile platforms Google Android and Apple iOS [26]. As a result, a developer has to maintain two code bases. Additionally, she needs to have deep knowledge in each of the platforms' subtleties.

The second approach to develop a mobile app is to use MCPD approaches. Such approaches allow building and deploying mobile apps for several mobile platforms from a single code base. MCPD approaches use different technologies for deploying mobile apps to multiple mobile platforms [14]. MCPD approaches can be classified based on their internal functioning [14]. Interpretive MCPD approaches (e.g., React Native) make use of web technologies, such as JavaScript, to render and display native user interface components at run-time. Hybrid approaches, such as Capacitor, display the mobile app within a native Web-View component, which is wrapped inside a native app. Approaches like Flutter integrate a complete rendering engine to generate UI components, which have a similar look and feel as native Android or iOS components.

PWAs are a rather new MCPD approach first introduced in 2015 [24]. The idea of PWAs is to build on top of standard web technologies (i.e., HTML, CSS, and JavaScript). Contrary to a standard website and although being served by and hosted on a web server, PWAs offer more sophisticated functionalities, such as, offline availability [1]. A PWA is a website that can be opened in a mobile device's web-browser. This website has implemented special functionalities that enable specific features, such as, push notifications, background sync and installation of the app [2]. As PWAs are websites with enhanced functionalities, they can also be run on a desktop computer, independent of the computer's operating system.

To implement these special features, PWAs make use of service workers [10]. A service worker is a JavaScript program that is loaded with the website, installed, and run in the background. For instance, to provide offline availability, a service worker intercepts network requests (e.g., loading an image) and serves these requests from a local cache.

For developing PWAs, a developer has several options to choose from. One option is to use common web-frameworks, such as, Angular, Vue, or React. Using such frameworks means to be dependable on standards prescribed by the framework. Alternatively, developers can use frameworkless approaches, such as, StencilJS or Svelte. These approaches compile PWAs in standard formats (i.e., web-components) reducing the load put on mobile devices executing the PWA.

Besides accessing a PWA via URL, marketplaces for apps start to include PWAs (e.g., Google Play Store [9] and Microsoft Store [19]). As such, a PWA can be downloaded and installed like any other mobile app.

Despite its advantages, PWAs still offer limited support for important functionality, such as, access to the file system, access to user data (e.g., calendar entries) and other platform dependent APIs [2]. Others name a possible higher energy consumption as one of PWAs' drawbacks [15].

3   Related Work

A comparison of the energy footprint of different MCPD approaches was presented by Corbalan et al. [6]. The authors based their investigations on three execution scenarios: intensive processing, video playback and audio playback. The study shows that the energy consumption varies strongly between the different scenarios and MCPD approaches. Moreover, native development does not have the lowest energy footprint in all scenarios.

Oliveira et al. [20] present another study, in which the energy efficiency and execution performance of common benchmarks implemented in JavaScript, Java and C++ were compared. The results show that JavaScript has a lower energy consumption in most benchmarks, but not in all. Additionally, they show that implementing parts of an Android app with JavaScript or C++ instead of Java could also save energy.

In [4], Ciman et al. compare the energy consumption of sensors (such as GPS or magnetometer) within apps developed with MCPD approaches and native apps for iOS and Android. The study shows that apps developed using MCPD approaches always exhibit a higher energy consumption than native apps. Furthermore, the authors mention that updating the UI demanded more energy than reading sensor data.

Two studies on the energy efficiency of service workers and networking in PWAs were conducted by Malavolta et al. [16,17]. In their first study, the results show that service workers do not have a significant impact on the energy consumption of PWAs regardless of the used network connection (i.e., 2G or Wi-Fi). The second study shows that an empty or populated cache has also no significant impact on the energy consumption of a PWA.

Previous research analyzed the energy efficiency of MCPD approaches regarding several aspects, such as processing or media playback [6], sensor usage [4] or benchmarks [20]. Energy-related aspects of networking and service workers of PWAs have been investigated by [16,17]. However, these previous studies do not investigate the energy efficiency of UI related aspects, which was identified as a research gap in the literature. As mobile apps are highly interactive in nature [27] and as experiments [21] show, UIs are responsible for a substantial part of the energy footprint of a mobile app, we consider the energy consumption of UI rendering and interactions a critical aspect for comparing PWAs with other mobile development approaches. Therefore we focus our study on the energy consumption of UI rendering and interactions.

4   Research Method

To answer the presented research questions, we implemented five versions of a sample contact management app using different mobile development approaches (Sect. 4.1). For each app, a series of repeatable and typical UI interaction scenarios (Sect. 4.2) was executed in a predefined test procedure (Sect. 4.5). During the procedure, the energy consumption of the different development approaches was collected (Sect. 4.3). The test scenarios were conducted on two different mobile devices (Sect. 4.4). The resulting data was used in a statistical analysis to answer our research questions (Sect. 4.6 and Sect. 4.7).

All the implemented apps, the interaction scenarios, the test procedure and the data analysis are publicly available as a replication package[2].

4.1   App Implementation Details

Five different mobile apps were implemented as the subjects of the study. Each app provides exactly the same functionalities, screens and UI elements. The look and feel of all the apps is strictly based on the Google material design guidelines[3] to make the implementations comparable with respect to the UI. One app was implemented using the Android SDK to serve as the native baseline. The other four apps were built using the MCPD approaches PWA, Capacitor, Flutter and React Native.

All the selected MCPD approaches are supported and used by large developer communities (e.g., visible on GitHub and Stack Exchange). Many successful apps found in app markets are developed with these approaches.

PWA and Capacitor. Both the PWA and the Capacitor app are based on the same web app. The web app was built with the Ionic web framework and the StencilJS web-component compiler. The Ionic framework provides reusable UI components, whose look and feel resembles the look and feel of native Android or

---

[2] https://github.com/stefanhuber/ICWE-2021.
[3] https://material.io.

iOS components. The framework comprises all the required functionality without the need for additional libraries.

For the PWA, we implemented a service worker and provided a web manifest to enable offline usage of the PWA and to make it installable on a mobile device. The service worker delivers all network requests from cache. As a result, no network requests were executed by the PWA allowing for a complete offline usage.

Capacitor is a wrapper around a web app inside an Android native app. Therefore, no additional changes were required to provide the web app inside Capacitor.

Flutter. Flutter offers a rich set of stateful and stateless widgets to build UIs, which mimic the look and feel of Android or iOS native UIs. The `Drawer`, `ListView` and `TextField` widgets were used to realize the screens. Navigation between screens was handled with the `Navigator` service.

React Native. React Native provides only a few core UI components. To build the contact app, several external libraries were required (i.e., `react-navigation`, `react-navigation-drawer` and `react-navigation-stack`). Besides the libraries the UI components `FlatList` and `InputField` were used to realize the screens. Also respective styling was applied to get the Material look and feel.

Native Android. The native Android app was implemented based on the Android SDK and no additional libraries were used. The two available screens were set up as an `Activity`. Navigation between Screens was implemented by using `Intents`. The views `NavigationView`, `RecyclerView`, `DrawerLayout` and `EditText` were used to create the screens.

4.2   Interaction Scenarios

To analyze the energy efficiency of the different development approaches, we created repeatable UI interaction scenarios using the Android UI Automator testing framework[4]. The automation framework was carefully selected based on the guidelines provided by Cruz et al. [7], to minimize the impact of the interactions on battery consumption. This framework allows scripting UI interactions that can be automatically executed on Android devices. The interaction scenarios were compiled and deployed on the test devices and could be started via command line interaction on the respective device.

Four interaction scenarios (i1, i2, i3 and i4), which comprise UI interactions commonly used within mobile apps, were implemented. These interaction scenarios are:

---

[4] https://developer.android.com/training/testing/ui-automator.

i1 Open the navigation drawer menu (change between first and second screen in Fig. 1) with a left-to-right swipe gesture and after one second close it with a tap outside the drawer menu. The interaction is repeated five times.

i2 Scroll down the list of contact entries (first screen in Fig. 1) with five consecutive bottom-to-top swipe gestures

i3 Tap on the top-right "Add Entry" menu icon (first screen in Fig. 1) to navigate to the entry form screen (third screen in Fig. 1) and after one second tap on the top-left back button to navigate back to the list screen. The interaction is repeated five times.

i4 Enter form data for the input fields "Firstname", "Lastname" and "Phone" (third screen in Fig. 1)

Fig. 1. Overview of the different screens of the implemented contact app

4.3 Energy Measurement

Android provides the `batterystats` tool, which collects battery related data on a mobile phone as timestamped usage data of hardware components, such as CPU, screen or Wi-Fi. Based on a power profile for each mobile device and power models, the energy drawn from the battery is estimated [12]. The energy consumption is estimated for the entire device and in a more fine-granular manner for each active app running on the device. For this study, the data for the active app was used.

The energy consumption is specified in milli ampere hours (mAh) of current drawn from the device battery. To be comparable to related research and to actually calculate the energy consumption, a conversion to Joule was done. Therefore, also the voltage was used from the collected battery statistics. For the conversion, the following formula was used:

$$Energy[J] = \frac{Charge[mAh]}{10^6} * Voltage[V] * 3600$$

4.4 Test Devices

The test cases were executed on two mobile devices running Google Android. We selected the devices with respect to their device class using the device's age, supported Android version and hardware configuration as proxies. Additionally, devices which at least support a big.LITTLE CPU architecture were selected, as this architecture already integrates energy optimizations. At the end, a lower end - LG Nexus 5X - and a higher-end device - Samsung Galaxy S9 - were used for the tests. The Android versions of the devices were updated to the maximum supported version of the manufacturer. Table 1 details the devices' specifications.

Table 1. Mobile device specifications

Class	Device	CPU	RAM	Android	Battery capacity
Lower-end	LG Nexus 5X	Snapdragon 808 4 × 1.4 GHz/2 × 1.8 GHz	2 GB	8.0	2.700 mAh
Higher-end	Samsung Galaxy S9	Snapdragon 845 4 × 2.7 GHz/4 × 1.8 GHz	4 GB	10.0	3.000 mAh

4.5 Test Procedure

The developed UI interaction scenarios were used to test the energy consumption of the developed apps on the test devices. In the test procedure, the following steps were executed:

1. The tested device was connected to a computer using USB and the device was prepared with all apps and the interaction scenarios.
2. The tested device was put into airplane mode and all open apps were closed and all services (e.g., GPS) were deactivated. Only Wi-Fi was enabled to communicate with the device via adb.
3. The test device's display brightness was set to approximately 50%.
4. The test device was fully charged, before the test started. After unplugging the device from USB, a Wi-Fi connection was established via adb from the computer, which controlled the entire procedure.
5. A python script running on the connected computer for controlling the mobile device via adb was started.

6. The script opened and closed each of the apps one after the other and executed all interaction scenarios (i1-i4) consecutively for each app on the device.
   (a) Before each interaction scenario, the `batterystats` tool (see Sect. 4.3) was reset on the test device using adb.
   (b) After each interaction scenario, data created by `batterystats` was collected for a latter analysis.
7. The python script was running in a loop for 30 times executing step 6, yielding 30 samples for each interaction scenario within each app on each device.

To answer RQ1 and RQ2 the test procedure was executed on each device, yielding an overall number of 1.440 samples. It must be noted that the same PWA was executed once in the Chrome web-browser engine and once in the Firefox web-browser engine, yielding 240 samples each.

4.6   Hypotheses Formulation

For the hypothesises of this study, the different mobile development approaches (i.e., PWA, Android native, Flutter, Capacitor and React Native) represent the independent variable. As the dependent variable we used the energy consumption in Joule during each interaction scenario for each development approach.

To investigate the differences in energy consumption of the PWA and other mobile development approaches as formulated in RQ1, the following two-tailed null hypothesis ($H1_0$) and corresponding alternative hypothesis ($H1_a$) were formulated:

$$H1_0 : \mu_{PWA(chrome)} = \mu_{MDA}$$

$$H1_a : \mu_{PWA(chrome)} \neq \mu_{MDA}$$

where $\mu_{PWA(chrome)}$ represents the mean energy consumption of the PWA execution in the default Chrome web-browser. μ_{MDA} represents the mean energy consumption of the other mobile development approaches. For simplicity, μ_{MDA} is considered as a variable for each of the four approaches (i.e., Android native, Flutter, Capacitor and React Native). Thus, the $H1_0$ hypothesis states that the energy consumption of the respective mobile development approach does not significantly differ from the PWA implementation with respect to the investigated UI interactions. The alternative hypothesis $H1_a$ states that the respective mobile development approach significantly differs from the PWA implementation in terms of the consumed energy.

Additionally, to investigate the differences in energy consumption of the used web-browser engine to execute the PWA as formulated in RQ2, the following two-tailed null hypothesis ($H2_0$) and corresponding alternative hypothesis ($H2_a$) were formulated:

$$H2_0 : \mu_{PWA(chrome)} = \mu_{PWA(firefox)}$$

$$H2_a : \mu_{PWA(chrome)} \neq \mu_{PWA(firefox)}$$

where $\mu_{PWA(chrome)}$ represents the mean energy consumption of the PWA execution in the default Chrome web-browser, and $\mu_{PWA(firefox)}$ represents the mean energy consumption in the Firefox web-browser. The $H2_0$ hypothesis states that the energy consumption of the PWA executed in Chrome and the PWA executed in Firefox have the same energy consumption. The alternative hypothesis $H2_a$ states that the respective consumed energy significantly differs between the two web-browsers.

$H1$ was tested for each of the four UI interactions with each of the four mobile development approaches against the PWA counterpart (executed in Chrome) on each of the two devices leading to an overall of 32 hypothesis tests. Similarly, $H2$ was tested for the four UI interactions on the two web-browser engines (i.e., Chrome and Firefox) and the two devices resulting in 8 hypothesis tests.

4.7 Data Analysis

The test executions on the two devices produced 1.440 samples for the energy consumption. Each sample consists of the energy consumed by one app executing one interaction scenario on one device in Joule.

To determine whether to use parametric or non-parametric statistical tests, we analyzed the samples' distributions using the Shapiro-Wilk test [25]. The threshold for significance was set to an alpha level below 0.05 ($\alpha = 0.05$). A result below the alpha level shows evidence that the data is not normally distributed. As 52% of the samples were not normally distributed, the non-parametric Mann-Whitney U test [18] was selected for testing the hypotheses.

Using the same data samples in multiple statistical tests increases the chances of Type-I errors. To counter this problem, we applied a Bonferroni correction [3]. This resulted in a final α value of 0.0125 to determine significance for hypothesis $H1$.

As a final step of analysis, the effect size was calculated by applying Cliff's Delta [5] on respective pairs (i.e., PWA executed in Chrome in comparison to the other mobile development approaches). Cliff's Delta is a non-parametric effect size measure that quantifies the statistical magnitude of the difference between two observed groups and goes beyond a p-value interpretation. The resulting effect size lies in the closed interval $[-1, 1]$. A value near 0 marks a high overlap between the values of the sample distributions of the two observed groups, which means a low difference between the groups. Whereas values near 1 or -1 mark the absence of an overlap of the sample distributions. The maximum delta of 1 or -1 occurs if there is no overlap of the distributions. In this study a positive value for Cliff's Delta means the observed mobile development approach has a higher energy consumption than the PWA executed in Chrome and a negative value means the development approach has a lower energy consumption.

5   Results

Figure 2 provides a descriptive overview of the results. The interaction scenarios (i1-i4) are displayed column-wise and the tested mobile device row-wise.

For each chart the y-axis represents the energy consumption in Joule, the x-axis represents the development approach.

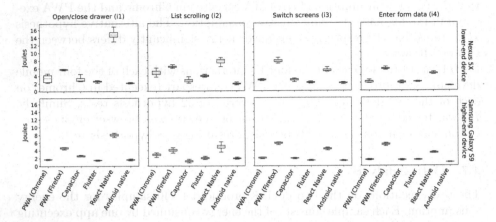

Fig. 2. Energy consumption (Joules) results of different UI interaction scenarios

The assessment of RQ1 shows a stark difference between the mobile development approaches. Figure 3 presents a heatmap, which shows the calculated effect sizes. Rows represent the respective interaction scenarios executed with the PWA in Chrome. The related mobile development approaches are listed column-wise. In the intersection, the respective effect size is listed. Additionally, the color values red (higher energy consumption) and blue (lower energy consumption) mark the direction of the difference.

The comparison of the PWA and React Native clearly shows that the PWA executed in Chrome always has a significantly lower energy consumption. All $H1_0$ hypothesises in the context of the PWA and React Native were rejected. Also the calculated effect sizes indicate a large difference, visible in the fourth column of the heatmaps in Fig. 3.

In contrast, the Android native development approach has a significantly lower energy consumption than the PWA with a large magnitude for all examined interaction scenarios on all mobile devices, except for the scenario i1 on the higher-end device. This can be seen in the last column of the heatmaps in Fig. 3. By interpreting the descriptive results, Android native in the scenario i1 on the higher-end device has a lower energy consumption than the PWA, but with no significance.

The Capacitor framework tends to have a lower energy consumption than the PWA executed in Chrome, however only 3 out of 8 tests have a significantly lower energy consumption. Scenario i1 on the higher-end device even has a significantly higher energy consumption for Capacitor with respect to the PWA. Displayed in the second column of the heatmaps in Fig. 3. Also, the Flutter framework tends to have a lower energy consumption than the PWA executed in Chrome as displayed in the third column of the heatmaps in Fig. 3. 5 out of the 8 statistical tests are significant.

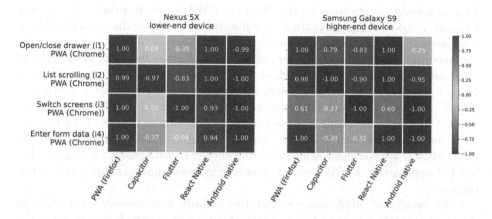

Fig. 3. Heatmap of the calculated Cliff's delta effect sizes

Considering RQ2 and the corresponding hypotheses, the results allow a rejection of all $H2_0$ hypothesises for all examined interaction scenarios. Therefore, the Chrome web-browser has a significantly lower energy footprint than the Firefox web-browser in all examined scenarios. Moreover, the magnitude of the difference between the two web-browsers is large when considering the effect size, as shown in the first columns of the heatmaps in Fig. 3.

6 Discussion

Prior work investigated different aspects of the energy consumption of mobile development approaches [4,6,16,17,20]. However, these studies do not focus on UI rendering and interaction scenarios, thus we have set up a set of testable interaction scenarios and focused our investigation on the energy consumption of UI related aspects.

When considering MCPD approaches, lower development cost, lower maintenance effort and ease of development [11] are common aspects, why developers prefer MCPD approaches over the native development approach. Practitioners face a difficult decision when selecting an MCPD approach over native development and intending to lower the energy footprint. The results of this study show that PWAs exhibit a higher energy footprint than native development. However, the results could help practitioners to choose a mobile development approach when trading-off the energy footprint with other non-functional requirements.

It is save to say that according to the results of this study, PWAs have a lower energy consumption than React Native and could be used as an alternative. It must be noted that PWAs miss some features that are provided by React Native (e.g., access to personal data, such as calendar entries). If such features are required, the PWA can be transformed into a hybrid app as demonstrated in this study by using the PWA within Capacitor. As this study shows, Capacitor also has a lower energy consumption than React Native. Capacitor even tends to have a lower energy consumption than the PWA. Capacitor uses a lightweight Chrome WebView implementation, which seems to minimize the energy footprint compared to the Chrome PWA even more.

According to this study, Flutter has the lowest energy footprint of the MCPD approaches. Flutter should therefore be the preferred MCPD approach with respect to energy efficiency, although for the entering form data UI interaction (i4), Flutter and the PWA show similar results. Moreover, if a PWA is packaged inside Capacitor, the results are even more comparable to the results of Flutter.

Therefore, regarding RQ1 we consider PWAs as a viable alternative to other MCPD approaches when considering energy consumption. Similar to other MCPD approaches, PWAs have a higher energy consumption than native development.

The results of RQ2 indicate that the default web-browser for PWAs on Android (Google Chrome) has a significantly lower energy footprint than the alternative web-browser Firefox. It has to be noted that when installing a PWA with Chrome, a WebAPK[5] is created and the PWA is transformed into a fully-fledged Android app. In contrast, for Firefox the PWA is stored as a web-browser bookmark with an icon on the home screen. A possible explanation for the energy overhead introduced by the Firefox PWA, could be that the WebAPK optimizes the Chrome PWA. Web-browser vendors like Mozilla could investigate the inter-operability and impact on the energy footprint when using WebAPKs for PWAs in their products. The lower energy consumption of Capacitor compared to the Chrome PWA is another indication that a more lightweight WebView component could lower the energy consumption.

There are threats to validity of this study, which should be considered in the context of our results. First, to allow for a comparison of the different development approaches by using the same interaction scenarios we developed sample apps. Throughout the implementation, we closely followed the documentation and best practices for the respective development approaches, additionally we strictly followed Google's material design guidelines to have typical and representative implementations. Second, we tried to cover a broad spectrum of mobile devices. Therefore, we carefully selected two devices from different device classes (lower-end and higher-end). Third, we used the built-in Android `batterystats` tool to calculate the energy consumption. We consider this tool an easy-to-use and easy-to-replicate approach for metering energy consumption. The tool uses models to estimate the energy usage. There are clearly inaccuracies when estimating the absolute energy consumption, however, we consider it adequate for comparing different approaches as the estimations are based on the utilization of the device's hardware components.

---

[5] https://developers.google.com/web/fundamentals/integration/webapks

7 Conclusion

Developing the same app for multiple platforms is a prominent challenge for practitioners [13]. In this study, we compared the energy efficiency of PWAs with other mobile development approaches. Additionally, the energy footprint of two different web-browser engines was examined while executing a PWA. The results showed that PWAs are a viable alternative for MCPD when considering energy efficiency. Also, the web-browser engine has a significant influence on the energy footprint of the PWA.

The study used self-implemented apps for comparing the energy efficiency of the various development approaches. An important direction for future work would be to use real world apps for experimentation. Moreover, this research focused on determining the differences in energy-efficiency of mobile development approaches. A detailed investigation on the root causes for higher energy footprints of some development approaches could be conducted. This could identify optimization opportunities for mobile software framework developers. Also this study only used Android as a mobile platform, integrating also iOS in such experiments would shed more light on the differences between mobile platforms.

References

1. Biørn-Hansen, A., Grønli, T.M., Ghinea, G.: A survey and taxonomy of core concepts and research challenges in cross-platform mobile development. ACM Comput. Surv. (CSUR) **51**(5), 1–34 (2018)
2. Monfort, V., Krempels, K.-H., Majchrzak, T.A., Traverso, P. (eds.): WEBIST 2016. LNBIP, vol. 292. Springer, Cham (2017). https://doi.org/10.1007/978-3-319-66468-2
3. Bonferroni, C.: Teoria statistica delle classi e calcolo delle probabilita. Pubblicazioni del R Istituto Superiore di Scienze Economiche e Commericiali di Firenze **8**, 3–62 (1936)
4. Ciman, M., Gaggi, O.: An empirical analysis of energy consumption of cross-platform frameworks for mobile development. Pervasive Mobile Comput. **39**, 214–230 (2017)
5. Cliff, N.: Dominance statistics: ordinal analyses to answer ordinal questions. Psychol. Bull. **114**(3), 494 (1993)
6. Corbalan, L., Fernandez, J., Cuitiño, A., Delia, L., Cáseres, G., Thomas, P., Pesado, P.: Development frameworks for mobile devices: a comparative study about energy consumption. In: 2018 IEEE/ACM 5th International Conference on Mobile Software Engineering and Systems (MOBILESoft), ACM/IEEE, Gothenburg, Sweden (2018)
7. Cruz, L., Abreu, R.: On the energy footprint of mobile testing frameworks. IEEE Trans. Softw. Eng., 1 (2019). https://ieeexplore.ieee.org/document/8862921
8. El-Kassas, W.S., Abdullah, B.A., Yousef, A.H., Wahba, A.M.: Taxonomy of cross-platform mobile applications development approaches. Ain Shams Eng. J. **8**(2), 163–190 (2017)
9. Firtman, M.: Google play store now open for progressive web apps (2019). http://bit.ly/3dKYSOp

10. Gaunt, M.: Service workers: an introduction (2016). https://developers.google.com/web/fundamentals/primers/service-workers/
11. Heitkötter, H., Hanschke, S., Majchrzak, T.A.: Evaluating cross-platform development approaches for mobile applications. In: Cordeiro, J., Krempels, K.-H. (eds.) WEBIST 2012. LNBIP, vol. 140, pp. 120–138. Springer, Heidelberg (2013). https://doi.org/10.1007/978-3-642-36608-6_8
12. Hoque, M.A., Siekkinen, M., Khan, K.N., Xiao, Y., Tarkoma, S.: Modeling, profiling, and debugging the energy consumption of mobile devices. ACM Comput. Surv. **48**(3), 1–40 (2015)
13. Joorabchi, M.E., Mesbah, A., Kruchten, P.: Real challenges in mobile app development. In: 2013 ACM/IEEE International Symposium on Empirical Software Engineering and Measurement, pp. 15–24. IEEE, Baltimore, MD, USA (October 2013)
14. Majchrzak, T.A., Biørn-Hansen, A., Grønli, T.M.: Comprehensive analysis of innovative cross-platform app development frameworks. In: Proceedings of the 50th Hawaii International Conference on System Sciences, pp. 6162–6171. Hawaii International Conference on System Sciences, Hawaii, USA (2017)
15. Malavolta, I.: Beyond native apps: Web technologies to the rescue! (keynote). In: Proceedings of the 1st International Workshop on Mobile Development. Mobile! 2016, Association for Computing Machinery, New York, NY, USA (2016)
16. Malavolta, I., Chinnappan, K., Jasmontas, L., Gupta, S., Soltany, K.A.K.: Evaluating the impact of caching on the energy consumption and performance of progressive web apps. In: 7th IEEE/ACM International Conference on Mobile Software Engineering and Systems 2020 (2020)
17. Malavolta, I., Procaccianti, G., Noorland, P., Vukmirović, P.: Assessing the impact of service workers on the energy efficiency of progressive web apps. In: Proceedings of the 4th International Conference on Mobile Software Engineering and Systems. IEEE Press, Buenos Aires, Argentina (2017)
18. McKnight, P.E., Najab, J.: Mann-Whitney U test. In: The Corsini Encyclopedia of Psychology, p. 1. American Cancer Society (2010). https://doi.org/10.1002/9780470479216.corpsy0524. ISBN: 9780470479216
19. Microsoft: Progressive web apps in the microsoft store (2020). http://bit.ly/3qXRAum
20. Oliveira, W., Oliveira, R., Castor, F.: A study on the energy consumption of android app development approaches. In: Proceedings of the 14th International Conference on Mining Software Repositories, pp. 42–52 (2017)
21. Pathak, A., Hu, Y.C., Zhang, M.: Where is the energy spent inside my app? fine grained energy accounting on smartphones with Eprof. In: Proceedings of the 7th ACM European conference on Computer Systems (2012)
22. Pinto, G., Castor, F., Liu, Y.D.: Mining questions about software energy consumption. In: Proceedings of the 11th Working Conference on Mining Software Repositories, pp. 22–31 (2014)
23. Pramanik, P.K.D., et al.: Power consumption analysis, measurement, management, and issues: a state-of-the-art review of smartphone battery and energy usage. IEEE Access **7**, 182113–182172 (2019)
24. Russell, A.: Progressive web apps: Escaping tabs without losing our soul. https://infrequently.org/2015/06/progressive-apps-escaping-tabs-without-losing-our-soul/ (2015)
25. Shapiro, S.S., Wilk, M.B.: An analysis of variance test for normality (complete samples). Biometrika **52**(3/4), 591–611 (1965)

26. Statista: Global smartphone sales by operating system from 2009 to 2017 (in millions). https://www.statista.com/statistics/263445/global-smartphone-sales-by-operating-system-since-2009/ (2018)
27. Vallerio, K.S., Zhong, L., Jha, N.K.: Energy-efficient graphical user interface design. IEEE Trans. Mob. Comput. **5**(7), 846–859 (2006)
28. Wilke, C., Richly, S., Götz, S., Piechnick, C., Aßmann, U.: Energy consumption and efficiency in mobile applications: a user feedback study. In: 2013 IEEE International Conference on Green Computing and Communications and IEEE Internet of Things and IEEE Cyber, Physical and Social Computing. IEEE (2013)

Ph.D. Symposium

Static Analysis of Large-Scale JavaScript Front End

Anton Karakochev[✉] and Gefei Zhang

Hochschule für Technik und Wirtschaft Berlin, Berlin, Germany
{anton.karakochev,gefei.zhang}@htw-berlin.de

Abstract. In modern web applications, the elaborate GUI of the front end is often developed with large-scale JavaScript frameworks. In such systems, the behavior of one HTML element is usually defined by code in different JavaScript functions scattered all over the source files, and a piece of code may also have influence on other functions and variables all over the source files. Therefore, the data and control flow of the front end may be hard to follow. We propose an automated approach to integrate the overall data and control flow of the front end into an overview model, which then provides us with an excellent starting point to application of formal methods to prove the correctness of the front end. Our approach is hence helpful for comprehension of the front end code and validation of its correctness.

1 Introduction

Modern web applications often have a rich front end with elaborate GUI, where several HTML elements, JavaScript functions and variables are involved in one single feature. In such systems, code that is scattered all over the source files may be working together and implementing the same feature, and a piece of code may have influence on other functions and variables spread throughout the source files. Therefore, the data and control flow of the application may be hard for the developer to follow. Moreover, such frond end systems are often implemented using a large-scale framework such as Angular [3], React [2] or Vue [16]. Since frameworks need to be generic, they usually make heavy use of advanced, dynamic features of the underlying programming language, which makes it hard for existing tools to analyze the source code of large-scale applications and prove their correctness by formal methods [15].

In the planned PhD research of Anton Karakochev, supervised by Gefei Zhang, we aim to develop techniques and tools to close this gap by

- integrating the overall data and control flow of the JavaScript front end into an overview model,
- developing automated analysis methods to proof the correctness of framework-based JavaScript front end.

M. Brambilla et al. (Eds.): ICWE 2021, LNCS 12706, pp. 483–489, 2021.
https://doi.org/10.1007/978-3-030-74296-6_36

In the following Sect. 2, we first discuss the state of the art in this area. Then we explain our research proposal in more details and show our preliminary results as well as a tentative plan for the future in Sect. 3. Finally, conclusions are drawn in Sect. 4.

2   Related Work

Static analysis of event-based and asynchronous JavaScript applications is explored in [12,13]. In [12] Sampaio et al. develop a formalism which enables reasoning about event-related APIs symbolically. Sotiropoulos and Livshits [13] present a calculus for modeling asynchrony and a callback graph that illustrates the execution order. These two approaches do not consider large frameworks. Our proposed approach does not rely on their semantics, we instead try to define rules which can be used for model checking or theorem proving.

Park, Jordan and Ryu [11] focus on the automatic modeling of library code. They propose an on-demand model using input samples, representing the analysis states, which are then dynamically executed and abstracted. In comparison, we do not analyze the library code dynamically, instead we model the behavior of the framework manually. This way, our approach is more suited to analysis of larger-scale framework based applications.

The detection of code issues using static analysis is explored in [1,7]. Liu [7] specifies nine issue patterns and proposes a tool capable of detecting and fixing them using pattern matching based on the abstract syntax tree and call graph of the code. Almashfi and Lu [1] present a tool which is able to detect fourteen code smells by building a control flow graph and performing a data-flow analysis. Instead of relying on predefined code-smell patterns, we aim to apply formal methods to validate the model.

State of the art frameworks for static analysis include SAFE [10] and WALA [14]. WALA offers various capabilities such as call graph construction and dataflow analysis. SAFE is designed as a playground for advanced research in JavaScript web applications, focusing on pluggability, extensibility and debuggability. Our proposed method uses neither and is currently based on the abstract syntax tree produced by ESLint [9].

3 Research Proposal and Preliminary Results

Fig. 1. Example: application "math for kids"

Consider the code given in Listing 1.1, which is based on the Vue framework and implements a simple application to provide math exercises to the user. Simply put, it poses math questions to the user, who can then input their answer and the application shows whether it's right or wrong, and does statistics of right and wrong answers given so far. A screenshot of the application is given in Fig. 1.

```
1  <template>
2  <div>
3   <div>
4    <form @submit.prevent>
5     <span>{{a}}</span> +
6     <span>{{b}}</span> =
7     <input v-model="answer"/>
8     <button
9      class="btn btn-primary"
10     type="submit"
11     :disabled="!may_check()"
12     @click="check_answer()"
13     > Check </button>
14    <button
15     class="btn btn-success"
16     disabled="1"
17     v-if="right === true"
18     > Right </button>
19    <button
20     class="btn btn-danger"
21     disabled="1"
22     v-if="right === false"
23     > Wrong </button>
24    <button
25     class="btn btn-info"
26     @click="new_problem()"
27     > New Problem </button>
28   </form>
29  </div>
30  <hr/>
31  <div>
32   <table>
33    <tr>
34     <td>Statistics</td>
35     <td>Right</td>
36     <td>Wrong</td>
37    </tr>
38    <tr>
39     <td />
40     <td>{{count_right}}</td>
41     <td>{{count_wrong}}</td>
42    </tr>
43   </table>
44  </div>
45  </div>
46 </template>
47
48 <script>
49 export default {
50  name: "MathForKids",
51  data() {
52   return {
53    a: 0, b: 0, c: 0,
54    answer: undefined,
```

```
55   right: undefined,              76      this.c ===
56   count_right: 0,                77        parseInt(this.answer);
57   count_wrong: 0,                78      this.right ?
58   };                             79      (this.count_right+=1)
59 },                               80      : (this.count_wrong+=1)
60 created: function () {           81    },
61   this.add_problem(); },         82    may_check() {
62 methods: {                       83      return (
63   add_problem() {                84      !(this.answer ===
64     let max = 100;               85          undefined
65     this.c =                     86      || this.answer==="")
66      Math.floor(                 87      &&(this.right ===
67       Math.random()*             88          undefined));
68       (max-1))+1;                89    },
69     this.a = Math.floor(Math.    90    new_problem() {
       random()*(this.c-2))+1;      91      this.add_problem(); },
70     this.b = this.c - this.a;    92    },
71     this.answer = undefined;     93 };
72     this.right = undefined;      94 </script>
73   },
74   check_answer() {
75     this.right =
```

Listing 1.1. Example: code

As is common in code based on this kind of frameworks, features of individual widgets are implemented by several snippets, usually scattered all over the source code. For instance, the behavior of the label Right, displayed if the answer of the user is right, is defined in lines 17, 22, 55, 72, 75 and 78, and the value the user input in line 7 has influence on the widgets Right, Check, and indirectly CountRight. Obviously, in realistic projects the overall data and control flow may get rather hard to follow, and the behavior of the application hard to reason about. On the other hand, the variables count_right and count_wrong do not influence each other, which may be important e.g. for test case generation,

In the planned PhD research, we propose to develop automated techniques to

- integrate the overall data and control flow into an overview model
- apply formal methods to the overview model and to prove the correctness of the application

3.1   Integration of Data and Control Flow

We propose to start from the source code and integrate all data and control flow into one visualization. To this end, we model how, in the application, the HTML elements and the JavaScript functions read and write JavaScript variables. For interactions between JavaScript functions and variables, we use parsing tools like ESLint [9], which reads JavaScript code and outputs an abstract syntax tree, and by analyzing the abstract syntax tree we can conclude whether a function writes a variable (if variable appears on the left hand side of an assignment) or reads a variable (otherwise).

Automatic analysis of how the HTML elements interact with JavaScript is a harder task. The interaction is actually implemented by the framework, and due to the dynamic and generic nature of frameworks, the code is usually difficult for existing analysis tools to analyze. Therefore, we follow the idea of [4] and simply model the behavior of the framework manually, that is, we hard-code the semantics of the *directives* and translate them into the overview model directly.

For example, in Listing 1.1, the directive v-model=" answer" in line 7 specifies a two-way data binding, that is, the value input by the user is automatically assigned to the JavaScript variable answer, and when the JavaScript code changes the value of this variable, the HTML element is also updated automatically. This kind of dependencies between HTML elements and JavaScript are translated by hard-coded framework specific rules as opposed to general-purpose JavaScript analysis tools.

3.2   Analysis

The overview model is an excellent starting point to further analysis. For example:

- "Reaching definition analysis" [8] between HTML elements would be interesting, which aims at revealing the values of which elements influence which other elements. In the running example, such analysis may reveal that the values of count_right and count_wrong do not influence each other.
- Now that we know how the HTML elements influence each other, it is a natural next step to discuss test coverage criterion and techniques of test case generation. In the running example, we could determine we need to test that after the user has input an answer then whether count_right or count_wrong will increase by 1.
- Also, we plan to apply formal methods, such as model checking or theorem proving, to validate the correctness of the application. For instance, we could model check or theorem-prove that according to the overview model, after the use has input an answer then whether count_right or count_wrong will increase by 1, but not both.

3.3   Preliminary Results

We have implemented a prototype [5] to generate an overview model, which we call *interaction diagram*, for applications based on the Vue framework and to generate test cases according to the test coverage criterion defined in [18]. We also have shown in [17] a possible modeling of the behavior of modern JavaScript front end using Temporal Logic of Actions [6] and some examples of model checking the model. However, automating this step, as well as applying other formal methods for stronger validation, are still subject to future research.

Tentative Plan. We plan to spend six months to enhance our current prototype, and another 24 months to develop techniques of applying formal methods to the overview model. For the final writing up of the thesis six to nine months are planned.

4   Conclusions

We have shown a research proposal to static analysis of large-scale, framework-based JavaScript front end. We aim to integrate the data and control flow of the application, usually defined in small parts, into an overview model and then verify properties of the model by formal methods. We have achieved promising preliminary results so far. When the research is finished, we plan to deliver full automated support for formal verification of framework-based JavaScript front end.

References

1. Almashfi, N., Lu, L.: Code smell detection tool for Java Script programs. In: Proceedings of the 5th International Conference on Computer and Communication Systems (ICCCS 2020), pp. 172–176. IEEE (2020)
2. Facebook: React - A JavaScript Library for Building User Interfaces. https://reactjs.org. Accessed 21 Feb 2021
3. Google: Angular - The Modern Web Developer's Platform. https://angular.io. Accessed 17 Feb 2021
4. Jensen, S.H., Madsen, M., Møller, A.: Modeling the HTML DOM and browser API in static analysis of JavaScript web applications. In: Proceedings of the 19th ACM SIGSOFT Symposium Foundations of Software Engineering and 13th European Software Engineering Conference (FSE/ESEC 2011), pp. 59–69. ACM (2011)
5. Karakochev, A.: Automatic interaction diagram generation of Vue.js-based web applications. Master's thesis, Hochschule für Technik und Wirtschaft Berlin (2021)
6. Lamport, L.: The TLA+ Language and Tools for Hardware and Software Engineers. Addison-Wesley, Boston (2003)
7. Liu, Y.: JSOptimizer: an extensible framework for JavaScript program optimization. In: Proceedings of the 41st International Conference on Software Engineering Companion, pp. 168–170. IEEE (2019)
8. Nielson, F., Nielson, H.R., Hankin, C.: Principles of Program Analysis. Springer, Heidelberg (2005)
9. OpenJS Foundation: ESLint - Pluggable JavaScript linter. https://eslint.org. Accessed 18 Feb 2021
10. Park, J., Ryou, Y., Park, J., Ryu, S.: Analysis of JavaScript web applications using SAFE 2.0. In: Proceedings of the 39th International Conference on Software Engineering Companion, pp. 59–62. IEEE (2017)
11. Park, J., Jordan, A., Ryu, S.: Automatic modeling of opaque code for JavaScript static analysis. In: Hähnle, R., van der Aalst, W. (eds.) FASE 2019. LNCS, vol. 11424, pp. 43–60. Springer, Cham (2019). https://doi.org/10.1007/978-3-030-16722-6_3

12. Sampaio, G., Fragoso Santos, J., Maksimović, P., Gardner, P.: A trusted infrastructure for symbolic analysis of event-driven web applications. In: 34th European Conference on Object-Oriented Programming (ECOOP 2020). LIPIcs, vol. 166, pp. 28:1–28:29. Schloss Dagstuhl-Leibniz-Zentrum für Informatik (2020)
13. Sotiropoulos, T., Livshits, B.: Static analysis for asynchronous JavaScript programs. In: Donaldson, A.F. (ed.) 33rd European Conference on Object-Oriented Programming, (ECOOP 2019). LIPIcs, vol. 134, pp. 8:1–8:30. Schloss Dagstuhl-Leibniz-Zentrum für Informatik (2019)
14. Sridharan, M., Dolby, J., Chandra, S., Schäfer, M., Tip, F.: Correlation tracking for points-to analysis of JavaScript. In: Noble, J. (ed.) ECOOP 2012. LNCS, vol. 7313, pp. 435–458. Springer, Heidelberg (2012). https://doi.org/10.1007/978-3-642-31057-7_20
15. Sun, K., Ryu, S.: Analysis of JavaScript programs: challenges and research trends. ACM Comput. Surv. **50**(4), 59:1–59:34 (2017)
16. You, E.: Vue.js - The Progressive JavaScript Framework. https://vuejs.org. Accessed 18 Feb 2021
17. Zhang, G.: Specifying and model checking workflows of single page applications with TLA+. In: IEEE 20th International Conference on Software Quality, Reliability and Security Companion (QRS-C), pp. 406–410. IEEE (2020)
18. Zhang, G., Zhao, J.: Scenario testing of AngularJS-based single page web applications. In: Brambilla, M., Cappiello, C., Ow, S.H. (eds.) ICWE 2019. LNCS, vol. 11609, pp. 91–103. Springer, Cham (2020). https://doi.org/10.1007/978-3-030-51253-8_10

Applying Predictive Analytics on Research Information to Enhance Funding Discovery and Strengthen Collaboration in Project Proposals

Dang Vu Nguyen Hai[✉] and Martin Gaedke

Chemnitz University of Technology, Chemnitz, Germany
{dang.vu-nguyen-hai,martin.gaedke}@informatik.tu-chemnitz.de

Abstract. In academic and industrial research, writing a project proposal is one of the essential but time-consuming activities. Nevertheless, most proposals end in rejection. Moreover, research funding is getting more competitive these days. Funding agencies are increasingly looking for more extensive and more interdisciplinary research proposals. To increase the funding success rate, this PhD project focuses on three open challenges: poor data quality, inefficient funding discovery, and ineffective collaborative team building. We envision a Predictive Analytics-based approach that involves analyzing research information and using statistical and machine learning models that can assure data quality, increase funding discovery efficiency and the effectiveness of collaboration building. Accordingly, the goal of this PhD project is to support decision-making process to maximize the funding success rates of universities.

Keywords: Research Information Management System (RIMS) · Linked data · Predictive analytics · Data driven decision making

1 Problem Context and Definitions

Writing a project proposal is a crucial and time-consuming activity in academic and industrial research. However, the success rates of funding worldwide are meager: only 14% were funded at the European Commission's Horizon 2020; the Australia National Health and Medical Research Council has been funding less than 20% of proposals it receives since 2017; and the US National Science Foundation had a success of just 25% in 2017 [13]. Some possible reasons are: (i) the subject is not relevant to an issue of regional or national importance, (ii) the funding agency is not the most appropriate source of funds for the proposed project, and (iii) the funding agency's priorities and interests may have changed [15]. Moreover, research funding is getting more competitive these days. Funding agencies are increasingly looking for more extensive and interdisciplinary research proposals, leading to the need for collaboration [14].

© Springer Nature Switzerland AG 2021
M. Brambilla et al. (Eds.): ICWE 2021, LNCS 12706, pp. 490–495, 2021.
https://doi.org/10.1007/978-3-030-74296-6_37

To increase the funding success rate, universities need to make the right research-intensive strategies: (i) understanding their research capabilities and strengths, (ii) finding potential funding opportunities quickly, and (iii) building the strongest possible team to work collaboratively on the project proposals [14].

To understand the research capabilities and strengths, the universities need to establish their own Research Information Management System (RIMS). It is an integrated system of research information, research outputs, grants, and research funds [9]. In addition, RIMS provides the central point for information relating to an institution's faculties, researchers and their research activities. Nowadays, many semantic web platforms with Linked Data as the main data model are widely used to implement RIMS: open-source platforms (VIVO[1], Profiles[2]) and commercial platforms (PURE[3], Converis[4]).

To find the potential funding opportunities quickly, the universities need to combine funding information (e.g. funder profiles, awarded grants, active funding opportunities) from multiple funding sources, and then integrated it into RIMS. In addition, the universities need to keep the information up-to-date. As a result, the universities will not miss any potential funding opportunities. "Targeted information on what grants are coming up can make a big difference" [14].

To build a collaborative team, the universities need to understand collaboration: what mix of skills and experience will be likeliest to success, which researchers will work well together, which partners will be strong fit for cooperation [14]. The research information can help the universities to build the strongest collaborative team so that "Getting those people to work collaboratively on a proposal is much more effective than one person leading, and then everyone adding their name once the proposal is written." [14].

2   Open Challenges

In this PhD project, we are going to focus on the following three challenges:

C.1 Poor Data Quality Research information of RIMS comes from many data sources, both internal (researchers, faculties, activities) and external (funding, publication, projects). The growing volumes of data and the increasing number of data sources can lead to possible data errors, duplicates, missing values, incorrect formatting and contradictions [2]. Additional, the rich data types, especially unstructured data (e.g., project description, funding program description) are hard to be processed and analyzed [3]. Moreover, data change very fast, and the "timeliness" of data is short, which can lead to outdated, inconsistent, and invalid information [3]. As a consequence of lacking a minimum level of quality, the universities will not able to make the right research-intensive strategies [3,6].

C.2 Inefficient Funding Discovery The fund-seekers use search skills and solid connections to find grants from funding sources [5]. Nevertheless, searching

---

[1] https://duraspace.org/vivo.

[2] https://profiles.catalyst.harvard.edu/.

[3] https://www.elsevier.com/solutions/pure.

[4] https://clarivate.com/webofsciencegroup/solutions/converis.

the funding opportunities in the long list of funding agencies (18,664 funders, according to Crossref Funder Registry [4]) is inefficient and time-consuming. A 2018 survey of more than 11,000 academic lab heads in the United States found that, respondents spent around 44% of their research time simply tracking down, preparing and dealing with grant applications [5]. Another study from the National Health and Medical Research Council found that most of this grant-related time is simply wasted, with little or no benefit to scientific progress [5].

C.3 Ineffective Collaborative Team Building Despite the fact that building the collaborative team, either across faculties or across sectors, can increase the key to success on the research proposals [14]; the collaboration choices generally depend strongly on the opinions and personal motivations of the researchers [12]. For example, researchers refer to collaborate with individuals from a similar organization due to similarities in organizational norms; or they prefer not to engage in collaborations with commercial partners due to concerns about research integrity, academic freedom [12]. As a consequences, these opinion-based decisions will lead to the ineffectiveness of collaborative team building [14].

3   Related Work

Prior studies most related to the open challenges raised in this PhD project focus on data quality assurance. Azeroual et al. [2] presented the methods to detect, analyze and correct the data errors in research information systems. The authors use three types of analysis: attribute analysis, functional dependency, and reference analysis to measure data quality before being fused into RIMS. In more recent work, Azeroual et al. [1] presented the implementation of text and data mining methods to ensure high research information quality. The main focus of this work is the unstructured data and its quality issues.

Guillaumet et al. [6] introduced "OpenAnalytics", the Business Intelligence solution developed by SIGMA for universities. Nevertheless, this solution focuses on research outputs and research impact. Moreover, it only introduces basic analytics types for visualization and reporting but lacks predictive analytics.

Finally, Elsevier Funding Institutional[5] is a commercial product, provides information on the active funding opportunities, awarded grants, and funding agencies profiles. Nevertheless, the product is more focused on the search and select functions, and it has a tight coupling with other Elsevier products.

4   Research Objectives and Contributions

According to [6] and our first impressions from existing literature, there is no holistic solution that can solve the mentioned problem. Therefore, in this PhD project, we envision the Predictive Analytics-based approach that runs on top of

---

[5] https://www.elsevier.com/solutions/funding-institutional.

RIMS. Predictive Analytics involves analyzing historical data and using statistical and machine learning techniques to develop models that can make recommendations, suggestions [10]. It is widely used in industries to enable organizations to make business decisions. Apart from business, it is also applied in higher education [11] and gained noticeable success. For example: Predictive Analytics help the University of Texas at Austin to rise its graduation rates from 53% (2013) to nearly 70% (2019) [7]. According to its success in different contexts, Predictive Analytics can be a promising approach to overcome all the challenges, especially (C.2) and (C.3). Hence, this PhD project is going to achieve the following objectives: (O.1) assure high data quality, (O.2) increase funding discovery efficiency, and (O.3) increase effectiveness of building collaborative teams.

O.1 Assure high data quality With the support of a data quality check, causes of quality problems can usually be detected [2]. For example, with the help of data profiling, the university can evaluate their research information and provide information about their quality, as well as examine the dependencies and redundancies between data fields and better correct them within their RIMS [2]. For textual data, we are going to adapt text and data mining quality techniques in [1] to analyze, quantify and correct the unstructure data and its quality issues. In addition, for the short "timeliness" data, we are going to develop the schedule jobs that run automatically to keep the research information in RIMS up to date.

O.2 Increase funding discovery efficiency After the funding information is integrated to RIMS, the discovery and search facilities supported by RIMS can help the universities find active funding opportunities quicker and easier. The historical information can also tell universities where they have been successful before. As the next step, we are going to develop Predictive Analytics models that can: (i) finding research topics of regional or national importance, (ii) recommending strong fit funding opportunities, and (iii) predicting the success of proposal applications. As a result, the models will actively suggest funding opportunities to the universities and increase the efficiency of funding discovery.

O.3 Increase effectiveness of building collaborative teams Instead of using opinion-based decisions, the universities can apply data-driven decisions for resource allocation. "If faculties can see which researchers have succeeded with which funders, they can significantly improve their chances of funding success." [14]. Therefore, we are going to build the models to analyze research information (expertise and skills, research projects, and funding information). Based on this, the models can recommend: (i) the most eligible experts who have experienced success with the funding agencies or have needed expertise and skill sets, and (ii) the suitable partners with good project partnerships.

With these research objectives, this PhD project will contribute: (i) the web-based Predictive Analytics-based solution that runs on top of RIMS, (ii) the Predictive Analytics models that can enhance the funding discovery and strengthen collaboration in the project proposals. At the end, this solution can support all researchers, in general, and the researchers from Web Engineering community, in particular, to improve the quality of their proposal activities.

5   Research Methodology and Preliminary Results

The main research method we use in this PhD project is the Design Science Research (DSR) methodology – the systematic problem-solving method for producing Information System solutions within a specific domain [17]. It comprises several phases, as depicted in Fig. 1. Moreover, DSR is iterative, allowing the predictive analytics models to be improved through various iterations as required.

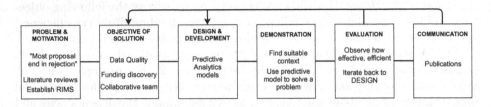

Fig. 1. Our envisioned DSR process model.

In the first year of this PhD project, we conducted a review to get familiar with the state-of-the-art in RIMS, Linked Open Data, Predictive Analytics, and Web Engineering. We presented the first contribution to Research Data Publishing in ICWE 2020 (SolidRDP [8]). Another project activity was establishing RIMS at the Chemnitz University of Technology which relies on VIVO semantic web platform. In addition, we contributed to the VIVO community[6] by sharing our development experience [16] at the VIVO Conference 2020.

In the future, the next step is to conduct a literature review to understand the state of problem context. In addition, we are going to identify the funding data sources and integrate this funding information into our current RIMS. Afterward, the main remaining tasks performed during the PhD work are: designing the architecture of the Predictive Analytics-based approach, demonstration (developing, validating, and deploying the models), evaluating the outcomes.

6   Conclusion

The competitive research funding and the need of research collaboration lead to the challenges in proposal activities, which includes funding discovery, collaborative team building, and data quality issues. To overcome the challenges, this PhD project envisioned the Predictive Analytics-based approach with the goal of supporting decision-making process to maximize the funding success rates.

Acknowledgements. This PhD project is supported by the project IB20 Fis Heavy/TU Chemnitz/259038, funded by the Saxon State Ministry for Science and Art. In addition, we would like to thank André Langer, Maik Benndorf and Sebastian Heil for their supports during the writing process of this Symposium.

---

[6] https://duraspace.org/vivo/community/.

References

1. Azeroual, O.: Text and data quality mining in CRIS. Information **10**(12), 374 (2019). https://doi.org/10.3390/info10120374, https://www.mdpi.com/2078-2489/10/12/374
2. Azeroual, O., Saake, G., Schallehn, E.: Analyzing data quality issues in research information systems via data profiling. Int. J. Inf. Manag. **41**, 50–56 (2018)
3. Cai, L., Zhu, Y.: The challenges of data quality and data quality assessment in the big data era. Data Sci. J. **14**, 2 (2015)
4. CrossRef: Funder registry factsheet. https://www.crossref.org/pdfs/about-funder-registry.pdf. Accessed 2 Feb 2021
5. Dolgin, E.: The hunt for the lesser-known funding source. Nature **570**(7759), 127–130 (2019)
6. Guillaumet, A., García, F., Cuadrón, O.: Analyzing a CRIS: from data to insight in university research. Procedia Comput. Sci. **146**, 230–240 (2019)
7. Kash, W.: Predictive analytics tools are boosting graduation rates and ROI, say university officials. https://edscoop.com/predictive-analytics-tools-are-boosting-graduation-rates-and-roi-say-university-officials/. Accessed 25 Jan 2021
8. Langer, A., Vu Nguyen Hai, D., Gaedke, M.: SolidRDP: applying solid data containers for research data publishing. In: Bielikova, M., Mikkonen, T., Pautasso, C. (eds.) ICWE 2020. LNCS, vol. 12128, pp. 399–415. Springer, Cham (2020). https://doi.org/10.1007/978-3-030-50578-3_27
9. Manu, T., Parmar, M., Shashikumara, A., Asjola, V.: Research information management systems: a comparative study. In: Research Data Access and Management in Modern Libraries, pp. 54–80. IGI Global (2019)
10. Mishra, N., Silakari, S.: Predictive analytics: a survey, trends, applications, oppurtunities & challenges. Int. J. Comput. Sci. Inf. Technol. **3**(3), 4434–4438 (2012)
11. Rajni, J., Malaya, D.B.: Predictive analytics in a higher education context. IT Prof. **17**(4), 24–33 (2015). https://doi.org/10.1109/MITP.2015.68
12. van Rijnsoever, F.J., Hessels, L.K.: How academic researchers select collaborative research projects: a choice experiment. J. Technol. Transfer 1–32 (2020). https://doi.org/10.1007/s10961-020-09833-2
13. Sohn, E.: Secrets to writing a winning grant. Nature **577**(7788), 133–135 (2020)
14. Thompson, L.: How to increase your institution's grant success rates. https://elsevier.com/connect/how-to-increase-your-grant-success-rates-with-insights-discovery-and-decisions. Accessed 24 Jan 2021
15. University, I.: Some reasons proposals fail. https://www.montana.edu/research/osp/general/reasons.html. Accessed 20 Jan 2021
16. Vu Nguyen Hai, D., Langer, A., Gaedke, M.: TUCfis: Applying vivo as the new RIS of the technical university of Chemnitz. Technische Informationsbibliothek TIB (2020). https://doi.org/10.5446/48014
17. Wieringa, R.J.: Design Science Methodology for Information Systems and Software Engineering. Springer, Heidelberg (2014). https://doi.org/10.1007/978-3-662-43839-8

A Web-Based Co-Creation and User Engagement Method and Platform

Andrea Tocchetti[1]([⊠])[ID], Lorenzo Corti[1][ID], Marco Brambilla[1][ID],
and Diletta Di Marco[2][ID]

[1] Dipartimento di Elettronica, Informazione e Bioingegneria, Politecnico di Milano,
Milan, Italy
{andrea.tocchetti,lorenzo.corti,marco.brambilla}@polimi.it
[2] Dipartimento di Ingegneria Gestionale, Politecnico di Milano, Milan, Italy
diletta.marco@polimi.it

Abstract. In recent years, new methods to engage citizens in deliberative processes of governments and institutions have been studied. Such methodologies have become a necessity to assure the efficacy and longevity of policies. Several tools and solutions have been proposed while trying to achieve such a goal. The dual problem to citizen engagement is how to provide policy-makers with useful and actionable insights stemming from those processes. In this paper, we propose a research featuring a method and implementation of a crowdsourcing and co-creation technique that can provide value to both citizens and policy-makers engaged in the policy-making process. Thanks to our methodology, policy-makers can design challenges for citizens to partake, cooperate and provide their input. We also propose a web-based tool that allow citizens to participate and produce content to support the policy-making processes through a gamified interface that focuses on emotional and vision-oriented content.

Keywords: Crowdsourcing · Gamification · Co-creation · Policy-making

1 Introduction

Over the past decades, a new form of governance has emerged to replace adversarial and managerial modes of policy-making. Engaging citizens in decision making is gradually proving to be a new way to overcome long-lasting symptoms of a democratic deficit in modern societies, such as the reluctance to publicly state one's opinion, declining voter turnout, and the diminishing participation in public debate within institutions. Governments and institutions are struggling to understand the real impact on innovation creation of such engagement processes, how they can be adequately developed and adopted [6,11]. The theory and practice of public policy are increasingly concerned with placing the citizen at the center of policy-makers' considerations, both as target and active agent. This new route focuses on opening up governmental structures to the external

The original version of this chapter was revised: this chapter was previously published non-open access. It has been changed to Open Access. The correction to this chapter is available at https://doi.org/10.1007/978-3-030-74296-6_50

environment and investigating the effect of the intensive use of data, information, and communications technology in the public sphere [7]. Public organizations are trying to learn how to encourage citizens to get involved in finding solutions to problems in the public sector for the sake of the common good. According to [1], the only way to meet and face these challenges is through the co-creation of new solutions with citizens.

This research proposes a method aimed at enabling large-scale citizen engagement and co-creation in support of policy-makers. The presented approach, as well as its implementation, is based on different principles and techniques, whose initial conceptualization has been reported in [10]. We report on our research plan and on the ongoing developments and continuous evolution with respect to the initial concepts.

2   Related Work

Most of the times, engaging citizens is a tough task, especially when it comes to the policy-making field. In recent years, many researchers and local administrations developed different methods and systems to achieve such a goal. Most of the developed solutions were digital, like platforms, social media and/or websites. "Love Your City" [9] allowed citizens to directly address to fellow citizens or authorities ("Addressing"), create solutions to a proposed problem ("Co-creating") and organize events ("Organizational"). "Decide" [3] was an online platform through which citizens could propose and vote new laws and opinions about the city proceedings, debate and rate how to redistribute the city's budget among projects.

Developed in the U.S.A., "MindMixer" [4] is an online platform through which citizens can express, support and comment public proposals. Its main functionalities involve submitting ideas, feedback, and photos, answering to questions on common themes and proposing their own solution to real life challenges.

Even though digital tools are more accessible and widespread, few European administrations opted for more tangible alternatives. Helsinki, Finland promoted public participation using a board game through which small teams of managers and front-line staff could learn together how to involve citizens in their work [2].

In Ovar, Portugal a method called "Participatory Budget" allowed citizens to express their support for different budget proposals [5]. The most interesting outcome was that people were asking friends and families to express their votes too. Inspired by this initiative, other cities pursued the same objective.

3   Co-Creation and User Engagement Method

3.1   The Evolution of the Policy-Making Process

In the traditional approach to policy-making citizens are perceived as passive actors. As can be evinced from Fig. 1, the active participation of citizens in the iterative formulation of a policy is able to enhance the overall outcome of such process by collecting direct feedback on the perceived impact of such procedure. However, this solution presents its own challenges when it comes to bridging the gap between policy-makers and citizens.

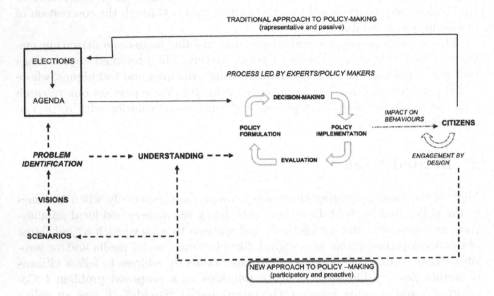

Fig. 1. Proposed co-creation process engaging both policy-makers and citizens.

3.2   The Research Method

In the attempt to face this problem, we devised a research plan implementing an incremental approach, where the work has been organized in four different steps:

- **Definition of the theoretical model** based on literature review and experts interviews;
- **Realization of a paper-based implementation** based on the theoretical model. The resulting physical mock-up has been tested by hosting workshops and gamified sessions, engaging experts in the social and policy-making fields to validate the engagement mechanisms. Tocchetti et al. [10] explains in details how such physical prototype was structured and how the experiment was carried out;
- **Development of a digital mock-up** featuring the core aspects deemed valuable based on the input of the physical phase;
- **Engagement of communities of policy-making experts** in the validation process of the digital mock-up.

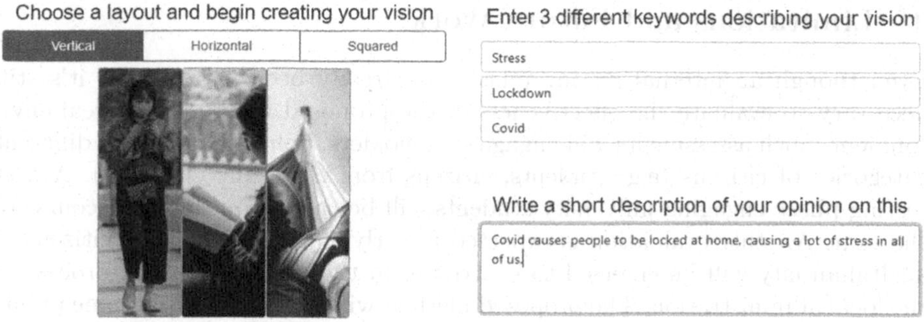

Choose a layout and begin creating your vision

| Vertical | Horizontal | Squared |

Enter 3 different keywords describing your vision

Stress

Lockdown

Covid

Write a short description of your opinion on this

Covid causes people to be locked at home, causing a lot of stress in all of us.

Fig. 2. Example of visual and textual content made by citizens

The preliminary feedback cycle contributed to identify some threats to the validity of our methodology. Therefore, policy-making experts were engaged in further discussion rounds. One of the aspects that has been under meticulous scrutiny is the emotional one. Due to its relevance and eventual impact on the design of the proposed interaction flow, this feature has undergone intense design cycles which led to a partial re-design of the mock-up to improve the emotional engagement of the citizens. The emotional facet has been modeled referencing the categorization of human emotions proposed by Plutchik [8]. In particular, the organization of people's emotions under eight categories, with three different intensities each, has been considered.

As most of the designed activities were successfully validated by the engaged policy-makers, a digital mock-up with the objective of improving the testing capabilities of the process has been developed. Further feedback on the final prototype have been collected to ensure that the principles validated in the physical prototype were correctly transposed into the digital one.

3.3 The Co-creation and User Engagement Solution

The approach and tool resulting from the research process engage citizens in a set of structured activities through which they are able to organize their thoughts in different formats. The interaction flow is structured to enable citizens to develop and convey their ideas through textual and graphical elements. In particular, the digital platform enables citizens to discuss about a variety of topics, through a series of gamified co-creation activities. The main goal is to detect moods, perceptions, and changes in the feelings of the users as they play and interact within the platform. The approach also leverages on empathy between players. Therefore, the proposed activities are aimed at structuring the thoughts of the citizens in an organized way, making them share, discuss, explore and converge on new lines of thought and visions for the future.

Thanks to its innovative content and interaction design, the proposed method is capable of capturing interesting signals from citizens about the topics of interest (Fig. 2).

4   Limitations and Future Work

Even though an internal testing phase has already been carried out, it's still necessary to evaluate the effectiveness of the proposed methods in a real environment. Such assessments will engage stakeholders, policy-makers and different categories of citizens (e.g. students, citizens from a specific city, etc.). A first testing phase engaging university students will be carried out over the course of the year. Another evaluation is expected in early summer, when the citizens of an Italian city will be engaged to contribute in the decision-making process of the local administration. The proposed method will be also tested in some public events and conferences attended by policy-makers. Finally, likely the most crucial aspect, the delivery of results to policy-makers will be addressed. This final objective will be accomplished via a data visualization dashboard. Its aim is to provide a comprehensive explanation of the content shared through the platform to the policy-makers, involving not only descriptive statistics but also analytical results about topics, questionnaires, keywords and textual comments shared by citizens within the process proposed above. The data collected will also be analyzed through machine learning algorithms to extract further knowledge that can be provided to policy-makers (e.g. by classifying the citizens depending on their feelings and shared content, it would be possible to determine the polarization of the citizens with respect to a specific topic).

The final objective will be to use the approach for creating and evolving policies, around which the community will converge and gather consensus.

5   Conclusions

In this paper, we described one of the aspects that both local and international administrations are currently trying to deal with, namely the engagement of the citizens in co-creating solutions to current problems. As a solution to such a challenge, we briefly exhibited a methodology through which provide policy-makers with insights on the thoughts of citizens, improving their decision-making capabilities. Over the rest of the year, the research will be enhanced with additional features. Furthermore, extensive experimentation will be implemented to test and validate the approach on real-world scenarios, engaging citizens and communities from different countries and with different socio-demographic characterization.

Acknowledgements. This research is partially supported by the European Commission under the H2020 framework, within project 822735 TRIGGER (TRends in Global Governance and Europe's Role) and project 101016233 PERISCOPE (Pan-European Response to the Impacts of COVID-19 and future Pandemics and Epidemics).

References

1. Bason, C.: Leading Public Sector Innovation (Second Edition): Co-creating for a Better Society. Bristol University Press (2018). https://doi.org/10.2307/j.ctv1fxh1w

2. BloombergCities. How Helsinki uses a board game to promote public partic- ipation, January 2018. https://medium.com/@BloombergCities/how-helsinki-uses-a-board-game-to-promote-public-participation-39d580380280
3. Sam DeJohn GovLab. Beyond Protest: Examining the Decide Madrid Platform for Public Engagement. May 2018. https://blog.p2pfoundation.net/beyond-protest-examining-the-decide-madrid-platform-for-public-engagement/2018/05/09
4. Ha, A.: MindMixer Raises $17M To Help Governments Connect With Their Communities - TechCrunch, September 2014. https://techcrunch.com/2014/09/02/mindmixer-raises-17m-to-help-governments-connect-with-their-communities/
5. Mak, H.W.: A Political Success Story: Gamification as Civic Engagement Tool, January 2016. http://www.gamification.co/2016/01/11/political-success-story-gamification-civic-engagement-tool/
6. Mazzucato, M.: Mission-oriented innovation policies: challenges and opportunities. In: Industrial and Corporate Change 27.5, October 2018, pp. 803–815. ISSN: 0960–6491. https://doi.org/10.1093/icc/dty034
7. Misuraca, G., Pasi, G.: Landscaping digital social innovation in the EU: structuring the evidence and nurturing the science and policy debate towards a renewed agenda for social change. In: Govern- ment Information Quarterly 36.3, pp. 592–600 (2019). ISSN: 0740–624X. https://doi.org/10.1016/j.giq.2019.02.004
8. Plutchik, R.: A general psychoevolutionary theory of emotion. In: Plutchik, R., Kellerman, H. (eds.) Theories of Emotion. Academic Press, pp. 3–33 (1980). ISBN: 978-0-12-558701-3. https://doi.org/10.1016/B978-0-12-558701-3.50007-7
9. Stembert , N., Mulder, I.J.: Love your city! An interactive platform empowering citizens to turn the public domain into a participatory domain. In: International Conference Using ICT, Social Media and Mobile Technologies to Foster Self-Organisation in Urban and Neighbourhood Governance, Delft, The Netherlands, 16–17 May 2013, May 2013
10. Tocchetti, A., Brambilla, M.: A gamified crowdsourcing framework for data-driven co-creation of policy making and social foresight. In: NeurIPS 2020 Crowd Science Workshop - CEUR Proceedings, vol. 2736, pp. 34–44 (2020)
11. Wegrich, K.: The blind spots of collaborative innovation. In: Public Management Review 21.1 (2019), pp. 12–20 (2018). 1433311. https://doi.org/10.1080/14719037

Posters and Demonstrations

Effectiveness Comparison of Email Addresses Recovery from Gravatars

Przemysław Rodwald(✉)

Department of Computer Science, Polish Naval Academy, Gdynia, Poland
p.rodwald@amw.gdynia.pl

Abstract. Internet was not designed for anonymity, but most users posting comments with unidentifiable pseudonyms hope to stay anonymous. On many websites, especially those powered by WordPress, the comments system is linked with the Gravatar service. That service uses email address, in obfuscated form (MD5 hash function), to provide users' avatars. This approach allows to deanonymize real emails of users. Emails, which according to EU law, are considered as a personal information. This article explains all stages and results of the real attacks on a three types on websites: national ones, security oriented national ones and global one. We compare the effectiveness of three types of attacks: brute-force, dictionary and hybrid in relation to the type of attacked website.

Keywords: MD5 hash function · Email recovery · Gravatar

1 Introduction

Gravatar is a widely used service for providing globally unique avatars. Avatar is an individual image uploaded by a user and linked with his email address. Unfortunately, Gravatar uses MD5 cryptographic hash function as a unique identifier for user's emails. A cryptographic hash function could be defined as an algorithm that maps data of arbitrary size to a fixed size string of bits (called hash). A hash function should be designed to be a one-way function - a function which is infeasible to invert. MD5 hash algorithm was designed by Ronald Rivest in 1991 and produces a 128-bit hash value [1]. Gravatar is the most popular but not the only service offering similar functionality, e.g. libravatar.org (MD5 or SHA256), evatar.io (SHA256) or dicebear.com (plaintext).

The results of recovering email addresses from Gravatar hashes was previously demonstrated a few time. First, in 2008, a user nicknamed abell [2] crawled 80000 MD5 Gravatar hashes from Stack Overflow webpage and was able to recover 10% of email addresses. Second, in 2013, Bongard [3] acquired 2400 MD5 Gravatar hashes from French political blog Fdesouche and was able to recover 70% of the email addresses. Rodwald, firstly in 2019 [4], showed how to prepare for the attack on Gravatar MD5 hashes and how to carry out it step by step. He showed results of a real attack on two polish language webservices

© Springer Nature Switzerland AG 2021
M. Brambilla et al. (Eds.): ICWE 2021, LNCS 12706, pp. 505–508, 2021.
https://doi.org/10.1007/978-3-030-74296-6_39

and revealed 65% of real email addresses. In 2020 [5] he adopted a small-scale
approach for the large-scale attack and was able to recover more than (1.25 M)
20% real emails of the Stack Overflow users.

2 Attacks on Gravatar MD5 Hashes

2.1 Targets

In order to provide more comprehensive comparison of effectiveness of attacks,
we decide to take into account three types of websites. The first group consists
of two national, general topic, web-services [4]: jakoszczedzacpieniadze.pl - Polish blog about saving money and swiatczytnikow.pl - Polish blog about e-books.
Those sites will be marked as *nat-gen-1* and *nat-gen-2* accordingly and *nat-gen*
together. The second group consist of two national, IT security oriented, websites:
niebezpiecznik.pl *nat-sec-1* and z3s.pl *nat-sec-2*, marked as *nat-sec* together. To
the last group belongs global IT service [5], Stack Overflow *global-it*.

2.2 Preparation Phase

Attacks had to be preceded by extracting Gravatar MD5 hash values. The structure of the HTML code of selected website has been analyzed and dedicated
web-crawlers prepared. As a result, a following quantities of unique MD5 hashes
were obtained: 13935 from *nat-gen-1*, 12321 from *nat-gen-2*, 50335 from *nat-
sec-1*, 18202 from *nat-sec-2* and 6016434 from *global-it*. Except of MD5 Gravatar hashes of users' emails some additional data were stored in the MySQL
database: nicknames for all sites and location for *global-it*. According to the proposed methodology [4,5] as a second part of the preparation phase an analysis
of most popular email providers, for particular country (Poland in our case) or
identified top the most popular user countries for *global-it*, has been carried out.
As a third step a username patterns analysis has been done. Table 1 gives a
summary of all identified most popular patterns. In the table the most popular
notation is used, where: ?d – any digit, ?l – any letter, ?s – one of the signs
{NULL . _}. To prepare a hybrid attack, based on patterns in the username part
of email address, searching for lists of national names and national surnames

Table 1. Username patterns

Pattern	Examples
$[lastname][?s][?d]\{0,4\}$	rodwald rodwald_1990
$[firstname][?s][?d]\{0,4\}$	paul paul07
$[firstname][?s][lastname][?d]\{0,4\}$	paulrodwald paul_rodwald2017
$[lastname][?s][firstname][?d]\{0,4\}$	rodwald.paul rodwald_paul77
$[?l][?s][lastname][?d]\{0,4\}$	p.rodwald p_rodwald33
$[lastname][?s][?l][?d]\{0,4\}$	rodwald_p rodwald_p01
$[nickname][?s][?d]\{0,4\}$	zipper oshin_82

has been done. For *global-it* this task involved not just one country, like in other cases, but earlier identified top the most popular user countries.

The final step, preparing for the dictionary attack, was the most time consuming one. The reason is the choice of our sources of emails. As the dictionaries we decided to use two sources of real leaked emails. The first one is known as a Exploit.in leakage and the size of the zipped file is larger than 10GB. The Exploit.in leakage has 805,499,391 rows of email address and plain text password pairs, but actually has 593,427,119 unique email addresses. The second one is more up to date source of emails, dated January 2019, called Collection 1–5. Size of the compressed files is larger than 870 GB. Once prepared dictionary of leaked emails could be used for attacking MD5 Gravatar hashes coming from different websites.

2.3 Techniques of Attacks

The attack itself has been carry out with the power of the hashcat software on dedicated rig (six overclocked GPU's MSI GeForce GTX 1080 8GB, total speed 65GH/s for MD5 hash algorithm) and is divided into three main approaches: dictionary attack based on leaked email addresses, hybrid attack and finally brute force attack. As a source for dictionary attack an extracted list of emails, coming from the two mentioned leakages, was used. Hybrid attack combines two elements: list of identified patterns presented in Table 1 and the list of the most popular national email domains. And finally, brute force attack attempts every possible combination of a given character set up to a certain length. We decided to check all possible usernames from 1 up to 8 chars long for *global-it* or up to 10 chars long for other services. As a domain part for this attack, all most popular domains were used as well as some disposable email (i.e. mailinator.com).

3 Results and Findings

The summary of our attacks is as follows: for *global-it* 20.88% (1256315 of 6016434) of all Gravatar MD5 hashes were broken and emails revealed; the effectiveness of individual attacks: dictionary - 14.78%, hybrid - 9.89%, brute force - 8.96%; for *nat-sec* 62.18% reversed MD5 hashes (31.79%, 19.12% and 47.58% accordingly); for *nat-gen* 64.27% recovered emails. Venn diagram for three types of attacks presents Fig. 1. The diagram shows that the attacks are complementary, the use of all three approaches gives the best results.

There is a significant disproportion among number of revealed emails for national websites (62.18% *nat-sec*, 64.27% *nat-glo*) and a global websites (20.88% *global-it*). The highest success rate for national sites could be reached with brute force approach where five the most popular email domains covers about 70% of all emails. For global sites dictionary attack is the most effective one. The key factor is the time-consuming preparation of appropriate dictionaries in advance. Comparing domain statistics among recovered email addresses between *nat-sec* and *nat-glo* there is a noticeable popularity of disposable emails, what could lead to a conclusion of higher cybersecurity consciousness among IT-security oriented users.

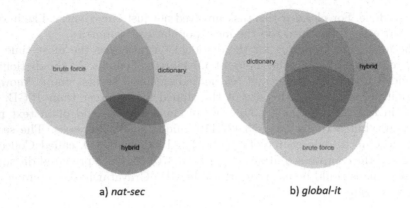

a) *nat-sec*   b) *global-it*

Fig. 1. Venn diagram for three types of attacks for: a)*nat-sec* and b)*global-it*.

4   Conclusions

It is worth pointing out that in many jurisdictions an email address is consider as a sensitive private data. For example in European Union an email address such as name.surname@company.com is an examples of personal data as well [6]. Such a data in many circumstances must be anonymized. For data to be truly anonymized, the anonymization must be irreversible. We prove in this article that the usage of MD5 hash function as an anonymization technique for email addresses is a bad idea. A usage of gravatar in places where deanonymization could be a problem should be withheld.

The article aims to increase the awareness of users publishing comments on various websites about the potential possibility of disclosing their real email addresses.

References

1. Rivest, R.: The MD5 Message-Digest Algorithm. RFC 1321 (1992). https://tools. ietf.org/html/rfc1321. Accessed 18 Jan 2021
2. abell: Gravatars: why publishing your email's hash is not a good idea (2009). http://www.developer.it/post/gravatars-why-publishing-your-email-s-hash-is-not-a-good-idea. Accessed 18 Jan 2021
3. Bongard, D.: De-anonymizing Users of French Political Forums. Technical report (2013). https://bit.ly/2XLhMNz. Accessed 18 Jan 2021
4. Rodwald, P.: E-mail recovery from websites using Gravatar. Bull. Military Univ. Technol. **68**(2), 59–70 (2019)
5. Rodwald, P.: Large scale attack on gravatars from stack overflow. In: Zamojski, W., Mazurkiewicz, J., Sugier, J., Walkowiak, T., Kacprzyk, J. (eds.) DepCoS-RELCOMEX 2020. AISC, vol. 1173, pp. 503–512. Springer, Cham (2020). https:// doi.org/10.1007/978-3-030-48256-5_49
6. European Commission: What is personal data? https://ec.europa.eu/info/law/law-topic/data-protection/reform/what-personal-data_en. Accessed 18 Jan 2021

A Web Tool for XQuery Debugging

Jesús M. Almendros-Jiménez[(✉)] and Antonio Becerra-Terón

Department of Informatics, University of Almería, 04120 Almería, Spain
{jalmen,abecerra}@ual.es

Abstract. This system demo shows how to debug XQuery programs using an algorithmic debugger developed for XQuery. The debugging process consists in the building of a debugging tree and the answering of questions Yes/No by the user about the results of Function calls and XPath expressions until a bug is found (or no more questions remain). Using the higher-order capabilities of XQuery several debugging strategies –children selection strategies– can be used, enabling the adaptation of the debugging to the program/query.

Keywords: Debugging · Database query languages · XQuery

1 Introduction

Declarative debugging (DD) [4] is a well-known debugging technique enabling to find program bugs. Also known as *algorithmic debugging*, it was proposed for logic programming [7], but it has been adapted to other programming languages (for instance, *Haskell* [5], *Java* [6], *Datalog* [2] and *SQL* [3]). DD is based on the navigation of the so-called *debugging tree*, where the root of the debugging tree is the main program and the result, and non-root nodes contain *partial computations* (usually, function calls) and their computed values. The children of each node correspond to subcomputations of the parent. The debugging process consists in the navigation of the debugging tree, in which an *oracle* (normally, the user) answers "Yes" or "No" to *debugging questions*, which are questions about the results of the partial computations. When the answers of the oracle to all the children of a given node are "Yes" and the answer to the parent is "No", a *bug* has been located in the code of the parent. Several *strategies* have been defined (see [8] for a survey), whose main goal is to reduce the time of the DD. They range from *top-down* to *bottom-up* traversal of the debugging tree, selection strategies of nodes, types of debugging questions, memorization of oracle answers and debugging tree transformations, among others. The order, number and complexity of debugging questions affect the *debugging process time*. Additionally, the reduction of the time to be built or the space consumed by the debugging tree have influenced the design of declarative debuggers.

This work was supported by the State Research Agency (AEI) of the Spanish Ministry of Science and Innovation under grant PID2019-104735RB-C42 (SAFER).

© Springer Nature Switzerland AG 2021
M. Brambilla et al. (Eds.): ICWE 2021, LNCS 12706, pp. 509–512, 2021.
https://doi.org/10.1007/978-3-030-74296-6_40

```
declare function local:min($t){
let $prices := db:open('prices')
let $p := $prices/prices/book[title = $t]/year
return min($p)}
-------------------------------------------------------------
declare function local:store($t,$p){
let $prices := db:open('prices')
let $p := $prices/prices/book[title = $t and price=$p]
return $p/source};
-------------------------------------------------------------
declare function local:min_price($t){
let $min := local:min($t) return
<minprice title='{$t}'>
{local:store($t,$min)}
<price>{local:min($t)}</price>
</minprice>};
-------------------------------------------------------------
declare function local:avg($rates){
let $n := count($rates) return sum($rates)}
-------------------------------------------------------------
declare function local:data($t){
for $b in db:open('bstore')/bstore/book[title=$t]
let $ra := local:avg($b/rate) where $ra < 5 return
if ($b[editor]) then ($b/editor,$b/publisher,<avg>{$ra}</avg>)
else ($b/author[position()<=1],$b/publisher,<avg>{$ra}</avg>)}
-----------------------------Query-----------------------------
<bib>{
let $mylist := db:open('mylist')
for $t in distinct-values($mylist/title)
let $d := local:data($t) where exists($d) return
<book>{$d,local:min_price($t)}</book>
}</bib>
```

Fig. 1. Example of buggy program (Color figure online)

Here we have adapted declarative debugging to XQuery. Let us suppose the XQuery program and query of Fig. 1. Here the query should extract the full data from 'bstore' of each book of a names list 'mylist' as well as the lowest price from 'prices'. The query should filter books with an average rating above five. With this aim, the query uses the following XQuery functions: *local:data* for getting the data of well-rated books (average rating above five); and *local:min_price* which returns the store and the lowest price. The later calls to auxiliary functions: *local:min* –for computing the minimum price– and *local:store* – for retrieving the store–. Additionally, *local:data* computes the average rate by calling the function *local:avg*. Intentionally, some *bugs* have been introduced (in red colour). From top to down, the first one uses a *wrong tag* year instead of price. In the second one, the average price is *incorrectly computed*. Also the *Boolean condition* for filtering average rating is incorrect – less than 5 instead of greater than 5– in the third one. Finally, the path on the document 'mylist' is incorrect –it should be *$mylist/mylist/title*–.

2 Debugging

A debugging session of the proposed debugger consists in the building of the debugging tree (see Fig. 2), and the answering of a sequence of questions with

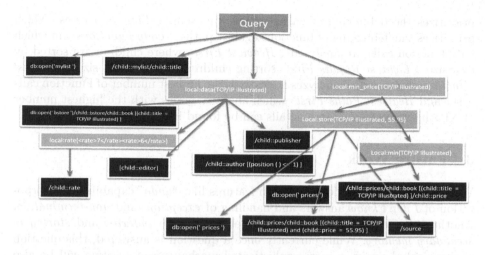

Fig. 2. Debugging tree

Debugging Questions		Please Select
▼ question		● ✓ ● ✕ ● ✗
▼ Can be		
the function call	local:data	
with arguments	TCP/IP Illustrated	
▼ equal to		
▼ author		
last	Stevens	
first	W.	
publisher	Addison-Wesley	
mrate	5.5	
▼ question		
Can be	db:open(' bstore ')/child::bstore/child::book [(child::title = TCP/IP Illustrated)]	
▼ equal to		
▼ book		
title	TCP/IP Illustrated	
▶ author		
publisher	Addison-Wesley	
rate	7	

Fig. 3. Debugging session

'Yes' or 'No'. Such questions are about the *results of the nodes* –which are *XPath expressions* and *Function calls*–. When the answers of the user to all the children of a given node are "Yes" and the answer to the parent is "No", a *bug* has been located in the code of the parent. The developed Web tool http://minerva.ual. es:8090/debxquery/ handles a graphical interface, and uses *grids* for improving the user experience (see Fig. 3).

The debugger has been implemented in XQuery, and the debugging tree is represented as a *XML tree*. It facilitates its building from a query and enables to use XQuery itself for the traversal of XML tree. The traversal function of the XML debugging tree is defined as a *higher order* XQuery function, which is *parameterized* by a *children selection function* in such a way that switching the children selection functions different user-defined strategies of debugging can be selected. Some built-in selection strategies are defined: *First Paths* –which prioritizes the debugging of paths against functions–, *First Functions* –which prioritizes the debugging of functions against paths–, *Only Functions* – in which only function calls are analysed–, *Heaviest First* –where children are sorted by tree size–, *Lightest Results First* –sorting children by the result size–, *Heaviest Functions First* –which analyzes nodes with the highest number of Function calls first– and *Heaviest Paths First* –which analyzes nodes with the highest number of XPath expressions–. More details can be found in [1].

3   Future Work

We plan to extend the debugger with features like *"undo"* capabilities, incorporation of *I don't know* answers and handling of *exceptions* and *non-termination*. Another planned improvement is the debugging tree *indexing* and *storing in secondary memory*. While currently once a question is answered, this question is never asked again, a more sophisticated mechanism of *trusting* will be also studied. Finally, we will study algorithmic debugging in other NoSQL database query languages.

References

1. Almendros-Jiménez, J.M., Becerra-Terón, A.: Declarative debugging of XML queries. In: Morales, J.F., Orchard, D. (eds.) PADL 2021. LNCS, vol. 12548, pp. 161–177. Springer, Cham (2021). https://doi.org/10.1007/978-3-030-67438-0_10
2. Caballero, R., García-Ruiz, Y., Sáenz-Pérez, F.: A theoretical framework for the declarative debugging of datalog programs. In: Schewe, K.-D., Thalheim, B. (eds.) SDKB 2008. LNCS, vol. 4925, pp. 143–159. Springer, Heidelberg (2008). https://doi.org/10.1007/978-3-540-88594-8_8
3. Caballero, R., García-Ruiz, Y., Sáenz-Pérez, F.: Algorithmic debugging of SQL views. In: Clarke, E., Virbitskaite, I., Voronkov, A. (eds.) PSI 2011. LNCS, vol. 7162, pp. 77–85. Springer, Heidelberg (2012). https://doi.org/10.1007/978-3-642-29709-0_9
4. Caballero, R., Riesco, A., Silva, J.: A survey of algorithmic debugging. ACM Comput. Surv. (CSUR) **50**(4), 1–35 (2017)
5. Faddegon, M., Chitil, O.: Algorithmic debugging of real-world haskell programs: deriving dependencies from the cost centre stack. ACM SIGPLAN Not. **50**(6), 33–42 (2015)
6. Insa, D., Silva, J.: An algorithmic debugger for Java. In: 2010 IEEE International Conference on Software Maintenance, pp. 1–6. IEEE (2010)
7. Shapiro, E.Y.: Algorithmic program diagnosis. In: Proceedings of the 9th ACM SIGPLAN-SIGACT Symposium on Principles of Programming Languages, pp. 299–308 (1982)
8. Silva, J.: A survey on algorithmic debugging strategies. Adv. Eng. Softw. **42**(11), 976–991 (2011)

Managing Versioned Web Resources
in the File System

Leon Müller and Lars Gleim[✉]

Databases and Information Systems, RWTH Aachen University, Aachen, Germany
{leon.mueller,lars.gleim}@rwth-aachen.de

Abstract. While the WebDAV standard provides a well-established read/write mechanism for Web resources, as well as version management through its Delta-V extension, the complexity of the underlying protocol limits its practical adoption. The W3C Linked Data Platform (LDP) more recently provides an alternative approach for simultaneous resource and semantic metadata management on the Web. In combination with the HTTP Memento protocol, it has recently been successfully employed in the context of interoperable data management. Inspired by file system interfaces for WebDAV, we present *factFUSE*, the – to our knowledge – first user-space application for the joint management of arbitrary computer files and semantic RDF data & metadata in the file system based on the LDP and HTTP Memento Web standards.

Keywords: Linked data platform · Semantic data management · FUSE · File system · Version management · HTTP memento protocol

1 Introduction

As the volume and variety of data that is produced every year keep growing, the challenge of efficient data management is becoming increasingly relevant. Especially since the beginning of the Corona pandemic, the need for distributed data management systems has become more apparent than ever. While popular distributed cloud storage services like Dropbox or Google Drive are readily available, they are not based on open Web standards and lack important interoperability features. Inspired by these services and version control systems such as Git, we developed factFUSE: a data management system based upon the W3C Linked Data Platform (LDP) [6] standard enabling the unified management of RDF and binary resources through a simple hierarchical mapping of Web resources into the classical file system, while providing simple version control mechanisms based upon the HTTP Memento protocol.

2 Mapping LDP Resources into the File System

Besides standardized HTTP CRUD operations for reading and writing Web resources, the W3C LDP specification [6] provides primitives to hierarchically

© Springer Nature Switzerland AG 2021
M. Brambilla et al. (Eds.): ICWE 2021, LNCS 12706, pp. 513–516, 2021.
https://doi.org/10.1007/978-3-030-74296-6_41

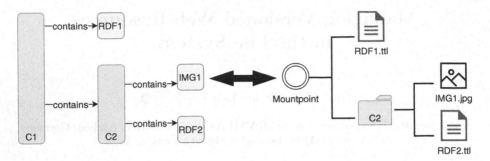

Fig. 1. Using the structural components of the Linked Data Platform Specifications, we can directly translate the containment relations in the LDP (left) to directory-child relations in the file system (right).

structure sets of RDF Linked Data resources, as well as arbitrary binary data, using containers that can contain RDF resources, binary resources and other containers. Based on the similarity of this organizational pattern with the traditional directory structure of hierarchical file systems, we define a straightforward mapping of LDP resources into the file system, as illustrated in Fig. 1. Containers are directly mapped to directories and other resources to corresponding file representations in the file system. While RDF resources are represented as text files containing a Turtle serialization of their triples, binary resources are displayed in their respective file format, as determined through their respective MIME-type.

Semantic Metadata. Each binary resource may further be augmented with RDF metadata which can contain semantic context information and metadata, stored in a dedicated metadata resource discoverable through a `describedBy` relation in the HTTP link header (implementing the LDP specification). Subsequently, this approach enables the flexible and extensible semantic enrichment of arbitrary binary resources and allows users to manage both RDF as well as arbitrary binary Web resources and their metadata inside the file system.

Persistent Identification. To allow for the persistent identification and referencing of individual resource revisions and keep a record of the resource revision history, we employ timestamped URLs according to the FactID scheme [1–3] to identify individual resource revisions and the HTTP Memento protocol [5], a standardized HTTP extension enabling time-based content negotiation to retrieve historical resource states, for version discovery and retrieval.

3   Implementation

factFUSE[1] is a NodeJS application implementing a custom user-space file system driver through JavaScript FUSE bindings[2]. The system is available as open-

---

[1] https://git.rwth-aachen.de/i5/factdag/factfuse.
[2] https://github.com/fuse-friends/fuse-native.

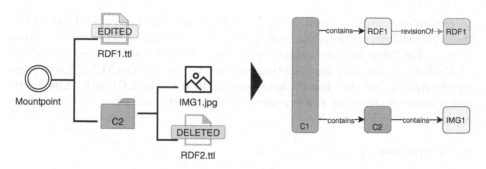

Fig. 2. Modifications to file representations are applied to the original LDP resource. Changes to resources are tracked by creating a list of revisions.

source for both macOS and Linux environments. It communicates with LDP servers through the *factlib.js*[3] library, which is part of the FactStack data management system [3]. CRUD interactions with resources in the file system are directly translated to corresponding LDP HTTP calls. factFUSE further supports subscribing to server-provided change-notifications in Activity Streams 2.0 format via WebSockets (as implemented by the FactStack system) to be informed about resource updates on the LDP and to apply them to the local file representations in near real-time. This makes factFUSE a tool that can be used to interface with LDPs, manage data sets containing both RDF resources and binary resources, and integrate previously unconnected data into the Web of Linked Data.

Versioning. factFUSE transparently handles resource versioning using the Memento Protocol [5] and assigns a persistent Memento URL – a FactID – to each revision according to the FactDAG data interoperability layer model [2] and the FAIR data principles [7]. New revisions of a resource are connected to their predecessor through a W3C PROV-O [4] `revisionOf` relation, which is added to the RDF metadata of the new revision. Our custom user-space file system supports all regular CRUD file system interactions, such as writing, creating, removing or renaming files. All interactions are translated into according HTTP calls and so changes that were conducted in the file system representation are applied to the LDP side. Users may discover and download previous resource revisions through a file context menu. Therefore, factFUSE transparently discovers the version history of the underlying Web resource from its respective TimeMap provided by the LDP HTTP server in accordance with the HTTP Memento specification.

Example. As described in Sect. 2, factFUSE maps LDP Resources and Containers to files and directories in the local file system. A selected LDP Container is mapped to a virtual root directory – the mount point – within the local file system. Once mounted, LDP resources are exposed below this root directory. In

---

[3] https://git.rwth-aachen.de/i5/factdag/factlibjs.

an example scenario, as seen in Fig. 1, after connecting factFUSE to the LDP the user can interact with the user-space file system and modify the resources with, or use them in, any desktop application. Figure 2 shows the state of the LDP after editing one, and deleting another file in the factFUSE file system representation and the changes have been applied to the LDP side. The modified resource is stored as a new revision, with a `revisionOf` link to the original resource.

4   Conclusion

In this paper, we have presented factFUSE, a user-space application for the joint management of computer files and semantic data and metadata. It is based upon the LDP, PROV and HTTP Memento Web standards and offers a novel solution for distributed data management and version control in a familiar environment – the file system. Through the mapping of LDP resources into the local file system, factFUSE offers a first step towards bridging the gap between traditional file system-based data management and semantic web management solutions.

factFUSE is available (see footnote 1) as open source software under the GNU AGPLv3 license to be evaluated by the community. The repository includes detailed installation and usage instructions, including screenshots of all the implemented features and interfaces in in-use scenarios, as well as pre-built binaries for macOS and the Ubuntu Linux distribution.

In future work, we plan to further extend upon the factFUSE concept in order to integrate flexible semantic metadata management into the traditional file system paradigm, ultimately working towards a tighter integration of Web resources, computer files and semantic knowledge graphs.

Acknowledgments. Funded by the Deutsche Forschungsgemeinschaft (DFG, German Research Foundation) under Germany's Excellence Strategy – EXC – 2023 Internet of Production – 390621612.

References

1. Gleim, L., Decker, S.: Timestamped URLs as persistent identifiers. In: MEP-DaW@ISWC (2020)
2. Gleim, L., et al.: FactDAG: formalizing data interoperability in an internet of production. IEEE Internet Things J. **7**(4), 3243–3253 (2020)
3. Gleim, L., Pennekamp, J., Tirpitz, L., Welten, S., Brillowski, F., Decker, S.: Fact-Stack: interoperable data management and preservation for the web and Industry 4.0. In: BTW 2021. Gesellschaft für Informatik, Bonn (2021, preprint)
4. Lebo, T., Sahoo, S., McGuinness, D.: PROV-O: the PROV ontology. W3C Rec. (2013)
5. Van de Sompel, H., Nelson, M., Sanderson, R.: HTTP framework for time-based access to resource states - Memento. IETF RFC 7089 (2013)
6. Speicher, S., Arwe, J., Malhotra, A.: Linked data platform 1.0. W3C Rec. (2015)
7. Wilkinson, M.D., Dumontier, M., Aalbersberg, I.J., Appleton, G., Axton, M., Baak, A., Blomberg, N., et al.: The FAIR guiding principles for scientific data management and stewardship. Sci. Data **3**, 160018 (2016)

Visualizing Web Users' Attention to Text with Selection Heatmaps

Ilan Kirsh[(✉)][iD]

The Academic College of Tel Aviv-Yaffo, Tel Aviv, Israel
kirsh@mta.ac.il

Abstract. Web analytics tools provide useful information about the interaction of users with websites, and particularly, on what captures the attention of web visitors on websites. User attention to areas of web pages can be visualized using heatmaps. Two types of attention indicators are commonly used in web analytics heatmaps: visibility duration of page sections in the browser's viewport and mouse activity on areas and elements of web pages. This work introduces a new type of user attention heatmap, which visualizes the frequency of text selection operations on websites. Selection is the first step in the process of copying text to the clipboard, but it is also used to highlight important points while reading, similarly to highlighting words on a notebook with a marker pen. As demonstrated and discussed in this paper, selection heatmaps provide interesting perspectives on user attention to paragraphs, sentences, and words on websites, and this could be useful in web analytics.

Keywords: Web analytics · Visualization · Heatmaps · Text selection

1 Introduction

Web analytics aims to shed light on how a website is used by its visitors, and particularly, what captures the users' attention [1]. In web analytics heatmaps, page areas that attract more attention are displayed with 'hot' background colors, such as shades of red, and areas that attract less attention with 'cold' background colors, such as shades of blue. Two types of attention indicators are commonly used in commercial web analytics: visibility time (page areas become visible and invisible as users scroll the page) and mouse activity (clicks and movements on page areas) [2,3]. A recent paper proposed to track and use copy operations of text to the clipboard by web users as a new source of data for web page heatmaps [3]. The usefulness and importance of heatmaps in web analytics are demonstrated and discussed in previous works [2,3].

This work introduces a new type of heatmap, which visualizes user attention to text as reflected by selection (or highlighting) operations. Text selection is often considered as merely the first step in copying text to the clipboard. However, analysis shows that the vast majority of text selection operations in this study's dataset are not followed by copying. Text selection can be used by

© Springer Nature Switzerland AG 2021
M. Brambilla et al. (Eds.): ICWE 2021, LNCS 12706, pp. 517–520, 2021.
https://doi.org/10.1007/978-3-030-74296-6_42

online readers to highlight points while reading, similarly to highlighting words in a book with a marker pen. Accordingly, selection heatmaps can extend the existing web analytics toolbox and may provide new perspectives on web user attention to elements of online text.

2   Implementation

Figure 1 illustrates the selection heatmaps implementation. At the top, we can see a standard HTTP client-server communication between a browser (on the left side) and a web server (on the right side).

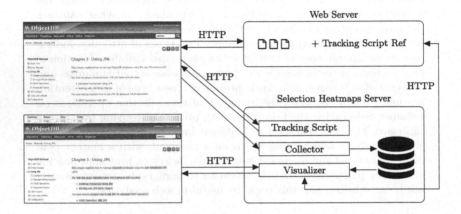

Fig. 1. Architecture of the selection heatmaps implementation

To track text selection operations, a reference to a *Tracking Script* is embedded in the website pages. As a result, when a web page is loaded it triggers a request to load the Tracking Script from the Heatmaps Server. Once loaded, the Tracking Script records text selection operations and reports them to the *Collector* component in the Heatmaps Server, which stores the data in a dedicated database. Following the common practice of web analytics, and to protect user privacy, all the collected data are anonymized.

User actions, such as clicking and moving the mouse, scrolling the page, and copying text to the clipboard, can be tracked by listening to JavaScript events in the browser. Text selection is different, as it does not trigger any JavaScript event. It is possible, however, to get information from JavaScript on which text is selected, if any, at any given point in time. Therefore, the implementation uses a timer to routinely check for text selections, at a rate of once every tenth of a second (which only adds a negligible performance overhead). This poses an additional challenge, as a single selection operation can be detected multiple times with different text strings, while a user extends the selection (and sometimes also shrinks it). Therefore, detected selections are filtered: selections that are substrings of the preceding or the succeeding selection are discarded.

Web analysts can examine the web pages with the selection heatmaps by visiting the website through the *Visualizer* component, which functions as a proxy server. The Visualizer retrieves the original web pages from the web server and converts them to heatmap pages by adding background colors and shades. The colors that this implementation uses are shown on the right side of the heatmap toolbar at the top of the web page (see the bottom browser image in Fig. 1), from the coldest color on the left to the hottest color on the right.

3 Demonstration

The selection heatmaps implementation was examined using pages of the ObjectDB website[1]. Web usage data were collected for six months, ending in June 2020. In total, 783,028 text selection operations were collected over 1,295,221 page views. Only a fraction of the selection operations were followed by copying text to the clipboard (there were only 109,525 copy operations).

Figure 2 demonstrates selection heatmaps for two lists. The explanations on the right side of these paragraphs attracted more selections than the class and method names on the left side. Some words, and noticeably the word 'exactly' (in both of its appearances), gained more selections than the other words. The similarity between the painting of the lines in these two paragraphs indicates repeating patterns. Possibly, users highlighted the explanations, and particularly the word 'exactly', to emphasize specific words to themselves while reading.

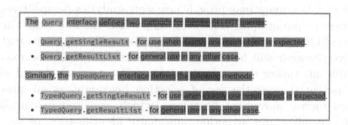

Fig. 2. A selection heatmap

Figure 3 presents heatmaps with the primary and secondary headers of two web pages. These examples demonstrate another pattern: words that are less frequent for the specific topic, or more unique, were selected more frequently. Common words such as 'Obtaining', 'Using', and 'Access' were selected less frequently than words that are specifically related to the context. The entire website is about 'JPA' (and database), thus 'Entity Fields' and 'Connection' are much more specific to these pages than 'JPA', and indeed, they were selected more frequently. Similar behavior is also identified when moving from the page and the primary header level down to page sections and secondary headers. In the

---

[1] www.objectdb.com.

'JPA Entity Fields' page, the word 'Fields' is very frequent, and not directly linked to any particular section of the page. Accordingly, the words 'Transient', 'Persistent', etc. (which are specifically related to certain sections of the page) were selected by users more frequently. This user behavior of selecting specifically related terms more frequently might be linked to the concept of Inverse Document Frequency (IDF) in Information Retrieval (IR). Terms that are generally less frequent in the context provide more information, and therefore, highlighting such terms might be more beneficial while reading.

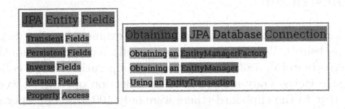

Fig. 3. Selection heatmaps for headers

4   Conclusions and Future Work

This paper introduces a new type of user attention heatmap, the selection heatmap, which visualizes the frequency of text selection operations across web pages. Selection heatmaps may provide new web analytics perspectives regarding user attention to paragraphs, sentences, and words on websites. The examples in this demo highlight interesting user behaviors with respect to text selection. Quantitative research will be needed to evaluate whether these examples represent significant, rather than causal patterns. Future work should also explore particular potential uses: the use of selection heatmaps as an alternative for conventional mouse movement heatmaps, which are used in commercial web analytics to visualize user attention; automatic identification of key sentences, for example for automatic text summarization; and automatic identification of important keywords in textual content, possibly as a complementary metric for Inverse Document Frequency (IDF) in Information Retrieval (IR).

References

1. Kaushik, A.: Web Analytics 2.0. SYBEX Inc., USA (2010)
2. Kirsh, I.: Using mouse movement heatmaps to visualize user attention to words. In: Proceedings of the 11th Nordic Conference on Human-Computer Interaction, NordiCHI 2020, Tallinn, Estonia, pp. 117:1–117:5. Association for Computing Machinery, New York (2020). https://doi.org/10.1145/3419249.3421250
3. Kirsh, I., Joy, M.: A different web analytics perspective through copy to clipboard heatmaps. In: Bielikova, M., Mikkonen, T., Pautasso, C. (eds.) ICWE 2020. LNCS, vol. 12128, pp. 543–546. Springer, Cham (2020). https://doi.org/10.1007/978-3-030-50578-3_41

City-Stories: Combining Entity Linking, Multimedia Retrieval, and Crowdsourcing to Make Historical Data Accessible

Laura Rettig[1]([✉]) [iD], Shaban Shabani[2,3] [iD], Loris Sauter[2] [iD],
Philippe Cudré-Mauroux[1] [iD], Maria Sokhn[3] [iD], and Heiko Schuldt[2] [iD]

[1] University of Fribourg, Fribourg, Switzerland
{Laura.Rettig,Philippe.Cudre-Mauroux}@unifr.ch
[2] University of Basel, Basel, Switzerland
{Shaban.Shabani,Loris.Sauter,Heiko.Schuldt}@unibas.ch,
Shaban.Shabani@hes-so.ch
[3] University of Applied Sciences Western Switzerland (HES-SO), Neuchatel,
Switzerland
Maria.Sokhn@hes-so.ch

Abstract. Digitized historical image collections as provided by individuals or memory institutions often suffer from limited or a complete lack of metadata In this paper, we present the *City-Stories* system that combines entity linking, multimedia retrieval, and crowdsourcing to make historical images searchable even across collections.

Keywords: Multimedia retrieval · Entity linking · Semantic data · Crowdsourcing

1 Introduction

Collecting, managing, and accessing historical data is essential for digital preservation of cultural heritage. This is particularly important for advanced applications that use digitized historical content shared across cultural heritage institutions and archives [6]. Sharing such data opens the door to several exciting possibilities. First, it makes it possible to integrate heterogeneous multimedia collections from different sources, formats, and metadata schemata, to ensure access via a homogeneous interface. Additionally, descriptive metadata opens the possibility to extract the context of the documents for meaningful concepts and to link the documents across media types and external collections. Second, integrated historic multimedia content allows for interactive approaches to retrieval which support different content and context-based query types such as

This work was supported by the *Hasler Foundation* in the context of the City-Stories project (contract no. 17055).
L. Rettig, S. Shabani and L. Sauter—These authors contributed equally to this work.

M. Brambilla et al. (Eds.): ICWE 2021, LNCS 12706, pp. 521–524, 2021.
https://doi.org/10.1007/978-3-030-74296-6_43

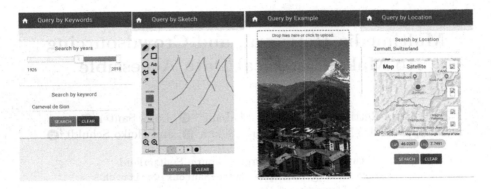

Fig. 1. Screen shots of City-Stories front-end supporting different query types.

keyword queries, query-by-example, query-by-sketch, semantic queries, spatio-temporal queries, and any combination thereof (Fig. 1). Third, these features allow the users of these applications to not only become content consumers but also content providers. Citizens own valuable private collections such as photo albums, audio, and video archives. Enabling crowdsourcing as a service allows them to share important content that can be of great public interest and contribute to the digital preservation of cultural heritage of their region. Moreover, by sharing their knowledge, citizens can play a crucial role in curating existing data.

In this paper, we present *City-Stories*, a hybrid system consisting of modules for multimedia retrieval, entity recognition and linking, and crowdsourcing for cultural heritage data. *City-Stories* enables the management, collection, and presentation of heterogeneous multimedia data in applications for cultural heritage, leveraging both content and metadata for the multimedia documents.

2   System Overview

The *City-Stories* system consists of three major components: (i) a module for *semantic data expansion*, (ii) a *spatio-temporal content browser* based on the *vitrivr* system, and, (iii) a *crowdsourcing and knowledge visualisation* module. During the offline phase, multimedia collections are extracted by a general data ingestion module and subsequently processed by the browser's underlying multimedia retrieval engine while simultaneously a semantic expansion is performed. In the online phase, additional information is gained via crowdsourcing, data that is further enhanced on-the-fly by the semantic data expansion module.

2.1   Semantic Data Expansion

The multimedia data present in this project is often accompanied by *textual metadata* (usually in the form of title and description of an item). In our previous work [6], we detail how we use *entity linking* to enrich the data presented to users with information from a knowledge base, specifically, WikiData[1]. In this component, we use textual metadata provided alongside media items in the DigitalValais[2] and Mediathèque[3] datasets to extract and link related entities. This allows us to enhance our data with relevant information on the entities present in both the metadata and in the knowledge base and enables linking data from further sources to the same entities for integration.

Due to the specificity of our data, we encounter many *rare* entities: Such entities are not recognized by our previous entity linking pipeline. However, using *word embeddings*, we can still infer relationships between entities in absence of entries to the knowledge base. In particular, since we are dealing with short textual information—too small to learn embeddings from the entirety of the *City-Stories* corpus—we employ methods that combine different textual sources for domain-specific textual information [4] and temporal term evolution [5]. For this, we localize the closest embedding (obtained via the aforementioned methods) in the vector space of an identified entity that is present in the knowledge base.

2.2 Spatio-Temporal Content Browser

City-Stories leverages a modified version of the *vitrivr* [2] content-based multimedia retrieval system, tailored to the search in historic multimedia collections. In particular, Cineast [3], *vitrivr's* retrieval engine, provides a plethora of query modes, of which *query-by-example* (QbE), *query-by-sketch* (QbS), *query-by-location* (QbL) and *query-by-time* (QbT) are enabled in *City-Stories*. QbE enables users to provide a sample image to be looked for. Using QbS, users might sketch the query freely or modify an existing image with a superimposed sketch. Spatial (QbL) and temporal (QbT) queries allow users to search for the time and/or place where historic objects have been captured.

QbS and QbE in *City-Stories* is based on a content-based similarity search along various features. Metadata for QbL and QbT are either extracted from the multimedia objects or provided externally. Often, historical documents lack appropriate metadata like EXIF for images and thus we heavily rely on additional data provided by the two other modules, either provided by human annotation or via semantic expansion. This data is stored in corresponding MongoDB and PostgreSQL databases, while the extracted multimedia retrieval features are stored in *vitrivr's* database CottontailDB [1]. The *City-Stories* system communicates with the *vitrivr* system via RESTful API, leveraging the OpenAPI standard[4].

2.3 Crowdsourcing and Knowledge Visualization

The crowdsourcing component of *City-Stories* allows platform users to share multimedia content. Citizens can share their private digitized historical

---

[1] https://www.wikidata.org.
[2] http://www.valais-wallis-digital.ch.
[3] https://www.mediatheque.ch/.
[4] https://www.openapis.org/.

collections and contribute to the digital preservation of cultural heritage of their region. The cross-platform capability enables users to share their collections from desktop or mobile devices and provide metadata that cover descriptive aspects of the shared items (title, description, tags, and categories) and the spatio-temporal properties (date and location).

The type of multimedia collections considered in *City-Stories* come without or only with little geographical and temporal information. For instance, finding the location and time where and when an image was taken is a rather challenging machine learning classification task. In contrast, humans can perform better especially if the annotation tasks are properly matched with annotators' capabilities. We deploy four crowdsourcing tasks and leverage the wisdom of crowds to improve the metadata of historical collections: i.) *Location-Finder*, used for finding the place depicted in images; ii.) *Year-Finder* for identifying the year images have been captured; iii.) *Annotation-Competition* for competitive image tagging, and iv.) *Validator* to validate automatically generated tags and image categories [7]. Gamification approaches are considered to incentivize the users participating in the tasks as well as for data quality control.

3   Conclusion

In this paper, we have presented the *City-Stories* system and how it seamlessly combines content-based retrieval with entity-based navigation and leverages the wisdom of the crowd for enhancing the metadata and extending the historical collections. It allows users to browse, perform different interactive query types and explore historical data from archives and museum collections.

References

1. Gasser, R., Rossetto, L., Heller, S., Schuldt, H.: Cottontail DB: an open source database system for multimedia retrieval and analysis. In: Proceedings of the 28th ACM International Conference on Multimedia. ACM (2020)
2. Gasser, R., Rossetto, L., Schuldt, H.: Multimodal multimedia retrieval with vitrivr. In: Proceedings of the International Conference on Multimedia Retrieval (2019)
3. Heller, S., Sauter, L., Schuldt, H., Rossetto, L.: Multi-stage queries and temporal scoring in vitrivr. In: Proceedings of the IEEE International Conference on Multimedia Expo Workshops (ICMEW) (2020)
4. Rettig, L., Audiffren, J., Cudré-Mauroux, P.: Fusing vector space models for domain-specific pplications. In: Proceedings of the 31st IEEE International Conference on Tools with Artificial Intelligence, ICTAI (2019)
5. Rettig, L., Hänggli, R., Cudré-Mauroux, P.: The best of both worlds: context-powered word embedding combinations for longitudinal text analysis. In: Proceedings of the IEEE International Conference on Big Data (2020)
6. Shabani, S., et al.: City-stories: a multimedia hybrid content and entity retrieval system for historical data. In: HistoInformatics@CIKM, pp. 22–29 (2017)
7. Shabani, S., Sokhn, M., Schuldt, H.: Hybrid human-machine classification system for cultural heritage data. In: Proceedings of the 2nd Workshop on Structuring and Understanding of Multimedia HeritAge Contents (2020)

SMOTE: A Tool to Proactively Manage Situations in WoT Environments

Daniel Flores-Martin$^{(\boxtimes)}$, Javier Berrocal , José García-Alonso ,
and Juan M. Murillo

Universidad de Extremadura, Badajoz, Spain
{dfloresm,jberolm,jgaralo,juanmamu}@unex.es

Abstract. The growing number of devices in the Web of Things (WoT) allows larger and more complex smart environments. These environments aim to provide the desired state for the people, adapting the devices to their preferences. The characteristics of the environment, the people and the devices generate a multitude of interconnections and behaviours in specific situations. However, managing these situations is not straightforward because of their changing nature. Tools are needed to identify and automate these interactions according to the desired conditions. In this demo we present **SMOTE** (**S**ituation **M**anagement f**O**r Smar**T** Environments), a tool for proactively managing situations in WoT environments, improving the management of different entities and reducing the effort for adapting devices to people's preferences.

Keywords: Web of Things · Smart-environments · Proactivity

1 Introduction

We live in a multi-device world connected to the Internet where we find different smart environments of heterogeneous devices. The WoT complements smart environments to reduce cost and risk for providers and consumers by combining multiple devices and information services. Also, it enables devices to use common and standardised languages for exchanging information.

One of the main challenges of the WoT is to provide interoperability and collaboration between devices transparently and automatically for people [5]. To this end, the WoT provides mechanisms such as the W3C Thing Description (W3C-TD) [3] that enables the description of devices. However, the interactions in the environment are not yet considered, limiting in many cases the collaboration among devices.

The Situation-Awareness paradigm already anticipated the concern for identifying the most suitable interactions in systems based on a descriptive view of the environment and individual [1]. These interactions are a fundamental aspect of the collaboration between devices and require information that is generated in WoT environments. This information is related to the characteristics of the devices, and is enriched through interaction with other devices. *When, where*

© Springer Nature Switzerland AG 2021
M. Brambilla et al. (Eds.): ICWE 2021, LNCS 12706, pp. 525–529, 2021.
https://doi.org/10.1007/978-3-030-74296-6_44

and *how* are considered traditional general aspects in the automation of a process. In WoT environments, these aspects represent specific properties such as spatio-temporal data, temperature or lighting level, for example. With this information, the interactions can be considered to generate and detect situations in smart environments and act accordingly.

In this demo we present SMOTE, a tool that identifies the devices and the situations in a given environment to act on it proactively. The information obtained from the devices and the environment is used to automatically detect the most suitable interactions to meet the desires of the users present.

2   SMOTE: Situation Management for Smart Environments

SMOTE is able to detect entities in a WoT environment, identify situations and modify the entities' behaviour to adapt them to the environment. The entities can be smart devices or people represented through their smartphones, which may have actions (operations that can change the environment) and objectives (the desired state of the environment). The description of these entities is done using an extended version of the W3C-TD specification [2], defined by the authors of this work to support the management of situations in WoT environments. For the identification and automation of situations, SMOTE is composed by two main parts: the **controller** and the **description manager**.

2.1   The Controller

The controller is responsible for detecting the entities in the environment, managing the interactions between them and adapting their behaviour when necessary. It is developed in NodeJS[1] and Python[2], and the communication with the entities is performed by using the MQTT protocol[3]. The processing of the devices' descriptions is done using Semantic Web techniques: an ontology based on the IoT-O ontology [4] to define the information contained in the descriptions of the entities, and the Owlready2 library[4] for its treatment (storing, searching and linking entities). The steps executed by the controller are:

1. **Description request.** When an entity is discovered, it is subscribed to the controller topic by using MQTT protocol and its description is requested.
2. **Description response.** Then, the entity publishes its description.
3. **Parse description.** The information of the entities is stored in the ontology. This ontology contains the classes needed to store W3C-TD models and match actions and objectives to meet the users' preferences.

---

[1] https://nodejs.org.
[2] https://www.python.org.
[3] https://mqtt.org.
[4] https://pypi.org/project/Owlready2.

4. **Check Situations**. The environment situations are constantly identified. This is done by comparing the information coming from the description with that stored in the ontology. At this point, two possibilities can arise: a previously defined situation is detected (4.a), or a new one is identified (4.b).
   - **4.a) Adapt the environment.** An existing situation is detected by getting the information related with where, when and how it is produced from the ontology. When discovered, the devices behaviour is adapted to achieve the desired state in the environment.
   - **4.b) Generate the situation.** The situation is generated by getting contextual information such as spatio-temporal aspects and the involved entities. Also, the detected objectives are matched with the available actions. Then, the situation is sent to all the entities to be identified in the future.
5. **Endpoint invocation**. Once the actions are identified their endpoints are invoked to perform the changes in the environment. This is done using the actions stored in the W3C-TD description of the entity.

2.2 The Description Manager

People' descriptions can be specified through a mobile application. This application allows people to perform CRUD operations over actions and objectives, to show situations and to display the complete description in W3C-TD format. This application can send the description to the controller and receive new situations automatically. The description is locally stored on the smartphones and it is automatically updated every time there is a change in it. In addition, device's descriptions can be provided by the manufacturer or obtained from external repositories to be included in the controller.

The process detailed above among the controller and the description manager is shown in Fig. 1. The source code of the implementation of the controller and of the mobile application is available in public repositories[5],[6].

3 Application

SMOTE was applied in a use-case based on a smart-office. The controller was deployed on a Raspberry Pi. Also, three members of the laboratory who stored their descriptions on their smartphones, were part of the environment, and a smart bulb (Xiaomi Yeelight) and a smart switch (Shelly v1) were used to adapt the lighting and turn a device on or off. In addition, a video was recorded.[7]

Although SMOTE has been applied in a smart-office, the biggest benefit is that it can be deployed in any environment that has IoT devices. All that is needed is a controller, which can be a Raspberry Pi, and to provide the necessary description of the IoT devices so that they can be used. Also, the same mobile application can be used in different environments.

---

[5] https://bitbucket.org/spilab/server-node-python-w3ctde.

[6] https://bitbucket.org/spilab/android-w3ctde.

[7] https://www.dropbox.com/s/bemodpkdc5v69rb/Video_W3CTDE.mp4.

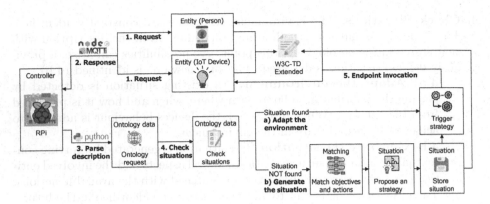

Fig. 1. General flow data of SMOTE

4 Conclusions

WoT environments are growing at an unstoppable pace due to the development of new and increasingly intelligent devices. This favours the emergence of ever-larger smart environments composed of devices capable of altering their state. Given the constant changes in these environments where entities are added or removed, the situations that can occur are numerous and need to be managed. In this demo we presented SMOTE, a tool that allows one to manage situations in real time to achieve the desired state of the environment according to objectives and actions, in a proactive and transparent way for the users.

Acknowledgments. This work was supported by the project RTI2018-094591-B-I00 and the FPU17/02251 grant (MCIU/AEI/FEDER, UE), by the 4IE+ project (0499_4IE_PLUS_4_E) funded by the Interreg V-A España-Portugal 2014–2020 program (POCTEP), by the Department of Economy and Infrastructure of the Government of Extremadura (GR18112, IB18030) and by the European Regional Development Fund.

References

1. Endsley, M.R.: Designing for Situation Awareness: An Approach to User-Centered Design. CRC Press, Boca Raton (2016)
2. Flores-Martin, D., Berrocal, J., García-Alonso, J., Murillo, J.M.: Extending W3C thing description to provide support for interactions of things in real-time. In: Ko, IY., Murillo, J.M., Vuorimaa, P. (eds.) Current Trends in Web Engineering. ICWE 2020. LNCS, vol. 12451, pp. 30–41. Springer, Cham (2020). https://doi.org/10.1007/978-3-030-65665-2_4
3. Kaebisch, S., Kamiya, T., McCool, M., Charpenay, V.: Web of things (WoT) thing description. Candidate recommendation, W3C (2019)

4. Seydoux, N., Drira, K., Hernandez, N., Monteil, T.: IoT-O, a core-domain IoT ontology to represent connected devices networks. In: Blomqvist, E., Ciancarini, P., Poggi, F., Vitali, F. (eds.) EKAW 2016. LNCS (LNAI), vol. 10024, pp. 561–576. Springer, Cham (2016). https://doi.org/10.1007/978-3-319-49004-5_36
5. Thuluva, A.S., Anicic, D., Rudolph, S.: Semantic web of things for industry 4.0. In: RuleML+ RR (Supplement) (2017)

Voice-Based Virtual Assistants for User Interaction Modeling

Marco Brambilla[✉][iD] and Davide Molinelli

Dipartimento di Elettronica, Informazione e Bioingegneria,
Politecnico di Milano, Milano, Italy
{marco.brambilla,davide.molinelli}@polimi.it

Abstract. In this work, we propose a virtual assistant that allows building models by means of voice commands. To demonstrate the generality of the approach, we describe three alternative strategies that apply voice-based support at three levels of detail: a fully-guided strategy; a pattern-based strategy; and an element-based strategy. We describe our implementation experience with the development of a design assistant covering the three strategies described above for OMG's IFML (Interaction Flow Modeling Language), in the context of user interaction design, including the integration with the Amazon Alexa assistant. We report our results that show how the assistant can bring advantages in terms of productivity.

1 Introduction

The design of the user interaction model represents one of the most delicate steps in the whole process of building and implementing a software system [2]. The objective of the work is focused towards the introduction of a form of artificial intelligence that could transform a passive support into an active assistance, able to communicate and guide the designer, understanding his commands, providing advice and building models automatically [4] . Other works aimed at this objective providing vocal assistant approaches for software designers [6,7].

In this paper we propose an approach and implementation of **a voice-based virtual assistant for model-driven development of user interactions and user interfaces**. While our solution is general and independent from the modeling language, to demonstrate the feasibility and advantages of the approach, the paper describes an implementation upon software models specified with IFML, the Interaction Flow Modeling Language [3,5]. The paper also reports our preliminary results that show how the assistant can bring advantages in terms of productivity.

2 Voice-Based Modeling Assistant

In the context of Model-Driven Development, a voice assistant can support designers with a different level of expertise, in a non-invasive manner, with the

© Springer Nature Switzerland AG 2021
M. Brambilla et al. (Eds.): ICWE 2021, LNCS 12706, pp. 530–533, 2021.
https://doi.org/10.1007/978-3-030-74296-6_45

Fig. 1. Overview of the voice assistant communication flow.

purpose of improving productivity and also the quality of the resulting models. Since modeling could be applied at different phases of the development and by different designers profiles, an assistant should be flexible and able to adapt to the trade-off between speed and precision in the design. The voice assistant can follow or lead the design process by interacting vocally with the designer, asking questions, reacting to his answers, and taking different decisions on the subsequent steps to follow in a dialogue based on these answers.

In order to offer different levels of support to the designer, we propose three different levels of assistance: a *fully-guided requirement-based strategy*, that produces complete designs starting from requirements, without the need of looking into the modeling at all; a *pattern-based strategy*, that lets designers specify solutions by selecting patterns and combining them together, thus obtaining quick and optimal designs; and an *element-based strategy*, that lets designers specify precise modeling structures with fine-grained granularity.

In this research we implemented *Model Creator*, an *Amazon Alexa* application (called *skill* in Alexa parlance) developed using the Alexa Developer Console, a suite made available by Amazon to define the *intents* of applications that make use of the voice assistant to execute tasks.

The implementation goes through a multi-step dialogue (see Fig. 2) and it progressively acquires all the information about the context and requirements, guiding the designer through a set of alternatives, so as to reach a point where a complete model of the application can be automatically generated (by exploiting also the template-based approach when needed).

The skill aims at supporting the design of IFML models, and integrates with *IFMLEdit.org*, an open-source, online framework for the specification of IFML models and the generation of code for web and mobile applications [1].

An intent specified by the user during the design process can be represented by a single interaction or a longer dialogue composed by multiple requests and answers. In the first case, the designer asks for the execution of a simple command, while, in the second case, the request is complex and the voice assistant demands the progressive acquisition of information. The reason is that any intent can require the fulfillment of mandatory and optional parameters. When the number of parameters is high, it is difficult to provide all the required values, by means of a single sentence. Moreover, some parameters may become mandatory, depending on the value assumed by other parameters. Therefore, the interaction is divided into multiple steps.

Fig. 2. In the guided mode, the voice assistant acquires the specifications through a multi-turn dialog before generating a complete model of the corresponding application.

The assistant is implemented as an Alexa skill that realizes a new voice-based front-end for the modeling editor. A communication flow between the skill and the modeling editor enables the voice-driven design process. This flow consists of the following steps, also depicted in Fig. 1: (1) The designer wakes up Alexa; (2) Alexa collects the voice stream containing the user request and sends it to the Alexa Voice Service that recognizes the command; (3) The skill is launched; (4) The modeling tool communicates back the result to the Alexa Cloud Service, that, in turn, elaborates the voice answer stream and sends it back to Alexa; (5) Alexa uses the speakers to communicate a feedback on the executed command and awaits the formulation of new commands or answers. For each new command (aka. intent) formulated by the designer, the process is repeated: the voice stream is sent to the Alexa Voice Service that identifies the intent and forwards the request to the modeling tool, which in turn executes the required operations on the model editor, and provides the respective feedback.

Some examples of usage of the assistant have been recorded in a video that is available online at: https://www.youtube.com/watch?v=00HoMz9Tq0A. For instance, the *Fully-guided Requirement-based Assistant* covers some typical business requirements and based on the decision of the designer at the requirement level we obtain a complete model of the application. The application scenarios covered in the current prototype include: e-commerce platforms, social network applications, blogs, and crowdsourcing systems. During the interaction process, the voice assistant initially asks for the scenario of interest and consequently changes the formulation of the next questions, starting a dialogue towards the ultimate intent of the user. At the end of the interaction, the assistant generates the complete and configured model that best fits the user's specifications. The progresses of the multi-turn dialog are visually managed and kept under control by means of a wizard panel (Fig. 2).

Table 1. Operations necessary to develop models with different assistants.

	No assistant or Element-based assistant					Pattern-based assistant (including configuration)						Fully-guided assistant (including configuration)					
	I	C	R	B	Total	I	C	R	B	Total	Saving	I	C	R	B	Total	Saving
E-commerce	200	97	927	219	1443	33	30	249	50	362	74.91%	1	0	249	0	250	82.67%
Blog	142	70	632	127	971	24	19	170	23	236	75.69%	1	0	170	0	171	82.38%
Social network	124	64	546	113	847	41	26	227	37	331	60.92%	1	0	227	0	228	73.08%
Crowdsourcing	107	49	478	101	735	22	10	139	6	177	75.91%	1	0	139	0	140	80.95%
Mean	-	-	-	-	-	-	-	-	-	-	71.85%	-	-	-	-	-	79.77%

3   Evaluation

We evaluated our approach by asking some designers to use the assistant in different configurations and application scenarios: an e-commerce application, a social network, a blog, and a crowdsourcing platform. Developers performed various kinds of operations:*Insertions (I), Connections (C), Refinements (R),* and *Bindings (B)*, i.e., links between IFML elements. Table 1 reports the total number of operations needed to build the model with the corresponding type of assistant, and the percentage of operations saved using the *Pattern-based support* and the *Fully Guided support* with respect to the basic *Element-based support*. On average, the *Pattern-based support* allows to save around 71% of operations, while the *Fully-guided support* can reach 79% of saving.

References

1. Bernaschina, C., Comai, S., Fraternali, P.: IFMLEdit.org: model driven rapid prototyping of mobile apps. In: 4th International Conference on Mobile Software Engineering and Systems, pp. 207–208. IEEE Press (2017)
2. Brambilla, M., Cabot, J., Wimmer, M.: Model-Driven Software Engineering in Practice. 2nd ed. Morgan & Claypool, San Rafael (2017)
3. Brambilla, M., Fraternali, P.: Interaction Flow Modeling Language: Model-Driven UI Engineering of Web and Mobile Apps with IFML. Morgan Kaufmann, Burlington (2014)
4. Cabot, J., Clarisó, R., Brambilla, M., Gérard, S.: Cognifying model-driven software engineering. In: Seidl, M., Zschaler, S. (eds.) STAF 2017. LNCS, vol. 10748, pp. 154–160. Springer, Cham (2018). https://doi.org/10.1007/978-3-319-74730-9_13
5. OMG: Interaction Flow Modeling Language (IFML), version 1.0. http://www.omg.org/spec/IFML/1.0.2015.
6. Soares, F., Araújo, J., Wanderley, F.: VoiceToModel: an approach to generate requirements models from speech recognition mechanisms. In: Proceedings of the 30th Annual ACM Symposium on Applied Computing, pp. 1350–1357. ACM (2015)
7. Stephan, M.: Towards a cognizant virtual software modeling assistant using model clones. In: 41st International Conference on Software Engineering: New Ideas and Emerging Results, pp. 21–24. IEEE Press (2019)

Tutorials

Similarity Search, Recommendation and Explainability over Graphs in Different Domains: Social Media, News, and Health Industry

Panagiotis Symeonidis(✉) [iD]

University of the Aegean, Samos, Greece
psymeon@aegean.gr
http://www.panagiotissymeonidis.com

Abstract. In this tutorial, we provide a rich blend of theory and practice regarding graph algorithms, to deal with challenging issues such as scalability, data noise, and sparsity in recommender systems. We also demonstrate real-life systems that use the graph algorithms for Social Media (http://delab.csd.auth.gr/moviexplain/), News (http://metarec.inf.unibz.it) and Health (https://drugrec.inf.unibz.it) industry along with user studies which were used to evaluate the acceptance of the users for these systems.

Keywords: Recommender systems · Graph-based algorithms

1 Introduction

In this tutorial, we provide a step-by-step analysis of graph-based methods to infer similarity and provide recommendations in heterogeneous information networks. In particular, this tutorial surveys important research in a new family of recommender systems aimed at serving multi-dimensional social networks. We describe the family of local-based (i.e., FriendLink [8], Friend Of A Friend (FOAF), etc.) and random walk-based algorithms (i.e., PageRank, SimRank, Katz, etc.) that can be used to provide contextual recommendations in multi-dimensional graphs, where there are many participating entities (users, locations, products, and the time dimension). Furthermore, we present the time-evolving graphs which incorporate session nodes to model the time dimension. Moreover, we will present methods that use meta paths to infer similarity among entities and how these meta paths can be used for explaining either the similarity among entities or the suggested item recommendations. We also present state-of-the-art graph neural networks, graph convolution networks, and graph embeddings (node2vec, metapath2vec, etc.) for similarity search and recommendation in graphs.

The remainder of the article is organized as follows. Section 2 describes preliminaries in graphs with a case study from News industry. We present the

© Springer Nature Switzerland AG 2021
M. Brambilla et al. (Eds.): ICWE 2021, LNCS 12706, pp. 537–541, 2021.
https://doi.org/10.1007/978-3-030-74296-6_46

related work of recommendation over graphs in Sect. 3. Section 4 describes real-world recommendation practices for different domains, such as Social Networks, and Medical industry. Finally, Sect. 5 concludes the paper.

2   News Industry Example Formulated as a Graph

In this Section, we give a basic introduction in multi-modal graphs, through a case study example from news industry. A network for an online news portal is a heterogeneous information network, containing objects from five types of entities $Q = \{U, S, A, C, L\}$: users (U), sessions (S), articles (A), article categories (C), and article locations (L). Each user u has one or more links to the sessions s. Each session s possesses one unique user u and one or more articles a, which were read by the user within the session. Finally, each article a can appear in one or more sessions s, belong to one news category and be assigned to one geographic location l.

Network schema serves as a template for a network and tells how many types of objects there are in the network and where the possible links exist. The network schema for an online news portal is shown in Fig. 1. More details about the network schema and the session-based graph algorithms which run over it can be found in [9].

Fig. 1. Online news portal network schema

3   Related Work

In this tutorial, we focus on local and global graph algorithms, which focus on the local nodes' structure, and the overall path structure of a graph, respectively. A local-based graph algorithm, known as FriendLink [8], is used in GeoSocialRec, which is a real location-based social netowrk[1]. A popular global-based graph algorithm has been proposed by Jeh and Widom [5] and it is denoted as SimRank. It builds on the concept of similarity in graphs, where two entities are considered similar if they are referenced by similar entities. Another graph-based algorithm for similarity search is Random Walk with Restart (RWR) [6],

---

[1] http://delab.csd.auth.gr/geosocialrec/.

which is a variation of the well-known PageRank algorithm. Another similarity measure that computes similarity in heterogeneous information networks is PathSim [10]. PathSim runs on meta paths and captures the subtle semantics of similarity among peer objects in a network. A meta path connects two peer nodes with a sequence of edges between different node types.

There are various meta paths that can be built on the USACL network, which is shown in Fig. 1. For example, if we start from the article type of the node, we can build the following paths: ACA, ASA, ALA, ASUSA, etc. The meta path framework provides a powerful mechanism for a user to select the appropriate similarity semantics, which can be also used for explaining later a recommendation.

Recently, graph embeddings have been used to infer similarities over graphs. For example, node2vec and DeepWalk [2] learn vector representations of nodes (i.e., node embeddings) with the goal to identify semantically similar nodes. Metapath2vec [1] extends the DeepWalk and node2vec algorithms for heterogeneous graphs by generating only meta path-based random walks. Moreover, there are deep neural network architectures, such as Graph Neural Networks (GNNs), Graph Convolution Networks (GCNs), etc., that iteratively propagate and aggregate node's feature and topological information from local graph neighborhoods using neural networks, to learn meaningful representations for graph data. For example, MCRec [4] is a graph-based extension of NCF [3], which uses as input the node embeddings that were constructed after applying a variation of the word2vec algorithm on node sequences. MP4Rec [7] is a GNN which is able to provide both accurate and explainable recommendations. To learn the local characteristics of the graph, it uses meta paths and the PathSim [10] algorithm.

4 Other Examples: Social Media and Health Industry

In the previous sections, we described graph-based algorithms for the news industry. However, these algorithms can be also applied to different recommendation domains.

For the health industry domain, a network schema for patients' treatment is shown in Fig. 2(a). As shown, for capturing patient's drug treatment, we would have a graph that consists of Patients (P), who undergo a Treatment (T) using Drugs (D) to target Genes (G) and may have harmful side Effects (E). Then, we can provide a hybrid meta path-based explanation to a medical doctor as follows: "We recommend for your patient drug D250, because: (i) it was prescribed to 6 other Patients (who have diagnosed the same disease with your patient) and took also similar Drugs with those of your Patient's current treatment (DTPTD), and (ii) It cures/targets similar Genes together with 5 Drugs that your Patient has already taken in his treatment (DGD)". More details can be found in http:// drugrec.inf.unibz.it.

For the social media domain, a network schema for online movies provider is shown in Fig. 3(b). As shown, it is very similar with the news recommendation network schema of Fig. 1. That is, instead of news articles (A), news categories

Fig. 2. (a) Drug treatment schema   **Fig. 3.** (b) Movies portal schema

(C), and Locations (L), it consists of movies (M), movie genres (G), and directors (D), respectively. More details can be found in http://delab.csd.auth.gr/moviexplain/.

5   Conclusion

In this tutorial, we focused on the graph-based models for the task of item recommendation. We also presented real-life systems that use the aforementioned graph-based algorithms for Social Networks, News and Health industry along with user studies which were used to evaluate the acceptance of the users for these systems.

References

1. Dong, Y., Chawla, N.V., Swami, A.: metapath2vec: scalable representation learning for heterogeneous networks. In: Proceedings of the 23rd ACM SIGKDD International Conference on Knowledge Discovery and Data Mining, pp. 135–144. ACM (2017)
2. Grover, A., Leskovec, J.: node2vec: scalable feature learning for networks. In: Proceedings of the 22nd ACM SIGKDD International Conference on Knowledge Discovery and Data Mining, pp. 855–864. ACM (2016)
3. He, X., Liao, L., Zhang, H., Nie, L., Hu, X., Chua, T.S.: Neural collaborative filtering. In: Proceedings of the 26th International Conference on World Wide Web, pp. 173–182. International World Wide Web Conferences Steering Committee (2017)
4. Hu, B., Shi, C., Zhao, W.X., Yu, P.S.: Leveraging meta-path based context for top-n recommendation with a neural co-attention model. In: Proceedings of the 24th ACM SIGKDD International Conference on Knowledge Discovery & Data Mining, pp. 1531–1540. ACM (2018)
5. Jeh, G., Widom, J.: Simrank: a measure of structural-context similarity. In: Proceedings 8th ACM SIGKDD International Conference on Knowledge Discovery and Data Mining (KDD'2002), pp. 538–543. Edmonton, Canada (2002)
6. Leskovec, J., Rajaraman, A., Ullman, J.D.: Mining of massive data sets. Cambridge University Press (2019)
7. Ozsoy, M.G., et al.: Mp4rec: explainable and accurate top-n recommendations in heterogeneous information networks. IEEE Access **8**, 181835–181847 (2020)

8. Papadimitriou, A., Symeonidis, P., Manolopoulos, Y.: Friendlink: link prediction in social networks via bounded local path traversal. In: 2011 International Conference on Computational Aspects of Social Networks (CASoN), pp. 66–71. IEEE (2011)
9. Symeonidis, P., Kirjackaja, L., Zanker, M.: Session-aware news recommendations using random walks on time-evolving heterogeneous information networks. User Model. User-Adapt. Inter. **30**(4), 727–755 (2020). https://doi.org/10.1007/s11257-020-09261-9
10. Yizhou, S., Jiawei, H., Xifeng, Y., Philip S., Y., Tianyi, W.: Pathsim: meta path-based top-k similarity search in heterogenuos information networks. In: Proceedings of the VLDB Endowment (VLDB'2011). Seattle, Washigton (2011)

High-Level Interaction Design with Discourse Models for Automated Web GUI Generation

Hermann Kaindl[✉] [ID]

TU Wien, Vienna, Austria
kaindl@ict.tuwien.ac.at

Abstract. *Interaction design* is considered important for achieving usable Web user interfaces. *Communicative acts* as abstractions from speech acts can model basic building blocks ('atoms') of communication, like a question or an answer. When, e.g., a question and an answer are glued together as a so-called adjacency pair, a simple 'molecule' of a dialogue is modeled. Deliberately complex discourse structures can be modeled using relations from Rhetorical Structure Theory (RST). The content of a communicative act can refer to *ontologies* of the domain of discourse. Taking all this together, we created a new discourse metamodel that specifies what discourse models may look like. Such discourse models can specify an interaction design. Since manual creation of user interfaces is hard and expensive, automated generation may become more and more important. This tutorial also demonstrates how such an interaction design can be used for *automated Web user-interface generation*. This is based on model-transformation rules according to the model-driven architecture. Based on AI optimization techniques, the graphical user interfaces (GUIs) are automatically tailored to a device such as a smartphone according to a given device specification. Since the usability of fully-automatically generated GUIs is still not satisfactory, unique *customization techniques* are employed as well. We also address *low-vision accessibility of Web-pages*, by combining automated design-time generation of Web-pages with *responsive design* for improving accessibility.

Keywords: Interaction design · Discourse models · Task models · Automated Web GUI generation · Customization · Low-vision accessibility of Web-pages

1 Intended Audience and Assumed Background

The target audience is interaction designers, Web designers, or project managers. Also educators can benefit from this tutorial.

The assumed attendee background is some familiarity with scenarios/use cases as well as interest in interaction design. There are no pre-requisites such as knowledge about Human-Computer Interaction in general.

2 Tutorial Structure and List of Topics Covered

This tutorial is a combination of lectures, group discussions and exercises.

© Springer Nature Switzerland AG 2021
M. Brambilla et al. (Eds.): ICWE 2021, LNCS 12706, pp. 542–546, 2021.
https://doi.org/10.1007/978-3-030-74296-6_47

In order to provide a common basis for participants with different background, this tutorial starts with an overview of background material. An overview of discourse-based modeling follows, which is brief but sufficient for understanding the generation and customization of GUIs. This section concludes with an explanation of the duality of task- and discourse-based interaction design.

Based on that, this tutorial shows how GUIs can be generated automatically and, in this course tailored to different devices (as specified). This tutorial also shows how customization can be integrated into such a generation approach, both through custom rules and custom widgets.

Last but not least, this tutorial explains how low-vision accessibility can be improved through a combination with Responsive Design.

2.1 Summary of Topics Covered

- *Background*

  - Interaction design
  - Task-based modeling
  - Speech acts
  - Conversation Analysis
  - Model-driven transformation

- *Interaction Design based on Discourse Modeling*

  - Discourse example
  - Communicative Acts
  - Adjacency Pair
  - RST relations
  - Exercise: Understand given model
  - Duality of Task- and Discourse-based Design

- *GUI Generation*

  - Process of user-interface generation
  - Generation of Structural UI Model
  - Generation of Behavioral UI Model
  - Weaving of structural and behavioral models
  - Optimization for tailoring to device
  - Examples of generated user interfaces

- *Customization*

  - Custom rules
  - Custom widgets

- *Improving Low-vision Accessibility*

  – Combination with Responsive Design
  – Accessibility evaluation

- *Conclusion*

3   Learning Objectives and Outcomes

In this tutorial, participants learn about an open and fully implemented approach to GUI generation from models at the highest level of the Cameleon Reference Framework, i.e., the Tasks & Concepts Level. These models focus on the specification of (classes of) dialogues in contrast to tasks for modeling activities that can be performed by the user or the application (system). Participants will understand a duality of these approaches. Participants also get an overview of both automatically generating and customizing Web GUIs.

4   Biography of Presenter

Hermann Kaindl is the head of the organizational unit entitled "Software-intensive Systems" of the Institute of Computer Technology and a Vice Chairman of the Senate at TU Wien. He joined this institute in early 2003 as a full professor. Prior to moving to academia in early 2003, he has gained nearly 25 years of industrial experience in requirements and software engineering as well as human-computer interaction at Siemens Austria. Kaindl is a *Senior Member* of the IEEE and a *Distinguished Scientist* Member of the ACM.

5   Tutorial History

Predecessors of the proposed tutorial have been presented by this proposer, e.g., at CHI'12, IEEE SMC'14, ACM SAC'15, RE'15, APSEC'16, eics'17, and ACM SAC'19 (most of them half-day). Each of these tutorials has been received very well by the respective audience. The number of attendees, e.g., at SAC'19 was 25. The most similar version was the one presented in a plenary session at eics'17, with even more attendees. These tutorials were based on the publications of this presenter as listed below.

The ICWE 2021 tutorial differs through its focus on Web GUIs, the inclusion of customization techniques, and low-vision accessibility of Web-pages.

References

1. Bogdan, C., et al.: Generating an abstract user interface from a discourse model inspired by human communication. In: Proceedings of the 41st Hawaii International Conference on System Sciences, HICSS 2008, Waikoloa, Big Island, Hawaii. IEEE (2008)

2. Bogdan, C., Kaindl, H., Falb, J., Popp, R.: Modeling of interaction design by end users through discourse modeling. In: Proceedings of the 2008 ACM International Conference on Intelligent User Interfaces, IUI 2008, Maspalomas, Gran Canaria, Spain. ACM Press (2008)
3. Falb, J., Kaindl, H., Horacek, H., Bogdan, C., Popp, R., Arnautovic, E.: A discourse model for interaction design based on theories of human communication. In: Extended Abstracts on Human Factors in Computing Systems, CHI 2006, pp. 754–759 (2006). ACM Press (2006)
4. Falb, J., Kavaldjian, S., Popp, R., Raneburger, D., Arnautovic, E., Kaindl, H.: Fully automatic user interface generation from discourse models. In: Proceedings of the 2009 ACM International Conference on Intelligent User Interfaces, IUI 2009. ACM Press (2009). Tool demo paper
5. Falb, J., Popp, R., Röck, T., Jelinek, H., Arnautovic, E., Kaindl, H.: Using communicative acts in interface design specifications for automated synthesis of user interfaces. In: Proceedings of the 21st IEEE/ACM International Conference on Automated Software Engineering, ASE 2006, pp. 261–264 (2006)
6. Kaindl, H.: Model a discourse and transform it to your user interface. In: Gross, T., et al. (eds.) INTERACT 2009. LNCS, vol. 5727, pp. 948–949. Springer, Heidelberg (2009). https://doi.org/10.1007/978-3-642-03658-3_125
7. Kavaldjian, S., Bogdan, C., Falb, J., Kaindl, H.: Transforming discourse models to structural user interface models. In: Giese, H. (ed.) Models in Software Engineering, MODELS 2007. Lecture Notes in Computer Science, vol. 5002, pp. 77–88. Springer, Heidelberg (2008). https://doi.org/10.1007/978-3-540-69073-3_9
8. Popp, R., J. Falb, D. Raneburger, H. Kaindl: A transformation engine for model-driven UI generation. In: Proceedings of the 4th ACM SIGCHI Symposium on Engineering Interactive Computing Systems, EICS 2012, Copenhagen, Denmark (2012)
9. Popp, R., Kaindl, H., Badalians Gholi Kandi, S., Raneburger, D., Paterno, F.: Duality of task- and discourse-based interaction design for GUI generation. In: Proceedings of the 2014 IEEE International Conference on Systems, Man, and Cybernetics, SMC 2014, pp. 3323–3328 (2014)
10. Popp, R., Raneburger, D., Kaindl, H.: Tool support for automated multi-device GUI generation from discourse-based communication models. In: Proceedings of the ACM SIGCHI Symposium on Engineering Interactive Computing Systems, EICS 2013 (2013)
11. Raneburger, D., Alonso-Ríos, D., Popp, R., Kaindl, H., Falb, J.: A user study with GUIs tailored for smartphones. In: Kotzé, P., Marsden, G., Lindgaard, G., Wesson, J., Winckler, M. (eds.) INTERACT 2013. LNCS, vol. 8118, pp. 505–512. Springer, Heidelberg (2013). https://doi.org/10.1007/978-3-642-40480-1_34
12. Raneburger, D., Kaindl, H., Popp, R.: Strategies for automated GUI tailoring for multiple devices. In: Proceedings of the 48st Annual Hawaii International Conference on System Sciences, HICSS-48 (2015)
13. Raneburger, D., Kaindl, H., Popp, R.: Model transformation rules for customization of multi-device graphical user interfaces. In: Proceedings of the 7th ACM SIGCHI Symposium on Engineering Interactive Computing Systems, EICS 2015, pp. 100–109 (2015)
14. Raneburger, D., Kaindl, H., Popp, R., Šajatovic, V., Armbruster, A.: A process for facilitating interaction design through automated GUI generation. In: Proceedings of the 29th ACM/SIGAPP Symposium on Applied Computing, SAC 2014 (2014)
15. Raneburger, D., Popp, R., Kaindl, H., Falb, J.: Automated WIMP-UI behavior generation: parallelism and granularity of communication units. In: Proceedings of the 2011 IEEE International Conference on Systems, Man and Cybernetics, SMC 2011, pp. 2816–2821 (2011)
16. Raneburger, D., Popp, R., Kaindl, H., Falb, J., Ertl, D.: Automated generation of device-specific WIMP-UIs: weaving of structural and behavioral models. In: Proceedings of the 2011 SIGCHI Symposium on Engineering Interactive Computing Systems, EICS 2011 (2011)

17. Rathfux, T., Popp, R., Kaindl, H.: Adding custom widgets to model-driven GUI generation. In: Proceedings of the 8th ACM SIGCHI Symposium on Engineering Interactive Computing Systems, EICS 2016, Brussels, Belgium (2016)
18. Rathfux, T., Thöner, J., Kaindl, H., Popp, R.: Combining design-time generation of web-pages with responsive design for improving low-vision accessibility. In: Proceedings of the ACM SIGCHI Symposium on Engineering Interactive Computing Systems, EICS 2018, Paris (2018)

Influence Learning and Maximization

George Panagopoulos[1][(✉)] and Fragkiskos D. Malliaros[2]

[1] École Polytechnique, Palaiseau, France
`george.panagopoulos@polytechnique.edu`
[2] Université Paris-Saclay, CentraleSupélec, Inria, Gif-Sur-Yvette, France
`fragkiskos.malliaros@centralesupelec.fr`

Abstract. The problem of maximizing or minimizing the spreading in a social network has become more timely than ever with the advent of fake news and the coronavirus epidemic. The solution to this problem pertains to influence maximization algorithms that identify the right nodes to lockdown for epidemic containment, hire for viral marketing campaigns, block for online political propaganda etc. Though these algorithms have been developed for many years, the majority of the literature focuses on scalability issues and relaxing the method's assumptions. In the recent years, the emergence of new complementary data and more advanced machine learning methods for decision have guided part of the literature towards learning-based approaches. These can range from learning how information spreads over a network, to learning how to solve the combinatorial optimization problem itself. In this tutorial, we aim to dissentangle and clearly define the different tasks around learning for influence applications in social networks. More specifically, we start from traditional influence maximization algorithms, describe the need of influence estimation and delineate the state-of-the-art on influence and diffusion learning. Subsequently, we delve into the problem of learning while optimizing the influence spreading which is based on online learning algorithms. Finally, we describe the latest approaches on learning influence maximization with graph neural networks and deep reinforcement learning.

Keywords: Influence maximization · Machine learning · Graph mining · Social network analysis

1 Introduction and Objectives

Social influence governs multiple aspects of our lives. From deciding the product you will buy and the restaurant you will visit, to adapting political ideas and getting infected from viruses, peer pressure and the amount and quality of the interaction with other people can be a deciding factor for a person's life. In the real world it can be used from epidemic containment [7] to diminishing the misinformation in social networks [3,10]. To this end, social influence is a concept worth studying and the problem of influence maximization is one of the most

© Springer Nature Switzerland AG 2021
M. Brambilla et al. (Eds.): ICWE 2021, LNCS 12706, pp. 547–550, 2021.
https://doi.org/10.1007/978-3-030-74296-6_48

challenging and timely in social network analysis. In its core, influence maximization is a combinatorial optimization problem that aims to find a bounded set of nodes in a network that can maximize spreading. This spreading might refer to political propaganda, product purchasing intent, a virus etc. Though the initial theoretical setting is rather well-studied, it suffers from some assumptions that restrict its effectiveness in the real world. For example, it has been observed that ignoring the structural impact of a node in influence relationships leads to inaccurate spreading prediction [1]. Moreover, the network topology alone is known to fail on predicting the spreading without temporal information [2,16] or content [4].

Recently, novel methodologies have emerged that either merge influence maximization with learning-based components from extraneous data, or fully transform it in a learning problem. In this tutorial, we are going to go through the literature connecting influence maximization with machine learning methodologies. These can be separated in the sections outlined below, which resemble solutions to the different problems pertaining to influence maximization. Methodologically this includes learning models ranging from recurrent neural networks and point processes, to multi-armed bandits, reinforcement learning and graph neural networks. From an algorithmic concepts, we delineate the basics of submodular maximization and performance guarantees, as well as heuristics and sketching. For each part of the tutorial, we aim to explain the most vital papers on the problem, discussing also some variants and extensions. The target audience of the tutorial includes (i) researchers in the area of machine learning, data mining, and web engineering with applications to social media and network analysis; (ii) graduate students interested in graph mining, algorithms, and machine learning; (iii) practitioners and members of industrial partners relevant to recommender systems, epidemiology, or marketing. The assumed background is sufficient knowledge of probabilities, graph concepts, and algorithm design.

Overall, we expect that the tutorial will be of great value for the ICWE community because of the aforementioned reasons on how timely is the problem. It could be argued that it is one of the most crucial problems in current social network analysis, with important implications in the real world. Its connection to the aforementioned fields as well as computational journalism renders it also rather interdisciplinary, hence its effect will be broad and lasting. The tutorial slides along with additional resources will be available online[1].

2   Outline of the Tutorial

In this section, we give a tentative outline of the tutorial. The proposed duration of the tutorial is half a day.

1. **Introduction**
   - What is influence
   - Exemplary applications

---

[1] http://fragkiskosm.github.io/projects/influence_learning_tutorial/.

– Metrics for influencer identification [22,28]
– What is a diffusion cascade
– Influence evaluation [25]

2. **Traditional Influence Maximization**
   – Influence maximization [17]
   – Faster heuristics [5]
   – Faster algorithms [20,27]

3. **Influence and Diffusion Learning**
   – The need for influence estimation [1]
   – Learning influence [11–13]
   – Influence Maximization with influence estimation [14,24,26]
   – Diffusion prediction using neural networks [15,21]
   – Diffusion prediction using point-processes [8,30]

4. **Learning Influence Maximization**
   – Learning combinatorial optimization [18]
   – Graph reinforcement learning for IM [9,23]

5. **Online Influence Maximization**
   – Multi-armed bandits with edge feedback [6,29]
   – Multi-armed bandits with node feedback [19]

6. **Summary and Open Problems**
   – Realistic influence maximization
   – Pointer to other tutorials and data

Acknowledgements. Supported by ANR (French National Research Agency) under the JCJC project GraphIA (ANR-20-CE23-0009-01).

References

1. Aral, S., Dhillon, P.S.: Social influence maximization under empirical influence models. Nat. Hum. Behav. **2**(6), 375 (2018)
2. Bakshy, E., Hofman, J.M., Mason, W.A., Watts, D.J.: Everyone's an influencer: quantifying influence on twitter. In: WSDM, p. 65–74 (2011)
3. Budak, C., Agrawal, D., El Abbadi, A.: Limiting the spread of misinformation in social networks. In: The WebConf, pp. 665–674 (2011)
4. Chen, S., Fan, J., Li, G., Feng, J., Tan, K.I., Tang, J.: Online topic-aware influence maximization. Proc. VLDB Endowment **8**(6), 666–667 (2015)
5. Chen, W., Wang, C., Wang, Y.: Scalable influence maximization for prevalent viral marketing in large-scale social networks. In: KDD, pp. 1029–1038 (2010)
6. Chen, W., Wang, Y., Yuan, Y., Wang, Q.: Combinatorial multi-armed bandit and its extension to probabilistically triggered arms. J. Mach. Learn. Res. **17**(1), 1746–1778 (2016)
7. Drakopoulos, K., Ozdaglar, A., Tsitsiklis, J.N.: An efficient curing policy for epidemics on graphs. IEEE Trans. Netw. Sci. Eng. **1**(2), 67–75 (2014)

8. Du, N., Dai, H., Trivedi, R., Upadhyay, U., Gomez-Rodriguez, M., Song, L.: Recurrent marked temporal point processes: embedding event history to vector. In: KDD, pp. 1555–1564 (2016)
9. Fan, C., Zeng, L., Sun, Y., Liu, Y.Y.: Finding key players in complex networks through deep reinforcement learning. Nat. Mach. Intel. pp. 1–8 (2020)
10. Farajtabar, M., et al.: Fake news mitigation via point process based intervention. arXiv preprint arXiv:1703.07823 (2017)
11. Feng, S., Cong, G., Khan, A., Li, X., Liu, Y., Chee, Y.M.: Inf2vec: latent representation model for social influence embedding. In: ICDE (2018)
12. Gomez-Rodriguez, M., Leskovec, J., Krause, A.: Inferring networks of diffusion and influence. TKDD **5**(4), 1–37 (2012)
13. Goyal, A., Bonchi, F., Lakshmanan, L.V.: Learning influence probabilities in social networks. In: WSDM, p. 241–250 (2010)
14. Goyal, A., Bonchi, F., Lakshmanan, L.V.: A data-based approach to social influence maximization. VLDB (2011)
15. Islam, M.R., Muthiah, S., Adhikari, B., Prakash, B.A., Ramakrishnan, N.: Deepdiffuse: Predicting the 'who' and 'when' in cascades. In: ICDM (2018)
16. Karsai, M., et al.: Small but slow world: how network topology and burstiness slow down spreading. Phys. Rev. E **83**(2), 025102 (2011)
17. Kempe, D., Kleinberg, J., Tardos, É.: Maximizing the spread of influence through a social network. In: KDD (2003)
18. Khalil, E., Dai, H., Zhang, Y., Dilkina, B., Song, L.: Learning combinatorial optimization algorithms over graphs. In: NeurIPS, pp. 6348–6358 (2017)
19. Lagrée, P., Cappé, O., Cautis, B., Maniu, S.: Algorithms for online influencer marketing. TKDD **13**(1), 1–30 (2018)
20. Leskovec, J., Krause, A., Guestrin, C., Faloutsos, C., VanBriesen, J., Glance, N.: Cost-effective outbreak detection in networks. In: KDD, p. 420–429 (2007)
21. Li, C., Ma, J., Guo, X., Mei, Q.: DeepCas: an end-to-end predictor of information cascades. In: The WebConf, pp. 577–586 (2017)
22. Malliaros, F.D., Rossi, M.E.G., Vazirgiannis, M.: Locating influential nodes in complex networks. Sci. Rep. **6**, 19307 (2016)
23. Manchanda, S., Mittal, A., Dhawan, A., Medya, S., Ranu, S., Singh, A.: Gcomb: Learning budget-constrained combinatorial algorithms over billion-sized graphs. In: NeurIPS (2020)
24. Panagopoulos, G., Malliaros, F.D., Vazirgianis, M.: Influence maximization using influence and susceptibility embeddings. In: ICWSM, pp. 511–521 (2020)
25. Panagopoulos, G., Malliaros, F.D., Vazirgiannis, M.: Diffugreedy: An influence maximization algorithm based on diffusion cascades. In: Complex Networks (2018)
26. Panagopoulos, G., Malliaros, F.D., Vazirgiannis, M.: Multi-task learning for influence estimation and maximization. IEEE TKDE (2020)
27. Tang, Y., Shi, Y., Xiao, X.: Influence maximization in near-linear time: A martingale approach. In: SIGMOD, p. 1539–1554 (2015)
28. Tixier, A.J.P., Rossi, M.E.G., Malliaros, F.D., Read, J., Vazirgiannis, M.: Perturb and combine to identify influential spreaders in real-world networks. In: ASONAM, p. 73–80 (2019)
29. Wen, Z., Kveton, B., Valko, M., Vaswani, S.: Online influence maximization under independent cascade model with semi-bandit feedback. In: NeurIPS (2017)
30. Zhao, Q., Erdogdu, M.A., He, H.Y., Rajaraman, A., Leskovec, J.: Seismic: A self-exciting point process model for predicting tweet popularity. In: KDD, pp. 1513–1522 (2015)

Correction to: Web Engineering

Marco Brambilla⬤, Richard Chbeir⬤, Flavius Frasincar⬤,
and Ioana Manolescu⬤

Correction to:
M. Brambilla et al. (Eds.): *Web Engineering*, LNCS 12706,
https://doi.org/10.1007/978-3-030-74296-6

In Chapter 10, the term "paths" was used instead of the term "operation." This has been corrected and the term "operations" is now used throughout the paper.

In Chapter 26, the email addresses of some authors have been corrected. The corrected email addresses are: dylan.vanassche@ugent.be, gertjan.demulder@ugent.be, and ben.demeester@ugent.be.

The updated version of these chapters can be found at
https://doi.org/10.1007/978-3-030-74296-6_10
https://doi.org/10.1007/978-3-030-74296-6_26

Correction to: A Web-Based Co-Creation and User Engagement Method and Platform

Andrea Tocchetti⬤, Lorenzo Corti⬤, Marco Brambilla⬤,
and Diletta Di Marco⬤

Correction to:
Chapter "A Web-Based Co-Creation and User Engagement
Method and Platform" in: M. Brambilla et al. (Eds.):
Web Engineering, **LNCS 12706,**
https://doi.org/10.1007/978-3-030-74296-6_38

Chapter "A Web-Based Co-Creation and User Engagement Method and Platform" was previously published non-open access. It has now been changed to open access under a CC BY 4.0 license and the copyright holder updated to 'The Author(s)'. The book has also been updated with this change.

The updated version of this chapter can be found at
https://doi.org/10.1007/978-3-030-74296-6_38

© The Author(s) 2022
M. Brambilla et al. (Eds.): ICWE 2021, LNCS 12706, p. C2, 2022.
https://doi.org/10.1007/978-3-030-74296-6_50

Author Index

Printed in the United States
by Baker & Taylor Publisher Services